# Pittsburgh

WITH A FOREWORD BY
RICHARD S. CALIGUIRI
THOMAS J. FOERSTER
ROBERT C. MILSOM

FEATURE ARTICLES BY
JOHN ALTDORFER
KEN FISHER
CHARLES LYNCH
BETH MARCELLO
ABBY MENDELSON

"PARTNERS IN PROGRESS" BY
JACK MARKOWITZ

THE GREATER PITTSBURGH CHAMBER OF
COMMERCE

CELEBRATING AMERICA'S MOST LIVABLE
COMMUNITY

WINDSOR PUBLICATIONS, INC.
NORTHRIDGE, CALIFORNIA

# Pittsburgh

## FULFILLING ITS DESTINY

Vince Gagetta

To Dee,
whose love, encouragement, and
patient understanding made it possible;
and Dave,
who will find his future here.

---

Windsor Publications, Inc.—History Books Division

Publisher: John M. Phillips
Editorial Director: Teri Davis Greenberg
Design Director: Alexander D'Anca

Staff for *Pittsburgh: Fulfilling Its Destiny*
Senior Editor: Karl Stull
Photo Manager: Laura Cordova
Assistant Editor: Marilyn Horn
Proofreader: Susan J. Muhler
Director, Corporate Profiles: Karen Story
Assistant Director, Corporate Profiles: Phyllis Gray
Editor, Corporate Profiles: Judith Hunter
Production Editor, Corporate Profiles: Una FitzSimons
Sales Representatives, Corporate Profiles: Clive Bates, Richard Dixon
Editorial Assistants: Kathy M. Brown, Marcie Goldstein, Pamela M. Juneman,
  Pat Pittman
Layout Artist: Ellen Ifrah
Layout, Corporate Profiles: Mari Catherine Preimesberger

Library of Congress Cataloging-in-Publication Data

Gagetta, Vince, 1932-
  Pittsburgh, fulfilling its destiny.

  "Produced in cooperation with the Greater Pittsburgh Chamber of
Commerce."
  Includes index.
  1. Pittsburgh (Pa.)—History. 2. Pittsburgh
(Pa.)—Description. 3. Pittsburgh (Pa.)—Industries.
I. Marcello, Beth. II. Mendelson, Abby. III. Greater
Pittsburgh Chamber of Commerce. IV. Title.
F159.P657G34   1986        974.8'86        86-22382
ISBN 0-89781-188-7

*Endpapers:* **Market Square circa 1930; courtesy, University of Pittsburgh**

*Title page:* **Golden Triangle, © Jack A. Wolf**

*Facing page:* **Concert at PPG Place, © Jack A. Wolf**

# Contents

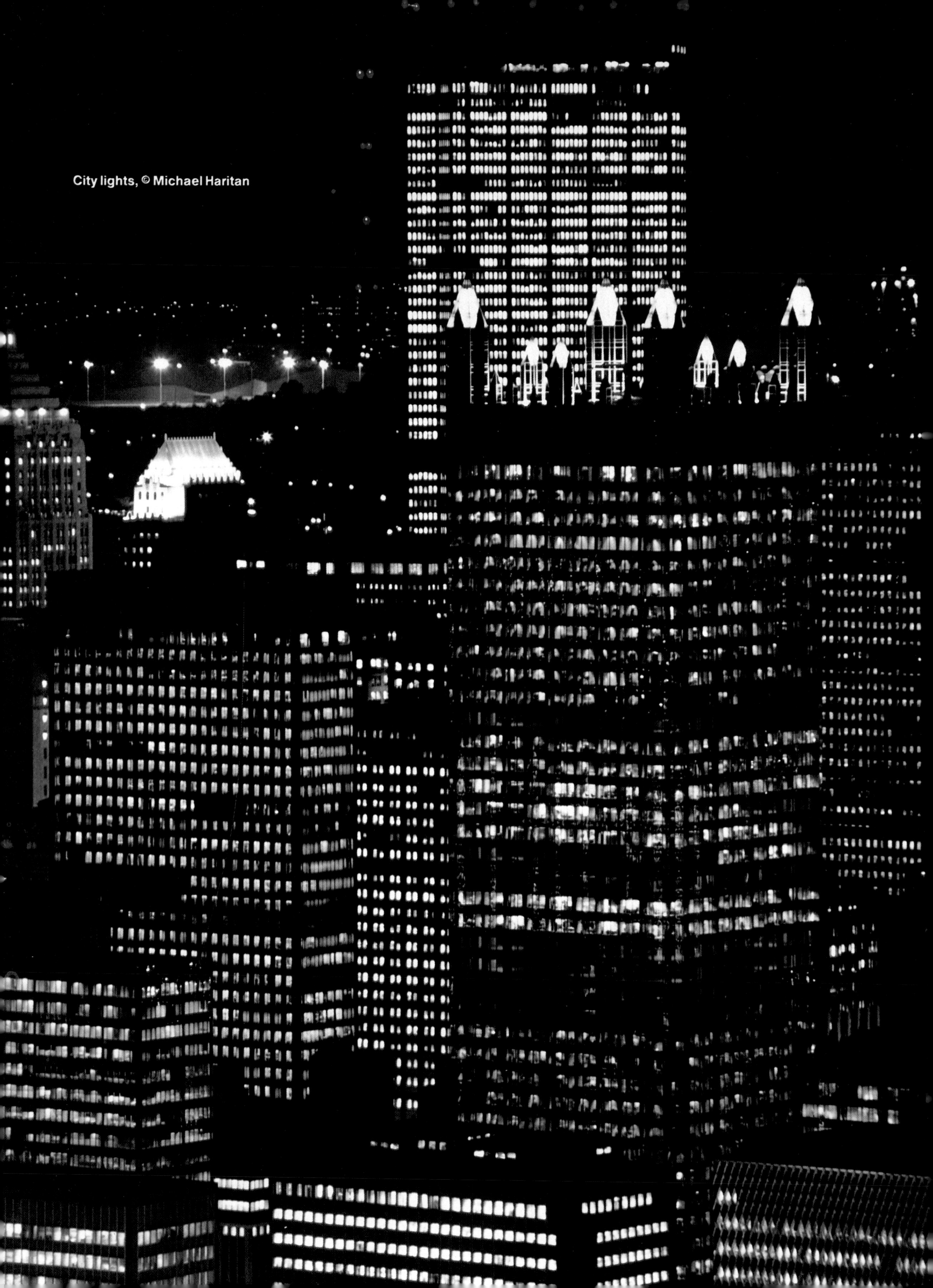

City lights, © Michael Haritan

# *Foreword*

RICHARD S. CALIGUIRI

With considerable pride we present this great new book showcasing Greater Pittsburgh.

*Pittsburgh: Fulfilling Its Destiny* is today's story of America's Most Livable Community—economy, image, and quality of life transformed and focused squarely on the goals for progress. The book details stunning changes and envisions a bright future. It is a testimony to the ever-present determination of Pittsburghers to realize their dreams.

Hometown readers will find in these pages the comfortable familiarity that predominates Pittsburgh living, for the book touches on nearly every important aspect of community life. Visitors and newcomers will enjoy learning about the city, Allegheny County, and the region. And those who have had little previous contact with Pittsburgh will find our community to be SURPRISING and EXCITING. *Pittsburgh: Fulfilling Its Destiny* reflects the deep values of our people, their honesty, and their commitment.

THOMAS J. FOERSTER

*Pittsburgh: Fulfilling Its Destiny* is a salute to the people of Pittsburgh, but it is also intended to show non-Pittsburghers the great things happening here. The book will enhance the perspective of everyone who reads it.

We would like to thank the authors of *Pittsburgh: Fulfilling Its Destiny,* the photographers whose works are displayed here, the Partners in Progress sponsors, Chamber of Commerce President Justin Horan, and all those who worked to bring this book to publication. Most important, we thank the citizens of Greater Pittsburgh for being themselves, our community's greatest asset.

Richard S. Caliguiri
Mayor
City of Pittsburgh

Thomas J. Foerster
Chairman
Allegheny County
Board of
Commissioners

Robert C. Milsom
1986-87 Chairman
Greater Pittsburgh
Chamber of
Commerce

ROBERT C. MILSOM

George Segal's "Tightrope
Walker" at Scaife Gallery,
© Herb Ferguson

# *Acknowledgments*

The author gratefully acknowledges the contributions made in the preparation of the manuscript by the following individuals: Jay D. Aldridge, John M. Arthur, William Block, Richard L. Burkman, Richard S. Caliguiri, Raymond R. Christman, Donald Clay, James Colker, Richard M. Cyert, David Donohoe, James R. Duffy, Tom Foerster, Charles R. Goetz, Daniel A. Goetz, Richard Gorman, Justin T. Horan, Jack Hoy, Robert Imperata, Donald Jones, Jacques Kahn, Warren Kimball, Jr., Alan R. Kugler, Leo R. McDonough, Hiram Milton, Wesley W. Posvar, Norman Robertson, John Robin, Jack Robinette, James C. Roddey, Richard P. Simmons, George M. Stewart, and Gerald J. Voros. Thanks are due also to the staffs of the Carnegie Library of Pittsburgh and the Oakmont Carnegie Library, as well as countless others whose information, advice, guidance, and direction provided much insight and understanding about Pittsburgh and its people.

**Gateway Center during the Three Rivers Arts Festival, © Herb Ferguson**

# PART

# 1

# Yesterday
# and Today

*This page:* Seven views of old Pittsburgh; courtesy, University of Pittsburgh

*Preceding page:* Grand Concourse Restaurant at Station Square, © Harry Edelman

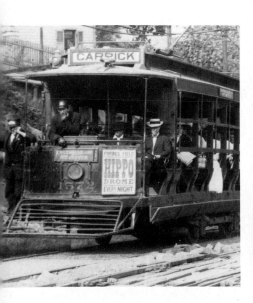

14

**Above, left to right:**
**Three Rivers Stadium,**
**© Herb Ferguson**
**Mt. Washington houses,**
**© Jack A. Wolf**
**Strip District street scene,**
**© Norm Schumm**

*Left:* **Pittsburgh today,**
**© Jack A. Wolf**

*Below, left to right:*
**Downtown subway, © Herb**
**Ferguson**
**Sixteenth Street Bridge,**
**© Jack A. Wolf**
**Mellon Square, © Michael**
**Haritan**

# CHAPTER *1*

## *Interlude*

Where the Allegheny and Monongahela rivers converge into the grand Ohio, a fortune-blessed city has willed a startling transformation. With civic pride, resilience, and a determined spirit, her citizens have produced one of the most dramatic and far-reaching transformations in twentieth-century urban America.

Pittsburgh isn't the Smoky City anymore. And visitors no longer liken her, as British writer James Parton did in the 1830s, to "Hell with the lid off."

The skies are bluer now, and the rivers run cleaner and clearer than they ever did in the glory days of steel, when Pittsburghers gladly suffered the Smoky City gibes, preoccupied as they were with the city's other, more glamorous nickname—Steel Capital of the World. This was the title that the locals wore with pride and spoke of with reverence. It was the title that the rest of the world recognized and envied and could not challenge.

When steel was king in Pittsburgh, the air was thick with the smoke and the stench of the mills, coke ovens, and foundries. When steel was king, coal was its vigorous and vital consort, its indispensable helpmate. Then Pittsburgh's rivers and railroads strained to satisfy the inexhaustible appetites of that mighty industry with their constant cargoes of coal, coke, and iron ore.

When steel was king, its realm was vast and awesome, covering almost all of southwestern Pennsylvania surrounding Pittsburgh and invading nearby areas of eastern Ohio and West Virginia as well. Boundaries and borders were irrelevant to the giant of steelmaking. As the hegemony of steel spread, local characteristics tended to blur, so that the look, feel, and smell of

one steel town was barely distinguishable from the look, feel, and smell of any other.

And everywhere that steel was made there was the dust—a thin layer of fine, gritty red dust that settled on everything and everybody, bringing rawness to the throat, tears to the eyes, and a grim, determined smile to the lips of those who stood up to the heat, danger, and challenge of steelmaking every day, producing what came to symbolize a rich, mighty, and powerful industry, the steel that proudly bore the stamp "Made in Pittsburgh."

When wives complained of the dirt and grit and odors that seeped into their homes and made housekeeping in Pittsburgh an exercise in drudgery, they were reminded—and not always patiently—that smoke in the smokestacks meant money in the bank. And money in the bank (it was never necessary to point out) meant food on the table, clothes on the back, shoes on the feet, and a chance, for the younger generation, of a better life away from the mills and rail yards and mines.

**Refinery, © Walt Urbina**

The smoke—at least most of it—is gone now, swept away by governmental and corporate action, driven off by the unyielding pressures of civic pride, as well as social and environmental concerns. And although the smoke and the smells were banished years before Pittsburgh's coveted title of Steel Capital of the World became obsolete, there are still some around who insist that the death knell for the area's "dirty but honest" industries was sounded by the first piece of smoke control legislation, enacted by the City Council in the early 1940s. The diehards are not swayed by the fact that after World War II, when city and state laws regulating air quality were first earnestly and effectively enforced, twenty years passed before the major markets for the American steel industry began shifting westward, away from the hills and hollows of the Pittsburgh area to the flatlands of Indiana and Illinois. The diehards maintain that smoke control—not changing markets or intensified competitive forces—killed Pittsburgh's steel industry. That is, smoke control and image.

Pittsburgh did have an image problem. The city emerged from the war years even grimier and dirtier than it had entered that era. And Pittsburgh's image as a mill town, a coal town, a railroad and river town, a gritty working town, was out of sync with the vision that civic, business, and government leaders then had for the future. Those leaders saw the need for a more hospita-

*Above:* **Roundhill country farm,** © Michael Haritan

*Left:* **Bridge into the city,** © Jack A. Wolf

ble environment, and the Pittsburgh of the 1940s and early 1950s, with its industrial slums and generally rundown condition, was not in any position to fulfill that need. They wanted a place where a man could go to his office Downtown and put in a day's work without bringing along a change of shirt to wear in the afternoon—his morning shirt having by that time been soiled by the soot and the grime of the city's mills and factories.

Two men are credited with instigating the massive effort (smoke control being only a part of it) that transformed the Smoky City into America's Renaissance City, that replaced industrial slums and eyesores with sparkling skyscrapers and parks and open spaces, that created a Golden Triangle out of what was once an urban sprawl. These two instigators—unlikely partners—were Richard King Mellon and David Leo Lawrence, the financier and the mayor. They had little in common, except power—and the will and know-how to use it.

Renaissances do, indeed, make strange bedfellows, and Mellon and Lawrence were unlikely bunkmates, to say the least. Mellon was a conservative Republican, millionaire, member of a distinguished patrician family, philanthropist, Protestant. Lawrence's origins were more humble; he was a liberal Democrat politician, pragmatist, iron-fisted product of the ward wars, Irish Catholic.

In other times, in other places, Lawrence and Mellon would scarcely have rubbed elbows. But in postwar Pittsburgh, its economy stifled by a thick layer of dirt and ugliness, the two rubbed more than merely elbows. They rubbed wills and flexed their considerable muscles, and what they willed was done. Of course they did not work alone: they commanded a small army of planners, dreamers, and visionaries, and led a powerful force of doers and achievers in the private and public sectors. The whole thing worked because Mellon and Lawrence had the power to make it work, no questions asked—and hardly any invited.

Lawrence and Mellon get most of the credit for creating a new and brighter Pittsburgh. Yet rumor has it that there was a formidable power behind one of the thrones. One apocryphal story has it that the real impetus behind Mellon's involvement was his wife, Constance Prosser Mellon, who reportedly gave her husband an ultimatum to get the stench and the filth of the city cleaned up. Otherwise she, and presumably her wealthy and

*Above:* **Painted faces,
© Jack A. Wolf**

*Facing page:* **USX corporate headquarters building,
© Herb Ferguson**

influential friends, would boycott the place, would refuse to venture Downtown to shop or socialize, and would take to their estates in peaceful, pastoral, pollution-free Ligonier, fifty-five miles to the southeast. In response her husband redoubled his efforts, and the unique public-private partnership of Mellon and Lawrence forged ahead—or so the story goes.

When the Renaissance came the smoke went, along with the dust, grime, and poisonous air. The effects of the ambitious $500-million program are still very much in evidence. In Pittsburgh now there is no need to keep streetlights burning until well past the noon hour in a valiant effort to cut through the smog and illuminate city sidewalks. Now one shirt normally lasts a full day in any Downtown office and remains clean and presentable enough to be worn into the evening.

No, Pittsburgh is not the Smoky City anymore. But with the smoke and the smell of steel production went the security and stability—more imagined than real, as it turns out—of Pittsburgh's economic past. Pittsburgh today, having achieved the

**Station Square, © Walt Urbina**

Renaissance of urban renewal, is a city at a crossroads, a region searching for a new destiny, an area tied emotionally to its past while it diligently pursues its future. For Pittsburgh and the Greater Pittsburgh area, this is a time of transition, a telling period of adjustment. This moment is the interlude between the acts of a great and powerful drama with the grandest scenes yet to be played.

Yes, Pittsburgh today is cleaner and brighter. It is also less dependent on the small group of closely related industries that previously controlled its economic well-being. And it is considerably smaller.

The nine-county southwestern Pennsylvania region that constitutes Greater Pittsburgh lost 6 percent of its population between 1960 and 1980. In a ten-year period ending in 1984, the City of Pittsburgh proper lost more than 56,000 residents, and the most recent census ranked Pittsburgh thirty-third in size among U.S. cities. As a metropolitan region, Greater Pittsburgh ranks fifteenth in size in the nation.

The area's declining population reflects dwindling job opportunities in the heavy industries that have traditionally served as Pittsburgh's economic base. Some 100,000 jobs were lost in the region from 1980 to 1983, and 91,000 of them were in manufacturing. Fully half of all jobs in the region's once-booming steel industry have vanished, probably forever. Today not a single ton of steel is produced within Pittsburgh's city limits, and little of it is being made in the surrounding area.

For Pittsburgh and Pittsburghers steel is but a memory of what used to be, of the glory days of a glorious industry, of good times and fat paychecks and hard but fruitful toil. The manufacture of conventional, or basic, steel is not likely ever to play the same role in Pittsburgh's economic future as it played in the area's past, when it was the predominant and preeminent industry, the one so many other industries depended upon.

But there is another steel industry, the specialty steel industry. Although production and employment in specialty steel have also declined over the past few years (as they have in just about every area of American manufacturing), this industry still plays an important role in Pittsburgh's economy.

In fact, American production of specialty steels, particularly stainless steel, is concentrated in Greater Pittsburgh. So the area can still lay claim to being a steel capital. It is—and has been—the Specialty Steel Capital of the World, a distinction and an honor that keeps Pittsburgh prominent among the world's industrial manufacturing centers.

Moreover, even basic steel still plays a role in Pittsburgh's economy, although the city's skies no longer glow red at night reflecting the mills' furnaces. Many area businesses and industries that were formed to serve basic steel still serve it, only now their best customers are far from home, in other parts of the country and in other parts of the world. While the basic steel industry in Pittsburgh is not the powerful and potent giant it used to be, companies and whole industries that grew up and grew rich in its service still prosper here.

It is ironic that many of the new steelmaking technologies that have enabled producers elsewhere to compete so successfully were developed in the Pittsburgh area. More ironic still is the widespread perception of the steel industry as hopelessly low-tech and out of date. In fact steel is fast developing into one of the most technologically advanced and demanding industries on earth. Pittsburgh, in its quest for a high-tech future, could do worse than concentrate on steel.

But in Pittsburgh now, steel has declined. The story of steel in this city having passed its climax, Pittsburghers are preparing a new script. And the best part of this new story is that it is true. In this scenario, declines in population, changing economic bases, shifts in industrial makeup, and geographic advantage are understood in an entirely different light.

A close look at population statistics as a measurement of economic activity reveals that in the twenty-year period between 1960 and 1980, when the population of the Pittsburgh area fell by 6 percent, the region's work force grew to a record high of one million. Four-fifths of these men and women are engaged in nonmanufacturing pursuits, ample evidence that the shift from a regional economy based on heavy industry and the manufacture of durable goods to a service-based economy has been fully realized. Pittsburgh may not be the Steel Capital of the World anymore, but neither do its economic fortunes rise and fall inexorably with those of a single industry.

Service is serving Pittsburgh well, even though wages in many such industries cannot match those provided by industrial firms, particularly in the areas of unskilled and semiskilled labor. Nor do service companies employ people in the vast numbers that steel mills used to. But as service businesses develop in the area, more professional and management-level opportunities arise, and they do carry with them heftier paychecks.

The impact of these service firms on Pittsburgh's economy is being felt increasingly. In recent years, both large and small companies engaged in service businesses have added an impressive 115,000 new jobs to the area's economy. In 1984 alone thirty-five new firms were established, bringing with them 2,335

new jobs and more than fifty-two million dollars in payroll.

Not only are the numbers changing, so is the composition of the work force. White collars have slowly overtaken blue as the predominant force in Pittsburgh's economy. Now white-collar workers outnumber their blue-collared colleagues by four to one, while in 1950 the ratio was one to one.

The fates destined Pittsburgh to be located in the northeastern United States, away from the sun and fun and the current golden opportunities of the Sun Belt. This may appear to be a disadvantage to Pittsburghers yearning for a resurgence of the economy. Yet fresh water is fast becoming the most valuable resource in the world, and Pittsburgh is blessed with what may be the world's best fresh-water supply. As severe water shortages and rationing measures beset other parts of the country, Pitts-

*This page:* Montage of Pittsburgh workers:
© Jack A. Wolf (top left),
© Herb Ferguson (top right and bottom)

*Facing page:* View from Bigelow Boulevard, © Mary Jane Bent

**Pittsburgh Steelers,** © **Herb Ferguson**

*Facing page:* **Scaife Gallery fountains,** © **Harry Edelman**

burgh, with its abundant water supply, and such efforts as a recently undertaken $240-million rehabilitation of the municipal system, will be poised to recapture its place in the economic sun.

Like many cities in the Northeast and Midwest, Pittsburgh has been identified as a low-tech area looking for a high-tech future. The glamorous worlds of technology and computer science seem marvelous indeed. Yet there are those who point out that Pittsburgh does not need to look forward to a high-tech future since it already enjoys a high-tech present. High technology is very much a fact of everyday life for the majority of companies doing business in Pittsburgh—and everywhere else in the world today.

Pittsburgh's ambitions to expand its high-tech capabilities are wisely tempered by a realistic assessment of the area's resources and talents and of the needs of the sought-after markets. It is unlikely, for example, that the Pittsburgh area will become a major center for computer hardware manufacturing. There are computer manufacturing firms flourishing in the area, but this industry has not shown signs of becoming a dominant force in the economy. On the other hand, the development of computer software for industrial applications is more in keeping with the needs and wants of the markets Pittsburgh is best prepared to service, and this activity is increasingly taking hold.

Pittsburgh is also making a name for itself as a center for the development and manufacture of industrial robots and for robot-

ics research. Extensive academic research in robotics technology, conducted at Carnegie-Mellon University, as well as practical applications of that technology by Pittsburgh firms pioneering the development of industrial robots, have added great luster to the area's economic crown.

Pittsburgh's high-tech future may not be unlimited, but it is bright. High technology is already playing a vital role in the economy, and the level of activity is definitely rising. Between 1981 and 1984, more than 400 high-tech firms set up operations in the Pittsburgh area, adding 40,000 new jobs to the economy. Pittsburgh continues to build on its considerable established strengths. It remains the third largest city for corporate headquarters in the United States, outranked only by New York and Chicago. Fifteen Fortune 500 industrial corporations call the city home.

Pittsburgh is second only to New York in the amount of investment capital controlled by resident corporations.

Increasingly, knowledge is becoming one of the area's most important and profitable products, and its economic worth may well surpass that of steel during that industry's heyday. The Pittsburgh area constitutes the third largest research and development center in the country and offers public, private, and education-based R&D facilities.

Banking in Pittsburgh is a $47-billion industry, and the city ranks as the fourth-richest financial center in the country. Its two largest banks are also the state's largest, numbering among the top 100 nationwide.

Health care, too, is a major industry. Health service industries employ some 85,000 people—a 50 percent increase over the last ten years. And the city is fast developing into a world-renowned center for organ transplantation.

Pittsburgh is the tenth-largest office market in the United States. Renaissance II, a $4-billion-plus program that has added several skyscrapers Downtown and is revitalizing city neighborhoods as well, put more than six million square feet of prime office space on the market, with another 1,800,000 square feet expected soon, along with 800,000 square feet of renovated space.

These big numbers befit a city of the size, scope, and importance of Pittsburgh. Even so, Pittsburghers have become accustomed to "thinking smaller" of late—not in ways that limit outlook, restrict ambition, or temper goals, but in recognition of the new opportunities that the future holds.

The giant corporations, which ruled the roost for generations and employed hordes of Pittsburghers, continue as a considerable presence—economic, social, and political. At the same time, small business is becoming the area's employer of record. Fully 90 percent of all new jobs are created by small business, and the small-business owner and manager, with an entrepreneurial outlook and enthusiastic spirit, is becoming a dominant force alongside the corporate elite.

"Thinking smaller" is a realistic approach to the problems and the challenges facing Greater Pittsburgh. Thinking smaller means playing to the region's great strengths, capabilities, considerable resources, and tremendous talents. It connotes control, assurance, and an understanding of marketplace forces. Thinking smaller means forgoing quick fixes to concentrate on permanent solutions. Thinking smaller calls for a firm sense of purpose, an understanding of the likely direction to pursue prosperity. It requires imagination, creativity, commitment, and dedication to realistic goals.

While "thinking smaller" is positive and realistic, "thinking small" is out of character, out of the question, for Pittsburghers. These are people who have been challenged by uncertainties, changing markets, economic instability, declining numbers, and an aging infrastructure. Yet Pittsburghers survive. They are doing what they know how to do best: battling back. Few cities could withstand the loss of 100,000 jobs in a four-year period. Yet Pittsburghers are on their feet, ready to fight on, to win back their lives and livelihoods by an act of collective will.

Pittsburghers—whether they live inside the city limits or in rural areas remote from the Golden Triangle—are a tough people, a people of character, stamina, and strength. Their toughness is born of hard work, a rugged industrial heritage, and determination. They have undergone periods of adjustment before and have enjoyed a number of revitalizations, some more successful than others. They have seen hopes dimmed, promises broken, opportunities disappear, and old orders by the dozens crumble. Mill hands, factory hands, farmhands, or hands that control the destinies of daring enterprises, Pittsburghers bring a rock-hard

*Above:* **Point State Park,**
© **Herb Ferguson**

*Right:* **Ethnic Parade,**
© **Herb Ferguson**

*Pages 36-37:* **Three Rivers
Regatta,** © **Herb Ferguson**

stability to the entire region. Among its many resources, both natural and acquired, this city has none more valuable, more key to its survival, more central to its hopes for renewal and development than its people.

Many Pittsburghers are of immigrant stock, and perhaps for this reason their dreams are for the future, not of the past. While they are dreamers and visionaries, they are distinguished by practicality and a firm grasp on reality. They are doers and achievers who rarely lose sight of their dreams for creating something better, for attaining something more. They seek only the chance to prove themselves. And together Pittsburghers bring to their city a tireless vitality, a powerful force for accomplishment that will soon overshadow all the glories of the past.

## Pittsburgh's *Lunchbagable* Downtown

By Abby Mendelson

When Rand McNally's *Places Rated Almanac* hailed Pittsburgh as America's Most Livable City, a number of factors were carefully measured: quality and cost of housing, education, medical care, and the like. Nevertheless, one of the factors that residents rate high but that rarely receives publicity is a Downtown that's small, walkable (or subwayable when the weather's bad), and, in the words of one office-tower denizen, "lunch-bag-able." Indeed, there are so many places to brown-bag it, to sit out under a sparkling blue sky and fleecy white clouds and eat lunch, that it is not uncommon to see one's entire office staff, from executive VPs to the guys in the mail room, munching and sunning in the early afternoon.

There's a good reason for the high number of quality public spaces in our human-scale Downtown. It is the product of careful—even soulful—urban planning, first accomplished during the original Renaissance in the 1950s. In fact, the city's first redevel-

Mellon Park picnic,
© Michael Haritan

39

opment project (and one of the very first in the nation) was predicated on the idea of placing a massive park at Pittsburgh's Point and building the adjacent Gateway Center office buildings in a context of greenery. Benches, fountains, and walkways abound.

The spirit spread throughout Downtown—and through the years. Now city ordinance requires that each new project must include open space, which is most often used for plazas of some sort, virtually all with benches or chairs.

There's good reason for this, says David Lewis, one of the city's premier architects and urban planners. Born in South Africa and now a longtime Pittsburgher, Lewis has worked all around the city, sensitizing people to the value of good architecture and urban design. He heads the firm that is codesigning and co-developing Liberty Center, the new hotel and office complex adjacent to the David L. Lawrence Convention Center.

''There are very few cities in America like Pittsburgh,'' Lewis says. ''Other cities do not use the topography and geography inherent in the land as form-giving features. They use geometry instead, and therefore their downtowns are infinitely expandable, limited only by man-made zoning.

''Pittsburgh, on the other hand, was shaped by this very powerful topography; it forms a mini-Manhattan on a spit of land.'' Lewis gestures: the Allegheny and Monongahela rivers come to the sharp Point. At the triangle's base, Downtown is hemmed in by the deep cut of the Hill. "Each of the rivers has its own grid," Lewis adds, "and the confluence of those two gives the city its macroscale, while individual design elements remain in microscale. The mix of those two is the key to making Downtown livable and a joy to walk around.

"The density makes it like a village. While Downtown is the hub of great corporations, the street life is that of a small town. There are parks and plazas full of people, and shopkeepers who know their customers. You can't go a block without running into someone you know. That is not only a joy, but it also makes Downtown safe.

"In a larger sense, Downtown's livable scale is more than pleasant. It also helps Pittsburgh remain economically viable. At one time Pittsburgh existed because it was resource-specific: it gloried in its coal and rivers. Now the city is a communications network, and to survive it must attract top people. A city has to be extremely livable to do that, and it has to have a comprehensive, livable downtown. And eating lunch outside symbolizes that like nothing else."

Of the numerous Downtown bring-your-own-lunch places, Lewis cites three as truly first-rate: Market Square, Heinz Plaza, and North Shore. This is not to overlook the many spots available where blankets may be spread out, such as the great expanse of Point Park, nor such notable favorites as Mellon Square, where sculpture and cascading waters provide the backdrop for summer noontimes spent listening to hot rock or cool jazz. Myriad lunchers perch on every bench, chair, and flower planter in PPG Place and throughout Gateway Center—even in the County Courthouse courtyard, dubbed Katie's Park, after the wife of a former county commissioner who championed efforts to turn an eyesore parking lot into one of Downtown's most charming parks.

*Market Square.* The site of a market that was torn down nearly thirty years ago, Market Square nestles comfortably next to the dark, mirrored majesty of PPG Place. Yet it retains a strong street-level shopping emphasis, with restaurants, taverns, and the like. It is literally a crossroads for bus routes and people, and at noon it is delightfully democratic, hosting everyone from

down-and-outers to up-and-comers. Many feed the pigeons, which perpetually circle the square. Although it is relatively small, Market Square has become a prime spot for noontime concerts, festive events, and rallies of all types—from politics to the Pirates, who came there to celebrate after the 1979 World Series.

"I love Market Square because of its mix of people," Lewis says. "It's extra rich, and so is the mix of businesses, from the hardware store to the fashion shop. And the pigeons! There's a direct correlation between informality, success, and pigeons. Because pigeons only go where people are lunching and eating popcorn and enjoying themselves. Pigeons are a measure of success."

*Heinz Plaza.* Pittsburgh lost a landmark five-and-dime store, to Heinz Plaza, a crisply designed and carefully appointed addition to Heinz Hall. It has five features that Market Square does not: trees, water (in the form of a wall-wide waterfall), food service, a lockable gate (for private parties), and flossy ambience. Heinz Plaza is always tastefully crowded, never dirty, and is a delightful place to spend the noon hour.

"One great attraction of Heinz Plaza," Lewis says, "is the presence and the sound of water. And with the trees you can sit in shade, filtered sunlight, or full light. And you can move the furniture into groupings, which is a plus."

**Left:** One Mellon Bank Center, © Jack A. Wolf

**Right:** Buffet under the balcony, © Jack A. Wolf

*North Shore.* Although not officially part of Downtown, North Shore is on the near North Side and a short walk across the Sixth or Seventh Street bridges. Featuring Allegheny Landing Park, North Shore is an urban square with a fountain, sculpture, and a long grassy slope down to the Allegheny River. The park was designed by landscape architect Jack Seay; the entire North Shore complex, including the office buildings, was designed by Lewis' Urban Design Associates. The area is nicely lit at night, and the river glows with the lights of Downtown. There is hardly a more beautiful—or more romantic—spot in the city.

The conceptual model for the North Shore design was "the Jeffersonian square, a public open space that provides a little piece of countryside within the city. There is always a central feature (in this case a fountain), diagonal paths leading to it, and containing lawns and trees. In addition, we ringed the North Shore with a white colonnade in homage to Jefferson. Then we let the plaza issue outward, to the meadow, to the Allegheny, and"—he gestures with a sweep of the arm—"to everything!"

*Abby Mendelson is a Pittsburgh-based writer and editor whose work has appeared in numerous local and national publications and includes a contributing editor's column in* Pittsburgh Magazine.

# *Thirty Ways to a Great Summer in Pittsburgh's Parks*

By Abby Mendelson

During the winter months, yes, there is always a long, snaky line of cross-country skiers traversing Pittsburgh's larger parks. And the early spring pastels and late fall foliage are wonders to behold. But let's face it: Pittsburgh's parks are the best in summertime. That's when the family can drop by a place like New Frick and stroll the nature trails in the hollow, watch a Little League baseball game on the upper field, follow the running course, race the pooch up the verdant hills, or unpack a picnic basket and let Junior work out on the slides, swings, and monkey bars. And it's all for free.

In some ways, though, the parks' best aspect is not what you can do in any one or another of them on a lazy Sunday but, instead, what you can do in all of them throughout the summer. The city's Department of Parks and Recreation (Citiparks) sponsors all the events, most of which are without charge (some have a nominal fee).

**North Shore, © Jack A. Wolf**

**Precision Jump Competition, Beaver Valley Sky Divers Club, © Herb Ferguson**

Here are thirty or so ways to spend your summer.

1. *Watch a movie.* The King Estate in Highland Park shows free art history films. Not a bad way to bone up on art.

2. *Shoot hoops.* You can practice layups and half-court hooks just about anywhere, or participate in the Invitational Basketball Tournament, for men over twenty-one.

3. *Launch a boat.* Free, at the South Side Riverfront Park boat launching ramp (where you can also fish).

4. *Eat.* At the Farmers' Markets they feature homegrown, home-baked, homemade produce, pies, cheese, and more. Five nights a week, four sites throughout the city.

5. *Watch a movie, part II.* Lawn chairs, blankets, and feature films in Schenley and Highland parks: Sundays, Tuesdays, and Wednesdays. The program runs the gamut from *Ghostbusters* to *Pee Wee's Big Adventure* to *The Hound of the Baskervilles*. Popcorn not included in the free admission.

6. *Find a bargain.* A flea market operates every Sunday at Allegheny Commons on the North Side.

7. *Shake, rattle, and roll.* There are noontime jazz, rock, reggae, or what-have-you concerts in Mellon Square, Market Square, the plaza in PPG Place, and Gateway Center.

8. *Smell the flowers.* Phipps Conservatory, Oakland, features a dazzling array of flowers and special events.

9. *Pitch horseshoes.* The Pittsburgh Senior Games have boccie, golf, darts, backgammon, horseshoes, and awards!

10. *Be entertained.* Five nights a week throughout the city there are free performances, including the Civic Light Opera, River City Brass Band, and others, such as Bounce the Clown,

Mademoiselle Ooo La La, and their dog Sparkplug.

11. *Swim.* There are only thirty-four free pools in the City of Pittsburgh, and they are open every day of the week during the summer. There are also swimming and lifesaving classes, and four swimming, diving, and water meets.

12. *Soar (musically).* The Pittsburgh Symphony plays half a dozen free concerts at the Point.

13. *Learn to lob.* Tennis classes, clinics, and courts are available all across the city. There are also leagues and tournaments, including the USTA-sanctioned Classic, the Family Challenge, the Lipton Tea Mixed Doubles, and more than you can shake a racket at.

14. *Hobnob with lions and tigers and bears.* Oh my, the new zoo has a natural-habitat-type exhibit with the above, plus elephants, snakes, sharks, and more.

15. *Grow a green thumb.* There's produce aplenty to go with gardening classes and a gardener's hotline. There's even the Great Tomato Race, which features a cash prize for the year's first ripe tomato produced within city limits.

16. *Pace yourself.* The Pittsburgh Marathon is only for the hardy. It's 26.2 miles of world-class hills, valleys, and cheering spectators.

17. *Fly a kite.* Anytime, anyplace, but most especially at Kite Flight, the annual competition with prizes for best decorated, highest flying, best performing, and more.

18. *Flip a flying disc.* Bring Bowser to the Ashley Whippet Invitational, where the best dog-and-human team will go on to the regional finals in Philadelphia.

19. *Find a bargain, part II.* The Antiques and Collectibles Fair convenes in Highland Park on the first Sunday of each month. Like the Pittsburgh Marathon, this is the real thing, organized by pros. (For gleanings from dusty attics, see item 6 above.)

20. *Run for daylight.* The Arco Jesse Owens Games are a full-day full-blown track-and-field meet for kids six to fourteen at South High Stadium.

21. *Roll your own.* The Great Ride is a noncompetitive family bike ride held in Schenley Park. It is more festival than race, and is hot—hot-air balloons, hot dogs, even hot T-shirts. There are bicycle touring events, from the fifty-miler to the six-miler, big-wheel competitions for kids, even an all-terrain trail tour for

those with stout hearts and friends who are chiropractors.

22. *Water the roots.* Pittsburgh is a grand conglomerate of neighborhoods, and there's a different community festival virtually every week in the summer. Places with names like Bloomfield, Beltzhoover, and Brookline celebrate their uniqueness, heritage, and, best of all, their food.

23. *Have Bach, Beethoven, and brunch.* No, the programs aren't limited to only those august composers—upstarts like Gershwin make it as well. There's no more pleasant Sunday morning than a concert in the Mellon Park Rose Garden, sunlight provided and victuals available for purchase.

24. *Start your engines.* The Pittsburgh Vintage Grand Prix features more than 100 pre-1959 sports cars racing over a 2.2-mile course in Schenley Park. Sanctioned by the Vintage Sports Car Club of America, it is the only authentic road course in the country. For those who can't bear such high-speed excitement, there is a display of classic cars.

25. *Brush up your Shakespeare.* Works of the Bard are performed on Flagstaff Hill, Schenley Park.

26. *Run for daylight, part II.* In some ways The Great Race, Pittsburgh's 10K race, is more club than competition, for the 1985 version had well in excess of 12,000 registrants. And it's short enough that everyone comes home a hero.

27. *Let the children play.* During the Pittsburgh Children's Festival of Performing Arts, there are stage productions, strolling players, international groups, and more.

28. *Play ball.* Softball teams abound, of course, but the premier horsehide event is "The Slickest Infield" competition. Four-person teams whip the ball around in an eighteen-move sequence of throws, pivots, and catches. Best time wins: four locations, two age groups, and both genders.

29. *Enter hands and feet.* There are no dogs at the Hackey Sack and Frisbee Festival. It's only people this time, and distance, accuracy, and catching count.

30. *Skip rope.* Double Dutch, the two-rope jump-rope competition, is recommended only for the nimble-footed.

... or go to the tot lots, recreation centers, basketball programs, and the open spaces, acres and acres of quiet green space where you can walk, think, run, collect leaves, eat a snow cone, and relax *ad infinitum*.

Before we bid *adieu* to summer fun in Pittsburgh, duty requires us to say that you can frolic in many public spaces other than city parks.

*The rivers.* Time was when the Three Rivers meant smoky coal barges and dour old salts. No longer. Allegheny County is a national leader in pleasure boat registration, and the seminal water sport event is the Three Rivers Regatta, a July weekend's worth of everything imaginable. From Formula One powerboat races to inner tubing to the howl-a-minute anything-that-floats contest, the Regatta is not to be missed.

*County parks.* Just as the city is covered in tree-filled parks, it is ringed by fine county facilities: such as spacious, bike-trailed South Park (with fairgrounds) and North Park (with stables), three monster wave pools (with artificial-turf sunning areas and rentable rubber rafts), Hartwood Acres (an estate turned outdoor performing arts center), and Boyce Park, which features skiing in the winter. But, hey, the parks are for *summer.*

*Above:* South Side playground, © Michael Haritan

*Facing page:* Churchill Golf Course, © Herb Ferguson

# Livability: A Measure of Satisfaction

It was March 1985 when Rand McNally's *Places Rated Almanac* appeared in the nation's bookstores. As far as many Pittsburghers were concerned, it was Year One, the start of something new and exhilarating for the entire Pittsburgh area. Subtitled *Your Guide to Finding the Best Places to Live in America,* the Rand McNally almanac rated Pittsburgh at the top of the list.

This recognition could not have come at a better time. With its image as an industrial superpower faded, the area needed a boost. A new title offered something to be proud of, something to brag about. The town that in years past had dubbed itself the Smoky City, Steel Capital of the World, City of Champions, now was being recognized and praised with a new name—America's Most Livable City—by one of the best-known publishers in the country.

The message was out at last. Pittsburgh is a fine place to live: a homey, pleasant, reasonable, comfortable, safe, unpretentious place. And despite its industrial history and heritage and image, a clean little town.

The place does grow on you. It is big enough to allow room for stretching and to satisfy a yearning for occasional anonymity, yet small enough to promote trust, honest relationships, and a happy familiarity. These qualities apparently won over the Rand McNally researchers and prompted Pittsburgh's selection for this honor. Small-town values and virtues, preserved in a big

**Outskirts of Pittsburgh,
© Jack A. Wolf**

city, had a great deal to do with winning the crown.

While joy abounded in Pittsburgh, its number-one ranking for livability was not cordially received by some other cities, which felt that they deserved the prize. Civic boosters elsewhere were not soothed by the assurances of Richard Boyer and David Savageau, authors of the *Places Rated Almanac,* that the "image of a smoky, noisy, blast furnace of a city" was long out of date. The choice of Pittsburgh, the authors conceded, might come as "a surprise" to uninformed out-of-towners.

Boyer and Savageau understated this point. Many were not merely surprised, they were startled, shocked, and in some cases downright outraged. How could any place without ocean views, year-round sunshine, heavy doses of cosmopolitanism and sophistication, and a blazing economy dare call itself most livable? The answer is that the Rand McNally research went beyond attributes that make good brochure copy, examining a range of factors that affect day-to-day quaiity of life. Put another way: year-round sunshine is nice, but it isn't everything.

The livability determination took into account climate and environment, housing, health, crime, transportation, education, the arts, recreation, and economics. In addition to its positive advantages in these areas, Pittsburgh scored well for its relative

***Above:*** Horse farm, © Jack A. Wolf

***Left:*** Up-close and porcine, © Norm Schumm

freedom from disadvantages associated with urban life. As the authors noted: "Pittsburgh's strengths lie as much in what it doesn't have as in what it does. Our number-one metro area heads an elite group of only nine places that have no rankings of 200th or worse in any of *Places Rated*'s nine major categories."

Perhaps the most telling conclusion of all reached by Boyer and Savageau was expressed by their observation that "Pittsburgh is remarkably like a small town in many respects, despite its great size. Values are traditional and simple, neighborhoods tight yet friendly."

In so many ways, Pittsburgh *is* a small town masquerading as a big city. In many ways, too, the town often seems a bit uncomfortable in that disguise, as if it were some sleepy midwestern hamlet that just happens to have a lot of tall buildings in its business section and hosts a lot of important corporate headquarters.

Topography has a lot to do with Pittsburgh's small-town look and feel. In the city itself, the hilly terrain and the merging of two large rivers into a great one create a hodgepodge landscape. The Golden Triangle, the city's central business district, being contained by water and the hills, is so compact that it can be encircled easily on foot in an hour's almost leisurely stroll.

This topography has made Pittsburgh a city of bridges and tunnels, a city of steep hills, of steep streets climbing those hills,

**West End, © Maurice Tierney**

and of houses clinging to the hillsides. Some are so precariously perched and so remote that they are reachable only by foot—assuming that feet are willing to climb several hundred steps from the nearest road or sidewalk.

It is a city segmented by topography into small, often isolated neighborhoods. (How isolated are they? There is one called Seldom Seen.) The City of Pittsburgh has eighty-eight officially designated neighborhoods, eighty-eight distinct and distinctive enclaves where many residents refer to and think of themselves in terms of their neighborhood identities first and as Pittsburghers second.

Many of these neighborhoods are of pronounced ethnic character, where despite intermarriage and increased mobility, the ethnic group's cultural values still mold the character of the place, still structure the neighborhood, still weave family ties that bind.

In some of these neighborhoods, at least until recently, homes were seldom sold outside the family, being instead passed on from generation to generation as family heirlooms, not merely

*Above:* **Buhl Planetarium and Institute of Popular Science,** © **Norm Schumm**

*Left:* **Market Square,** © **Norm Schumm**

**Above:** Filipino woman at the Pittsburgh Folk Festival, © Herb Ferguson

**Right:** Scandinavian cooks at the Pittsburgh Folk Festival, © Michael Haritan

places of residence. Generations of Pittsburghers have lived not only on the same street in the same neighborhood but often in the same house. This practice is one that naturally tends to bond a person to a place and create uncommonly strong and durable loyalties. It also contributes to the city's atmosphere of livability.

Many of the city's neighborhoods have managed to maintain and protect their particular values, identities, and ethnic cohesiveness despite years of pressure and the inroads of "Americanization." Unfortunately, economic forces are threatening such cohesiveness in ways that social forces never could. As job opportunities for the blue-collar young dwindle, and the lure of economic stability beckons from elsewhere, some of the younger generation are leaving family, neighborhood, and city for work. Such migrations may be casually accepted in some locales, but they are not in keeping with the tone and character of Pittsburgh and its neighborhoods.

The pride and cohesiveness of Pittsburgh's neighborhoods can also be seen in the small cities, towns, and villages that abound throughout the surrounding area. Whereas topographical features segment the city into eighty-eight neighborhoods,

**Pittsburgh Folk Festival featuring Lebanese, Italian, and Polish cultures, © Herb Ferguson**

governmental boundaries divide up the entire region into small and fiercely independent municipalities.

Some of the larger towns of the region provide a measure of leadership and contribute direction in matters municipal; nevertheless, smaller towns usually act independently of their larger neighbors—sometimes wastefully so—and are stubborn in their determination to control their own fates. The City of Pittsburgh, for example, sets the tone of governmental leadership for the region in general and for Allegheny County in particular, but the 130 smaller cities, towns, and townships in the county steer their own courses, sometimes contrary to the course set in City Hall. Such cases can lead to confusion, redundancy of services, and a formidably contentious bureaucracy at several levels. These can present problems, especially for outsiders looking in. To insiders, however, there are benefits, not the least of which is the pervasive sense of belonging that is only possible in a small social/political structure. There is, after all, a great deal of comfort to be taken from the fact that it is *your* police department answering your call, *your* fire department on duty to pro-

*Facing page:* **Elliott neighborhood, © Michael Haritan**

*Below:* **Fountain at the Point, © Jack A. Wolf**

*Above:* **West Park card game,** © **Jack A. Wolf**

*Right:* **South Side playground,** © **Michael Haritan**

tect you, *your* municipal official watching out for your interests, not some indifferent stranger from a centralized and remote authority.

Such municipal fragmentation does not always contribute to governmental efficiency. But efforts to unite the various municipalities into larger units have met with rejection. *Metropolitanism* continues to be one of the dirtiest words in the political lexicon of Pittsburgh, and it is likely to remain so, even though the economic forces that are thrusting change onto Pittsburgh's city neighborhoods are compelling municipal officials all over the region to accept certain hard facts. They know, for example, that they cannot any longer afford to deprive their constituencies of the benefits of closer cooperation, especially in the sharing of costly services.

The trick is to achieve closer cooperation without destroying the small-town character of the place. It is that small-town look and feel that accounts for Pittsburgh's uniqueness. It is what makes most Pittsburghers stop to help strangers find their way. It is what makes Pittsburghers take great pride in being more congenial than cosmopolitan, more caring than cautious, more sincere than sophisticated.

The small-town side of Pittsburgh character is what makes converts out of so many who have settled here from other places, often reluctantly at first. The tale has become a cliche from so many tellings: rising young executive is offered a transfer to Pittsburgh as a step up the corporate ladder; much agony, weeping, and gnashing of teeth among said executive's family and friends; horrid nightmares of life in the foul air and polluted environment of a dirty mill town; family dragged kicking and screaming to the airport for the flight to the dreaded Smoky City; promises to get out of town and on with the career in another town in a hurry. The oft-told tale, of course, has a happy ending. Rising young executive and family spend the first few weeks in Pittsburgh in openmouthed astonishment. The place is nothing like they have been led to believe: the skies are clean, and the natives walk in an upright position. After a couple months they are confirmed Pittsburgers, and after a few years they wouldn't dream of living anywhere else.

This scenario happens frequently enough in Pittsburgh that it is sometimes hard to separate the native-born from the more recently arrived—perhaps because the newer arrivals are like those religious converts who sing the loudest come hymning time and proselytize most fervently for their newly found faith. Those once-reluctant immigrants often become the town's biggest boosters.

The combination of factors that prompted Pittsburgh's selection as America's Most Livable City didn't include year-round sunshine. Meteorological records show that, on the average, Pittsburgh basks in uninterrupted sunshine only fifty-nine days a year. The Rand McNally researchers gave Pittsburgh a plus for having a "variable continental climate" but registered a minus for its "wet, cold winters" and its "occasional humid summer days." Even with such a marginal report card, however, Pittsburgh weather ranked eighty-seventh on the livable places list of 329 municipalities, ahead of such sun-and-fun spots as Fort Lauderdale and Daytona Beach, Las Vegas, and Phoenix, as well as such winter wonderlands as Denver and Colorado Springs.

Pittsburgh's winters can be cold and wet, its summers hot and muggy at times. But the town's location has rescued it from meteorological ignominy: it is a little to the south of the snow belt that girds Cleveland and Buffalo, and a bit to the north and west of the weather system that visits unbearably muggy summers on Philadelphia and Washington, D.C.

**Church in North Hills,**
**© Herb Ferguson**

Although the preponderance of cloudy days did not seriously dent Pittsburgh's livability standing, the city did fall in the ratings on the score of housing conditions. Boyer and Savageau used three factors to determine these rankings: average annual mortgage payments, real estate taxes, and utility payments. According to the authors, the average Pittsburgher pays his mortgage banker $5,738 each year, foots a property tax bill totaling $986, and forks out $1,375 to utility companies to heat, cool, and illuminate his castle. More than 43 percent of all homes in the area were built before the Second World War, and the average home price at the time of the survey was $60,500.

That average home-cost figure, incidentally, is quite reasonable. Only one of the top ten metropolitan areas in the final ranking, Louisville, had a lower average cost than Pittsburgh; St. Louis matched Pittsburgh, but the remaining seven top finishers recorded higher home costs.

Home costs in the Pittsburgh area have traditionally been below those of other cities its size, and houses are consistently rated among the most affordable in the country. There are many housing bargains to be found, and those moving into the area (especially from the West Coast and areas of Connecticut within commuting distance of Manhattan) marvel at how much house for the money can be bought in Pittsburgh.

The Rand McNally researchers toting up the scores for the livability sweepstakes rated the area a surprisingly high 185th in the economics category, which is based on average household income (adjusted for taxes and cost of living), rate of income growth, and rate of job expansion.

Pittsburgh was found to have lower-than-average housing costs but slightly higher than average food costs. The second finding was disputed in a later study done by newspaper food editors, however, who found the area to be the fifth lowest for food prices in the United States.

The Rand McNally researchers found that the average household income in the Pittsburgh area was almost $33,000—just a few dollars shy of the national average. This figure rose almost 45 percent in the five years preceding the study.

**Oakland park in winter,
© Herb Ferguson**

In the jobs category, researchers found that there were still more blue-collar jobs than the national average, despite the transformation from an industry-based economy to one reliant on service. They also concluded that the unemployment threat was "moderate," indicating that the area may have taken most of its job-loss lumps already and that the future holds some promise.

It should be pointed out that the city's economic ranking in the 1985 edition of the *Places Rated Almanac* was higher than it was in the preceding edition published in 1982. In that earlier work, Pittsburgh was ranked 232nd among 277 metropolitan areas, fifty-two fewer than the more recent survey. So it can be argued that, at least by the standards and criteria used by the *Places Rated Almanac,* Pittsburgh's economic outlook is improving.

Continuing improvement is also being forecast by local officials for another category—transportation—in which Pittsburgh ranks very respectably. Even so, most Pittsburghers, especially those living and working in the city and in Allegheny County, are not convinced that the rating adequately takes into account certain transportation drawbacks, known as Pittsburgh's "Four

*Top:* **University of Pittsburgh football fans,** © **Herb
Ferguson**

*Bottom:* **Concert at the
Smoky City Folk Festival
© Joel B. Levinson**

*Clockwise from top left:*
**Shadyside cafe,** © Jack A.
Wolf
**Three Rivers Regatta,**
© Herb Ferguson
**East Allegheny baseball
team,** © William Metzger;
courtesy, Neighborhoods
for Living Center
**Tailgate party at polo
match,** © Mary Jane Bent

P's''—patterns, potholes, PAT, and the Parkway.

Street patterns are a particular problem in Pittsburgh. The topography, especially that of Downtown Pittsburgh, as well as hills, valleys, rivers, and streams, present a challenge to frustrate the most ingenious traffic engineer and the most creative road builder. The triangular shape of the central business district creates a traffic funnel that is narrowest at its most critical point. Since there are rivers, there must be bridges, and the hills create the need for tunnels and more bridges, all of which significantly limit traffic-pattern and road-construction possibilities.

The shape of the Golden Triangle virtually dictates against the establishment of an ordered and logical grid system for Downtown streets. This shape, as well as traffic patterns established in simpler, less congested times, has created a complex and sometimes bewildering street system, particularly where the Golden Triangle narrows approaching the Point. Sixth Avenue, for example, does not become Sixth Street when it crosses Liberty Avenue (the Triangle's principal east-west thoroughfare and the dividing line between "street" and "avenue" designations), but rather runs into Seventh Street. Sixth Street is fully a half block to the west, and when *it* crosses Liberty it becomes Market Street.

This problem brings to mind the old joke about many older cities in which streets tend to meander haphazardly. The streets, they say, follow paths made by a drunken rider on a horse in the early days of settlement. In Pittsburgh, the joke goes on to say, the horse was drunk as well.

There is evidence that motorists' complaints are being heeded, however, at least in the city. Some changes in Downtown traffic patterns are likely to be made after the major construction and street-repair programs in the Golden Triangle are completed. The city is also undertaking a major signage improvement program, which includes erecting new signs above the streets, eliminating clutter introduced by unnecessary and illegally erected "private" signs, and erecting more visible and less confusing signs directing motorists to major roadways and bridges leading out of the city.

The second "P" is for potholes, which perennially bedevil anyone who drives in the area. The potholes bloom each winter. They result, the experts say, from topography and the continual freeze-thaw cycles that are part of the place's climatic heritage.

## *Roads and Bridges: A New Route to the Future*

By Ken Fisher

**Golden Triangle, © Jack A. Wolf**

It's a popular item of Pittsburgh folklore to tell friends about driving home from vacation on smooth highways, then hitting a big pothole just after crossing the Pennsylvania border. This tale sums up the frustration of Pittsburgh motorists who have spent many years dodging potholes and crossing bumpy bridges with rusted railings and dilapidated sidewalks.

Like all man-made things, highways and bridges have a finite life. How long they last depends upon such factors as their design and materials, climatic conditions, and the weight and frequency of the traffic they carry. The decaying infrastructure of highways and bridges is a national problem. But the severity of the problem, at least in the early 1980s, may have been greatest within Allegheny County, where there are more than 1,300 bridges—nearly one for every mile of highway.

Highway and bridge infrastructure problems in Allegheny County had become so severe during the 1970s that:

Stop signs had to be erected in the middle of Wildwood Road in suburban Hampton Township, north of Pittsburgh, so that traffic could drive slowly, one side at a time, around the crippling potholes.

Steel-hauling trucks heading for Duquesne Works were forced onto a nine-mile detour around the weight-restricted Thompson Run Bridge. The additional round-trip mileage increased the cost for transporting goods by $1.2 million annually, according to company estimates.

A worker repairing a bridge on the Parkway East, the second busiest highway in the state, lost his jackhammer while repairing a hole. He poked a hole right through the deck.

But road conditions began to improve dramatically in the 1980s as Pennsylvania resolved to set its transportation system back on its feet and establish preventive maintenance programs. During each succeeding spring over the past five years, pothole patching is finished earlier and earlier. And the state's $1.4-billion bridge repair program has become a model for the nation. Transportation officials from around the world gather in Pittsburgh each June to discuss bridge problems and learn from Pennsylvania's experiences.

Pothole problems will always exist, but they're not as bad as they were a decade ago, when a combination of neglect, geology,

*Above:* **West End Bridge at sunset, © Jack A. Wolf**

*Facing page:* **Crosstown Express, © Norm Schumm**

topography, weather, and heavy weight of vehicles combined to virtually decimate the highway and bridge infrastructure.

Pittsburgh's geology is an important factor in these infrastructure problems, says Roger Carrier, a soils engineer who for six years administered the Pennsylvania Department of Transportation (PennDOT) District 11 office in Allegheny County. Carrier says that Pittsburgh's road system, which today carries autos and heavy tractor-trailer trucks weighing as much as 80,000 pounds, essentially follows the same routes as mountain streams and trails blazed by the pioneers. And the ruggedness of the southwestern Pennsylvania terrain has given the region the greatest density of bridges per road mile in Pennsylvania. Moreover, soil and rocks beneath the asphalt don't allow underground water to drain properly. Thus, the water weakens the roadway base and in some cases washes it away. Water does its greatest damage in winter. It remains beneath the road or in cracks on the surface; it then expands in freezing temperatures, cracking the asphalt so that chunks of the road surface break loose during the spring thaw. It is clear that those pioneer dirt paths were never meant to support today's high axle-weights and traffic volume of 50,000 vehicles each day.

While these factors were causing the bulk of the infrastructure to crumble during the 1970s, state highway engineers were concentrating on building replacement roads. Unfortunately, the state ran out of money for new highways, so the partially completed new road system became a patchwork quilt of concrete strips. Motorists had new highways but nowhere to go on them.

The most prominent of these unfinished, unattached segments of a regional road system was the East Street Valley Expressway between Downtown and the junction of Interstate 79 in Franklin Park, in the county's North Hills. Ramps on the northern end of the Fort Duquesne Bridge over the Allegheny River and on the Crosstown Boulevard next to the Civic Arena stretched into the air, connecting to nothing. Moreover, the Allegheny Valley Expressway dead-ended against hillsides in northwestern Allegheny County. Ohio River Boulevard dropped from an eight-lane to a two-lane road on the city's North Side, and the Bloomfield Bridge was left abandoned between the Bloomfield and Oakland neighborhoods.

After a decade of neglect, the state began in the early 1980s

**South Side through Birmingham Bridge, © Michael Haritan**

to reconstruct and finish Pittsburgh highways as the newly elected Governor Richard Thornburgh made it a priority to put the transportation system back in order. PennDOT adopted the theme "maintenance first" under Transportation Secretary Tom Larson's "do it right" policy.

For six straight years, a flush of fresh revenue has been raised through increased state gasoline taxes, higher fees on truckers, and a flat tax on the wholesale price of gasoline. Targeting an additional source for transportation funding, the Greater Pittsburgh Chamber of Commerce organized western-Pennsylvania support for state revenues to be matched by federal highway and bridge money, with the state and federal governments contributing 10-percent and 90-percent shares respectively. As a result of the efforts of business, labor, and government leaders working with the legislature, Pennsylvania has moved from last place to first among all states in the amount of federal highway and bridge monies received for six consecutive years.

In other action at the state level, lawmakers changed the way maintenance money was allocated to Pennsylvania's sixty-seven counties: PennDOT developed a formula for maintenance money based on the number of miles, volume of traffic, and condition

**Busy highways, © Jack A. Wolf**

of roads in a county. Since Allegheny County's high mileage, heavy traffic, and poor roads weighed heavily in the new formula, it was the biggest recipient of much-needed maintenance money from the state. During 1975-1976, maintenance accounted for only 28 percent of PennDOT's total budget. By 1981-1982, however, maintenance expanded to 49 percent.

A total of more than $7.7 billion of gasoline taxes has been converted to subsidies to maintain, restore, and rebuild the state's highway and bridge network between 1979 and 1986. Total maintenance expenditures, including restoration on the interstate highway system, have averaged more than a billion dollars each year.

In addition to fundamental maintenance duties, such as patch-

**Smithfield Street Bridge,**
© Jack A. Wolf

ing potholes, cleaning drainage ditches, and erecting safety guard-
rails along highways, significant repair projects were initiated to
improve the primary highway system. The Penn-Lincoln Parkway
East (Interstate 376), the second busiest highway in Pennsylvania,
was rebuilt one side at a time and in two parts over four construction seasons in a unique federally sponsored project. The
U.S. Department of Transportation subsidized a traffic plan for
commuters that included a train, park-and-ride lots in the eastern suburbs, timed traffic signals, van pools, and off-duty patrol
officers to direct traffic. It was the first time in the nation's history that highway money was used for anything but road construction.

The Westinghouse Bridge was closed for nearly a year while
its historic concrete arch was repaired and a wider concrete
deck installed. Traffic was maintained in single lanes for more
than one year on the Liberty Bridge, which carries traffic from
the Liberty Tunnels into the Golden Triangle.

Nor was new construction forgotten. Work started on completing the missing highway links of limited-access roadways
that had been planned and started ten to twenty years earlier.
The $400-million East Street-Valley Expressway project was the
first to advance from the drawing boards to construction. More
than a dozen contracts were required at one time to construct
the multi-lane highway as a north-south bypass to Interstate 79.

**Gateway Center subway station, © Herb Ferguson**

As part of that effort, PennDOT undertook the Crosstown Boulevard Expressway, the most complicated project ever undertaken by the state. It involved coordination with the transit agency, a railroad, the city highway department, business owners, private developers, and utility companies.

The unfinished Allegheny Valley Expressway got the green light, too. Earth moving was so massive for that project that bulldozers shoveled enough to fill Three Rivers Stadium five times up to its roof. And the Bloomfield Bridge project cleared environmental, financial, and legal hurdles so that its construction could proceed.

But even with this record pace of highway construction activity and with the fresh reserves of money available through gasoline taxes, the distressing deficiencies in the infrastructure have yet to be completely eliminated.

To fix its roads, the state budgeted an additional $600 million strictly for maintenance during 1986. But to continue steady progress toward improving the condition of highways and bridges, spending levels will have to be increased by at least 5 percent each year until 1990, in order to provide an additional $300 million specifically for maintaining the infrastructure.

To raise that it will be necessary to look beyond the traditional sources of transportation dollars, such as gasoline taxes, license fees, and truck assessments. Legislation permits the formation of transportation partnerships between the state and local governments and the private sector. These partnerships enable the pooling of funds required for transportation improvements that might otherwise be delayed. Such was the case with erection of the overhead ramp from the Parkway Center Mall on the Green Tree-Pittsburgh border onto the Parkway West. The ramp installation was financed not by PennDOT but by the mall developers.

Additional revenues will be necessary to keep the state's bridge repair program on pace with the problem. In 1983, Pennsylvania began a six-year program to rehabilitate or replace nearly 1,000 deficient bridges at an estimated cost of $1.4 billion. PennDOT

**Highway transportation,
© Herb Ferguson**

estimates that a second billion-dollar bridge program could rebuild another 2,000 bridges over six years.

Another solution to the transportation funding dilemma is to relieve traffic on older roads by constructing new ones with toll revenues. A $3.7-billion toll-road program to expand the Pennsylvania Turnpike in western Pennsylvania will complete two missing links: the Beaver Valley Expressway (Route 60) through Beaver County and the Greensburg Bypass in Westmoreland County. A third extension, the Mon Valley Expressway, is planned to connect Pittsburgh with Interstate 70 in Washington County. And a fourth would be U.S. 219 between Ebensburg and Interstate 80.

These turnpike extensions and the Southern Expressway near

*Above:* **Bridge into the city,** © Jack A. Wolf

*Facing page:* **Crosstown Express,** © Norm Schumm

Greater Pittsburgh International Airport are among the last new-highway projects planned for southwestern Pennsylvania. Penn-DOT's outlook for the future will continue an emphasis on maintaining the infrastructure rather than on expanding the state's 44,000 miles of highways.

The war on potholes will never end in a final victory. But if the number of telephone calls to the state's pothole complaint line is a barometer, PennDOT is at least gaining the upper hand in the battle. Since instituting its pothole hotline in 1981, the state has seen the number of complaints drop to about one-third of the first year's total of more than 1,700 calls.

Like homes, highways and bridges require periodic repairs and restorations. So it's natural that just as a home owner regularly repairs a leaking roof or a cracked ceiling, PennDOT routinely maintains its roads and bridges. Pennsylvania just learned the hard way that it is much easier and far less expensive to repair the infrastructure than to replace it.

*Ken Fisher reports on highways, bridges, and public transportation for the Pittsburgh Post-Gazette.*

**Phipps Conservatory during Spring Flower Show,**
**© Joel B. Levinson**

Traffic experts also report that Pittsburgh's pothole problem is no worse than that experienced throughout the Northeast and is significantly better than in some cities.

Potholed or not, Pittsburgh's roadways and bridges have elicited complaints for many years. Many of the area's roads are in substandard condition, and maintenance too often seems to be undertaken on a crisis basis. As a result of years of neglect, a lot of the area's bridges (and remember that Pittsburgh is a city of bridges) carry weight restrictions that limit their ability to move traffic.

Many Pittsburghers blame state government for the widespread neglect that characterizes road and bridge construction and maintenance. PennDOT, the Pennsylvania Department of Transportation, receives the brunt of the criticism, by those who claim that the Pittsburgh area has been ignored in favor of the more easily maintained roads in the eastern flatlands around Philadelphia and the area surrounding the state capital in Harrisburg, where legislators who control the agency's budget are wont to congregate.

Things are changing, however, and PennDOT has been committing greater resources to the Pittsburgh area. Major bridge

**Old Economy,** © **Mary Jane Bent**

replacement and rehabilitation projects have been undertaken in the past few years, and a two-year project that virtually rebuilt the Penn-Lincoln Parkway was completed in fall 1985. The I-279/I-579 project linking Downtown Pittsburgh with Interstate 79 north of the city is expected to be completed in 1988. State officials call this 13.5-mile, $500-million expressway project the most difficult new highway construction project ever undertaken by PennDOT.

Another of the Pittsburgh "P's"—PAT, or the Port Authority Transit—influenced the livability rating. The mass transit arm of the Port Authority of Allegheny County, PAT operates one of the largest public transportation systems in the country, using more than 900 buses, 60 trolleys, 38 light-rail vehicles, and an incline (a second incline is privately operated) to carry 300,000 passengers a day. Many of the street trolleys are being replaced by new light-rail vehicles to be integrated into Pittsburgh's new subway system.

More than half of all area residents who commute to Downtown Pittsburgh to work use public transportation, and 50 percent of all shoppers in the central business district get there by bus or trolley. Those percentages are likely to increase now that the city's short (1.1 mile long), compact (three Downtown stations) subway system is completed and operating. The subway, opened in 1985, is part of a $560-million light-rail transit system that serves the southern suburbs. In addition, plans are under consideration to expand this light-rail system to serve city neighborhoods and suburbs to the east and north of Downtown.

Pittsburgh's principal east-west vehicular traffic artery is the fourth "P"—the Parkway or, more formally, the Penn-Lincoln Parkway. The Parkway East extends fifteen miles from Downtown to Monroeville where it links up with the Pennsylvania Turnpike. The Parkway West extends about the same distance, terminating at Greater Pittsburgh International Airport. Rush-hour traffic conditions on the parkway, in either direction, can usually be described in just one word: clogged.

Despite some transportation shortcomings, the average commuting time in the Pittsburgh area is among the shortest for any major U.S. metropolitan area: just over fifty minutes. The Rand

**Station Square depot,
© Norm Schumm**

McNally research revealed that commuters in only one other area, Minneapolis-St. Paul, took less time to travel to and from work each day.

A fifth "P" could well stand for parking. Public parking in center-city lots and garages is both plentiful and relatively affordable by big-city standards. Ample inexpensive parking is also available across both the Allegheny and Monongahela rivers from Downtown.

Overall, the *Places Rated* authors ranked Pittsburgh seventy-sixth in the country for transportation, using as measurements daily commuting time, public transportation, freeway traffic, interstate highways, airline service, and rail service. A major factor in the relatively high ranking had to be Greater Pittsburgh International Airport, or Greater Pitt, as it is more commonly referred

**South Side from Duquesne Heights, © Mary Jane Bent**

to. The airport is a focal point in the region's transportation scheme, so much so that plans to revitalize several areas in the region include provisions for direct-route access to the airport, considered a critical ingredient for economic recovery.

Greater Pitt is an important Northeast airline hub and serves as the operational center for USAir, a company that had its beginnings in the Pittsburgh area. Greater Pitt is the twelfth-busiest airport in the country, ranking immediately after New York's JFK airport, with more than 206,000 takeoffs and landings per year. The airport, to maintain its ability to serve the Pittsburgh area, the Northeast, and the nation in the future, must enhance its capacity and facilities. Improvement plans include a new $414-million midfield terminal and other improvements.

**Right:** Fallingwaters, © Herb Ferguson

**Below:** Three Rivers Arts Festival, © Mary Jane Bent

**Civic Arena, © Herb Ferguson**

The new airport facilities could be used to welcome skeptics flying into town to see why Pittsburgh ranked so highly in the *Places Rated* arts category. Those skeptics want to know how a shot-and-beer town could possibly rank twelfth in the land for the quality of its arts and cultural environment and ninth among the thirteen largest metropolitan areas in the country.

Obviously, the raters found that while Pittsburghers do enjoy their shots and their beers, they also enjoy the world-ranked Pittsburgh Symphony Orchestra, the constantly improving Pittsburgh Opera, and the Pittsburgh Ballet. There are more than 200 active performing arts groups in the area, about evenly divided between theater and dance groups. Included in that number are forty-five classical music groups, about a dozen of them symphony orchestras. Pittsburghers enjoy browsing in the area's thirty-nine art galleries and taking in its sixty museums and landmarks. Carnegie Institute is a local favorite, attracting visitors to its museums of art and natural history. And the public library system here is among the largest in the world.

Pittsburgh's prominence as a center for culture and the arts was well hidden for many years by the presumed layers of soot and dirt, part of the city's image as a rough-and-tumble factory town. Nevertheless, the heritage has always been there, as has the enthusiastic and generous support of business and industrial leaders. Andrew Carnegie, who made his fortune in Pitts-

Bridge over Manchester,
© Jack A. Wolf

**University of Pittsburgh football halftime show, © Michael Haritan**

burgh, left a sizable portion of it there as well. He nurtured his interest in library endowment here, and the first American library he endowed still stands in Braddock, in the shadows of a USX Corporation mill that once carried the Carnegie-Illinois Steel Company name.

Pittsburgh has traditionally benefited from the generosity of civic-minded and culturally inclined business leaders. Others besides Carnegie have made substantial contributions to the local cultural scene. Their familiar names include Heinz (Heinz Hall for the Performing Arts), Benedum (Benedum Center), Frick (Frick Art Museum), Buhl (Buhl Science Center), Scaife (The Scaife Galleries), Phipps (Phipps Conservatory), and Mellon (Mellon Institute), among many others.

If Pittsburgh's prominence in the arts and culture was well hidden from the world for many years, so was its image as a likely place to pursue recreation. Even though industrial and commercial river traffic tonnages made Pittsburgh the busiest inland port in the country for many years, Pittsburghers have made good use of the area's abundant waterways for recreational purposes. Traditionally, the number of pleasure boat licenses issued in Allegheny County every year is among the highest for any county in the United States.

Water is not the only sporting attraction, of course. The area supports 134 golf courses, more courses per capita than any other metropolitan area in the U.S. And state, county, and municipal parks throughout the region contribute to the quality of life.

Because of these resources, Pittsburgh was ranked ninetieth in the nation for recreation by the *Places Rated* researchers, and ninth among the thirteen largest metropolitan areas. This good standing in part derives from the city's three professional sports teams: the baseball Pirates, the football Steelers, and the hockey Penguins. Pittsburghers consider the area a solid sports town, but their failure to support some teams with less-than-outstanding records casts some doubt on that proclamation.

The Pittsburgh Pirates are a good example. After several unspectacular seasons, local fans were staying away from games

**Polo match, © Jack A. Wolf**

in record numbers. The John Galbreath family and Warner Communications, Incorporated, owners of the franchise (one of the oldest in professional baseball), decided in early 1985 to sell the team. Out-of-town buyers, thinking to move the team to another city after the sale, expressed the most interest. But pressure by City Hall and civic leaders, alive to the considerable economic advantages of retaining the team, prompted the owners to hold off the sale until local buyers could be found. A consortium was formed late in the year, and with financial help from city government, agreement was reached for the team's local purchase.

The public—all those fans who had been staying away from Pirate games in droves—rallied behind Mayor Richard Caliguiri's efforts to save the franchise for the city, perhaps to salvage their reputations as avid sports fans as well.

The success of the Pirate deal will depend upon the team's attracting fans in sufficient numbers to make it a paying proposition. Since the presence of major league sports teams in an area contributes to quality of life, it also affects a place's livability rating, whether measured formally, as in the *Places Rated Almanac,* or informally. Pittsburgh may not be a significantly less attractive place to live should the Pirates, or any other profes-

**Carnegie-Mellon University dorms, © Michael Haritan**

sional sports team, leave town, but major league teams give the place a major league image, and that image attracts business, induces companies to set up shop, and generally contributes to the overall well-being of the area and the people who live there.

So, of course, does the quality of health care a community provides, and in this category Pittsburgh is rapidly moving into the medical big leagues. Fifty hospitals in the nine-county region treat more than 750,000 patients a year. The *Places Rated* researchers found that the area has 213 physicians per 100,000 people. The quality of care, the availability of top-ranked facilities, and other related factors earned Pittsburgh the ranking of fourteenth best in the nation in health care and eleventh among the thirteen biggest U.S. metropolitan areas.

For many years, Pittsburghers have stayed in hospitals longer and have used hospital facilities more than those in much of the rest of the country. One reason why could be health care costs, which are among the most affordable in the country. Pittsburgh earned a rating of "excellent" for care affordability in the *Places Rated* survey, a rating equaled only by Washington, D.C., among the thirteen biggest metropolitan areas.

Most of the region's premier health care facilities are located in the city of Pittsburgh, as are the principal medical research and teaching facilities. The area's eleven teaching hospitals, medical school, four cardiac rehabilitation centers, and hospice are all located within the city limits.

**Highland Park Zoo,**
**© Michael Haritan**

The University Health Center of Pittsburgh, affiliated with the University of Pittsburgh and its medical school, serves as the heart of the region's medical treatment and research capability, although outstanding work in patient care and medical research is conducted outside the center as well. Doctors working in the city have made Pittsburgh a world leader in organ transplantation.

The city's reputation for health care excellence is beginning to attract attention. Patients are coming to Pittsburgh from outside the area for quality medical care. Until recently, about 5 percent of patients admitted to Pittsburgh's hospitals were from outside the area; the percentage is gradually increasing, along with Pittsburgh's reputation as a medical treatment center.

The area also enjoys a fine reputation for educational opportunities and schools and for the quality of the programs offered. Pittsburgh's highest ranking—seventh in the country—came in education. Criteria for evaluation were teacher-pupil ratios in the public schools, the amount of support given to an area's public schools, and the options available for higher education.

The four-county Pittsburgh area had the smallest public school population of the thirteen biggest metropolitan areas in the coun-

**Parade, © Herb Ferguson**

try—322,000 pupils in 631 public schools in 80 school districts. Among metropolitan areas with populations of two million or more, the Pittsburgh area ranked fourth in teacher-pupil ratio (13.83 to 1) and eighth in the amount of support given public schools ($3,079 per pupil). Among the thirteen biggest metropolitan areas, only Washington, D.C., gave more support to public school students.

The high ranking in education reflects heightened awareness of the needs of the area's public schools. It also reflects the success of efforts undertaken to improve the school systems, particularly the Pittsburgh Public Schools, which serve the city and the neighboring borough of Mount Oliver. Quality has improved considerably in the past few years, particularly because of the success of such initiatives as the city's magnet schools program in the middle school grades. Magnet schools are established to emphasize particular subjects or academic disciplines—languages, computer science, fine arts, performing arts, classical studies, and so on. The success of the magnet school program can be measured by the fact that applicants exceed available spaces in the schools, and parents have been known to stand in line for days to enroll their children in particular schools.

The public schools of the Pittsburgh area were not always the focus of so much attention or innovation. For years the city and much of Allegheny County had a very large and active parochial school system, which served a large segment of the student population, both in the primary and the secondary grades. While the area's sizable Catholic population has a strong tradition of supporting parochial schools, such support has waned in recent years as operating costs of schools, both public and private, have risen significantly.

Economic pressures have also contributed to an increased awareness of the value of post-secondary education. In the past, area residents have not taken advantage of educational opportunities after high school, trailing below national averages in this regard. Educators blame this situation on two factors: the lack of a strong educational tradition among the blue-collar families that dominated the population for so many years, and the ready availability of good-paying jobs in the mills, mines, and factories—jobs that required no extensive schooling to secure and maintain. The decline in this category of jobs has made younger Pittsburghers keenly aware of the importance of a post-secondary education and more eager to pursue academic training beyond the twelfth grade.

The Pittsburgh area can readily accommodate any such increased interest. There are twenty-nine colleges and universities in the nine-county region and about fifty vocational/technical schools ready to help prepare residents in their pursuit of job stability and improved earnings. Eight four-year colleges and universities operate in Allegheny County—seven of them within the city's limits—along with the two-year, three-campus Community College of Allegheny County. The University of Pittsburgh operates three regional campuses, in addition to its main campus in the Oakland section of the city; Penn State University has regional campuses in the area as well.

Those schools not only provide wide-ranging educational opportunities, they are also increasingly involved in nonacademic pursuits that have the potential to bring great benefit to the region. The area's colleges and universities are becoming active centers for training and retraining of the unemployed, for municipal revitalization, and for local economic development programs. Many serve as focal points for new ideas, new approaches, and new strategies that will aid in the region's economic recovery and further its quality of life.

Pittsburgh's performance compared to the twelve other major metropolitan areas was even better in the category of crime, a consideration that many feel is among the most important to a city's livability.

The relatively low crime rate may reflect Pittsburgh's small-town inclination and the values that go with it. The area ranked seventy-eighth in the nation on the *Places Rated* list, and only Nassau-Suffolk, New York, was rated freer from crime among the thirteen largest metropolitan areas. The significance of this ranking is heightened by the poor showing of the eleven others on the big-city list: they were all ranked in the bottom half, and many of them were near the very bottom of the list.

Since the *Places Rated* rankings were determined, the crime picture in Pittsburgh has apparently improved even more. A Federal Bureau of Investigation report of October 1985 showed that although serious crime in cities this size had risen by 7 percent in the first half of 1985, Pittsburgh experienced a decline of more than 12 percent in that period, which represented the single largest decrease in serious offenses reported for the past nine years in the city.

Earlier in 1985, published reports based on FBI statistics indicated that Pittsburgh was the safest large city in the nation. Commenting on Pittsburgh's low-crime environment, a city police official said, "I believe, naturally, that the police have done a good job in controlling crime, but I think the real answer lies in the makeup of the people living in Pittsburgh."

Pittsburghers, with their small-town values, their close family ties, their ethnic heritages, their friendly nature, their helping attitudes, and their concern for others, make the difference. They make this a safe place and attractive place.

It all adds up to the fact that Pittsburgh is a great place to live. But who would want to visit? Apparently a lot of people do. Since Boyer and Savageau bestowed their Most Livable crown, the Greater Pittsburgh Convention and Visitors Bureau reports a significant increase in interest from out-of-towners who want to hold their meetings and conventions in Pittsburgh. There are even those who are coming for vacations and pleasure trips. Of course, no one expects Pittsburgh to become a major tourist attraction. But then, no one ever expected it to become the best place in the country to live, either.

# CHAPTER III

# The Market Surveyed

*Facing page:* Sixth Street
Bridge from North Shore,
© Michael Haritan

*Pages 98-99:* Heinz Chapel,
© Maurice Tierney

The fates have blessed Pittsburgh with an uncommon abundance of riches and resources. Impressive coal reserves helped make Pittsburgh an industrial power in post-Revolutionary America, and its rivers made the city an important early shipping and transportation center.

Pittsburgh's earliest entrepreneurs harnessed the resources, tamed the rivers, and forged for themselves mighty industrial empires of iron, steel, coal, coke, glass, and aluminum. Many of those empires still play influential roles not only in Pittsburgh's economy but also in the economies of the nation and the world.

The city's strategic location, in the western foothills of the Allegheny Mountains where the Allegheny and Monongahela rivers meet to form the Ohio, was the key to the area's early prominence as a commercial and industrial center. After the Revolutionary War, as pioneers set out to seek new adventures, new lives, and fortunes on the western frontiers, the town of Pittsburgh became the Gateway to the West. It was to Pittsburgh that pioneers gravitated after their long and dangerous journey over the mountains. And it was Pittsburgh that welcomed them, rested them, fed them, and bolstered them with provisions for their trek across the flatlands.

It was location that earned Pittsburgh a prominent place in the early history of the republic. It was chosen as the site for the signing of the infant nation's first treaty with an Indian tribe—a treaty with the Delaware Nation, solemnized at Fort Pitt on September 17, 1778.

Location was what impressed young George Washington about

*Right:* **Fort Necessity historic reenactment, © Herb Ferguson**

*Facing page:* **Century Inn in Washington County, © Herb Ferguson**

the place at the rivers' fork that was one day to become Pittsburgh. It was location that attracted the early settlers, inspired the entrepreneurs, gave refuge to westward-traveling pioneers, and helped make Pittsburgh an industrial pacesetter in the nineteenth century and an industrial colossus in the twentieth.

In 1753 George Washington, twenty-one years old and holding the rank of major in the Virginia Militia, came upon the area during a surveying expedition. Seeing the potential for the site, Washington recommended that a fort be built at the confluence of the rivers. In a letter to Governor George Dinwiddie of Virginia (what is now Pennsylvania was part of Virginia in those days) Washington wrote that the location was "extremely well situated for a fort, as it has absolute control of both rivers."

His advice was heeded, and Fort Prince George was built at the site the following year. Control of the rivers and the land surrounding them was of paramount importance to the Virginians and to their British superiors, and Fort Prince George gave them the advantage they needed in their ongoing struggle with the French.

However, the French knew a thing or two about the impor-

tance of strategic location, and they determined to take control of the territory by taking the fort. The French captured Fort Prince George in July 1754, renaming their prize Fort Duquesne.

It took the British four years to reclaim the fort, which was destroyed in the conclusive battle that finally drove off the French. The British rebuilt the fort in 1759 and rechristened it Fort Pitt, in honor of William Pitt, Earl of Chatham and British prime minister.

Pittsburgh's early settlers knew a thing or two about location themselves, and they were well aware that the safest place to pitch one's tent and eventually to build one's dwelling was in the shadow of a well-equipped, well-defended fort. With the passage of years, a sizable settlement grew up around Fort Pitt.

The British were long gone by the time the townsfolk got around to incorporating Pittsburgh as a borough in 1794. By that time the town's first newspaper, the *Gazette,* and its first institution of higher learning, the Pittsburgh Academy, were thriving. Both were established in 1787, and both still exist today; the *Gazette* as the *Post-Gazette* and the Pittsburgh Academy as the Univer-

sity of Pittsburgh. By 1816 the town had grown and spread, and the charter of incorporation was amended, making Pittsburgh a full-fledged city.

And it all started with a prime location. Of course, it also helped that the area around Pittsburgh was rich in the natural resources needed by industry. Besides the coal, which fed Pittsburgh's furnaces and was valued also as an export commodity, there was sand for the many glassworks in the area. And not too many miles away there was oil.

Colonel Edwin L. Drake's fabulous oil strike of 1859 in Titusville, about 100 miles northeast of the city, signaled the beginning of a boom in the Pennsylvania crude fields that proved astonishingly beneficial to Pittsburgh. Location again played the key role. Pittsburgh applied its expertise as a transporter of goods to a vast river-fed market to become a major refining and shipping center.

It seemed only natural that Titusville's oil would end up in Pittsburgh. Barreled at the wellhead and shipped by barge to Oil City via Oil Creek, the crude was there loaded onto bigger barges

*Right and facing page, top:* Forbes Street; right, courtesy, University of Pittsburgh; facing page, © Herb Ferguson

*Below:* North Side's Carnegie Library in 1909; courtesy, University of Pittsburgh

*Facing page, bottom:* Allegheny Center and Pittsburgh Public Theater, © Herb Ferguson

*Above:* Cathedral of Learning site, Fifth Avenue toward Forbes; courtesy, University of Pittsburgh

*Facing page:* Cathedral of Learning, © Herb Ferguson

*Below:* Caldwell Street; courtesy, University of Pittsburgh

for the trip down the Allegheny to Pittsburgh's refineries. By 1871 there were sixty petroleum refineries operating in the city, refining a daily total of 36,000 barrels of oil. Thus Pittsburgh became a far more important petroleum center than the northern towns that actually produced the crude and serviced the wells.

The two primary factors that upheld the city's prominence were strategic location on the rivers and proximity to large and rich markets. Neither of these factors was taken lightly in nineteenth-century Pittsburgh. They were strengths to be exploited at every opportunity, and they contributed mightily to economic development. An 1870 publication, *Pittsburgh: Its Industry and Commerce,* summed up their importance:

*No city in the Union possesses greater natural advantages, greater resources, or better facilities for transportation than Pittsburgh.*

**Right: Old hardware store; courtesy, University of Pittsburgh**

**Facing page: Strip District vendor, © Norm Schumm**

**Forbes Street; courtesy, University of Pittsburgh**

*Her natural position, her inexhaustible coal fields, her river and rail communication, her central location and her proverbial industry, combine to render her the foremost manufacturing center in the Union.*

"Smokestack industries" dominated Pittsburgh's economy in the 1870s. The city and its entrepreneurs took full advantage of everything at their disposal to create an industrial citadel whose economic influence would be felt well into the twentieth century.

Published accounts of the day show clearly why Pittsburgh's claim to the title of Smoky City would come to be largely unchallenged by any other area in the country. Operating in the city at the time were thirty-two iron mills, nine steel mills, forty-eight foundries, eleven brass foundries, twenty-seven machine shops, twenty-six tanneries, sixty-eight glass factories, thirteen brickyards, and dozens of other assorted foundries, mills, shops, and factories, of virtually every kind and description.

No one thinks of Pittsburgh today as a tobacco center, but it was in the 1870s. The book mentioned above on the city's industrial makeup noted that at that time Pittsburgh was in "the

**Pittsburgh neighborhood; courtesy, University of Pittsburgh**

**Playground; courtesy, University of Pittsburgh**

foremost rank among the northern cities engaged in the manufacture of tobacco." Ten factories processing tobacco were then
located in Pittsburgh and the city of Allegheny, now Pittsburgh's
North Side, along with "some 140 other facilities engaged in
other branches of the trade."

Not everyone, however, was engaged in heavy industry or the
tobacco trade in the Pittsburgh of the 1870s. Many were employed in enterprises designed to meet the more fundamental
needs of the populace. At the time there were fifty-two brew-
eries, eight distilleries, and one coffin factory.

The foundation for all the industrial and commercial activity of

*Facing page, clockwise from top left:*
Carnegie Museum, © Herb Ferguson
Royal American Regiment at Point State Park, © Herb Ferguson
Vintage Grand Prix at Schenley Park, © Herb Ferguson

*Left:* Incline, © Jack A. Wolf

*Below:* Smoky City Folk Festival, © William Metzger; courtesy, Neighborhoods for Living Center

**Historic home thriving as a restaurant in Lawrence County, © Herb Ferguson**

the 1870s was laid much earlier. What we call Pittsburgh was not much more than a wide settlement in the road (or on the rivers) when the locals began flexing their industrial muscles.

In 1793, a year before Pittsburgh's incorporation as a borough, the area's first iron furnace was erected by George Anshutz in what is now the Shadyside section of the city. The furnace, which produced mostly castings of stoves and grates, went out of business after about a year because of a shortage of wood for fuel, of all things.

Glassmaking in the area was undertaken in earnest in 1795 when General James O'Hara and Major Isaac Craig established a glassworks on what is now the South Side. Peter William Eichbaum, a German-born craftsman, was superintendent of the works, which apparently suffered through many reverses before a product was manufactured successfully. On that occasion, General O'Hara is reported to have said: "Today we made our first bottle. It cost us just $30,000."

# Carnegie Institute: A Wise Extravagance

By Abby Mendelson

It is safe to say that Pittsburgh simply would not be the city it is without Carnegie Institute. Built eighty years ago at a cost of six million dollars, it would be impossible—both because of cost and craftsmanship—to duplicate or replace today. With its opulent Music Hall, landmark free library, aggressive Museum of Art, and world-class Museum of Natural History, the institute has been nothing less than the cornerstone of all things cultural in Pittsburgh. None of the subsequent twentieth-century development of Pittsburgh arts and culture—key factors that make the city unique and so livable—would have been even conceivable without Carnegie Institute. Pacesetter, standard-bearer, with fit material for a lifetime's study and enjoyment, Andrew Carnegie's five-acre soot-blackened-stone "American palace of culture," as he called it, stands as a monument to the vision and generosity of its founder and guide.

At the age of thirty-three, steel magnate Carnegie found himself making the unheard-of salary of $50,000. Vowing to take no more, the American who was second in wealth only to J. Pierpont Morgan said he would "spend the surplus each year for benevolent purposes." When in 1881 he found Pittsburgh culture "dormant," he offered to build a library, and then he couldn't stop. By 1907 the edifice had swelled to nearly its present size, and it included the music hall and two museums. Carnegie himself stressed what he called the "noble quartet": science, music, literature, and art. According to his plan, the four are represented by statues, placed in front of the institute, of Galileo, Bach, Shakespeare, and Michelangelo.

For the institute that stood behind the sculptures, Carnegie demanded the best. There was fine marble, for example: sixteen different kinds were employed, 6,000 tons all told, including more white Pentelic in the halls of sculpture and architecture than were in all other American buildings combined. He bought so much of it, in fact, that the government of Greece actually considered banning its export. And the buildings were modern. Twenty-five thousand electric lights (3,000 in the Music Hall

**Above:** Scaife Gallery,
© Herb Ferguson

**Right:** Scaife Gallery,
© Jack A. Wolf

foyer alone), 200 miles of wiring, and the world's largest switch-board. There was wall space sufficient to hang 1.75 miles of paintings. And so on. Carnegie shrugged off the cost, dubbing his largesse "wise extravagances."

On Friday, April 12, 1907, the official dedication was marked nationwide by organized discussions of such topics as litera-ture, character, and international peace, conducted in 500-odd Carnegie-sponsored music halls. So strong was Carnegie's feel-ing that the people should share in access to education and cul-ture that he turned down a British knighthood the following year, explaining that the title "Sir" would violate his democratic prin-ciples.

The institute has expanded a bit since Carnegie's time. The lecture hall gets a lot of use for various events, and the film sec-tion is immensely popular. Because the music hall has been fairly quiet of late and because the library has a life almost of its own, most people think of Carnegie Institute in terms of its two museums, Art and Natural History. And rightly so, for the insti-tute claims one of the world's foremost dinosaur displays—of brontosaurus and *Tyrannosaurus rex,* among others, the "big bones" that so delight children. There is also a marvelous mixed bag of materials on Indians and Egyptology, unique casts of At-tic friezes, mountain goats, and more. In the art museum are collections of the French Impressionists and Postimpressionists, nineteenth-century Americans, and contemporary art; traveling shows (Celtic art, for example, or Cartier-Bresson's seminal photography); and the triennial International, originated by Andrew Carnegie, which brings to Pittsburgh the latest, hottest, and best from around the world.

Since art is so costly, the Museum of Art's director John R. Lane has wisely decided to specialize and to continue building upon both the museum's permanent collection and that donated by the late Sarah Scaife, whose name graces the new galleries. Those two collections feature such important artists as Claude Monet, whose *Water Lillies* measures twenty by seven feet, Edgar Degas, Vincent van Gogh, John Singer Sargent, Henri Matisse, Willem de Kooning, Piet Mondrian, Georgia O'Keefe, and Pittsburgh-born Mary Cassatt. There are others, of course, including Winslow Homer's *The Wreck,* a prizewinner in the first International of 1896 and the initial work purchased by the mu-

seum. (At that time, the museum also purchased Whistler's *Sarasate,* and thereby became the first American public gallery to own a Whistler.)

In the forty-ninth International, in 1986 the museum purchased seventeen works for the permanent collection, making for what one local art critic termed a stellar year. Chief among them was Richard Serra's outsize steel box *Carnegie,* Anselm Kiefer's *Midgard,* and George Baselitz' *The Mocking.*

Serra's sculpture stands outside the museum's Scaife Galleries entrance; indeed it seems to be institute policy to use every available inch of space. Jean Dubuffet's movable, cartoonish *The Free Exchange* stands in the Scaife foyer, and George Segal's "The Tightrope Walker" stands suspended over another entrance foyer. A mobile by Alexander Calder swings over a grand staircase—and there's even a mini-cafe, called Under the Stairs, featuring wine, cheese, fruit, and the like, under the long steps leading to the Scaife Galleries.

There are 10,000 objects on display on the natural history side, and the most dazzling is certainly the Hillman Hall of Minerals and Gems, donated by a premier Pittsburgh family. The

hall has 2,500 specimens, 400 of which appear in a mirrored vista. Specials include nineteen selections of gold, a 197-carat opal (believed to be the largest in any museum collection), a 500-pound amethyst geode, and a touchable meteorite.

To keep Carnegie Institute vigorous, new director Robert Wilburn has put together the One Hundred citizens committee, comprising top people from various facets of the Pittsburgh community. One recommendation is the upgraded use of the music hall: the 9,000-square-foot marble and gold foyer is often employed for receptions (where it accommodates 2,000 standees or 500 banqueters) and exhibitions (medieval fairs to antique auto shows). Inside, the hall has been graced by the talents of a variety of great artists, from Victor Herbert to Luciano Pavarotti.

And *Carnegie Magazine,* while given to thumping the house tub, turns a consistent eye to art and culture in the city. Plans are under way to expand the magazine's role, shaping it into the true arts forum that Pittsburgh greatly needs.

After all, the institute sees for itself a lofty role in Pittsburgh's future. "We collect," director Wilburn says, "we preserve, we exhibit. We educate and entertain an entire population."

## *Three Rivers Arts Festival*

***Above:* Beribboned dinosaur at the Three Rivers Arts Festival, © Mary Jane Bent**

***Facing page:* Balloons, © Walt Urbina**

By Abby Mendelson

Truth is, it's hard to say who has a better time at the Three Rivers Arts Festival, the kids, the adults, or festival director John Brice.

The 1986 edition was the twenty-seventh in an annual series that began as a weekend event in late spring and is now a full-blown three-week art festival in June. Kids—joyous, giggling children, hordes of them—were treated to face painting, countless encounters with jugglers and clowns, and scrumptious foods of all kinds. Instead of the blue tent of years past, there was the Castle, a scaffolding covered in red, blue, and yellow nylon banners with eight discovery rooms where children explored a magic kingdom replete with great beasts!

This year's tantalizing, thoroughly charming theme was Dinosaurs and Dragons. With help from Carnegie Institute's Museum of Art and Museum of Natural History, kids found no Loch Ness monster; instead they found the Three Rivers Creatures, three

120

giant aquatic beasts fashioned by Pittsburgh artists. And the kids got the thrill of adding wooden scales and other finishing touches to the finny leviathans.

The festival kept up the participation theme throughout much of the children's programming. The Dinosaur Dig, for example, had junior-size paleontologists digging for bones in a sand-table bone bed, then attaching them to dinosaur outlines. And to top it off, all of the bone sleuths received official dinosaur hunting licenses.

There was more, of course. Kids fed plant bean bags to a diplodocus and meat bean bags to an allosaurus. Courtesy of the Carnegie Library, they read about dinosaurs at the book display and listened to read-alouds on what was here (and what wasn't) millions and millions of years ago. They stood, scared and pointing, as a masked *Tyrannosaurus rex* wandered through their midst. And they listened to dinosaur rock, music and puppets that further enhanced the theme.

Nor was that all. Aside from the great lizardy beasts, there were special concerts, including famed children's songster Barry Louis Polisar. He's the one who sings such real-life ditties as ''He Eats Asparagus, Why Can't You Be That Way?'' and ''I Don't Think My Teacher Likes Me.'' As the titles might indicate, Polisar's songs struck chords of understanding for kids and parents alike.

Others focused on different educational messages. Lynda Martha Dance Company, for example, performed Grimms' fairy tale *The Little Tailor*. Puppets taught lessons about litter, recycling, and conservation. And there were storytellers, banjo players, even marimba players. And it was all free, of course.

For the rest of us, there were cool, early summer evenings, free concerts in parks packed with thousands of attentive people, food and plenty of it, art on display, art being made, and crafts for sale. The festival brought more than 600,000 visitors, who accounted for the sale of more than $40,000 worth of art and equally robust sales of souvenir T-shirts, posters, and catalogs.

At its softest focus, the Three Rivers Arts Festival is an easy-to-approach catchall, featuring performers from around the country, exhibits of art by locals and out-of-towners, foreign and non-commercial films that would not otherwise be widely seen, roving entertainers, and endless food booths—overall, a wonderful

*Left:* Frog men, © Jack A. Wolf

*Below:* Garden Mart, © Mary Jane Bent

and relaxing in-town festival. In terms of physical space, including the various gallery spaces, the festival covers a good portion of city, including the South Side, Regent Square, and Shadyside. It belongs to the entire metropolitan area, for virtually every Pittsburgh corporation, media outlet, and political entity sponsors some portions of it.

In 1986 an impressive 371 artists showed 599 works, and less than a quarter were based in Pittsburgh. "The competition is very intense," explains festival director John Brice. "That may not be good for us," admitted one local rejectee, "but it is good for the city."

In 1986 the pavilions were easier to traverse than they had been in years past, and the art was chosen by more prestigious jurors—Lynn Gumpert, for example, the senior curator of New York City's New Museum of Contemporary Art. And none of the artists argued with the fact that 1986 generally meant *more*: more locations, more prize money ($32,000 in cash awards), more special exhibitions with separate catalogs, more artists in action (fifty demonstrating daily), more banners (nearly three dozen of them), more of just about everything.

Then there were the showcases, important exhibitions of individual artists or groups. Among them was a showing of Tom Otterness' funny, figurative metal sculptures. Otterness, a thirty-four-year-old Kansan now living in New York, specializes in robots with comic and sexual overtones. His rigid, seriocomic metal men and women always invoke a smile and a nod of recognition.

The year's major group exhibition—one of the elements for which the Three Rivers Arts Festival is justifiably developing a national reputation—was titled "Connections: Works in Fiber." The works were eclectic and eye-catching, a feast for the imagination, worthy of many delightful viewing hours. It was a very special and rare show, and a few of the pieces were brilliant, such as Polish artist Magdalena Abakanowicz' *Seated Figures,* seventeen headless bodies sitting on bare tubular frames along a wall. Other notables included Ohioan Kathleen Moore Farling's woven wire *Kiva Ceremonial Vessel,* Ohioan Janice Lessman-Moss' wood-and-linen tapestry *Passing Dream IV,* New Yorker Lois Bryant's Mondrianesque *Water Bugs Series #8,* and New Yorker Katherine E. Knauer's *Air Force,* a work in painted cotton with planes, guns, stars, and angels—a riot of color, form, and

message.

On stage there were more than 170 performances, from folk to rock to jazz to the Pittsburgh Symphony. The opening act was jazz guitarist Stanley Jordan, whose unique, finger-tapping technique makes him sound like an entire string band instead of a solo act. Then came surf singers Jan and Dean, folk doyenne Judy Collins, and soul legend Smokey Robinson. The festival provided a cornucopic earful many times over.

Somehow it all gets whipped into shape by John Brice, formerly the director of a South Bend, Indiana, art center. He came to take his new year-round Pittsburgh job in November 1982, and from all accounts has not stopped moving since. You may have seen him during the festival, a shirt-sleeved young man with walkie-talkie and clipboard, lending a hand wherever needed. From the time early commuters arrive in town until after the last nighttime concert stragglers depart, he is there. He'll help move heavy equipment, or shinny up a tower to facilitate a sound check. And it's all worth it, to Brice and everyone else. Because spread all over town for three weeks is the Three Rivers Arts Festival. It stops everybody—but everybody—in their tracks to peek and taste and consider the arts. For that alone, and for the truly festive spirit it brings to Downtown, Pittsburgh's Super Bowl of the Arts deserves high praise and yearly eager anticipation.

The financial risks incurred in the glassmaking enterprise did not deter others from investing in businesses and industries in the infant settlement. Thomas Perkins, a jeweler, opened the city's first department store, at Third Avenue and Market Street, in 1800, and he induced John Hammond, a shoemaker, to lease space in the store from him. And the borough of Pittsburgh was only seven years old when George Cochran started making chairs there and William Cecil opened a leather-goods factory. A tin-plate business was opened in 1802 and an ironware works in 1803, and the first cotton factory inside the borough's limits began operating in 1804.

In 1807 the world's first flint-glass factory was founded in Pittsburgh by George Robinson and Edward Ensel. The partners sold it a year later to Bakewell's, where the world's first glass-crystal chandelier was cut in 1810. The chandelier was sold for $300 to one Mr. Kerr, who hung it in his inn. In the following year, the first steamboat to ply America's western waterways was built and launched in Pittsburgh. Also in 1811, the first iron cannon to be made west of the mountains was forged here. These were the first of many "firsts" credited to industrialists, business owners, researchers and inventors, and entrepreneurs of the Pittsburgh area.

The first-ever iron mill to puddle and roll iron was started in Fayette County in 1817, and the world's first file factory opened in Pittsburgh in 1829. In 1835 the world's first cast-iron bridge was erected over Dunlap's Creek in Brownsville; it was eighty-five feet long and twenty-five feet wide. Ten years later John Augustus Roebling built the first wire-cable suspension bridge, over the Allegheny River in Pittsburgh, completing the bridge at a total cost (including the removal of an old wooden bridge at the site) of $62,000. Roebling was quite a resourceful fellow. He owned the factory that produced the seven-inch iron cable, and he invented the machine that wound the cable.

Steel was just a glimmer in some industrialist's eye when the city's first blast furnace was installed by Graff, Bennett and Company in 1860. That steelmaking was to play an important role in Pittsburgh's economic future could be discerned rather readily, for soon after Graff and Bennett got their furnace under way, two other men, whose names eventually became synonymous with steel in southwestern Pennsylvania, got into the act.

Benjamin Franklin Jones and James Laughlin erected a blast furnace of their own in the city, and by 1870 they had seven furnaces operating in Pittsburgh. By 1877 Andrew Carnegie's mills were breaking production records and setting the new standard of quality with the manufacture of Bessemer-process steel. These mills were to be included among the steelmaking and processing facilities assembled in 1901 to create U.S. Steel, the world's first billion-dollar corporation. Thus was the foundation of the city's glory as Steel Capital of the World so firmly established.

At about the same time that Jones and Laughlin were making steel, another Pittsburgher, Henry John Heinz, was hard at work shredding horseradish and peddling it door to door. By 1869 Heinz had enough business to open a food-processing factory in Sharpsburg, just outside the city limits, and thus made it into the record books as the world's first commercial producer of foodstuffs. The site of that first factory is less than ten miles from the H.J. Heinz Company's principal North Side plant, still in operation today, and within view of Heinz's worldwide headquarters in Downtown Pittsburgh.

Natural gas was used for the first time ever to fuel an iron-making operation at the Rogers & Burchfield mill in Leechburg, Armstrong County, in 1873. A year later Rogers and Burchfield were also to start the world's first factory for the manufacture of black plate, tin, and terneplate.

The first large-scale production of plate glass took place in 1883 in Creighton, just northeast of the city. It was produced by the New York City Plate Glass Company, which, after recapitalization a few months later, changed its name to Pittsburgh Plate Glass Company. Today the company is known as PPG Industries, Incorporated, and it still keeps its world headquarters in Downtown Pittsburgh in an architecturally dramatic building complex called PPG Place.

Another major industry also got its start in Pittsburgh, as the year 1885 saw the first commercial production of aluminum. The Pittsburgh Reduction Company later became the Aluminum Company of America, or Alcoa. Alcoa also made history when it moved its headquarters into the world's first aluminum-faced building, the thirty-story Alcoa Building, which was completed in Downtown Pittsburgh in 1953. About three million pounds of

aluminum were required in the construction of the building, which incorporates all-aluminum elevators, electrical wiring, and conductors.

Westinghouse Electric and Manufacturing Company, which maintains its headquarters in Pittsburgh (under the shortened name of Westinghouse Electric Corporation), and is today the largest employer in the greater Pittsburgh area, was the first to produce electric meters on a commercial basis, and it did this in a Pittsburgh factory in 1888.

While Pittsburgh is not the center for the automotive industry today, it was an early manufacturer. The first American-made truck was designed and built in 1898 by the Pittsburgh Motor Vehicle Company, later the Autocar Company. A company brochure described the first effort as "a delivery wagon which can be made of any size or design, that will be fitted with five- to eight-horsepower motors. Complete with motors it will weigh from 900 to 1,400 pounds—so simple in construction that any driver of ordinary intelligence can operate it with more safety than he could drive a horse."

This list of noteworthy events and notable firsts could go on and on. But Pittsburghers did not concern themselves only with the manufacture of durable goods and with heavy industries. They found time for other pursuits as well, and in doing so they made a bit of history.

The Republican party held its first national meeting in the city February 22, 1856, to plan its first national convention, and the very first national labor union of any importance, the Federation of Organized Trades and Labor Unions, was organized here in 1881. Later the organization changed its name to the American Federation of Labor. And the Steelworkers' Organizing Committee, which eventually grew into the giant United Steelworkers of America, held its first meeting in the Grant Building in Downtown Pittsburgh on June 21, 1936.

Two other labor firsts occurred in Pittsburgh. On the positive side, George Westinghouse, inventor of the air brake, was the first factory owner to give workers a half day off on Saturdays; he did it at his Pittsburgh plant in June 1871. On the other hand, it was in Pittsburgh that Chinese migrant laborers in the United States were first exploited: one William Kelly "induced" twelve Chinese to work in his foundry in 1854 for what were reported to have been "extremely low wages."

On a cheerier note, moving pictures made history in Pittsburgh when Harry Davis opened the Nickelodeon on June 19, 1905. It was the first theater in the world devoted exclusively to motion pictures. The ninety-six-seat cinema, managed by John P. Harris, made a profit of $1,000 during its first week of operation.

Pittsburgh was also a broadcasting pioneer. The world's first commercial radio station KDKA was licensed here on October 27, 1920, and the country's first community-owned public television station, WQED, went on the air here in 1953. Less than a week after KDKA went on the air, it made the first broadcast of presidential election results—the Harding-Cox race. KDKA, still broadcasting from Pittsburgh, became the first radio station to go to 50,000-watts power. It was the first to broadcast a religious service (from Calvary Episcopal Church in Downtown Pittsburgh on January 2, 1921), a tennis match (the Davis Cup match between Australia and Great Britain, from Allegheny Country Club in Sewickley, on August 4, 1921), and baseball play-by-play (Pittsburgh Pirates versus the Philadelphia Phillies, August 5, 1921—a game the Pirates won 8-5).

It is appropriate that sporting events were so prominent in KDKA's early broadcasting schedule, because they are prominent in the city's history. The first black player to play on a white baseball team played under the name J.W. (Bud) Fowler; his real name was John Jackson, however, and he played for a team in New Castle, Lawrence County, in 1872.

Pittsburgh opened the world's first fireproof baseball stadium, Forbes Field, on June 30, 1909, and to celebrate the Pittsburgh Pirates defeated the Chicago Cubs 3-2.

A year earlier, the University of Pittsburgh's football team was the first ever to have players wear identifying numbers on their jerseys. Unfortunately, the device did not help the Pitt team, as they lost on December 5, 1908, to Washington and Jefferson College, 14-0.

Although some would dispute the claim, there is sufficient proof to establish that the first professional football game ever played—a game in which at least one participant was a paid performer—was played in the Pittsburgh area on September 3, 1895; the contest, which took place in Latrobe, Westmoreland County, pitted the Latrobe YMCA squad against the Jeannette

Athletic Club.

Other notable and noteworthy Pittsburgh firsts include the U.S. Postal Service's putting the two-digit zip code system into service in Pittsburgh in 1943. The push-button telephone was introduced to the world here in 1963. The first drive-in gasoline station was opened by Gulf Refining Company in the city's East Liberty section in 1913 (and it is reported that the station, which stayed open all night and provided free crankcase service, sold thirty gallons of gasoline on the first day). And Gulf Oil made another bit of automotive history in 1914 when it produced and distributed the world's first automobile road map—a map of roads and routes suitable for automobile traffic in Allegheny County. The first assembly plant to be operated in the United States by a foreign auto manufacturer was established by Volkswagen in the mid-1970s in nearby New Stanton.

Rounding out the city's illustrious association with things automotive is this item: Pittsburgh was the scene of the world's first armored-car holdup. It happened March 11, 1927, when the notorious Flatheads, a band of local ne'er-do-wells, dynamited a truck carrying the Pittsburgh Terminal Company's payroll—all $104,250 of it—on a road about seven miles from the city. Reports of the day indicated that the gang escaped with the loot, leaving five guards seriously injured in the explosion.

The industrial glories Pittsburgh can claim are, for the moment at least, mostly things of the past. There is not much talk around town these days of industrial firsts, nor are there many remembrances of those days of automotive glory. Pittsburgh is different today than it was when steel reigned supreme and coal was king. Things have changed, but location is still the city's greatest blessing, and Pittsburghers know that location—the factor that brought their city to prominence in the first place—will emerge again as its critical and true strength.

Pittsburgh today is still ideally situated, in the right place at what could be the right time, to ply its trades, practice its professions and its crafts, make and ship goods, provide vitally important services, mine resources, build, farm, sell, finance, heal, and teach. For within 500 miles of the Pittsburgh area lie some of the richest and ripest markets in the world.

Inside that 500-mile radius live more than half the people of the United States and Canada. Nineteen metropolitan areas with

**Three Rivers Regatta,**
© Walt Urbina

populations of one million or more are located in that market territory, as are a dozen of the country's top twenty-five metropolitan retail markets—where more than half the retail sales in the United States are rung up—and twenty-two of the country's thirty-five major industrial markets. Moreover, the people who control 55 percent of all the personal income in the United States live within Pittsburgh's 500-mile reach, and fully 58 percent of all the manufacturing activity in the United States takes place in that area.

But demand for Pittsburgh's steel has dwindled as markets have shifted westward. And Pittsburgh's coal is too rich in sulfur to be environmentally acceptable for many contemporary uses. Depressed, too, are the markets for many of the area's other key commodities, aluminum and glass among them. So how does Pittsburgh propose to serve this rich and tempting marketplace lying so close at hand?

By doing what the town's earliest entrepreneurs did: exploit ing the area's considerable strengths and resources; making maximum use of the skills, talents, and industriousness of the almost three million people who live and work in the locale known as Pittsburgh.

It is a large and diverse area stretching over a large chunk of southwestern Pennsylvania. When you say *Pittsburgh* you can mean a lot of things and a lot of different places.

Pittsburgh is the City of Pittsburgh proper, of course, a city that covers a fifty-seven-square-mile area centering on the Point, where the Ohio River is formed and begins its westward wanderings. This city is the capital of Allegheny County and is the largest municipality in southwestern Pennsylvania—in all of western Pennsylvania, for that matter. And Pittsburgh is indisputably the region's economic, governmental, and social hub. Some 403,000 people live in the city's eighty-eight neighborhoods.

The designation *Pittsburgh* is also frequently used to refer to all of Allegheny County. The county covers 728 square miles and is home to almost one and a half million people. They live in 130 separate, and very independent, municipalities, each with its own ordinances and regulations, its own governmental structure, its own police and fire departments, its own road and maintenance departments, and its own fierce sense of individual identity.

Then there is something called Greater Pittsburgh, an amorphous area, the boundaries of which hardly anyone agrees upon. One interpretation designates Greater Pittsburgh as a four-county area surrounding the city, and that is the definition used by many of the area's marketing and civic organizations. The area encompasses Allegheny, Beaver, Washington, and Westmoreland counties, where almost 2,300,000 people live, and where a good deal of the area's economic and commercial muscle resides. Other designations, however, include Butler County in that geographic assemblage, since it is closer to the city than some of the areas in the other four counties. Still others insist on adding Fayette County to that number as well. With the addition of the last two counties named, Greater Pittsburgh encompasses six counties and includes an area in which almost two and a half million people reside.

There are still others, however, who take a sprawling nine-county area around the city to constitute a Pittsburgh "region." This regional designation encompasses areas somewhat removed from the city hub but where the influences of the city of Pittsburgh and of Allegheny County are still strongly felt.

The Pittsburgh region is made up of three counties in addition to the six mentioned above; they are Armstrong, Greene, and Lawrence. These counties bring the total population of the nine-county Pittsburgh region to almost three million.

There are a million people in the region's work force. They don't make as much steel anymore, and they don't mine as much coal. Fewer of them are involved in the endeavors that made the area an industrial giant until the late 1970s. But they are working, and they constitute a larger work force than was supported in the glory days of steel and coal.

In 1953 more than 44 percent of the area's workers were involved in manufacturing; the comparable group today is slightly over 16 percent. Despite that decline, though, there are still more than 7,000 different products made in the Pittsburgh area, and manufacturing still accounts for a sizable share of local paychecks.

Manufacturing's economic clout in the area is revealed by statistics for Allegheny County. A U.S. Department of Commerce report issued in May 1985 states that although manufacturing occupations were only the third largest category of jobs among workers in the county (after general services and retailing), total payrolls for those occupations exceeded all other employment categories. When it came to financial contribution to the county's work force, manufacturing occupations outdistanced all others, including general services; retailing; transportation and public utilities; contracting and construction; finance, insurance, and real estate; wholesale trade; and mining.

A recently compiled economic profile of the Pittsburgh area indicates that primary metals production and other manufacturing will probably continue to decline during the decade of the 1980s. The two categories together are expected to provide employment for about 21 percent of the area's work force by the year 1990 whereas they employed 41 percent of all the workers in 1955, and 25 percent as recently as 1981. The report also forecasts that service jobs and trade, both wholesale and retail, should continue to replace primary metals and other manufac-

**Pittsburgh Seminary,**
**© Herb Ferguson**

turing throughout the decade and will employ 60 percent of all area workers by 1990.

Government, which employed about 8 percent of the work force of Pittsburgh in 1955, had grown to 12.5 percent by 1981 and is expected to inch up slightly, to 12.7 percent, by the end of this decade. Mining and construction, an employment category that accounted for slightly more than 7 percent of area jobs in 1955, and which dropped to 5.7 percent by 1981, is expected to recover in the decade ahead and rise slightly by 1990 to a little more than 6 percent.

Today, according to the Commerce Department report, only 21 percent of workers in Allegheny County and 15 percent of workers living in the City of Pittsburgh are engaged in manufacturing; not many years ago those percentages would have been more than double.

One indication of how great a turnaround Pittsburgh's economy has undergone is the fact that education is now a major employer in the area, and higher education is the region's second-largest industry. The University of Pittsburgh ranks as the largest employer in the City of Pittsburgh, with almost 8,000 faculty and staff on the payroll. And local education employs more than 50,000 people throughout the region.

An impressive twenty-nine colleges and universities—including two of the nation's premier research universities, Carnegie-Mellon University and the University of Pittsburgh (known to the locals as Pitt)—serve the region, and about fifty vocational and technical schools help Pittsburghers develop their talents to earn a living with solid, salable skills. All told, more than 100,000 students are enrolled in post-high-school education, more than 75,000 of them in schools in the four-county area around the city.

Research conducted at many of these academic institutions combines with the considerable research and development endeavors carried on by many of the business and industrial firms in the area, making Pittsburgh a major world research center. More than a billion dollars is spent every year on R&D in the area, and such activity is estimated to contribute over fifteen billion dollars to the region's economy. More than 25,000 scientists and technicians are employed in Pittsburgh's more than 170 research centers and laboratories, and one out of every fifty people engaged in science in the United States lives and works in western Pennsylvania. The professional engineers working in the region constitute the fifth-largest pool of engineering talent in the nation, according to an economic profile published in 1985 by the Greater Pittsburgh Chamber of Commerce.

Moreover, most of the corporations headquartered in Pittsburgh maintain and operate R&D facilities in the region. About seventy scientific and technical societies either have headquarters here or maintain chapters in the area.

These scientists and technicians are some of the over 34 percent of all Pittsburgh-area white-collar workers categorized as professional and technical, one of the highest such rankings in the United States.

Pittsburgh's scientific and research capabilities have a strong heritage, and from it the area is building on its already impressive reputation as a health-care and medical teaching and research center. There are more than fifty hospitals in the region, supported by a $12-billion infrastructure, and by member hospitals of the University Health Center of Pittsburgh. Affiliated with the University of Pittsburgh and its School of Medicine, the Health Center has earned international acclaim as a medical treatment, research, and teaching organization and is fast becoming one of the country's major organ transplantation facilities as well. The world's first combined heart and liver transplant, for example, was performed at Presbyterian University Hospital, one of the Health Center's member institutions. Almost 4,000

*Facing page:* **Fireworks over Sixth Street Bridge, © Michael Haritan**

students are in training in the Health Center and in Pitt's health-profession schools.

Medical research being conducted at the university and in the Health Center has already yielded impressive results. Synthetic insulin was developed there, and the first successful polio vaccine was developed in 1954 by Dr. Jonas Salk while working in the University of Pittsburgh's Virus Research Laboratory. At Pitt Dr. Klaus Hofmann produced the first synthetic cortisone-producing hormone. And Pitt's medical school's Department of Orthopedic Surgery was responsible for the first successful metal implants in human bones.

Carnegie-Mellon University, Pitt's Oakland neighbor, is a world leader in computer science and robotics engineering, research, and development. CMU's Robotics Institute, established in 1980, does advanced R&D on artificial intelligence and on robots that "think, see, and act."

Several small companies, many of them spinoffs of CMU's Robotics Institute, are actively engaged in robotics research and engineering, as well as in manufacturing robots for industrial applications. This is an area in which Pittsburgh's Westinghouse Electric Corporation has long been a world leader.

Pittsburgh is making a very serious commitment to high-tech activities as well as to other endeavors that are transforming the area from a one-industry, blue-collar locale into one where the work force wears mostly white collars. Pittsburgh is backing the high-tech commitment realistically with capital investment; training and retraining programs; R&D efforts at both the corporate and the educational levels; and the strong, proven leadership capabilities of every segment of the community, in the areas of business, education, religion, and government.

Pittsburgh has also renewed its commitment to the area's most valued and productive resource, the people themselves. It is, after all, the people, with their history and heritage of industriousness, their instinct for survival, and their willingness to face realistically the challenges of change, who will eventually accomplish Pittsburgh's reemergence as an economic power. They recognize that although the glory days of steel and of heavy industry are history, their city and their entire region have the potential to emerge again stronger and more vital than ever before.

CHAPTER **IV**

# Governing Principles

"What the hell," Harry S. Truman wanted to know, "is a prothonotary?"

President Truman asked the question with characteristic bluntness, upon being introduced to the prothonotary of Allegheny County. This was during a campaign visit to Pittsburgh in November 1948.

A prothonotary, Truman was told, is clerk of civil courts in Allegheny County and chief record keeper of the civil court system. In Allegheny County, it is an important political post. The title, which has its origins in British usage, is more traditional than practical and is only rarely used in the United States.

The soon-to-be reelected president reportedly was highly amused that Pittsburghers, residents of a busy, bustling, booming industrial behemoth of a town, would insist on referring to one of their top elected officials and powerful politicians by such a quaint title. A clerk of courts is a clerk of courts, and there should be no doubt about it in anyone's mind, he seemed to suggest. *Prothonotary,* indeed. (This reaction from a man who had once won election in his native Missouri to a political post that entitled him to be addressed as "judge," although his duties were those of a county road commissioner.)

Harry Truman's amused reaction at being introduced to the prothonotary was tempered by his realization that the clerk of the civil courts was—and still is, for that matter—a political power to be reckoned with in Pittsburgh. In fact, the candidate was eager to court the favor of the prothonotary—and every other Democratic official assembled to greet him that day. He knew

*Facing page:* **Cathedral of Learning and fountain, © Norm Schumm**

that their support would be backed by the votes of the multitudes, because Pittsburghers had abandoned their traditional Republicanism with a vengeance in the 1932 election that sent Franklin Roosevelt to the White House, and the elapsed years had not dampened their ardor for the Democratic party. Upon being so instructed by the party leadership, most Pittsburghers could be counted on to deliver a straightforward, straight-ticket performance at the polls, come election day. Pittsburgh voters in the 1940s were unstintingly Democratic, and Harry Truman knew it.

That was the political picture in post-Depression, post-Hoover, post-war Pittsburgh. And that picture could well be described as a still life, for little of substance has changed in the forty years since. Oh, the voters are not so unquestioningly loyal today. Even the staunchest Democrat splits a ticket now and then, if just for appearance's sake. But the Democratic party still rules the political roost in Pittsburgh, in Allegheny County, and throughout most of southwestern Pennsylvania.

One-party political domination has never guaranteed political peace and harmony, however. Just because Democrats occupy most of the political perches in the area's roost does not mean that they all coo like lovebirds all the time. Intraparty feuds are frequent and on occasion have been of extended, even interminable, duration—although hatchets are publicly buried and differences conveniently forgotten when required in the interests of party unity.

Some have observed that Pittsburgh Democrats fight among themselves so much because they can't find enough Republicans to fight with. And Pittsburgh Democrats, it seems, like nothing better than a good, rousing, bloody, no-holds-barred family fight every once in a while, just to keep the juices flowing and to make things interesting.

Case in point: Pittsburgh City Council is a nine-member body united by the common bond of Democratic membership and divided by just about anything else one could think of. There has not been a Republican seated in council chambers, on the fifth floor of the City-County Building on Grant Street, since 1934, except as a visitor. With no Republicans to fight with, council members have had little choice but to fight among themselves, as well as with heads of various city departments, bureaucrats,

*Above:* Steelers fans,
© Joel B. Levinson

*Left:* Pittsburgh Steelers,
© Michael Haritan

*Facing page:* Pittsburgh
skyscrapers, © Herb
Ferguson

**Carnegie-Mellon University,**
**© Maurice Tierney**

political appointees, and other elected officials. The battles frequently involve matters that would only rarely merit mention in political science textbooks.

Fortunately, City Council does get its act together with sufficient regularity so as not to hamper unduly the passage of necessary legislation. Despite the frequent bickering, members of council have gotten the job done when circumstances commanded their attention.

Pittsburgh City Council members are elected at large by voters from throughout the city, who cast ballots for the entire slate. Some Pittsburghers have become very vocal in their opposition to at-large election of council, contending that their neighborhoods and their interests would be better served by district elections. Those disgruntled citizens point out that a majority on council are from the East End of town, and representatives on council from some sections of the city have been as rare as Republicans (which is to say nonexistent). The debate over at-large versus district elections was fueled anew during the 1985 election when, for the first time in many years, no black was elected to a council seat, giving Pittsburgh the dubious distinction of being the only major northern city without black representation on its legislative body. District election would not only assure minority representation on council but would result in better and more diverse representation for various neighborhoods, supporters contend. But the forces favoring retention of the at-large system (which include the mayor and most of the political establishment in Pittsburgh) are powerful and not likely to surrender their position without a battle, one that could wear on for years.

The City of Pittsburgh has a strong-mayor government, a form that bestows much power, including most of the decision-making prerogatives, upon the mayor. This governmental structure allows a strong individual to control the course of events, to have the dominant voice in political matters, to horde or share power as is deemed fit, and to hold a strategic position in virtually all dealings both inside and outside the political structure. As the current mayor of Pittsburgh, Richard S. Caliguiri, puts it, "A mayor of Pittsburgh is empowered to form some very strong partnerships."

Strong partnerships have been a political tradition in Pittsburgh. They predate the days of David Lawrence's term of office, although the Lawrence years still serve as the standard by which such liaisons are judged by Pittsburghers. Certainly, there had been public-private partnerships in Pittsburgh before that time, but when David Lawrence and Richard King Mellon forged their partnership in the 1940s, they joined together in a force that not only changed the face of the city, in its first Renaissance, but changed its destiny as well.

Virtually every mayor since has emulated that public-private partnership, successfully or not. When Caliguiri was elected mayor in 1977, after having served on City Council for twelve years and having defeated the endorsed Democratic candidate in the mayoral primary, relations between City Hall and the business and corporate community may have been at their lowest ebb since the Lawrence years. Caliguiri saw a rekindling of the fire in which earlier public-private partnerships were forged to be his biggest challenge and his first priority.

There are not many cities in which the Democratic mayoral candidate can hope to attract votes from the Democratic electorate by promising to reestablish strong ties with the business community. But doing so, Caliguiri won the election handily, and

the same posture of public-private cooperation has helped him win reelection twice. Political realities in Pittsburgh are such that Democrat Caliguiri can openly court the Republican corporate and business power structure, and be openly, enthusiastically, and generously supported in return, while still enjoying the overwhelming support of the predominantly Democratic electorate. He might be said to have the best of both worlds: he is as comfortable and welcome in the quiet, richly paneled corridors of power in the Duquesne Club as he is at a boisterous neighborhood celebration in the heavily Italian neighborhood of Bloomfield.

The reason the electorate is not suspicious of the mayor's close associations with the business community and with those who normally support Republican politics is, he insists, because everything is out in the open. There are no hidden agendas, no secret promises, no shady dealings, no under-the-table arrangements. He repeats what others often say: Pittsburgh is a small town and (referring to the leadership of both the public and private sectors) "We all know each other; we are like family here."

And in a family, when times get tough, you can call on other family members for help. That is what Caliguiri did immediately after being elected mayor in 1977.

The mayor remembers it well: "One of the first things I did then was to go to the Conference [the Allegheny Conference on Community Development, representing Pittsburgh's corporate and business interests] and ask for help and support. Of course, I knew most of the people involved with the Conference from my time on City Council, but I wanted them to know that I wanted to work closely with them, that I needed their support and the city needed their support for the great rebuilding job that had to be done. So I took that message to them in person."

The visit paid off, both for Caliguiri and for the city. With the enthusiastic support of the city's business and corporate community, plans were made for another round of building and redevelopment. For the most part these plans centered on projects in the central business district and on the shores of the Monongahela and Allegheny rivers, although they also included projects in some city neighborhoods. The result: Pittsburgh's skyline was transformed again, for the second time in twenty years. This series of construction and renewal projects came to be known col-

*Facing page:* **One Mellon Bank Center, © Herb Ferguson**

151

*Above and facing page:*
**Liberty Center construction,**
**© Michael Haritan**

lectively as Renaissance II.

Caliguiri was confident that the business and corporate communities in general would not turn their backs on him when he sought their help and support. In seeking their assistance, he was in keeping with the hallowed Lawrence-Mellon tradition, a tradition no one in Pittsburgh treats lightly. Caliguiri's initiative reestablished the equal partnership between the public and private sectors, a coalition that profoundly affects the way Pittsburgh is governed. The private-sector partners who pledged their support to Caliguiri in 1977 (and continue to make good on that pledge today) hold no official seats in city or county government, nor have they stood for election to any such seats. Nevertheless, many of Pittsburgh's business leaders must be considered to share in the governing process, because without their support, influence, and financial clout, some vital projects would not be undertaken and completed, and some of the hope for the future would be lost. Things are made to happen in Pittsburgh when public and private sectors, Republican and Democrat, work cooperatively. Of such efforts are renaissances made.

Pittsburgh is, after all, the "City of the Ten-Minute Renaissance"—or at least that's the way a reporter for the *New York Times* saw it. The reporter came to town a few years ago to do a story on the transformation of Pittsburgh from a grimy mill town to a very attractive headquarters city. He interviewed business, civic, and government leaders and was obviously impressed with what he saw and heard. Commenting on the unusual degree of public-private cooperation and the easy access to the seats of power in both sectors, the reporter observed that in New York it takes thirty days to get ten people together in a room to fix a traffic ticket; in Pittsburgh, on the other hand, in ten minutes you can get thirty people together to plan a renaissance.

This exaggeration is not so great as is might appear. Important and far-reaching efforts, such as an urban renaissance, can be planned and executed with less red tape and thus more speedily in Pittsburgh than elsewhere because, as the mayor points out, this *is* a small town, and everyone who is anyone really *does* seem to know everyone else. Once there is agreement that something must be done, action follows fast.

This is true despite the fact that the structure of power has changed dramatically since the 1940s and 1950s. No politician to-

day commands the unquestioning loyalty that David L. Lawrence could—and did. No corporate official today can unilaterally commit virtually unlimited funds and manpower to a development program, however noble and beneficial, as Richard K. Mellon could—and did. Reshaping a city—changing its look and restructuring its economy—is not something that can be done with a handshake and a promise, as it was when Lawrence and Mellon shook hands and made promises. The governing philosophy these days, in political entities and in business organizations, is that of shared power, of distributed rather than concentrated authority and responsibility.

Over the years many of Pittsburgh's corporate leaders have always exercised their considerable influence on how the place was governed and how the economy was structured by virtue of sheer force of numbers—the numbers being the size of their industrial payrolls. And despite recent plant closings and employee layoffs, especially in the steel industry, many corporate

leaders whose companies have been forced to cut back employment and production still enjoy high visibility and considerable influence, and their companies continue to be vital to the area's economic growth and well-being. Pittsburgh is, after all, the third largest corporate headquarters city in the United States, and fifteen Fortune 500 industrial companies maintain their headquarters here. The influence they exert cannot be measured solely in terms of local production. Even though USX Corporation (formerly U.S. Steel) is no longer Pittsburgh's top industrial employer, the corporation—the nation's fifteenth largest— maintains its corporate headquarters in Pittsburgh. And its chairman, David M. Roderick, continues to hold a position of civic and political power in Pittsburgh. The same can be said of the chief executives of other locally headquartered firms, despite their curtailment of production activities in the area.

As one member of middle management at Rockwell International Corporation is fond of observing: "We don't make anything in significant numbers here, we have little in the way of payroll outside the executive offices in Pittsburgh, and we are not a productive force to speak of. But Pittsburgh is home and it's where we keep the money, the money that comes from all operations all over the world. So who's to say we don't contribute to the economic well-being of Pittsburgh?"

Thus, it is safe to say that the amount of power and influence big business has in Pittsburgh has not diminished appreciably since the Lawrence-Mellon era; it has merely been diffused. Richard King Mellon held an inordinate amount of power in his hands alone, and so did David Leo Lawrence. Today, however, power and influence are shared. Business people still influence the way the pace is managed and governed; it just takes more people to do so.

Finding those people has apparently not been a problem in Pittsburgh. Corporate chief executives have always sat on the key boards and committees, making their voices and opinions heard, contributing guidance and advice. Civic involvement has not been confined exclusively to the top echelon of Pittsburgh's corporate community. Traditionally, bright stars from lower ranks of management have been earnestly recruited to participate in civic and governmental activities in Pittsburgh. Community service continues to be a requirement for corporate advancement here: no one can expect to ascend to corporate leadership without a consistent record of community involvement, civic enrichment, and organizational leadership. In Pittsburgh, the road to the top of the corporate hierarchy is paved with good civic intentions, backed by public service.

The voice of small business has recently become more influential in political and civic affairs. As small businesses assume more prominent roles in the economic life of the area, as they continue to make significant contributions to the economy and take up at least some of the employment slack left by plant closings, their stature in the community grows, and so does their level of participation in the political structure.

Some small-business leaders want an even stronger voice in government and in formulating plans for Pittsburgh's economic future. Small business, they contend, is carrying the load of economic revitalization and shouldering the burdens of business leadership without sharing in the benefits. Big business is still

**Hilton Hotel brunch, © Herb Ferguson**

**View from North Side,**
**© Mary Jane Bent**

influencing the course of events in Pittsburgh out of proportion to its contribution to the local economy, these small-business people insist, and they are determined to see the power structure changed.

They are not likely to be ignored, since economic reality is on their side. Currently, small business is creating most of the new jobs in the area, establishing a firm economic foundation for the entire region. Small business is contributing to the quality of life as well as to the livelihoods of an increasingly large number of Pittsburghers, and small business is eager to help manage Pittsburgh.

**Towers, © Michael Haritan**

Those who manage the city and its surrounds, the front-line political leaders, have found Pittsburgh to be very manageable. It is a compact city, being much smaller both in population and in geography than most U.S. cities of similiar importance. It works to the city's benefit that most Pittsburghers cherish small-town values and seek to be governed accordingly.

Pittsburgh's city government and its elected officials respond accordingly, often appearing and functioning as a small town's government might. There is surprisingly little aloofness in City Hall and council chambers. Even most city bureaucrats are reasonably pleasant, and some of them are exceedingly so. Of course there are some callous and uncooperative functionaries, but Pittsburghers generally get decent and friendly treatment when they undertake business with city departments.

The small-town character of Pittsburgh results in an unusual accessibility of officeholders. In Pittsburgh, people do not have to have a great deal of political pull to obtain an appointment, lodge a complaint, or get a rise out of government. Mayor Caliguiri makes a point of attending neighborhood and ethnic functions regularly and boasts that he marches in more parades than

*Above:* Winter scene,
© Walt Urbina

*Left:* Brookline snowfall,
© Michael Haritan

most area band directors. He sees such activities as functions of his office, and the mayor is not alone in that regard. Other elected city officials are often seen in the neighborhoods, mingling and meeting the people. A very visible government presides over Pittsburgh. This visibility and accessibility give the governed—or at least those who avail themselves of the opportunity—a direct link with those who govern, which is something rare in big-city politics.

The same scenario is followed in Allegheny County government as well. The county, encompassing as it does 130 separate municipalities of various sizes, relies on a small-town approach to governance. Years ago county government was innocuous and unobtrusive, which is to say that it functioned as do most county governments in this part of Pennsylvania, performing the services that individual municipalities could not or preferred not to perform for themselves. In recent years, however, Allegheny County government has become a powerful force for economic and social development. When the downturn in the steel and basic metals industries occurred, for example, county government

*Above and facing page:*
**Meadows racetrack,**
**© Jack A. Wolf**

*Above:* **Pirates baseball,**
**© Jack A. Wolf**

*Above, right:* **Motocross,**
**© Michael Haritan**

*Center:* **Marathon finish**
**line, © Jack A. Wolf**

*Facing page, clockwise*
*from top left:* **Joggers, fish-**
**ing at Fox Chapel, and**
**resting at Schenley Park,**
**© Jack A. Wolf**

*Above:* **Cathedral of Learning reflection,** © **Michael Haritan**

*Right:* **Field Hockey at Fox Chapel High School,** © **Harry Edelman**

established and helped fund early programs for training the unemployed and underemployed—programs that were conducted in the county's community college. County government established the area's largest public transit agency, arranging to buy out dozens of small private transit operations and merge them into the Port Authority of Allegheny County. County government operates the two airports that serve the region, Greater Pittsburgh International and Allegheny County Airport. And county government owns a countywide hospitalization system for chronically ill elderly residents.

County government also provides Republican party members an opportunity to share in governance. State law mandates minority representation on boards of county commissioners, and in this part of Pennsylvania *minority* usually means Republican.

Even though the Allegheny County Board of Commissioners has had a two-to-one Democrat-Republican ratio for as long as most can remember, voting does not always follow party lines. (That would be too simple and too predictable.) The two Democrats will often split on a vote, providing the Republican member with the opportunity to flex some political muscle and cast the deciding vote. This happens more often than one might expect in a place where Democrats dominate so overwhelmingly. In fact, for most of the 1975-1979 term, Commissioner Robert Peirce, a

Republican, teamed with Democrat James Flaherty in a strategy that effectively neutralized the second Democrat (and the most senior member of the board), Tom Foerster. Foerster managed to survive the ordeal, surviving both Flaherty and Peirce as commissioners as well. He is currently serving his fourth consecutive term as an Allegheny County commissioner.

The Board of Commissioners of Allegheny County government today comprises Tom Foerster as chairman; Peter Flaherty, former Pittsburgh mayor (and brother of former county commissioner James Flaherty); and Barbara Hafer, who has used her term to gain statewide recognition as well as local clout while effectively serving her county constituency. Hafer has been identified as the second most politically powerful female politician in Pennsylvania, following a city councilwoman in Philadelphia. In 1986, after only a few years in public office, Hafer was a serious contender for the Republican nomination as lieutenant governor.

The government of Allegheny County has emerged as an innovative and powerful economic and social force virtually out of

165

necessity rather than mandate. As Commissioner Foerster has said, "We had little choice. So much of what we did we took on ourselves." In some cases the county has taken the initiative when precedent or direction from the state level was lacking. One example is the establishment of one of the country's first Model Cities programs in the Turtle Creek Valley. "We saw that logically we were the only ones, the only governmental entity— the only entity of any kind—that could fulfill that need. There was a need for aggressive action. Someone had to do something. So we did it. We knew there were risks, but they were risks we had to take."

John Robin, now chairman of Pittsburgh's Urban Redevelopment Authority and a legendary political figure in the area for years (he was David Lawrence's civic adviser, political strategist, and first link with the Republican industrialists in the planning of the first urban Renaissance of the 1940s and 1950s) has also contributed his evaluation of county government:

*The character of county government generally and Allegheny County government in particular has been changing over the years. At least in Allegheny County, government is ending up being the lowest common denominator in the decision-making process. When there is no one else to do the job, to take on the task, county government is stepping in, and really has to step in, to do it. We are fortunate that we have the machinery and the interested, concerned people in both city government and the county administration who are up to the job and are committed enough to take it on.*

More and more the county emulates the city in forging liaisons with the business community. Robin points out that because the area's business and corporate leadership is necessarily more restrained than it used to be, because the power to act, to commit, to authorize, and to command is more dispersed than it was in the 1940s and 1950s, the burden for action is increasingly

**Above:** University of Pittsburgh football, © Herb
Ferguson

**Right:** Halftime, © Jack A.
Wolf

falling on the public sector. "Political leaders in both the city and county government must take a greater and more active role because they do not have the private sector to fall back on as they once did," Robin says.

Economic adversity has done something for the political and governmental structure of the Pittsburgh area that decades of pressure could never do: it has forced all the small independent political and governmental structures to examine where they are, where they are going, and how they hope to survive. For the first time in memory, municipalities are cooperating, planning together, purchasing together, working together—not necessarily because they want to, but because they have to. They are sharing services ranging from police protection to computer purchasing. They are jointly hiring financial experts and budget planners. And they are participating in programs that they would not have considered a decade ago because such cooperation implied metropolitanism, which in turn implied loss of power and ultimately loss of independence.

Much of the encouragement and expertise for improved cooperation has been coordinated with the support of the business community. The Greater Pittsburgh Chamber of Commerce, through its Public/Private and Intergovernmental Cooperative Programs, is the leading organization assisting local government in providing services more efficiently and cost-effectively. The Chamber's Loaned Executive Consulting Programs began in the late 1970s with ComPAC, the Committee for Progress in Allegheny County, and continued two years later with ComPEP, the Committee for Progress and Efficiency in Pittsburgh. ComPAC and ComPEP utilized business expertise to streamline and improve the day-to-day management operations of county and city government and today are documented as saving the taxpayers of the region more than twenty-four million dollars per year.

Additional Chamber-sponsored programs, conducted at no cost to local governments, are continuing to improve the management and delivery of public services in the region, with the really big payoffs to the taxpayers to come in the years ahead. A three-year Local Government Financial Forecasting Project was recently completed providing the City of Pittsburgh, Allegheny County, and the Pittsburgh Board of Education with state-of-the-art computer software for performing long-range revenue and expenditure projections. COGNET is a computer networking capability currently being established among the county's 130 municipalities and eight Councils of Government. The Chamber has launched a loaned executive program requested by the Community College of Allegheny County to advise on a five-year plan for the upgrading of the college's computer system.

The Chamber has also launched a Risk Management Task Force for the City of Pittsburgh to evaluate and recommend how the city should update and maintain insurances and generally upgrade its risk management. The Pittsburgh School District is now being advised by another Chamber Loaned Executive Task Force on the development and implementation of a performance-based compensation system for its employees.

And finally, a Chamber task force assigned to study the Port Authority of Allegheny County completed recommendations covering labor relations, cash management, budgeting, legal ser-

vices, purchasing, construction, and risk management. More than 2,500 man-hours were devoted to this study, which is dramatically improving the day-to-day operation of the Port Authority and proved to be an important document leading to the passage of PAT labor reform legislation at the state level.

Recently the Chamber signed a three-year agreement with the Board of Directors of the Intergovernmental Cooperation Program (ICP) to provide administrative support for ICP and will combine the program with its existing Public/Private Cooperative Program.

Pittsburgh, Allegheny County, the Pittsburgh area, and the entire Pittsburgh region are likely to benefit greatly from this new era of cooperation. The forces that emerge from the cauldron of economic necessity are likely to forge a stronger, more powerful, more representative coalition, a unified effort that will not diminish the individualism and spirit that make up the unique character of Pittsburgh.

# Pittsburgh Plays Hardball to Keep the Bucs

By Charles Lynch

For a time it appeared as if the once-perfect marriage of Pittsburgh and the National League baseball Pirates was about to break up and fade into the history books. But the Pittsburgh Pirates live on today. And they will continue in this town for the foreseeable future, because of a uniquely Pittsburgh demonstration of civic pride, through which the public sector in partnership with private interests has taken responsibility for this important civic asset.

Here's the story. The shocking news about the Pirates emerged in November 1984 when then Pirates president Dan Galbreath stated that his family's thirty-eight-year association with the team was to come to an end. After years of multimillion-dollar losses, they were giving up hope. The faltering franchise was up for sale, Galbreath said.

The Pirates had been losing money—big money—for years. The main problem was that the home attendance was down; the team was just not generating sufficient interest in the community. In fact, the Pirates had lost six million dollars in 1984, and many millions more since winning the world championship in 1979.

Dan Galbreath, president of the Pirates, was in tears at the press conference held to announce the sale in the Pirates' executive boardroom in Three Rivers Stadium. He told reporters, "I love baseball, and as a matter of fact, our whole family loves the game."

The Galbreaths represent what almost amounts to a throwback, the older generation of respectable and civic-minded baseball owners. By all accounts they are honorable people, true sportsmen who have done much for baseball and for Pittsburgh. They have been a family in baseball not to make money but for the love of the game. That was, until 1984, when the time had come for a change.

The selling of the Pirates had been postponed once before, in January 1983, when Warner Communications paid six million dollars for 48 percent of the stock, joining the family as a partner. The Galbreaths, of course, didn't need a *partner*, but they

*Facing page:* Great Race, Boulevard of Allies, © Michael Haritan

**Pirates baseball, © Jack A. Wolf**

did need to straighten out the franchise. However, Warner's interest in baseball ownership didn't last, and the following year its stock was put up for sale. Instead of buying back the Warner holding, the Galbreaths decided to sell out completely.

Dan Galbreath announced, "In light of the many other business and personal commitments that our family now has, we are not in a position to repurchase the Warner stock." He added, "Because of the situation, we have concluded reluctantly . . . that we will sell our interest in the Pirates."

John Galbreath, Dan's father, was part of a four-man group that bought the Pirates from Bill Benswanger for an estimated $2.23 million in 1946. Benswanger in turn had inherited the club from his father-in-law, Barney Dreyfuss, in 1932. In 1950 John Galbreath and Thomas P. Johnson became the dual owners until 1982, when Galbreath took sole possession. Throughout his period of ownership, John Galbreath maintained a low profile and remained happily in the background. In fact, he was so obscure that when he attempted to enter the Pirates' clubhouse at Forbes Field after their 1960 World Series victory, a guard tried to keep him out.

There's no doubt that the Pittsburgh Pirates are deeply rooted in the region's economy and culture. Over all those years, baseball became an integral part of summer living for generations of fans living in the Tri-State area.

Pittsburgh, especially in television views of the Golden Triangle, received national attention when the Pirates won the world championship in 1979. In that year, the Greater Pittsburgh Chamber of Commerce estimated that baseball-related spending in Pittsburgh was $33.4 million. A 1985 estimate pegged the area's financial stake in baseball at more than $36 million each year. The Pirates provide almost 1,000 jobs and millions of dollars for the city treasury and in business for restaurants, bars, hotels, Port Authority Transit, parking lots, and other concerns.

And there is no doubt that the Pirates contributed to the overall factors that gave Pittsburgh the distinction of being named the nation's most livable city. The Pirates, like the Steelers, are an enormous promotional tool. While there's no statistical measurement or financial graph that can measure community pride, it's there just the same, big as life. The *Places Rated Almanac,* which rates the quality of life in 329 cities in the United States, credits major league baseball as the most important spectator sport. In the 1985 edition, Pittsburgh moved into first place. There is an important and clear-cut relationship between franchises and cities whose mutual interests are one and the same—survival and progress.

In the team's ninety-nine-year history, the Pirates have played their home games at four different ball fields (Union Park, Exposition Park, Forbes Field, and Three Rivers Stadium) and have won nine league titles and five world championships. Three Rivers Stadium has become a focal point for city planners, who hope to develop the surrounding property into a major recreational area. Early plans have called for a hotel, a children's theme park, restaurants, a shopping mall, and business offices. Much of the success of the project, however, will depend upon the Pirates fans attending the eighty-one home games each year.

In 1982 the Pirates negotiated a new lease at Three Rivers Stadium. This move was described by Dan Galbreath as necessary to ensure the team's continued presence in Pittsburgh. The team claimed that the city had not lived up to certain promises in constructing the stadium. The Stadium Authority then took over the management of Three Rivers Stadium and agreed to undertake major construction improvements, including a new computerized scoreboard. During the same year, as additional support for the franchise, fifteen local corporations agreed to spend fifteen million dollars over a ten-year period for medallions at the stadium. Corporate owners of the ornamental medallions are: Allegheny International, Coca-Cola, Dollar Savings Bank, Dravo Corp., Equibank, Gulf Oil (now Chevron Corporation), H.J. Heinz Company, Mellon Bank, National Steel Corporation, Pittsburgh National Bank, PPG Industries, USAir, U.S. Steel (now USX Corporation), Warner Communications, and Westinghouse Electric. But the public commitment and corporate support were not enough.

Despite the concessions and public concern, the Pirates were still in financial trouble. There was immediate interest, however, from moneyed organizations around the country in buying the Pirates—and moving them out of Pittsburgh. Fortunately for the city and for Mayor Richard Caliguiri, the city's lease with the team was binding on all present and future owners of the team. That lease stipulates that the Pirates will play all of their home games at Three Rivers Stadium through the year 2011.

Equally important is a provision that gives the city and the Stadium Authority the right to approve any sale of the Pirates to new owners. For Caliguiri it became a personal challenge of the utmost importance to keep the team in town. The mayor emphasized over and over again that the team would stay in Pittsburgh.

In response to the threat, the mayor, Governor Richard Thornburgh, and concerned district business people began a campaign in February 1985 to boost attendance at Pirates games, so necessary to keep the club in Pittsburgh. At a news conference in the offices of the Greater Pittsburgh Chamber of Commerce, Thornburgh asserted that "Pittsburgh wouldn't be Pittsburgh without the Pirates." The big push was on to save the team. Thornburgh added, "It is important that all the region's business and civic leaders rally behind the team in order to keep it in Pittsburgh. We can't take this ball club for granted. I'm afraid some of us have done so."

Some 2,500 member companies of the Greater Pittsburgh Chamber of Commerce and other chambers of commerce in the tri-state area were asked to participate in a season ticket drive to help promote game attendance. The companies received a letter from Governor Thornburgh, Mayor Caliguiri, and then Chamber Chairman W. Bruce Thomas, and Chamber President Justin Horan urging them to buy season tickets. And three area chambers—Airport Area, Butler County, and New Castle—offered their support in selling tickets.

In response to the mayor and governor's plea for help, a group of Pittsburgh businesses contributed by offering their services free to potential local buyers of the team. The firms, who also participated in the ticket-buying campaign, were the Price Waterhouse accounting company; the law firm of Eckert, Seamans, Cherin & Mellott; and the advertising firm Ketchum Communications, Incorporated.

As part of the sales campaign, the Smaller Manufacturers Council, headquartered in Pittsburgh, made a commitment to ensure that 13,000 youngsters would see a Pirates game in 1985.

Two months later, on April 12, 1985, the Pirates beat the St. Louis Cardinals 6-4 at Three Rivers Stadium before an excited opening-night crowd of 47,335. It was the largest crowd at the stadium since August 17, 1980, when 49,417 fans watched a Pirates-Montreal Expos doubleheader, and it was the largest audience for a Pirates opener since 1976. The fact that the club was up for sale and faced a possible move to another city might have had something to do with the attendance. Fans had become aware.

It's not often that one sells a professional baseball club, and as the season dragged on, with the team playing poorly and attendance lagging, it became apparent to the Galbreaths and city officials that the sale would be tougher than imagined. The asking price, between thirty-five and forty million dollars, may have been a factor. But if the franchise could be turned around and operated in Pittsburgh at a profit, then the price would seem to be a steal.

In June a frustrated and disappointed Dan Galbreath said he would begin considering offers from groups that might buy and move the club out of Pittsburgh. In the seven months that the team had been up for sale, Galbreath said he hadn't received a single offer from anyone in the Pittsburgh area.

Other offers, however, came from New Jersey, Denver, Tampa, St. Petersburg, Indianapolis, Buffalo, Vancouver, and Washington, D.C. But the city was determined and ready to move into court to keep the franchise.

At about the same time, the new baseball commissioner Peter Ueberroth came to Pittsburgh and declared himself to be "absolutely committed to keeping the Pirates in Pittsburgh." Ueberroth met privately with Caliguiri and leaders of several Pittsburgh-based corporations in the Duquesne Club. Before he departed, the commissioner said he had "a good feeling" about baseball's future in Pittsburgh. He assured his listeners that he would block any attempt to move the team from the city.

About a week after Ueberroth left town, the chairman of Westinghouse Electric Corporation said he was willing to organize a group of local corporations to buy the Pirates. Douglas D. Danforth, who helped arrange the commissioner's visit to the city, said the mayor had asked him earlier to see what corporate executives could do to keep the franchise in Pittsburgh. David Roderick, chairman of U.S. Steel (now USX Corporation), was one of the corporate leaders involved in the strategy.

Finally, eleven months after the Pirates were put up for sale, a deal unique in major league sports was struck; a private-public partnership assembled by Caliguiri and his staff reached agreement on October 2, 1985, with the Galbreath family to buy the Pirates. The mayor's proposal, with its twin goals of local ownership and keeping the team in town, had been intended as a last-ditch effort to save the team if a private local buyer could not be found.

The partnership also announced that Malcolm M. Prine, Chairman of Ryan Homes, Incorporated, would be president and chief executive officer of the team. Dan Galbreath said that he was "immensely pleased" with the deal, and he reiterated his family's commitment to sell the team to a local group, with intentions of keeping the franchise in Pittsburgh.

Dan Galbreath, with his father seated near him said, "Today, with a somewhat sad heart, but with some enjoyment, too, we are announcing an agreement to sell the baseball club." He added, "My family and I, along with our partners at Warner Communications, take a great deal of satisfaction in knowing that the Pirates are going to be run by a group of people committed to excellence and to maintaining the tradition of this great baseball franchise." The completion of the sale ended the Galbreath family's involvement in the ownership of the team, a long and glorious era that started in 1946 and included World Series championships in 1960, 1971, and 1979.

A happy Caliguiri told reporters, "I am confident that interest in the Pirates will soon be revived and that the Bucs will be competitive again and contenders for many years to come." The mayor also praised the Galbreaths for their "selfless and personal dedication to major league baseball and this community." The *Post-Gazette* stated in an editorial that this agreement represented the mayor's finest hour.

The long-awaited, final step in the acquisition came on March 17, 1986, when the Pittsburgh City Council approved a $20-million loan for the baseball team.

In accepting the money from Caliguiri at a press conference on April 26, 1986, Prine stated, "The money is not a gift from the city. It is a redevelopment loan to improve an industry." The new Pirates president explained, "The Pirates generate 1,000 jobs and two million dollars in taxes."

The group of investors, called Pittsburgh Baseball Associates, invested twenty-six million dollars toward buying and operating the team. Pittsburgh Baseball Associates includes: J. David Barnes (Mellon Bank), Joe L. Brown, Mayor Richard Caliguiri, Dr. Richard Cyert (Carnegie-Mellon University), Douglas Danforth (Westinghouse Electric), Eugene Litman (Litman, Litman, Harris, Portnoy & Brown), Howard Love (National Intergroup), John McConnell (Worthington Industries), Thomas O'Brien (PNC Financial Corp.), Charles Parry (Alcoa), Malcolm Prine (Ryan Homes), David Roderick (USX), Vincent Sarni (PPG Industries), Frank Schneider (Schneider, Inc.), and Harvey Walken (H.M. Walken Co.).

Taking everything into consideration, the sale package, so important to Pittsburgh's economy and prestige, was the product of strong public and private sector leadership, coalescing in the mayor's office. Mayor Caliguiri might have given up his determined crusade to keep the team in Pittsburgh. But he persevered, shrugged off criticism, and delivered the goods. The Pirates have survived, as has an important part of Pittsburgh's history. So Pittsburgh and the Pirates are still a team, like hot dogs and baseball.

*Charles Lynch, a Pittsburgh native, has been a staff writer for the* Post-Gazette *for more than twenty years.*

CHAPTER **V**

# The Challenge of Change

Art really does reflect life. And when it has to, art exaggerates life a little to make a point. After a while the artistic version, especially if it is popularized on television or other mass media, may even replace the reality, so that we can begin to believe, for example, that the TV serial *Dallas* realistically portrays Dallas, Texas. *Miami Vice* becomes our image of Miami, and *Naked City* represents New York. On the other hand, Pittsburgh really is *Mr. Rogers' Neighborhood*. No doubt about it.

Despite television's reliance on exaggeration, the neighborhood that Pittsburgher Fred Rogers created here as the setting for his acclaimed children's television show comes astonishingly close to reflecting what this city and its citizens are all about. And the people who populate Pittsburgh share many of the same characteristics that Rogers gave his neighborhood's fictional characters. They are, for the most part, decent, trusting, unassuming, gentle, generally conservative in both manner and dress, dutiful, thoughtful, concerned about upholding their values, courteous, respectful and respectable, friendly, obliging, and—above all—neighborly.

The distinctive character of the populace is a result of the demands the city and the region have made upon the people, as well as of the heritages and ethnic backgrounds of the people who were and still are attracted to the place. These characteristics are, on the whole, endearing and desirable, and they make Pittsburghers endearing and desirable neighbors. Nevertheless,

**Boy's view of the city**
© **Michael Haritan**

they have also helped to create some of the problems that to-day plague the city and that have made economic recovery here slow and frustrating.

Generally speaking, Pittsburghers are conservatives who come by their conservatism naturally. They learned their economics lessons from that most demanding teacher, the Great Depression of the 1930s, and their economics textbooks were the mills and the mines, where even in the best of times the threat of extensive layoffs or a strike were always present.

It is no wonder, then, that risk taking and adventurousness do not typify the average Pittsburgher. Why take risks when there were good jobs waiting in the mill or the mine for almost every-one, even those with only limited skills and a high school educa-tion? And when, as was bound to happen, the strike or layoff came, there was always the family to be counted on for help un-til things got back on track again—and of course they would, because the mill and the mine would be here forever, and Pitts-burghers would always have a place to work.

Pittsburgh has no great tradition of reverence for education.

German (left) and Serbian costume at the Pittsburgh Folk Festival, © Herb Ferguson

German (left) and Serbian costume at the Pittsburgh Folk Festival, © Herb Ferguson

Those who came to the area to work the mines, the mills, the foundries, the rivers, and the railroads were generally without much formal education, so they were without an educational heritage to pass on. Few of them appreciated the need for seeing to it that their offspring became educated beyond the legally mandated limit or, at best, beyond high school. After all, there were good, well-paying jobs available. A young man could go to work in the mill or the mine the day after he graduated from high school and earn more than someone starting out in an office job Downtown after four years of college. What if the white-collar office job had a brighter and more prosperous future? Well, the mill and the mine were here and now, and if there was one lesson more valuable than any other that Pittsburghers could teach their young, it was simply: make it while you can, and tomorrow will be taken care of by the savings account, the family, and the labor union.

This approach to life helped mold Pittsburghers, making many of them better followers than leaders, better employees than employers, better supporting actors than leading men and women. Even today, most Pittsburghers seem happier traveling in the middle of the road rather than in the fast lane. They are, for the most part, disciples of the safe and sane. They tend to buy dark-colored automobiles (which they usually pronounce "auto-MObiles") and favor sensible shoes and wash-and-wear shirts. Not each and every one of the them, of course. There continue to be those not reluctant to take the risks—emotional as well as financial—required to start and operate enterprises, to help lay

**Jewish Festival** *sukkah,*
© **Joel B. Levinson**

a solid economic foundation for the region, to create opportunities for themselves and others, to serve as the economic backbone and leadership of Pittsburgh. But the style of the place and its spirit, the forces that have given Pittsburgh its character, have for the most part been those of the followers, not the leaders, the risk avoiders, not the risk takers.

As a result, there has been in Pittsburgh a reluctance to change. It seems that the old order is often considered the best order. In fact, many think that the old way is not only the best way but the only way. Certainly there have been dramatic changes in the look of Pittsburgh, especially in its Downtown skyline, but not so much in the feel and style of it. After all its surface changes, Pittsburgh is still a small town with tall buildings in one part. And although that makes it a very desirable place to live, it does not always make for economic success in today's highly competitive marketplace.

Even so, there are hopeful signs that Pittsburghers' almost inbred resistance to change is itself undergoing change. In response to the economic conditions that have virtually overthrown their basic industries, Pittsburghers are becoming more realistic about themselves, their town, their jobs, their futures, and the economic foundation that supports all of these things. They are becoming more realistic about what has to be done to make Pittsburgh a vibrant and dynamic place once again.

The harsh glare of this new reality is causing—or allowing—

the people who call Pittsburgh home to see things in sharper definition. After years of what can only be described as a deluded optimism, a vocal majority of steelworkers in the area no longer hold firm to the belief that any day now the mills will be open and booming again and Pittsburgh's skies will be filled once more with the sweet stench of heavy-metal prosperity.

It is not an easy admission to make for those who have long helped keep this town moving economically, but the fact is that there are now more people working in high-technology industries in Pittsburgh than there are making steel or producing other basic metals. Steelworkers, who in the 1950s represented 20 percent of the area's work force, now hold only 4 percent of the area's jobs. So there are more ex-steelworkers than steelworkers here now—a fact that, even for the most dedicated optimist, tends to force things into realistic perspective.

Steelworkers are not the only ones who are, however reluctantly, beginning to accept the reality of the situation as it exists in the 1980s. The area's coal miners, too, know well how dispiriting the outlook is for them. Coal production and employment in the Pittsburgh area are at their lowest levels in almost a century, and there is little hope that coal will rebound until well into the last decade of this century. The prospects for those in the aluminum, glass, and heavy metals industries are virtually as limited, and Pittsburghers who currently work the rivers or the rails are not encouraging their children to follow in their occupational

*This page, top:* Aerial ride at Kennywood Park, © Herb Ferguson

*Below:* Children at Highland Zoo, © Michael Haritan

*Facing page, top left:* Chinese dancers at the Pittsburgh Folk Festival, © Michael Haritan

*Top right:* Polish costume at the Pittsburgh Folk Festival, © Herb Ferguson

*Center:* Time out for fishing, © Herb Ferguson

*Bottom:* Pittsburgh Marathon open to all, © Maurice Tierney

footsteps.

While the situation has been critical for several years, the Pittsburgh working man and woman are finally beginning to accept it. This has led to a metamorphosis, currently taking place. Older Pittsburghers are no longer encouraging their children to stick it out a little longer in the old hometown in the hope that things will turn around, that unskilled and semiskilled jobs in heavy industry, so abundant before, will be available again. Now they are sending those children—who are often the best, brightest, and best educated—to live and work among strangers in far-off places where there are more immediate prospects for employment, more opportunities, more hope.

The ones who stay are not doomed to a future of forced idleness and low-paying employment, of course. There are still good prospects in the new industries that are growing up, the new businesses that are taking hold, the new enterprises that are carving out a place for themselves in Pittsburgh. There are still good-paying jobs to be had in Pittsburgh, and a person

*Facing page:* **Steel Plaza Fountain, © Michael Haritan**

*Below:* **Pittsburgh Folk Festival, © Michael Haritan**

Aboard the *Liberty Belle,*
© Jack A. Wolf

need not brave the heat of the mill, the danger of the mine, or the numbing noise of the foundry to hold one of them. But there are fewer of them than there used to be, and the competition is, and will continue to be, intense. This is a classic hallmark of an economy in transition.

The people undergoing the greatest difficulty in handling the transition are the middle-aged Pittsburghers, the men and women who started on the job immediately after high school and believed they had made the right decision to ensure job security and a carefree retirement. Many of them are now forced to realize that without a skill that is easily transferred to jobs in the increasingly complex, high-technology enterprises becoming established here, without a great deal of formal education, and without the will or perhaps the opportunity to undergo retraining, they face poor prospects for the remaining years of their working lives.

Thus, the change that is taking place in Pittsburgh is taking its toll. For so many traditional close-knit families, it means break-ups and separations. For older Pittsburghers, it means disappointment that the secure world they thought they were creating with their labor, a world where they and their families would live close together in comfort, is being destroyed. For the middle-aged it means lost opportunity and the realization that hard work and honest toil are no longer guarantees of a better life and financial security in the years ahead. And for many of the young it means separation, moving from old, familiar neighbor-

Lithuanian women and Irish-
man at the Pittsburgh Folk
Festival, © Herb Ferguson

hoods, severing family ties that have been forged over generations.

Pittsburghers do no treat such things as family ties, neighborhoods, and job security lightly. Traditionally, these are not people who change jobs on a whim; they took great pride in staying
with the same employer for thirty or forty years or more. Some
have by custom eaten Sunday dinner in the same house in the
same neighborhood since they were infants. These are not people who casually turn their backs on a family member in trouble.
Pittsburghers are their own kind of people. They do not take
easily to change, especially change that disrupts the familiar, un-
settles the family structure, and challenges old values.

But the requirements of survival make such change inevitable.
Without change there is little hope for a future reasonably free
of economic uncertainty. The trick will be to achieve the necessary change in a reasonable, rational way, to approach change
realistically and to base the responses to its challenges not
on desperation but on opportunity. The challenge will be to ef-

**Jewish Festival, © Joel B. Levinson**

fect change while utilizing the resources that form the core of the area's economic capabilities, resources that have made change feasible in the first place.

Because change is inevitable, however, does not mean that it is always greeted with unbridled enthusiasm. There are those who suggest that service industries and businesses might eventually accommodate the area work force but will never provide the large paychecks of heavy industry. While those critics may be right, the realities of the situation have pushed Pittsburgh to pursue development of the service sector.

To someone who has put in twenty years in the mill and has been rewarded generously for his labors, the thought of seeking employment in the service sector when the mill shuts down forever is both discouraging and unnerving. Almost invariably, this twenty-year mill veteran will equate service with fast food establishments and a minimum wage. But service is much more than that: service is banking and the law, insurance, communications, marketing, and research—all areas in which Pittsburgh has traditionally been strong and is becoming stronger.

Commencement at Carne-
gie-Mellon University,
© Michael Haritan

Of the ten largest employers in the Pittsburgh area at the
start of 1986, only two—Westinghouse Electric Corporation and
United States Steel Corporation (now USX Corporation)—were
manufacturers. Of the remaining eight, five were service concerns: the University of Pittsburgh (which is also the largest
employer in the City of Pittsburgh), Mellon Bank, USAir, Giant
Eagle (a food retailer), and the May Company, which operates
Kaufmann's department stores locally. The three other top-ten
employers were government—local, state, and federal.

Only sixteen of the fifty largest employers in the Pittsburgh
area were engaged in producing goods at the start of 1986.
The rest, with the exception of the three government listings,
were all securely anchored in the service sector. So even if a
displaced mill hand, for example, is reluctant to flip Big Macs for
McDonald's (the eighteenth biggest employer in the area, according to published reports) or Big Boy hamburgers for the locally owned Eat 'N Park restaurant chain (number twenty-four
on the top-fifty list), there are a considerable number of other
employment opportunities.

More important, considering the world economy and the international marketplace, service seems to be the area's best economic bet. From all indications it offers Pittsburghers the most
hope and appears to make the best use of the region's available
talent and abundant resources. And among those resources, the
most plentiful and most valuable is undoubtedly the people who

**Carpatho-Russian costume at the Pittsburgh Folk Festival, © Herb Ferguson**

live here.

Can Pittsburghers, with their reputation as steelmakers to the world, adapt to service industries, in which the best-paying jobs most often put more strain on the brain than on the muscles? Can the people of this region, with their rich history of involvement with and dedication to the labor movement, function effectively in industries that have traditionally resisted unionization? Can a labor force conditioned for the most part to dealing with things of bulk and weight change focus and be comfortable working with things of little heft—or no heft at all, in the case of intangibles? Can a worker who is used to the grime, the noisy activity, and the challenging danger of blue-collar employment find comfort in an antiseptic environment? The answer is *Certainly,* for this is a matter of economic survival, and Pittsburghers have a heritage of survival.

Of course, service is not the only alternative. It is not as if a smokestack will never again emit a reassuring puff into Pittsburgh's atmosphere. It is not as if the last ton of coal or steel or the last pound of machined material has been dispatched from a Pittsburgh facility. The steel production that once was centered in the Pittsburgh area may have moved away, closer to steel's market, but there are still many steel-related jobs going strong in the region. Steelmaking as Pittsburghers knew it and practiced it may never return to the region, but new, efficient, and effective steelmaking technology, much of it being developed in the Pittsburgh area, could well turn the shadow of what once was a proud and productive industry into a vibrant and profitable enterprise once again.

Some of the most exciting research being done in the Pittsburgh area involves the two commodities most closely associated with the area: steel and coal. Perhaps the most promising factor is that Pittsburgh has not totally abandoned the industries that have contributed so much to the region's economy and to the world. As much as things have changed, as much as the emphasis has switched from industry to services, and as eager as most Pittsburghers are to adapt to the new ways and meet the demands of new enterprises, there is still a feeling of confidence here that the qualities and capabilities that made this place the muscle of industrial America can now be used to turn around the economic fortunes not only of the Pittsburgh region

**Bulgarian (left) and Ukrainian dancers at the Pittsburgh Folk Festival, © Herb Ferguson**

but of the entire country as well.

That confidence is backed by solid evidence of performance. Robotics research being conducted at Carnegie-Mellon University here is changing the way America and the world produce goods and operate production facilities. Dozens of companies are being spun off from the academic research activities of the university, and these are among the most promising new firms in the area.

The University of Pittsburgh now operates one of the largest and most sophisticated industrial research centers in the country. Just a few miles northeast of the city, the center, formerly the principal research facility for Gulf Oil Corporation, was donated to the university by Chevron Corporation after the California firm acquired Gulf. Through the center, the university plans to provide smokestack industries in the United States with the same type of research and technological assistance as Stanford University has contributed to California's Silicon Valley, and as Massachusetts Institute of Technology has provided the firms that populate Route 128's high-tech complex outside Boston.

But isn't service to Smokestack America an exercise in futility? Are not we as an entire nation committed to the razzle-dazzle of high technology, and not to the grit and grind of manufacturing? Aren't steelmaking and iron making and coke mak-

**Highland Fling Festival at Highland Park, © William Metzger; courtesy, Neighborhoods for Living Center**

ing passe? Hardly. After all, what is needed, the experts say, is not necessarily the total abandonment of the nation's production facilities but new ways and new techniques to produce goods more efficiently and profitably. There is hope for Smokestack America, and that means there is hope for Smokestack Pittsburgh, too.

What might be required to make heavy metal production a profitable enterprise once again is not a change of focus but a change of direction, a change of technique and approach. Recently, a great-nephew and biographer of Andrew Carnegie was asked what he thought Uncle Andrew would do were he alive today and seeking an investment opportunity. Given the state of the steel industry, what would Carnegie invest in during the 1980s? The response was immediate. Uncle Andrew would, after studying the market, studying the industries that are touted as being the best bets for the future, and studying the international marketplace, do what he did the first time opportunity presented itself: get into steel. It seems that Andrew Carnegie usually put his money and his talent into things that everyone else had written off. He would see great potential in steel today, his nephew insists.

He would undoubtedly see great potential in Pittsburgh as well. For Pittsburgh has the elements that people like Carnegie—people of power who plot the course of industry—appreciate: a willing work force with a heritage of industriousness, an acceptance of the need to work for what is to be gained, and a spirit that can turn adversity to advantage. It is that spirit that will ultimately set the town back on the road to economic recovery.

It seems certain now that Pittsburghers are ready to accept the challenges of change, ready to adjust to a new order, ready to pursue new goals. Pittsburghers are realizing that the challenge of change is the challenge of opportunity. They are beginning to understand that they are not at fault for the turn of economic events that has eroded an entire industry. And they have begun to look upon change not as a defeat but as a chance to eclipse even the most glorious days of their impressive industrial history.

Pittsburghers have begun taking a fresh new look at themselves, their circumstances, and their prospects. Traditional foes, labor and management, still glare at each other menacingly across the bargaining table as they always have in Pittsburgh, but there now seems to be a deeper appreciation of each other's stance and position; they understand that their fates are intertwined.

The challenge of change is improving attitudes without diminishing spirit and will. The challenge of change is focusing on new enterprises without abandoning the robust and vital industrial history and heritage of the past. The greatest challenge is first accepting the necessity for change, and then being willing to pursue the best, most effective, and beneficial course. Pittsburgh and Pittsburghers are at last accepting the challenge. The sun is rising in Mr. Rogers' neighborhood.

## Unique Information Center Helps Pittsburgh Newcomers Find a Home

By Beth Wagner Marcello

Finding a place to live in Pittsburgh, a city of more than eighty diverse neighborhoods, would be a formidable task for a new resident if it weren't for the Neighborhoods for Living Center, a city agency that helps newcomers find a neighborhood to settle in.

Unlike a real estate sales agency, the center doesn't list or sell specific properties. Instead, it "sells" city neighborhoods by promoting the features that make them attractive, thereby helping newcomers choose a neighborhood that suits them before they contact a realtor. The center has extensive information—including brochures, news clippings, census data, and histories—about every one of Pittsburgh's communities. What it doesn't have on file, its four staff members (each of whom lives in a different city neighborhood) are eager to share from their firsthand experiences.

In short, the center provides information on almost every aspect of a neighborhood that may be a factor in a person's decision about where to look for an apartment or buy a home.

Do you have to be close to an elementary school? Is the convenience of walking from home to work Downtown a priority? Do you want the challenge of renovating a historic Victorian mansion or turn-of-the-century row home? Center staff can pinpoint where the best housing bargains are, as well as locate Pittsburgh's most prestigious addresses. The staff also knows where Pittsburgh's cultural and nightlife centers are, where newcomers are likely to find old, well-built, three-story homes or newer ranch-style houses, what neighborhoods have busy shopping districts and are close to schools, churches, and synagogues, and what communities have the best access to major highways.

In addition, the center offers information about the ethnic makeup of the city's neighborhoods, the percentage of owner-occupied homes in a neighborhood, whether an area has an active community group that represents residents in public forums, what the crime rate and average housing values are, and how they've changed in recent years. Moreover, the center will often introduce newcomers to current residents who can answer questions and offer personal viewpoints about living in their neighborhoods.

A one-of-a-kind office developed in 1979 by Mayor Richard Caliguiri to encourage investments in Pittsburgh's neighborhoods, the Neighborhoods for Living Center is recognized internationally as a model for marketing older, urban neighborhoods. A division of the city's Urban Redevelopment Authority, the center promotes Pittsburgh's neighborhoods as good places to live through brochures and other publications, tours, slide and video presentations, and publicity campaigns. Its premier event, NeighborFair, is held each spring with the Pittsburgh Home and Garden Show at the city's David L. Lawrence Convention Center, Downtown.

NeighborFair is a celebration of neighborhoods in which nearly two-thirds of the city's volunteer community groups design individual booth displays outlining why their areas are great places to live, work, and play. City departments, like Parks and Recreation and the Police, Fire, and Emergency Medical Bureaus, also create and staff fun and interactive exhibits that illustrate their special contributions to city life.

Some 100,000 visitors attend NeighborFair each year. Since it began in 1983, many homes have been purchased by buyers who were convinced at the show to choose a particular city neighborhood. Because of the fair's success, and the demand for information about it, the center produced a video in 1985 that explains how NeighborFair is coordinated. Since then, several neighborhood celebrations, patterned after Pittsburgh's, have been held in major cities across the country. In 1986 Pittsburgh received two prestigious awards from the U.S. Conference of Mayors recognizing NeighborFair as an outstanding public-and-private-sectors partnership and honoring Mayor Caliguiri for his active role in the show.

Through events like NeighborFair, as well as by reaching out to prospective residents in other ways, the center promotes Pittsburgh as a progressive, culturally rich metropolis. But it does more than spread the word: the center's staff works behind the scenes as well, helping neighborhood groups with projects that enhance the quality of life in the city and, consequently, make Pittsburgh more marketable.

Pittsburgh's neighborhood organizations are typically nonprofit volunteer groups of residents that sponsor a variety of inter-neighborhood activities, such as block watches and block parties. They also speak up for city programs that will benefit their communities and, in the long run, increase property values. These groups frequently play significant roles in economic development activities by influencing plans for programs that will affect their neighborhoods.

To reinforce the mostly volunteer efforts by neighborhood organizations, the center invests time and money in projects that help them attract new residents and make current residents proud of the community. For instance, the center often works with community groups to develop newsletters or newspapers that inform residents about neighborhood happenings; it also helps organize and publicize community house tours and festivals.

The center also involves itself in various campaigns to benefit many neighborhoods at once. In 1986 it conducted a study of the way crime in city neighborhoods is reported by the local media and how the reporting shapes the image of city living and affects individual communities.

Most of Pittsburgh's eighty or so active neighborhood groups believe the help they get from the center has a positive impact. In an evaluation completed in 1985, community groups agreed that the center has enhanced the image of city living, encouraged new investment in their neighborhoods, improved the quality of information available to the public about their neighborhoods, and helped them improve communication with other government departments and agencies.

The center offers an array of publications, most of them free, including colorful brochures about more than twenty-five neighborhoods. A newsletter highlighting activities and developments in Pittsburgh's neighborhoods is produced monthly. Other publications include a map of city neighborhoods; a book that presents narratives about each neighborhood and details the facilities and amenities of each; and a "Househunter's Checklist," a handy brochure that helps in keeping track of the features of as many as five homes at once.

Because Pittsburgh's neighborhoods are so numerous and diverse, center staff say there is one that's nearly custom-made for every newcomer. Big houses or small, old or new, sprawling lawns or tiny yards, full of shops and nightlife or quiet and completely residential—there's a Pittsburgh neighborhood suited to everyone's personality, budget, and needs.

For information about living in Pittsburgh, call (412) 391-1850, or write to the Neighborhoods for Living Center, 517 Court Place, Pittsburgh, PA 15219.

*Beth Marcello is a full-time staffer at the Neighborhoods for Living Center of the Urban Redevelopment Authority of Pittsburgh.*

*Facing page:* **Birmingham Bridge overlooking South Side,** © **Harry Edelman**

## SOUTH SIDE

When Pittsburgh was known as a shot-and-beer town, South Side was a stereotypical neighborhood. It was first and always ethnic at heart.

South Side residents were immigrants, mostly from eastern Europe. The Poles, Ukrainians, Serbs, Lithuanians, Greeks, Britons, Germans, Croatians, and Slovaks who settled there lived their new lives in America much as they would have in the Old World, still cooking halusky and halupki, kruszcyki and pierogi, still carrying on the religious customs of their ancestors. They worked in the steel mills and factories along the banks of the Monongahela River—they worked hard to feed and clothe their families—and they socialized in the bars scattered on East Carson Street.

Their neighborhood, called Birmingham, grew rapidly since the river offered a convenient and fast mode of transportation for industrial enterprises. Dr. Nathaniel Bedford, one of Pittsburgh's first physicians, laid out a simple pattern of streets in Birmingham—those running from east to west were given numbers; those running north to south were named for his father-in-law's family. Sarah, Mary, Jane, Sidney, Paige, and Wharton streets still exist on South Side's "flats." On the "slopes," modest frame homes, built at every angle into the hillside, still seem to dangle dangerously on the mountain, yet they are sturdy enough to be handed down from one generation to the next. The homes on the slopes are two stories high on the side that fronts the street and four stories on the side that now offers a magnificent view of corporate Pittsburgh.

But Pittsburgh's image has changed, and so has South Side's. The mills on the Mon no longer employ the thousands they used to, and that's been a tough lump to swallow for South Siders. Residents weren't making what they were used to either, and when folks began shopping in suburban malls rather than in their neighborhoods, the businesses along the mile-long length of Carson Street began to fold.

Thanks, though, to the grit and determination of lifelong South Siders who were not about to let their neighborhood collapse, and to the forward-thinking philosophy of community groups and local government, South Side was not left to die; in fact, just the opposite is happening. The cooperative goal, however,

**Above:** South High School
Stadium, © Herb Ferguson

**Right:** Carson Street,
© Herb Ferguson

South Side festivities,
© William Metzger; cour-
tesy, Neighborhoods for
Living Center

isn't to make South Side better than it was, only to allow it to adapt to the needs of the 1980s, to reuse its past to serve future generations.

In 1982 the South Side Local Development Company was founded to help stimulate interest and facilitate economic development in the neighborhood. A nonprofit organization funded in part by the city, the LDC has been a paramount influence behind South Side's comeback. It petitioned for and received national historic designation for a large portion of East Carson Street; this classification lures history buffs to the neighborhood and gives current and potential business owners tax breaks and the opportunity to apply for low-interest loans to rehabilitate their storefronts.

Dozens of new businesses and trendy eateries dishing out everything from French to Chinese to Mexican cuisine have opened on the South Side. The cluster of artists, craftspersons, and antique dealers who discovered their niche in the tall, narrow commercial structures that front East Carson has grown. South

Side Hospital, an active community institution, built a modern, 255-bed facility in the flats; another hospital, St. Joseph's, was renovated to provide apartments for older residents. A new shopping center opened on the site of a former steel mill, and the city built the million-dollar Riverfront Park between 17th and 26th streets to give residents recreational access to the river.

Neighborhood landmarks, like the Market House, have been renovated and put to new use, and nearly a dozen historic churches reflecting the neighborhood's rich cultural heritage are open for tours every summer. Projects like these, residents say, not only preserve beautiful and historic structures, they also safeguard the memories of lifelong South Siders.

In addition—and largely due to the success of the Local Development Company and the cooperation among the many community groups committed to the revival of South Side—the neighborhood was named in 1985 to participate in the National Trust for Historic Preservation's prestigious Main Street Program, a designation that community leaders believe will spur further commercial development. As part of the program, several projects are under way to increase available housing in the neighborhood, since additional residents will mean more shoppers to support East Carson Street businesses.

South Side is already on the verge of becoming a mecca. Whereas in the old days South Siders seldom crossed the bridge into town because everything they needed was on Carson— today its location is a prime attraction to commuters. This convenience and affordable rents are generating interest in the neighborhood as a place to do business. The simple Victorian row houses in the flats are drawing young professionals who find real urban living exhilarating; as a result, property values are increasing.

Yet South Side is still ethnic and still retains its Old World charm. Women in babushkas still make pierogis on Thursdays and Fridays at St. John Ukrainian and on Thursdays at St. Vladimir; kielbasa and sauerkraut are standard fare at community dinners.

South Side is still a typical Pittsburgh neighborhood, one where family ties and commitment to traditional values live on. It's a neighborhood, like so many others, that is succeeding in its search to find new ways to prosper while preserving its past.

## ALLEGHENY WEST

In the late 1800s it was called Millionaires Row, because a stretch of Ridge Avenue in Allegheny West was believed to be home to more millionaires per square foot than any other place in the world. Pittsburgh legends like Andrew Carnegie, H.J. Heinz, Harry K. Thaw, and Gertrude Stein lived and worked in the neighborhood. Mary Roberts Rinehart used it as the setting for her mystery novels. In Allegheny West, Mary Cassatt painted and Stephen Foster composed.

Close to burgeoning Downtown and surrounded by lush, quiet parks, the neighborhood lured the wealthy. But eventually they

**Snow cones for sale in Allegheny West, © Mary Jane Bent**

moved to country estates, and by the time of the Depression the grand old mansions were turned into boardinghouses, many mismanaged by absentee landlords.

But what represented doom for the neighborhood in the first half of the century became opportunity in the 1970s for those with energy, an eye for the historic, and a desire to be within walking distance of Downtown. Homes in desperate disrepair were bought cheap. The new owners invested money and lots of "sweat equity" to restore the old row homes to their original grace. Today they could sell out at a profit. But most aren't doing so, because over the years that it took to rewire, replumb, and refinish their Richardsonian and Romanesque town houses, they developed a love for the neighborhhood and an attachment to their neighbors.

Only four blocks wide and home to fewer than 800, this North Side neighborhood is Pittsburgh's tiniest. Small size in this case doesn't indicate lack of strength, however, since the Civic Council in Allegheny West is one of the most active volunteer neighborhood groups in the city. The attention residents first gave to refurbishing their homes they now give to preserving their neighborhood as a good place to live and bring up a family. To its credit, the council was instrumental in securing city dollars to help subsidize the young buyers who wanted to fix up what were eyesores and neighborhood nuisances; today the group continues to support developments that maintain the cultural diversity and architectural integrity of this historic district.

Through word of mouth and two annual house tours that have become traditions in Pittsburgh, residents are encouraging others to move to the area. In May and December, those who have lovingly restored their homes open them to visitors. And since many of the renovators also collect antiques from the Victorian

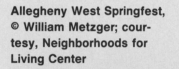

**Allegheny West Springfest, © William Metzger; courtesy, Neighborhoods for Living Center**

era, the tours are an interior designer's delight.

At Christmastime it's a candlelight event, where guides don old-fashioned dress and lead visitors through drawing rooms lavishly decorated for a nineteenth-century holiday. Period furnishings and ten-foot pine trees with heirloom ornaments fill the homes. Dining tables are set for holiday dinners with fragile antique china and crystal. Freshly cut greens, just-baked cookies, wood smoke, and pomanders create a fragrant atmosphere, and even the decorative gas streetlights are embellished with holiday ferns and bright bows.

The tour showcases the spirit and energy that new and long-time residents have devoted to preserving the area's landmark structures, now gleaming examples of how an old neighborhood can serve a new generation. And when Allegheny West is decked out for the holidays, potential buyers find it hard to resist.

## MT. WASHINGTON-DUQUESNE HEIGHTS

There's the view. From atop "the Mount," Downtown beams. The sun reflects from the rivers and from the glass and metal of corporate skyscrapers, and on a clear day you can see landmarks miles away. At night, the Golden Triangle sparkles romantically. Some say the view of Pittsburgh from atop "the Mount" at night is the most breathtakingly beautiful sight of any city in the world.

And what hundreds of thousands of tourists, lovers, and photographers climb the hillside to see every year, residents enjoy every day.

Though the view is certainly a fringe benefit of living in Mt. Washington and Duquesne Heights, the two communities that merge on the hilltop, it is probably not the main reason that 15,000 people live there. Convenience is a more substantial incentive, for residents are just a downhill ride away from Downtown or any of Pittsburgh's major traffic arteries. "We're accessible to everything, not only to Downtown, but to Route 51, and Parkway West and East," noted one Mt. Washingtonian, a traveling sales manager who depends on the neighborhood's location to speed his transport to clients all over the region.

In addition, the Mount and the Heights are the only neighborhoods in Pittsburgh that feature operational inclines. There are two, the Monongahela and the Duquesne; they scale the side of

*Facing page:* **Renovated Mt. Washington home, © Michael Haritan**

*Below:* **Overlook in Mt. Washington, © Jack A. Wolf**

the mountain and offer an alternative to driving or the bus. Residents say there is something intrinsically *urban* about commuting by incline, and because they're traffic-jam-free, inexpensive, and "they go in the snow," the inclines are the preferred mode of transportation by many who travel to and from Downtown daily.

The history of the Duquesne Incline includes a neighborhood success story, and many of the old-timers who ride it do so for reasons that run deeper than a simple desire to get from one place to another. When the always-dependable but taken-for-granted incline was shut down in the early 1960s, residents reacted with all the community spirit and energy they could muster. In a campaign that inspired everyone from the Boy Scouts to the business association, they held bake sales, card parties,

and fund-raising drives to obtain the $15,000 needed to reno-
vate the aging incline. Today, the century-old funicular is operated by a nonprofit neighborhood group called the Society for
the Preservation of the Duquesne Incline, and the line's maintenance and repair expenses are covered by the seventy-cent
one-way fare, by sales from the souvenir shop at the upper station, and by corporate and individual contributions.

You'd expect a neighborhood that offers both unparalleled
convenience and a spectacular vista to be pricey. And it is, for
those who live in the luxury condominiums and mansions that
span Grandview Avenue, which offers front-row views to Fourth
of July fireworks and Light-up Night (a luminary extravaganza
held each November to signal the start of the holiday season).
But the homes that cascade down the other side of the moun-

tain offer the same conveniences and some of the best values in the city. The housing is an eclectic mix, and prices range from $30,000 to more than $450,000. There are small frame dwellings that sit close together as well as newer ranch-style homes with spacious yards; the quaint town houses of Chatham Village, the nation's first cooperative housing community; stately, vintage Victorians with oak flooring, stained glass, fireplaces, and treasures that ambitious renovators long for; and rental properties for every taste and budget.

The neighborhood is diverse not only in architectural style but in the style of living of its residents, a feature that keeps the community lively and interesting. Picture tycoons in tuxes and their ladies in gowns alighting from limos in front of the condos and four-star restaurants on Grandview, while women in aprons and babushkas scrub their stoops and sidewalks a block away down the hill. The convenience and view attract newcomers from all over the world, yet many residents are from families who have lived there for generations, descendants of the east-

ern Europeans who mined in the neighborhood and dubbed it "Coal Hill." These longtimers still retell the saga of General George Washington, who during the Revolutionary War is said to have climbed the Mount to survey the forks of the Ohio River. According to legend, the president-to-be proclaimed the village to have a "grand view."

Washington wouldn't recognize the neighborhood or the view today, but the residents whose roots are embedded there have adapted to new developments and to the growing skyline. On a summer night, they mingle with tourists who stroll along Grandview Avenue. They'll offer advice about neighborhood restaurants. They'll explain that the inclines really are safe, and yes, residents do use them to commute everyday. They'll snap photos for couples and families, so that no one is omitted from a picture of Pittsburgh taken from the Mount.

And like the occasional spectators, Mt. Washingtonians marvel with pride at the stunning view of Pittsburgh. However, their admiration is an emotion felt everyday.

## SQUIRREL HILL

"I always feel real *urban* when I'm in Squirrel Hill. It's the kind of neighborhood where you go to a deli for brunch on Sunday morning to read the *Times.* And then you ride your ten-speed to Schenley Park. You go to Squirrel Hill when you want to see a foreign flick or the newest releases, or look for a rare, out-of-print book, or buy a bike part or bag of onion bagels.

"It doesn't matter what you wear in Squirrel Hill or who you are or what your background is—you fit in. Or at least you're certainly not out of place."

Colorful and cosmopolitan, Squirrel Hill might be the closest thing to New York City in Pittsburgh. You're as likely to run into the mayor in Squirrel Hill as you are a Korean medical student carrying a ragged backpack; you're as likely to see a famous Pittsburgh personality or sports star as you are a leftover flower child in tie-dye. Squirrel Hill is peppered with kosher delis that give this neighborhood a flavor like no other Pittsburgh community has.

**Squirrel Hill shops, © Mary Jane Bent**

Squirrel Hill is an emporium, so compact and complete that you could dispense with your Volvo if you wanted to—and many do, since finding a parking space on Saturday morning is as surprising as winning the lotto. Businesses, services, restaurants, and take-outs line the intersecting Forbes and Murray avenues. You can American Express that $5,000 sequined evening gown and have your button-downs starched at the Chinese laundry there, slurp a Haagen-Dazs, or pig out on a pizza that's been consistently rated among the best in the area. People come from across the East End to take a number and wait in line at the two bakeries, which offer everything from Russian rye to strawberry pie.

Squirrel Hill, located about fifteen minutes east of Downtown, is the city's largest, most populous neighborhood, and it features the greatest housing values as well. The housing stock is old, mammoth, and handsome. Many have been subdivided, and there are numerous small apartment buildings that attract young marrieds, internists, students, and professors because of the neighborhood's proximity to the universities and medical complexes in Oakland. Although the homes are carefully kept and the grounds manicured throughout Squirrel Hill, the section com-

monly referred to as "north of Forbes" is the showplace. Some of Pittsburgh's most prestigious addresses are here, where ten-bedroom, ivy-clad mansions with beech-shaded, landscaped lawns bespeak inherited wealth.

Squirrel Hill's living space is sandwiched between Schenley and Frick parks, so residents have plenty of ground for play. In winter they toboggan, cross-country ski, or ice skate at Schenley, which features one of the city's three outdoor rinks. In summer they picnic, run, tan, bike, hike, and play tennis. Exceptional recreational facilities—coupled with a collection of exclusive private schools, yeshivas, and fine public schools, including Taylor-Allderdice High School (frequently named among the best urban public schools in the nation) make Squirrel Hill a desirable place to live and raise a family.

*Above:* Forbes and Murray avenues, © Harry Edelman

*Facing page:* Winter scene in Squirrel Hill, © Michael Haritan

## NORTH POINT BREEZE

Its wide, Parisian-style boulevards with center islands of flowering fruit trees and grassy spaces are the most distinctive characteristic of North Point Breeze. Add to that its collection of historic, well-appointed homes—which range from Civil War row houses to 1920s villas, from Victorian gingerbread to noted Pittsburgh architect Frederick Scheibler's modernistic landmarks—and the fact that it's probably the most racially integrated neighborhood in Pittsburgh, and you'll understand why so many young home buyers moving back to the city are choosing to live in North Point Breeze.

Located in Pittsburgh's East End near the borough of Wilkinsburg, North Point Breeze has a rich past that gives it a commanding presence today. Much of the neighborhood was developed after the Civil War, when noted industrialists like H.C. Frick, Andrew Mellon, and George Westinghouse moved there from their urban mansions to build more spacious country estates. They dubbed the area Point Breeze after a popular watering hole of the same name located at the crossroads of the com-

**North Point Breeze home,
© Michael Haritan**

**North Point Breeze homes,
© Michael Haritan**

**North Point Breeze home,**
**© Michael Haritan**

munity. Only recently did residents of the northernmost section of Point Breeze, the area across Penn Avenue, attach the geographic distinction to the name of their neighborhood.

Much lore surrounds the area's first and famous residents. For instance, legend has it that when Westinghouse discovered natural gas on his property in 1884, people miles away were able to read their evening newspapers by the light of the flame the gas fed. The Westinghouse estate, called Solitude, is now a much-used neighborhood park.

Residents have researched and documented the history of many homes in the neighborhood. The block bounded by Penn Avenue, Thomas Boulevard, and Murtland and Lang avenues was once H.J. Heinz's estate, called Greenlawn. Two structures still standing on Meade Street were part of the property. One was built around 1890 and, after the turn of the century, housed one of the first cars in Pittsburgh, a 1903 model that Heinz bought in Paris. The other was a small museum, built around 1916, that exhibited the magnate's souvenirs from foreign trips. It is said that ivory and watches were displayed there, as well as remnants from the Great Wall of China, Roman aqueducts, and the Appian Way, and lava from Pompeii. In addition, two neighborhood structures are known to have been the homes of George Westinghouse's son and personal physician.

In 1885, after the introduction of the trolley made getting around convenient, a six-block area of North Point Breeze became one of the first planned suburban communities in the country. Its main streets, Thomas and McPherson, were named after Civil War generals and designed to resemble French boulevards with their floral islands. Half of the houses in North Point Breeze were erected between 1880 and 1890 and owned by some of Pittsburgh's leading citizens, including company presidents, vice-presidents, and school board members. Reminiscent of an era when building meant handcrafting, the homes are graced by wide verandas, wood-paneled rooms, stained-glass windows, and solid construction, features that today's renovators seek out.

**North Point Breeze home,**
**© Michael Haritan**

What made up a secluded, suburban sanctuary a century ago is now a thriving and fashionable inner-city neighborhood. Residents swear by the convenience and cultural diversity of North Point Breeze, home to an almost equal number of white and black families, making it a racially balanced community.

Although the neighborhood is close to Downtown and convenient to shopping in Squirrel Hill and Shadyside, it is completely residential, and has no commercial district of its own. This has been known to deter some potential home buyers, and as a result residents say they have had to become more aggressive and creative in marketing their venerated mansions. Through the North Point Breeze Coalition and the Good Neighbor Club, the locals work together with realtors and officials to maintain the quality of the neighborhood.

They have also sponsored a variety of events and tours that show off the neighborhood's houses. Most recent was a series of "musicales" that gave nonresidents an opportunity to visit some of the most beautiful homes in Pittsburgh. During these events, classical music was played while wine and Brie cheese were offered. The concerts have the added benefit of giving neighbors a chance to mingle and strengthen social relationships that help unify the neighborhood and maintain it as a good place to live and invest in.

## POLISH HILL

You can spot Polish Hill from miles away by the copper-green onion domes of the Immaculate Heart of Mary Church, which seems to watch over this tiny community of Polish descendants.

The presence of the eighty-year-old Roman Catholic church is even more magnificent, more powerful and compelling up close on Brereton Street. Said to have been patterned after St. Peter's Basilica in Rome, the church was built during the evenings between July 1904 and December 1905 by Poles who worked twelve-hour shifts in the mills, railroads, and factories down the hill along the Allegheny River. Though the church is ornate and massive (seating 1,800), it does not impose on its surroundings. In fact, it seems to link arms with the narrow row homes marching up and down the street on either side. There are no paved parking lots to set the church apart, for most of the parishioners walk to Mass. There are no spacious manicured grounds; only a sidewalk separates the edifice from the street.

As well as being physically in step with the feel of the neighborhood, it is emotionally one with the neighbors, for nowhere in Pittsburgh is the Church more predominant in daily life than in Polish Hill. Many attribute this influence in the neighborhood to one figure, Father John Jendzura, the priest who has shepherded the parish for more than a quarter-century. A soft-spoken man, slight of build, Father John is the driving force behind the community and its accomplishments. He encourages young adults in Polish Hill to remain in the community and raise families of their own there, and he works hard to ensure that young people have plenty to do by promoting youth groups and a church-sponsored baseball team. He is often a spokesperson for the Polish Hill Civic Association, a neighborhood group that encourages community pride and works to see that residents get a fair return on their tax dollars through developments in the neighborhood.

Packed with row houses that have been updated with siding and decorative brick, Polish Hill is a family neighborhood with staying power. Outsiders recognize Polish Hill as one of Pittsburgh's typically ethnic, tightly woven communities—many drive through it on a Downtown shortcut between Bigelow Boulevard and Liberty Avenue. But to the generations of Poles who live there, and to the new and not necessarily Polish families that

*Immaculate Heart of Mary Church; above, © Herb Ferguson; left, © Jack A. Wolf*

227

**Polish Hill street scene,
© Norm Schumm**

are moving in and renovating inexpensive former storefronts, the neighborhood offers a stability hard to come by.

It is often called "the neighborhood that time forgot," for life moves slowly in Polish Hill. Original cobblestone streets still wind up and down past century-old homes in which women still make kluski and pierogi and other favorites from recipes invented ages ago. Mass is still said in Polish once a week at the church, and the traditional Easter ham is still bought for a reasonable price from Chester, the neighborhood butcher.

While it is stable, it isn't stagnant. Residents, through the Civic Association, are always looking for ways to enhance the neighborhood and create new homes for the generations who want to stay and raise their families in Polish Hill. The neighborhood group recently purchased a parcel of secluded land and encouraged a developer to build eight new town houses, intended to lure back some of the young people who moved elsewhere because of a lack of available housing. During the ground-breaking ceremony, Father John acknowledged the spirit of the residents, saying that they "have an amazing energy for making things happen in the community. Our people make Polish Hill the best place to live in the city, don't you think?"

He added, "Oh, I know we have competition from other neighborhoods, but we'll take them on. We work hard at being the best."

## BROOKLINE

A charming slice of small-town Americana in a big and influential city, Brookline is ten minutes due south of Downtown and as laid-back as Petticoat Junction. Except for Brookline Boulevard—a small business district that creates much of the community's hometown atmosphere—this is a neighborhood of older brick homes with front and back yards (a rarity in most cities), tree-lined streets, and sidewalks where neighbors walk their dogs.

From the Little League to the Lions to the American Legion, Brookliners are generally a patriotic bunch who get pleasure from familiar traditions. The neighborhood's only landmark is a World War I cannon that sits near the war memorial in a triangular parklet between Brookline Boulevard and Chelton Street. A weekly tabloid that reports news, features the activities of the Area Community Council, and highlights local births, marriages, and service news builds pride among neighbors. A Memorial Day parade and Junefest, a community carnival held at one of the area's two parks, are annual events that exemplify community spirit.

**Brookline stores, © Norm Schumm**

Whatever daily bustle there is in Brookline is on the Boulevard, where neighbors drop off their dry cleaning, visit the library, meet for a beer. One look at its row of quaint storefronts and diagonal on-street parking spaces and you'll realize that nostalgia is not necessarily a thing of the past. Brookliners needn't venture far to shop, for nearly every daily need can be met by the dozens of family merchants who have flourished here for generations. There are pharmacies, banks, pizza pubs, florists, a deli, and a supermarket. A swirling, candy-cane-striped pole still identifies the barber shop. The hardware store has been in business for decades, and cakes and cookies from the local bakeries have tempted dieters at neighborhood weddings, confirmations, and first communions for years.

*Above, and facing page:*
**Brookline homes,**
**© Michael Haritan**

As in many small towns where customs live on, the Boulevard at Christmas is dressed to the nines with wreaths in every storefront and strands of tinsel, bells, balls, and bows that span the thoroughfares. Church chimes peel out carols, and when it snows, Brookline is postcard perfect.

The professionals who are choosing to buy their first homes and raise their families in Brookline say the neighborhood is perfect year round. They may have been accustomed to large yards and ample living space in the suburbs where they grew up, but now they want the convenience that only an urban neighborhood can offer. In Brookline they get both.

"I want to have space to grow fresh vegetables in my back yard, but I don't want to be forced to jump in my car every time I need a loaf of bread, and I don't have time to spend two or more hours every day commuting to work," explained one new resident. Many young families add that Brookline is a great place to raise children, since the neighborhood still has public elementary and middle schools and several parochial schools that most kids can walk to.

**Brookline business district,
© Norm Schumm**

## BLOOMFIELD

At Donatelli's, a homey Bloomfield grocery that's known for its imported cheeses and spices and homemade pasta and sausage, it isn't unusual to overhear a fast-paced conversation in Italian between shopper and shopkeeper. Perhaps they reminisce about the old country or share secrets of loved ones in southern Italy. Or, *mamma mia,* bicker over the price of a pound of proscuitto!

Everyone seems to know one another—or is made to feel that way—at the bakery, the gift shop, and the pharmacy, too. These neighborhood businesses all thrive on the loyal patronage of the second- and third-generation Italians who flocked to Bloomfield in the early 1900s to put down American roots. Folks like Victor Santucci, a local restaurateur who immigrated to Bloomfield in 1947 and whose speech is still peppered with a touch of Italian, have never lived anywhere else in the United States. Barber Dan Cercone, fondly called "the mayor of Bloomfield," and Lenny Malvin, the druggist who has given many neighborhood youths their first job, know their customers and their customers' families by name.

Much business in this East End neighborhood is still done the old-fashioned way, for many of the 161 small shops and markets that line an eight-block stretch of Liberty Avenue are family-owned and operated. The impersonal business practices of generic suburban malls have never invaded Bloomfield, where customers, even unfamiliar ones, are treated like special friends. "Go on, take a taste. How else will you know if you like it?" the man in the white apron urges, pushing a thick slice of freshly made pepperoni on a carpet of waxed paper across the deli counter. "So you don't have the money today—so you pay me tomorrow," a storekeeper assures a longtime trusted customer.

Residents say they can get everything from shoes to a haircut, from widgets to bootleg albums, from ravioli al dente, overstuffed with ricotta and dripping in thick, red meat sauce, to a dental exam on Liberty Avenue. Culinary institutions, like Del's and the Pleasure Bar, which have been in business for more than forty years, are known for their down-home atmosphere, mouth-watering Italian dishes, and enormous portions. They not only serve the locals but attract hearty appetites from across Pittsburgh.

But the Avenue is more than a thoroughfare, more than a place where residents shop and dine and make their living. It's very much the pulse of the community; it's where everyone meets, where everything happens. St. Joseph's, a parish that's nearly a century old and the site of many community bingo sessions and spaghetti dinners, is on the Avenue, and one weekend each summer the area around the church is blocked from traffic for

*Above:* **Friendship School, © Joel B. Levinson**

*Facing page:* **Bloomfield, © Harry Edelman**

an old-fashioned street fair. The young congregate on the Avenue at the Plaza Theater; the older citizens hug and greet lifelong friends in Italian and catch the latest family gossip and political scuttlebutt. Bloomfielders keep tabs on one another on the Avenue, and many say that for decades this communication has kept the neighborhood a stable, tightly knit place to live and raise a family.

Although it has a decidedly Italian flavor about it, Bloomfield (once a field of blooming flowers) was originally settled by Ger-

mans in the mid-1800s. Joseph Conrad Winebiddle, a wealthy industrialist and Revolutionary War veteran, developed it into residential lots, and the Germans who worked in his tannery along the Allegheny River in neighboring Lawrenceville built their Bloomfield homes in the compact style of the villages they left behind in Europe.

These small, frame row houses with cement front stoops are still bunched in the narrow, one-way side streets off Liberty Avenue. In 1850 there were only 13 structures in Bloomfield; today there are nearly 6,000 making homes for more than 11,000 residents. From the street the houses appear tiny, but they're surprisingly spacious and sturdy. Meticulously maintained, they have been passed from one generation to the next, a family tradition that has enabled Bloomfield to preserve its ethnicity but has, unfortunately, prevented new young families from moving in.

"We don't have a covert plan to keep people out," one resident explained, but "there's a strong line of communication between neighbors here, so if a house on the street is going on the market, the word gets around, and someone's son or daughter buys it before the For Sale sign ever gets put out."

Even if the Bloomfield grapevine is more effective than a real estate agency, it doesn't mean that there are no buying opportunities in the neighborhood. Although residents maintain that it's rare to find a renovated, single-family house on the market, there are a few turn-of-the-century charmers waiting for some handy do-it-yourselfers to move in and restore them.

But Bloomfield offers more to new residents than well-built homes and a bustling, self-contained business hub. Bloomfielders have a community spirit that's both energetic and contagious. They're actually quite smug about their annual Halloween parade, the largest in the city, and they boast of their Youth Athletic Association. In fact, residents will tell you that through the Citizens Council, they have acquired a professional Astroturf playing field for the teams. They're quick to point to celebrities who've gotten their start in the neighborhood, like Baltimore's National Football League hero Johnny Unitas, who played for the Bloomfield Rams, and makeup designer Tom Savini, who created special effects for thrillers like *Night of the Living Dead* and *Creepshow.* And old-timers still talk of the days when Pittsburgh native Gene Kelly danced on Lorigan Street for nickels.

## WEST END-ELLIOTT

It's surprising that even the most humble of homes in Elliott has a view that is vibrant, breathtaking and . . . well, surprising! You'd not expect to uncover such a vista atop the steep, wooded, narrow Belgian-block side streets that seem to wind endlessly. Yet at the top there's a panorama that is just as fabulous (but available at a quarter of the cost) as a similar view from a condo in a better-known neighborhood.

Granted, it's harder to get to the view from Elliott. And West End-Elliott residents say that's fine with them. Still, thousands traipse through the community to get to Rue Grand Vue and the Overlook every Fourth of July and Light-up Night, two Pittsburgh traditions that residents recently decided to join rather than beat.

Though they don't really object to the annual trek of photographers and spectators through the neighborhood, residents simply wish that visitors would pay more attention to the community they're climbing through. So now, in an organized fund-raiser,

**West End-Elliott homes,**
**© Michael Haritan**

City lights, © Michael Haritan

*Facing page:* **West End-Elliott backyard, © Michael Haritan**

the West End-Elliott Business Associates offer visitors a "taste" of the neighborhood each year. Treats like Wabash wienies, Crucible crunch, Chartier's chocolate, Lorenz lollies (named for neighborhood streets), Pittsburgh potable, and Temperanceville tarts (Temperanceville was the original name of the community), are served up along with a menu of information about the neighborhood.

West End and Elliott are two distinct neighborhoods in Pittsburgh's western section. They have joined in their efforts to promote the area as a good place to live and do business. West End, the neighborhood in the valley, is primarily commercial, while Elliott, atop the hill, is a middle-class residential community. As a team, the neighborhoods offer convenience, affordable and well-built housing, and a collection of shops and services to meet most needs in a business district that's being restored, building by building, to its turn-of-the-century style.

In the early nineteenth century, the communities were called Temperanceville, a name drawn from the stipulation on all property deeds that liquor should never be sold on the premises. Today community leaders are reviving the name (without the ban on alcohol) to call attention to the area's historic significance.

The name is catching on, inspiring renovations that are, in turn, attracting new businesses and shoppers to the neighborhood. New commercial enterprises are adopting the theme. There's Temperanceville Antiques, a spacious store filled with artifacts and collectibles; it has been renovated inside and out so beautifully that the details of the rehabilitation are almost more eye-catching than the merchandise. Temperanceville Tavern, a charming and popular establishment in spite of the contradiction in terms, serves residents and patrons from throughout the area.

Elaborate Victorian detailing—like cut-stone facades, heavy oak doors, and hand-painted scrollwork—which would be very expensive to create today, is being cleaned and refurbished on

**Backyard garden,
© Michael Haritan**

storefronts throughout the valley. Not everything in West End is turn-of-the-century grace, however. Scattered along Wabash, Steuben, and South Main streets, the major commercial areas, there are still vacant structures, affordable opportunities for entrepreneurs looking for the charm and security of an established neighborhood business hub and the convenience of being close to Downtown, without the high rents.

Opportunities abound in the neighborhood, residents say, and those who live and work in West End-Elliott—persistent, vocal, and longtime advocates of the neighborhood's attractions—are playing a vital role in the community's rebirth. A coalition of area

community groups formed the West End-Elliott Joint Project, and with help from the city they hired a full-time staffer to work on a comprehensive plan for economic development of the valley. The organization is promoting the area to attract more shops and shoppers and is working with current and potential business owners to get low-interest city loans for advancing the spirit of renovation.

West End-Elliott residents are natural and eager promoters of their neighborhood; they say they have a lot to brag about. Besides a healthy and growing business sector, the homes in this neat, friendly neighborhood are a bargain. Mostly two-story, three-bedroom frames, some can be had for as little as $32,000, and many feature a picturesque view of the Golden Triangle. Perhaps the brochure the community group distributes to prospective residents says it best:

*"If you lived in West End-Elliott, you could still shop in neighborhood stores—family-owned stores where the personal touch is most important. There's a neighborhood shopping area at the top of the hill with pharmacies, grocery stores, a butcher shop, and a hardware store, florists, a dairy, barber and beauty shops, and neighborhood restaurants. And in the valley is Temperanceville, the historic district with everything else you might need. From printing to pizza, from furniture to framing, from collectibles to carpeting, it's all here. And if you lived in West End-Elliott, you wouldn't have to leave the neighborhood to take advantage of it."*

## THIRTY-FIRST WARD

There's a long, narrow piece of Pittsburgh that reaches southward from the shores of the Monongahela, then vanishes into
the city's wooded hillsides. On older maps, this winding wedge
of woodedness is called the Thirty-first Ward. But as you drive
along Mifflin Road, the neighborhoods's main artery, there are
signs for four neighborhoods—Hays, Lincoln Place, Gates Manor,
and New Homestead—the little pockets of Thirty-first Ward tranquillity that nearly 6,500 Pittsburghers call home.

The peacefulness of the Thirty-first Ward is a haven for some.
The quiet tree-lined streets, the frequent forests and wide open
spaces, and the occasional cornfields and vegetable gardens

**Thirty-first Ward backyard,
© Michael Haritan**

are a pleasant alternative to the fast-paced world of Downtown,
only twenty minutes away. Although the houses are diverse in
style, many would nestle as well on acres of farmland as they
do in this urban neighborhood. And residents delight in their solitude. They have the best of both worlds, all the convenience
and cultural amenities of big-city living in a pastoral setting.

Although the Thirty-first Ward probably has more down-home
country atmosphere than any other neighborhood in the city,
the community is by no means a rural one. The area's serenity
is interrupted by Mifflin Road, a commuter route dotted with restaurants, services, and shops. The thoroughfare also links the
Thirty-first Ward with downtown Pittsburgh, Century III mall, and
the southeastern suburbs, an advantage that residents say is in-

**Watering garden, © Michael Haritan**

valuable.

Despite such access to other areas, the Thirty-first Ward is quite self-contained. Nearly everything residents need is right at hand—convenience stores, parks, churches, and the new Thirty-first Ward Citizens Council. Residents say that the group was organized not to address a specific concern but simply to attract more attention to the neighborhood. "We just want to make people more aware of the Thirty-first Ward," one neighborhood leader explained. "Everyone knows about the ethnicity of South Side and Lawrenceville and Polish Hill, and everyone knows about shopping in Shadyside and Squirrel Hill, but no one knows much about the Thirty-first Ward."

Since it began in 1983, the council has participated in several promotional events and developed a brochure that is distributed to potential residents. Though there is no exact count of how many new families have moved to the neighborhood because of the Citizens Council's efforts, residents note that more city services are available to the community since they became active.

And like the residents of so many Pittsburgh neighborhoods, who believe their community is really the best, those who reside in the Thirty-first Ward say that their area is every bit as special as those that get more frequent publicity. But that's okay, residents say. After all, they don't want a mad rush of development in the neighborhood, only a little attention. As one resident concluded, "It's the people who live here who make the neighborhood a nice place to be. Everyone gets along with everyone here, and there are a lot of organized activities for families, like Little League and softball. We're pretty much a quiet family neighborhood, just a nice place to live."

*Facing page:* **Sunset,** **© Michael Hartian**

*Below:* **House in the country, © Michael Haritan**

## MANCHESTER

Community leaders in Manchester still pinch themselves when they walk down Liverpool Street, just to be sure they're not dreaming. Today Liverpool, like many of the streets in this North Side neighborhood, is a wonderland of red-brick sidewalks, evenly placed street planters, and vast, three-story brick homes that sit in rows, each with matching front porches and gingerbread detailing—lots of gingerbread, which has been carefully repaired and painted to look the way it did when Manchester was home to well-to-do industrialists at the turn of the century.

A decade ago, however, Manchester was a nightmare. Some called it urban blight, others called it a ghetto. Most of the stately old mansions and row houses then were rat-infested shells, abandoned when more than 10,000 fled the neighborhood between 1965 and 1975. The rest were dilapidated, unsafe, and near condemnation, homes inhabited only by the very poor. Beset with high crime and problem bars, covered with broken glass and unsightly weeds, ten years ago Manchester was a far cry

**Manchester street scene, © William Metzger; courtesy, Neighborhoods for Living Center**

*Above:* **Detail of renovated Manchester home,** © Jack A. Wolf

from the prosperous borough it was in its heyday.

Named after the industrial town in England, Pittsburgh's Manchester was originally home to some of the area's most influential citizens. By 1901 it was an industrial powerhouse, where more than a dozen factories employed residents and made money for their founders. LaBelle Steel and Iron Works, McCloy Nail and Key Factory, Pittsburgh Locomotive and Car Works, Benson Pump Company, and Hutchinson Oil Works were just a handful of the successful enterprises located in early Manchester.

In the 1950s, however, as with many urban neighborhoods across the country, city residents were attracted to newer homes and spacious living in the suburbs. The flight from Manchester was compounded by the construction of a highway that divided the neighborhood, left many homeless, and ultimately prompted the exodus that pushed the community to the depths of decay. The population plummeted from 15,000 to just over 4,000, and some say that as many as twenty families left each week.

Soon afterward, urban renewal came into vogue, and the battle between demolitionists and preservationists in Manchester was fueled. Residents favored preservation for fear that if properties were razed, new construction wouldn't be started, and the land, once home to their friends and families, would remain vacant and misused. Eventually many structures were demolished, and in their place, suburban-style ranch houses, though completely out of sync with the historic district, were constructed

Manchester street scene,
© Mary Jane Bent

and sold. Yet fortunately for those who live in the beautifully restored homes on Liverpool, Lexington, and Pennsylvania avenues today, the residents persisted. They staved off the bulldozer, and through an organization that came to be known as the Manchester Citizens Corporation, they exercised sole responsibility for managing more than thirty million dollars in city grants and loans for rehabilitation.

The tenacity, energy, and leadership of the Manchester Citizens Corporation produced Pittsburgh's first black historic district and what is probably the first black urban-preservation neighborhood in the nation. To ensure the quality of each renovation, the MCC established strict guidelines governing rehabilitation of the neighborhood's historic structures and new construction. In addition to promoting renovations, the group supported the development of new town homes and condominiums in Manchester, as well as construction of the first passive solar energy units in Pennsylvania. A pilot project completed in cooperation with Carnegie-Mellon University, the Sheffield Street solar town homes were designed to harmonize with the neighborhood's predominantly Victorian architectural style.

Because of the community spirit and the pride of neighborhood residents, who refused to let their community die, Manchester today is a showplace. The hundreds of historic renovations completed in Manchester are stunning testimonies to what can be achieved when government funding for urban preservation is paired with grass-roots ambition, drive, and dreams.

## Pittsburgh Style Goes Beyond the City Limits

By John Altdorfer

The suburban areas of Greater Pittsburgh extend well past the city's borders. Outside of the city proper, throughout Allegheny County, in 129 politically defined and clearly distinct communities, nearly one million people make their homes. Ten desirable places to live—to the north, east, south, and west of the city— are described here. They represent the diversity of Allegheny County and depict the high quality of life that each contributes to the genuine character of the region.

*John Altdorfer, a lifelong resident of the Pittsburgh area, is managing editor of* Pittsburgh Magazine.

**River recreation in Allegheny County, © Jack A. Wolf**

BELLEVUE

Thirty years ago, for pleasant entertainment you could stroll along Lincoln Avenue, chow down on chow mein at a Chinese restaurant, slurp a hot fudge sundae for dessert at the soda fountain across the street, and take in a movie to round out the evening. Things were like that in Bellevue then, and they're pretty much the same today.

Just seven miles northwest of the city on Ohio River Boulevard (known as the "Bullvard"), Bellevue is a pleasing combination of urban convenience and suburban comfort. Its 10,128 residents live peacefully inside the mile-square borough. Streets are clean, wide, and safe. Children play on close-trimmed lawns of well-tended homes that are a testament to the community's pride and stability. Shoppers frequent the more than 100 businesses along Lincoln Avenue, some entering their seventh decade. Five parks, a community center, and a swimming pool offer numerous recreational possibilities. A short block off the business district, a towering elm (the oldest in the state, at 390 years) provides shade and repose for the weary pedestrian. You might not expect all this within a fifteen-minute drive of the glimmering glass towers of Downtown. But then Bellevue has always

View from Bellevue,
© Michael Haritan

been a pleasant surprise.

Like other communities along the north shore of the Ohio River, Bellevue was originally settled by Revolutionary War veterans who were offered parcels of land at low rates in exchange for their service in battle. Although the first tracts went up for sale at twenty cents an acre in 1785, nearly two years later less than half the land was sold, because of less-than-friendly Indians who weren't quite ready to surrender the territory that an early French settler said had a "beautiful view" of the lush hills and valleys. Eventually farms sprang up throughout the countryside. By 1850 a number of Pittsburgh residents had forsaken the city for clean and quiet Bellevue, which was then still a part of its present-day neighbor Ross Township. Seventeen years later the town split from Ross in a dispute over the distribution of tax dollars used to pave roads and build sidewalks.

Just a sleepy village of 300 residents in 1867, Bellevue was quickly transformed into a residential community by the completion of the Pennsylvania-Baltimore Railroad. The first storefront opened for business on Lincoln Avenue in 1873, when Dr. George Langfitt hung his shingle on the corner of a building he later shared with a drugstore, a grocery, and a butcher shop. At the turn of the century, as the first streetcars clanged through town, Bellevue's population had grown more than tenfold.

Today Bellevue continues to be a thriving town. In a recent survey of customer households more than 50 percent said that the primary reason for being in "downtown Bellevue" was for shopping. And 87 percent of those surveyed said they shopped in Bellevue at least once a week.

While other towns boast of their shopping districts, Bellevue can let the facts speak for themselves. Along a quarter-mile stretch of Lincoln Avenue, there are five restaurants, two shoe stores, a book and record shop, two hardware stores, a butcher shop, three pharmacies, two supermarkets, a dress shop, a men's clothing store, five banks and savings and loans, two ice cream parlors, two bakeries, a two-screen movie theater, two automobile dealerships, and more pizza shops than in any other city except Rome. You get the idea—if you want it, Bellevue probably has it.

More than a shopper's paradise, Bellevue is a community of deep-rooted beliefs and cultural diversity. Eleven churches represent every major faith, including Jehovah's Witnesses. The Andrew Bayne Memorial Library, located in a six-acre park in the heart of town, houses more than 19,000 cataloged books and dozens of magazines and periodicals. Many young artists and professionals call Bellevue home, thanks in large part to low rent and housing prices. (The average price of a single-family dwelling is below $45,000.) Perhaps Bellevue's main strength is its stability. Its residents are employed mainly in the service and retail fields, and because a significant number of those people work in the town itself, Bellevue is in many ways self-sufficient.

Bellevue cares for its own, too. Twenty-three civic organizations attend to the town's young, old, and needy. The problems of the handicapped youngster are tackled by the expert staff of St. Peter's Child Development Center, one of the area's finest schools for exceptional children. More than forty physicians, covering the gamut of medicine, and a major hospital are within Bellevue's boundaries.

The Indians have vanished, and the farmlands have given way to parks and shops and houses. Streetcars no longer rumble down Lincoln Avenue. But nearly 200 years later Bellevue remains the same—vital and desirable. We should all be so lucky.

## FOX CHAPEL

It's not hard to figure out why Fox Chapel has long been one of the most attractive and exclusive suburbs in the Pittsburgh area. A short drive across the Highland Park Bridge from the city's East End neighborhoods and just six miles from Downtown, this sprawling borough of 5,045 residents is a pleasant maze of quiet country roads that wind past secluded estates separated by acres of lush woodlands.

Fox Chapel has fought hard to keep development in the community to a minimum. It has no industrial or commercial zones. (A nearby shopping mall bears the borough's name—the prestige factor is high—but is actually located in O'Hara Township.) Land use is limited to residential buildings, schools, churches, and private recreational clubs.

In 1930 signs of commercial encroachment began to threaten. First, Allegheny County considered building an aquatic amusement park with a 500-foot pool (to accommodate an anticipated 17,000 splash-happy swimmers), a harbor on the Allegheny River, an amphitheater, and numerous picnic groves. Then plans were announced for the construction of a dog-racing track. While many saw the proposed projects as possible financial windfalls, especially with the onset of the Depression, the leaders of Fox Chapel acted to prevent their completion. They convinced the county commissioners that the water park would create unmanageable congestion and warned the racetrack developers that they would be arrested and prosecuted if they attempted to build. In fact, the borough has defeated most foes who have challenged its zoning laws. Today Fox Chapel is a classic example of what can be done to preserve an environment of natural spaciousness in the shadow of a busy metropolis.

The rewards of the battle are plentiful. Homeowners enjoy the privacy afforded by zoning laws that, in most cases, require dwellings to be built on a minimum of one to three acres. Many of Pittsburgh's corporate and civic heads, as well as sports and entertainment luminaries, live here to escape the fishbowl of public life. Accordingly, real estate prices are among the highest in the county, with the average value of a house being more than $170,000.

But the benefits go beyond the monetary. Fox Chapel has more than 200 acres of parks reserved for activities such as

hiking and bird watching. The most famous of the parks is the Trillium Trail, where thousands of blossoming trilliums cover the ground each spring with a blanket of white, purple, and pink. And for the true naturalist, there's the Beechwood Farms nature preserve—90 acres of meadows, thickets, pine plantations, and meandering streams. Henry David Thoreau would have loved this place.

If your recreational pleasures are a bit more active, don't fret. McCahill Park, a five-acre expanse, has two baseball diamonds, a basketball court, and two large fields used mostly for touch football and rugby. Golfers can play the links at two private courses. There is also a members-only racquet club.

Fox Chapel is more than parks. Its schools are ranked among the best in the state. The system features a perceptual motor development program in the elementary grades, while the high school offers advanced placement and accelerated courses designed to prepare students for college. A measure of the success of the schools is the number of college graduates living in the borough. More than 65 percent of Fox Chapel's residents have at least an undergraduate degree, and 68 percent of them are employed in managerial and professional positions. The average salary of this work force is more than $57,000.

In case you haven't guessed yet, Fox Chapel is an island of Republicanism in the Democratic sea of Allegheny County. Three out of four people here have registered their allegiance to the GOP. Ronald Reagan would definitely love this place.

Incidentally, Fox Chapel's name has nothing to do with those furry red creatures that decorate the community's hand-painted road signs. It seems that in 1889 well-to-do settler, John Fox, left a plot of land to his daughter, Eliza Fox Teats. Shortly thereafter a local Methodist congregation called on Eliza to donate part of the land for the site of the group's chapel. Eliza complied, and the structure was named in honor of her father—hence, Fox Chapel.

Though its population has increased nearly 66 percent over the past two decades, the 8.5-square-mile borough shows few signs of becoming overcrowded. Strict zoning laws and the desire of Fox Chapel's people and government to maintain their privacy and the rustic tranquillity of the community will see to that.

Fox Chapel parks in autumn and winter, © Mary Jane Bent

*Facing page:* **Monroeville Mall, © Herb Ferguson**

## MONROEVILLE

Monroeville is many things to many people. First, it is a shopper's mecca. There isn't a red-blooded, credit-card-toting consumer in Allegheny County who hasn't made a pilgrimage at least once in his or her lifetime if not once a week to the Miracle Mile, that fabulous stretch of U.S. Route 22 jammed with a cornucopia of malls, plazas, restaurants, hotels, and factory outlets.

Monroeville is a center of industrial and scientific research for many of Pittsburgh's major corporations. Since 1953, USX Corporation (formerly U.S. Steel) has operated a facility here for developmental work on raw materials used in making steel as well as in the company's chemicals and plastics divisions. More than 10,000 people are employed in Monroeville by Westinghouse, including 1,300 at the firm's Nuclear Center, where work is being done on improving the performance of the nation's power plants. The Loppers Company, a manufacturer with special engineering and construction capabilities, has its Science and Technology Center here.

Monroeville is a pleasant and affordable place to live. Though the first image of the area might be one of overwhelming commercial and industrial development, many fine homes with generous lawns can be found in settings that are almost pastoral. (Monroeville was primarily an agricultural region until the early 1950s.) Most of the housing is relatively new, and prices for a single-family home average about $60,000.

Monroeville is a cultural and recreational center. It has a community college, a library, an art gallery, and a symphony orchestra. Residents can relax and play in more than 1,500 acres of municipal and county parklands that include a wave pool and skiing trails and slopes.

Monroeville is also the site of a beautiful Hindu temple. Sri Venkateswara Temple took Indian craftsmen three years to build on a wooded hillside overlooking the Parkway East. The granite used in the construction of this delicately sublime structure was imported from India, as were the statues inside.

Monroeville is more than meets the eye. Commerce, industry, and community coexist harmoniously within its 19.5 square miles. Once known as Wallurbia and later described as "being of little importance," it has grown at an unbelievable pace over the past three decades.

Incorporated in 1951, Monroeville's large tracts of inexpensive land drew the attention of companies looking to expand their office and research facilities. As thousands of professionals with families entered the area, they began looking for homes near their jobs. Housing developments sprouted overnight, reaching a peak of activity between 1962 and 1972. By the mid-1970s the community had more than 30,000 residents.

The demand for homes, apartments, and office buildings remains high. New businesses are being courted by the Monroeville Area Industrial Development Corporation, a nonprofit group that works with the Monroeville Chamber of Commerce to welcome potential clients to the area. Convention activity is strong as a result of an exposition center with easy access to more than 2,000 nearby hotel rooms.

No longer just a suburb and not quite a city itself, the Monroeville of the 1980s might be best described as a satellite community. With a short, wildly successful past, Monroeville can look ahead to even more growth and prosperity in the future.

**Monroeville Marriott,**
**© Herb Ferguson**

## MOON TOWNSHIP

Because Moon Township is the oldest chartered community in Allegheny County, one might expect it to be steeped in history. Well, it does have its fair share of lore and legends about marauding Indians and frightened but persevering settlers, but most of what's happened here has occurred in the last thirty-five years.

After receiving its papers back in 1788, Moon Township, which is believed to have gotten its name from the crescent-shaped bend of the Ohio River that forms its northern boundary, went about the business of tilling the 143 square miles of land within its borders. Farming remained the main occupation of the area until the late 1800s.

Though Moon has shrunk drastically from its original size, it is still the sixth-largest community in the county at twenty-four square miles. The area, though only sixteen miles from Pittsburgh, was virtually undeveloped well into the middle of the twentieth century. Then several things happened to spark a period of growth that would change the face of Moon.

First, the commissioners of Allegheny County decided that the region needed a new, modern airport to handle the forecasted boom in air traffic. After considering several sites, they tabbed more than two square miles of land in Moon for building Greater Pittsburgh Airport, which was inaugurated in 1954.

At that time many city dwellers, tired of the grind of urban life, were heading for the serenity of the suburbs around Pittsburgh. The completion of the Parkway East and Beaver Valley Expressway aided this migration and boosted Moon's population from 7,000 in 1950 to 21,000 in 1980, according to U.S. Census figures. Nevertheless, despite a 200-percent increase in population and the mushrooming of hotels, car rental companies, restaurants, and shopping centers near the airport, more than 6,000 acres of the township's 15,000 acres are vacant.

Of the land that is developed, more than 40 percent is for residential use. The majority of residences are single-family homes that are fairly well spread out over the township. Duplexes, apartment buildings, and other multifamily dwellings are abundant, although they tend to be concentrated in a few areas. Most of the housing in Moon is less than thirty years old, and home prices are reasonable at an average of $64,000.

Moon Township is a family-oriented community. Nearly half

the families have children under eighteen. Moon is also a young community. The median age is twenty-eight, and nearly a fifth of the population is between the ages of twenty-five and thirty-four.

Moon Township is also the home of a branch of Robert Morris College, a fully accredited four-year school well regarded for its business program. Located on a secluded bluff just minutes from the airport, the campus also boasts a basketball team, the Colonials, that has gone to the NCAA playoffs several times in the last few years.

During its thirty years of rapid growth, Moon was often hard-pressed to provide and maintain the public services its residents needed. Today, however, it has a full-time police department, a volunteer fire department, and a municipal water and sewer authority. In addition, the township maintains a 150-acre park and three golf courses.

As Moon Township nears its bicentennial, it can look forward to a period of stability and moderate growth. Plans are now under way for the construction of a midfield terminal at Greater Pittsburgh International Airport. To handle the increase in auto traffic, an additional expressway has been proposed. As access to the airport and to the city is improved, more people are expected to move into the area, although at a rate much lower than previously experienced, and this growth will be guided by long-term community planning efforts now under way.


## MT. LEBANON

Mt. Lebanon makes no apologies for the many advantages it has to offer. "You can find communities that have lower tax rates," says a Chamber of Commerce brochure given to potential newcomers, "but you won't find a community anywhere that gives as much benefit for the tax as [Mt. Lebanon does]. We invite you to find out if this is so." With a tax rate that is among the highest in the county, what exactly will your dollar buy in this township of 34,000 people that dares you to do better?

Number one is a quality education. Mt. Lebanon students earn consistently high marks on standardized national tests, and 85 percent of the district's pupils go on to college. The district ranks in the top thirty in the country among public and private schools in terms of the number of National Merit Scholars, and 75 percent of the faculty holds master's or doctoral degrees. The per-pupil expenditure is high ($5,518), while the student-teacher ratio is low (18 to 1). The municipal library is considered by many to be the finest of its kind in the county; with more than 90,000 books and 200 periodicals, its circulation exceeds 350,000 volumes a year.

Safety is another plus. Mt. Lebanon's crime rate is one of the nation's lowest. More than 50 percent of its forty-three police officers have college degrees. An added bonus is a fire-fighting force that includes fourteen full-time personnel and thirty-five volunteers. And eleven skilled paramedics are on call to respond to medical emergencies.

Residents also enjoy an extensive parks and recreational system. The Recreation Center, located in the main municipal park, is a sports fanatic's dream come true. The largest facility on the premises houses two indoor skating rinks, including a full-size hockey rink where the Pittsburgh Penguins and other NHL teams often practice. Also in the park is an olympic-size swimming pool with a separate diving area and a children's pool. The center also has fifteen clay and synthetic-surface tennis courts. The prestigious National Amateur Clay Court Championships and West Penn Tennis Tournament are held here each July. Past participants have included such greats as John McEnroe, Vitas Gerulaitas, and the legendary Big Bill Tilden. The center also has baseball and soccer fields and an exercise trail. Elsewhere around town there are many more tennis courts and athletic fields and a 100-acre, nine-hole golf course.

Still not convinced that this place is worth it? Jump into your car and discover why for yourself. Cross over the Mon River on the Liberty Bridge, tunnel through the Liberty Tubes, then take West Liberty Avenue to the edge of Dormont, to the point where Washington Road begins. Stop. You are in Mt. Lebanon. What you see is this: a bustling business district that is the equal of any in the area—save Downtown Pittsburgh itself. Over there is an antique shop specializing in country-style furniture and collectibles. Next door a gaggle of long-legged dancers strut into a studio. A little farther down the street is the bookstore, which has been there for more than a quarter of a century. Down the block people are lining up outside the theater for a first-run movie. Take note: there are more than forty shops and boutiques—not to mention numerous physicians' offices, banks, and restaurants—flanking Washington Road. Impressive, you think, but what you really want to know is how people live around here.

On just about any street in Mt. Lebanon, you are likely to encounter a pleasing blend of graceful older homes and bold contemporary-style dwellings. Set well back from the tree-lined streets (there are more than 9,000 trees in Mt. Lebanon) are many fine examples of Colonial, Tudor, and Cape Cod design. There are even a few farmhouses that recall the community's rustic past. Though many of the edifices are more than sixty years old, housing prices are steep. While the average price of a home is a little higher than $70,000, many others are worth as much as three to four times more. It takes a very upwardly mobile type to live in this neighborhood.

The typical Mt. Lebanonite is thirty-five years old and has an income a bit higher than $40,000. He or she is a college graduate and probably works in a managerial or professional position. He or she owns a home or condo, which is shared with a spouse and child. And he or she is a Republican.

Because residents are interested in preserving the special appeal Mt. Lebanon holds, they are active in community affairs. They keep up on what's happening around town by reading the latest issue of *Mt. Lebanon* magazine, a monthly publication operated by the township and distributed free of charge.

In short, the average Mt. Lebanon resident is successful, confident, and involved. These people want the best for themselves and their families, and they feel Mt. Lebanon offers just that.

Everything has its price, the old saying goes, and excellent schools, safe neighborhoods, and the convenience of being twenty minutes from Downtown do not come cheap. Then again, Mt. Lebanon told you so.

## SEWICKLEY

Imagine you are in a Norman Rockwell painting. Young couples sit in wicker rockers on the wraparound porches of their elegant Victorian and Georgian homes, perusing the latest edition of the Sunday *Times*. The kids and the dog take turns chasing one another around the spacious yard, occasionally scampering through a mound of fallen leaves. Down in the village center, three elderly men rest on a bench near the town's sole traffic light, observing the trickle of traffic passing by. On their way back from the tack shop, neighbors stop in front of the fish market and chat about the upcoming harvest festival. That man over there—the one in the khaki dungarees, duck shoes, flannel shirt, and goose-down vest—looks as though he stepped right out of an L.L. Bean catalog. You ask yourself, can this be for real?

It is if you're in Sewickley. This tiny community of 4,700 residents was a picture of Americana even before its incorporation in 1853. Long before the first white settlers arrived, the Asswikales Indians, from whom Sewickley is believed to have taken its name, roamed the area's bountiful forests and fished along the banks of the mighty Ohio. Later, as British and French expeditions stretched the frontiers of the New World westward, such notables as George Washington passed through. (No, he did not sleep here. Sewickley may be the only town in the United States that lays no claim to his slumbers.) Because it was on the main road between Pittsburgh and Erie, Sewickley soon became a major stopover for stagecoach passengers and pioneers in their Conestoga wagons headed for the great Northwest.

Some of these travelers, lured by the charm of the valley and wary of the long journey ahead of them, stayed on to build their homes and farms.

Many opened inns to feed and lodge other more determined but weary pilgrims on their treks. As commerce on the Ohio increased, riverboat captains as well as captains of industry built homes and summer cottages here. Today many of those "cottages" are called mansions.

By the time the first train steamed into town in 1851, the personality of Sewickley was well defined. Though much of the town's population was made up of wealthy businessmen and their families, a sizable community of service and working-class people, who tended to the needs of their more prosperous neighbors, lived there as well. Even now Sewickley retains this livable mix of social and economic classes.

Though staunchly conservative, Sewickleans are tolerant. During the tumultuous 1960s, high school students staged several walkouts to protest the Vietnam War. Yet the most severe reprimand was a heartfelt homily from the school's principal on the responsibility of accepting the consequences of one's convictions and actions.

Today the biggest controversy in the town revolves around whether the police officers on the beat are spending too much time talking to the citizens they are protecting from the practically nonexistent crime in the borough. Another debate, much older than the police story, is whether the town was actually named after those western Pennsylvania Indians or after the Indian word *seweekly,* meaning "sweet water."

Though only a suburb twelve miles northwest of the city, Sewickley seems to have suburbs of its own. The adjoining communities of Osborne, Edgeworth, and Sewickley Heights, home of many of the wealthiest people in the country, view the borough as their center of shopping, worship, medicine, and recreation.

More than fifty boutiques, markets, newsstands, and clothing stores are situated along Beaver and Broad streets, Sewickley's main thoroughfares. There are even two mini-malls: the Nickelodeon is housed, of course, in an old movie theater, and the Carbarn Shops are in the giant garage of a former auto dealership.

The Quaker Valley school district operates two elementary schools, a junior high school, and a senior high school for its 1,870 students. And the Sewickley Academy, a private coeducational institution, is well regarded for its college prep curriculum.

Sewickley Valley Hospital, a modern 236-bed facility, serves the entire Ohio Valley with one of the most up-to-date critical-care units in the area. Parents of handicapped youngsters can take advantage of the fine service provided at the D.T. Watson Rehabilitation Hospital.

Organized sports leagues of all kinds, for kids and adults, abound in Sewickley. If you're more inclined to individual sporting pursuits, the YMCA offers a multitude of programs. The Y also has one of the largest indoor pools in the area, and three private country clubs offer the finest in golf and tennis.

Maybe the best thing about Sewickley is that it is about as big as it will ever get. Although people live comfortably here, nearly every available bit of land has been developed. Most homes are older and in very good condition, with prices running anywhere from $35,000 to $450,000—examples of both sometimes only a few hundred feet apart on the same street. Don't expect to find a buyer's market, though—folks tend to stay a while. Over the past fifty years, the population has fluctuated between 4,500 and 6,000. People do move, but a few blocks' distance is often the extent of it.

As more and more of the country becomes suburbanized (falling prey to what writer Joan Didion describes as "the malling of America"), Sewickley still has that friendly small-town atmosphere. "This is a community of people and homes," says one longtime resident, "not a jumble of prefab plywood boxes thrown together out in the middle of nowhere that people call a neighborhood. I know my neighbors. I went to school with them. I worked at their parents' businesses during the summer. I like the variety Sewickley offers. I can drive to my office in Pittsburgh in less than half an hour. By the same token, I can ride by bicycle five minutes out of town and be in some of the most beautiful surroundings in the country. Sewickley is unique. You just can't find many places like this anymore."

## OAKMONT
Michael Bright came to Oakmont in 1820, attracted by the area's wooded valleys and solitude; he built a log cabin and later opened a pottery business. About a millennium or two before Bright's arrival, the Adena Indians lived here, taking advantage of the plentiful fishing in the Allegheny River. Though the ensuing centuries and decades have wrought a few changes, neither Bright nor the Indians would have trouble recognizing Oakmont today.

Nearly 100 years after its incorporation in 1889, Oakmont's natural assets are still enticing residents and visitors alike. On any given weekend during the late spring, summer, or early fall, you're likely to discover fishermen lounging at the river's edge, enjoying a relaxing day in the sun. You may find families picnicking in the community's thirteen-acre park. Or perhaps you'll spend the day watching the annual regatta, capped off by a mirthful parade of small pleasure craft and luxurious yachts decorated with colored lights.

What was once a quiet little village of 1,600 people is now a quiet, slightly larger town of 7,000. Split nearly in half by a single set of long-abandoned railroad tracks that run through the heart of its business district, Oakmont consists of a long, flat stretch of land along the river on one side of the tracks and a hilly section on the other. Homes on either side of the tracks are generally well into their middle age but tend to be in excellent condition. Because Oakmont is nearly 100-percent developed, there are only a few newly built houses. Turnover in real estate is small (the average price of a home is around $50,000), reflecting the fact that most people are content to stay just where they are.

Perched on the south bank of the Allegheny River, Oakmont is a pleasure seeker's paradise. Riverside Park, a rambling thirteen-acre complex, has four baseball diamonds, a football field, and an ice-skating rink. In addition, a quarter-mile track encircles five tennis courts, volleyball and basketball courts, horseshoe pits, and a fine playground for the kids, chock-full of swings, slides, tunnels, and monkey bars. For the boater it is possible to sail as far as fifty-five miles upstream, as well as all the way down the Allegheny, Ohio, and Mississippi rivers to the Gulf of Mexico.

Oakmont is the self-proclaimed golf center of the state, thanks to the eight courses in and around the town. The most famous of these is the Oakmont Country Club, the site of many professional tournaments, including the National Open and the PGA Championship. There are also several fine public courses.

Community spirit has always been high in Oakmont, in large part a result of its small size; it covers a scant 1.4 square miles. When Riverside Park was proposed, residents raised $75,000 for its construction, and they pitched in to do most of the work themselves. A $60,000 community center was built with the help of donations from the townspeople. In 1966 a group of citizens rented a small bus to provide extra shuttle service from regular bus lines to banks, shops, and doctors' offices. A decade later, a van equipped with a hydraulic lift was purchased to serve Oakmont's elderly and handicapped. Both vehicles are still running, financed by personal contributions and grants from service clubs.

Oakmont is a balanced community. Its population is an equal mix of young and old. Though residential development accounts for most of the land use in town, there are several light industries and a small but diverse shopping strip. While it has the atmosphere of a summer retreat, Oakmont is close enough to Pittsburgh to partake of a cosmopolitan flavor. All in all, despite a few small changes, it wouldn't be stretching the imagination much to say that the Adena Indians and Michael Bright would still feel right at home in Oakmont.

## ROSS TOWNSHIP

Pinning a label on Ross Township is nearly impossible. On one hand, it's the northern cousin of Monroeville's Miracle Mile business strip. Along a two-mile stretch of McKnight Road, one of the two main arteries that run through Ross Township (Perry Highway is the other), is a crazy clutter of shopping malls, movie theaters, fast-food joints and restaurants, bowling alleys, gas stations, car washes, video stores, and office complexes. Nearly every imaginable service or product can be bought here. On the other hand, a short detour off McKnight will put you smack-dab in the middle of some of the coziest neighborhoods that western Pennsylvania has to offer.

Like Monroeville, Ross experienced the greatest part of its expansion, especially in commercial development, after World War II. Most of the growth resulted from the construction of McKnight Road in the late 1940s and from numerous reconstructions and widenings in the ensuing years. Much of the land in the township's eastern half, where the massive, multilevel malls now stand, was used for farming just a little less than four decades ago. In fact, the site of the newly opened Ross Park Mall, a gigantic three-story retail center that will eventually house 190 stores, was an agricultural holdout until the early 1980s.

Over on Ross' western reaches, however, it's a different story. Here you'll find a trio of communities that have managed to retain their individual identities, despite having long ago been annexed by their giant parent.

Tiny Perrysville flanks Perry Highway, also known as Route 19. Both the town and the road were named in honor of Commodore Oliver Perry, who defeated the British at the Battle of Lake Erie during the War of 1812 and who passed through the area via stagecoach on his way to the battle. Residents of Perrysville appreciate its rolling, winding streets and wide, manicured lawns. The homes are a pleasing potpourri of aluminum-sided split-levels, wood-frame Cape Cods, and red-brick Gothics. There is a fine old elementary school and a small business district within ten-minute walking distance from most streets. Many of the

**Ross Park Mall picnic,
© Michael Haritan**

area's young professionals and their families have made Perrysville an ever-more-popular choice for planting their roots.

Laurel Gardens, however, has a distinctly different personality. Located at the top of what may well be the highest hill in North Hills, it is a twisting, often confusing maze of streets and alleys that dip and climb along the contours of the roller-coasterlike terrain. The houses here are modest, well-kept, and clustered together. While their neighbors in Perrysville relax on Wolmanized decks or sun themselves by the pool, the people of Laurel Gardens are more likely to unwind by pitching horseshoes in the backyard. Twenty-five years ago Laurel Gardens was the working man's idea of the American Dream come true. Today the dream lives on.

North Bellevue is practically an island unto itself. Tucked between West View and Bellevue, it is separated from the main body of Ross Township by a 500-foot-wide ravine. While the residents of this diminutive neighborhood (there are just six short streets) enjoy the convenience of nearby Bellevue, they also receive the benefits of being part of a much larger and wealthier township.

The North Hills school district, which serves Ross, is consis-

**Ross Park Mall picnic,
© Michael Haritan**

tently rated as one of the best in the state. Some of the facilities featured in the junior and senior high schools are a planetarium, fully equipped radio and TV studios, and an olympic-size swimming pool that is often open to the public after school hours. In the lower grades, individualized courses and instruction are provided to students who need a bit more special attention. Ross residents can take advantage of free lending privileges at the Northland Library, of which the township is a supporting member.

Though the school system is a big plus for both newcomers and longtime Ross residents, the township presents a host of recreational opportunities as well. There are parks throughout the area, with most communities having at least one small area devoted to recreation. The Ross Community Park, nestled in a small wooded valley, features several miles of hiking trails, a fishing pond, and many picnic groves. With a few weeks' notice, the park's handsome, spacious lodge can be rented for reunions, receptions, and parties.

Because Ross is basically a commuter suburb, several Port Authority bus routes carry thousands of office workers and shoppers Downtown. Even so, a rising number of firms are relocating to the many commercial and research buildings that are springing up along McKnight Road.

Continued growth is certain for Ross. New malls are in the works, and housing developments seem to spring up magically overnight. An extension of U.S. Interstate 79 is due to be completed by fall 1987, running parallel to Route 19 and cutting travel time between the township and Pittsburgh. More people and more businesses will be moving in—yet Ross will probably continue to confuse those who want to label it, and satisfy those who live and work there.

## WILKINSBURG

To many people Wilkinsburg is a question mark. Is it the easternmost community of Pittsburgh, sharing many of the city's urban advantages and disadvantages, or is it a busy suburban community of well-kept homes and hardworking merchants?

From its early days, Wilkinsburg has been something of an enigma. While most towns in the area were built along the Ohio, Allegheny, and Monongahela rivers or on the many tributary streams, Wilkinsburg is not near any significant body of water. Nor did it come into being as an extension of Pittsburgh. Until the latter part of the nineteenth century, great stretches of unoccupied land separated Wilkinsburg from the city. Though these factors would have hampered—even snuffed out—the development of most towns, they are exactly the reasons why Wilkinsburg progressed.

Located almost midway between the shores of the Monongahela and Allegheny rivers and just seven miles from the heart of Pittsburgh, Wilkinsburg became a major stopover for people and goods coming from and going to the city. Passengers on stagecoaches and wagon trains checked in for a night's lodging on the way west—which usually meant Ohio in those days. As the 1850s approached, farmers and ranchers from the outer edges of the county capitalized on Wilkinsburg's proximity to Pittsburgh. Crops were brought to market in town to be sold to city produce merchants. Cattle were herded into a large stockyard near what is now the intersection of Penn and Grant avenues, to be auctioned off to buyers who later led their purchases to the slaughterhouses in nearby East Liberty.

Then, during the 1880s and 1890s, the first great eastward exodus of city residents began. While the rich favored the pastoral retreats of Homewood or Schenley Farms in Oakland, the less affluent ended up in Wilkinsburg. By 1885 more than 2,500 people called Wilkinsburg home. Shortly afterward, a movement was started to incorporate the swelling village as a borough.

Following nearly three years of heated debate between residents who wished to form a borough and those who didn't, Wilkinsburg received its papers in 1888. In a similar scenario, the opposing faction had gone to the state supreme court fifteen years before to put an end to Wilkinsburg's two-year stint as part of the city of Pittsburgh. It seems that these folks liked living in a small town.

The advent of the streetcar and the automobile, however, defeated any attempts to keep Wilkinsburg small. As commuters found that the distance to the city was dramatically reduced by these modern contraptions, Wilkinsburg blossomed. The once-tiny village soon annexed land from neighboring communities. As more and more people moved in, Wilkinsburg established its own library. (Andrew Carnegie said he would build a branch of his free public library there if a suitable site could be found, but civic leaders neglected the proposal for so long that the philanthropic Scot withdrew his offer.) A symphony orchestra was formed. Wilkinsburg was as much like a city as the city it was a suburb of.

This period of prosperity and growth continued through the early part of this century, peaking around 1950, when Wilkinsburg was perhaps the most desirable neighborhood outside of the city. Its business district was patronized by shoppers from all parts of the county. Nearly 5,000 passengers a day were boarding trains at the Pennsylvania Railroad's historic station. Families found this to be a good place to raise the kids. But as Wilkinsburg and its residents were enjoying their good fortune, another eastward migration was beginning. The relatively virgin lands of Monroeville and destinations farther east were beckoning.

Meanwhile, the twin urban plights of poverty and racial tension spilled over into Wilkinsburg. Middle-income people fled the advancing decay and crime of once-pleasant and safe streets. Businesses moved to the malls or shut their doors for good. Wilkinsburg, it seemed, was dying.

But while some people were busy performing the last rites on Wilkinsburg, others were not quite ready to call it quits. Working together, the borough government and several community organizations began mapping strategies to revitalize their community.

After some uneven progress with rehabilitation projects of the 1960s and 1970s, Wilkinsburg is striving diligently to restore itself to its former glory. The Wilkinsburg Development Corporation has drawn up a five-year plan, beginning in 1986, to rebuild the borough's business district. Sidewalks are being repaired and replaced. Trees and shrubs are being planted along the borough's main street, Penn Avenue, and its offshoots. Contractors are busy sprucing up the faces of the many elderly but elegant structures in the heart of the business district. Efforts are also being made to upgrade the school system, often a central concern of families moving into a new location.

So far the plan is working well. New businesses are offering shoppers an eclectic mix of choices. On any given day, people can be seen browsing in a vintage-comic-book store, buying vegetables at an Asian grocery that supplies produce to many Pittsburgh restaurants, or having a hot pastrami sandwich at a small deli.

Families are once again discovering the pleasures of Wilkinsburg. Though housing prices are climbing in many of the city's eastern neighborhoods, great bargains are easy to find here. Most homes are large and upward of sixty years old, and prices in the low $40,000s are common. One of the borough's more popular areas is Blackridge, a quiet neighborhood with newer housing, similar to many suburban, planned communities. And with the Parkway East and the Port Authority's bus expressway nearby, access to the city is still fast and easy.

Some questions still remain. Should Wilkinsburg try to compete head-on with the suburban malls and specialty shopping areas of the city, such as Shadyside, or should it offer a well-rounded selection of shops and services to conveniently meet the demands of its residents? Should it develop into a homogeneous neighborhood of young professionals, or should it remain a neighborhood of diverse races and cultures? The answers aren't easy, but Wilkinsburg is working hard to find them.


## UPPER ST. CLAIR

It's hard to believe that Upper St. Clair was named after a man who ended a once-glorious life in abject poverty and obscurity. After all, this bedroom community ten miles south of the Golden Triangle is one of the most prosperous and well-known neighborhoods in all of western Pennsylvania. But before we get to the history and civics lessons, let's get a few facts straight about this place.

First of all, there is no *Lower* St. Clair. Well, it did exist a hundred years ago or so, but the City of Pittsburgh gobbled it up somewhere along the way. No one seemed to care much about it then, and hardly anyone gives the matter a second thought anymore. Next, Upper St. Clair has no commercial district to speak of. Part of a large mall is in the township, but don't expect to revel in your serendipitous discoveries of quaint little boutiques and trendy restaurants on Main Street. They're just not there.

What Upper St. Clair does have is money. The median household income—the combined salaries of husbands and wives and any other significant wage earners under one roof—is $47,322. In comparison, the same figure for all of Allegheny County is in the mid-teens. There is no truth to the rumor, however, that the township is considering changing the official spelling of its name to "Upper $t. Clair."

Once one of the largest municipalities in the area, Upper St. Clair now covers a modest 6,378 acres, of which 43 percent has been developed for residential use. In 1762 John Fife, the township's first settler, bought 1,000 acres from some Indians for a pair of long underwear. Today such a purchase would cost an arm and a legging. Because zoning laws require homes to be built on at least a third of an acre, the price of a house in Upper St. Clair is high, running from an average $93,000 all the way up to $400,000 and more. Check your financial portfolio before thinking about establishing your nest here.

Between 1960 and 1980, Upper St. Clair's population skyrocketed from a little more than 8,200 people to 19,000—an increase of 130 percent. Basically, the reason was the area's rural atmosphere and the improvements in the roadways connecting it to the city. Another spur to the township's growth was its reputation for providing a wide range of services to its residents. This is one of the safest communities in the area, thanks in large part to a twenty-five-member police force. The township also operates 130 acres of parks and a year-round recreational program, including many activities for older adults, and a three-hole executive golf course.

Education is a top priority, and as one township official says,

the reputation of Upper St. Clair is the main selling point in convincing newcomers to settle here. During the 1985-1986 school year, the Upper St. Clair school district had an operating budget of almost eighteen million dollars. More than half of that total was devoted directly to instructional purposes, and an average of twenty-five dollars per day was spent per pupil. The money appears to be well spent, as 90 percent of the district's students pursue formal education after graduation. Daytime adult-education courses are also offered.

While we're talking school, maybe it's time to take a look at the chronicles of Upper St. Clair. The township was named for Arthur St. Clair, a Scot who settled in the area in the 1760s. After serving in the British army, St. Clair achieved the rank of major general in the Continental forces during the Revolution. His credentials, though, are somewhat questionable. Only the intervention of General George Washington prevented his being court-martialed out of the military following an ignominious surrender of Fort Ticonderoga to the redcoats. But St. Clair's spirit was not as easily vanquished. In 1791 he led his forces into battle against an Indian tribe, in what would later be called the worst defeat ever suffered by an American army.

Although Upper St. Clair may carry the name of one of history's all-time losers, this community is definitely one of the area's biggest successes. Good schools, efficient municipal services, and a quiet way of life are strong attractions to the corporate heads and many professionals who live here. As one township official puts it, "We planned things to turn out this way, and we'll do everything that's necessary to maintain the status quo."

# PART

## II

## TOMORROW
## AND BEYOND

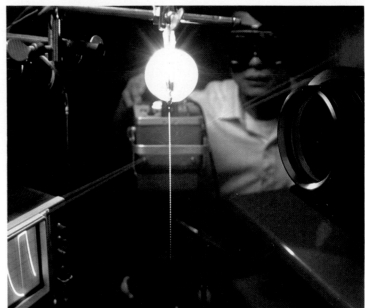

*Preceding pages:* Pittsburgh burst of energy, © Michael Haritan

*This page, clockwise from top left:*
Lunchers at Pitt Cathedral and Heinz Chapel, © Jack A. Wolf

Laser experiment, © Bill Redic; courtesy, Robotics Institute, Carnegie-Mellon University

Allegheny Observatory in winter, © Michael Haritan

Computer education in Pittsburgh public schools, © Michael Haritan

*Facing page, clockwise from top left:*
One Mellon Bank Center entrance, © Michael Haritan

Robotics Institute research, © Bill Redic; courtesy, Carnegie-Mellon University

One Mellon Bank Center, © Herb Ferguson

Fishing at Lake Arthur, © Jack A. Wolf

Carnegie-Mellon commencement, © Michael Haritan

Allegheny Observatory in spring, © Michael Haritan

280

# VI

# The Entrepreneurial Style

Entrepreneurs are curious people, certainly different from the masses who are placed here to do the world's work. Entrepreneurs are a breed apart. They think differently than the rest of us. They perceive the world in a different light, a light that creates for them shimmerings and shadows that the rest of us either never see or, if we do, ignore because we cannot comprehend them.

Entrepreneurs tend to be restless, eager, and impatient, sometimes intolerantly so. Rarely can they comprehend why the rest of us are not driven by the same fierce internal force, not prodded on by the same needs, not guided by the same burning energies as they are.

Entrepreneurs are dreamers, even though most of them deny it and protest their commitment to rigid, unbending practicality. But without their dreams they are merely tightly wound coils of boundless, ambitious energy, desperately anxious to explode, undirected and lost.

As different as most of them are from the rest of us, they usually are quite similar in some curious way to one another— so similar that they and their stories are often indistinguishable one from the other.

Most stories of successful entrepreneurs and their ventures have a familiar ring to them, a familiarity that comes from repeated tellings of the same tale. There are always tales of sacri-

*This page:* **Caucus at Mellon Square,** © Michael Haritan

*Facing page, clockwise from top left:*
**Three Rivers Arts Festival,** © Herb Ferguson

**Flying in from Mt. Washington,** © Herb Ferguson

**Bicycle race,** © Michael Haritan

**University of Pittsburgh engineering student,** © Herb Ferguson

**Study at University of Pittsburgh,** © Joel B. Levinson

*fice and struggle, of meager earnings and thoughtless creditors, of intoxicating highs and depressing lows, of toil and trouble, and of the ever present but unthinkable thoughts that haunt their nights: that tomorrow or the day after or the year after will find their bubble burst and their savagely fought for gains lying in ruins.*

*It is sometimes impossible to distinguish the teller from the tale, the entrepreneur from the enterprise, so closely are they woven together, so bound up are they in each other* (From *Daniel A. Goetz: A Man & His Company,* by Vince Gagetta).

Not every Pittsburgher is an entrepreneur, hopes to be an entrepreneur, or wants to be an entrepreneur. There are literally thousands of Pittsburghers who cannot even define the word. But fewer and fewer of them can any longer ignore the concept of entrepreneurship and its spirit of enterprise and daring, its inherent requirement of risk taking. To overcome the unbending realities of a steel-diminished economy and to forge for themselves a hope and a dream and a future, Pittsburghers are going to have to begin in larger numbers to *think* like entrepreneurs.

Pittsburghers tend to think of Pittsburgh in corporate terms and to measure commercial, industrial, and business enterprises on the large scale: the giant steel mill, the huge foundry, the sprawling mine with its miles and miles of hidden tunnels and

*Above:* **Marathon kick-off at PPG Place, © Mary Jane Bent**

*Facing page:* **Phipps Conservatory, © Herb Ferguson**

passages, the twenty-barge river tow, thousands of workers absorbed by a factory's single shift.

They tend to forget their entrepreneurial heritage. Yet the history of big business in Pittsburgh originates with such single-handed empire builders as George Westinghouse, H.J. Heinz, Andrew Carnegie, Andrew Mellon, Frank and Ralph Dravo, Henry Oliver, Edwin Drake, John Roebling, Benjamin Franklin Jones, James Laughlin, Claude W. Benedum and a host of other risk-taking, restless, eager, impatient, energetic individuals who founded the enterprises that grew to vast wealth, power, and prominence. As much as any other place, Pittsburgh owes what it has and what it has become not to giant corporations but to the people who formed them, to individuals, to entrepreneurs.

There are those who argue that the heyday of the entrepreneur is past. Things are too difficult and complicated nowadays, the argument goes, for the individual to make it big. Even the person with the best idea, the best business plan, the most solid financial backing, the hungriest and eagerest market, and the

**View from North Shore,**
**© Michael Haritan**

most tireless will can these days create no more than a shadow of what that same person with those same attributes could have created a century ago. So what is the point of pursuing the entrepreneur's dream?

The point, of course, is economic survival. For what is needed here and now is not necessarily a rebirth of individual business ownership as the foundation stone of the region's economy but a rebirth of the spirit of the entrepreneur, a rekindling of the ideals that so enflamed the pioneering individuals of an earlier age.

Not every Pittsburgher is destined to be his own boss, manage and operate his own enterprise, and own the key that opens the business's doors in the morning and locks them at night. On the other hand, it isn't necessary to fulfill the dictionary definition of entrepreneur in order to think like one, act like one, and work like one.

What Pittsburgh needs in the late 1980s is not a huge throng of entrepreneurs but more people who have the entrepreneur's attitude and outlook, who have the entrepreneur's drive to make things happen. Economic revitalization in the Pittsburgh of the late 1980s is a matter of approach, a rediscovered style of business—the entrepreneur's style.

That style can give the people power. The entrepreneurial style and spirit can give them initiative, strength, and the courage of self-reliance. Style is sometimes a means of concealing the absence of substance, but where Pittsburghers are concerned it can be the molding of substance into a more powerfully creative force. Style is what separates the potential successes from the passively failed, the risk takers from the risk avoiders, the self-reliant from those who prefer to rely on others to solve their problems.

The concept of entrepreneurship is most often linked to business endeavors, but in Pittsburgh the entrepreneurial style and spirit need not, should not, and must not be so limited. To make a substantial difference in Pittsburgh's economic future, its principle must also be applied rigorously to government, education, labor, and institutions in the public, private, and non-profit sectors.

Pittsburgh is served by a governmental bureaucracy that func-

**Mural at Scaife Gallery,**
**© Jack A. Wolf**

tions rather efficiently at most times. It is a rare kind of bureaucracy: it tends to help rather than hinder, and has a record of accomplishments that are a source of justifiable pride. Government's methods, policies, and procedures may not always be the most modern and sophisticated, but they do manage to serve the needs of the people.

To its considerable credit, the leadership of local government—notably in the City of Pittsburgh and the County of Allegheny, but certainly not limited to those political entities by any

*Above:* PPG Place at Christmas, © Herb Ferguson

*Right:* North Park ice fishing, © Michael Haritan

means—has worked to foster a more businesslike, and therefore more entrepreneurial, approach to governance and municipal management. Routinely in recent years, political leaders have actively sought the help, advice, and hands-on assistance of the business community and have used it to the great benefit of the region. The business community, to its credit, has demonstrated a full willingness to participate in the community.

Business owners, managers, corporate executives, and retired business leaders serve on boards, commissions, and councils and actively give of their considerable talents and expertise. They are helping make government more responsive, more efficient, and more entrepreneurially oriented. They come from every level of the business community. By training and experience they are planners, policy makers, and budget makers, and they have given of themselves unselfishly and unstintingly. It must be said that without the help given to governments and government agencies by business people in Pittsburgh, many of the region's most hopeful and ambitious plans and programs for revitalization would never have been born, and few would stand much chance of being completed successfully.

The people who manage and operate governments and agencies, in the course of their close association with the Pittsburgh business community and with some of the most prominent and respected members of that community, have gained new perspectives and skills with which to address issues, solve problems, and manage more effectively. Their increased exposure to effective business methods, policies, and practices has helped make many of them better and more creative managers. In Pittsburgh we have a corps of non-bureaucratic bureaucrats.

Their number is small but growing as they demonstrate how the application of sound business practices and proven business methods to the operation of their units, agencies, and departments very often results in more efficiency, increased economy, and the more effective delivery of services. They care about the bottom line and about performance. Willingness to take the initiative, openness to bold ideas, hard-bitten practicality—these are entrepreneurial traits by which Pittsburgh's non-bureaucratic bureaucrats are benefiting the region.

If Pittsburgh's governmental style has a decided business look and feel, and if entrepreneurial attitudes and approaches

Race at auto gala, © Herb Ferguson

are making important inroads here, it is because of the very close ties that have been formed between government and business. Pittsburgh is one of the few cities of its size in the United States where the chief executives of the region's leading businesses and industries gather regularly to meet with government leaders to address realistically the problems facing the area and to seek realistic solutions to those problems.

The process has created a shadow government of sorts, a widespread organization of concerned and committed business leaders, representing both big and small business, who are willing to lend their own and their companies' capabilities and expertise to the cause of making Pittsburgh a better governed, better managed place.

There is no question that government units and agencies in Pittsburgh, the big ones as well as the small ones, are recognizing the advantages of a more entrepreneurial approach. At the same time Pittsburgh's big-business community also continues to seek out new ways to adapt the entrepreneurial style to their own very large operations.

Intensified competition, market displacements, and a continually changing international economy have altered the face of corporate Pittsburgh, as they have altered the face of corporate America. Economic realities have compelled fundamental changes in Pittsburgh's biggest, richest, and most established corporate giants. Gone are the freewheeling days when markets and profits were both sure and growing, when staffs were large and far flung, when the corporate structure could support overmanning and tolerate operational inefficiencies. Corporate executives now can no longer hide behind phalanxes of underlings and the very bigness of their organizations.

As Pittsburgh's economic fortunes have slipped and slid over the past half decade, so have the economic fortunes and the general well being of many of the biggest names in the Pittsburgh corporate hierarchy. Some of the most successful companies in the area are now searching eagerly for ways to streamline themselves, make their operations more profitable and more competitive, and breathe new life into their organizations.

Increasingly, Pittsburgh's big-business leaders have taken to emulating their small-business colleagues in the quest to control their economic destinies. After lifetimes of thinking big, equating bigness with power and power with profits, big-business executives are beginning to recognize the need to scale down both their expectations and their corporate structures. All of a sudden thinking entrepreneurially is very definitely in.

Pittsburgh's corporations, or at least many of them, have undergone massive reorganizations and undertaken new marketplace approaches. The reorgnizations have not only significantly reduced the size of headquarters staffs among Pittsburgh's corporate elite but have also placed new emphasis on performance and made new demands on every level of management.

Executives now are being forced to manage more efficiently with fewer resources and smaller budgets. Managers are being held more acutely responsible for the successful operations of their units, departments, sections, and facilities. Now it is performance and not seniority or longevity that is rewarded in the management ranks.

Managers seeking direction on how to achieve more with less, on how to redirect the course of their enterprises, are looking more and more to their roots—specifically, the roots of their corporate organizations. They are beginning to appreciate what went into the establishment and early successes of their corporate organizations and adopting the principles and approaches of their corporate founding fathers. To succeed in corporate

*Above:* **Slippery Rock Creek, © Herb Ferguson**

*Pages 296-297:* **Marathon finish line at Point State Park, © Herb Ferguson**

Pittsburgh, executives and managers are learning to be entrepreneurs.

For some it is a return to a familiar role. Not all Pittsburgh corporate executives by any means have spent entire careers in the quiet elegance of the corridors of corporate power. Many are quite familiar with the hardships and the heat, the dirt and the danger of foundry floor and blast furnace. Many cut their managerial teeth operating small businesses of their own. Many others came up through the ranks, honing their skills and their craft at every step along the way. These appear to be the most confident that they can again make a significant and valuable contribution to the economic well-being of this place called Pittsburgh. They see the challenge and they know full well what they and their corporate organizations must do to meet the many challenges of becoming profitable once again.

To meet those challenges Pittsburgh's corporate managers are rethinking their options and refocusing their initiatives. They

*Above:* **Corner of Oliver Street and Smithfield,**
**© Michael Haritan**

*Facing page:* **PPG Place at dusk, © Michael Haritan**

fully realize the importance of funneling every available resource into their revitalization efforts. The development and adoption of new and more sophisticated technology are, of course, of primary concern to the area's producing companies. New management techniques, new approaches, new twists to old methods, and a new willingness to adapt, adopt, and take risks are part of every corporate manager's portfolio in the Pittsburgh of the 1980s.

As much as they must identify and incorporate the new, however, Pittsburgh's corporate managers must also rely heavily on the old, on the tried and proven. They must now commit themselves to doing whatever it takes. Much of the time it comes down to an individual effort. Executives and managers individually are directing efforts that only a few years ago would have been directed by management committees. That requires the individuals to be far more resourceful than was required in the past, to take more risks, to manage more directly, to accept responsibility for a wider and more diverse area of operations, to

*Above:* Strip District vendor, © Norm Schumm

*Left:* Sixth Street and Smithfield, © Michael Haritan

*Facing page:* Fort Pitt Bridge, © Norm Schumm

delegate wisely, to show great strength of leadership, and to have the utmost courage of their convictions—in short to manage entrepreneurially.

A new word has been coined to describe corporate managers who act and work and think like entrepreneurs; they are called *intrepreneurs.* The term refers to those in large corporate structures committed to, or at least charged with, adapting entrepreneurial principles and practices to their areas of responsibility. Within the new theoretical framework, intrepreneurs manage their units, departments, or facilities as if they were sole proprietors or at least limited partners. They evaluate and directly apply appropriate methods that will benefit the operation and make that operation efficiently profitable.

As is the case with government locally, the success rate for applying the entrepreneurial style and spirit to big business here is difficult to determine. Not every operation adapts easily to the entrepreneurial approach. And there are those who argue that large corporate structures cannot operate effectively in the entrepreneurial style—at least not without even more dramatic restructuring than has already occurred.

It must be expected that large corporations, like huge ships steaming ahead at full speed, cannot easily make a sharp change in course. In Pittsburgh, big companies have operated so profitably and successfully in the past that it is unrealistic to imagine that fundamental changes in style and approach are likely to occur quickly or quietly. Just as unrealistic, however, is any notion that these large corporations can operate in the late 1980s as they did in the 1960s. Whatever compromise may be reached in the operations of those companies—or at least some of them—it is highly likely that entrepreneurship will have to be considered and adapted to some degree.

Small business, of course, has a less difficult time with the concept of entrepreneurship and the maintenance of the entrepreneurial style. After all, small business and entrepreneurship are practically interchangeable terms. In Pittsburgh, small business is becoming a greater and greater force for change and revitalization. Increasingly, the area is relying on small business to provide its economic base, its financial stability, and its source for employment. Fortunately, small business is responding positively to these demands and has demonstrated that it is able to take on more than its share of the efforts now under way.

Many small-business practitioners also want more recognition for the entrepreneurial principles that have served business and the Pittsburgh market well and long. In addition, they want rewards for those who take entrepreneurial risks, establish enterprises where none others dared, work unreasonably long and unusually hard to ensure the success of those enterprises, create job opportunities in their communities, and contribute positively to economic revitalization of the area. The rewards advocated by small-business leadership would be in the form of more favorable and creative tax incentives, more financing assistance at realistic and reasonable borrowing rates, fewer regulations, and more positive cooperation by government in the creation of a fertile environment for businesses to grow and prosper in.

Those rewards, they say, will not only help ensure that small business continues to make significant contributions to the region's economy but will also encourage the widespread practice of entrepreneurship and the entrepreneurial spirit—qualities that are critical to Pittsburgh's economic future. Without those rewards, they say, the number and quality of those willing to be entrepreneurs, to take business risks, to undertake the financial burdens of establishing new businesses, and ultimately to energize the region's economy will be considerably lessened.

True to the exemplary spirit of entrepreneurship, Pittsburgh entrepreneurs are not sitting back and waiting for someone to hand them their rewards. They are pursuing their goals and best interests actively, using their organized strength to make inroads and to effect change. New small businesses, particularly those involved in high-technology enterprises, are emulating their entrepreneurial predecessors, Pittsburgh's earliest business and industrial pioneers, by recognizing that they have enormous economic clout and realizing that they have the brains and the collective will to use it effectively.

**Allegheny County countryside, © Herb Ferguson**

The late-1980s entrepreneur in Pittsburgh has options that most of his predecessors did not have. Only in rare instances are they obliged to locate their enterprises here. The world is their marketplace now, and there is no preeminent steel industry here to hold them close by. The high-technology firms particularly are free to go wherever they please, to shop around for the best offer when deciding where to site their facilities. With no industrial need binding them to Pittsburgh, it can be said that many of the region's companies and firms are here because they like it here, because they find the place livable, because they like the people and the small-town atmosphere. Nevertheless, it is vital to the future of Pittsburgh that such enterprises and such entrepreneurs be encouraged with business incentives as well to operate here and create their successes here. Since government reflects the will of those who are governed, the people of Pittsburgh have an obligation to help ensure their own economic futures by encouraging government to make Pittsburgh a place suitable and conducive to the establishment, development, and growth of such entrepreneurial enterprises.

But first Pittsburghers will have to be shown and convinced that entrepreneurs and the entrepreneurial approach to both business and government, big and small, are vital to their future well-being and economic prosperity. It is not enough to explain the facts of entrepreneurial life to them. It is not enough to tell them that their economic futures depend very heavily on how well the region is able to attract new entrepreneurs and new enterprises worthy of their support and encouragement. They must be shown the benefits of the entrepreneurial approach and of entrepreneurship. It must be demonstrated to them that a return to the basic principles and philosophy of the entrepreneur can mean jobs and economic security in a region sorely in need of both. There has to be a greater and deeper awareness of what Pittsburgh can be, if only the entrepreneurial forces that spawn businesses—daring the often cruel economic fates—are encouraged to flourish here. And there must be awareness of what Pittsburgh will be if they are not.

**Lions at Highland Zoo,**
**© Michael Haritan**

The entrepreneurial style and spirit must become the Pittsburgh style and spirit if the region is to take full advantage of its business and economic potential. That means it must be a pervasive style and spirit, not limited to business only, or small business only. To achieve its maximum potential the entrepreneurial approach has to cut across all lines and engulf all Pittsburghers: the employee as well as the employer, the governed as well as those who govern.

There are those who doubt that Pittsburgh, with its reputation as a tough labor town, would accept wholeheartedly the concept of entrepreneurship in the workplace. But Pittsburgh labor is nothing if it is not realistic. And the realities of the marketplace require acknowledgment, at the least, of the new forces that govern Pittsburgh's economy. Organized labor has the wisdom and practicality to accept that ways must be devised to accommodate changing conditions. That does not mean that organized

*Left:* **Strip District vendor,
© Norm Schumm**

*Facing page:* **Heliport
© Herb Ferguson**

*Pages 308-309:* **"Pittsburgh
Variations" Allegheny Land-
ing at North Shore,
© Michael Haritan**

labor is powerless to act in the best interests of its membership.
It does not mean that unions are an anachronism and that they
cannot continue to be a vigorous economic force in Pittsburgh.
But is does mean that labor must change its style and its approach if it hopes to be a force for change and for good in Pittsburgh—just as business and government and every other sector
of the local economy must change and adapt to the realities of
life in the 1980s.

Organized labor and entrepreneurship are not mutually exclusive elements. They can coexist here. It will, however, take a
great deal of creative effort and some imaginative approaches to
make the match work. And it will work so long as unions do not
attempt to dampen the entrepreneurial spirit and impose unrealistic and unreasonable restrictions on the work place, and so
long as management does not attempt to discourage the legiti-
mate interests of employees and impose unrealistic and unfair
demands on workers.

Organized labor can be a force for very positive change in the
Pittsburgh economy, there is no doubt about that. And there is
no doubt that the principles of entrepreneurship will play a pivotal role—perhaps *the* pivotal role—in redirecting the economic
forces that have gripped this region the past few years. Entrepreneurship and the entrepreneurial spirit represent the future of
Pittsburgh and the future hope of every Pittsburgher.

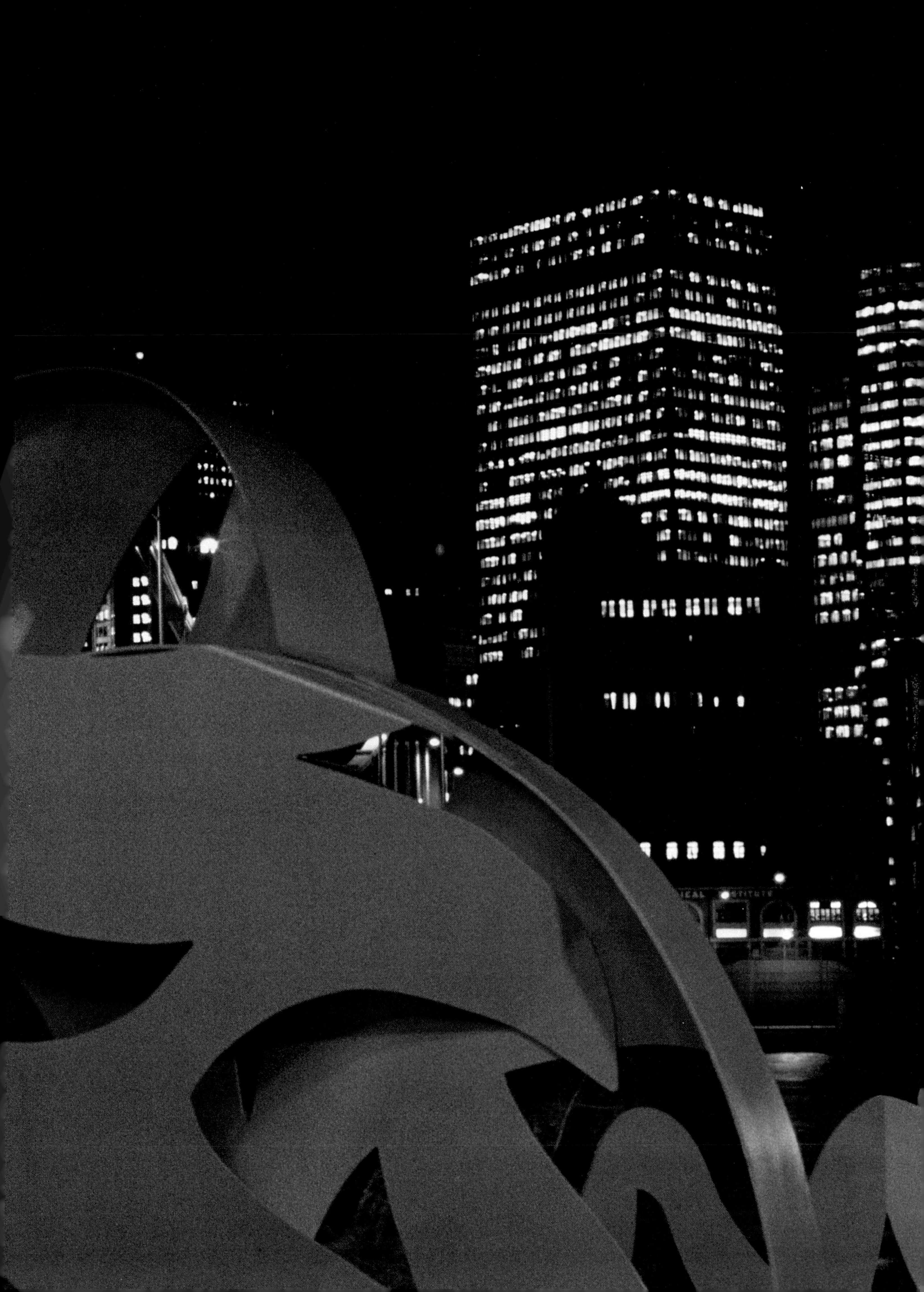

**Pittsburgh Symphony in concert (two views), © Herb Ferguson**

# Pittsburgh Symphony Lets Its Long Hair Down

By Abby Mendelson

The familiar, cartoonish faces stare out of full-page newspaper ads with a kind of bemused integrity. "The Doctors Are In," the ads say, "Take the Music Cure."

What's this? The stodgy old Pittsburgh Symphony, everyone's favorite civic repository of high culture, is offering composers like Bach, Beethoven, and Brahms as soothers of the day's ills.

Says Lou Spisto, symphony marketing director, "The old notion that a consumer does himself a lot of good just gracing our hall wasn't going to work. Instead, we needed to communicate what we could do for him. The whole campaign"—which was buttressed by TV ads that featured casually dressed people attesting to the power of the symphony to lift them out of their daily routine—"is saying, 'we're accessible. We're fun. We're enjoyable.' And it was targeted at a specific level—those people who work hard and are stressed. 'The Doctors Are In' says to these people, 'here are the composers; let's have some fun.'"

The campaign was developed *pro bono publico* by a local ad agency and has worked well, for the 1985-1986 season was more than 90 percent sold—a jump of more than 12 percent in one year. "That growth," Spisto adds, "is phenomenal."

310

**Pittsburgh Symphony at Heinz Hall; courtesy, Pittsburgh Symphony**

The numbers are also proof that the public has apparently forgotten the much-publicized infighting that brought about the abrupt departure of wunderkind maestro Andre Previn only two years earlier. Perhaps, in the face of almost daily finger pointing, it was time to stress music's own bottom line: not high art but simple enjoyment.

The symphony has a lot more going for it than merely relaxing the day's tensions. Tradition is as much a part of the Pittsburgh Symphony as sheet music; while watching such energetic contemporary conductors as Michael Tilson Thomas or Michael Lankester, one is reminded of the grand maestros of the past ninety years. There was the flamboyant Irish Victor Herbert (1898-1904), for example, and the romantic Hungarian Fritz

Reiner (1938-1948), and the patient German William Steinberg
(1952-1976). And one felt the ghosts of great visiting batons as
well, including Richard Strauss conducting *Till Eulenspiegel* and
Edward Elgar with *Enigma Variations.* And then there were the
legendary soloists: Pablo Casals, for one, and Vladimir Horowitz.
And Gershwin, Rachmaninoff, Bernstein, Bartok—and too many
more to name.

The symphony entered a period of doldrums during the 1960s
when the orchestra was critically respected but unsensational.
Although it was (and still remains) richly endowed by local foundations and corporations, there were the twin problems of dull
programs and empty seats. In 1971 the symphony's fortunes
were energized by relocation to the opulent and smartly refurbished Heinz Hall at Sixth and Penn avenues Downtown. The
Howard Heinz Endowment donated ten million dollars to remake
the old Penn Theater, a 1927-vintage vaudeville-cum-movie-
house. Rechristened as Heinz Hall, the new facility had nearly
3,000 seats, fittings of marble, velvet, crystal, and gold leaf, and
two fifteen-foot-high chandeliers in the grand lobby, and was
hailed as the crowning jewel of the Pittsburgh Renaissance.

In 1976 symphony stock soared again as newly hired Andre
Previn breathed new life and interest into the orchestra. It was
hoped that the celebrity of Previn would revive interest, and it
did for a while. Yet his great range of talents—as composer,
conductor, jazz pianist, and four-time Academy Award-winning
film score arranger—never translated well to Pittsburgh. To
many, Previn never seemed to be here. In 1984, after eight years,

Previn and the Pittsburgh bade each other farewell.

Currently the symphony is headed by Lorin Maazel as its Principal Guest Conductor and Music Advisor; he is a former child prodigy who first conducted at the age of twelve in 1943. Signed with the Pittsburgh Symphony through 1988, Maazel has expanded the orchestral repertoire and added three European tours. Michael Lankester, the Conductor in Residence, is known for his pops work and the "Music Here and Now" series.

Marshall Turkin, the symphony's managing director, greatly expanded symphony services to attract nontraditional patrons, with children's concerts, composers' symposia, and numerous outreach programs. All in all, these efforts expanded not only the role of the symphony but the audience as well.

Further innovations grew out of Lou Spisto's market research. "We conducted surveys to find out specifically why some subscribers left, why some stayed, and why some who fit our demographic profile weren't subscribing at all," Spisto recalls. A high number wanted more varied programming and greater package flexibility. Spisto answered with a mix of ticket packages, including such innovations as a brunch program and the Mozart Room, an eighty-seat restaurant available for subscribers' preshow dining. "People's lifestyles have changed," he adds. "We had to make subscribing attractive."

Every subscriber is invited to the symphony's season-opening gala, and those who buy ticket-plans for twelve or more concerts attend private postconcert receptions with orchestra members and guest artists. Then there's the Thursday night series called "The Smart Set," aimed largely at singles. Each program is prefaced by an informal presentation on the evening's contents, and is followed by a party. "We've taken our lowest-selling night and turned it into our fastest-selling night," Spisto says.

In addition, he's instituted a corporate campaign, in which local businesses use tickets as employee bonuses, as gifts to customers and clients, and as a vehicle for selling Pittsburgh to potential employees.

It has all paid off—with more to come. Yet while Spisto is happy with the current numbers, he continues to look ahead. "The most important thing," he says, "is that we're building a base for the future of the Pittsburgh Symphony."

# *Pittsburgh Opera: Hitting the High Notes*

By Abby Mendelson

If Tito Capobianco were not the general director of the Pittsburgh Opera, then surely that august organization would have to invent him. Charming, talented, and immensely popular, Capobianco has come to personify his organization in a way that no one else has. Although some might accuse him of grandstanding—his name, face, and voice appear everywhere, from gossip columns to billboards to radio ads—he has given the Pittsburgh Opera a recognizable persona. Indeed, no one in Pittsburgh can roll out titles like *Cosi Fan Tutte* or *Il Trovatore* like the continental-sounding Capobianco. (Actually, he is Argentinian. Go figure.) "People have to know you, identify you," he said when he initiated his raised-awareness campaign. "I had to become part of the community immediately."

For Capobianco, it wasn't hard. Arriving in July 1983 to assume the post of general director, he set forth a new administrative and marketing plan, based on a broader organization and higher-quality productions, and was quickly rewarded with the opera's best advance sales in five years. In part because he is known for three decades of opera-world connections—including conducting stints at the Met and La Scala and friendships with major talents like Joan Sutherland and Rosalind Plowright—and because he has the kind of clout and contacts to make major changes virtually overnight, he was able to shape performers and programs to his vision of quality. True believers and, perhaps more important, those who were previously only marginally interested have responded the best way they can—by continuing to buy tickets.

And to a town used to the late Gurdon Flagg raising opera money by putting the arm on a few of his wealthy friends, Capobianco candidly announced that the business of opera is also business. When asked what he meant, Capobianco pointed to his own operation. At his previous post in San Diego he had a support staff of twenty-one. When he came to Pittsburgh, he found a mere three, to handle every function from marketing to artistic development to accounting. By comparison, that's only forty-seven fewer people than the front office of the San Francisco

**Above:** Pittsburgh Opera in performance; courtesy, Pittsburgh Opera

**Right:** Ballerinas; courtesy, Pittsburgh Ballet

Be quiet! Here come the gypsies.

OpTrans; courtesy, Pittsburgh Opera

Opera.

Typically, Capobianco spoke his mind, and his candor was refreshing. "Development and fund-raising are number one," he told the opera board upon arrival, "because in the long run a community decides on the kind of opera company that it wants. I can only show the way. This city will have the opera company it is willing to pay for.

"Quality and excellence—these things go together with money. No matter how good your intentions, your talent, your background, if you don't have the economic support, you can't do it. I am confident of a brilliant future for opera here—*if* we get community support. Because it is the proper moment for Pittsburgh. But it will cost money, and we will need full community support. Because we have to rebuild the confidence of the community in the product we offer."

Faced with an annual endowment of roughly $800,000 (the symphony, by comparison, has roughly $40 million), Capobianco first moved to broaden the fiscal support base for the opera. As such, he initiated a slew of membership categories, with prices ranging from $25 to $30,000. After all, he explained, ticket sales cover only 40 percent of cost; memberships do the rest. "Every time we raise the curtain, we need $100,000 in the bank," he said. Ticket prices remained reasonable, ranging from eight to thirty-four dollars. And if the budget ballooned to three million dollars, even that new number was quite low by contemporary standards.

**Pittsburgh Opera in performance; courtesy, Pittsburgh Opera**

Various ticket packages were made available as well, including the special Tuesday Plan: patrons first dine at a top-rated Mount Washington restaurant with an unparalleled view, then are driven to Heinz Hall for the performance, and return afterward for coffee, dessert, and conversation with the artists.

But the Pittsburgh Opera's success is based on more than handouts, special packages, and fluff. Capobianco has been highly successful in bringing world-class singers, directors, set designers, and conductors. The artistic improvement, as well as the spirit, has been obvious. On his first day on the job, Capobianco took his case to the opera's first line of defense: the chorus. "I came here for one purpose," he said, "to give Pittsburgh one of the finest—the *finest,* not the biggest—opera companies in America." Then Capobianco asked for, and got, one extra musical and stage rehearsal for each opera—without pay. "Every time the Pittsburgh Opera curtain is raised, it should be a national event," he said.

And if not a national one, then at least an event on the cusp of greatness. Indeed, critics have already spoken of the Pittsburgh Opera as joining the ranks of the Chicago, San Francisco, and New York City opera companies. And for the viewer, perhaps the single biggest change is OpTrans, an English translation of key dialogue that is projected above the stage on a three-by-twenty-eight-foot screen. In 1985-1986, the first full season with OpTrans, 1,200 new subscribers were added to the rolls.

To get OpTrans started, it was of course necessary to spend some money for the equipment. Capobianco rarely passes up the opportunity to remind the city of how much art costs. In a September 1985 guest editorial called "The Arts—Big Business in Pittsburgh," written for local business magazine *Executive Report,* Capobianco pointed out that opera is the most labor-intensive of the arts, incorporating music, ballet, theater, and the visual arts. *La Traviata,* for example, employed 153 in cast, chorus, orchestra, and technical staff—not to mention front office, ushers, ticket takers, and so on.

Yet even a large number like that doesn't seem to faze Capobianco, or his patrons. Since Capobianco came, the Pittsburgh Opera has grown from twenty-seventh to fifteenth largest in the U.S. and looks to be in the top ten within two years, by its fiftieth anniversary in 1988.

With the addition of the new Tuesday-night early curtain series, Pittsburgh Opera attendance reached an all-time high of 45,765 customers. That's about 10,000 less than are drawn to a single Steeler game but a good figure for a regional opera company (albeit one that draws from as far as Jamestown, New York).

This year, the forty-eighth season, Capobianco is hoping for sellouts for each threesome of performances. He has plans to add an additional Sunday matinee series in 1987, once the opera moves into Benedum Center for the Performing Arts, a refurbished, block-long theater on Penn Avenue east of their current Heinz Hall home. Luciano Pavarotti agreed to perform at a 1987 season-opening fund-raiser, and Capobianco began to move tickets—eighteen months early. "Luciano's concert signals a new era of opera in Pittsburgh," he announced with typical ebullience.

At Benedum, he added, "there would be no limit to the dream of opera in Pittsburgh. It could be the best opera house in America and a blessing for the city. We could then exchange productions with the opera companies of San Francisco and Chicago and have the proper space and time to improve our product.

"After all, the arts give you another perspective in life. For in the arts, nothing has a limit. And in opera all the arts come together. So everything is possible in opera—*everything!*"

## The Night Club Scene

By Abby Mendelson

In their own way, night clubs are as much a part of city life as the daytime activity in stores and restaurants. In places like New York or New Orleans, the club influence is more pronounced than in a nine-to-five business town like Pittsburgh. Yet Pittsburgh has a surprising number of night spots that feature live music.

Pittsburgh club life goes back many years. During jazz's heyday, the city had premier clubs that produced such greats as George Benson, Ahmed Jamal, Billy Eckstine, and others. In fact, Downtown, Herron Hill, and the East End were dotted with clubs and lounges. By the early 1980s, jazzman Walt Harper had grown weary of running his Market Square Attic, a tiny, charming room, and impressario Will Shiner felt the drain of operating Shadyside's Encore, small, smoky, and thoroughly splendid. For a time jazz showcases seemed a thing of the past.

Yet jazz will never die—at least not in Pittsburgh. After a few years' hiatus, Harper reopened Downtown, in a 100-seater in the new office-retail complex, One Oxford Centre, where he continues to play and showcase such favorites as Mel Torme, Nancy Wilson, and Charlie Byrd. Over his four decades in the business, Harper has made his name synonymous with easygoing, intelligent jazz. And Shiner came back virtually overnight (although on a limited basis), featuring jazz at Brendan's—a decidedly upscale restaurant that replaced the Encore on Walnut Street. Indeed, when one hears Harold Betters' sweet trombone wailing into the night, one might think the Encore had never gone away. Betters is part of a noted musical family. His brother Jerry recently ran his own club and now has a regular gig at an Allegheny riverside spot called the Crow's Nest.

And many jazzmen with day jobs get their licks in at such night spots as the Balcony, also on Walnut Street, and Figgins, a part of the wholly redone North Shore.

There are a couple of raucous East End rock clubs—with total seating somewhere around 300—called Electric Banana and the Decade. While they both feature the best of the local rock talent, the latter has something of a reputation for the unexpected. Witness last year's sudden surprise appearance of Bruce Springsteen, who dropped by to play a couple of numbers after blowing away a sold-out Three Rivers Stadium.

In Pittsburgh there is one room that showcases all kinds of music, from rock to reggae, bluegrass to boogie, folk to jazz to zydeco. Graffiti is a made-over warehouse on the edge of Oakland, adjacent to Shadyside, a five-minute ride from Highland Park and Squirrel Hill—in all, the heart of the disposable-income district.

Graffiti is owned and operated by Tony DiNardo, a thirty-three-year-old father of six who's been in the club business since his teens. DiNardo started out with the fondly remembered Antonino's and the Portfolio, both on South Craig Street in the shadow of Carnegie Institute and right in the middle of the Oakland arts scene. Some four years ago DiNardo shifted his operations to Graffiti and never looked back. Combining a 65-seat club with a 400-seat showcase room, he's been able to draw some of the best small-hall talent from around the world—Celtic folksingers to Soviet jazz trios to English, American, and Canadian rock stars.

DiNardo is a somewhat anomalous figure in the high-power world of clubs, for he speaks in a calm, considered way. "To run a club like this," he gestures at the empty stage, "you need a little bit of life behind you. [Translation: you have to have established a line of credit with your suppliers and credibility with booking agents.] You need an understanding of mankind. [You can't start a fight in your own place.] And you have to come to harmony and realize that music cuts across a lot of borders. [You can't put on only what you like or you'll go broke in a week.] In my own case, I've always felt that I have a calling. Overall, in fact, I'm really trying to be an asset to Pittsburgh.

"You know, music means people's spirits becoming one. And that's an experience that can't be thrown away. That experience is what we work hard for. People dream—and artists bring them there."

CHAPTER **VII**

# The Forces of Change

In the summer of 1985, in a dramatic demonstration of the co-operation between business and government, a powerful coalition was forged to reshape and renew the economy of the Pittsburgh region. The resulting plan was called "Strategy 21," a blueprint for a vital economic structure that will carry the region into the twenty-first century. This comprehensive plan has garnered the broad and varied constituency needed to effect change on a heroic scale—and this is the scope of change required by the insistent fiscal realities confronting Pittsburgh today.

This magnitude of vision didn't come easily to beleaguered Pittsburghers. Pittsburghers, after all, have tended to treat change much in the same way they do the weather: they have talked about change for as long as anyone can remember but have felt helpless to do anything about it—until now.

Once, not too long ago, many Pittsburghers thought the industries that established this place as a production capital recognized around the world would continue to provide the firm foundation of the region's economic base. Certainly, they agreed, there was ample evidence that someday Pittsburgh *should* become less dependent on a small handful of basic industries for its economic lifeblood. Certainly, they agreed, it was desirable to augment the area's prospering smokestack industries with some strong, secure service businesses, less sensitive to the ebbs and flows of the industrial marketplace—but no one ever suggested that those smokestack industries would have to be *replaced*.

Pittsburgh a city of bridges,
© Jack A. Wolf

*Below left:* Balloons at
Point State Park, © Michael
Haritan

*Below right:* Downtown
street scene, © Jack A.
Wolf

*Facing page, bottom left:*
Bob Quarter sculpture,
© Michael Haritan

*Facing page, bottom right:*
Research at University of
Pittsburgh chemistry lab,
© Herb Ferguson

Even as the telltale signs of industrial and economic decline emerged unmistakably at the close of the 1970s, many Pittsburghers still felt that they had a choice about change, that they could dictate the pace of change and control the forces that regulated that pace.

Then, in the early 1980s, the moment of truth arrived, and with it came the awful realizations: this was no longer the Steel Capital of the World; Pittsburgh's coal, with its high sulfur content, had been judged unfit for widespread commercial application; and the precious products of the area's mills, mines, factories, and foundries were no longer in great demand. The marketplace had turned fickle, and Pittsburgh's choice about change was suddenly Hobsonian. Forty years of thinking about change and talking about change and arguing the relative merits of change became, almost overnight, a pointless realization that there was no choice but to change. The only way out of the economic stranglehold, locked on the town by international industrial competition and evolving markets and business philosophies, was a dramatic alteration in the fundamental economy of the entire region.

Basic metals production, as Pittsburgh had practiced it for generations, was a thing of the past. Pittsburgh had to find a new way to meet the payroll and keep its work force working.

Fortunately, there was a base to build upon, a structure that could be manipulated by the forces of change. Though it had gone virtually unnoticed, the gradual development of Pittsburgh's service businesses had progressed for years, so in fact the area had a well-established and widespread service segment already in place. Already there were as many white collars worn in the Pittsburgh work place as blue. Even in the metals industries and other manufacturing segments of the local economy, clerical, professional, and technical employees were equaling in number—and sometimes surpassing—those involved in actual production. Even before the headlines proclaimed clean air and relatively unpolluted skies were no longer a rarity, that the Smoky City image had disappeared, likely forever, the number of Pittsburghers working in offices, classrooms, laboratories,

**Phipps Conservatory,
© Jack A. Wolf**

hospitals, research facilities, restaurants, banks, and other such environments had surpassed the number of those toiling in mill, mine, and factory. Steel and coal and manufacturing had so dominated the place for so long that no one paid much attention to the service industries that had gained a strong foothold in Pittsburgh's economy. The truth was that Pittsburgh hadn't been a one-industry or two-industry or basic-industry town for years, although only a few people had realized it.

So Pittsburgh did not have to start from scratch when the need to change its economic structure became painfully apparent. Formidable strengths and resources were much in evidence in the area, and these could be called upon during the course of revitalization. What had to be done—and done quickly—was to mobilize the forces that could effect the needed change, that

329

**Peafowl, © Jack A. Wolf**

could energize the strengths and marshal the abundant resources, that could focus the area's energies and efforts on common and well-defined goals.

Leadership was needed to harness the forces of change. Such a leadership rose from the ranks of government. Local government, with considerable assistance from the state, proved to be the unifying factor to bring together the various and often competing segments of the community and the economy. Government's role was frequently referred to by Allegheny County Commission Chairman Tom Foerster as the common denominator in the equation of economic change.

With big business in Pittsburgh waging a fight for survival, small business struggling to organize itself, labor seeking to slow the steady erosion of its power base and to organize the increasingly white-collar work force, and with the area's civic, religious, and educational segments playing supporting roles, government has assumed the mantle of leadership in the cause of economic revitalization—or has had that mantle thrust upon it

330

by the urgency of events.

It is a role that most agree only government could play effectively. Only government—or the sum of the efforts of the area's governmental bodies and agencies—has the comprehensive constituency and support needed to effect change of such a massive order. And only government, acting on behalf of all the segments that it represents, has the necessary legislative power to overcome obstacles, circumvent opposition, and forge needed consensus.

Government can be the maker of the grand plan and the plotter of the noble cause. Government can also be the deal maker, and this capability can be the most important when economic revitalization is at issue.

But government can only function effectively as a force for change if all parties agree to support and participate in the unified effort. In Pittsburgh such a consensus has been reached. The business community, civic leadership, and the public have all supported government's assumption of leadership. Pittsburgh's long tradition of close cooperation between business and government, coupled with the power amassed by the Democratic party after generations in office, have made such leadership a natural occurrence.

And government has responded forcefully. The most dramatic example of local government's power to engineer change came in the summer of 1985, when the political leadership of the City of Pittsburgh and the County of Allegheny joined forces with the University of Pittsburgh and Carnegie-Mellon University to formulate the Strategy 21 plan—a comprehensive program for reshaping the local economy over the next fifteen years. This blueprint for a new economic structure has four major goals:

1. to reinforce Pittsburgh's traditional economic base as a center for metals industries and as a corporate headquarters;
2. to convert underutilized land, production facilities, and work force to new uses, especially in the areas of advanced technology;
3. to enhance the quality of life in the region and attract new residents while increasing tourism; and
4. to expand opportunities for women, minorities, and the structurally unemployed.

**Squirrel Hill grocery, © Herb Ferguson**

Achieving this ambitious and expensive vision for economic revitalization will cost an estimated two billion dollars to implement—in 1985 dollars. The private sector, the same sector called upon to provide the bulk of the financing for Pittsburgh's first Renaissance in the 1940s and 1950s, is expected to pick up the larger share—$1.1 billion—of the tab. Local, state, and federal government treasuries are being asked to assume responsibility for the remainder.

Not everyone agrees that Strategy 21 is the best or the only approach to economic revitalization. Many think it too broad, seeing it as an unwieldy collection of improvement and modernization projects, none of them startlingly bold or different, and most of them relying for support—both financial and legislative—on state and federal lawmakers, who have earned a reputation for recalcitrance when it comes time to approve plans and commit to funding.

But the plan's supporters (and they are many) point out that Strategy 21 has a good chance to work because its approaches are so basic and its assessments and goals so realistic. Many, if not most, of the twenty-five economic development projects in-

**Above:** Farmers Market, North Side, © Mary Jane Bent

*Left:* Strip District vendor, © Norm Schumm

cluded under the umbrella of the plan had been proposed and individually championed at an earlier date, at which point they had been strongly supported by various segments of the community. Strategy 21's bold achievement was to bring the twenty-five projects together into a comprehensive and realistic package. It is comprehensive because it took into consideration the value of the individual projects on the region's economy as a whole; it is realistic because it not only proposed projects but made recommendations for their funding as well.

Strategy 21 also represents the first time that city, county, business, civic, and university officials have aligned their considerable political muscle in a bid for state funding to get the individual projects, and the plan as a whole, off the ground.

Community leaders and opinion makers have rallied quickly and enthusiastically around Strategy 21. The day after the plan was announced, on June 14, 1985, the *Pittsburgh Press* editorialized:

*This has about it the solid ring of the old Allegheny Conference on Community Development in the days when projects tumbled*

333

*out so fast one was hard put to keep up. For the first time since the economic plight of this region became so distorted, we have a list of things we can do to put the Pittsburgh-Allegheny County-Western Pennsylvania economy on a stronger foundation.*

Framers of the plan say Strategy 21 could add 36,000 jobs to the region's economy. And although the bulk of the development projects proposed by the plan are clustered in the City of Pittsburgh and Allegheny County—the economic center of the area—most agree that a ripple effect will carry its economic benefits throughout the region.

If Strategy 21 has a focal project, one with unmistakable regional impact, it is the proposal for improving, modernizing, and enlarging Greater Pittsburgh International Airport. Construction of a new midfield terminal is seen as critical to making Pittsburgh a truly regional hub of transportation. The plan also stipulates the construction of an expressway near the airport to open up more than 1,000 acres of unused land for development and to improve access to the facility from the area's busiest, most

*Facing page:* Chatham Center, © Herb Ferguson

*Below:* Downtown fountains, © Jack A. Wolf

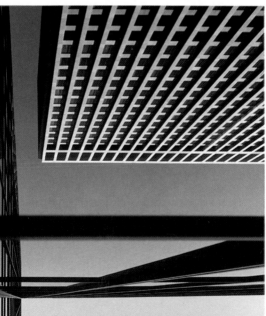

*Above:* **United Steelworkers Building, © Herb Ferguson**

*Left:* **Oliver II Building, © Walt Urbina**

*Facing page:* **PPG Place, © Michael Haritan**

heavily traveled roadways, particularly the Pennsylvania Turn-pike.

Other roadway and transportation improvements are envisioned, including desperately needed work on the highway system in the Monongahela Valley, where the untimely demise of the steel industry has wreaked particular havoc.

Local officials are already comparing Strategy 21 to Pittsburgh's Renaissance of the 1940s and 1950s, but they emphasize that the plan for the twenty-first century is much broader in scope and potentially more far-reaching in its impact.

And just as the first Renaissance was considered at the time to be an extreme measure, undertaken by a city desperate to modernize itself, Strategy 21 was also born of desperation. Proposals made to the state legislature by various local officials were falling on deaf ears, because individually these proposals lacked region-wide support. Area members of the legislature complained that they were unable to garner the necessary votes to assure critical state funding for individual projects on a piece-meal basis when other sections of the state were taking a more

**One Oxford Centre, © Norm Schumm**

comprehensive and considered approach. What was needed, the lawmakers told Allegheny County Commissioner Foerster and Pittsburgh Mayor Caliguiri, was a unified plan for action. At that point Foerster and Caliguiri, with the support of the business community, sought out the economic planners and strategists at the University of Pittsburgh and Carnegie-Mellon to put the plan together.

The planners had a lot to work with. Many of the projects considered essential to regional economic revitalization had been clearly identified. And in many cases strategies and schedules had already been devised. In fact much of the thrust for Strategy 21 came from earlier economic development plans and strategies. The first such recommendation had its origin in the late 1970s with the Committee for Progress in Allegheny County (ComPAC), a group organized by the Greater Pittsburgh Chamber of Commerce and Allegheny County to study the operations of county government. In addition to its cost-saving recommendations to the county, the Chamber group suggested that a broader effort be mounted to address economic development in a comprehensive way.

In 1981, at the suggestion of the Ad Hoc Committee organized following the Chamber study, the Allegheny Conference on Community Development agreed to take on responsibility for developing a unified strategy for regional economic development. It proceeded to form the Economic Development Commit-

**One Mellon Bank Center,**
**© Maurice Tierney**

tee and targeted nine areas of concern crucial to the region's
economy: advanced technologies, manufacturing, services, corporate headquarters, international trade, infrastructure, human
resources, business climate, and quality of life. The task forces
assigned to these areas included more than 200 representatives
of the community. The Economic Development Committee issued its final report in November 1984.

The report recognized additional steps needed to improve the
region's business climate in the areas of state and local tax policy, labor, and the availability of business capital and financing
assistance. "The primary thrust [of the strategy]," the framers
said, "must involve direct attempts to step up business activity
and job growth, thereby developing a more productive and larger
economy."

They cited a number of state-level initiatives for business tax
reform, pointing out that much had already been done to establish a favorable business climate for the region. For example,
Pennsylvania's Corporate Net Income Tax was reduced from
10.5 percent in 1984 to 8.5 percent in 1986. This key reduction
of the tax burden on business is freeing hundreds of millions of
dollars for private investment in jobs and economic expansion.

341

**City lights, © Herb Ferguson**

Two other major changes identified by the Committee were the passage of a predictable-formula base for calculating Pennsylvania's Capital Stock and Franchise Tax and the establishment of the "S Corporation" tax option, enabling many small-business owners to pay the lower personal income tax rather than the corporate tax rate.

Improving the region's infrastructure was identified by the Economic Development Committee as another ingredient to economic revitalization. Areas targeted include increased state and federal funding for roads and bridges, construction of a new airport terminal and related access roads at Greater Pittsburgh International Airport, dedicated funding for the Port Authority of Allegheny County, lock and dam repair and replacement on the Pittsburgh area rivers, and water and sewage system improvements throughout the region.

Clearly a sound infrastructure is essential to economic growth. And progress is being seen on several fronts.

With a predictable funding mechanism now in place in Penn-

## Leadership Pittsburgh: Two Views of Community Service

Sponsored by the Greater Pittsburgh Chamber of Commerce, Leadership Pittsburgh is a program that strives to broaden the leadership base of the community. Entering its third year in 1986-1987, Leadership Pittsburgh identifies, brings together, and further educates emerging leaders from all sectors, using the city and region as the classroom. Participants, who devote one day each month to intensive learning sessions, gain insight to the key issues and challenges facing the community.

Edwin V. Clarke, Jr., one of the founding fathers of Leadership Pittsburgh and a past chair on the organization's steering committee, is a retired senior executive vice president of corporate resources at Westinghouse Electric. Born and raised in the Pittsburgh area, he graduated from the University of Pittsburgh with a degree in industrial engineering and later attended the Harvard School of Business. Clarke now resides in Sewickley with his wife, Kathryn. "I'm extremely enthusiastic and bullish on the future of Pittsburgh," he says. "We are going through a difficult economic period, but I think we'll come out with a brighter economic infrastructure. I think we'll end up being a model city."

Faith Gallo, a 1986 participant in Leadership Pittsburgh, is the publisher of *Pittsburgh Magazine.* A graduate of Syracuse University, she also attended Tufts University and the University of Edinburgh in Scotland. Before joining *Pittsburgh Magazine,* she worked on various publications in New York and Washington, D.C. Active in many of the city's cultural organizations, she serves as a board member for the Pittsburgh Dance Council and the Three Rivers Arts Festival. She is also a board member of the Better Business Bureau of Western Pennsylvania, the Golden Triangle YMCA, and the City and Regional Magazine Association.

Q: How did you become involved with Leadership Pittsburgh?
Clarke: It started when I was chairing the Pittsburgh Chamber of Commerce. Justin Horan, who is the full-time president of the Chamber, told me that he had heard about similar programs in Cleveland and Cincinnati, and we thought maybe we ought to take a look at them. We talked to people in the programs in both cities. They spoke so highly of it, and the programs had

such good results that we decided there was a place for it in Pittsburgh.

Gallo: I have friends who participated in Leadership Baltimore and Leadership Denver, and they were so enthusiastic about those programs that I became interested when I heard Pittsburgh had a similar group.

Q: What do you see as the overall goals of Leadership Pittsburgh?

Clarke: Our key goal is to broaden the base for leadership in the Pittsburgh area. Pittsburgh has been a basic industry town with much of the leadership provided essentially through the industrial sector. We are trying to broaden that to have people not only from business, but from the colleges and universities, from government, from the arts, from foundations, from all aspects of the city's infrastructure. To achieve that goal, the program has a process of requesting applications. The selection sub-committee reviews the applicants and chooses a predetermined number, making sure that no one segment of the community dominates the group.

Gallo: I see its goal as finding and educating people for community leadership. In the past the Pittsburgh area has benefited by a strong coalition of government and industry. Leadership Pittsburgh brings together people of diverse backgrounds who can address the needs of the community.

Q: How is Leadership Pittsburgh different from other community-oriented organizations?

Clarke: It's different in that its whole mission is to acquaint people with the key issues of the community and to expose them to the leaders of those issue areas. The program gives the participants a unique opportunity for dialogue in terms of the direction and resolution of those issues.

Gallo: I see it as an education. It has a specific goal of improving the leadership in this city. I don't know of another organization in the city that has that specific goal.

Q: What type of person is interested in Leadership Pittsburgh?

Clarke: There are two basic types. One is the person who is already involved in some kind of a committee or board activity and wants to be involved in a more significant way. The second is a person who has basically been career-oriented and now has an additional interest in making their contribution to the community in which they reside. Leadership Pittsburgh provides that opportunity.

Gallo: Anyone interested in serving the community would do well to be a member of the class. Someone looking for networking possibilities, which are enormous, would be interested in the program. People on the outside know about the class and tap participants to help community organizations.

Q: What type of commitment is expected of participants? Do they find it very demanding?

Clarke: The commitment is for one day a month for eight months. This can be a problem because most of these people are in fairly responsible career jobs. If an attorney has to be in court on a particular day, he has a very difficult decision to make. So there have been some schedule problems.

Gallo: I found it demanding as far as the time and my attention, but I liked that. In fact, I tried to devote more of myself to it than just going to the classes. I served on a couple of committees. I was co-chairman of the mid-year retreat. That took a lot of time, but it was rewarding.

Q: How do participants benefit from Leadership Pittsburgh with respect to their roles in the community?

Clarke: We put together a booklet at the end of each class that contains alumni profiles that indicate each person's areas of interest in the community. Then when an organization wants to find a new board member, or someone to head up a fund drive, they can look in the book to select someone.

Gallo: It presents many opportunities to the participants. All anyone has to do is respond to those opportunities. Most of the people in the class are not shy, retiring types. They will hear of something that will pique their interest and go after it. Many of the participants also benefit from the networking that develops out of the classes. It also creates an atmosphere of concern and duty towards the city.

Q: How does it help in their careers and personal lives?

Clarke: I don't know of any particular instance where somebody has come back and said as a result of the program he or she had been promoted. That really is not our intent. We're operating under the assumption that when people are already growing in their organizations, Leadership Pittsburgh is merely another aspect in their development.

Gallo: In my case, as publisher of *Pittsburgh Magazine,* it helped me to learn more about the history of the city, its politics and neighborhoods, and to address in the magazine the issues relevant to the city. One classmate told me that the program changed his life. He said he felt intimidated at the beginning of the class because so many of the participants had advanced degrees. But by the time the year was over, he realized he had become an active and valuable member of the class.

Q: Are you pleased with the results of Leadership Pittsburgh so far?

Clarke: Yes. I've gotten more satisfaction from this program than from any other organization I've had the pleasure of being involved with in this city. I get a good feeling just from meeting some of the bright young people who clearly have the potential to be not only the present, but the future leaders in the community.

Gallo: Yes, it was a great experience for me because I was a relative newcomer to the city. It really taught me a lot about Pittsburgh. The city's magazine will benefit, too.

Q: Has Leadership Pittsburgh had any effect on the city already?

Clarke: I think it's entirely too early to tell if it's had an effect. But a lot of people are talking about the leadership program, and I get inquiries about the program at meetings I go to. So it's beginning to pick up a reputation.

Gallo: It's certainly had an effect on everybody who's been in the program. Our class hopes to put together a project we can all work on to benefit the city.

Q: What is the best part of the program?

Clarke: The networking potential that it creates. These people will end up in responsible positions. Since many of them will be personally acquainted, that should create an ambience of great cooperation in the future of the city and the metropolitan area.

Gallo: The learning that goes on and the people you meet and work with were the high points for me.

Q: How could the program be improved?

Clarke: By simply refining the process to deal with and get feedback from the students is one way. Another is by making sure the issues studied are indeed key issues. We also need to have people from the labor movement become more involved.

Gallo: By intensifying the search for participants with more diverse backgrounds. The Chamber is working to recruit more women and more blacks. Also by continuing efforts to improve the curriculum. I know from being co-chairman of the mid-year retreat that the staff at the Chamber constantly strives to do so.

Q: What would you like to see Leadership Pittsburgh accomplish in the future?

Clarke: I'd like to see it be instrumental, as we look down the road ten years, in the emergence of people in the key leadership activities of the community. Leadership Pittsburgh can make a significant contribution in broadening the base of leadership for the future of this area. I feel very strongly that we will achieve that.

Gallo: I'd like to see its graduates in roles which foster economic growth in the area and improve the quality of life for everyone here. Downtown revitalization is important, but so is the Mon Valley. The alumni will, hopefully, be working on both.

One gratifying thing to see was how quickly the alumni put together the Brett Hardt Scholarship. Brett, a 1985 Leadership Pittsburgh graduate, was recently struck and killed by lightning. The alumni met to establish a scholarship in his honor for future participants in the Leadership Pittsburgh program.

Most of the people are very community-oriented. They're concerned people who want to put something back into this community, and I think they will.

*Left:* Station Square shops, © Norm Schumm

*Facing page:* Schenley Park in autumn, © Herb Ferguson

sylvania, major highway and bridge construction and rehabilitation projects and renewed emphasis on maintenance are dramatically improving the region's vital transportation links. Additionally, the Port Authority has just completed construction of the 10.5-mile, half-billion-dollar Light Rail Transit System, which serves Downtown (as a subway) and the densely populated South Hills communities.

Locks and dams constitute another area of concern that is receiving considerable attention. Formed under the leadership of the Greater Pittsburgh Chamber of Commerce, DINAMO/OVIA is working to assure a viable river navigation system by expediting cooperation for modernization of the locks and dams in the Ohio River Basin. This organization's strength comes from the broad base of its membership, which includes representatives of industrial, commercial, and financial interests and labor unions, as well as state governments concerned about regional and national implications of the Ohio Valley's inland navigation system.

The 1984 economic development strategy also called for the formation of a seed-capital fund to provide start-up financing for new companies. It urged using the area's universities and

**Heinz Hall for the Performing Arts, © Herb Ferguson**

the entrepreneurs already in business to create job-producing opportunities through commercialization and application of academically conceived and created technology. It also proposed that a smaller-business assistance program be created, and it sought to form a high-level committee charged with attracting growth-generating businesses to the region.

Seven other areas were dealt with in the Economic Development Committee's plan. In total there were more than 100 specific recommendations. The plan did even more, however, than provide the framework for the broadly supported Strategy 21 program that followed. It succeeded, many concur, in cementing the credentials of the Allegheny Conference on Community Development, the Greater Pittsburgh Chamber of Commerce, and other business organizations as a solid force for revitalization of the economic structure of the Pittsburgh region.

The Allegheny Conference on Community Development, born of the fabled first Renaissance, is a natural focal point for the planning of the renewal effort. For implementation, groups such as the Greater Pittsburgh Chamber of Commerce, the Pennsylvania Economy League, Penn's Southwest Association, and the Greater Pittsburgh Convention and Visitors Bureau all work

**Frick Fine Arts courtyard,
© Herb Ferguson**

closely with government. The membership rosters of these organizations, although no longer confined to representatives of
corporate giants, include the most powerful business people in
the region—men and women who control awe-inspiring financial
resources and who influence the course of efforts to change the
area's economic destiny.

Pittsburgh's position as a headquarters city—the third largest
headquarters city in the United States after New York and Chicago—virtually guarantees the continued significance of major
corporations in the economic life of the region. Some of their
mills, foundries, and mines may stand idle here, and their role
as the region's major employers may have diminished over recent years, but the fact that their leadership is located here and
that their worldwide decision making is stamped "Made in Pittsburgh" make them a still-potent force. It is inconceivable that
any significant change in the economic structure or strategy of
the Pittsburgh region could be made without the approval and

*This page, top to bottom:*
**Mime at Three Rivers Arts Festival, © Mary Jane Bent**

**Science exhibits at Buhl Planetarium and Institute of Popular Science, © Maurice Tierney**

**Halloween festivities at East Hills School, © Mary Jane Bent**

*Facing page:* **Roller coaster at Kennywood Park, © Herb Ferguson**

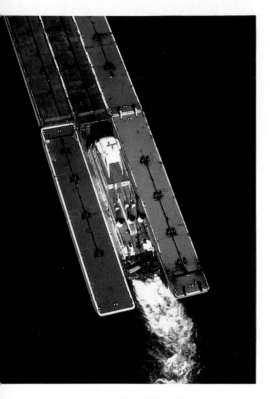

**Barge on the Ohio, © Herb Ferguson**

support of the big-business community.

If significant change is inconceivable without the support of big business, it is unimaginable without the support of the small-business community. This segment of the regional economy is growing faster than any other. Indeed, in many sections of the region, it is the only segment growing at all.

The small-business leadership in Pittsburgh is determined to make its voice heard and have its opinions heeded. They are a force to be reckoned with, small-business owners and operators insist, and they can boast a history of performance and accomplishment—a *recent* history at that, as opposed to that of big business, which is measurable now in decades past.

The record, these leaders say, speaks for itself. And it is an impressive one: companies with twenty or fewer employees created more than half of all new jobs between 1977 and 1981, and the figure in more recent years is even more emphatic. Firms with annual sales of under five million dollars employ 80 percent of all workers in the Pittsburgh area, and those firms introduced 40 percent of all new services and products in the Pittsburgh market.

Small business, closely managed and controlled, has the flexibility needed for innovation and creation—flexibility larger companies often lack. And small businesses can be more successful in introducing new products and services and in developing new ideas, because they are not hampered by shareholders demanding high short-term returns on their investments, the thinking now goes.

A newly emerging force in Pittsburgh's small-business community is represented by black citizens. According to the U.S. Census Bureau, there are 1,879 black-owned businesses operating in a four-county area around Pittsburgh (Allegheny, Beaver, Butler, and Westmoreland), and they take in almost fifty-four million dollars annually in gross receipts. Most of these firms are located in the City of Pittsburgh, and 1,068 of them have thirty-three million dollars in gross receipts a year.

Most of Pittsburgh's black-owned firms are in what the U.S. Census Bureau calls a ''selected services'' category, which includes such diverse business operations as advertising agencies, building services companies, funeral homes, barber shops and beauty parlors, and rooming houses. The vast majority of them are sole proprietorships. In Pittsburgh the number of black-owned businesses has not grown significantly since 1977, according to the Pittsburgh Regional Minority Purchasing Council, an organization that helps put minority vendors in touch with corporate purchasers. But those who have been observing the economic scene in Pittsburgh closely are quick to point out that the number has not declined during that time, either—a period during which bankruptcies and other business failures were not uncommon throughout the region.

If small business is a force for change and revitalization in the Pittsburgh area (and no one doubts that it is), the leading edge of that force has to be firms engaged in what can be categorized as high technology. Pittsburgh's vision of a high-tech future differs little, if at all, from the dreams being dreamed by practically every other city or region that has seen its economic fortunes decline in recent years. For Pittsburgh the difference may very well be that the dream is based on a realistic assessment of the resources available here, and there have been enough developments in Pittsburgh's high-technology industries over the past few years to make such dreaming worthwhile.

**Reflection on architecture,
© Mary Jane Bent**

While no one with feet firmly planted in reality expects Pittsburgh to develop into another Silicon Valley or Route 128, that does not mean that Pittsburghers cannot realistically count on businesses that rely heavily or solely on high technology to play a major role in the restructuring of their economic future.

Yet Pittsburghers do not really have to wait for a high-tech future because, in fact, evidence reveals that they have a high-tech present. Consider some facts: while the total number of jobs in a four-county Pittsburgh area grew by only one-tenth of one percent between 1984 and 1985, high-tech employment during that time was estimated to have risen more than 18 percent. Between 1983 and 1984 high-tech employment in nine southwestern Pennsylvania counties around Pittsburgh rose by more than 34 percent, and sales by companies engaged in high-technology enterprises were up by almost 36 percent.

Since 1980 at least eighty new companies have been founded in the region that are engaged in such fields as electronics, computer hardware and software production, automation, and advanced materials development, according to the Pittsburgh High Technology Council, an organization representing most of the

high-tech firms in the area.

Surprisingly, the almost 40,000 men and women who work in high-tech firms in the Pittsburgh region outnumber those currently engaged in steelmaking in what was once the Steel Capital of the World. Penn's Southwest Association, a regional development organization spun off from the Allegheny Conference on Community Development many years ago, estimates that high technology now accounts for about 20 percent of all the manufacturing in the region. And the association estimates that at least 400 high-tech firms now operate in the nine-county region.

If these growth and development patterns continue at a reasonable pace, high technology could create between 6,000 and 7,000 jobs in Pittsburgh every year. Thus, it is high tech that is putting muscle in Pittsburgh's small-business community, an economic segment that until recent years depended heavily upon servicing the steel and other heavy metals industries.

The impact that small business as a whole has on the economic life of any community is limited by the size of the companies themselves. Small and independent companies, accustomed to operating on a small and independent basis, generally cannot significantly influence an economic system. But when such businesses join together in groups to espouse their causes, address their concerns, and magnify their individual voices, they become a force for action and for change. Having operated for so long in the shadows of the town's giant corporations, Pittsburgh's

**Scaife Gallery garden,
© Herb Ferguson**

small firms have recently come to recognize the importance of united efforts and unified action. Working through such long-established organizations as the Greater Pittsburgh Chamber of Commerce and newer ones such as the Smaller Manufacturers Council and the Pittsburgh High Technology Council, small business is aggressively emerging as a force in itself for lobbying legislators and raising issues and concerns. Small business is becoming one of the essential principals in any and all efforts to influence economic events in Pittsburgh.

Much of the development in Pittsburgh's emerging high-technology segment has been the result of work and research carried out in the area's colleges and universities. As a result, Pittsburgh's academic community has taken on a new role for change and revitalization. And while developments that helped

*Left:* **Westinghouse Building,** © **Herb Ferguson**

*Right:* **Gateway Center,**
© **Herb Ferguson**

spawn many of the area's high-technology enterprises can very
often be traced to the region's two principal research universities, Carnegie-Mellon and the University of Pittsburgh, other educational institutions have made considerable contributions to
the effort to move the region off dead economic center.

Schools like Carnegie-Mellon and Pitt have been able to influence change and incubate new businesses and industries because they have both the resources and the tradition to conduct
basic research. Carnegie-Mellon's Robotics Institute, its extensive and sophisticated computer programs, and its new Software Engineering Institute are natural creators of technologies
and products that can provide new opportunities for entrepreneurs and new jobs for the work force.

The Software Engineering Institute, funded by the Department
of Defense, will conduct research into military applications for
computer software. It will also serve as a center for developing
commercial software technology and moving it into the marketplace. Carnegie-Mellon officials forecast that as many as 25,000
jobs will result from the institute's efforts scheduled to com-
mence within five years after it goes into full operation, in 1987.

About the same time that Carnegie-Mellon was informed that
the school was the successful bidder on the $103-million Soft-
ware Engineering Institute project, University of Pittsburgh officials were learning that Chevron Corporation, which had acquired

Pittsburgh-based Gulf Oil Corporation in 1984, had decided to donate Gulf's expansive research and development center in nearby Harmarville to the university. Now called the University of Pittsburgh Applied Research Center, it will serve as a place where businesses can conduct research and where new companies can lease facilities needed to undertake sophisticated technological development of products and processes. Pitt officials hope the center will provide the technological and research assistance Pittsburgh's smokestack industries—and the smokestack industries throughout the country—need to revitalize themselves. Employment at the center is expected to reach 2,000 by the early 1990s; beyond this, however, the potential for the creation of new spin-off companies and jobs is enormous.

The two research-oriented universities have also entered into joint working arrangements on certain projects, and in January 1986 they were successful in establishing a supercomputing facility in Pittsburgh. The Pittsburgh Supercomputing Center, which the two universities will operate in conjunction with Westinghouse Electric Corporation, was established with a $40-million grant from the National Science Foundation. The schools, corporations, the State of Pennsylvania, and Cray Research, Incorporated, are providing operating funds, and a $40-million Cray supercomputer has been purchased for the center, which is the most advanced of five national supercomputing centers. This facility is important to Pittsburgh's revitalization efforts because it provides the area with a powerful resource, not only for conducting all manner of research but for attracting businesses and industries.

As impressive as the accomplishments of Pitt and Carnegie-Mellon have been, these institutions are by no means the only members of the Pittsburgh academic community making significant contributions to economic rebirth. Without exception, each of the region's twenty-nine colleges and universities are stepping out of their traditional roles to provide resources, personnel, and facilities.

Almost without exception, the schools have established small-business consulting services, centers for entrepreneurial development, and business research facilities. And each is involved to some extent in programs to train and retrain Pittsburgh's underutilized work force, helping prepare Pittsburghers for the next generation's labor market. In many of the areas of the region that have been hardest hit financially, academic institutions are bringing people together, stimulating ideas, infusing hope, and providing some structure upon which to build a more promising economic future.

Economic hard times have provided Pittsburghers with incentives to awake to the benefits of education. Traditionally the populace has not been greatly concerned that succeeding generations reach ever-higher levels of academic achievement. Plentiful and well-paying jobs in the semiskilled and unskilled industrial work force gave a false confidence that one need not have a decent education to do well.

For the most part, those attitudes are changing. Scholastic endeavors at all educational levels, from kindergarten through graduate school, are gaining new prominence as a valuable resource for the region's economic well-being. And the educational institutions themselves have adjusted their attitudes, have taken on new roles, have gone beyond their walls to reach out to a region and to a community that desperately needs their resources. In doing so they have established themselves as powerful instruments of change.

Another segment of the Pittsburgh community has found that it possesses considerable influence outside its walls and confines. The leaders of the region's religious community have

traditionally exerted significant influence within their church juris-
dictions. Relatively recently, however, those leaders have risen
up as a force for addressing economic concerns with the same
vigor they have for generations brought to moral and religious
concerns. Pittsburghers, with their ethnic heritages and small-
town values, have generally maintained close ties to their religious leaders and church organizations. As times grew hard and
the region's economic outlook dimmed, the church, temple, and
meeting hall were often turned to as safe havens, as places for
comfort and stability.

Religious leaders have recognized both the need and the opportunity for their involvement in the process of change. Although together they are not as well organized as some other
forces, church leaders wield the strength of their large constituency, so vital to change, and they have the concern for their
flocks that gives them the impetus to work unstintingly for transformation.

In their recent efforts to provide the framework for growth, to
marshal the forces that will effectively bring about renewal and

**Computer Center, © Jack A. Wolf**

create a new atmosphere for economic revitalization, Pittsburgh-ers have found that they have at their disposal staggering re-sources—financial, entrepreneurial, economic, philosophical, psychological, and moral. They are also beginning to appreciate that they themselves constitute the greatest, most potent re-source, the most powerful force of all.

Over the past several years, Pittsburghers have come to un-derstand that they themselves must be the architects of revital-ization. For so many who relied on the benevolence and stability of large companies for their livelihood, this need for greater self-reliance has been viewed with considerable alarm. For so many whose lives and hopes were shattered when the mills and mines and foundries shut down forever, life has become a matter of virtual day-to-day survival.

But Pittsburghers are surviving, and now they are beginning to do more than that: they are changing, and influencing the course of change, for the entire region. They know now that there is life beyond the blast furnace and that they have the strength and resources to bring that life into being.

## Destination Pittsburgh

By Abby Mendelson

Lanky, mustachioed Rich Gorman had good reason to smile at the fifty-first annual meeting of the Greater Pittsburgh Convention and Visitors Bureau, held in the Pittsburgh Hilton. After all, 1985-1986 convention business booked in Pittsburgh topped the $100-million mark, a whopping 20 percent increase over the previous year. Gorman happily told the assembled throng that the revenue from 200-odd conventions and nearly 200,000 hotel-room nights meant a rise in spending of more than 38 percent. It all meant more than $100 spent each day per convention delegate.

Why the sudden upsurge? Rand McNally's Most Livable City rating and renewed marketing efforts didn't hurt, of course. But still it was surprising for a city not otherwise known for tourism—like San Francisco, say—to be doing so well at attracting both convention delegates and visitors. Gorman, just finishing his rookie season in 1986, and Bob Imperata, a longtime hand at the Visitors Bureau, are in the process of turning around what was once a fairly stodgy public-service agency. They're beefing up the number and quality of sales calls on convention planners, upgrading publications, and designing tourist packages to increase the area's visibility and attractiveness as a tourist center. In 1985, for example, the Visitors Bureau conducted nearly 100 travel agent tours. And a related ad campaign in USA Today netted more than 6,000 responses.

People in these parts are wont to clap Gorman and Imperata on the back and tell them what a splendid job they're doing. They respond that it's easy—once people discover the real Pittsburgh. The area's attractions sell themselves. Here is a trio of extras that put Pittsburgh over the top as a desirable stopover for visitors.

1. Kennywood Park. Clean and safe, and spruced up every year, Kennywood Park is a premier amusement park that is a short drive from Downtown—and a day's solid family entertainment. From gentle kiddie rides to gut-wrenching roller coasters to the flip-you-like-a-flapjack Laser Loop, Kennywood rates high among residents and visitors alike, and for the cognescenti an

annual outing is simply *de rigeur.* Typical of many are the comments of one Mellon Bank vice president, who was lured from New York in part because of Pittsburgh's livability, and who never misses a chance to pile his wife and two children into the family car and head for what some have called The Roller Coaster Capital of the World.

"With the exception of some of the megaparks," he says, "like Disneyland or Six Flags, Kennywood is one of the best amusement parks I've ever seen. I like the fact that the park adds a first-rate new ride every year, like the Raging Rapids or the Ferris wheel. And of course there's my own favorite, the Thunderbolt. I don't know of any other traditional roller coaster that fast and that steep. And when it climbs that big hill and makes that turn, *wow!*—you think you're going right into the Monongahela River. With Kennywood here," he concludes, "there's simply no reason to go anywhere else."

2. *Weekends.* The Visitors Bureau promotes a weekend package to the short-stay business market. It highlights the various civic virtues, stresses that Pittsburgh is within 600 miles of the majority of the population of the United States and Canada, and, best of all, features reduced weekend rates at selected hotels. "You can come to Pittsburgh on business," goes one trial slogan, "but you'll stay for fun."

Billed as a play package, it appeals to the road-and-office-weary exec of either gender who likes such amenities as out-of-town shopping, dining, an abundance of the arts, plentiful golf courses, river sports, college and professional teams, and the like. And then there are the virtues of just getting away. "I've been to a lot of cities," offered one transplanted Downtown exec, "and Pittsburgh is a great getaway spot. If you stay Downtown, you get the whole city within a safe, clean, *short* walk. At the Hilton, right at the Point, there's nothing better than waking up early Sunday morning with a cup of good coffee and watching the mist rise off the Ohio River. What a sight!"

3. *History.* Pittsburgh, standing west of the Allegheny Mountains, was an important fort and frontier trading town, so there is much to interest the history buff. For the military-minded, the area is rich in forts and battlefields dating from the time of the French and Indian Wars. No single area is richer than the Point, which was scouted by a young Virginian named George Wash-

ington and later became the site of two forts—one French, the other British. Still standing is the Fort Pitt Blockhouse, built in 1764; nearby is the Fort Pitt Museum. As an added attraction, the Royal American Regiment reenacts noisy, smoky battles.

There are many exhibits and much architecture to remind the visitor of the city's great industrial heritage. There is stunning nineteenth-century architecture all over town, from Fourth Avenue (the heart of the financial district, dubbed Pittsburgh's Wall Street) to the hillsides, from onion-domed ethnic churches to H.H. Richardson's Courthouse, a masterpiece of Romanesque architecture in stone. There are also country estates, neomedieval castles, covered bridges, country stores, and historic trails galore. And of course there are those two glorious pieces of moving history, the Monongahela and Duquesne inclines (1870 and 1877, respectively), which transport visitors and commuters up the nearly 800-foot sheer cliff of Mount Washington, where the definitive cityscape of Downtown Pittsburgh shimmers across the Monongahela River.

CHAPTER *VIII*

# A New Renaissance

The glory days, some say, are over. But Pittsburgh is too young yet, with too much to do and too much to offer, to be counted among the casualties of America's industrial decline. It has only been a couple of hundred years since the place was settled after all. Pittsburgh is still a teenager worrying about what it wants to be when it grows up.

Formed in the wilderness, Pittsburgh had a colonial infancy and a rowdy and restless childhood, when its industrial muscles were first formed and flexed. Then came its precocious adolescence, when with youthful exuberance—brashness, even—it made itself steelmaker to the world. Only now is Pittsburgh reaching maturity, entering adulthood. It is ready now to go to work and make another name for itself in twenty-first-century America. Pittsburgh has begun to come of age.

The story of Pittsburgh during the latter years of the 1980s is a tale of two towns, of two economies that have existed side by side over the past decade: the traditional nineteenth-century heavy industry economy, which is in steep decline, and the emerging, technology-based twenty-first-century economy, which is in sharp incline.

Some wanted to write the final act of the Pittsburgh story; they wanted to ring down the curtain when heavy industry left center stage and no other single industry swept in from the wings to take over the starring role in the region's economy. The Pittsburgh drama is now without a reigning star, but happily there are several young and exciting industries auditioning enthusiastically for leadership roles; it is apparent now that top

billing will likely be shared billing. As Pittsburgh prepares itself for the economic resurgence, it will need an ensemble cast on stage, a cast that no longer relies on a single star to make performance a twenty-first century hit.

When steel was in the spotlight, there was room for no other player, and it filled the stage with its overwhelmingly powerful presence. It was such a spellbinding performer that it lulled Pittsburghers into a dream state of false security. As they sat back and watched, Pittsburghers were mesmerized into thinking that the grand old star could play out the hero's role forever. Steel gave its Pittsburgh audience a show the town will never forget.

The city will not and should not forget steel and coal and the other heavy industries that made it an industrial behemoth. Neither can it linger too long in the past, however. This is a time for looking ahead, for planning a future. Economists seem to agree that Pittsburgh will end up healthier economically, since it will no longer rely so heavily on a single industry or on a small group of similar industries as its economic base. Spreading the burden will strengthen the foundation, the economists say, thus echoing what many local observers have been preaching for decades.

As Pittsburgh enters its economic adulthood and prepares to practice what has been preached, it seems in remarkably good shape. This is a place that lost 7 percent of its manufacturing jobs in just three and a half years at the start of this decade, yet saw the total number of jobs in the work place actually increase by 4 percent and saw per capita income rise by 8 percent in the same period. This is also the place where personal income grew by almost 6 percent in 1984, when the area was plagued by an almost 10-percent unemployment rate. Such apparent contradictions are actually very strong indicators that reports of the area's imminent demise are, in fact, gross exaggerations.

There are still Pittsburghers who see a return to the traditional steelmaking practices in the exisitng facilities as the area's only good hope for economic revitalization. Some are still convinced that steelmaking will somehow, someday, make a significant comeback here and will once again prove to be a force for large-scale employment. But time and the realities of the marketplace are taking their toll, and the numbers of such true believers are dwindling.

*Facing page:* **Point State Park © Michael Haritan**

This is not to say that the manufacturing base faces complete annihilation in Pittsburgh's future. To the contrary, the maintenance of the region's manufacturing base is often seen as a key element of revitalization. Whatever manufacturing is likely to be carried on in the Pittsburgh of tomorrow, however, it will almost certainly be on a smaller scale than Pittsburghers have been accustomed to, and it will be more technologically oriented as well. In the past much of the region's manufacturing base operated in support of the steel industry, and for the most part, that market has been lost. Manufacturing activity here is likely to be dominated by smaller, so-called light manufacturing companies operating plants with employment rolls measured not in the thousands, as in the past, but in the tens and twenties and fifties. And most of these concerns will probably be located in

modern facilities in industrial parks.

Specialty steel is likely to remain a rising star in Pittsburgh's economic future, because of certain advantages over conventional steel. Labor is a smaller component of costs; specialty steel's higher price is attributable to the very high priced raw materials—nickel and chromium, for example—used in its production. Transportation costs of both raw materials and finished product are lower in the specialty industry, which means production facilities do not need to be very near customer markets. And what may be the telltale advantage is the fact that the specialty steel industry has kept pace with new technology. These factors help ensure the continued presence and increasing prominence of specialty steel in Pittsburgh's future—provided, industry leaders say, they are allowed to compete fairly with foreign producers.

How well the specialty steel industry is able to compete in the international marketplace and how successfully other industries in Pittsburgh's manufacturing sector revitalize themselves, make themselves more capable technologically of competing in an increasingly sophisticated and competitive environment, will

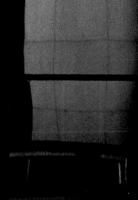

NATIONAL STEEL CENTER

largely determine how much and what kind of blue-collar job opportunities will exist here over the next twenty years. There is a future for smokestack industries in this country in this century—and in the next. The nation's dwindling production capability may well be an opportunity in disguise, the chance for a place like Pittsburgh, with its industrial heritage, its production-oriented and disciplined work force, and its extensive facilities and resources for manufacturing to take up the slack (a slack that is national in scope and of increasing concern to America's governmental and corporate leadership) and become once again a vital center for such activity.

Not that the manufacturing and industrial production sectors of tomorrow's economy are likely to dominate as steel and heavy industry did for so many years. In the long run Pittsburgh will likely count more on its brain than its brawn, count less on its muscle than on its intellect. Knowledge, in fact, could be its most important product, knowledge in various forms: new information, new technology, new insights, new solutions, new applications.

In the past Pittsburgh was able to count on familiar combinations of letters when it examined its economic base: USS for

**City from North Side,**
**© Mary Jane Bent**

United States Steel, J&L for Jones & Laughlin Steel, LTV for J&L's successor company, PPG for Pittsburgh Plate Glass, ALCOA for Aluminum Company of America, and PRR, B&O and P&LE for the railroads that crossed the land, to name only a handful. Now, although some of the old combinations are still serving the region very well, Pittsburghers are looking to a new combination of letters: R&D—letters that could spell prosperity for Pittsburgh.

Research and development and the application of new and advanced technologies are likely to fuel an industrial resurgence in Pittsburgh—as well as elsewhere across the country. It will be R&D that breathes new life into old industries and creates the new industries that could someday dominate the world's economies. The application of new technologies to old and established (and in many cases obsolete) industries is in itself becoming a new industry. Pittsburgh, with its history of industrial productivity and with its extensive resources and capabilities in manufacturing as well as research, is uniquely qualified to assume a leadership position in this emerging enterprise. In doing so it could profit two ways: by becoming a developer and exporter of new technologies and by utilizing those new technologies and adapting them to its established, older industries in an effort to revitalize them and make them profitable once again.

Should that happen, it would be good news for the local blue-collar work force. However, even a return of manufacturing and industrial production jobs to the area will be no guarantee that the glory days will return. It is most likely that revitalized older industries will need fewer blue-collar workers in their operations and will therefore be more selective. New technologies will require fewer unskilled and semiskilled workers. The blue-collar jobs that will be available in any revitalized older industries will be more technologically and intellectually demanding. Education and training will become qualifications as important for blue-collar jobs as they have traditionally been for white-collar positions.

If Pittsburgh does realize its potential, becoming *both* a center for the development of new manufacturing and industrial technologies and processes and a focus of their widespread adoption and use, the region's older industrial and manufacturing concerns could be revived to a state of renewed competitiveness. This undoubtedly will add a whole new dimension to the region's economic future.

Manufacturing is not the only segment of Pittsburgh's economy that stands to benefit immensely from technological advances and from breakthroughs generated by research and development. Coal could use even more help; without technological assistance, coal is not likely to recover from its current slump and will not emerge as a major factor in the region's economic redevelopment anytime in the foreseeable future.

Western Pennsylvania coal, Pittsburgh coal, can use all the technological help it can muster. The industry statewide is currently suffering through its most disastrous time in modern history; records indicate that 1985 was the worst year for both coal production and employment in the state in 100 years. A headline in the February 26, 1986, *Pittsburgh Press* told the tale: "We're at Rock Bottom, State Coal Firms Say."

The industry is likely to remain there unless it can be rescued by effective R&D and technological improvements for both production and use. As recently as 1979 Pennsylvania was ranked the third-largest coal producing state in the country; it now ranks fourth. As many as 39,000 Pennsylvanians held coal min-

**Walking along the Ohio Pyle, © Jack A. Wolf**

**University of Pittsburgh,**
**© Herb Ferguson**

ing jobs in 1978; by 1985 that number had been cut by more than half, to 19,000—the lowest statistic since 1877. Coal output throughout the state declined by 31 percent in the last decade alone, the same period in which national coal production rose 33 percent.

Because of its high sulfur content, Pittsburgh coal's best customers were the area's steel producers. This coal is not regarded as suitable for electrical generation, an industry that utilizes most of the coal mined and marketed in this country. Since Pittsburgh coal has lost its traditional steel market, it is a valuable resource in search of an application. Research already under way could provide that application. There have already been reports that improved burning methods will make Pittsburgh's bituminous coal not only suitable for power generating plants but also less expensive to burn than lower-sulfur, western coal.

Other research is being conducted to develop technologies for improving mining techniques and efficiency. These technologies are also expected to create opportunities for industrial, commercial, power, and home-heating applications. Much of the research is being conducted locally, and many of the anticipated technologies will carry Made in Pittsburgh labels. If efforts in

these areas prove successful (and there are strong indications that they are already beginning to bear fruit), Pittsburgh coal could become a significant factor in the region's revitalization and once again provide excellent employment opportunities for Pittsburgh's work force.

Of course, new processes and new technologies alone will not do the job of revitalizing older industries and make manufacturing and coal profitable again. Other changes will have to be made. To some extent both labor and management will have to alter their traditional tactics of confrontation and their postures of opposition. New attitudes and approaches must accompany any new technologies and processes if there is to be an industrial revival. Change cannot occur in a vacuum; revival cannot take place without give and take among all participants.

Over the years Pittsburgh has earned a reputation—well deserved, in not a few cases—as a tough labor town. The labor climate here has not always been warm and sunny. There have been serious and often bloody battles fought in labor wars in Pittsburgh's mills, mines, and factories. And even when management and labor, the bosses and the bossed, quit confronting one another physically (and sometimes violently) at mill gate or

379

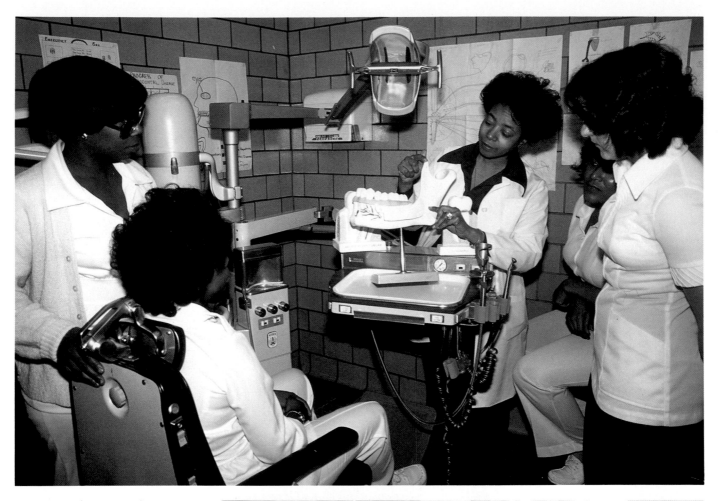

*This page:* **Dental assistant training and pottery class in Pittsburgh public schools, © Michael Haritan**

Art class in Pittsburgh public schools, © Michael Haritan

mine portal, they merely moved their antagonisms and their open distrust to the bargaining table, with predictable results.

Obviously, the whole structure of and approach to labor relations in Pittsburgh have needed to change. And both structure and approach have undergone significant change over the past several years. As the economy has faltered, as jobs have been lost and as job opportunities dimmed, organized labor has seen its power diminished. Shutdowns and threats of shutdowns have created a new atmosphere at the bargaining table, one that is likely to endure for at least the immediate future. Unions have been asked to make sacrifices, to give up benefits they fought and bargained for long and hard, in order to avert more shutdowns and to prevent the loss of even more jobs. But in the final analysis—or at least as final as circumstances permit—labor has given more than it's gotten. Despite givebacks and concessions, the plants and mines continued to close, the jobs continued to move away.

In the face of these hardships, Pittsburgh is achieving a measure of labor peace and cleaning up its reputation as a tough and sometimes brutal labor town. This is not to say, however, that organized labor will not be a factor in determining Pittsburgh's economic future, just as it continues to be a factor today, despite dwindling membership and the decline of the heavy metals and mining industries, unionism's traditional bastions.

Nor can the blame for Pittsburgh's poor reputation as a labor town be laid on organized labor alone. Certain managements have done their share to help establish that unsavory reputation. It is fair to say, from a historical perspective at least, that neither labor nor management has covered itself with glory in the area of labor relations. Undoubtedly this sorry state of affairs will require continued improvement if Pittsburgh hopes to shed its bad-labor-town image, as it certainly must in order to keep companies and industries here and to attract new ones to the region.

There are very hopeful signs that progress is being made in this area and that Pittsburgh could emerge from the 1990s with

**Chemistry class in Pittsburgh public schools, © Michael Haritan**

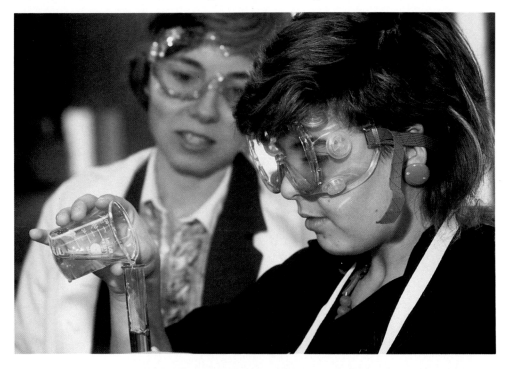

a much more positive labor image. The economic climate has forced new rules on labor relations, rules that affect participants on both sides of the bargaining table. The reluctance of both sides to change attitudes and alter hardened postures is diminishing, however slowly. It has finally dawned on Pittsburghers that everyone stands to benefit when negotiations are conducted in an atmosphere of mutual understanding, mutual trust, and mutual respect—with the emphasis on the *mutual.*

Organized labor is still likely to play an important role in Pittsburgh's future economic revitalization. For their part, unions will step up their efforts to organize the new companies and the new industries emerging on the local scene, both to reestablish their sphere of influence and to replace the membership lost in the decline of the steel, basic metals, and coal industries. Some of that organizing may actually be aided and supported by business. There are in Pittsburgh business owners and managers who see union or labor groups as necessary, not as necessary evils. One theory of management holds that it is easier and more efficient for management to operate if there is an established labor organization in place, to serve as a conduit for information between management and the labor force, an arena for settling disputes, and a mechanism for promoting cooperative efforts that are of mutual benefit to employer and employees. Those who sit across the bargaining tables of tomor-

**Duquesne University computer repair course, © Michael Haritan**

row are likely to realize that labor negotiations do not *have* to be conducted on an adversarial basis. The entire region can only benefit as a result, and tomorrow's Pittsburgh will be a stronger, more competitive, and healthier economic entity.

An improvement in Pittsburgh's labor climate, real or perceived, could significantly affect the region's ability to attract new business and industries, as well as attract the continuing inflow of capital needed for economic revitalization. Pittsburgh's financial community of commercial banks, investment banks, and venture capitalists is thought to be willing and able to finance revitalization efforts throughout the region. It will be counted on to provide the financial fuel for the establishment of new busi-

**Greater Pittsburgh International Airport, © Joel B. Levinson**

nesses, the making over of old industries, and the development of new products and technologies.

In 1980 a critical shortage of venture capital was identified as one of the most serious obstacles to economic stability and growth in Pittsburgh. Economists and leaders of the business community alike saw the shortage not only as a detriment to revitalization efforts but as an indication of a lack of faith in the region's economic future on the part of the financial community, especially the local financial community. If local bankers and venture capitalists were unwilling to invest in Pittsburgh or unable to carry a heavy share of the investment load, then why would others outside the region put up the money? The answer to that question was as obvious as it was ominous.

Fortunately, the investment climate has changed. New venture capital firms have been organized and venture capitalists have become more confident about the future of Pittsburgh. They have begun investing more vigorously in both new and established enterprises. In just three or four years after what may have been the low point for such investments, the situation almost completely reversed itself; today it appears that capital in a

variety of forms and from a variety of sources is available for business establishment, expansion, and development.

There are indications that this very positive condition will continue into the 1990s and beyond. The local financial community has demonstrated its willingness to invest extensively in the region, and its involvement has attracted the interest and active participation of bankers and venture capitalists from other parts of the country and the world. Pittsburgh is now considered to be a good investment. It will be seen as an even better investment in the years ahead, as efforts to stabilize and revitalize the economy move forward to fruition.

The financial segment of the Pittsburgh economy will no doubt continue to occupy a leadership position in the reshaping of the region. That segment has been and is expected to continue as one of the most robust of all the local economic segments. Pittsburgh's emergence as a prominent financial center and its ranking as the fourth-richest money center in the United States is one of its brightest accomplishments. Money is a growth industry in Pittsburgh today, and there is no reason to expect its prominence to diminish tomorrow.

Finance serves as a prime example of the contributions a service industry can make to an economy, even one that depended so long and exclusively on nonservice endeavors for its sustenance. The success of Pittsburgh's financial segment—a textbook example of what service is all about—should help pave the way for Pittsburgh's full embrace of other service businesses and industries in the 1990s. By that time most Pittsburghers will have become accustomed to the fact that service

**"Gatan" electron microscope, © Herb Ferguson**

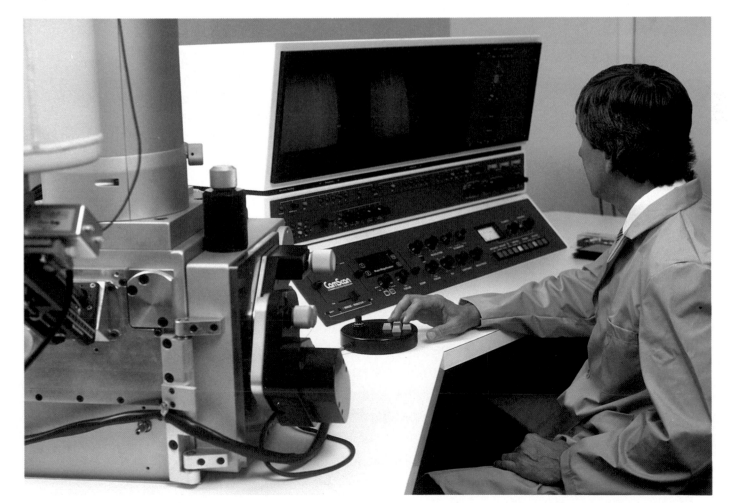

## Putting Brain Behind Pittsburgh's Brawn

By Vince Gagetta

Pittsburgh, like virtually every city in America, dreams of a future made secure and prosperous by technology and the development of businesses and industries that are referred to by that most magical of descriptions: high tech. The world of high technology promises marvels and riches to those who are smart enough to harness its awesome power and enterprising enough to exploit it. High tech appears to be the hope of the future, and a way to recapture the glories of our industrial past.

High technology is usually thought of as something to be used in the pursuit of one goal or another, as a means to an end. However, it is not the mere utilization of technology that holds the most promise for revitalization and renewal. Rather it is the development of technology that will be the essential. The richest spoils will fall not to the users but to the developers, to those who discover the ways, means, and methods of making things more economically and doing things more efficiently. The people who take a leadership role in this development process will be the ultimate victors.

Pittsburgh appears to have some significant advantages over many areas in this regard. The region's industrial and manufac-

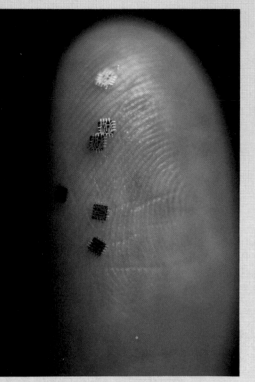

*Above:* Computer micro-chips, © Michael Haritan

*Below:* University of Pittsburgh Chemistry Department research on lasers, © Herb Ferguson

turing heritage provides both the foundation upon which techno-logical development efforts may be laid and the facilities in which to test and perfect such developments. Also present here are the sources of capital to finance development. Another factor is the presence of a large, experienced, skilled, and willing work force that is both trained and trainable, one that forms the core labor pool for enterprises that emerge from research efforts. And certainly there is the need.

The key ingredient, however, may well be Pittsburgh's aca-demic centers. There exists in Pittsburgh a strong, established, resourceful, and multi-disciplined academic community—really an academic force for change and development—willing to and very capable of providing such efforts with learned guidance, impetus, and astute leadership.

The Pittsburgh region's twenty-nine colleges and universities, along with the legion of technical and training schools, compete very actively for students and resources. But for all their com-petitiveness, the schools are most eager to join in cooperative efforts not only to enhance the educational and training oppor-tunities for the region's residents but also to serve as vehicles for realistic economic revitalization efforts.

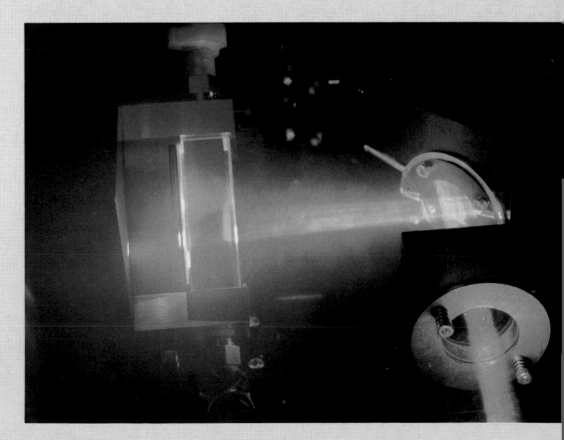

**Robotics research; courtesy Robotics Institute, Carnegie-Mellon University**

The ten schools that make up the Pittsburgh Council on Higher Education—Carlow College, Carnegie-Mellon University, Chatham College, Community College of Allegheny County, Duquesne University, LaRoche College, Pittsburgh Theological Seminary, Point Park College, Robert Morris College, and the University of Pittsburgh—not only cooperate closely in developing and sharing academic programs and learning opportunities for their students, they also provide the city, Allegheny County, and the region with a solid structure that is the foundation of many of the economic renewal and business development efforts currently under way.

The two research universities in Pittsburgh dominate the academic scene and provide the region with its most potent and most direct resources for technological development. Both the University of Pittsburgh, with its demonstrated strengths in the health sciences and biotechnology, and Carnegie-Mellon University, with its outstanding capabilities in computer science and robotics, are the region's strongest links with high-technology

development and its best bridges between the industrial past and technological future.

CMU's robotics research is an outstanding example of what the future might hold for Pittsburgh if Pittsburghers are able to harness the technological wonders available right now. The university in late 1980 inaugurated its Robotics Institute, believed to have been the first academic department in the United States totally dedicated to the study and development of usable robots. The institute is at the leading edge of robotics research and development, not only in the United States but in the world. The institute's researchers and scientists are combining skills, expertise, and knowledge from both academe and industry as they work to advance the science of robotics and develop the technology and the equipment that promise to change the way the world works.

Robots, of course, are already important elements in most industrial and manufacturing processes. They have for years been counted on to perform many of the tasks—the skilled as well as the mundane, the routine, and the dangerous—to produce goods more efficiently, more cost effectively, and more competitively. As industrial competition throughout the world intensifies

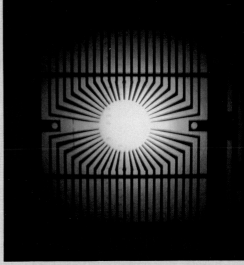

*Above:* Computer circuit,
© Herb Ferguson

*Left:* Remote core sampler,
© Mary Jo Dowling; cour-
tesy, Robotics Institute,
Carnegie-Mellon University

on a continuing basis, the means and methods of production will have to be made even more efficient and economical, and the robot's role will become even more important. Ideally, robots will replace humans and free them for more meaningful and reward-ing work, helping make men and women more resourceful, more creatively productive, and able to contribute more significantly to the world's well-being.

Production applications are not the only realm in which robots are being utilized. Many beneficial applications of the science of robotics are in health care. For example, robotics technology like that being developed at CMU is making life more livable for the physically disabled. This is just one aspect—regarded by many as the most rewarding—in a fast-developing field.

It is not enough, however, to build a better robot and have the world beat a path to your laboratory door. A robot is merely a device, a mechanical or electrical contraption. It has to be told how to perform its tasks. The science of instructing robots in what to do and how and when is as important to robotics tech-

nology as the development of the hardware. Both CMU and Pitt have made tremendous strides in the development of artificial intelligence, the robot's "brain" so to speak. Breakthroughs by scientists and researchers at both universities have resulted in the awarding of joint grants as well as individual grants.

As exciting as the outlook has been for robots and robotic development in Pittsburgh, it was made even more exciting recently with the arrival of the supercomputer. In January 1986 Pitt and CMU together with Westinghouse Electric Corporation were given a grant by the National Science Foundation to establish the country's fifth—and most powerful—supercomputing center. The center's awesomely powerful computer allows scientists and researchers to perform complex calculations in a single day that previously took weeks or even months. The supercomputer is a fantastic resource for academic and industrial research, both basic and applied, and in only a few months of actual operation has achieved remarkable results in several important areas. Its presence in Pittsburgh could be the most dramatically significant factor in this region's revitalization. As a tool to allow for the faster, more efficient development of technology, it serves as a powerful magnet to attract vital new businesses, industries, and highly talented scientists and academicians.

All of the area's efforts in high-tech development and technological application provide Pittsburghers with a new source for economic strength and stability. Like many such technological enterprises before it—at CMU, Pitt, and other schools throughout the region—the Robotics Institute has spun off new enterprises that apply the knowledge and information gained from academic research and development. Without doubt, these are among the most promising and potentially profitable of the businesses and industries of tomorrow taking shape today. Their development means that Pittsburgh's young need not search elsewhere for meaningful careers with meaningful futures, that Pittsburgh's skilled work force will find opportunities anew.

That mission is certain to be enhanced with the merger in the summer of 1986 of Carnegie Institute and Buhl Science Center. The merger joins together Pittsburgh's premier scientific education organizations and links the Carnegie complex in Oakland with Buhl's planetarium and exhibit spaces on the city's North Side into a formidable exhibition and education system.

may not be the only economic game in town, but it is certainly the most promising one. By that time the young Pittsburghers who twenty years ago would have sought employment at the mill or the foundry or the mine will be eagerly looking for work in banking, law, insurance, food, research, one of the high-tech companies, or the burgeoning heatlh-care industry. And they will be good jobs. In the long run service promises to serve Pittsburgh very well as an economic foundation. And Pittsburghers will be far better off in the 1990s and in the twenty-first century because they are recognizing service for the good it is and the good it can do.

Moreover, the Pittsburgh of tomorrow will very likely continue to be an important headquarters city. Not only do the corporations that have been based here for many years show every sign of continuing their presence but foreign companies are also increasingly locating their U.S. headquarters here. Some who study Pittsburgh's economic climate closely are convinced that

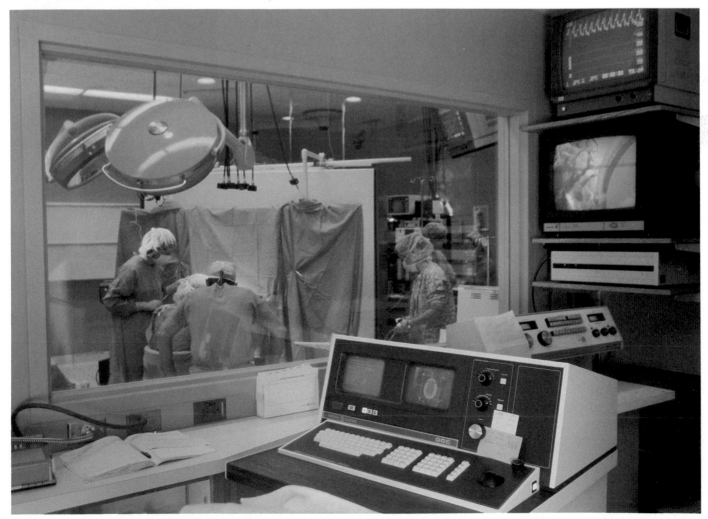

the area's continued ability to attract foreign firms to locate their American headquarters, sales offices, and production facilities here is *the* single best hope for economic growth in the region.

The presence of foreign firms and foreign funds will certainly add to the continued diversification of the region's economy. In fact, the area's economy has been undergoing steady diversification for many years. The process is already much further advanced than many Pittsburghers imagine and represents the city's hope for economic stability, revitalization, and growth. Diversity will be the keystone of tomorrow's Pittsburgh.

The transition from yesterday, with its industrial prosperity based on the unquestioned dominion of one of the most important industries in the world, to the less-well-defined, less-secure Pittsburgh of today has not been a pleasant one. Pittsburgh has not been accustomed to a disadvantageous economic position—the entire region experienced a forty-year period of only mildly and infrequently interrupted stability and growth between 1941 and 1980. For that reason, the area's widespread industrial decline of the early 1980s, coming as abruptly as it did, created all the more alarm and damage. That Pittsburgh has been able to adjust as well as it has, to recover substantially, and to pose itself on the threshold of what is almost unanimously agreed to be a powerful resurgence, is a tribute to its resilience, its spirit, its determination, and the strength of its citizens.

There is a new renaissance on the horizon for Pittsburgh, a renaissance that carries the promise of rivaling the ones that have gone before. The initial Pittsburgh Renaissance was the nation's first publicly sponsored and privately financed urban-renewal project. It transformed the look of the place and cleared away the debris of 100 years of determined industrialization. Renaissance II was a refurbishing, a home-improvement project that gave the place a new sparkle and a new shine. The next renaissance will likely be carried out over a longer and less-defined period and will work to transform and renew the spirit of Pittsburgh.

Pittsburgh in the year 2000 will probably look much the same as it does now. There will be fewer people if current trends continue. The U.S. Commerce Department's Bureau of Economic Analysis forecasts that the Pittsburgh metropolitan area will lose

*Above:* **Allegheny General Hospital, © Jack A. Wolf**

*Facing page, top:* **The Mercy Hospital, © Jack A. Wolf**

*Facing page, bottom:* **Neurosurgery team, © Herb Ferguson**

**Beribboned at the Three Rivers Arts Festival, © Mary Jane Bent**

about 30,000 people by the time the twenty-first century rolls around. That decline of more than 1.5 percent will move Pittsburgh from fourteenth to twenty-second place among the nation's largest metropolitan areas.

Also by the year 2000 the area's work force should actually grow more than 14 percent. Some 130,000 jobs will be added to the work force over those reported in 1983, as Pittsburgh continues to recover from the Great Recession and the untimely demise of the steel industry. Per capita personal income is expected to increase by 31.5 percent by the time Pittsburghers are preparing to pop their champagne corks on New Year's Eve 1999. And it is estimated that total personal income for the area will grow by almost 30 percent over the 1983 figure, to nearly thirty-four million dollars. These are statistics *not* generally associated with cities in decline.

The economic transformation of Pittsburgh will not likely affect the things that make Pittsburghers what they are and make Pittsburgh the type of place it is. Despite disruptions and dislocations brought on by the search for solid employment oppor-

**Shannopin Country Club,
© Michael Haritan**

tunities, Pittsburgh is very likely to remain very much a family town with strong family ties. Pittsburghers, even displaced ones, will probably not miss out on those traditional family gatherings; they will just have to travel a little farther to get to them.

As the face of the region changes over the years, its small towns and city neighborhoods will probably remain much the same. Pittsburghers, even those who live in or near the heart of the city itself, can be counted on to retain their small-town values. They are values too precious to be casually discarded, and they are the values that give Pittsburghers a special quality, that set them apart, that invigorate and ennoble them.

Those values will continue to serve Pittsburghers well as they

*This page, clockwise from top left:*

**Investment Bank,
© Maurice Tierney**

**Kaufmann Clock, © Jack A.
Wolf**

**Beechview homes,
© Michael Haritan**

*Facing page:* **Alcoa Building, © Maurice Tierney**

*Above:* **Ninth Street Bridge,**
**© Mary Jane Bent**

*Facing page:* **Fireworks**
**over Three Rivers Stadium,**
**© Herb Ferguson**

prepare themselves for the twenty-first century. They will provide Pittsburghers with strength and a sense of purpose and will
help them keep things in perspective, help them realize that it is
not they themselves that must change but their economic structure. Those values will help all Pittsburghers remember that no
matter where they live in this big and vital place, they have much
to offer to the nation and the world: talents, great resources,
and spirit—most especially spirit.

Spirit will carry Pittsburgh through. Spirit has made this town
and its people a dominant economic and industrial force in the
past, and the same spirit will create a new Pittsburgh.

It is no easy task to transform a place so that it can survive
and prosper once again. The years ahead are not likely to be
easy. There are no guarantees of success, no ironclad assurances that all plans will work and all efforts will be successful.
But Pittsburghers love a fight and have been at their best not in
celebrating victory but in striving for it. They are determined to
succeed.

# CHAPTER *IX*

## *Partners in Progress*

Recorded in this book is the story of Pittsburgh today. Her economic base is changing and strengthening, and so is her image. Rand McNally's "most livable community in America" is well positioned for the future and capitalizing on every opportunity.

Change is not new to the region. Every great wave of the continental economy has passed through the site that George Washington thought "extremely well situated for a Fort." Pittsburgh emerged from the forest originally as a "service center," a few huts and a trading post with the Indians.

Then came its gateway role to the West; boatbuilder and provisioner of immigrants; small manufacturer of axes, nails, calico, and harness; as well as the forger of tools, arsenal of the Civil War. Blessed with coal, limestone, navigable rivers, a hospitable attitude toward capital, and a location central to the industrial and agricultural heartland of America's East and Midwest, the area was superbly situated to bring iron ore by lake and rail and to mount the greatest steel-producing capacity on earth.

The heavy manufacturing industries that created the "Workshop of the World," that brought paychecks and public confidence for more than a century, have been joined by a newly emerged economy. Pittsburgh's most striking statistic of the mid-1980s was a crossover: service and high-technology industries forged well ahead of steel and manufacturing as the chief employers.

Another impressive fact is that from 1974 to the present, the private sector—in such areas as health, financial, and legal—has added many thousands of jobs. In short, the "Steel City" is conforming to the characteristics of America as a whole, with approximately one in five workers employed in manufacturing, and moving into new sectors where its presence will be felt around the world.

This elegant statistical congruence was not easy, however, and Pittsburghers do not kid themselves about what it means. From the loftiest boardrooms to the employment services bulletin boards, there is a healthy realization that today all the world is a workshop, and all the world is a marketplace.

The vagaries of "trade policy" and the bouncy U.S. dollar can make a company competitive one season, orderless the next. No market or technical leadership can ever again be taken for granted—and certainly no customer. In order to prosper, businesses, regardless of size, need a constant infusion of fresh ideas; but a town must be livable and exciting to attract the most talented people. In today's market demands, quality of life is quickly becoming one of the most significant factors in a favorable business climate. Quality of life is one of Pittsburgh's greatest assets.

The following chapter profiles Pittsburgh area businesses and organizations. Each has chosen to support this publication, and contributes to its perspective on an economy and quality of life in a time of important transition. In these stories lie the clues and outlines to the "new" Pittsburgh and the commitment that is assuring the region a vibrant future.

# GREATER PITTSBURGH CHAMBER OF COMMERCE
## IMPROVING THE CLIMATE FOR WESTERN PENNSYLVANIA BUSINESS

For more than 120 years the Greater Pittsburgh Chamber of Commerce has operated on a simple, commonsense credo. Where there is economic vigor and a favorable business climate, there is the soundest basis for a fulfilling community life, comprised of stable families; cultural institutions that are well-supported; and public facilities and neighborhoods that please the eye, lift the heart, and impart to thousands the feelings of "home."

Thus it was that when Pittsburgh won the "Most Livable City" accolade of the 1985 Rand McNally *Places Rated Almanac,* it came as no surprise to the Greater Pittsburgh Chamber of Commerce. No surprise—but of course a matchless opportunity to give credence to what its residents have always known: that the city on the three rivers is a great place to live, to work, to raise children, and to do business.

An early result of winning the place race was "Celebrate Pittsburgh," an unforgettable weekend, November 23 and 24, 1985, whipped up in an astonishingly short time by the efforts of the Chamber, the city, Allegheny County, and more than 250 companies and individuals who contributed freely their time, resources, and talents. To cap it off, 3,000

Pittsburghers dined at the David L. Lawrence Convention Center and honored 70 of the region's most eminent sons and daughters—who came home from far and wide as the community's special guests.

This book is another Pittsburgh celebration.

The Chamber sponsored it, but financial support from the businesses and institutions whose stories are told in "Partners in Progress" really made it happen. No end of help came, too, from the enthusiasm of Pittsburgh mayor Richard S. Caliguiri and Allegheny County Commission chairman Thomas J. Foerster in "getting the word out."

The Chamber itself has operated continuously since 1874. It is the largest organization speaking out in behalf of local businesses and their employees. Its 1986 membership roster includes many thousands of business owners and managers in southwestern Pennsylvania. More than 80 percent of the membership consists of small to medium-size firms, with fewer

---

*Clyde Hare's "Winter Dawn on Pittsburgh" depicts the stunning renaissance and breathtaking beauty of the city. One of the great centers of global commerce, Pittsburgh is poised for an ever brighter future.*

than 50 employees. Consequently, Chamber policy positions serve to bring together a wide range of perspectives; and, upon achieving a consensus, it develops powerful momentum in civic matters.

Although the organization employs a full-time staff of 27 and has convenient offices at Three Gateway Center, the Chamber's chief asset is the talents of its membership—especially when applied to specific tasks through a well-focused internal committee system. A Loaned Executive Task Force, for example, directed the scrutiny of business people to nine different areas of Port Authority Transit operations; its findings provided the factual background for the momentous PAT labor reform legislation of 1986. And ongoing Chamber programs seek to further intergovernmental cooperation among neighboring municipalities. The objective of these programs is to generate cost-effective improvements in the day-to-day operations.

Says Greater Pittsburgh Chamber of Commerce president Justin T. Horan: "If we in Pittsburgh can maintain our close relationships between public and private sectors, the potential is for hundreds of millions in future tax savings—and a better life for all the people of the region."

# THE WESTERN PENNSYLVANIA HOSPITAL
## A FRIEND FOR LIFE

The Western Pennsylvania Hospital, familiarly known as "West Penn," is a hospital that has grown with Pittsburgh from an era of primitive medicine to scientific wonders, from horse-drawn ambulances to helicopters, and from a treatment center for Civil War wounds to the scene of over 500 open-heart surgeries a year.

Officials at the institution remain constantly on guard against equating old with good. They have the history; however, they also know that only by maintaining in the front line of progressive care will patients of the twenty-first century still be declaring, "They saved my life at West Penn."

In 1848 a group of community leaders received the first charter for a public hospital west of the Alleghenies (in Pittsburgh), but it was five years later when the institution actually opened, with 100 beds and 12 physicians. In 1865 West Penn was designated the area's veterans' hospital; hundreds of Civil War soldiers received treatment there en route to their homes.

Other achievements in the early decades included sponsorship of the region's first medical college in 1883 (it later became the University of Pittsburgh School of Medicine), and the first school of nursing training male nurses in 1892. West Penn has graduated more than 4,600 nurses over the years.

The hospital's present facility was built on Friendship Avenue in

*It was the fastest way to get there—in the 1890s.*

the city's Bloomfield neighborhood in 1912. Striking in its angled design of radiating wings—and designated a historic landmark in 1973—it has progressively enhanced its scope and effectiveness. West Penn is now a 568-bed regional-referral center and advanced metropolitan teaching institution, a community of 2,300 employees and 500 physicians.

A parent company, The Western Pennsylvania Healthcare System, Inc., was created to enable distinct entities such as The Western

Pennsylvania Hospital, The West Penn Hospital Foundation, and West Penn Corporate Medical Services to better perform in a highly regulated industry.

Several Pittsburgh "firsts" are credited to West Penn: the city's first intensive care unit, 1959; its first ambulatory care facility (Mellon Pavilion, 150 medical staff physicians in private practice), 1970; and the first hospital heliport (scene of 250 air transports a year), 1971.

Other notable achievements of West Penn include the operation of the region's largest and most comprehensive burn/trauma center; 130 babies born per average month in the obstetrics department; a major referral neonatal intensive care unit, which serves more than 100 other area hospitals; and a multidisciplinary team approach that has brought the cancer care center one of the region's heaviest caseloads. These endeavors, however, are just a few of many leadership positions in West Penn Hospital's continuing history of medical advancement and excellence in patient care.

*With modern additions, parking, and ambulatory care facilities, West Penn Hospital, as it is familiarly known, serves a broad region from the city's friendly Bloomfield neighborhood.*

405

# PITTSBURGH NATIONAL BANK
## KEY PLAYER IN A DYNAMIC ECONOMY

Heavy manufacturing down, service industries up.

All of heartland America rides that employment seesaw, and there may be no more striking example of the upside than Pittsburgh National Bank.

It's a historic irony that midway through the past century the enterprising B.F. Jones and James Laughlin established in Pittsburgh both a steel works and, with other investors, a bank. After many a glorious decade the mills of the Jones & Laughlin Steel Corporation are shrinking now along the city's rivers; the name itself has melted into the ladle of mergers in seething industry. However, the bank goes on. In fact, it's in a state of competitive dynamism, its 3,400 employees key players in a regional transition from the boom-bust cycles of the past to a diversified future of services and advanced technologies.

The grandest epoch of America's first industrial revolution still lay ahead on January 28, 1852, when the Pittsburgh Trust and Savings Company opened its doors with a capital of $150,000. Two years later the fledgling enterprise moved into one-half of the ground floor of a newspaper building at Fifth Avenue and Wood Street, where the bank's modern headquarters—its fourth on that site—still stands.

The location is one of the Downtown's busiest, most historic corners. In an earlier day the Mansion House, a pioneer hotel there, had entertained the Marquis de Lafayette during the old revolutionary's triumphal American tour of 1825. Long before that it had been a patch in the lordly domains of colonial founder William Penn, and was sold by his descendants in 1786 for about $90. Reassembled for a bank expansion in the early 1900s, the slivers of Downtown turf fetched well over one million dollars.

When the National Bank Act

Robert C. Milsom, chairman and chief executive officer of Pittsburgh National Bank.

George J. McClaran, president of Pittsburgh National Bank.

was passed in the Civil War, in part to push the sale of government bonds, Pittsburgh Trust was early in line for a charter. It became the First National Bank of Pittsburgh in 1864, and the modern institution still serves under the articles of that prized franchise, Number 252.

The city's population grew more than fivefold in the latter half of the nineteenth century. In the fertile soil of the "steel center of the world," scores of banks sprang up, flourished, and seldom failed in that era's numerous "panics." Three that survived to become additional forebears of Pittsburgh National were the Peoples Savings Bank, founded in 1866; Fidelity Title and Trust, 1886; and Pittsburgh Trust Company, 1893. A corporate genealogical chart would show the bloodlines of at least 60 smaller institutions.

The truly formative merger, the one that aligned the institution's modern direction, came in 1959. That brought together the by now awkwardly titled Peoples First National Bank and Trust Company

and the Fidelity Trust. The former was strong in its retail branch network and emerging ambitions in commercial banking, the latter in its personal trust portfolios.

Newly named the Pittsburgh National Bank, the combined organization had 52 offices, not quite one billion dollars in assets, and a management under Frank E. Agnew, Jr., its first board chairman. Determined to bid for a growing share in the nation's commercial banking markets, it was greatly aided by the savings habits of the hometown folks.

"Pittsburgh always has generated a good deposit base," explains Robert C. Milsom, who became bank chairman in 1985. "We had to find ways to put those deposits to work."

In bankers' terms, the strategy that developed could be stated as providing "differentiated financial products and services in defined geographic markets to particular market segments and customer groups." What Pittsburgh National did was specialize. It made itself expert in growth industries—par-

*Thomas H. O'Brien, president and chief executive officer of PNC Financial Corp.*

ticularly those in an entrepreneurially hungry state for financing—and used these special lending capabilities to enter national markets, eventually as a syndicator of large loans and provider of cash management and other sophisticated services. Cable television and fast-food operations were two important fields of expertise; the bank's Emerging Companies Group constantly seeks out more.

Meanwhile, the regional office network has more than doubled, to 115; foreign offices were strategically placed to assist the overseas business of U.S. corporate customers; and the 30-story bank headquarters, completed in 1972, was augmented by other facilities in Pittsburgh to handle computer operations, systems development, and general services.

In 1982 the enactment of statewide multibank holding company legislation found Pittsburgh National, under then-chairman Merle E. Gilliand, eager to grow by merger. Management had already identified partners with superior market shares in other regions of the state. Within a month Gilliand

had an agreement with Philadelphia's Provident National Bank to form a new holding company, PNC Financial Corp. Since then Erie's Marine Bancorp, Scranton's Northeastern Bancorp, and central Pennsylvania's Hershey Bank have joined—each retaining, however, as Pittsburgh National does, its highly valued "local" market identity and management. By the mid-1980s, under president and chief executive officer Thomas H. O'Brien, PNC could address the new age of interstate banking as one of the nation's 30 largest bank holding companies, with nearly $19 billion in assets. Pittsburgh National accounted for $9.1 billion of that figure.

*Rising sheer in 30 stories of pink granite and glass, Pittsburgh National Bank's fourth home, and third building of its own, at Fifth and Wood, also serves as headquarters for its state-spanning holding company, PNC Financial Corp.*

Still, more important than size is profitability. Both bank and holding company consistently earn above one percent on assets, a benchmark that is gospel in small banks but rarely achieved by giants—a tribute to the institutions' unremitting attention to "asset quality," or, in other words, good loans.

Pittsburgh National chairman Milsom and president George J. McClaran are determined that a larger bank must not become an impersonal bank. Computers and automated teller machines may enhance the smooth handling of routine transactions; but the kind of services that offer growth potential in the era of deregulation, such as investment banking and personal trusts, clearly demand the human touch. "Our main thrust is to have all our people identify quality with service," says Milsom. "It's still a people business."

# PRICE WATERHOUSE
## LARGEST OF THE BIG EIGHT IS A TIRELESS MARKETER

It is an accounting firm over 120 years old, of a probity sufficient to be entrusted with the envelopes of the Academy Awards, and with more than eight solid decades in Pittsburgh. Still, Price Waterhouse takes nothing for granted.

This emphatically includes its top market share among the "Big Eight" accounting firms in the Golden Triangle. Occupying approximately 60,000 square feet at 600 Grant Street, PW's local staff of 275 employees audits the books of more of Pittsburgh's *Fortune* 500 tier of corporations than any other accounting firm. However, that implies no invitation to relax the oars, in the view of David W. Christopher, who has worked for Price Waterhouse since 1951 and has headed its Pittsburgh opera-

tions as partner-in-charge since 1976.

Under Christopher's direction, PW has actively sought new business. "Price Waterhouse Steps Out," stated a headline in an issue of Pittsburgh's *Executive Report* magazine in 1986. The article detailed not only an aggressive search for new clients in advanced technology fields but also a spirited use of advertising, including billboards, and a bold participation in matters of nonprofit public interest as well as a commitment to significant growth in management consulting.

Typical of PW's approach was the new division it created to serve western Pennsylvania's smaller businesses. This represented quite a shift. The Price

Waterhouse image—valuable but limiting—has traditionally been that of auditor to the eminent. However, when it opened a satellite office in Oakland in 1984 to serve the university area's growing cluster of high-tech companies, PW rented a simple storefront on South Craig Street.

"We wanted them to come in shirtsleeves, work with our microcomputers, and talk about their business," explains Christopher. "We didn't want them to have to come to 600 Grant Street and our art work and walnut furniture." The endeavor was successful. By mid-1986 PW had added 40 high-tech clients that exceeded $250,000 in annual billings. However, PW Pittsburgh continues to emphasize its interest in major

*Some of the accounting firm's employees in the ultramodern Pittsburgh headquarters of Price Waterhouse at 600 Grant Street.*

corporations; it audits more SEC companies than any other Pittsburgh firm.

Does it help to be instantly recognized as the guardian of Academy Awardee's identities until the suspenseful moment when a star says, "May I have the envelope, please?" Christopher gladly admits that it does. The movie industry connection and the positive image create a conversational icebreaker that has launched many a serious business relationship.

If PW's energetic marketing in Pittsburgh comes as one surprise, the sheer size of its international organization is another. With more than 360 offices in 95 countries, Price Waterhouse's total accounting, auditing, tax, and management consulting force comes to approximately 28,000—more than 7,000 in about 100 offices in the United States alone.

The first stone in this foundation was laid by Samuel Lowell Price, who began performing independent audits in "The City" of London in 1850. His partnership with Edwin Waterhouse dates from 1865, and their clerks were serving British clients on the American shore in 1870; however, independent U.S. operations did not get under way until 1890.

An assignment to examine the accounts of subsidiary companies in a then-new United States Steel Corporation launched Price Waterhouse's first Pittsburgh office in May 1902, with six employees. On June 30, 1905, the office issued its first separate report on a local client's financial statement—the Western University of Pennsylvania, which had not yet changed its name to the University of Pittsburgh. Business expanded during the long tenure of J.C. Moresby White, who served as senior partner in Pittsburgh from 1916 to 1948. One remarkable assignment came in 1931 to examine the City of Pittsburgh's Department of Supplies; that examination led to the conviction of Mayor Charles H. Kline and his supply department chief for disbursement irregularities. In March 1933 the mayor had to resign to avoid serving a six-month jail sentence.

Meanwhile, a 1932 highlight was Price Waterhouse's assignment to act as auditor for Gulf Oil Corporation. A few years later the work load was large enough to justify a second partner in the office. In 1953 PW became one of the new Gateway Center's first tenants. The firm's 1957 staff numbered 78. A stellar event of 1969 was the appointment of PW as auditor for Westinghouse Electric Corporation.

By 1975 PW's Pittsburgh employment had reached 200, and the need for larger quarters prompted the move to 600 Grant Street. The following year Robert G. Nichols moved up to regional partner, and Christopher became partner-in-charge in Pittsburgh.

A first for any Price Waterhouse office was Christopher's staff addition, in 1978, of a Pittsburgh director of practice development—charged with actively soliciting clients by direct selling, advertising, and the organization of seminars on such subjects as employee benefits and tax planning. The post is held by Stephen U. McCloskey, a non-accountant—by design. "Big Eight accountants are conservative," says Christopher. "You can't take guys and girls with green eyeshades and expect them to be salespeople." He emphasizes that the underlying principle of PW is to market "high-quality service, not the cheapest."

While PW's billings remain confidential, Christopher foresees continued growth in its small-business and high-tech divisions, as well as in management consulting, for which the staff doubled from 1985 to 1986 and is expected to double again by 1988.

Another facet of Price Waterhouse's marketing aggressiveness has been its willingness to take forward positions in community service. Helping to catch a crooked mayor is nice but negative. The business image brightens much more when you help to save the Pirates, as Price Waterhouse did, along with other civic and business leaders, in the mid-1980s. The accounting firm may never see a direct return, to be sure, on the more than $100,000 in financial services it contributed.

"You can't evaluate it that way," says Christopher. "We like what is good for the community. It took us only about 30 seconds to say yes to that one."

# HEYL & PATTERSON, INC.
## A CENTURY OF PROVIDING MUSCLES TO INDUSTRY

As America roared toward industrial maturity near the end of the nineteenth century, Pittsburgh's iron, steel, coal, and shipping industries were forced to cope with unprecedented, ceaseless flows of materials. It was inevitable: The "workshop of the world" had to become supreme in the skills of manipulating massive physical resources.

Heyl & Patterson, Inc., an engineering venture born in the large-tonnage boom of a century ago, has prospered by solving the problems of fast, efficient, safe handling of materials and processes for a wide variety of industries. The company's designs, intended to meet future challenges, have often become present standards.

It was Heyl & Patterson's continuous bucket elevator unloader that showed the electric power utilities how to empty barges of coal at up to 4,000 tons an hour. A similar design was created to unload grain barges throughout the grain industry.

Entrepreneurship was the magnetic force that brought the firm's two founders together in 1887. Edmund W. Heyl and William J. Patterson (both native Pittsburghers) met, formed an enterprise, and began as manufacturers representatives to sell chain and buckets to coal producers, haulers, and dealers. Soon they were producing their own, better equipment. They became materials-handling specialists, serving the steel and coal interests of western Pennsylvania, Ohio, and West Virginia; and they left a company legacy of energy, risk-taking, and industriousness.

Led by entrepreneurs, inventor/engineers, and astute financial men, the organization has had only five presidents through its first century. Although many employees and retirees hold stock, four families have provided most of the ownership and leadership,

and two of these still continue in those roles.

Heyl & Patterson's history records many firsts. It built glass-making factories; 350-ton cranes for the Navy; hydro-cyclones for the processing of slurries; and traveling ore bridges, some of which were shipped as parts and assembled by women in the Soviet Union during World War II.

H&P holds world leadership in the production of rotary rail car dumping systems, fluid bed dryers for coal, and bucket-elevator barge unloaders. A rotary car

*Edmund Wendell Heyl*

*William Joshua Patterson*

dumper grips an entire rail car and turns it over like a child emptying a beach bucket. Going that feat one better, engineers combined a dumper with a train indexer for Heyl & Patterson's unit train unloading system. It moves the entire train, positioning each car—without uncoupling the train.

This car-dumping technology has also been adapted for the notoriously slow-flowing wood chips of the forest products and paper industries. The company's traveling hammermill frees hopper gratings clogged by frozen coal or

other large-lump materials.

Inventiveness is a company tradition. The firm built its first ship unloader in 1904, and a half-century later it supplied the machinery to "make the roof go around" for the famed retractable dome at Pittsburgh's Civic Arena. H&P's Bradford Breaker of 1892

*The Heyl & Patterson headquarters in RIDC Park West.*

may have been the first modern coal-cleaning device. Decades later the corporation was pioneering "hydro-cyclones" to classify, clarify, separate, and concentrate such materials as coal, minerals, and phosphates. Its shipyard cranes won the Navy's first "E" for excellence awarded in western Pennsylvania in World War II.

Heyl & Patterson's earliest home was in an industrial building—long since razed—in Downtown Pittsburgh. After several moves the organization built its own headquarters in 1980—an airy, modern, two-story structure, which was one of the first in RIDC Park

*The Heyl & Patterson warehouse and the complete line of process equipment parts.*

West, near the airport. Other facilities are a warehouse and research center in the O'Hara Township RIDC Industrial Park; a fabrication plant at Merritt Island, Florida (where H&P has served the space agency); and an office of the firm's Renneburg Division in Baltimore, which specializes in chemical and food-processing equipment.

"We provide full-service engineering and involvement in all phases of a project," explains H&P president Harry R. Edelman III. This means starting with a feasibility study; performing design and engineering; then specifying, purchasing, and scheduling the delivery of construction materials and fabricated components. The corporation, in fact, remains involved right through plant start-up, and beyond. Parts and service for the after-market have always been company mainstays.

Heyl & Patterson separates its products into four groups for market purposes:

Process Technology produces a variety of restless-sounding devices, such as froth flotation cells, cyclones, sieve bends, fluid bed dryers, rotary dryers and coolers, calciners, kilns, mixers, mills, presses, granulators, and centrifuges.

A customer who needs a grab bucket unloader, continuous unloader, bucket wheel stacker reclaimer, ship barge unloader, or scraper reclaimer comes to H&P's Bulk Transfer Group.

The Inspection Group performs bridge and crane inspections and certifications and other specialized mechanical and structural inspection services for various makes of equipment.

The Customer Service Group is the source for technical services and custom-engineered replacement parts and services.

Coal and steel have never ceased to be major client industries, but now there are many more: aluminum, docks and ports, power, phosphate, food, potash, chemicals, minerals, sewage, cement, and lime.

Heyl & Patterson, Inc., finds it noteworthy that employees of many ancestries have been major contributors over the years— Polish, Slavic, German, Irish, English, Scottish, and Indian, among others.

"The ingredients of success have been innovation, risk-taking, and responsibility," says Edelman, "but in every case it was people who brought us those things. And the people have been a microcosm of the Pittsburgh melting pot."

*Heyl & Patterson's rotary railcar dumping system is shown here dumping coal from an aluminum rail car.*

411

# BLUE CROSS OF WESTERN PENNSYLVANIA
## MEETING A VITAL COMMUNITY NEED

Blue Cross of Western Pennsylvania was the first nonprofit prepayment health care plan in the commonwealth. It came into being during the Great Depression of the 1930s, part of a national pattern to create a new solution for meeting medical costs in a period of financial hardship.

During that period many people found it impossible to pay for medical attention, however acutely needed; and hospitals stood on the brink of financial ruin. Experts warned of a crisis coming to both the sick and the healers.

Various public-spirited Pittsburghers joined forces in 1935 to address this emergency. With Buhl Foundation financing they set up a study committee, which made a then-daring recommendation: that western Pennsylvania's hospitals "combine to offer group hospitalization." The following year some institutions did so, forming the Hospital Council of Western Pennsylvania. The new organization's

first acts were to appoint a committee on group hospitalization and to apply to the Buhl Foundation for $20,000 financing for the proposed innovative program.

Meanwhile, Governor George H. Earle and the state legislature were being urged to support enabling legislation to establish nonprofit hospitalization programs in Pennsylvania. Thus, State Representative Herbert B. Cohen, who was house majority leader, introduced the Nonprofit Hospital Plan Act. Passed in the spring of 1937, the initiative provided for nonprofit hospitalization programs to be regulated by the Pennsylvania Insurance Department.

In Pittsburgh, steps were already under way to prepare articles of incorporation. The Insurance Department gave prompt approval, and Common Pleas Judge Elder W. Marshall issued a charter. On September 15, 1937, the Hospital Service Association of Pittsburgh, as it was called then, came into

being.

A month later, from rented offices on the eighth floor of the Farmers Bank Building—now the 301 Fifth Avenue Building—the association's six employees began offering Pennsylvania's first group hospitalization plan. It provided 21 days of inpatient care—at a premium cost of 72 cents monthly.

The first Blue Cross agreements took effect January 1, 1938. Experts predicted an eventual enrollment of 75,000 persons; that target was passed within a year. By the fifth anniversary membership had reached 500,000. In 1945 when, for the first time, a program be-

*Members of the executive committee of Blue Cross of Western Pennsylvania (seated, left to right): George C. Greer, chairman of the board; Eugene J. Barone, president; Raymond R. Wingard, secretary of the board; and Nancy T. Brown. Standing (left to right) are Leo R. McDonough, Richard L. Reinhart, Charles L. Sewall, and John H. Satterwhite. Not present is Keith K. Kappmeyer, vice-chairman of the board.*

*Blue Cross chief executive officers have been: (left) Abraham Oseroff, 1938-1956; (right) William H. Ford, 1956-1974; (above) Howard W. Gindele, 1974-1984; and (below) Eugene J. Barone. since 1984.*

came available to persons not covered through a group, the association enrolled its millionth subscriber.

Growth was also stimulated by the offering of companion programs of the Medical Service Association of Pennsylvania, which later became known as Pennsylvania Blue Shield. As early as 1940 western Pennsylvanians could receive coverage for both hospital and doctors' services.

The new approach enabled the area's residents to prepay hospital expenses and, in turn, to receive services as needed in participating Blue Cross facilities. It was the familiar insurance principle. Hospitals were assured of payment at rates approved by the state insurance department. In 1938, its first full year, the Association had agreements with 23 participating institutions; two years later the roster included almost all hospitals in the 29-county area now served by Blue Cross of Western Pennsylvania. The widespread acceptance of the program necessitated the opening of branch offices to serve hospitals and subscribers in Erie, Altoona, Johnstown, and Butler. Official recognition of the ex-

tended geographical reach came in 1963: The organization was renamed Blue Cross of Western Pennsylvania (BCWP).

Although the social and economic climate of the region has changed over the past half-century, the Blue Cross commitment has not. The unique strength of community risk-sharing—a Blue Cross concept from the start—enables BCWP to offer benefit plans for the total population. Commercial health insurers generally concentrate on selected risks; the Blue Cross idea is to

spread individual risks through the community. The better risks, in effect, give voluntary financial support to the higher-risk subscribers—a result of the enabling law. Under the stated mission of nonprofit hospitalization programs, BCWP has a public service to perform: ensuring accessibility to health care. That means developing administrative and support programs that other insurers might shun as unprofitable.

BCWP routinely offers coverage to high-risk individuals not covered by group plans; to businesses with as few as two employees; to the elderly, the unemployed, underemployed, and economically disadvantaged; and to the disabled. Of course, the cost is partially subsidized. However, historically free of the need to show a profit or to pay most federal and state taxes, BCWP has been able to return to its subscribers—in the form of benefits—over 96 cents of each premium dollar.

BCWP is an active link in the progress now being made voluntarily to manage health care costs. By 1990, for example, a "managed care" program—developed and marketed nationally by BCWP and

The main concern was affordability. Thus, BCWP developed products that offered options keyed to individual need and circumstance.

For nongroup customers the corporation offered a variety of benefit packages appropriate to various income levels. Its staff also developed—and, in cooperation with Pennsylvania Blue Shield, put into place—the nation's first private health insurance program

*The extensive and cumbersome central records department of the 1950s (inset) has been replaced with sophisticated computer systems.*

its affiliate, Health Related Services, Inc., is expected to be included in all Blue Cross of Western Pennsylvania products.

There is another dimension to the good management of inpatient services. To help solve the dilemma of unused beds in hospitals, Blue Cross of Western Pennsylvania established a million-dollar fund called SPARK (Stimulating Planning, Rationalization, Know-how) to encourage such institutions to find cost-effective alternative uses for their excess capacity. New BCWP-developed patient

classification and cost-weighting approaches also show promise of yielding many benefits.

While perhaps no one is in a position to declare just what proportion of community income is "appropriate" for health care, the consensus in the mid-1980s was that current costs were too high.

exclusively for youngsters. The Caring Program for Children receives support from Blue Cross and Blue Shield subsidized rates, religious and community groups, and tax-deductible contributions made to the Western Pennsylvania Caring Foundation. The aim is to guarantee the children of unemployed (and marginally employed) persons greater access to primary, preventive health care.

For groups, new programs became available with a wide selection of options, regardless of group size. Employers can choose from several benefit, cost-sharing, and cost management options, including various coinsurance and deductible amounts. Preadmission

*David P. Lyle is executive vice-president and chief operating officer of Health Related Services, Inc. It is a Blue Cross affiliate that offers health care cost management services.*

review, continued-stay review, and second surgical opinions are potent tools to manage costs. In addition, groups may select hospitals and physicians to function as "designated providers."

Preferred Provider Organizations (PPOs) and Health Maintenance Organizations (HMOs) have grown to become viable participants in "the new health care." Blue Cross management recog-

Hospital Service Week merited a mayor's proclamation in the early 1940s. In camera range before the signing were (from left) Dr. George L. Wessels, president, Hospital Council of Pittsburgh; Arthur E. Braun, banker; Abraham Oseroff, vice-president, Hospital Service Association of Pittsburgh; M.A. Silver, general manager, Warner Bros. Theaters; and (seated) Mayor Cornelius D. Scully.

nizes them as competitive facts of life. Hence, active research is under way to incorporate the best of both concepts into the management of health care services and costs.

BCWP also has expanded in another direction: forming or acquiring subsidiary and affiliate members of its Family of Service Companies. Those businesses have been established to offer products and services to complement existing product lines. The for-profit ventures enable the corporation to offer packages of products and services that are competitive in today's changing marketplace. Profits from the companies also may be used to subsidize community

rates and to carry out community programs. The for-profit and the nonprofit corporations enable BCWP to more effectively carry out its mission: to make available affordable health care protection to the largest number of western Pennsylvanians at the lowest-possible cost.

The Blue Cross Family of Service Companies includes Standard Property Corporation, a subsidiary that owns real estate to provide accommodations for BCWP and its affiliates; Consumer Service Casualty Insurance Company, a casualty insurance firm authorized to underwrite and sell insurance for personal legal services and other lines of insurance; and Health Related Services, Inc., a company organized to provide a broad range of health care cost-management services.

Also included are Pen-Wel, Inc., a subsidiary that functions as a third-party benefits administrator and data-processing service for self-insured benefit programs; Penn West, Inc., a subsidiary that serves as agent for established life insurance carriers and provides the convenience of a single source of employee benefit programs; and Keystone Health Plan West, a jointly owned health maintenance organization (HMO) of Blue Cross of Western Pennsylvania and Pennsylvania Blue Shield.

Nonprofit members of the Family of Service Companies are Pittsburgh Research Institute Center for Health Services Research, a scientific research organization established to engage in health care research and provide for the systematic collection, exchange, and public distribution of knowledge in the health care field; Western Pennsylvania Caring Foundation, Inc., a corporation established to support programs designed to improve the quality, awareness of, and availability of health care for the economically disadvantaged or the elderly; and the Health Educa-

Hospital costs were the subject at Pittsburgh Mayor Cornelius D. Scully's "Radio Round Table" on Station KQV during World War II. From left: Abraham Oseroff, Blue Cross president; William N. Robson, Round Table director; Mayor Scully; and Dr. W.W. McFarland.

tion Center, a corporation established to encourage, support, and promote health and the prevention of disease and disability in western Pennsylvania.

A 33-member board of directors oversees the affairs of BCWP. The directors are elected to three-year terms and each represents a cross section of public interests. The chairman of BCWP's consumer advisory council also attends board meetings as a non-voting participant. The Blue Cross president and chief executive officer reports to the board and is charged with carrying out board directives for all divisions, subsidiaries, and affiliates.

It is clear to the management of Blue Cross of Western Pennsylvania that there is perhaps no field in which change has become more the rule of life than in health care. Pioneering has its risks, but Blue Cross feels an intense responsibility to innovate—not to be bound by the past, but to build on it, continually striving for the twin goals of community service and sound business practice.

The management and 1,700 employees of this unique Pittsburgh-based organization have distilled the challenge of addressing tomorrow's health care needs into four corporate attitudes. They can be briefly stated: "never give up," "want to do," "can do," and, simplest of all, "caring."

# KIRKPATRICK & LOCKHART
## THEY WANTED TO KEEP IT SMALL

*George D. Lockhart*

*Robert L. Kirkpatrick*

Founded by seven young lawyers on the eve of the first Pittsburgh Renaissance, Kirkpatrick & Lockhart has provided legal services to the Pittsburgh community throughout the period of Pittsburgh's rebirth and renewal.

The founding partners of Kirkpatrick & Lockhart were originally associated with Reed Smith Shaw & McClay but left that firm in the early 1940s to enter military service. Returning to Pittsburgh at the end of World War II, the seven lawyers decided to establish a small general practice firm of their own, and in 1946 they began practice under the name of Kirkpatrick, Pomeroy, Lockhart & Johnson. Today Kirkpatrick & Lockhart is one of the largest law firms in the country, with more than 200 lawyers and offices in Washington, D.C., Miami, and Boston as well as Pittsburgh.

The founding partners of Kirkpatrick & Lockhart believed that lawyers should have a broad grounding in the law, and they brought to their new endeavor experience in a wide variety of legal fields—corporate law, banking, municipal finance, estates and trusts, real estate, bankruptcy and reorganization, railroad and public utility law, and litigation in federal and state courts. That breadth of experience and their associations within the Pittsburgh community soon attracted clients to the new firm.

After a few months the firm moved from temporary offices in the Union Bank Building to quarters in the Oliver Building, where Kirkpatrick & Lockhart is still housed. The firm's first major project, however, came from an unexpected direction—the Wabash Terminal fire. That fire created a tangle of legal problems that engaged many of the firm's lawyers, just as it provided the occasion for

the renewal of the Golden Triangle and the creation of Point State Park and Gateway Center.

Since that time Kirkpatrick & Lockhart's practice has been rooted in the activities and life of the greater Pittsburgh community. The firm has advised a growing body of clients, including major corporations and financial enterprises; smaller businesses, partnerships, and entrepreneurial groups; governmental units and municipal authorities; educational, medical, charitable and civic organizations; foundations; and individuals. In the course of serving its clients, the firm has helped create such Pittsburgh landmarks as Three Rivers Stadium and Station Square.

Kirkpatrick & Lockhart's contributions to the Pittsburgh community have not been limited to the legal services it provides to its clients.

Kirkpatrick lawyers have devoted substantial amounts of time to charitable, educational, governmental, civic, and professional groups in areas of their particular interests. From the firm's ranks have come a governor of Pennsylvania, a justice of the Pennsylvania Supreme Court, a chief judge of a United States District Court, judges of the Allegheny County Court of Common Pleas, and other public officials, both elected and appointed.

Today Kirkpatrick & Lockhart serves clients whose operations are national or multinational in scope. Whether they produce stainless steel or robots, ingot molds, computer software, or health care programs, the firm's clients face practical legal problems that cut

across disciplines, embrace disparate areas of substantive law, and require legal services in various locations throughout the nation and the world. In rendering those services, Kirkpatrick & Lockhart draws upon lawyers from its different offices—lawyers who work together to meet client needs. The firm continues to believe that its lawyers must have experience in varied areas of the law, but it knows that the growing complexity of society and increasing legislative activity of governments at all levels require increased specialization. Breadth of experience and specialized skills are both necessary resources for a client faced with an increasingly complex legal world and diverse, and sometimes conflicting, legal

*Members of Kirkpatrick & Lockhart assemble on the occasion of the 1984 partners' meeting.*

requirements.

In light of the past 40 years Kirkpatrick & Lockhart knows that change is inevitable. Pittsburgh has changed since 1946, and Kirkpatrick & Lockhart has changed—and grown—with the city. But Kirkpatrick & Lockhart knows that some things must remain constant in the practice of law: responsibility, competence, integrity, and hard work. These qualities have been the hallmarks of Kirkpatrick & Lockhart since its founding. They are the standards against which the firm measures its future.

# LANDMARK SAVINGS ASSOCIATION
## EMBRACING THE CHANGING REGION FROM ITS DEEP PITTSBURGH ROOTS

Pittsburgh and Landmark have a lot in common. The 1980s have challenged the city and its surrounding region to adapt to changing markets, and Pittsburgh has responded by evolving into a service and high-technology center. Landmark has also embraced change. In 1984 it converted from a mutually owned savings association to a public financial institution owned by stockholders.

Landmark has also become the first savings association in Pittsburgh to offer both consumer and commercial loans. With assets of $1.5 billion and branch offices serving five counties, it is the fifth-largest FSLIC-insured institution in Pennsylvania.

Just like Pittsburgh, Landmark Savings, in its modern form, represents a coming together of many dissimilar origins, peoples, and strengths. It was formed by merging four associations that had already put down deep roots in diverse neighborhoods: Suburban Savings Association, Second Federal Savings and Loan, Friendship Federal, and Mt. Lebanon Federal Savings and Loan.

The oldest family tree belonged to Suburban. It began in 1882 with the chartering of the Twenty-seventh Ward Building and Loan Association. In those days the interest rate paid on savings was one-half of one percent. A loan cost one percent. The driving force behind a building and loan was the idea of neighbor helping neighbor to make the dream of owning a home come true. In time, the Twenty-seventh Ward B&L merged with several others—Columbia Building and Loan No. 3, Crailo B&L of Crafton, Josephine Dime, and Schillers/Glocke B&L—to become Suburban Savings Association.

Second Federal's roots went back to 1925. Originating as the Lang Avenue Building and Loan Association, in Pittsburgh's venerable East End section of Home-

wood, it was initially a part-time operation with desk space in a small real estate office. As one of its early presidents, J. Fred Reinhardt, recalls: "The association was made up of ordinary people, who would get together when one of the members wanted to build a house. We would vote on the request and, if everything was in order, we gave them the money." Long afterward, in his lively nineties, J. Fred Reinhardt would be a director emeritus of Landmark.

In 1934 Lang Avenue B&L became only the second thrift institution in Pittsburgh to receive one of the prized federal charters that commenced a new era of confidence for American savers. Five years later Lang took the name of Second Federal Savings and Loan Association, and began full-time

*J. Richard Eshleman, president and chief executive officer.*

operations in an independent office at North Homewood Avenue and Idlewild Street. The association's rapid growth after World War II made a move to the Golden Triangle essential. In 1954 Second Federal purchased the old State Theater at 335 Fifth Avenue. It became Second Federal's headquarters, and now serves as the headquarters and main office of Landmark.

The forerunners of Friendship Federal also date back to the seedbed era of building and loans: Friendship B&L, founded in 1891; Eagle B&L No. 2, 1895; and New Century, 1903. All conducted business as part-time, independent operations until 1920, when they opened for full-time operation in Pittsburgh's Bloomfield section. In 1939 the three organizations

merged under a federal charter to form Friendship Federal Savings and Loan Association.

Synonymous with Friendship Federal is the Knapp family. J.C. Knapp was secretary of all three forerunners to Friendship Federal. In the 1920s his son C. Elwood Knapp joined the operation. When C. Elwood Knapp became chairman of Friendship Federal in 1971, his son, Richard E. Knapp, became president. Today, Richard E. Knapp is the chairman of Landmark Savings Association.

Friendship Federal eventually moved to Pittsburgh's East Liberty, then branched to Butler, Greensburg, Penn Hills, and Shaler Township.

The origins of Mt. Lebanon Federal were early suburban. Farmland in the South Hills first began being rapidly developed into housing tracts in the 1920s. Tiny villages such as Dormont and Mt. Lebanon mushroomed along the trolley routes that linked downtown Pittsburgh to the southern reaches of Allegheny County. Construction of the Liberty Tunnels and the Liberty Bridge caused land values south of the city to skyrocket; and one of the partici-

*Richard E. Knapp, chairman of the board.*

*Times have changed. Clothing styles, equipment, and even the business of banking have transformed dramatically over the years. But friendly service and personal attention remain at the root of Landmark Savings Association, where "People To People Banking" is more than just a slogan.*

pants in this era of growth was the foresighted Lehigh Building and Loan, which received a Pennsylvania charter in 1922 and established an office on West Liberty Avenue, Dormont.

Like most B&Ls of that period, Lehigh shared space with a number of real estate firms. This was a logical arrangement. A prospective home purchaser would talk with the real estate people, walk across a hall and become a member of the building and loan institution, and borrow the funds to complete the deal.

As the southern suburbs grew, so did Lehigh. It became a member of the Federal Home Loan Bank of Pittsburgh in 1933. Even the Depression did not halt the rapid pace of the South Hills, and in 1937 Lehigh B&L converted from a state to a federal charter as the newly named Mt. Lebanon Federal Savings and Loan. South Hills brothers Wallace and Guy Bland played a significant role in the development of this association.

All these traditions came together in 1982 to form Landmark Savings Association. Since then, Landmark has tailored innovations to meet the changing financial needs of Pittsburgh businesses and of Pittsburgh people. Landmark now offers products and services to meet all the financial needs of young professionals, entrepreneurs, small and mid-size businesses, and families.

But Landmark's basic values hold firm through change, just like Pittsburgh's. The people of Pittsburgh still approach life with a friendly, neighborly attitude, and will always work with dedication and sincerity. That's the way Landmark does business and will always do business. That's the essence of the Landmark slogan, "People To People Banking."

People to People. That's Pittsburgh. And that's Landmark Savings.

# PPG INDUSTRIES, INC.
## HOW TO LIVE TO BE 100—BY NEVER STANDING PAT

Technological wonders melt into the stream of modern life. Yesterday's marvel is absorbed in the pace of a richer today, while tomorrow will certainly want more and better. It requires an act of will not to take for granted the beauty and efficiency of window-walled skyscrapers and the routine miracle of chemicals that purify water and increase food supplies, of car colors that gleam through punishments of sun and spray, and patio doors that won't come crashing down.

A long honor roll of such contributions to the quality of everyday living could be drawn from the restless enterprise of a single Pittsburgh-based company, PPG Industries, Inc.

Now into its second century—an era in which it sees immense opportunities in the "globalization" of rising living standards—PPG today is a diversified corporation of

John Pitcairn's financing and cost controls, enhanced by a genius for diversification and growth, dominated PPG's crucial first three decades.

Firm-jawed pioneer enterpriser John B. Ford saw three plate glass factories fail before his dream survived with PPG. He died in 1903 at age 92.

*Opened in 1883, the first plant at Creighton, Pennsylvania, had become a mass of crowded factories along the Allegheny River by the early 1900s.*

more than \$4.3 billion a year of worldwide sales. It has also provided a textbook case in how to live to be 100—by constantly opting for paths of risk and growth through technological change. Although it is among the world's largest manufacturers of flat glass,

and the U.S. leader in an annual market of four billion square feet, the company long ago stopped making plate glass, the product that gave it birth.

In 1883 plate glass was the latest word. Formed between iron rollers, which inevitably marred

Vincent A. Sarni became board chairman and chief executive officer of PPG Industries, Inc., in 1984. Once head of the firm's chemical operations, he sees extensive business globalization under a "blueprint for the decade."

Forty-story One PPG Place, world headquarters of the corporation, caps a 5.5-acre complex in Pittsburgh's Golden Triangle. Office space totals 1.5 million square feet, with retailing occupying 70,000 square feet in the $200-million development.

and clouded its surface, it had to be laboriously ground and buffed. The steam-driven factories of Europe first mechanized that process, with the result that glass for the proliferating storefronts of America was totally imported.

John Baptiste Ford passionately wanted a piece of that business. Born in 1811 in Danville, Kentucky, a tireless frontier enterpriser, by turns saddle-maker, boat-builder, forger of plows, and operator of a fruit jar factory, he imported workmen and machinery from England and manufactured America's first plate glass in 1867 in a plant in New Albany, Indiana. But insufficiently capitalized, the entrepreneur lost that factory, scraped up funds for two more, and lost those as well. By 1880, penniless at age 69, he borrowed $100 and traveled to Wall Street for one last chance.

Somehow he found backers. By the next year the New York City Plate Glass Company, capitalized at $600,000, was erecting a factory at Creighton, Pennsylvania,

along the Allegheny River some 20 miles northeast of Pittsburgh. The site was blessed with a willing labor force, good access to markets by land and water, and proximity to glass sands and clays as well as natural gas deposits. Ford counted on that cheap, clean fuel to impart a more controllable heat than Europe's coal-gas furnaces could, and thus give his product an edge in strength and durability as well as cost.

The plant began producing on February 20, 1883—the world's first major industrial facility to rely on natural gas. But again Ford's dream had emptied his pockets. This time additional working capi-

tal was brought in by Pittsburgh investors, led by John Pitcairn, a Scots immigrant who had prospered in railroads. Reincorporated as the Pittsburgh Plate Glass Company on August 24, 1883, with Ford's son, Edward, as president, "PPG," as the infant firm quickly became known, soon had a market foothold.

Timing certainly helped. It was a

421

watershed era. America was maturing from a predominantly agricultural to an urban and industrial society. Demand for glass was soaring. The combination of the Fords' enthusiasm for quality production, under the disciplined cost controls imposed by Pitcairn, proved successful. In time the strong-willed partners clashed. Eventually the Fords cashed in their interest—but not before PPG, now with four plants in the Allegheny Valley, had centralized its headquarters in Downtown Pittsburgh in 1895, with a capital that had grown to $10 million.

Behind the trim mustache and goatee of the cost-accountant, John Pitcairn had the soul of an empire builder. To assure the supply of a critical glassmaking ingredient, he built a soda ash plant at Barberton, Ohio, in 1900. It became the root of PPG's chemical operations, today a billion-dollar manufacturer of industrial, agricultural, and specialty products. A half-interest in a paint company (Pitcairn noticed that glass and paint sold at the same hardware stores) led to what is now PPG's Coatings and Resins Group, whose annual sales are now more than $1.5 billion. In 1902 the company made its first international investment, the purchase of a glass plant in Belgium. Further expansion came in 1910 with the construction of a pioneering glass research and development laboratory in Creighton.

When Pitcairn died in 1916, he left a company poised to take advantage of immense growth possibilities—a fact evidently perceived by his patient heirs. Nearly 70 years later, in 1985, they sold the 15.4 percent Pitcairn block of stock back to the company for $529.8 million.

By the time of the auto and construction booms of the 1920s, PPG was already a large producer of sheet glass as well as plate, and a leader in devising continuous-

A "quality circle" of employees inspects an auto windshield at PPG's Greensburg, Pennsylvania, glass fabrication plant near Pittsburgh. This group devised a better way to attach the rearview mirror "button" to the glass.

ribbon production processes as opposed to the old "batch" methods. The need for safety glass in cars was met with the "Creighton process," which produced more economically a laminated sandwich of two glass panes with a plastic interlayer. The company's fast-drying lacquers helped Detroit solve its major bottleneck of that era, the slowness of the paint lines.

The Depression hurt, but even in grim 1933—the corporation's 50th year—shareholders received a dividend, maintaining a string of annual payouts unbroken from 1899 to the present. Meanwhile, PPG introduced fast-drying house paint and the first green-tinted solar glass, a forerunner of today's Sungate "low-emissivity" glass products that control solar and heat flows with a scarcely visible whisper of sophisticated coatings. A new mode of transportation challenged the company's glass

lamination technology; in 1935 PPG outfitted the first successful airliner, the DC-3, and remains today the Free World's largest supplier of aircraft transparencies.

After World War II the firm became the nation's second-largest producer of chlor-alkali "workhorse" chemicals. It developed double-paned insulating glass; lead-free house paints, decades ahead of federal regulation; long-life acrylic enamels for industrial coatings, appliances, and residential siding; and easy-to-apply Pittsburgh Paints with a latex base. In 1952 came a fiber glass operation, which spearheaded developments in textiles, belted tires, and reinforced plastic for boat hulls and auto bodies.

In the closing years of the firm's first century, management teams led by such chief executive officers as David G. Hill, Robinson F. Barker, and L. Stanton Williams completed a virtual revolution in glassmaking. All the old plate and sheet lines were phased out in favor of the "float" process, in which molten glass runs unceasingly onto a mirrorlike bath of molten tin, cooling and solidifying as it streams forward to acquire a sparkling surface finish. Nearly as total was the market sweep won by PPG's technology in electrodeposition, "painting with electricity." More than half of the Free World's autos nowadays are dunked in a charged bath of paint, the ionized particles flocking to every corrosion-prone crevice of the exposed metal.

By 1968, when company sales topped one billion dollars for the first time, it was obvious that Pittsburgh Plate Glass Company had become a misleading name. The official change that year to PPG Industries, Inc., however, represented no breaking of ties to the hometown. Although a full-fledged multinational organization, with 80 plants wholly or jointly owned in a dozen countries, PPG remains one of Pittsburgh's largest sources of paychecks. It employs 4,500 persons in the city and suburbs, including the staffs of four of the company's eight research centers—for glass, coatings and resins, fiber glass, and environmental services. Even the original Creighton plant received a $20-million modernization in the mid-1980s, as a first-class producer of auto windshields.

However, the corporation's most striking investment in the future of Pittsburgh was a new world headquarters completed in 1983 on a 5.5-acre site in the Golden Triangle—PPG Place. Coming in the midst of the city's Renaissance II (of which one critic hailed it as the "brightest star"), it is a crystal splash of office towers, stores, and "people" places. The six-building complex is at once a showcase of modern materials technology and a recollection, in its clusters of spires, of some of the most traditional architectural expressions of the aspiring spirit.

From his office on the 40th story of One PPG Place, with its floor-to-ceiling views of Pittsburgh's rivers and hills, board chairman Vincent A. Sarni speaks of a "blueprint for the decade" under which the company's business is expected to grow significantly by the mid-1990s. The company has goals for continued growth in sales, productivity, and return to shareholder in order to rank among America's 100 top-performing industrial corporations.

To achieve this goal PPG knows it must move at a more rapid pace than the U.S. economy. This undoubtedly implies the addition of at least one new major business. For all their dynamism, glass, paint, and chemicals—in America at least—have to be viewed as low-growth, mature operations. Hence PPG is establishing new directions, geographically and technologically.

The company has entered a

An array of light bulbs simulates the effect of the sun's heat on a panel of float glass at PPG's glass research center at suburban Harmarville, near Pittsburgh.

long-term agreement with the Research Institute of Scripps Clinic, in La Jolla, California, to pursue basic studies in biotechnology. PPG expects that by the year 2000 it will have poured $120 million into this endeavor, which could benefit both the firm and the world's food supply. Living cells may perhaps be employed as microscopic factories to make chemicals and pest-fighting, crop-enhancing agricultural products.

No less exciting is "globalization," a view of the earth as a boundless marketplace, most effectively served by an array of wholly owned or partnership factories and marketing facilities in many countries. To Sarni this means not only investing in the economies but also becoming a

part of the diverse cultures where PPG operates. "We're not just asking ourselves where we can ship things," he says. Thus, some of the firm's recent advances in chemicals production have flowed from joint research with Japanese and Italian companies, and PPG looks forward to opening, in 1987, its first joint venture in float glass manufacturing in the People's Republic of China.

America's trade problem—solved by yesterday's Fords and Pitcairns with ingenuity and courage—calls for similar market-opening answers today, in Sarni's view. He feels that the United States must press other countries to lower protectionist barriers rather than to raise its own.

"Other countries need to develop their standard of living and quality of life," states the chairman of PPG Industries, Inc. "The only way to do that is by building an industrial base. That's how we did it!"

# GATEWAY CENTER
## MODERN PITTSBURGH BEGINS WITH GATEWAY CENTER

In the early 1950s The Equitable Life Assurance Society of the United States invested the first millions of what was to become a total of $150 million in the renaissance of dingy, desolate Pittsburgh Point, where the Allegheny and Monongahela rivers come together to form the Ohio—and suddenly 20 years of plans and promises took on the ring of reality.

Those were exciting days, and Arthur Van Buskirk, the Allegheny Conference's anchorman for the post-World War II transformation of the Smoky City, remembers them well. "When it actually began to happen," he recalls, "when people saw it start, they felt their city was finally about to be reborn, and they were right."

In the largest urban-renewal project ever undertaken without the use of public funds, Equitable Life financing transformed that forbidding industrial slum into today's resounding commercial and aesthetic success. The six handsome office towers initially financed, owned, and operated by the company, and the lush, park-like settings in which they were placed, gave Pittsburgh a beautiful, vibrant new heart in which more than 10,000 people work today.

Recently, Equitable completed a $25-million improvement program at Gateway Center, which saw dramatic atriums created, lighting upgraded, plazas redone, and building exteriors cleaned. Significant value has been added to the interiors of the buildings for tenants in the form of life safety improvements, a new independent steam-generation plant, a computerized energy-management system that handles four Gateway Center buildings, telecommunications, and other shared tenant services. The 750-car Gateway Center garage has been completely rebuilt, another phase of the improvement program. All of this is the giant financial services company's way of making a good thing even better.

"If you could pick the ideal location for new offices in this city, we think it would still be Gateway Center hands down," says Thomas McKeown, the center's general manager under Equitable Real Estate Investment Management, Inc., the insurance firm's subsidiary that manages more than $23 billion in assets for pension clients, offshore investors, and its parent corporation.

Equitable's original decision to invest in the future of downtown Pittsburgh was largely predicated on the unique partnership of state, local, and private interests in the huge project. Pennsylvania had committed to develop the 36-acre Point State Park, while the new Urban Redevelopment Authority was ready to condemn 23 adjacent acres—and 93 dilapidated buildings. Meanwhile, local firms were signing commitments for office space on the strength of architects' renderings.

One, Two, and Three Gateway Center added one million square feet of office space to the market, resulting in a temporarily overbuilt situation. Equitable, contending

*The six handsome office towers of Gateway Center (shown are One, Two, and Three) stand amid lush, park-like settings, giving Pittsburgh a vibrant new heart in which more than 10,000 people work today.*

with several years of sluggish market conditions, sold off parcels for the Bell Telephone and State Office buildings. But the firm stuck by its guns and brought Gateway Center to fruition through its financing of the Hilton Hotel and subsequent completion of Equitable Plaza with its multilevel underground garage, Gateway Towers, Four Gateway Center, Five Gateway Center (owned by the United Steelworkers of America), and Six Gateway (owned by Westinghouse Electric Corporation).

Gateway Center offers four parking garages, numerous restaurants within three blocks, matchless suburban access via bridges and a subway station, enclosed walkways between buildings, great flexibility of floor plans, and professional on-site management by Equitable Real Estate experts.

# EQUITABLE GROUP & HEALTH INSURANCE COMPANY
## HELPING EMPLOYERS AND EMPLOYEES TO BETTER PLAN BENEFITS

In 1911 a new type of low-cost life insurance came into being to protect workers' families under a single master contract: group insurance. The Equitable Life Assurance Society of the United States was its creator. A Pittsburgh agent wrote one of the first policies at a major firm. Thus, the city of Pittsburgh could be considered one of the pioneers in insurance, and it still is filling a major role in the development of new and innovative products.

The Equitable continued to pioneer extensions of the risk-spreading principle: the first group accident and sickness insurance in 1921; and later, hospital expense, surgical benefits, and group annuities. By the 1980s the organization was serving 1,500 large group clients, with an annual premium or premium equivalent income of four billion dollars.

This vast business is now conducted by Equitable Group & Health Insurance Company, an unincorporated division of the parent firm currently deepening its commitment to the mid-size and large employer market of 100 or more employees.

"We don't think the solution is prepackaged benefits, an off-the-shelf plan that doesn't really serve particular client needs," says Francis J. McGrath, Jr., regional vice-president for Equitable Group & Health's large Pittsburgh-based operations. "A group representative works with clients or prospects to design plans with options that boost productivity and morale—and also help contain costs and risks."

As a major headquarters city, Pittsburgh has been a key location for marketing, notes McGrath. It houses one of the firm's six Strategic Business Unit operations serving clients in group life, disability, and medical benefits throughout the East. There are also three benefit-paying offices, a Pre-Admission Review operation

in Greentree, and a medical and disability case-management office. A service center in Moon Township is involved in underwriting risks, issuing sales proposals, and writing contracts; and the marketing office in Three Gateway Center works with agents, brokers, and consultants to maintain and expand the client base. In total, Equitable Group & Health employs 700 people in the Pittsburgh area.

Major clients include a number of the city's most prestigious enterprises, "and some have had group coverage with us for more than 70 years," says McGrath. However, it is the most recent years, the late 1970s and early 1980s, that have caused deepest concern about health-cost escalation. This is a field in which The Equitable has again taken the lead.

Its health care cost-management program in Pittsburgh has begun putting reins on costs through pre-admission review of hospital stays, second opinions on surgery, and medical and dental case-management. Guiding employees to become more knowledgeable consumers of health care and to adopt healthier life-styles are also inherent in the overall effort.

"The latest development," says

The Pittsburgh executive staff of Equitable Group & Health Insurance Company (from left to right, on the left): Francis J. McGrath, Jr., regional vice-president; J. Robert Mitchell, regional financial officer; Michael P. Brady, regional marketing officer; Ray J. Colleran, regional account officer; and J. Garvey Jones, group benefits manager. On the right (left to right, front row): Patricia A. Burke, director, PAR Services; and James D. Bachman, regional benefits officer; and (left to right, back row): Robert J. Balash, divisional group manager; and Steven M. Noe, manager, client services.

McGrath, "is the joint venturing with Health Corporation of America forming a new Company, EQUICOR, an Equitable HCA Corporation. This is enabling us to move quickly into managed care by working with local providers of medical care here in Pittsburgh, the surrounding communities, and throughout the country to establish preferred provider organizations (PPOs) as well as health maintenance organizations (HMOs). It is vital to provide, not only traditional indemnity products, but also managed health care options that will be beneficial to the communities."

# THE HARRIS/DUDDY AGENCY
## CHANGING PITTSBURGH SCENE BRINGS INSURANCE OPPORTUNITIES

The Harris/Duddy Agency is the bearer of an insurance tradition that goes back more than 100 years, but is now perhaps into its most exciting days.

Chartered in Pennsylvania in 1859, The Equitable Life Assurance Society wrote its first Pittsburgh business in 1862, and won market domination after establishment of the famous Woods Agency in 1880. Led by Edward A. Woods—who had left school at age 15 to sell insurance—the Pittsburgh firm was the industry's leading sales organization for many years, the pioneer of group life, and the home base (in 1926) of the leading female life underwriter in the world, Bertha Strauss, who had started as a secretary.

In time The Equitable had four agencies in Pittsburgh, which were consolidated in 1981 in the present Harris/Duddy Agency in Four Gateway Center. It is a large organization—150 agents and 50 staff personnel—with a market area of five states. All are employees of The Equitable; however, the office operates as a partnership, under veteran Chartered Life Underwriters Robert C. Harris and Thomas J. Duddy, Jr.

"Pittsburgh is an outstanding town for the insurance business," says Duddy, noting both the strong sense of ethnic family responsibility and the awareness of fringe benefits in a corporate center. "People understand the 'hidden paycheck'," he says. One result is that counseling of business insurance, deferred compensation, and similar programs—particularly at middle- and high-management levels—has become a major opportunity for knowledgeable agents, especially as their product lines have grown far beyond traditional life and health insurance limits.

"Our people are 'registered reps,' like stockbrokers," states Duddy. "But many investors never see a stockbroker's face. Most business is over the phone. The insurance agent is still somebody who's close to the family situation."

Pittsburgh's economic transition, marked by spin-offs of new companies and other forces of change, have brought the Harris/Duddy Agency a strong growth impulse from the start. A new business generally has entrepreneurial lives to insure, if only for the creditors' sake. "The importance of key people, especially in fledgling companies, is extremely high," explains Harris.

The agency's growth rate has been spurred in part by four major tax law changes since 1976 and by increasing awareness. Harris calls these coverages, which include tax-sheltered accounts and incentive accounts, "the power of money accumulating."

"Anybody who hasn't talked to a good insurance agent in a few years doesn't realize that he or she has a briefcase full of new concepts," advises Harris. Twenty years ago a young agent faced a lot of rejection. Now there's a buying public out there that's never been more receptive."

---

*The management team of The Harris-Duddy Agency. In the back row (left to right) are district managers Robert J. Spagiare, Joseph E. Kovacic, Michael A. Paul, Philip J. Schulte, Antonio Bolea, and Thomas E. Hafner. Center row (from left) are district managers Robert J. DeAngelo, Thomas G. Gillingham, and Steve J. Linkowski. The two agency managers, Thomas J. Duddy, Jr., CLU, and Robert C. Harris, CLU, are seated in front.*

# KIDDER, PEABODY & CO., INC.
## LATE START BUT FAST GROWTH IN PITTSBURGH

Thomas C. Ryan remembers with a smile, "We moved into a building loft, "un-rehabbed," on Wood Street near the Monongahela River. On the ground floor was a political headquarters—a great harbinger of success!"

Such was the humble entry into Pittsburgh of one of the nation's most prestigious investment banking institutions. It was May 1980, and Kidder, Peabody & Co., Inc., was 115 years old. "Ralph DeNunzio told me they had wanted to come here for years," says Ryan, "but had never found the right people."

DeNunzio is president of Kidder, Peabody, a Wall Street leader that has become a rarity in the financial world. While large and diversified (mid-1980s totals nine billion dollars in assets, 5,700 employees, 65 U.S. offices, six overseas), it remains privately held and free of mergers, the concern of some 460 stockholding executives fully occupied in the day-to-day business. That group now includes Ryan and several Pittsburgh vice-presidents: Charles W. Chewning, Jr., Richard A. Hay, and J. Philip Russell.

This team, plus Boyd S. Murray and Robert C. Wetmore, had seen long service with the former Moore, Leonard & Lynch, Inc., a 102-year-old regional brokerage that merged in 1978 with a na-

tional "wire house," which in turn was acquired the year after, bringing disenchantment. "We didn't want to be in a branch of a branch," explains Ryan, then a 23-year veteran and department head. He arranged a meeting with DeNunzio, a friend from several financing syndications over the years, and Kidder, Peabody had found its Pittsburgh vehicle.

The connection flourished. From three employees that first day, the staff has increased to 65. The loft has long since been left behind for spacious quarters in the Golden Triangle's tallest building, 600 Grant Street. All four of Kidder, Peabody's core businesses are pursued there—investment banking, brokerage, market making, and tax-exempt financing—with access to the firm's famed research staffs in New York and, increasingly, London and Tokyo, for the era of burgeoning international investments by multinational corporations.

Determined from its first day to be "more than just a sales office" the organization immediately commenced making markets in municipal securities (a product in which it holds one of the top places in the nation in sales to individual investors). Later the Pittsburgh office managed bond underwritings up to $50 million for Carnegie-Mellon

University, local authorities, and hospitals.

Determined to continue its policy of penetrating the tri-state area, Kidder Pittsburgh opened a separate office in Wheeling, West Virginia, on January 1, 1986. This office, headed by Robert C. Hazlett, Jr., a former Wheeling banker, is expected to establish a growth pattern similar to its big brother in Pittsburgh.

From Kidder, Peabody's perspective, Pittsburgh is a market not in decline but in a transition, posing enormous opportunity for financial services. The city's role as a medical center alone implies portfolio attention to physicians and corporate practices, financing of health care facilities, and the spinoff of medically related companies from hospital and university think tanks.

"We look for a period of growth comparable to what Pittsburgh experienced at the beginning of this century, but in different directions," says Ryan. "It's a time to set up new companies here. Just the old principle again: buy low and sell high."

*Kidder, Pittsburgh senior management meets with resident officer Thomas C. Ryan to review Kidder research.*

# MELLON BANK
## HELPING PITTSBURGH GROW FOR MORE THAN A CENTURY

Since 1869 Mellon Bank has been instrumental in financing Pittsburgh's commercial and industrial growth. The bank has been closely connected with the conception or development of Pittsburgh's major financial and industrial corporations. In a very real sense, American economic history is the history of Mellon Bank.

The founder, Thomas Mellon, was an attorney and judge of the Court of Common Pleas of Allegheny County. Mellon retired from law at age 56 to open the private bank of T. Mellon & Sons. He had gained banking experience through board memberships and by aiding two sons in forming The East End Bank.

Mellon's bank occupied a two-story brick building. While the structure was modest, the firm's lending policy was ambitious. In 1871 the judge lent $10,000 to Henry Clay Frick, who was interested in building coke ovens for a growing Pittsburgh steel industry. A long-standing Mellon-Frick relationship developed. The rapid increase of business by 1871 required the firm to move to new quarters at 514 Smithfield Street. By 1874 deposits were nearly $600,000.

Mellon gave his son Andrew a one-fifth interest in the firm. When the judge retired in 1882, Andrew became sole proprietor. In 1887 Richard B. Mellon, Thomas' youngest son, joined Andrew as an equal partner. R.B. had gained banking experience in North Dakota.

Displaying the optimism shown in the Frick loan and reinforced by its ability to weather the nation's financial panic of 1873, T. Mellon & Sons continued to facilitate capital growth for Pittsburgh industry. In 1889 the Mellons financed the Pittsburgh Reduction Company's aluminum production venture. Pittsburgh Reduction is known today as ALCOA.

Andrew Mellon and Henry Frick joined a venture that formed the

*Thomas Mellon founded Mellon Bank after retiring as an attorney and judge of the Court of Common Pleas of Allegheny County. Courtesy, Mellon Bank Historical Resource Center*

Union Transfer and Trust Company, an organization to specialize in corporate securities transfers. Mellon was elected president of the new entity. The securities business was disappointing; the firm was saved from dissolution through an expansion of services into the

*R.B. Mellon (center, seated), son of the founder and president of the bank at the time of this 1922 photo, is flanked by W.S. Mitchell (left) and A.C. Knox (right), vice-presidents. Standing (left to right) are B.W. Lewis, cashier; A.W. McEldowney, vice-president; E.M. Foster, assistant cashier; and H.S. Zimmerman, cashier. Courtesy, Mellon Bank Historical Resource Center*

general trust business. The institution's name was changed in 1892 to the Union Trust Company of Pittsburgh. After directing Union Trust's entry into commercial banking in 1894, Andrew Mellon withdrew from its daily operations.

An era of sustained growth and innovative commercial lending began in 1895. Numerous businesses significant in the nation's modern industrial development were financed over a 20-year pe-

riod: the Carborundum Company, Crucible Steel, Gulf Oil, and the Koppers Company. Other Mellon-funded concerns included Union Steel, Standard Steel Car, and McClintic-Marshall Construction.

T. Mellon & Sons' evolution mirrored Pittsburgh's industrial vigor. In 1902 the bank incorporated and joined the national banking system. Mellon National Bank was chartered; the firm assumed T. Mellon & Sons' assets and lia-

*The bank had occupied assorted locations until, in the 1920s, an impressive structure was erected at 514 Smithfield to consolidate operations. The lobby is shown here. Courtesy, Mellon Bank Historical Resource Center*

bilities. In a further consolidation of Mellon interests, Union Trust acquired the shares of Mellon National. Operations were expanded in 1903 with the acquisition of Pittsburgh National Bank of Commerce and the establishment of a foreign bureau to promote international operations of Pittsburgh businesses.

Andrew Mellon served three U.S. Presidents as Secretary of the Treasury and later served as Ambassador to Great Britain. R.B. Mellon managed the family's interests. The 1920s were marked by important signs of Mellon's growth. Deposits reached $100 million. The bank constructed an impressive structure at 514 Smithfield Street to replace the assorted buildings into which Mellon operations had spread. The Mellbank Corporation, a bank holding company, was organized. Frank Denton, who A.W. had met in Washington,

was sent to Pittsburgh to administer Mellbank.

R.B. Mellon died in 1933; his son, Richard King, succeeded him. In the economically troubled 1930s Mellon acted to shore up the nation's finances. Mellon Indemnity Corporation was organized to issue bonds on Mellbank's member banks. Mellon Securities Corporation was established to underwrite and distribute general market stocks and bonds—the Union Transfer and Trust spirit was alive.

In 1946 Mellon National Bank and Union Trust merged to form the Mellon National Bank and Trust Company. R.K. Mellon served as chairman, Denton as chief executive officer. In 1955 Mellon pioneered as an international leader in banking applications of computers and telecommunications. The bank continued expanding its horizons while focusing on a commitment to support Pittsburgh's growth. The Melbank Regional Clearing House, a check-clearing service, was established for Mellon's correspondents.

Continued growth led the firm in

1972 to establish Mellon National Corporation, a one-bank holding company. Mellon National Bank and Trust Company became Mellon Bank. Pennsylvania's legislature voted in 1982 to allow statewide banking, and in 1983 Mellon merged with the Girard Company. Philadelphia-based Girard was founded in 1835 and in 1981 had acquired Delaware's Farmers Bank, an early U.S. financial institution. Both of these institutions have long and proud histories of their own.

Mellon employs more than 14,000 people in 500-plus locations worldwide. Major subsidiaries include Mellon Bank (Central), Mellon Bank (Delaware), Mellon Bank (East), Mellon Bank International, Mellon Bank, Mellon Bank (North), and Mellon Financial Services Corporation. Mellon has domestic offices in no fewer than 12 states and foreign locations in 16 countries. Since 1869 Mellon's banking facilities have consistently symbolized optimistic support for the Pittsburgh's industry and people. T. Mellon & Sons' original building at 145 Smithfield Street could today fit in the lobby of One Mellon Bank Center, Mellon Bank's newest headquarters building and a familiar landmark on Pittsburgh's skyline.

*The Union Trust Building. Courtesy, Mellon Bank Historical Resource Center*

# ALCOA
## PROVIDER OF MATERIALS FOR A NEW CENTURY

Alcoa is a Pittsburgh company born in invention and nurtured in risk-taking. In 1886 young Charles Martin Hall economically unlocked aluminum, one of earth's most abundant metals, yet paradoxically held in one of nature's tightest chemical bonds. Hall's liberating invention led to the birth of the aluminum industry with the founding, in 1888, of Alcoa.

Since then the company has grown into a worldwide enterprise that continues to nourish the spirit and processes of innovation. Few materials producers even closely approach Alcoa's investments in research and development and creative marketing.

Heeding the omens of global overcapacity in metal production, Alcoa's management, under chairman Charles W. Parry and president C. Fred Fetterolf, has determined that future profits will have to

*An inspector checks an aluminum skin quality sheet at Alcoa's Davenport, Iowa, Works.*

*Advanced ceramic parts, such as these housings for semiconductor chips used in computers, will be made by Alcoa.*

come from higher value-added, fabricated products of aluminum— as well as ceramics, advanced composites, new alloys, and chemicals that have made the aluminum company more accurately a materials company.

Alcoa Laboratories stands among the world's leading light metals and advanced materials research organizations, set in the midst of 2,300 acres of rolling countryside in Upper Burrell, Westmoreland County, approximately 20 miles from the Golden Triangle. The facility employs 1,200 scientists, technicians, and support people.

Alcoa is pursuing new directions as well through research into materials, joint ventures, and carefully selected acquisitions—for example, in production of fiber-optic telecommunications cable. A part-

nership with Metal Box America, Inc., will produce plastic packaging that allows perishable foods to be stored for extended periods without refrigeration. "Aluminum-intensive" autos for the 1990s are the motivating force in another international undertaking.

Thus, already an enterprise of more than five billion dollars in an-

nual sales and 40,000 employees, Alcoa foresees a second century at least as challenging as its first.

Despite its natural abundance, aluminum, as a usable metal, was a mid-1800s exotic: $545 a pound! True, costs were gradually reduced—the 100-ounce aluminum cap placed atop the Washington Monument in 1884 was a bargain at $225—but most usage was still restricted to expensive novelties.

That was the challenge that captivated Charles Martin Hall even as a chemistry student. Upon graduation he continued experimenting in a woodshed laboratory behind his parents' home in Oberlin, Ohio. On February 23, 1886, Hall ran an electrical current from a battery into a carbon crucible containing a bath of the molten mineral, cryolite. Alumina, a nonmetallic oxide, had been dissolved in the cryolite; and Hall's process of electrolysis formed small, silvery globules of nearly pure metal.

To protect his invention and prove his discovery "commercial" in a plant-size test, Hall, who was only 22, needed backers. His search led to an important meeting in Pittsburgh with Alfred E. Hunt. Captain Hunt was a 33-year-old metallurgist and an experienced steel works manager. He quickly grasped the potential of Hall's achievement.

Hunt gathered a small group of Pittsburgh businessmen—George Clapp, Robert Scott, Horace Lash, Millard Hunsiker, and Winfield Sample—and formed a capital pool of $20,000. On July 31, 1888, they incorporated the Pittsburgh Reduction Company to develop the Hall process in a little factory on Smallman Street in the city's Strip District. The operation drew its electricity from a 125-horsepower engine with two dynamos.

Hall and the company's first employee, another recent graduate named Arthur Vining Davis (who would eventually become an Alcoa board chairman and live into his

nineties), worked 12-hour shifts. By Thanksgiving they had poured their first commercial-grade aluminum. At first they averaged 30 to 50 pounds of daily production, locking up any unsold metal overnight in the company safe. Rapid improvements in technique lifted the output to nearly 50,000 pounds in 1889. By 1900—long after the Smallman Street facility had been outgrown—annual production would be seven million pounds.

Charles Martin Hall, who, at age 22, discovered the electrolytic process that forged the aluminum industry.

New and larger plants were sited near abundant hydroelectricity, and in 1907 the firm was reincorporated as Aluminum Company of America. Credit for developing the metal as a worldwide commodity clearly must go to Hall's backers and generations of successors. The shy inventor himself had little commercial flair. He remained a vice-president and one-third stockholder until his death in 1914 at the age of 51.

Alcoa added mining and shipping interests over the years to ensure its raw materials supply and finished and semifinished goods production. The company constantly created and encouraged new uses for the light metal in transportation, construction, energy, and packaging markets. Dur-

The Alcoa Building from Mellon Square Park, Pittsburgh.

ing World War II the company built and operated more than 20 plants for the U.S. government, which sold all but one of them to competitors after the war. Expanding internationally, Alcoa has concentrated development in Australia and Brazil.

On its home grounds Alcoa has long played an important role in Pittsburgh's educational, cultural, and health and welfare organizations—in part through grants from Alcoa Foundation, which was established in 1952 and is now the largest permanently funded corporate foundation in the United States.

Alcoa participated famously in Pittsburgh's downtown renaissance of the 1950s. It erected its 31-story headquarters at Sixth Street and William Penn Way not only as a statement of faith in the city, but also as an expression of the age of aluminum in architecture. Curtain wall sheathing, reversible windows, and a daring use of materials throughout have combined to keep the corporate command post refreshingly up to date.

From the Alcoa Building on a clear day, company observers assert, you can see the next century.

# ALLEGHENY LUDLUM CORPORATION
## DEDICATED TO QUALITY SPECIALTY STEEL

Allegheny Ludlum Corporation in its modern form is a private corporation that came into being as recently as December 26, 1980. However, it is a very old new company. As a pioneer in specialty steel the firm is responsible for the great achievement of commercializing stainless steel on a low-cost basis in the United States; and long before that its ancestral furnaces took part in making America free and saving the Union.

Today's Allegheny Ludlum is one of the world's largest manufacturers of flat-rolled specialty steel, the producer of more than 180 grades for a vast range of consumer, industrial, and defense applications. While the steel business overall has declined, specialty steel needs continue to grow. The leading-edge participants simply have never permitted themselves to fall into technological sloth or obsolescence.

By spending a higher percent-

R.P. Simmons, chief executive officer at the AOD Furnace.

age of its funds on research and development than the industry norm, Allegheny Ludlum has turned a profit every year since going private. This has meant continual, salutary change—in an enterprise that pays closest attention to product quality, productivity, market development, and capital improvements. During the 1960s about 10,000 employees produced average annual sales of $280 million. In the mid-1980s those figures improved to 5,500 employees and sales over $740 million, a productivity leap of nearly 400 percent. Today's steadier employment base remains one of the largest in the Pittsburgh metropolitan area. It has particular importance for the Allegheny-Kiski Valley, which receives infusions of nearly $200 million in payroll and taxes.

While it's not a company that looks back, Allegheny Ludlum could trace half its ancestry to a business formed in 1854 to operate a furnace—which was even then a century old—in Pompton, New Jersey, near Paterson. The apparatus had formerly been utilized by Pompton Furnace, an enterprise known to have produced iron in 1750. It supplied cannonballs to the Continentals during the Revolutionary War. The great

chain that George Washington ordered stretched across the Hudson to blockade the British fleet was made in Pompton's foundry: four-foot links of iron six inches thick. (A "cousin" operation, Troy Iron Works, made the plate of the *Monitor,* the "cheese box on a raft" that fought the *Merrimac* in history's first battle of ironclads in the Civil War.)

In 1854 James Horner acquired Pompton Furnace to make file steel and handmade files. James Ludlum joined the firm as a salesman; and in 1864 it became Horner & Ludlum, a partnership, with Pompton Tool Steel added to the product line. Ludlum took over in 1875 as president of the renamed Pompton Steel and Iron Company, then making steel springs for railroad cars, which became the Ludlum Steel and Spring Company in 1898. Nine years later the Corning family interests of New York State took control of the firm's finances during a troubled period in business. They moved the operation from its ancient site in north Jersey to a new plant at Watervliet, New York, not far from Albany. It remained headquartered there until a 1938 merger with Allegheny Steel Company brought this survivor of a great colonial ironworking tradition into Pittsburgh regional history.

The oldest limb of the organization's Allegheny branch was the West Leechburg Steel and Tin Plate Company, established in 1897. Captain Alfred Hicks (he had won his bars in the Civil War) was president of the firm, and H.E. Sheldon was a director. In 1900 Sheldon and Hicks withdrew from the West Leechburg firm and organized a rival, the Allegheny Steel and Iron Company. The two men chose a site about 10 miles downstream—that is, west on the Kiskiminetas and south on the Allegheny—at Brackenridge for their first small plant, which consisted of one open-hearth furnace, a bar

The management team consists of (seated) R.P. Bozone, president; R.P. Simmons, chief executive officer; and (standing) R.K. Pitler, senior vice-president and technical director; and R.C. O'Sullivan, senior vice-president and chief financial officer.

The 120-ton-capacity argon oxygen decarburization furnace, Brackenridge.

The continuous caster at Brackenridge.

The pilot process of stainless steel strip cast directly from molten metal, Research Center, Natrona Heights.

Above: The new state-of-the-art annealing and pickling facility, West Leechburg.

Right: Optical metallography at Research Center in Natrona Heights.

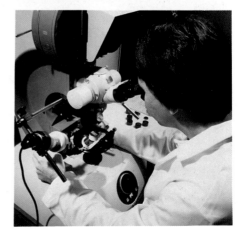

mill, and four sheet mills. The modern Allegheny Ludlum still operates its world-class facilities on that excellent river valley tract.

In May 1905 Allegheny Steel Company was formed to succeed Allegheny Steel and Iron, with a capital of $300,000. The new firm made itself a pioneer in the "high technology" of its day. Technology has never been alien to the thinking of the most progressive metals manufacturers, and specialty steels—particularly the U.S. edge in technology, which is granted by virtually all the world competitors—has been the single argument for fair trade that has been pressed most emphatically by such leaders as Allegheny Ludlum chief executive officer Richard P. Simmons. The entire industry was born of the effort to improve on "basic" steel, not to mention the brittle iron of the 1700s, by alloying the metal with rarer ingredients such as chromium and nickel. These additives improved its resistance to wear and corrosion—vital for a host of applications in chemical, transportation, utility, and food-manufacturing processes— as well as to impart a glitter to the eyes of auto buyers and housewives.

In 1922 Allegheny Steel pioneered, with General Electric, in the first melt of low carbon, 12-percent chromium stainless, called Ascoloy. Later the two companies established "18-8" steel—representing those percentages of chromium and nickel in the alloy—

as "Super Ascoloy," the standard for the industry. "Allegheny Metal" was originated for the manufacture of stainless products in the home, such as flatware. Silicon iron alloys with unusual electrical applications and magnetic alloys such as "Mumetal" were developed as early as 1902 and 1903, but found their true markets in the building and industrial booms of the 1920s. Tool steels, valve steels, and superalloys followed as natural outgrowths of intense experimentation.

The Depression in the 1930s brought a fearful winnowing to the Pittsburgh steelwork district. Orders plunged far below the survival level for many of the firms. On August 1, 1936, Allegheny Steel Company merged with its old rival, the West Leechburg Steel Company; two years later, on August 10, 1938, Allegheny Steel and Ludlum Steel, the New York descendant of Pompton Furnace, joined to form the Allegheny Ludlum Steel Corporation.

At the time of the merger, Ludlum had assets of approximately $11 million, Allegheny about $20 million. The surviving organization was Allegheny Steel, based in Pittsburgh, which was renamed Allegheny Ludlum Steel Corporation. The nomenclature would soon be-

Richard P. Simmons, chief executive officer of Allegheny Ludlum Steel Corporation, at the firm's AOD (argon oxygen decarburization) vessel in Brackenridge.

Complete truck (top) and passenger car (bottom) exhaust systems made from stainless steel ensures corrosion resistance, durability, and gasoline efficiency.

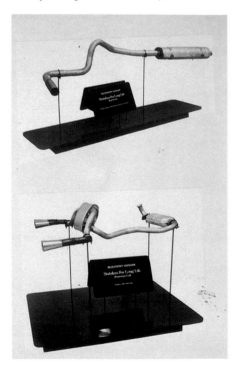

come synonymous with leadership in the technology, manufacturing, and marketing of specialty steels.

During World War I, pre-merger by at least 20 years, both firms had each been heavily engaged in production of military materials. In World War II the entire output of Allegheny Ludlum Steel went to the war effort.

The company's products—and, even more so, its ceaseless development of new products—paved the way for revolutionary advances in the automotive and aviation industries. In a pleasant neighborhood of Natrona Heights, a suburb overlooking the Allegheny River a mile or two from the great Brackenridge steel plant, Allegheny Ludlum established the first, and still one of the largest, research center in the specialty steel industry. Its commitment to research and development has never waned; and preeminence in metals research continues to be a high-technology asset of the Pittsburgh region.

Allegheny Ludlum began diversifying in the 1950s, and by the early 1970s the firm was bidding for a new image as Allegheny Ludlum Industries; yet the steel division always came through as the bulwark of sales and profits. In 1980 the parent organization, now Allegheny International, Inc., sold the

specialty steel group to a nucleus of managers and outside investors for $223 million. Once more the proud name of Allegheny Ludlum Steel Corporation was retrieved, this time by a privately held, entrepreneurial company.

Today's sophisticated stainless steels and high-temperature alloys serve vastly upgraded markets. The "jewelry shop" stainless of the 1920s, for cutlery, surgical instruments, and luxury utensils, and the demonstration metal of the 1930s—an all-stainless auto, even an all-stainless airplane (built and test-flown for 1,000 hours)—have all been forerunners of advanced materials critically needed in industry, the home, automobiles, defense, aviation, and space. The specialty steel industry continues to be a frontier of technical innovation.

In 1986 Allegheny Ludlum repurchased the last stock held by its former parent firm and opened new executive offices at Six PPG Place. It is determined to maintain America's world leadership in specialty steel manufacture.

# DELOITTE HASKINS & SELLS
## SERVING NEW INDUSTRIAL GENERATIONS

Pittsburgh was irresistible at the turn of the century for a recent phenomenon—nationwide accounting firms. Ambitious to be where the industrial action was, Haskins & Sells established an office—its sixth—in the former Farmers Bank Building, at Fifth Avenue and Wood Street. The year was 1903, and the organization offered what are recognized today as basic accounting and auditing services.

Not until the 1930s, with passage of the Securities Act and the Securities Exchange Act, did the services of professional accountants assume so pervasive an economic role. The new laws opened an epoch of federal regulation of business, requiring standards of accounting and financial disclosure as well as independent audits of all corporations offering securities to the public. It was during that decade that Haskins & Sells began serving Rockwell International, PPG Industries, H.H. Robertson

Deloitte Haskins & Sells' offices in One PPG Place, and its collection of regional art displayed there, reflect the firm's commitment to western Pennsylvania and to the area's cultural life.

*Client service teams, comprising professionals with audit, tax, and consulting skills, meet to discuss ways to serve clients effectively. They also work together to plan a comprehensive service plan for their clients.*

Company, and Duquesne Light—a client list since augmented by Mobay Corporation, National Intergroup, L.B. Foster, Carnegie-Mellon University, and many others.

The Pittsburgh office needed more space in 1952 and became one of the early tenants of Gateway Center. That same year the British firm of Deloitte, Plender, Griffiths & Company merged its United States offices with those of Haskins & Sells. Long a close working relationship, the union became official in 1977 with worldwide adoption of the Deloitte Haskins & Sells name.

An important extension of the firm's services in Pittsburgh occurred in the early 1980s with the formation of two additional groups: emerging business services and management consulting. The emerging business group, which views the entrepreneur as a key player in the economy, has grown rapidly by tailoring services to varied needs of developing companies. The consultants in Pittsburgh specialize in information systems: helping a client design a data-processing or telecommunications network, for example, or in improving computer security.

Traditional services also are

constantly adapting. For example, the tax group helps multinational clients plan and evaluate the tax consequences of moving employees to foreign countries; auditors now make extensive use of microcomputers and progressive audit techniques.

With expansion demanding larger quarters, the firm moved to PPG Place in 1984, where its collection of regional art—paintings, photographs, sculpture, textiles, and ceramics—reflects a commitment to the region's cultural life. The firm also maintains an office in McKeesport, to meet the needs of governmental and commercial clients there.

Deloitte Haskins & Sells' most recent Pittsburgh expansion makes a forward-looking commitment as well. Opened in 1985 amid the Oakland ambience of university-based research and entrepreneurial opportunity, the firm's high-technology office is especially set up to serve an entire new generation of industries.

# CONSOLIDATED NATURAL GAS COMPANY
## FROM WELLHEAD TO BURNER TIP

Consolidated Natural Gas Company is Pittsburgh's seventh-largest corporation in terms of revenues, more than $3 billion a year by the mid-1980s. It is a holding company whose subsidiaries operate in every phase of the natural gas business. Consolidated wholly owns five distribution companies, two exploration and production operations, and an interstate transmission company that form one of the nation's major integrated gas systems.

At every level—from wellhead to burner tip—Consolidated is a significant factor in the natural gas industry.

As a distributor, it's among the four largest gas utilities in the nation. It serves more than 1.5 million customers in the tri-state region. Most know Consolidated best, in fact, by the names of its local distributors. The Peoples Natural Gas Company, for example, has provided energy to Pittsburgh and western Pennsylvania for more than 100 years. Three Ohio distributors—The East Ohio Gas Company, Cleveland; West

Consolidated Natural Gas Company is one of the largest gas and oil producers in the country, with production properties throughout the United States and in Canada. Photo by Gary Gladstone

Consolidated drilled the largest gas well in the history of the Gulf of Mexico from this platform about 90 miles off the Louisiana coast. Photo by Bill Farrell

Ohio Gas Company, Lima; and The River Gas Company, Marietta—and their West Virginia counterpart, Hope Gas, Inc., of Clarksburg, all have similar standing in their states' economic and energy development.

Consolidated Gas Transmission Corporation, a large interstate pipeline, furnishes most of the gas sold by the five distributors and also by nonaffiliated utilities across New York State. Recently its role has been growing. It now supplies gas to New England, metropolitan New York, and New Jersey, and, prospectively, to the Baltimore and Washington areas.

Consolidated is a substantial force in exploration and production—one of the largest gas producers in the United States. Two subsidiaries that are not utilities conduct its search for both gas and oil. CNG Producing Company, based in New Orleans, operates in the Gulf of Mexico and most major onshore U.S. basins. CNG Development Company functions exclusively in the Appalachian Region.

A key strength of Consolidated is its operation of the largest natural gas storage facilities in the

country: old gas fields—26 of them—deep in the porous Appalachian rock, which the company has converted for underground storage. With 840 billion cubic feet of capacity, these cost-efficient facilities enable Consolidated to buy gas economically year-round, store it in summer when demand is low, and withdraw it throughout the heating season—a reliable service that takes the bite out of winter, when customer demand substantially exceeds the supply of gas flowing into the region. More than once, this storage has been able to feed emergency supplies to utilities outside its own region that were struggling to cope with a weather disaster.

In a formal sense, Consolidated was founded in 1942; but its line of descent goes back nearly a century to John D. Rockefeller's Standard Oil Company and the origins of the natural gas industry.

Consolidated operates 94 compressor stations along its more than 6,000 miles of interstate gas transmission pipelines.

Drilling in the Appalachian mountains still provides vital gas supplies for Consolidated, which traces its roots to John D. Rockefeller's early gas and oil drilling in West Virginia in the late 1800s. Photo by Camille Vickers

Standard Oil formed, merged, and acquired various firms engaged in exploring the Appalachian Region for gas and developing the fuel's first commercial markets. Those enterprises today are the cornerstones of Consolidated's system. For example, the East Ohio, Hope, and River utilities grew from Standard Oil's plan late in the nineteenth century to build an integrated system of gas production, gathering, and distribution from West Virginia to Ohio. The technology was primitive by today's standards, and crossing the Ohio became an engineering feat. Laying a pipeline under rivers, around swamps, and through upland wilderness strained men and machines to their limits.

Meanwhile, another element of the future Consolidated was in the making. Two Pennsylvania entrepreneurs, attracted by large gas finds near Pittsburgh, set up a company to drill for the energy and pipe it to the city. Their successful venture, The Peoples Natural Gas Company, was later sold to Standard Oil.

With the breakup of Rockefeller's original company in 1911, all of these gas operations came under the umbrella of the Standard Oil Company of New Jersey—forerunner of today's Exxon. In 1930 "Jersey" organized a pipeline to supply utilities in New York State, and thus put many of the pieces of the present Consolidated system in place. There they remained until 1943 when, in order to avoid becoming a regulated utility under the Public Utility Holding Company Act, Jersey spun off its gas concerns as a totally independent company. This action resulted in the formation of Consolidated Natural Gas Company.

One quality it inherited was the expansive spirit. Vigorous efforts to add customers and operating territory marked the firm's first two decades. Aggressively creating demand, Consolidated also built up supply. It made purchases from newly formed pipeline companies, and it joined the march to explore for gas in the Gulf of Mexico. At the same time, it was developing the storage capacity to serve a growing market. All of these activities tested and polished the organization's skills for the difficult years that were to follow.

In the late 1960s Consolidated was one of the first gas operations to foresee and act against the coming shortages. It diversified

437

A network of underground gas storage fields in four states helps provide adequate supplies of gas to Consolidated customers in winter. The 26 fields operated by Consolidated constitute the largest gas storage network in the country. Photo by Gary Gladstone

opment of an "off-system" market in the late 1970s by selling gas under short-term contract to nonaffiliated pipelines and utilities. More recently it established a strong foothold in the Northeast. Twenty utilities are buying under long-term contracts in New England, New Jersey, and New York City; and the Baltimore-Washington market appears to be next.

New business serves two purposes: It expands Consolidated's earnings base and value to shareholders, and contributes to a high operating level that helps keep the firm's gas rates down. Those dual concerns have also spurred the organization to take innovative paths in its traditional markets. During the shortage period it

Consolidated has always encouraged its customers to use the most efficient and economical gas equipment. Here, the burner design on a new, high-efficiency gas furnace is being tested. Photo by Bill Farrell

its supply sources and pressed ahead with one of the industry's largest exploration programs. Thus it was able to maintain a high level of reliable service to customers.

The shortages have faded, but the benefits remain. Multiple supply sources enable Consolidated to purchase gas at least cost. Large volumes are under contract, and much of this includes inexpensive older vintages. The result is long-term assurance to customers of ample, attractively priced gas. Eleven trillion cubic feet of gas are dedicated to Consolidated's use. This is equivalent to 16 years of supply versus a gas industry average of 10 years.

Consolidated is employing its advantages of supply and strategic location—between the major producing and consuming areas— to broaden the scope of its sales. The company pioneered the devel-

Gas bound for Consolidated's markets in New England, New Jersey, New York, and in the Baltimore and Washington, D.C., areas passes through facilities such as this one in western Pennsylvania. Photo by Camille Vickers

helped large industrial customers find additional gas supplies that could be carried to them through the Consolidated system—so-called "self-help" gas. This has now evolved into a full-fledged transportation service, providing large users the opportunity to shop for gas on the spot market

and to employ Consolidated to bring it to their door.

The company is also directly helping customers improve their productivity and efficiency. Several million dollars have gone into a novel program organized by Consolidated to demonstrate the latest gas-using technology to industrial and commercial customers. These are not laboratory demonstrations: The equipment goes into actual use, in office buildings, shopping centers, and factory production lines.

The result is that Consolidated's industrial and commercial representatives are now actually high-tech experts. Able to evaluate new gas-using processes, they professionally advise the decision-makers of industry. A unique team of "industry specialists"—engineers who have acquired a detailed knowledge of the equipment and processes in a broad range of regional industries—are on call

Consolidated's five gas distribution utilities serve more than 1.5 million customers in Ohio, Pennsylvania, and West Virginia.

throughout the firm's service territory to help solve the energy problems of customers.

A strong local economy also means a vigorous market for gas. Consolidated is prominent in the Pittsburgh area's economic development activity. It works in harmony with regional and municipal agencies to attract and retain businesses—a highly competitive arena. Consolidated's results are impressive. It has helped engender nearly 2,500 jobs annually in the past several years in western Pennsylvania alone. It also has taken the lead in forming a coalition of utilities, transportation firms, and local development agencies to promote western Pennsylvania in the national marketplace.

The Consolidated Natural Gas Company Foundation has the same broad goals in view. Its agenda is longer-term, however— a strengthening of the institutions that contribute to quality of life and the region's ultimate appeal as a business center. Organized in

1984, the foundation supports the tri-state area's education, social and economic development programs, and the arts. Its work is funded entirely by Consolidated's profits and reflects the tangible bond between the company and its operating territory. Profit growth has also rewarded shareholders, of course; in recent years Consolidated's combined return—stock price appreciation plus dividends— has ranked with the highest in the gas industry.

This success can be traced directly to the company's aggressive marketing, its expansion of sales into new geographical regions, and the impressive spread of its exploration and production.

The roots of this production that were planted in the Appalachians during the Rockefeller era have now proliferated into most of the country's principal gas and oil basins. Consolidated first drilled in the Gulf of Mexico in the 1950s. It is now a sizable offshore operator, participating in more than 100 producing fields in the Gulf and as lease operator in half of these. In 1985 a Consolidated gas well set a new Gulf of Mexico production record: more than 100 million cubic feet of gas per day.

The company has also pushed its search for gas and oil inland across the continent, and extended its gas sales from coast to coast. If expansion has been a leading motif of the 1980s, there has been renewed commitment to local production as well. CNG Development Company, formed in 1982, and headquartered in Pittsburgh, serves as an important source of Appalachian gas for customers throughout the region.

Altogether, Consolidated's exploration and production activities cover nearly five million acres of gas and oil properties. They range from the Appalachians to the Rockies and southward to Texas and the Gulf, that immensity of water dotted with steel-legged

islands. More critical than the size and daring of these operations, however, are their consistently solid results. Against a backdrop of declining national reserves, Consolidated increased its gas reserves to over one trillion cubic feet and its oil and condensate reserves to more than 26 million barrels.

Consolidated Natural Gas Company has achieved a pace of progress that could be measured from almost any point in its history. Possibly the most illuminating comparison, however, might be with that fledgling company of 1942. The spin-off Consolidated, substantial enough in its time, had assets of $211 million, annual revenues of $62 million, and net profit of $11 million. Today it is in the range of $4 billion in assets, revenues above $3 billion, and earnings of more than $200 million.

A computerized service dispatch system helps Consolidated's utilities provide faster service to customers.

# THE PEOPLES NATURAL GAS COMPANY
## CLEAN ENERGY ENTERS ITS SECOND CENTURY

Buried beneath the streets and lands of western Pennsylvania lie more than 7,000 miles of Peoples Gas pipeline, a network that represents the growth and progress of The Peoples Natural Gas Company since its founding in 1885. Today Peoples Gas, an employer of 1,400, delivers clean-burning natural gas to more than 322,000 residential, commercial, and industrial customers in Pittsburgh and the surrounding area of western Pennsylvania.

Natural gas has played a leading role in the development of the entire region. The smokeless fuel has encouraged industrial expansion; created thousands of jobs; heated homes, offices, schools, and stores; and improved the air of the once "Smoky City."

Pittsburgh's gas industry began in 1878 with the discovery of natural gas in Murrysville, some 15 miles to the east, by two brothers—Michael and Obediah Haymaker.

By 1883 the gas was being piped under its own pressure from wells in Murrysville to 16th Street in Pittsburgh. As the leaders of an industrializing nation, such local residents as Andrew Carnegie soon learned the significance of this fuel that burned more cleanly and cost less than coal. In 1885 Joseph Newton Pew and Edward O. Emerson founded The Peoples Natural Gas Company, which soon expanded its service area; and by 1929 the region consumed one-eighth of the entire United States' usage of the fuel.

The utility, which became part of Consolidated Natural Gas Company in 1943, made important technical innovations during the late nineteenth and early twentieth centuries. One was the natural gas compressor station, a device that allowed the fuel to be pumped to market under controlled conditions. Invented by Joseph Newton Pew, compression marked the first

step toward long-distance, cross-country transportation of the versatile fuel.

World War II profoundly changed the gas industry. Steelmaking Pittsburgh emerged from the war exhausted and filthy. The Smoky City, properly so called in those days, was the scene of hundreds of industrial and domestic furnaces that burned volatile coal. More than 700 coal-burning locomotives chugged into and out of Pittsburgh every day. Soon after the war, however, a determined group of civic leaders, led by banker Richard King Mellon and Mayor David L. Lawrence, gave a powerful push to legislation that helped transform the Smoky City into the "Renaissance City." Railroads began using diesel fuel, and industrialists and home owners re-

*A clean, smoke-free Pittsburgh skyline— thanks to natural gas.*

The Peoples Natural Gas Company was the first gas utility in western Pennsylvania and among the first in the United States to use computer graphics for mapping.

placed coal-burning furnaces with natural gas. Within two years Peoples Gas saw a 77-percent rise in gas-heating installations. Such magazines as *Time* and *Fortune* praised Pittsburgh as the "Cinderella City of the East."

The expansion of Peoples Gas continued through the 1950s and into the 1960s, when the initial signs of an energy crunch emerged. At that time federal regulatory action controlled the price that drillers were allowed to charge for their gas, causing prices to be held unrealistically low. Since it no longer was profitable to explore for gas, there was a decline in the number of new wells drilled—although demand soared to an all-time high for the underpriced but premium fuel. Eventually the government eased industry restrictions, which invited more realistic prices at the wellhead and the resumption of gas exploration.

Today western Pennsylvania's declining heavy industrial base has required that new markets and

new uses for gas be developed. Peoples Gas has been successful in burning natural gas with coal, compressing natural gas to power fleet and service vehicles and equipment, and promoting cogeneration, the production of both steam and electricity. Benefits include increased efficiency in the use of energy, maintenance of environmental emissions standards, and new cost-effectiveness for the consumer.

This Harper's Weekly *drawing depicts the first gas well in Murrysville, Pennsylvania.*

Peoples Gas has traditionally searched for better ways to serve its markets. The principal objectives of customer service are assuring the safe delivery of adequate gas volumes to customer premises, helping to maintain safe gas service on those premises, and helping customers to get satisfactory performance from their gas appliances. Prompted by its commitment to those goals, the firm was the first gas utility in western Pennsylvania and among the first in the United States to use computer graphics for mapping. With the Facilities Information Management System (FIMS), all field maps and distribution maps have been transferred to a computer. Thus, the company's operations and service people can make emergency decisions and repairs accurately and speedily. Another high-tech computer system monitors every cubic foot of gas flowing through the firm's 16-county pipeline network; it collects data from the field on pressure, volume, and temperature, ensuring an adequate supply at all hours to all customers.

Now into its second century, The Peoples Natural Gas Company is ready, says president Jack B. Hoey, "to meet the challenges of the future with a constant eagerness to serve."

Peoples Gas has traditionally searched for better ways to serve its markets.

# UNION NATIONAL BANK OF PITTSBURGH
## RESPONDING TO PEOPLE'S NEEDS

The rivers and forests of western Pennsylvania in the 1850s abounded in deer, beaver, muskrat, squirrel, and fox. Hunters and trappers could bring in their skins and be paid on the spot at McCune and Youngs, a leather tannery and fur shop on Market Street in "Pittsburg," then a trading, shipping, and manufacturing center of 50,000 residents.

Cash on the barrelhead could be a mixed blessing, however. Wise minds knew the sort of perils that might befall a backwoodsman with full pockets in the big town after "one too many." To avoid exposing all their coins to the urban temptations, McCune and Youngs' patrons began leaving a portion for safekeeping at the tannery.

Such was the commonsense origin of Union National Bank of Pittsburgh. A century and a quarter later a multibank holding company approaching three billion dollars in assets would still retain a special instinct for the personal and business opportunities of its home region. Despite an imposing capital base, fully modernized services, and professional management teams that had succeeded generations of "family bankers," Union National came to the threshold of interstate banking in the mid-1980s with a characteristically independent approach. It wasn't tempted to spread too far too fast.

"We're optimistic about western Pennsylvania and the tri-state area," says board chairman Robert F. Patton. "It's going to take some time to develop, but we foresee a more service-oriented, broader-based economy."

Union National was founded in 1857 by John Robison McCune, a Pittsburgh leather merchant who had been born 31 years before in rural Beaver County, northwest of the city. Apprenticed to a tanner at 14 years of age, the energetic young man became a partner and later sole owner of McCune and Youngs. The firm's sturdy safe be-

*John Robison McCune, founder.*

*Charles Lockhart McCune*

came such a popular depository that McCune organized what he called the Diamond Savings Bank. A few months later, August 18, 1857, he renamed it Union Banking Company.

In one year the bank declared a dividend; in another it had a state charter, a new office at Fourth Avenue and Market Street, assets of $67,979.61, and a diversified board of directors—respectably listed by vocation. There was a ship chandler, grocer, merchant, planer, and a future department store magnate—whose trade was given as "Notions, Trimmings, Etc."—Joseph Horne. The bank's directors a half-century later included two who gloried in the simple billing of "captialist"; H.K. Porter, "locomotives"; Thomas M. Armstrong, "cork manufacturer"; and H.J. Heinz, "pickles."

Having acquired its national charter, Number 705, on February 1, 1865, the institution erected a handsomely pillared, three-story building at Fourth and Market five years later. The official seal proudly displayed a Union eagle on guard within a sturdy, arching, leather belt.

A 21-story office building, then Pittsburgh's third largest, rose

on the corner of Fourth Avenue and Wood Street to house Union National in 1906. The bank and holding company are still head-quartered there. In 1914 came a million-dollar cash dividend from surplus, the bank's first sale of stock, followed by the hiring of its first female tellers and bookkeepers to replace men entering World War I.

Union National kept its head above the financial wreckage strewn by the 1929 stock market crash and ensuing Depression. Then the St. Patrick's Day flood of 1936 brought a crisis of a different sort. Pittsburgh's rivers crested waist-high in the main banking floor, and basement vaults were engulfed. The human response became the core of legend. Neighboring institutions offered dry space. Bank employees' families and friends pitched in to dig out, mop up, and throw away. Careful hands stripped valuable documents one by one from the dripping piles and ironed them dry on laundry mangles.

By the end of World War II, Union National had $84 million in assets and strong commercial relationships—but only one Downtown office with an insignificant retail

*Front row (left to right): Fred H. Gardner, senior vice-president and chief financial officer, Union National Corporation; George F. Kesel, president and chief executive officer, Union National Corporation; Robert E. Patton, chairman of the board, Union National Corporation; Robert H. Stevenson, senior vice-president, secretary, and general counsel, Union National Corporation. Center row (left to right): John R. Echement, president and chief operating officer, Union National Bank; William E. Walker, chairman of the board and chief executive officer, Union National Bank. Back row (left to right): Gayland B. Cook, president and chief executive officer, Keystone National Bank; Roy E. Buchman, Jr., chairman of the board and chief executive officer, McDowell National Bank.*

*Union National Bank occupied the corner of Market Street and Fourth Avenue from 1859 to 1905. This modest structure housed its office until 1870.*

base—when Charles L. McCune became president in 1946. Grandson of the bank's founder, son of one of its presidents, he had successfully wildcatted oil leases in Oklahoma and Texas—selling out his holdings to Texaco (and thereby becoming that firm's largest shareholder) before returning to Union National full time. By turns jolly and cantankerous, strong-willed and sentimental, the white-thatched occupant of a desk on the mezzanine above the main banking floor remained president for 25 years—while assets grew tenfold to $837 million, and the number of offices to over 50. Ac-

quisitions and retail services developed apace.

A merger that gave McCune special delight—he joined the jackhammer crews that tore into the dividing walls—was the 1964 link-up with Commonwealth Bank and Trust Company, neighbor and friendly rival from 1906 when the two headquarters had gone up side by side simultaneously.

Later chief executives Richard D. Edwards and, since 1977, president George F. Kesel completed the progress into the mainstream of state and national banking. The formation of Union National Corporation as a holding company on February 8, 1982, opened the way to strategic mergers with other independent, strongly regional institutions, beginning with Keystone

National Bank, Punxsutawney; McDowell National Bank, Sharon; and First Financial Group, Washington, Pennsylvania. By the mid-1980s the offspring of John R. McCune's leather shop employed some 1,900 persons.

President Kesel and chairman Patton see no letup in the competitive fervor of the age of banking deregulation. For customers that will mean "a growing variety of financial products," backed, at Union National, by an unbroken tradition of meeting the needs of the community that now extends some 130 years.

# THE WESTIN WILLIAM PENN
## PITTSBURGH'S "GRAND HOTEL"—PAST AND FUTURE

*Coal and steel magnate Henry Clay Frick, seated on the porch of his summer home, Eagle Rock. Pittsburgh's landmark hotel was his last great project. Courtesy, Carnegie Library of Pittsburgh*

If there is any group of patrons that yields to no other in admiration of The Westin William Penn, it's the architectural critics. "The image of everything that the older-established American hotel should be," James D. Van Trump, patriarch of art historians has called it. "An example of high-style, early twentieth-century architecture," says another, "one of the grandest in the nation and one of the best preserved of its era . . . Pittsburgh's great public living room."

History can be a chilling traveling companion, of course. For guests of the age of jet, computer, and credit card, the delights of The Westin William Penn aren't only in its richly evocative past but in its elegant—and expensive—present. A $30-million program of building renovations, parlayed by a new team of management representing the world's most distinguished hotel-keeping style, is destined to carry Pittsburgh's landmark hotel fresh and alive into the twenty-first century.

"Landmark" isn't used loosely. In 1985 the 70-year-old hotel won a place on the U.S. Interior Department's National Register of Historic Places. The designation has been both a glory and a burden. Remodelers may not "deface" a national landmark. Thus, when the dictates of decor and modern heating and air conditioning signaled replacement of all the hotel's hundreds of windows, the contractor had to ensure the metal framing was ordered in the original color.

The film of age has been lifted from towering facades of limestone, brick, and terra cotta, the "deep reds and cool grays" of the Georgian style that give The Westin William Penn, in the eyes of one connoisseur, "great presence even amidst the behemoths of Downtown." Occupying an entire city block, the hotel has replaced all its perimeter sidewalks—a sixth-mile hike for fitness enthusiasts—and less visibly, but vitally, its entire electrical and plumbing systems.

A more intimate improvement emerged gradually, floor by floor, in the 1984-1986 period that resulted in hundreds of larger guest rooms. The conjurer's trick was accomplished by reducing the rooms in number from 840 to 595. The average 40-percent expansion, combined with all-new carpeting and fabrics, and furnishings by Drexel and Henredon, has essentially created the city's most modern accommodations for the corporate or pleasure travelers. The hotel also has 35 meeting rooms, 18 hospitality rooms, and 47 suites varying in size to 3,000 square feet. A contemporarily themed restaurant and bar off the lobby, some general freshening of all public rooms, corridors, and crannies—in fact, countless individual touches—will flesh out what is now viewed as an ongoing process akin to the community's own renaissance.

The establishment has often mirrored the moods of Pittsburgh. Its construction and later expan-

*The smiling pickman's name has been lost, but wielder of the shovel at the hotel's 1914 ground breaking was Henry P. Haas, president of the Pittsburgh Real Estate Board. Photographer was the veteran Frank E. Bingaman of the long-gone Pittsburgh Sun-Telegraph. Courtesy, Carnegie Library of Pittsburgh*

Westin is the oldest operating hotel management company in America. It was founded in Seattle in 1930 as Western Hotels—the streamlined, less limiting name was adopted in 1981—and it owns or manages over 50 hotels or resorts, with a total of 28,000 rooms, in 10 countries; and more are under construction. Two of the firm's proudest properties are the Plaza, in New York, and San Francisco's Westin St. Francis. Since 1970 an autonomous subsidiary of UAL, Inc. (which also owns United Airlines and Hertz Corporation), Westin has enjoyed a long association with Alcoa in other cities. The aims of both companies blended in Pittsburgh. Already committed to a $30-million wager on the future of its hometown hotel, the aluminum producer wanted the best independent management of its huge investment. For its part, Westin saw the improvement program, bankrolled by a Pittsburgh industrial leader, moving the

*Tea time or cocktails—where better than in the elegant lobby Palm Court of The Westin William Penn?*

*Set amid the city's towering corporate headquarters, The Westin William Penn also faces Mellon Square, an oasis of greenery and quiet in Pittsburgh's Golden Triangle.*

sion marked two great eras in civic and national optimism; but in other times local residents who met, dined, entertained, and married there had reason to fear for the survival of their city's supreme exponent of the age of the "grand hotel."

Probably not since its earliest days, however, has the treasure been in stronger hands. The facility is owned by Alcoa Properties, Inc., a subsidiary of Pittsburgh-based Aluminum Company of America, which placed it under a 20-year management contract with Westin Hotels in March 1984.

Pittsburgh's supreme Grand Ballroom, on the famed 17th floor of The Westin William Penn.

The Urban Room, a masterpiece of Art Deco, and a memorable place to meet—or to marry.

establishment in exactly the direction of top-of-the-line elegance that the firm itself had long identified as its market niche.

"All Westins are deluxe and first-class," said Robert L. Hawes, veteran hotelman who won the nod as first general manager of The Westin William Penn. "The owners are clearly making a statement here, renewing a tradition that made this great place the focus of social, business, and entertainment life in the city."

That was exactly what Henry Clay Frick had envisioned. The famed industrialist and art collector (1849-1919) had long since made fortunes in coal, steel, and real estate, but he believed that Pittsburgh needed excellent accommodations to match its economic and industrial progress. In what would prove to be his last major investment, he hired Janssen and Abbott, the city's foremost architects, to create "the greatest hotel between New York and Chicago."

It opened in March 1916—after what the *Gazette Times* unrestrainedly hailed as "months of tireless energy, the employment of every known art and craft, the calling into service of every engenuity of man. . .a house of a thousand guest rooms, without need of candles. . ." The presidential suite was occupied by "Coal King" Frick himself.

The mammoth structure, facing William Penn Way, did contain 1,000 rooms—on 23 floors shaped like the letter "E". A back-to-back E-shaped addition, built in 1928-1929 that faced Grant Street, added 600 rooms and indeed for a time made the hotel the country's largest outside New York or Chicago. However, the 1930s brought receivership, and later decades saw a succession of ownerships until the sale to Alcoa in 1971. That acquisition finally ended what historian Van Trump recalled as "a period of anxiety for those of us who loved the old hotel and were fearful it might be sold for its site." No idle fear, that.

Facing Grant Street on one side—the Golden Triangle's red-brick boulevard of banks, courts, and corporations—and the jewel-like park of Mellon Square on the other, The Westin William Penn does occupy what may be the community's most prestigious

446

block. It's a five-minute walk to any of 18 well-known corporate headquarters, and an easy stroll to David L. Lawrence Convention Center, Heinz Hall for the Performing Arts, and other amenities of one of the country's most compact and humanly scaled Downtowns.

The grand hotel is also its own community—with more than 400 full-time employees, including 70 with over 35 years of service, dozens of highly skilled craftspeople, and professionals. Executive chef Bernd Liebergesell, who joined Westin in South Africa in 1974, has won culinary honors from Hawaii to Houston to Denver.

Whether meeting, dining, staying overnight, or holding a once-in-a-lifetime family event, The Westin William Penn is a place where service is framed in memorable am-

The Canada Room, one of 35 meeting facilities suitable for gatherings serious or social.

biences. "The interior spaces are extraordinary evocations of their time, conveying the scale, force, and power of the world of financiers and industrialists," notes the citation of the National Registry. "The main lobby, crowned by the massive carved ornate plaster relief ceiling, is one of the most remarkable spaces of its kind, handsomely complemented by the adjacent dining rooms."

More splendor greets the eye on the hotel's celebrated 17th floor. The gilded Grand Ballroom of 1916 offers exciting perspectives of the city through great arched windows. Light sparkles from crystal chandeliers, and a spacious balcony encircling the waist of the tall room enhances a seating capacity of 1,200. Adjacent is the darkly glittering Urban Room. This masterpiece of Art Deco, a style that came to fruition in the 1920s, was installed by Joseph Urban—a renowned theatrical designer who often fulfilled the extravagant visions of producer Florenz Ziegfeld. With its black Carrara glass walls, its gold-curlicued ceiling mural of a never-never Eden 'neath a Persian "tree of life," the Urban Room has achieved a rare distinction. It is a designated Pittsburgh landmark in

its own right.

Characteristically, every floor has its subtle charms and indulgences. While no room has been left unrenovated, the business traveler—or the sybarite on a 50-percent-off weekend package—will find the original solid wooden doors, brass hardware, and bathrooms of marble. One of the more elaborate suites provides a wet bar, jacuzzi, and a grand piano. More than 50,000 square feet of space are available for conventions and meetings. Whether the group is 10 people in a private business huddle or 1,000, The Westin William Penn makes the optimum spot to gather.

Alone or in a part, at the business day's end, or at the start of an evening's entertainment, there is the special charm of afternoon tea—or the cocktail hour, as one prefers—amid the potted palms, the discreet clink of ice cubes, the mellow piano (formerly owned by Andre Previn), and the spectacular Georgian lobby of a hotel that is for the past, the present, and the future.

Under the arches of the Terrace Room, long a favorite place to dine.

# NATIONAL INTERGROUP, INC.
## FORGING A NEW FUTURE IN DISTRIBUTION

Just as Pittsburgh is moving away from an economy dominated by steel, so has one of the city's largest enterprises, National Intergroup, Inc. (NII), forged a new course for the future. There is little resemblance today between NII and its predecessor, National Steel Corporation.

Since 1980 National Intergroup has redeployed assets in a thoroughgoing restructuring. The result is that by 1986 steel accounted for only 12 percent of corporate assets. The major portion—nearly 63 percent—stood with businesses involved in distribution services.

Founded in 1929 as National Steel Corporation, the Pittsburgh-based firm quickly made a reputation as an aggressive innovator. It was quick to adopt technology, and its steel plants became showcases for the industry. As a specialist in sheet steels, National reaped the rewards of the post-World War II boom in cars, houses, and appliances. That prosperity continued for more than 35 years. Then substitute materials and low-priced imports seriously began

biting into demand and prices. Markets shrank; profits slowed to a trickle. Steel had become a worldwide commodity.

National's management team recognized that dramatic changes would have to be made, and in the early 1970s the company diversified into the aluminum business. It built a jointly operated smelter, and acquired aluminum fabricating and rolling companies that specialized in sheet and foils. It also expanded its metals distribution activities to most states east of the Rockies.

As a springboard to faster change, excess coal properties were sold in 1980. The resulting cash was redeployed far outside the world of metals. National acquired a West Coast financial services firm. Renamed First Nationwide Financial, this property grew in the next five years from $5 billion to $11 billion in assets by expanding operations to New York, Florida, and Hawaii. Later it would play a major role in yet another stage of restructuring.

Meanwhile, with aluminum and financial services as partial counterweights to steel's cyclical nature, National turned to the hard task of scaling its steel operations to the new global realities. First it downsized its largest steel plant, at Detroit, by nearly 40 percent, matching production capability to reduced demand.

Then, and more innovatively, it made a daring suggestion to the workers at its second-largest steel plant in Weirton, West Virginia. They were told they could buy the entire works and operate it under an employee stock ownership plan. The employees enthusiastically approved, and they created the largest ESOP in the nation, as well as one of the world's most successful steel plants.

Thus, in three years National trimmed its steelmaking capacity from 12 million to under 6 million annual tons—but more important,

Howard M. Love, chairman and chief executive officer.

cut its costs and capital needs and enabled its remaining steel plants to run at higher, more efficient rates.

In 1983 National Intergroup, Inc., was organized to serve as parent firm for National Steel and its former subsidiaries and divisions. Each business then became a stand-alone entity in legal and operating terms. This step paved the way for further redeployment of assets into operations of greater opportunity.

NII, in 1984, sold a 50-percent interest in National Steel to Nippon Kokan K.K., of Japan, for $273 million in cash. National Steel thus became the largest international joint venture of its kind with direct access to the most advanced technology.

The substantial cash from the sale to Kokan became NII's ticket to move into the distribution industry—which is virtually free of the problems posed by imports, excessive government regulation, high labor costs, or heavy capital investment. Wholesale drug and pharmaceutical distribution in par-

Computer controls on National's steel and aluminum lines are improving quality and productivity.

ticular promises faster growth, greater cash flow, and improved earnings.

NII's strategy materialized in three bold actions.

In August 1985 it acquired The Permian Corporation for $172 million. Headquartered in Texas, Permian provides distribution and other services to oil lease holders and refineries in 16 states. It operates 600 trucks and 5,000 miles of pipeline, gathering and moving crude oil to long-established customers. The firm is not directly involved in oil exploration, production, refining, or product marketing; its earnings come from distribution and services. The excellent cash flow is a boost to NII's other restructuring activities.

Late in 1985 NII completed the sale of its 81.4-percent interest in First Nationwide Financial to Ford Motor Company. The $401-million sale price, plus the $25 million received from a public offering,

brought a satisfying return on the $241-million purchase five years earlier.

Finally, culminating a two-year effort to secure a strong position in the drug distribution industry, NII acquired the FoxMeyer Corporation in early 1986 for $343 million. This gives National Intergroup a new core business with excellent growth and profit potential.

*Over 600 trucks distribute oil to refinery customers of The Permian Corporation, acquired by NII in 1985.*

FoxMeyer is America's third-largest pharmaceutical wholesaler. Its customers are independent and chain drugstores and hospitals. *Forbes* magazine ranked Fox-Meyer 71st in sales growth among 1,004 American companies in 1985—and in growth of sales and earnings per share in the drug industry, a solid first. Through its distribution centers more than 25,000 products are shipped daily to thousands of outlets throughout mid-America. It also franchises the exclusive Health Mart program, supplying more than 350 locally owned drugstores with merchandising, decor, and brand-label products to compete with the large chains. FoxMeyer's acquisition of Ben Franklin Wholesale Company, supplier to more than 1,300 franchised variety stores and 300 other accounts, added yet another growth path.

National Intergroup, Inc., is virtually a new company—with a dynamic future in the new Pittsburgh.

*NII's acquisition of FoxMeyer Corporation in 1986 created a new core business—wholesale pharmaceutical distribution to drugstores, chains, and hospitals.*

# BELL OF PENNSYLVANIA
## SERVING WITH TOMORROW'S TECHNOLOGY

A newspaper advertisement of 1878 offered the first clue to a service that would have unimaginable impact on how Pittsburgh works and lives.

The awkwardly named Central District and Printing Telegraph Company had offices in the First National Bank building at Fifth Avenue and Wood Street. It announced that it would serve as agent for "Prof. Bell's (Talking) Telephone, by means of which conversation can be carried on over a line of Telegraph. . . . The conditions being right, it will give entire satisfaction."

Alexander Graham Bell had invented the device that made talking possible by wire two years previously. Subsequently, business people such as Pittsburgh's Thomas B.A. David, in their own parts of the country, helped to establish the telephone as the essential convenience of everyday communication.

Born in Pittsburgh in 1836, David earned pennies as a newsboy, learned telegraphy at age 14, and joined the Union Army in the Civil War. He is credited with setting up the first field telegraph to serve with an army on active duty in America. A veteran manager at

Western Union, he established the Central District and Printing Telegraph firm to provide communications in Pittsburgh by Morse instruments and machines printing messages on ticker tape. The telephone came in as a supplementary service. The directory that first year (1878) in Pittsburgh listed 108 subscribers.

There was no stopping Bell's wonderful voice carrier. In part, the telephone's triumph must be credited to armies of quick-fingered operators "plugging in" and disconnecting conversations all day and to the hardy men clanking up and down "telly poles" to hang the mazes of overhead wires necessary to bring people together in those early days. Veteran operator Mary Wilhelm, who lived into her nineties, remembered starting in 1905 at 35 cents a day; promoted to chief operator, she was raised to one dollar. By the time of her retirement in the late 1940s, she headed a large central service facility of 600 operators. Far fewer persons are employed in that capacity today: Advanced switching technology has long since taken over nearly all local and long-distance calls.

David's CD&PT enterprise belat-

*This photograph was taken in 1889, just 13 years after the telephone was exhibited at the Centennial. It was then known as the old Allegheny Central Office; its name was later changed to Cedar. Courtesy, The Pittsburgh Press*

edly recognized its true growth business by name in 1913, when it became the Central District Telephone Company. Five years later it merged into a then-new, Phildelphia-based Bell Telephone Company of Pennsylvania, and thus passed into history.

More history was made on January 1, 1984, when the epochal divestiture of American Telephone & Telegraph's local service firms. Bell of Pennsylvania became a subsidiary of the multistate, $19-billion Bell Atlantic Corporation—a diversified giant—maintaining a

business strategy keyed to communications market growth and technological innovation. Its network, which now serves approximately one million subscribers in the Pittsburgh area, is characterized by software-controlled switching systems, high-speed digital transmission, and fiber optics.

Pittsburgh, for example, was one of the first major cities to achieve "all-electronic" switching. This offers many benefits: greater reliability, a host of communications options, higher system productivity, and hence substantial cost economies that ultimately reward consumers. Electronic switching enables phones to be more versatile. On the near horizon are telephones programmable to accept calls only from a list of specific sources, display the calling number, automatically redial the last number tried, ring with a special tone from designated numbers, and originate a trace of annoying calls.

"Stored program" electronic switching opened numerous sophisticated options to business customers. With state-of-the-art CENTREX service they can make changes in their own networks, and give least-cost routing to

*Bell employs the latest technology to monitor the performance of vital customer networks.*

long-distance calls. In addition, CENTREX permits subscribers to eliminate masses of switching equipment from their offices. The equipment stays in the Bell central office, monitored and maintained around the clock. With a new Integrated Services Digital Network (ISDN), users can send and receive voice, data, and image signals over a single line, simultaneously.

Bell of Pennsylvania also has taken the lead in applying the technology of fiber optics. Even the engineers of Thomas David's time would recognize the principle of telephone conversations and data being transmitted as electrical impulses over copper wire. However, with fiber optics, voices and data move as bursts of laser-powered light on fibers of ultrapure glass, fine as hair. As early as 1981 such a system was pioneered with a 40-mile link between Pittsburgh and Greensburg, the seat of Westmoreland County to the east; it was then the longest interoffice fiber-optic transmission system in the nation.

Bell achieved another national first with a light-wave network linking several major locations in Downtown Pittsburgh. Configured like a star, the hub being at Bell's Seventh Avenue building, the company's "Lumicom" network puts the great potential of fiber-optic connectivity at the very doorsteps of the city's large and medium-size businesses.

With annual revenues of more than a half-billion dollars in the Pittsburgh area, and 3,500 employees in district operations, Bell of Pennsylvania is committed to keeping the region in the vanguard of the most advanced telecommunications capability available. Thomas David's original promise of "entire satisfaction" still prevails.

*The city of Pittsburgh and a Bell of Pennsylvania telephone crew share a night of reflections by the Monongahela River.*

# USX CORPORATION
## CHANGING WITH ITS CITY IN A COMPETITIVE WORLD

No business enterprise has been more dramatically linked to the life of the Pittsburgh region than USX Corporation, formerly U.S. Steel. The corporation's deepest roots are there, and from the start Pittsburgh served as its operational headquarters. In 1971—with the opening of the largest office building between New York and Chicago, the 64-story steel-clad skyscraper at 600 Grant Street— the company established its administrative headquarters in the Golden Triangle as well.

Among the industrial firms that make Pittsburgh a world-class headquarters city, USX, with annual sales well above $20 billion, is the largest. This giant corporate presence has meant more than towered offices, steel mills and rail lines, coal mines, chemicals plants,

Andrew Carnegie (1835-1919), founder of The Carnegie Steel Company, whose merger with Federal Steel Company formed the nucleus of United States Steel Corporation.

Elbert H. Gary, first chairman of United States Steel Corporation, who served from 1901 to 1927.

The Edgar Thomson Plant of the USS Mon Valley Works in Braddock, Pennsylvania.

warehouses, research labs, and real estate developments. To a surprising extent USX "built" Pittsburgh, its skyline and river crossings. The steel for most of the city's skyscrapers and bridges

was melted, formed, fabricated, and erected by the organization and its American Bridge Division. The company and its foundation have helped to build the community's cultural as well as physical profile with extensive support of arts and education.

Another parallel has been un-

mistakable between the legendary "City of Steel" and the mightiest operation in the industry. In the 1980s both were rapidly changing in response to demands in a world marketplace that showed little regard for economic rigidity. Even as Pittsburgh's economy was diversifying to a broader base of service industries and advanced technology, U.S. Steel restructured itself to major positions in oil and gas, joint ventures in steel, and superior financial strength overall. The name change to USX Corporation in July 1986 reflects that new, diversified profile.

The corporation's history traces from some of Pittsburgh's—and the world's—greatest empire-builders. One was surely Andrew Carnegie (1835-1919), the quintessential immigrant success story. At age 13 he arrived in Pittsburgh from Scotland virtually penniless and rode the industrial boom of the post-Civil War era to immense fortune, philanthropy, and personal influence that continues to this day through institutions he endowed for education and peace. It was the canny Scot's decision to retire from active money-making at 65

David M. Roderick, chairman of the board of directors and chief executive officer of the USX Corporation.

that set the stage for U.S. Steel's corporate creation in 1901.

The Carnegie Steel Company owned dozens of regional facilities, including the coal mines and ovens of the H.C. Frick Coke Company. Fayette County's Henry Clay Frick (1849-1919) had also built his firm from scratch, and in 1882 he became Carnegie's chief partner. A third member of the team was Charles Schwab. He had gone to work for Carnegie Steel at age 17 as a stake driver at one dollar a day; by age 35 he was company president.

The other major scene in the corporate drama unfolded in the Midwest. In 1898 the Illinois Steel Company had consulted Chicago attorney Elbert H. Gary about the purchase of a short-line railroad. Judge Gary (as he was known after serving two terms on a county bench) advised that the firm truly needed more than a railroad. He suggested a "rounded proposition"—the whole range of manufacturing and support operations. Asked to organize such an all-embracing enterprise, Gary helped

to form the Federal Steel company and became its president. The firm was the largest steel producer west of Pittsburgh. However, the fully "integrated" industry that he envisioned had to await the merger of the Federal and Carnegie interests.

The epochal deal came after two years of discussions and after Schwab and Gary had convinced eminent Wall Street banker J.P. Morgan that fully integrated steel-making from ore mine to customer's door was a feasible way to spend $492 million. A group headed by Morgan purchased Carnegie's interests for approximately that sum, and United States Steel was incorporated on February 25, 1901. Its authorized capital of $1.4 billion constituted the largest venture ever launched to that time.

Carnegie and Federal Steel became the nucleus, but the new firm also included McKeesport's National Tube, Cleveland's American Steel & Wire, and other companies that made tinplate, hoops, and sheet steels. Soon afterward the fledgling giant acquired American Bridge Company and Lake

Superior Consolidated Iron Mines. Gary became the first board chairman (holding the post until his death in 1927); Schwab was named president.

In 1902, its first full year of operation, the firm produced 10.9 million tons of raw steel, or just about two of every three tons melted in American steelmaking furnaces. Since then it has remained the country's largest steel producer—an aggregate 1.3 billion tons for rails and automobiles, appliances, roofing and siding, and weight-carrying structures that range from a coat hanger to the Verranzano-Narrows Bridge.

U.S. Steel played crucial roles in two world wars. It supplied allied forces with the metal sinews of ships, trucks, tanks, and guns. Employees and equipment met unprecedented goals; the Western Pennsylvania plants gained fame as "Victory Valley."

Change has been a continual phenomenon over the decades.

The Irvin Plant of USS Mon Valley Works in Dravosburg, Pennsylvania.

While the corporation never really stood pat in its operations or organization, the 1980s brought a sharp acceleration of the restructuring process. Pressure from foreign producers and stateside mini-mills forced a drastic downsizing and streamlining throughout the domestic steel industry.

In USX's case the shrinking process was more than balanced by an aggressive broadening of the firm's asset base under the leadership of Pittsburgh-born David M. Roderick, who in 1979 became the organization's 10th board chairman. The major thrust has been to make USX a leading competitor in the oil and gas industries. In 1982 it acquired Marathon Oil Company, then the nation's 17th-largest oil producer. The diversification momentum continued in early 1986 with the acquisition of Texas Oil & Gas Corp. of Dallas, a leading natural gas firm principally operating in the Southwest.

Such acquisitions in no way lessen USX's dedication to steel and other ventures that offer competitive returns, chairman Roderick has often stressed. "But we are now broader-based, less vulnerable to a downturn in any one business," he says. "Therefore, each of our business segments is stronger."

The company's current presence in the Pittsburgh area reflects the new balance. Without question, its steel capacity is down from the immense proportions of old. But the Mon Valley remains an active part of USX's steelmaking unit, USS. Its Clairton Works is a major producer of coke from coal, not only for the iron-making blast furnaces of Pittsburgh but for USS plants in other states. The Edgar Thomson Plant in Braddock was Andrew Carnegie's first "greenfield" works, in 1875; repeatedly upgraded, it remains the primary source of iron and steelmaking for USS' Mon Valley operations—feeding slabs primar-

USX Corporation headquarters in Pittsburgh.

ily across the river to the Irvin Plant in Dravosburg, where they're finished into sheet and strip. Irvin is one of the country's major suppliers of steel for appliances.

USX operates a variety of business interests in its hometown area: A mining company subsidiary administers three coal mines and two preparation plants in Washington and Greene counties. Research activities continue at the Technical Center in Monroeville. The Chemicals unit of the U.S. Diversified Group, another division of USX, makes plasticizers and resins at Neville Island for such varied end-uses as paints, pesticides, and pleasure boats; while its Tar-Ben plant at Clairton extracts a host of byproducts from the coking process. The U.S. Diversified Group's Supply Division service center on the North Side is one of a national network to supply products quickly and conveniently to customers. American Bridge not only erected the centerpiece skyscrapers of Gateway Center in Pittsburgh's 1950s renaissance but several stars of Renaissance II as well, including One Mellon Bank Center, One Oxford Centre, and PPG Place; it also

constructed the massive Crosstown Expressway bridge and approaches.

A Realty Development Division operates nationwide, with a dramatic local example in West Mifflin's Century III Mall—built on a reclaimed slag dump. Other Pittsburgh-based subsidiaries are a credit company and an engineering and consultant group.

In nonbusiness terms, too, USX adds hugely to Pittsburgh's now proverbial livability. Annual contributions in the millions of dollars are one way, but thousands of employee hours of volunteer service given to boards and agencies is another. Company and foundation grants support a broad array of charities and social services, educational institutions, and the region's superb variety of performing arts.

Pittsburgh and USX have created a team in which the corporation has taken pride from the beginning of the twentieth century, and there seem to be no bounds to an enduring community of interests.

# MATTHEWS INTERNATIONAL CORPORATION
## SINCE 1850 A LEADER IN "IDENTIFICATION MARKETS"

More than 136 years of staying ahead technologically has kept Matthews International Corporation in the forefront of an immensely diverse, yet also expertly specialized, industry. The public knows Matthews as a maker of rubber stamps, bronze plaques, or elegant building signs; and manufacturers know it as a supplier of machinery and inks for product and package marking. The firm took the lead in the development of super accurate methods for producing bar code symbology, thus helping to make automated checkout counters a reality.

The connecting theme is identification.

This unique Pittsburgh enterprise began in 1850, when John Dixon Matthews arrived with stencils, signs, and marking devices. An engraver from the steel mills of Sheffield, England, he was selling a revolutionary idea: that product recognition increased sales. A pioneering nationwide business developed. By the late 1800s the firm was providing the first stencils for the revolutionary advance of corrugated paperboard packaging. Later, its vulcanized rubber printing plates led to flexographic printing and high-speed container marking; just as its bronze plaques, then a half-century-old product line, led in 1927 to the first flush grave memorial, which irreversibly changed the cemetery industry.

Incorporated in 1902, Matthews now operates four divisions serving distinct markets. Graphic Systems makes printing plates in plants strategically sited in the nation to serve manufacturers of corrugated and flexible packaging; its output also includes creative graphics, bar code film masters, and computerized printing programs. Marking Systems supplies the means for marking all types of products and materials by printing, indenting, embossing, and etching. Identification Systems operates five foundries in the United States

and one in Canada to produce building signage and memorials. Matthews International Trading Company is a fourth division, which markets globally, selling Matthews' products as well as those of other manufacturers.

The firm's greatest innovation internally was a decision taken in the mid-1950s to become employee-

*Personal memorialization in the form of flush, bronze memorials are handcrafted for memorial parks.*

tion, not unlike Pittsburgh itself. It has added new software and electronic engineering skills to the craftsmanlike know-how that has so often adapted to challenge.

*Matthews International Corporation offers a broad range of industrial marking systems.*

owned. Years ahead of any other large local company, it identified employee control as a key motivator in improving customer service.

Matthews, which employs 1,260 people, is a corporation in transi-

Thus, the firm's research and development effort is already deep into tomorrow's identification technologies: ink jet printing, computer-aided printing processes, and improved automatic identification systems, to name a few. Market planners are looking at totally new industries as well, seeking opportunities for technology transfer.

# WESTINGHOUSE ELECTRIC CORPORATION
## THE FUTURE IS NOW

Westinghouse Electric Corporation has spent very little time during its 1986 centennial in reflection. "If we weren't continually changing, we wouldn't be as strong as we are today—we might not even be here," states Douglas D. Danforth, the company's 11th chief executive officer.

The achievements of Westinghouse—from its victory in the 1890s' "battle of the currents" through the infancy of radio, television, and nuclear power to today's radars and robots—have become the essence of economic history and the progress of mankind. The challenge to chairman Danforth and his second-century team is to pilot the organization, with its 115,000 employees and nearly $11 billion in sales, into the "winner's circle"—the top 5 or 10 percent of America's best-performing companies, measured by quality of products and services, management excellence, and financial results.

Inherent in this strategy is to be "the key player in the markets we serve," explains Danforth, citing

An 1890 switchboard was equipped with alternating-current apparatus made at the company's Garrison Alley plant.

A rarely photographed George Westinghouse, at about the time he founded the company.

current leadership in nuclear power, defense, relays and meters, transport refrigeration, construction products, industrial systems, and materials. The corollary is also true. Lacking a strong presence in a particular business, Westinghouse will look at selling, withdrawing, or forming a joint venture with another firm. Indeed, the corporation has been in the forefront of advocating, and making, multinational joint ventures rather than relying on protectionism as the model for U.S. and global prosperity.

Westinghouse is committed to research and development; in the mid-1980s its expenditures on such projects averaged a quarter-billion dollars a year, much of it spent in the campus-like research center on the hilltops of suburban Churchill. The Pittsburgh area's largest private employer, the firm currently manufactures several thousand products but derives nearly half its business, with typically higher profit margins, from services.

However, manufacturing was

what George Westinghouse, at 39, had in mind on January 8, 1886, when he was granted a charter to organize an operation to make equipment for generating and distributing electricity by alternating current. Born in upstate New York in 1846, the tireless tinkerer and teenage Civil War veteran had won his first patent at age 19—and there would be 360 more. Already an established manufacturer of air brakes and other railroad equipment, he put his new Westinghouse Electric Company in a used plant in Downtown Pittsburgh's Garrison Alley. By year-end the firm had 200 workers, 13 products, and $175,000 in annual sales.

In promoting alternating current as the only practical means of transmitting electricity more than a mile or two from a power plant, the enterprising businessman challenged the enormous prestige of Thomas A. Edison. The great inventor was a stubborn believer in direct current; he feared that no insulation could contain the high voltages envisioned by the Pittsburgh upstart. The showdown came at Chicago's Columbian Exposition of 1893. Westinghouse daringly underbid Edison's General Electric for a contract to light the great fair. When the switch was thrown, the nearly 200,000 lamps of the "City of Light," safely and spectacularly ablaze, effectively ended the debate. Within weeks the Pittsburgh firm had a contract for three huge generators to harness the power of Niagara Falls. The large-scale electrification of America—and the world—was under way.

In succeeding decades Westinghouse Electric proved to be a cornucopia of innovations: the first steam turbine for a U.S. electric utility, the first automatic electric range, iron, and percolator. The primitive radio transmitter that company engineer Frank Conrad wired up in his garage evolved

*Solid-oxide fuel cells, a project of the Westinghouse Research and Development Center, offer promising market opportunities, from home to outer space.*

into KDKA—the pioneer commercial broadcasting station of the world in 1920—and the billion-dollar Westinghouse broadcasting business of the 1980s. Company engineer Clinton Hanna's tank-gun stabilizer was honored as one of the half-dozen inventions that helped the Allies win World War II. In the 1950s Westinghouse built nuclear reactors for the first atomic-powered submarine and the first commercial-scale nuclear generating station at Shippingport, Beaver County, which reliably supplied electricity to Pittsburgh for a quarter-century. It was succeeded by a more powerful Westinghouse-built unit.

The organization went on to world leadership in nuclear power and to major contributions in national defense and the space effort. When Neil Armstrong set foot on the moon in 1969, the moment was captured forever by a Westinghouse TV camera.

Through most of its first century, the firm's growth was driven by the virtually unbroken expansion of electric power. That changed in the mid-1970s as skyrocketing fuel prices forced consumers and industry to conserve. Public utilities were encumbered with excess capacity. Electrical apparatus sales plunged.

Westinghouse responded with aggressive diversification. It moved out of some old, low-growth businesses—including lamps and consumer appliances—and concentrated on such opportunity markets as commercial and defense electronics, land and community development, and waste-to-energy systems. A dearth of new U.S. power plant orders might have wrecked the nuclear industry, despite the atom's many environmental and economic advantages; however, the undaunted Westinghouse Nuclear Center at Monroeville, Pennsylvania, successfully built the world's strongest service organization to manage, refuel, and retrofit existing power plants. The fissioning atom remains, for Westinghouse, a profit maker.

The company's first factory in Garrison Alley has long since departed in the brick dust of urban change. Even the valley-filling East Pittsburgh Works, begun in 1895, has shrunk with changing markets to a fraction of its former immensity. Yet a strong forward impulse pervades the corporation's all-electric headquarters building overlooking the Monongahela. "We need to be mindful that the future is now," says Danforth. "What we do today is the foundation for Westinghouse's next 100 years."

*The management committee oversees diversified interests of a multinational giant. From left are (seated) Leo W. Yochum, board chairman Douglas D. Danforth, Robert F. Pugliese; and from left (standing) John C. Marous, Jr., Thomas J. Murrin, Daniel L. Ritchie, Paul E. Lego, and Douglas D. Stark.*

# BURT HILL KOSAR RITTELMANN ASSOCIATES
## A HALF-CENTURY OF EXCELLENCE IN ARCHITECTURE

Pittsburgh's largest architectural firm has made its mark with some homely virtues. Burt Hill Kosar Rittelmann Associates is known for hands-on engineering and technical skills, a seeming wizardry at energy conservation, and a passion for meeting schedules and completing projects within budget.

But Ralph H. Burt points out that these are just the components of good design. "It isn't either-or," says Burt.

The headquarters that BHKRA created in 1982 for L.K. Comstock Engineering Company brought honors both for imaginative design and diminutive electric bills. The 10-story structure on a basically tight lot at 912 Fort Duquesne Boulevard achieves the look of a spacious setback by its "reverse pyramid" configuration, while an atrium showers daylight into the interior. Yearly total energy costs run about half the average per square foot for other similar Pittsburgh office buildings.

"Ornate Landmark Gets Loving Care," was *Engineering News-Record's* headline to a 1985 report on the $30-million restoration of Two Mellon Bank Center, with Burt Hill as architect. The former Union Trust Building, an early 1900s Flemish Gothic treasure, has not only been updated to "first-class 1980s office space," the magazine said, but has undergone complete exterior renovation.

BHKRA's largest hometown project to date is Liberty Center, the $137-million complex at Pitts-

*University of Pittsburgh Medical/Surgical Research Facility*

burgh's second "Point"—Grant Street's acute terminus at Liberty Avenue—a team effort with UDA Architects, with The Architects Collaborative as consultant. The hotel and office towers of earth-tone walls and sky-tinted glass, linked by retail arcades, seem to

*Liberty Center Hotel and Office Tower*

derive visual power from the very angularity of the site. The structures achieve the sort of focus that the meeting of the two great avenues has always needed.

Liberty Center's completion in 1986-1987 will see Burt Hill Kosar Rittelmann Associates across the threshold of its second half-century. Notwithstanding its longevity, the firm's fastest growth has been recent, a parallel to the city's Renaissance II.

BHKRA, which now has five offices, did not actually set up its first desk in Pittsburgh until 1971, when its total employment was 19; it's now 165. Architect Edwin Howard launched his solo practice in 1936 in Butler, a county seat 30 miles north of Pittsburgh, with

*Mellon Independence Center, Philadelphia*

*Pittsburgh Office and Research Park*

*Comstock Center*

*Two Mellon Bank Center (formerly Union Trust Building)*

*Two Chatham Center*

Ralph Burt and Alva L. Hill joining in 1952 as apprentice architects after graduation from Carnegie-Mellon University. Burt is now chairman of the firm, and Hill serves as vice-chairman. John E. Kosar, president, and P. Richard Rittelmann, vice-president/treasurer, came aboard in 1959 and 1969, respectively. The corporation was given its present name in 1978.

Activity in Pittsburgh stepped up sharply after Prudential Insurance selected BHKRA in 1979 to design Two Chatham Center, the first of the Renaissance II wave of new buildings to come on line. The architects moved their Pittsburgh staff to 300 Sixth Avenue and were soon expanding, with a big jump in growth in 1983 with the acquisition of Paul Planert Design Associates. Annual billings by the mid-1980s stood at nearly $10 million for the total firm.

Much of the firm's activity has taken place far from the Golden Triangle. Long active in Florida's market for retirement facilities, BHKRA has broadened into resort housing and retail projects.

An assignment in 1967 to design an ideal Florida community for retirement and continuing care resulted in Shell Point Village at Fort Myers, still regarded as a model for life-care communities, and still growing. BHKRA's Fort Myers office also serves The Landings, a $150-million condominium community developed in village clusters. The architects' 1979 design for Oxford Development's luxury shopping mall, the Bell Tower,

won awards for its tasteful recreation of the Florida Spanish era.

BHKRA's expertise in historic restoration led to an appointment in early 1986 as principal architect for the Mellon Independence Center in Philadelphia, an endeavor that represents a $70-million transformation of the former Lit Brothers department store—unoccupied since 1977. It will become a modern 450,000-square-foot regional banking headquarters, with 500,000 square feet of additional tenant and retail space behind its elegant, block-long nineteenth-century facade.

A three-year contract to supply technical services to the U.S. Department of Energy spurred the opening of BHKRA's Washington office in 1980; it has gone on to tackle energy-related projects for other federal agencies as well as other private- and public-sector

*Ariel Tower, The Landings, Fort Myers, Florida*

work. Research and development continue to be basic underpinnings at Burt Hill Kosar Rittelmann Associates, in fields ranging from solar engineering to the pioneering of graphic tools for energy-conscious design and new products for the building industry.

"Excellence in architecture for us means a combination," explains Ralph Burt. "It means creativity, quality, and cost effectiveness. All three are necessary for a successful project."

# HUSSEY COPPER, LTD.
## FOSTERING A PROGRESSIVE PARTNERSHIP

When the president of Hussey Copper stops beside a worker in the mill to say he has heard "the average has been slipping lately," the man is likely to break into a broad smile. He knows it's not a typical complaint about falling production, merely commiseration over a bowling score.

There's very little that's typical about Hussey Copper, Ltd., or its chief executive, Roy Allen. In a metals industry plagued by steady shrinkage in recent years, Hussey stands out as a growth story. From its headquarters plant in Leetsdale, northwest of Pittsburgh, the company ranks as one of the nation's leading suppliers of copper and copper alloy products in sheet, strip, bar, and plate forms—with annual sales of approximately $80 million in the mid-1980s, and higher projections ahead.

Allen explains it as a phenomenon of attitude.

"Hussey is a progressive company. We've been able to create an atmosphere here that eliminates the friction between labor and management," he says. "We're all in this venture together, working for the same goals. I know everybody talks about cooperation. Here we have it, and it works. It's a partnership. It shows in the

work we do and the service we provide."

Recent history demonstrates that. Since new management came to Hussey in 1979, productivity at the Leetsdale facility has increased more than 70 percent: a dramatic statistic given the state of the copper industry. A sense of direction and a feeling of pride have been restored to a firm that has seen wide swings of prosperity over the course of almost 130 years.

Hussey is the second-oldest rolling mill in the country. It was established in 1848 and had a precocious infancy. The business was so successful that its founder, Dr. Curtis Grubb Hussey, a quintessential Renaissance man—physician, art collector, entrepreneur, politician—declined a second term in the Pennsylvania legislature in order to give more time to his flourishing trade in copper.

After Dr. Hussey's death in 1893, however, his successors made a string of poor management decisions, bringing the business almost to bankruptcy. Then in 1931, under J.P. Lally's direction, it was acquired by Copper Range Company, a Michigan min-

*Roy D. Allen, president and chief executive officer.*

ing concern and that combination clicked. The new corporate entity, Hussey Copper Range, was able to pay off its bank debts at the depth of the Great Depression. Strong leadership had reversed the company's decline, and a similar pattern has marked the 1980s.

To Roy Allen—who came up through the manufacturing ranks—hands-on, engaged management involves leadership by knowing and doing rather than directing and delegating. "I've worked on the floor in the plant," he says, "and I know how important it is to have management that knows who you are. It builds trust—both ways."

A significant clue can be found in labor agreements that management has been able to work out with the United Steelworkers and other unions. When the new executive team took over in 1979, Hussey was locked in a long, debilitating strike. Allen needed the union's cooperation to keep the Leetsdale plant alive, and he received it. Vital help also came from Mellon Bank. More recently the company and union agreed to extend the existing contract, and the support of the rank and file was overwhelming.

Productivity at Leetsdale is up,

*Hussey Copper's high-speed rolling mill with automatic gage control.*

morale is high, and the effects are visible in customer service. The corporation's motto is "Be The Best At What We Do." And with a customer list that includes Westinghouse, General Electric, Square D, AT&T, Siemens-Allis/ITE, and the country's leading copper and brass distributors, numerous measures and programs are under way to ensure equally first-class service.

Thus, the firm features "Hustle" delivery. That is a shipping schedule to meet customer's just-in-time production requirements from Hussey plants at Leetsdale and at Eminence, Kentucky; or from one of three regional depots at Eminence and at Cranbury, New Jersey, and Hillside, Illinois. Having strategically located inventories enables the organizaton to respond to the shifting needs of regional and industrial markets:

*The top management team at Hussey Copper: from left (seated) Joseph C. Scripko, vice-president/finance; Roy D. Allen, president; Frederick P. Drango, vice-president/ sales and marketing; (standing) Eugene S. Fabiny, vice-president/materials management; Ralph A. Stragand, director of marketing; and George W. Hessler, vice-president/manufacturing, Leetsdale.*

construction, communications, electrical equipment, electronics, transportation, machinery, marine, defense, and metals distribution. Sales employees and manufacturers' representatives around the country staff a national sales effort directed from Leetsdale.

Hussey has developed a Statistical Process Control system to maintain and improve quality levels company-wide. SPC employs a common "language" of statistics to coordinate a great variety of work disciplines, everything from accounting to metallurgy, to monitor the firm's results—the objective being not to detect slips in quality after the fact, but to prevent them.

Many of Hussey's 310 employees work at the Leetsdale mill, and the firm considers itself deeply committed to the Pittsburgh area. Its capital reinvestment program puts profits back into the home plant and the economy of the region, and its major suppliers are Pittsburgh firms. The relationship between city and company was cemented in May 1984 with the purchase of Hussey Copper by management and a group of Pittsburgh-based investors.

With a business that is national

*Copper coils awaiting shipment at Hussey's Leetsdale depot.*

in scope, the corporation makes it a point to locate all its production in the United States and to purchase all raw materials domestically. Hussey's people have taken the restoration of the Statue of Liberty particularly to heart. The copper sheet, which is rekindling Liberty's torch high above New York Harbor, was a donation of Hussey Copper, Ltd.

"Of all our national symbols, Liberty is the most powerful," said Allen. "It's a symbol of a way of life that welcomes everyone. People of different backgrounds, with different ideas, coming together, living together, working together. Now *that*—that's what we call a partnership."

# ST. FRANCIS HEALTH SYSTEM
## PROVIDING CARE FOR BODY, MIND, AND SPIRIT

The largest hospital in western Pennsylvania, and the fourth-largest private employer in Pittsburgh, is the major subsidiary of St. Francis Health System. The medical center—at 750 beds, 2,790 employees, and a mass of hilltop buildings in the Lawrenceville-Bloomfield section—has a major economic impact on its host community.

It is also an institution that has taken the lead in shaping new organizations and techniques to reach toward the ill and the troubled who do not, or cannot, come knocking at its door. Apart from its broad range of medical surgical specialties, St. Francis offers health assistance programs to industry, a separate 210-bed psychiatric and rehabilitation unit, apartments for the elderly, and one of the nation's first facilities to treat the heartbreak of teenage drug abuse. As a retired president of the hospital,

*The St. Francis complex dominates the skyline of the Lawrenceville-Bloomfield section of Pittsburgh.*

*The original St. Francis Hospital was established in 1865.*

Sister M. Adele Meiser points out: "We have an institution that's unique in caring for all three—the body, the mind, and the spirit."

The major surprise at St. Francis, however, in view of its religious origins and more than 120 years of caring tradition, is that it is nonsectarian and privately owned. It is indeed administered

by the Sisters of the Third Order of St. Francis—approximately 65 nuns, or some 2.5 percent of the total staff—but it is not funded by the diocese of Pittsburgh. Rather, the institution relies for financial

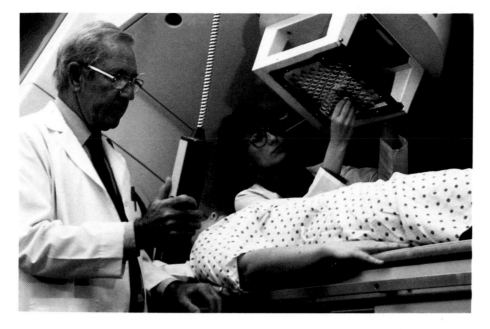

*The MeVatron machine being used to treat oncology patients.*

support on the general community and on those of its subsidiaries that were set up to provide profit-making services.

St. Francis started small, in 1865. Its first home was just that, a modest frame house in Pittsburgh's Lawrenceville, then so rural that horses plowed in neighborhood fields. The Civil War had just ended. The city's factories were turning from munitions to farm implements, springs, and carriage frames. Three nuns of the Franciscan order in Buffalo, New York, arrived in Lawrenceville in response to a plea from the residents for a hospital.

Sisters Mary Elizabeth Kaufmann, Magdalen Hess, and Stephanie Winkelmann made a 15-bed facility out of the house on 37th Street. They were armed with prayer books and faith as well as a sound nursing education. Under the leadership of Sister Mary Elizabeth, the first administrator, within a short time the tiny hospital-in-a-house proved too small for the demand.

Dr. Phillip Weisenberger, a Lawrenceville physician, donated six acres along 44th Street—as well as a larger house that stood on the property and could be converted to hold 30 beds. It was the Weisenberger tract that formed the core acreage of today's St. Francis Medical Center. An imposing three-story brick building—dedicated in September 1871—contained 120 beds, a chapel, dispensary, reception rooms, and a half-basement. The total cost was $49,208.57. The 30-bed house remained useful as an isolation pavilion.

In 1884 St. Francis became the only hospital in the city licensed to treat mentally ill women. Admission of male mental patients followed. The growing institution also was one of the nation's first to recognize and treat alcoholism as a disease rather than "a physical allergy or mental obsession." And a "free dispensary" for medical and surgical care opened in 1908 for the indigent.

The early decades brought renovations, razings, and new buildings; the addition of a laboratory and a school of nursing; and periodic leaps of advancement in standards—from hot and cold running water to wider corridors, fire escapes, "cross ventilation," fireproof building materials, food lifts, and refrigeration. There were parallel medical innovations: in 1915 Pittsburgh's first electrocardiograph machine, imported from En-

gland, and subsequent advances in anesthesia and in radiation therapy. Years afterward some of the city's first successful open-heart surgery was performed in operating suites at St. Francis.

The hospital's centennial decade, the 1960s, witnessed the opening of the only comprehensive Department of Rehabilitation Medicine between New York and Chicago, a heart catheterization laboratory, and departments of community mental health and inhalation therapy. The addition of a school of practical nursing made St. Francis the first general hospital to train both registered and practical nurses. The institution continues as a major teaching hospital affiliated with the University of Pittsburgh School of Medicine in such disciplines as respiratory care and anesthesia, along with numerous internship and residency programs.

St. Francis replaced its X-ray department in 1975, installing, among other equipment, the city's first computerized axial tomography, or CAT scanner. Through a consortium with the NMR Institute, nuclear magnetic resonance imaging also became available: a diagnostic technique that projects an internal picture of the body through radio waves and magnetic fields. In 1986 St. Francis opened its Imaging Center for outpatient diagnoses. Mammography, ultrasound, fluoroscopy, and radiology procedures are performed in a comfortable office setting.

Its long experience in treatment of drug and alcohol addiction spurred St. Francis in 1980 to open the tri-state area's first Adolescent Chemical Dependency Unit. Only the second facility of its type in the country, it is a 28-bed unit where youths who have fallen into serious abuse problems can be helped on an intensive, inpatient basis.

Demands of a changing health care environment provided the impetus, at the end of 1983, to launch an expansion unlike any in the hospital's history, an $83-million patient care building program that was to have lasted three years. The response proved overwhelming from corporate Pittsburgh and

*Today neurosurgery is accomplished using state-of-the-art laser equipment.*

from the hospital's own personnel and auxiliary. The result was that the major improvements opened ahead of schedule, in 1986. The endeavor included a nine-floor psychiatric building, a 12-floor addition for laboratory services, expanded patient care units and support services for operating rooms and nursing, and the Gurdon F. Flagg Medical/Surgical Addition. An interesting touch architecturally and in terms of

utility is the Liberace Lobby Concourse. It is named for the pianist entertainer, who donated for its construction. Critically stricken once on a concert trip to Pittsburgh, he became a great favorite during convalescence and credited St. Francis with saving his life.

The clustered hospital campus in Lawrenceville, impressive as it is, does not limit St. Francis' mission. It reaches throughout Allegheny County. Six satellite centers

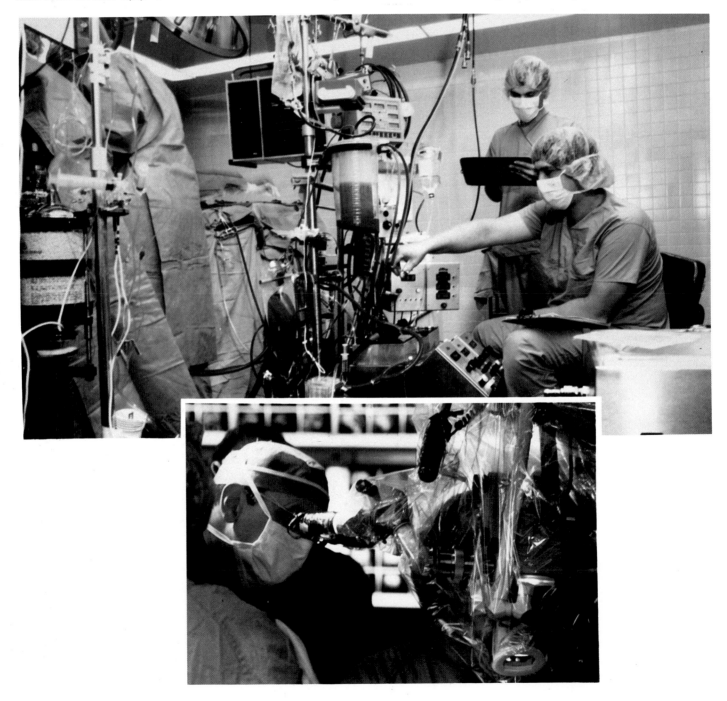

bring mental health services to adults and adolescents in as many scattered communities. Family health centers in Cranberry Township and Sharpsburg provide obstetrics and gynecological care, general medicine, ophthalmology, pediatrics, immunizations, physical exams, laboratory tests, and health education.

It is estimated that 33 percent of the U.S. population will be 65 or older by the year 2010. Sister M. Rosita Wellinger, chief executive officer of the medical center reports, "St. Francis expects to be ready, through its Geriatric Health Services." Already in operation is St. Francis Plaza, a high-rise, 100-unit apartment building for the low-income, elderly, and handicapped. Located on 44th Street, it is connected to the hospital by a small bridge. Residents are encouraged to use the medical services, chapel, and cafeteria. In addition, plans are taking shape to work with a citizens' group to revitalize the surrounding neighborhood.

Physical changes are the most easily visible. However, the hospital's organizational structure also changed dramatically in 1983, prompted by federal legislation that sharply altered the system for health care reimbursement. DRGs—diagnostic related groups —forced all hospitals to trim costs, streamline operations, purge unneeded beds, and explore alternate financing.

The result was creation of St. Francis Health System, now the parent of seven corporate entities. They are St. Francis Medical Center, St. Francis Financial Corporation, St. Francis Diversified Corporation, St. Francis Health Care Services, St. Francis Endowment, St. Francis Health Foundation, and Pennsylvania Health Choice Plan.

According to Sister M. Sylvia Schuler, president and chief executive officer of St. Francis Health System, the new organization enhances the hospital's traditional mission of care for the sick, because subsidiaries that compete in certain appropriate commercial markets are able, hopefully, to return profits. An example is HAPPI. That is the Health Assistance Program for Personnel in Industry, a Pittsburgh "first" in comprehensiveness. It includes treatment for worker injuries but more than an ounce of prevention, too: preemployment physicals, periodic examinations for managers, and health promotion seminars.

St. Francis Executive Health Center, in the National Steel Building, 20 Stanwix Street, Downtown, is a health club unlike any in the city. For active adults serious about improving their condition, it provides cardiopulmonary fitness training, diagnostic testing, medical rehabilitation, and educational wellness programs.

One of Lawrenceville's newest structures is St. Francis Medical Office Building. Convenient to the medical center, it connects by a pedestrian bridge over 44th Street to the parking garage—which serves as automotive gateway to the entire campus. The medical building contains 69,000 square feet of office space and is managed by St. Francis Diversified Corporation, whose chief executive is John R. Arnold, a former Sears, Roebuck group manager who also heads St. Francis Health Services. The eight-floor parking and office complex is topped by a heliport for Angel One, the hospital's air transport system operated through the Center for Emergency Medicine.

St. Francis has established a preferred provider organization (PPO) under the guidance of M. Daniel Splain, chief executive officer, to meet the health care needs of its own employees. Physician office visits and inpatient hospitalization are completely covered so long as service is provided by participating hospitals and doctors. Not limited to its own employees, however, the program also has been made available to corporate Pittsburgh.

The business community relies on St. Francis' extensive expertise in substance abuse prevention, intervention, and aftercare. The Adult Chemical Dependency Treatment Unit was designed particularly for working men and women. It focuses on early intervention in substance abuse. Fourteen days, half the average length of stay, reduces productivity loss. A joint venture between St. Francis and Saltworks Theater Company has put a touring show on the road. It presents to student and adult audiences brief, absorbing drama that underlines the detrimental impact of chemical dependency.

Such activities and alliances are more than cost-effective; they move in the direction of improved community health, says John R. Arnold. He points out, for example, that in momentous 1983 St. Francis's Department of Home Health joined in a bold venture with several other hospitals. They set up two corporations, Hospital Home Health Services and Complete Home Care Services, to provide special nursing attention and medical equipment in the home. Both units are able to achieve definite savings to the patient—under home conditions, which typically are far more familiar and comforting than institutionalization—while at the same time yielding a moderate profit to the sponsoring hospitals.

Some other important St. Francis affiliations are with the Keystone Regional Spinal Cord Injury System and the Center for Emergency Medicine of Western Pennsylvania, with its superb land and air transport.

St. Francis, the diamond in the rough of 1865, has become a multifaceted gem in Pittsburgh's setting as a world medical center.

# HORNE'S
## QUALITY AND FASHION LEADERSHIP SINCE 1849

An enterprise was launched with a notice in the *Daily Gazette* February 20, 1849, that stated ". . .and the business will hereafter be conducted under the style of JOSEPH HORNE & Co., at the old stand No. 63 Market, between Fourth Street and the Diamond." The old stand consisted of three floors and a basement, each measuring 18 by 60 feet. It stood until PPG Place succeeded it in 1982. An early advertisement called attention to "long & square shawls of every quality," and the "embroidered chemizetts" promoted the first year could have been ancestors of the perennially popular T-shirt.

Horne's little shop for trimmings and fancy goods appealed to both townspeople and country trade. Pittsburgh was home to 46,601 native Americans, Germans, English, Welsh, Irish, Scots, Africans, and French in descending order of census count. Ribbons sold at six and a half cents a yard, embroidered cuffs at 50 cents to $1.25, and handkerchiefs for eight and a half cents to $2.50.

Joseph Horne Co. soon expanded into curtain fringes, umbrellas, comforts, and "gents. Berlin, buck and kid gloves, gents. super silk

*An 85-foot decorated tree on the Penn and Stanwix corner of Horne's Downtown store has heralded the Christmas shopping season since 1953.*

shirts and drawers, gents. Saxony fancy cravats, &c., &c." Catering to the customers were 11 employees and the 23-year-old proprietor, who had come to Pittsburgh three years earlier from his native Bedford, Pennsylvania.

What historic foresight to launch a business in 1849! Prospectors struck gold in California, whistling the merry tune of Pittsburgh's Stephen Foster, "Oh, Susanna." Thoreau published his *Civil Disobedience*, and another revolutionary idea won a patent—the safety pin. The U.S. government organized the Department of the Interior. A woman received a med-

*Joseph Horne (1826-1892), pioneering Pittsburgh retailer, set an innovative tone in the store that bears his name.*

ical degree for the first time in America. The Great Chinese Museum opened in New York, whetting the appetite of fashion for the styles and materials of exotic places. And Amelia Bloomer thundered in print against the male chauvinists of her day.

A month after Horne's opened, Zachary Taylor was inaugurated 12th President of the United States. Since then 28 successors have occupied the White House—and Horne's has grown exponentially. The first expansion was next door, into spaces renumbered 77 and 79 Market Street. In 1871 the store moved to Liberty Hall on Penn Avenue, a building originally occupied by Mercy Hospital and (after Horne's moved out) by the Thaw Library and the famed Bijou Theater. Customers' carriages could be driven around the corner to the Red Lion Stables on Sixth Street. Joseph Horne Co. now boasted a doorman.

During his 43 years at the helm, merchant Horne directed his firm's expansion into a complete department store and the move to Penn Avenue and Stanwix Street, its Downtown site to this day. However, he died in 1892, before the wondrous emporium could be completed.

The new store opened the next year, a steel-frame structure with five hydraulic elevators, an integral power plant, and the first pneumatic tube system in town: bills and orders whooshed in cannisters through windy pipes to and from bookkeeping. Offered for sale were such specialties as Worth fashions, French corsets, perfume extract at 25 cents per ounce—decanted into the customer's own vial—and a quarter-acre of millinery assembled from Paris, London, and the store's own workshops on the premises. The chief dressmaker crossed the sea by ship to Paris twice a year to tune into the latest word in fashion.

Unhappily, the great store's early decades were marred by disasters. There were fires in 1897 and 1900, and a flood in 1907 that swirled water as high as three feet on the sidewalks; major damage was somehow kept outside, the story goes, by "hard work, common sense, and oakum." Then in the St. Patrick's Day flood of 1936, the rivers filled the magnificent street floor and raised a watermark to the mezzanine above. Hard work, indeed, to clean up from that one!

Early delivery services could make a history of their own. In

*Customer service concerns president O'Connell every day—but he wears the banner during "At Your Service" days before Christmas.*

1865 a onetime slave trundled packages in a wheelbarrow. A bright red and black horse-drawn wagon performed delivery and drayage chores in 1871. A crew of boys augmented the service in the next decade. If they had packages to carry as far as the fashionable homes on Wylie Avenue, they were given fare for the public horsecars, but they generally pocketed the coins; in Downtown's wagon-clogged streets

*Bravo!—Horne's trend-setting shops for fashion. President O'Connell confers here with E.B. Pepper, buyer.*

*Horne's at South Hills Village is a proto-type for store renewals.*

Horne's that ran the first sales commercial on the country's first commercial radio station, KDKA. In 1937 the establishment became Pittsburgh's first completely air-conditioned department store. A fully funded pension plan and a group life insurance plan for employees were introduced in 1944. An unprecedented broadening of the spectrum of regional retailing was originated the following year, with Horne's opening of Pittsburgh's first suburban department store, in Mt. Lebanon.

The geographical extension has continued, first in the suburbs, then to Erie, Pennsylvania; and subsequently to three Ohio locations—Southern Park Mall in the Youngstown area, and Randall Park Mall and Great Lakes Mall near Cleveland. The opening of a Century III Mall and Ross Park Mall units in November 1986 made Horne's a 15-store operation. The Westgate store in Fairview Park, Ohio, near Cleveland, will add a 16th in March 1987.

Joseph Horne Co. remained privately owned by two families, the Hornes and the Burchfields, until 1928, when 40,000 shares of common stock were issued to the public. The only corporate tie was to Associated Merchandise Corporation, a group for the exchange of ideas and quantity purchasing, which the Pittsburgh store had helped to found in 1903. In 1965, the year that Horne's sales hit a then-record $83 million, Associat-

*Art, furnishings, and curios from around the world are offered in Collector's Gallery.*

walking was quicker. By the turn of the century, packages were being expressed to Beaver, Sewickley, and other suburbs by train, then by wagons posted at the depots. Horne's introduced the city's first department store motor delivery in 1903, a Conrad two-cylinder steamer. Within a few years came gasoline-powered Oldsmobiles. Long-distance service was inaugurated with an epic journey in 1919. A truck, accompanied by a mechanic, delivered furniture to New York City—an 800-mile round trip—in only six days.

Changing times brought new methods of conducting and attracting business. In 1920 it was

President O'Connell and senior vice-president Rossin inspect an architectural view of the Century III store, opened in October 1986.

ed Dry Goods Corporation of New York acquired the firm through an exchange of stock.

The late 1960s and the following decade were years of struggle for quality retailers. The economy ran a jagged course of erratic growth and recession. Inflation skyrocketed. Baffling competition arose from chain specialty stores, discounters, and mass merchandisers. By the early 1980s Joseph Horne Co. felt it was time for some considerable rebuilding of relationships with its customers. In 1982 store president Joseph Vales became corporate executive vice-president of ADG, and in 1983 Robert A. O'Connell arrived as president and chief executive officer.

"I knew about Horne's," says O'Connell. "I knew it was an elegant store that prided itself on good service and fashion leadership, and was fairly traditional in appeal."

There has been a change in that latter impression. Horne's self-conception is now "contemporary and classic, sophisticated and lively," with a focus on "moderate-

to upper-income customers of all ages and life-styles." The company is committed to being the leading quality and fashion department store in the market. Thus, merchandise is being continually upgraded, and departments redeveloped for distinctive character.

Some recent additions include a department called Bravo!, featuring advanced fashions for misses, juniors, and men; Club 5'4" for petites; Women's Club, for large sizes; and Weekenders, with prestigious to pop sportswear. Says Philip Rossin, senior vice-president/sales promotion: "Our inventory has increased; there is more merchandise, and it's better edited. We're carrying more of the lines that people want."

The firm's role as leader in the industry annually reaches its most glittering hour at The Symphony Fashion Gala. Cosponsored by The Pittsburgh Symphony Association, the event is believed to be the largest benefit fashion show in the nation. It fills Heinz Hall twice, with a total audience of some 6,000, and during a 22-year period has raised more than a million dollars for the orchestra. Other organizations allied with Horne's in major community events on a regular basis are the Pittsburgh Ballet, the Pittsburgh Public Theater, Children's Hospital, Easter Seal Society, Kidfest, Ketchup Kids, High School Festival of Arts, the Make-A-Wish campaign for critically ill children, and numerous women's groups for breakfast fashion shows.

Horne's is currently undergoing extensive remodeling. The South

Hills Village store has been thoroughly transformed; a similar sea-change is on tap at Northway Mall, and the Monroeville Mall store will be crowned with a skylevel. A new look is considered inevitable for the Downtown store, likely incorporating a walkway over Penn Avenue to the recently completed office complex, Fifth Avenue Place.

President O'Connell considers Horne's earnings and prospects to be at all-time highs. At 15 units the chain employs 3,400 full-time people and an equal number of part-timers and extras. Sales percentage increases at the suburban stores have risen sharply, according to the weekly figures compiled by the University of Pittsburgh, and the Century III store is expected to add impetus to that trend. For additional capital strength Horne's parent firm, ADG, continues to register healthy and substantial growth. In 1985, when Pittsburgh won the accolade of America's "most livable" city, Horne's raised its sales record above $200 million and increased its market share by 2 percent for the third consecutive year.

The feeling around Horne's is that the best is yet to come. "We hope that as we get better, our customers will expect even more of us," says O'Connell. "Their expectations must become our realities."

World of Electronics beams state-of-the-art entertainment.

# DUQUESNE UNIVERSITY
## AN INFLUENCE ON THE THINKING OF A CITY'S LEADERS

They could smell the aroma of bread in the ovens as they climbed the stairs, the original students at what would later become Duquesne University. It was October 1, 1878, and there were 40 students, all young men; the pioneering coeds would not appear for another 30 years. Gathering on the second floor of a building near the present site of Pittsburgh's Civic Arena—above a bakery—they launched into the study of classical, scientific, commercial, and religious subjects. It was the first day of classes at the Pittsburgh Catholic College of the Holy Ghost.

The college was the dream of a small group of German priests and Brothers from the Congregation of the Holy Ghost. Previous attempts to bring Catholic higher education to Pittsburgh had failed. But after

*Duquesne University Campus as it looked in 1924. Old Main, the building in the center foreground, still stands.*

a diocese was established in the city, the university's founders resolved that there should be an opportunity in the growing industrial center for a church-related education.

The new institution took root and held. Within a few years came the beginnings of a campus, in this case incorporating a rare touch of hands-on labor. The Administration Building that rose in

1885 contained bricks fashioned by the Holy Ghost Brothers from the area's own rock and clay. And Old Main still stands, but is now part of a 39-acre campus on "The Bluff," which overlooks Pittsburgh's Downtown, between Forbes Avenue and the Monongahela River.

During its first 60 years the school's enrollment grew to more than 4,000 students as the children of immigrant parents sought the benefits of advanced education. In 1911 the institution was granted university status by the Commonwealth of Pennsylvania. It was the first Catholic institution in the state to achieve that rank. A few months later its name was changed to Duquesne University. The Marquis de Duquesne had been governor-general of French Canada in the eighteenth century, and it was under his influence that Catholic observances first reached the Pittsburgh area. At about the time of the name change, Duquesne also became the first Catholic coeducational university east of the Mississippi.

The needs of a growing student population were met through the College and Graduate School of Liberal Arts and Sciences, and the schools of Business and Adminis-

*Old Main is part of a 39-acre campus on "The Bluff" today. Its Gothic lines are in marked contrast to the modern structures that predominate.*

tration, Education, Law, Music, Nursing, and Pharmacy.

In 1937 came the founding of a unique extracurricular activity, the Duquesne University Tamburitzans, the nation's first university-based folk ensemble. "America's Youth Ambassadors," as they've been called, the "Tammies" have toured the world with their shows of folk music, song, and dance traditional to Eastern Europe, the homelands of many of Pittsburgh's ethnic people.

The post-World War II years brought more growth to The Bluff. WDUQ-FM came into being as the city's first educational college radio station. The basketball Dukes won the 1955 National Invitational Tournament (NIT) when it was considered the championship of college basketball. Duquesne also joined the elite of NCAA Division I schools in 1986, when the Dukes won their 1,000th basketball game.

Duquesne University continued to expand its facilities and its pro-

---

*In 1911 the school was granted university status, officially adopted the name of Duquesne University, and became the first Catholic coeducational university east of the Mississippi.*

grams for 25 years under two presidents, the Reverends Henry J. McAnulty and Donald S. Nesti. It is now western Pennsylvania's largest private church-related university, guided by what Father Nesti calls "five overriding principles." These principles are a commitment to excellence, particularly in academics; a recognition of abiding moral, ethical, and religious values in the education of the whole person; service to the community; a broadening of students' international and intercultural perspectives; and outreach to the disadvantaged.

Today Duquesne University offers 6,500 undergraduate and graduate students more than 100 programs leading to degrees on the associate, baccalaureate, master's, doctoral, and professional levels. The student body represents nearly every U.S. state and 40 foreign countries.

The component schools of the institution have achieved a number of milestones in quality. From the College of Liberal Arts and Sciences, for example, 100 percent of recent graduates recommended by its Pre-Health Professions Committee have been accepted by schools of medicine, dentistry, and osteopathy. The School of Business and Administration is metropolitan Pittsburgh's chief source of accountants. Thirteen members of the Pittsburgh Symphony teach at the School of Music. In the 1980s the School of Pharmacy achieved 100-percent job placement for its graduates. And 28 percent of all practicing attorneys in western Pennsylvania are alumni of the School of Law, including numerous lawmakers, state and federal judges, and justices of the State Supreme Court.

The Graduate School of Liberal Arts and Sciences enjoys international renown in a branch of contemporary philosophy and psychology known as "existential phenomenology." The school's In-

*Duquesne University, on the shore of the Monongahela River, has the skyscrapers of Downtown Pittsburgh as a backdrop.*

---

stitute of Formative Spirituality studies the effect of religious values on human development amid the pressures of contemporary society.

The university's participation in the life of Pittsburgh takes many forms through its Center for Economic Education, the Institute for World Concerns, the Duquesne History Forum, the Mid-East Music Festival, and the Division of Continuing Education, which offers popular programs in accounting, paralegal, and financial analysis.

In 1985 the institution completed its most ambitious fund-raising program ever—the $20-million Strategies for a Second Century campaign. This success was gratifying but not surprising. After more than 100 years Duquesne University is a Pittsburgh institution, deeply akin to the community in which its graduates have made a mark in fields ranging from business to the arts, government, education, law, communications, and health and social services. Of Duquesne's 39,000 living alumni, approximately 60 percent have put down roots within a 50-mile radius of The Bluff.

# THORP, REED & ARMSTRONG
## EXPANDING IN NUMEROUS AREAS OF THE LAW

Thorp, Reed & Armstrong, one of Pittsburgh's largest law firms, traces its origin to 1895, when A. Leo Weil and Charles M. Thorp established the partnership of Weil and Thorp. This firm had a continuous existence for 25 years, being dissolved in 1920, when Charles M. Thorp; his son, Charles M. Thorp, Jr.; and W. Denning Stewart established the firm of Thorp & Stewart. Charles M. Thorp had a long and successful career, leading the firm through many changes until his death in 1942.

In 1920 Thorp & Stewart became one of the first tenants of the new Union Arcade, later the Union Trust Building. With its industrial orientation, the firm prospered. In 1921 Roy G. Bostwick, a trial lawyer with an active interest in community affairs, joined the firm. Earl F. Reed became a partner in 1923, and five years later Thorp, Bostwick, Stewart & Reed relocated to the Grant Building.

It was in 1929 that the firm was retained to incorporate National Steel Corporation, thus establishing a client relationship that has continued into the firm's second half-century. National Steel, an amalgam of scattered tinplate, sheet mill, and raw materials interests, was the creation of Ernest T. Weir, for whom Weirton, West Virginia, was named, and George M. Humphrey, later Secretary of the Treasury to President Dwight D. Eisenhower. Earl F. Reed, a brilliant trial lawyer of prodigious energy, served on the executive committee of National's board for many years while continuing an active trial practice with the firm.

The company's practice continued to reflect the nature and the growth of the Pittsburgh community. Earl F. Reed served as counsel for David L. Lawrence, Pittsburgh's mayor during the city's postwar renaissance. The firm carried Jones & Laughlin Steel Corporation's challenge to the constitutionality of the National La-

bor Relations Act of 1935 to the United States Supreme Court. In a very real sense the firm's labor group helped write the first case in the book on labor relations.

A partner who began his preceptorship under Earl F. Reed in 1933 recalls working with Reed on the Poland-Ontario coal cases, involving the ownership of a vast

*Thorp, Reed & Armstrong, a law firm established in 1895, continues to serve local and national clients from its modern headquarters in One Riverfront Center, a Renaissance II structure.*

block of coal in Greene County, Pennsylvania. Allotted a scant eight minutes for argument before the Pennsylvania Supreme Court, Reed covered, in those eight min-utes, the years of development of the case and the numerous legal issues involved, including the murky Rule Against Perpetuities. The Supreme Court ruled for Reed's client and upheld the judgment.

The firm became Thorp, Reed & Armstrong in 1947. Clyde A. Armstrong, a well-known college athlete and onetime semipro base-ball player, was an aggressive liti-gator and a specialist in libel law, representing *The Pittsburgh Press.* His son, Clyde W. Armstrong, con-tinued the firm's antitrust practice, which was developed to serve the corporate clients of Charles M. Thorp, Jr., and acted as the head of the firm's litigation section until his death in 1985.

Sixteen lawyers comprised the Thorp, Reed & Armstrong of 1947, providing a range of corporate services that emphasized labor re-lations, litigation, taxation, and fi-nance. Since then the trial staff has engaged in legal contests be-fore courts and administrative agencies throughout the nation—including antitrust, environmental, and product liability cases suc-cessfully concluded only after years of effort. A present partner vividly recalls a contest before the Alle-gheny County Board of Viewers, in which the firm represented the former Pittsburgh Railways Com-pany in its struggle for fair value from Port Authority Transit on its 1964 takeover. The case was set-tled only after 198 days of hear-ings.

Several fast-growing areas of the law have fueled Thorp, Reed & Armstrong's expansion in the past 20 years, including environmental regulation, tax-free financing, em-ployment rights, pensions, and "toxic tort" litigation. The growth in its practice has lead to geo-graphic expansion. The firm opened an office in Washington, D.C., in 1976, and its Sarasota, Florida, of-fice now employs eight lawyers on matters related to the business and banking interests of Pittsburgh clients, and to the service and technology of emerging Florida companies.

In 1983 Thorp, Reed & Armstrong relocated its headquarters to three floors of One Riverfront Center, one of the first buildings completed in Pittsburgh's Renaissance II. Now comprised of some 70 law-yers plus support staff, the firm has a client base that continues to reflect the interests and growth of Pittsburgh and of the region. Its clients include not only major in-dustrial corporations such as oil and chemical companies, but also newspapers, financial institutions, commercial developers, waste-management companies, health care institutions, pharmaceutical manufacturers and distributors, and other diverse and growing businesses.

To serve those clients and the community, Thorp, Reed & Armstrong has developed exper-tise in specialized fields. Among its lawyers are individuals trained in accounting, engineering, and computer science. Former judges and public officials provide practi-cal experience in solving clients' problems. Continuing the tradition of public service established by Charles M. Thorp and Earl F. Reed, Thorp, Reed & Armstrong's lawyers act as directors and advi-sors to a number of local charities and to religious, social, and edu-cational institutions.

As Pittsburgh's business commu-nity is augmented by new service and high-technology companies, Thorp, Reed & Armstrong contin-ues to develop its expertise in those areas of law that it believes will be critical to the future of those companies and to the future of Pittsburgh.

# FISHER SCIENTIFIC
## HOUSE OF 80,000 LABORATORY PRODUCTS

*"The Alchemist,"* probably the world's best known scientific picture. The 1648 original hangs in the Fisher Collection.

(1986 sales, $675 million; 4,100 employees; a product line of 80,000 items), Fisher remains a company with a uniquely personal flavor. For most of its long existence, it was managed by Pittsburgh-born Fishers—in shirtsleeves.

It was in 1902 that Chester Garfield Fisher—a 20-year-old engineer recently graduated from the University of Pittsburgh—opened a supply house, in a loft building at 711 Penn Avenue, to equip local laboratories. The increasing role of chemical analyses in the steel industry had made a dependable supply of laboratory apparatus

Personnel in laboratories are continually striving to improve every article of food, clothing, and shelter that mankind uses. Health care, transportation, national defense, and the communications industries all constantly draw new light from research.

The drama of the laboratories unfolds behind the scenes rather than stage-center, which may be why one Pittsburgh company—Fisher Scientific—despite its familiar headquarters at 711 Forbes Avenue, remains a bit mysterious in its own hometown. However, the organization is no mystery to the world's scientists. While sitting in the firm's granite lobby, one might see the Emperor of Japan's personal physician (a distinguished hematologist) pass through on a visit to the company's museum. It contains Dutch and Flemish masterpieces depicting early laboratories—scenes familiar to almost every science student on the planet, because these famous paintings have been reproduced for textbooks and laboratory walls in every country.

When Nigeria's Ministry of Edu-

*Fisher glassblowers make the sensitive electrodes to measure acidity in everything from champagne to shampoo.*

cation wanted to introduce a new generation to science, it relied on Fisher to equip 150 teachers' colleges. Eventually, 640 tons of laboratory materials were transported to Africa in 18 air freighters—not the sort of order ($12 million) that a school board places every day, or that an ordinary scientific supplier could begin to fill.

Contrary to its size and scope

and high-purity chemicals vital; yet, prior to young Fisher's enterprise, there had been no commercial source in the region.

The little operation soon outgrew its birthplace. It moved

"uptown" in 1906 to its present location, which has now grown to an edifice of seven interconnected buildings. The business expanded steadily until 1914, when the war in Europe abruptly cut off its chief sources of supply. Undaunted, Fisher set up his own facilities for research and development and for manufacturing.

*Young entrepreneur Chester G. Fisher at his company desk in 1902.*

The step proved to be important in the coming "battle of the laboratories." Almost forgotten today is the panic that followed the first German gas attacks in 1917. Fisher was able to rush a complete research laboratory to the Allied Expeditionary Forces. Put in place outside the "east wall" of Paris, the lab analyzed the contents of gas bomb duds; and effective countermeasures were soon developed. (A generation later, in another scientific "battle," the firm would be the chief laboratory supplier to the Manhattan Project for the atomic bomb that swiftly ended World War II.)

Many products developed by Fisher in the first two decades of the twentieth century improved on the earlier European models. One was the world's first electrically heated, thermostatically controlled laboratory incubator, which replaced the erratic gas models. Another was the little Fisher burner, hailed by *Encyclopaedia Britannica* as one of the most important ad-

*Robot Maxx-5, controlled by personal computer, reads bar codes and performs accordingly, protecting human colleagues from laboratory hazards.*

vances since the original Bunsen burner.

The company's first out-of-town operation opened in 1925 in Montreal, the forerunner of dozens of branches in the United States, Canada, and worldwide. Although the appliance plant in Indiana, Pennsylvania (east of Pittsburgh), provides .3 million square feet of state-of-the-art production, the Fisher burner is still made by hand; no machine can assemble its 100-opening grid so precisely.

Far more sophisticated is the firm's Computer-Aided Titrimeter, or CAT, which automates quality-control processes in everything from petrochemicals to wines to baby food. The Histomatic is a microprocessor-controlled machine that prepares human tissues for microscopy, vital in the diagnosis of cancer and other pathologies. Maxx-5 is the most advanced laboratory robot to date. A reader of bar codes affixed to beakers and flasks, it prepares samples accordingly for analyses—thereby freeing human colleagues for less routine chores.

The Fisher catalog, a biennial production, is the largest catalog in the scientific and health care industry—over 2,000 pages, and weighing seven pounds. The first edition, written entirely by Chester Fisher, had 400 pages. It included finely detailed etchings of such products as "Otto's Acetometer, for Determining the Percentage of

Acetic Acid in Vinegar; on Wooden Base. Each, $0.60." The 1986 version features prices more in keeping with its sophisticated contents; the Genesis 21 Analyzer, for the automated testing of patient samples in medical labs, is $99,255.

Chester Fisher led his company for more than 50 years. He was joined in 1929, 1938, and 1944, respectively, by sons Aiken W., Benjamin R., and James A. In 1975 Edward G. Perkins became the first president outside the family, followed in 1982 by Thomas P. Lawton.

The Fisher family has served the community through the Allegheny Conference, Western Pennsylvania Hospital, Children's Hospital, the Child Guidance Center, Carnegie-Mellon University and other institutions; and the James Fishers have been developing a collection of twentieth-century American paintings intended for Carnegie Institute's Museum of Art.

If in some future century those modern works—as did the seventeenth-century paintings in the company museum—require restoration, they may well be examined with Fisher instruments and cleaned with Fisher chemicals, in a laboratory.

# CONSOLIDATION COAL COMPANY
## ENERGY FROM THE EARTH'S ABUNDANCE

Consolidation Coal Company headquarters is located at modern Consol Plaza, Upper St. Clair, in suburban Pittsburgh.

Coal is one of civilization's oldest energy fuels. It was burned in China 3,000 years ago. It has been used in America since Colonial times. As the world's most abundant fossil fuel, it will be a mainstay in supplying the world's energy for many years to come.

Coal's future will involve vastly more technology than its past. Gone are the pick and shovel. And in their place are automated longwall mining systems with microprocessors to guide the cutting heads through the coal seam, and technologically sophisticated transportation systems and processing plants to prepare the product for growing global markets.

In Pittsburgh, there is a leader in the coal industry. It has been part of that industry for more than 120 years and it has grown with the demand for this vital energy resource. Pittsburgh is the home of Consolidation Coal Company. Consol, as it's familiarly called, is the nation's second-largest producer of the "rock that burns." In a typical year it will produce 40 to 50 million tons from the earth,

serving the electric power, steel, and industrial markets of the United States and the world with high-quality steam and metallurgical coal. Individual markets fluctuate, but coal's total usage is a growth phenomenon. From an estimated 1985 level of U.S. consumption at 903 million tons, the demand for American coal will reach the billion-ton-a-year level in the 1990s.

Consol's production for its entire first year—37,678 tons—could have been loaded on three modern coal trains. That was in 1864, and the Union was winning the Civil War. The firm had been incorporated in 1860 when several property owners in the Georges Creek region of western Maryland voted to "consolidate" their holdings. But it wasn't until after the war that mining operations could seriously begin.

The company's general office was at 71 Broadway in New York, and Frederick H. Wolcott was its first president. The initial 1,000 shares of stock had been quickly subscribed; in May 1864, with mining actually under way, it was sim-

ple to raise the capital stock to six million dollars. Wall Street was bullish on coal. The postwar railroad and industrial booms were foreseen as inevitable. Two early New York directors of the organization were Warren Delano and James Roosevelt, grandfather and father of a future U.S. president.

By 1869 Consol was the leading producer of so-called Cumberland coal, shipping 287,605 tons. The Baltimore & Ohio Railroad purchased a large stake in 1875, and for 30 years the two firms often shared officers and directors. In 1901 Consol shipped its first coal to Japan. It was clear that western Maryland mines alone could not satisfy the global demand, prompting the company to purchase West Virginia's Milholland coal field in 1902; the 37 mines of Fairmont Coal in West Virginia the following year; and various eastern Kentucky properties in 1909 and 1910.

The 1920s brought record-breaking foreign trade, railroad freight movements, and rising prices and wages. By 1927 Consol was investing three million dollars a year on cutting and loading machines, underground transportation, and safety improvements. (Today its capital expenditures are 10 times higher on safety-related programs alone.)

The intensified demands of World War II spurred the company to buy additional mines and also to launch the industry's first major coal research program. Within months of V-Day, Consol and Pittsburgh Coal—then the nation's two largest producers—merged on November 23, 1945, to become Pittsburgh Consolidation Coal, headquartered in the Golden Triangle. A year later the new corporation acquired the Hanna Coal Company's bituminous fields in Ohio.

*Highly productive and safe, the longwall mining method produces nearly 50 percent of the coal from Consol's underground mines. Shearers move back and forth across an exposed face of coal 500 to 600 feet long while steel shields protect workers. Chain-driven conveyors carry the coal away.*

The postwar era brought a revolution in marketing and environmental standards. Competitive fuels and smoke control permanently deflated the railroad and home-heating markets, and Consol focused on development of coal for electric power generation—today's greatest single usage. Acquisitions in the 1950s, notably of the Pocahontas Fuel Company, secured a powerful position in low-volatile metallurgical coal, ideal for the making of coke to produce steel. "Pittsburgh" was removed from the company's name in 1958, and another large acquisition in 1962, Truax-Traer, added capacity in Illinois and North Dakota. By its centennial in 1964, Consol and its predecessor companies had mined more than one billion tons of coal.

Two years later came a momentous merger into Continental Oil Company, now Conoco, which in 1981 was acquired by the DuPont Company. The coal operation moved its headquarters to Consol Plaza in suburban Upper St. Clair in 1978; and in 1982 B.R. Brown was elected chairman and chief executive officer of Consol and president of coal operations of Conoco.

Consol now mines coal in most of the major coal-producing regions of the United States, plus Alberta, Canada, operating or supervising 32 deep and surface mines and employing about 10,000 persons. Predominantly an underground mining company, it has compiled one of the industry's consistently best safety records.

Today computers monitor the processing of coal in preparation plants in Pennsylvania and West Virginia, and 1986 saw a pioneering installation of a longwall shearer automation system in a southwestern Pennsylvania mine.

As early as the 1940s, predating most environmental regulation, Consol was reclaiming surface-mined land. Today it reclaims more acres per year than it disturbs, returning mined-out areas to

*Wheat is harvested on land reclaimed after surface mining. Each year Consol reclaims as many acres as it disturbs in surface mining.*

*B.R. Brown, Consol chairman and chief executive officer, confers with associates at a mining operation. The firm mines coal in nine states and Canada.*

grazing, farming, and recreational uses.

Also a pioneer in converting coal to liquid and gas fuels, Consol developed the world's first system for transporting coal in a water mixture, called slurry. In 1957 coal slurry from a Consol mine in eastern Ohio began feeding a power plant near Cleveland, and in 1979 the firm led the industry in transporting coal slurry from an underground mine to a preparation plant.

The technological frontier that Consol is exploring most avidly today, in collaboration with the Conoco Coal Research Division, at Library, south of Pittsburgh, is the improvement of combustion methods: in short, to make coal a cleaner-burning product. Impurities can be removed before, during, and after the combustion of coal in the furnace—when millions of years of locked-up energy is released to do the work of today and tomorrow.

# OXFORD DEVELOPMENT COMPANY
## PROVIDER OF EXCITING CHANGES TO SUBURBS AND CITY

It has been Oxford Development Company's destiny to change the patterns in which Pittsburghers work, shop, meet, and entertain. Just as the city of steel was turning to the broader growth opportunities of a service economy, Oxford was pioneering the industrial "plants" of the new era—the regional shopping malls and office buildings in which so much of modern economic activity takes place.

Oxford Development grew out of a predecessor company, Don Mark Realty, which represented family partners in various residential and commercial properties in Pittsburgh's Oakland section. By the early 1960s the partnership was setting its sights on more ambitious endeavors.

The partners had foresightedly obtained 90 acres of farmland on the west side of a major South Hills intersection—Washington and Fort Couch roads—even as two major department stores, Horne's and Gimbels, were striving to develop acreage on the east side for an enclosed mall. Despite the two first-class "anchors," the shopping center developers of that era doubted whether smaller tenants could be assembled under the same roof with the giants, especially so far out in the suburbs that sheep still grazed across the road.

The partners read the market differently. They swapped their own tract for the Horne's-Gimbels property and almost at once began to build. The result was the instantaneously successful South Hills Village. It opened in 1965 as the area's first mall with multilevel outdoor parking, making two floors of stores equally accessible to the occupants of 5,000 automobiles. Within a few months one million square feet of space was fully occupied by 120 tenants. The "regional mall" concept clearly worked, and shopping and travel

*The Frick Building and the Grant Street lobby.*

patterns around Pittsburgh would never be the same.

The developers did not go into a restful state of rent collection. What they had learned in Pittsburgh's southern suburbs could be applied on the east, where Monroeville—nexus of the Parkway, Turnpike, and Route 22—had become the natural focus of growth. In that case, however, all the potential had to be in the eye of the enterprising beholder. "There was no site," recalls Jack R.

*James H. Reed Building (center).*

Norris, Oxford's executive vice-president. "You were looking at wooded hillsides and a deep ravine."

Three years and seven million cubic yards of earth moving later, Monroeville Mall opened its many doors. The 1.3-million-square-foot facility and its related parking and annexes occupy 80 acres; but in fact, 260 developable acres had been gouged and filled, equivalent to two-thirds of Downtown Pittsburgh. Having created this value, Oxford has been steadily capturing it. A hotel, apartment houses, fitness clubs, office buildings, and additional retail facilities have moved in under its master plan extending into the 1990s. Oxford also expanded southward to develop malls—and more—in Florida and West Virginia. It built the new Village Square Shopping Mall in 1982 on its original acreage across Fort Couch Road—with a different marketing strategy, featuring discount outlets.

By that time Edward J. Lewis had long since become Oxford's leading executive personality. A native of Ellwood City and a practicing lawyer, Lewis served as a member of the Pittsburgh Parking Authority and various civic institutions. He had a strong interest in transferring the firm's expertise into the central city. His chance came in 1978. Two prime blocks of county-owned land, between Grant and Smithfield streets and

Third and Forbes avenues, came up for public sale. Oxford invested in a grand architectural plan, then was the successful bidder for two precious acres in the heart of Pittsburgh.

Ground was broken in July 1980; by April 1982 the first ten-

*One Oxford Centre.*

ants were moving into One Oxford Centre. The quick build was important. Lewis' firm earned a full year's marketing lead by beating the relatively leisured construction pace of its Renaissance II competition. Its 46-story cluster of aluminum and glass octagonal towers not only wrote one of the boldest statements on the skyline (it is Pittsburgh's third-tallest structure) but the atrium of the first five floors, traversed by glass-walled elevators, created a new elegance for shopping and dining with 50,000 square feet of fashionable retail space.

By 1986 One Oxford Centre was 94-percent occupied with corporate headquarters (Duquesne

Light, Joy Manufacturing, and Westinghouse Credit), several major insurance, law, financial, and accounting tenants, as well as Oxford Development's own headquarters staff on the many-windowed top floor.

In order to protect the Grant Street flank of a future "Two Oxford Centre," Lewis's firm purchased the marbled, brassy, 80-year-old Frick Building and thoroughly rejuvenated it. To help win Duquesne Light as an office tower tenant, Oxford took over the utility's own lease, which had seven years to run, on a rather nondescript structure at 600 William Penn Way. Sensing a hidden beauty in the place, Oxford purchased it from Mellon Bank, and, in partnership with Reed Smith Shaw & McClay as a long-term tenant, transformed it into a splendid showcase for the big law firm, the James H. Reed Building. Another relic, the old Frank & Seder and later Swindell-Dressler building at 441 Smithfield Street, also has been purchased and renovated. In addition, the firm hired on as manager for One Oliver Plaza.

Oxford Development Company has become the largest private owner, developer, and manager of property in Downtown Pittsburgh.

Lewis evidently means to extend that lead. As chairman, president, and chief executive officer, he hopes to establish Oxford as developer in at least one other city by the early 1990s, but he has much unfinished business locally. There is Two Oxford Centre to be constructed and a lush spread of suburban "inventory" to fill—300 acres in the North Hills' Pine Township, well-connected to Route 19, Interstate 79, and the long-awaited I-79 Bypass, pushing north out of Pittsburgh in the late 1980s. Judging from its record, Oxford Development Company will provide the essentials needed to attract motorists traveling those thoroughfares.

# MELLON STUART COMPANY
## COMMITTED TO THE BUILDING OF PITTSBURGH

*Mellon Institute for Industrial Research, completed in 1937 with 62 limestone columns 42 feet high, remains today the largest single installation of such monoliths in the world.*

Mellon Stuart Company has grown to be one of the nation's most creative general contractors and construction managers, while often raising the skyline of its own restless home city. Since early in the century the firm has put its signature on many of Pittsburgh's most famous buildings.

Since 1980 Mellon Stuart's nationwide contract volume has regularly exceeded one billion dollars. The firm also has erected two corporate headquarters of its own in the past quarter-century, in each case sparking a localized renaissance in the surrounding neighborhood. The new executive offices

*The Gulf Building was constructed by Mellon Stuart in the mid-1930s and topped the Pittsburgh skyline for a generation.*

at One NorthShore Center—set in a landscaped plaza decorated with statuary and floodlit at evening— enjoys a dazzling view across the Allegheny to the Golden Triangle, whose towers the company's workers helped to create in steel, stone, and glass.

The corporation came into being in 1917 by the merger of two complementary contracting firms. The Robert Grace Company had specialized since 1910 in railroad, tunnel, and bridge construction; the James L. Stuart Company in office buildings, power plants, and reinforced concrete work. James Stuart served as first president until ill health caused him to sell out in 1921 to his partner, Thomas A. Mellon, who had been associated with the Grace firm.

Mellon was a scion of the prominent banking family, but he had struck out on his own into the grittier business of construction. The 1920s boom in the economy spurred the establishment of offices in Chicago and New York. The $1.5-million Union Station and Standard Club were major achievements of that era in the Windy City, while numerous commercial projects went up in New

York. When the Depression took hold, the Chicago and New York licenses were allowed to expire in 1933 and efforts were concentrated in Pittsburgh, where Mellon Stuart erected the Gulf and Koppers Buildings on opposite sides of Seventh Avenue at Grant Street, a harmonious grouping that would top the city's skyline for a generation.

Meanwhile, in Oakland's civic center, the Mellon Institute for Industrial Research, completed in 1937, posed a construction challenge of a different sort: 42-foot-high limestone columns, 62 of them, which remain to this day the largest single installation of such monoliths in the world. A laborer on that project was young Edward P. "Ned" Mellon, who had joined his father's operation in 1930 in an entry-level position. When the founder retired in 1947, his son became chairman. Sensing the need for more technical expertise at the helm, Ned recruited Donald "Don" C. Peters from a vice-presidency and directorship at Crump, Inc., to join Mellon Stuart as president in 1951.

During the 1950s, under Peters' direction, Mellon Stuart developed a method of controlling costs from the initial design stage of a project and called it "ABC" (Advanced Budget Control). The decade proved prosperous. Branch offices sprouted anew to administer contracts at a distance from Pittsburgh. By 1955 the firm was using an employee incentive program and quarterly bonuses as a spur to performance, and since the early 1960s it has been employee-owned.

When a new headquarters was built for the company's staff of 30 in 1963 in the New Chateau Street

West redevelopment area, more than 10 additonal firms awarded construction contracts to Mellon Stuart and followed the firm into the neighborhood. A similar contagion positively took hold on the North Shore in the 1980s.

Ned Mellon retired in 1972; Don Peters became chairman, and his brother, Robert "Bob" N. Peters, president. The latter had joined the organization as a field engineer and risen through increasing responsibilities from estimator to vice-president of operations.

Reorganized as a holding corporation of several diversified activities, Mellon Stuart enjoyed unparalleled growth in the 1970s. A cherished Pittsburgh project was the transformation of the faded Penn Theatre, a 1920s palace, into Heinz Hall for the Performing Arts. In 1980 the company's contract volume crossed the billion-dollar mark; Don Peters retired, Bob Peters became chairman and chief executive officer; and David F. Figgins, an expert on construction systems and a Mellon Stuart employee since 1957, became president.

In Pittsburgh, Phase One of the NorthShore complex, two new office buildings and the renovation of a warehouse into a third office building for the Limbach Company, were completed in 1983. Mellon Stuart relocated its own 150 headquarters employees to NorthShore Center, and proudly watched as the new Allegheny Landing Park beautified the riverbank and additional structures underwent renovation nearby.

In more recent years Mellon Stuart has completed the spectacularly spired, six-building PPG Place in Pittsburgh's Downtown; given new life to such old lofts and warehouses as Commerce Court and Fort Pitt Commons; erected eight office structures for L.B. Foster Company; expanded or renovated major facilities for Allegheny General, South Side, and

Divine Providence hospitals; and reestablished an office in Chicago. Mid-1980s projects include most of the major reshapings of the Golden Triangle skyline: the Liberty Center hotel, office, and retail complex; Fifth Avenue Place, an office-retail tower; and the 32-story CNG headquarters building.

Mellon Stuart Company sees a vast opportunity for creative construction in Pittsburgh's metamorphosis from a grimy past to "the most livable city." Providing facilities for an entire new generation of advanced manufacturing and service firms—along with research, education, health care, and cultural activities—is Mellon Stuart's vision for the strongest growth period in its history.

*In recent years Mellon Stuart has completed the spectacularly spired six-building PPG Place in Pittsburgh's Downtown.*

Below: *Exterior of NorthShore Center, headquarters for Mellon Stuart Company, and (inset) a view of the lobby to the firm's offices taken from a vantage overlooking the fourth floor.*

# FIRST FEDERAL OF PITTSBURGH
## CONSISTENTLY IN FRONT

*The bank's original headquarters building at 600 Grant Street, now the home of USX Corporation.*

First Federal of Pittsburgh, founded with investments of $7,500 in savings during the Great Depression, has forged ahead to leadership in the thrift industry by often making itself, literally, "the first."

The institution was the first federally chartered savings and loan association applicant in Pennsylvania, and apparently the first in the nation to provide construction loan financing—the credit advance to the builder, which ensures the completion of the house. In time, First Federal became the state's initial savings and loan establishment to exceed the $100-million mark in assets. In the 1980s it became the first in Pittsburgh to raise its own Downtown skyscraper headquarters, a $100-million project destined by location and design to be one of the most prominent in the Golden Triangle.

First Federal began with an idea—and persistence. A group of determined local residents, headed by Robert Jones, believed that home building could be one of the keys to reviving the Depression-stung economy. Establishment of the Federal Home Loan Bank system in 1932 seemed the answer to a prayer. Jones personally hand-delivered his group's charter application to Washington; in fact, a bank official came out and con-

gratulated him for being the first applicant.

However, the effort was followed by months of inaction, only to end with rejection. It was found that Allegheny County had no need for a federal savings and loan association because there were already 200 state-chartered operations. Yet, not a single one advanced funds to build homes—even though, then as now, the primary purposes of an S&L were to encourage thrift and to help people purchase homes. Jones investigated and found the only type of construction loan available was "a small advance after the roof was completed, which was to finance

payroll only."

Jones proceeded to sell his idea to the objecting state S&Ls in countless personal meetings. The intent wasn't to invade their market but to supplement it, he argued. Loans would be approved before a house was begun, with funds released as the work progressed—and "only after personal inspection and approval of material and workmanship."

In the end Jones and attorney Samuel M. Jackson convinced the Federal Home Loan Bank Board itself: It granted a charter on June 5, 1934, two years after the application. (In later times the FHLB's counsel would single out First Federal as "the originator of construction financing," which today is virtually a universal practice.) Not surprisingly, a number of lumber and building supply companies subscribed the first $7,500 in savings as working capital to launch the new association. By the first annual meeting, on January 7, 1935, this sum had grown to $14,685, in 84 savings accounts.

Some of the figures from those early days seem to leap out of a different dimension. Two important early employees—Howard Nichols and Madlyn Schavonne, who each would stay 30 years or more—worked gratis in the period before First Federal received its charter, then went on the payroll at re-

*The first branch office in the Empire Building, site of the new Fifth Avenue Place.*

spective salaries of $112.50 and $70—per month. Of course, savings deposits of less than a dollar were also common.

By 1938, when the institution moved to the old American Bank Building at 600 Grant Street after outgrowing earlier quarters, assets had risen to $1.3 million; and by 1944, the 10th anniversary, to $5.3 million.

Thrift and home building both flourished after World War II. First Federal at the 20-year mark had $39 million in assets. It opened its first branch in 1955 and four years later entered its first nationwide mortgage participation syndicate, launching an activity that now exceeds $500 million in portfolio. Also in 1959, Jones retired as president—after what he called ''two years of frustration and 25 years of active service, which afforded me untold pleasure and satisfaction in accomplishment.'' His successor, Harold L. Tweedy, presided into the early 1970s through an era of growth in services, locations, and operating challenge.

A merger that extended First Federal into Pittsburgh's burgeoning South Hills in 1964 also raised it above the $100-million mark in assets—and the base has multiplied more than 22 times since. By the mid-1980s the association had more than $2.5 billion in assets, 65 offices, 700 employees, over 400,000 accounts—and much more competition.

Andrew R. Evans, the association's board chairman, who has been chief executive officer since 1976, believes that the opening of markets to state-spanning financial institutions and to aggressive non-bank service providers, will inevitably mean fewer, larger institutions; more mergers; and more advantages to consumers.

In 1968, after its Grant Street executive office was purchased and razed to make way for the headquarters of U.S. Steel, now

*An artist's rendering of the imposing Fifth Avenue Place, the new headquarters location for First Federal of Pittsburgh. Completion is expected in 1987.*

USX Corporation, First Federal moved its headquarters to 300 Sixth Avenue. Envisioning ''a major headquarters presence in Pittsburgh'' since the mid-1970s, its fruition of the dream was made possible by the association's own farsighted purchase of the old Empire Building (at the strategic corner of Liberty Avenue and Stanwix Street) and the purchase and later demolition of the venerable Jenkins Arcade, on the same block.

The new $100-million Fifth Avenue Place, a joint venture of First Federal and The Hillman Company, will contain two floors of executive offices for each of those firms in a 31-story tower offering 690,000 square feet of office space and 46,000 for retail stores.

A showcase branch of First Federal itself will invite attention from the plaza's busy pedestrian traffic.

Chairman Evans believes that Pittsburgh's economy shows a vitality in new technologies and services, which, among other positive effects, should help fill this beautiful new building. He also sees good news for consumers in the practically certain prospect that more competition in financial services will ''keep pricing to a minimum on loans, a maximum on deposits.''

## #1 COCHRAN PONTIAC-GMC TRUCKS
### A COMMITMENT TO SERVICE

"Dealership is a better word than dealer," says Robert "Bob" W. Cochran. "It takes everybody."

Included in that group are the 141 employees—sales, service, and administrative—who have made #1 Cochran Pontiac-GMC Trucks the Pittsburgh area's largest single seller of vehicles at retail. The Monroeville agency has put a lock on first place since 1978 (and among the Pittsburgh zone's 106 Pontiac dealers, long before that).

The company averages between 140 and 165 sales each week—and that's without any figure bloating by large fleet sales. Cochran does cater to a few small fleets, but basically it serves individual family decision-makers. The firm's record year, 1978, moved 8,591 vehicles, at the crest of the region's steel-based prosperity. Although the ensuing recession in the mill valleys unquestionably put a multi-year crimp in auto sales, the agency's founder (who sold his first car in a mill town) seems certain that his dealership will one day leave the old sales record in a cloud of dust, and that new industries will restore the local community as they have another hard-hit manufacturing center. "What it took Boston 30 years to accomplish I think Pittsburgh's going to do in 10," he states.

In terms of how a great market is served, having dealt over 100,000 vehicles through the years—more than enough to comfortably carry every resident in the city—Cochran returns again and again to the idea of teamwork, of an organization that retains customers by the manner in which they are taken care of after the contract is signed. "If you don't service the vehicle, you don't sell the vechicle," he says flatly.

A Pittsburgh native, Cochran went to college, served in the Army, and covered three states as

a salesman for Lance, Inc., the snacks manufacturer, for three years. On a friend's suggestion he applied to C.A. Clark Pontiac, in North Braddock, and was hired as a salesman. That was 1956, and he was 25 years old. Four years later he was general manager.

*Some of the 141 employees who have made #1 Cochran Pontiac-GMC Trucks the Pittsburgh area's largest single seller of vehicles at retail.*

The Clark agency was owned by a Westinghouse accountant who had acquired it as an investment but could not give it full-time attention. The physical set-up was cramped: showroom, service garage, and outside lot all occupied less than one acre. However, the agency enjoyed the loyalty of its mill town customers and the contagious work ethic of service people accustomed to dealing with men who knew their machines. In 1959, when Cochran became manager, the firm had 30 employees and sold 333 vehicles. Two years later it topped 400 sales for the first time; and in 1965 exceeded 1,000—some of which had to be parked at a drive-in theater, while the service department was forced to shuttle vehicles from rented garage spaces all over town. Owner C.A. Clark died in June 1965, and his general manager decided to take the plunge into ownership, risking the assets of a young family for the bank financing to make it Cochran Pontiac, Inc.

Tougher by far, though, was the decision two years later to move the dealership to Monroeville. General Motors wanted the fast-growing suburb "covered," and Cochran Pontiac clearly needed more space; but it meant a quadrupling of overhead, "a huge gamble," as Bob Cochran saw it, for the rent, taxes, utilities, and staff to man a 64,000-square-foot bare-walls building, on six acres, which had housed a discount appliance vendor and a farmer's market.

The move was officially made January 1, 1968—after several weekends during which employees voluntarily ferried cars, files, furniture, and equipment to the new location at 3772 William Penn Highway. The extra effort was characteristic: Employee loyalty is rarely an accident. Cochran Pontiac's success has been tracked right along with a lucrative profit-sharing formula, and the firm has made it a principle never to lay off a single worker in a slack time.

"We find ways to keep things going," says Clyde F. Treloar, executive vice-president and general manager. When new car sales dip, there's usually a boost to used cars, for example, and hence to the need for mechanical reconditioning. A long view of how to satisfy customers can also be a business-cycle leveler. "You sell a person one car at a time," notes Treloar. "If your price and service are right, the relationship builds each time."

The Monroeville move proved to be spectacularly right. Two large additional acreages later were acquired—for predelivery vehicle preparation and some future expansion, respectively. In 1969, impressed that one in three U.S. households owned a light truck, Cochran Pontiac obtained a GMC Trucks franchise; and later, its only auto import, Isuzu (mostly because General Motors is a heavy investor in it), as well as Vixen motor homes and recreational vehicles.

The Cochran family—wife Marge (longtime secretary/treasurer of the Oakmont Presbyterian Home) and three children—have all been part of the operation. A son-in-law, Peter Tsudis, is one of the firm's sales managers. "Everybody who goes to our house seems to end up driving our vehicles," Cochran confesses.

The entrepreneur is quite optimistic on the future of a leading-edge auto agency, but believes increasing competition inevitably must winnow the ranks of small dealerships. With modern cars utilizing as many as 10 on-board computers, the equipment and training necessary for proper service has risen to a new level of complexity. General Motors raised the competitive stakes substantially in 1986. It offered GM rustproofing, lifetime guaranteed, at no additional charge.

"With the price of cars today," explains Cochran, "auto ownership has to be viewed as an investment. You've got to have a real protection plan, and customers will come to the people who take care of their investment the best."

# PORT AUTHORITY OF ALLEGHENY COUNTY
## TWO MISSIONS THAT FLOW TOGETHER

*Dedicated on July 3, 1985, PAT's Downtown subway carried an astounding one million riders after only six weeks of operation. The popularity of the subway created a mid-day rush hour and resulted in the establishment of a new Downtown shuttle service utilizing three new light rail vehicles approximately one year ahead of schedule.*

Transportation has played an integral role in the development of southwestern Pennsylvania. Pittsburgh owes its location to the rivalry between Europe's great eighteenth-century powers, Britain and France, because both coveted the Ohio River Valley's access to the continent's interior. The raw pioneer settlement served as "Gateway to the West," and much of the early flow of people and goods that filled the heartland of America went downriver by keelboat and barge, inevitably creating a center of manufacturing, trade, crafts, and commerce at the Ohio's headwaters.

From the primitive rafts and carriages of yesterday to today's modern air-conditioned buses and light rail vehicles, transportation has served critical needs for millions of area residents joined, but also separated, by a deeply carved topography of hills, streams, and valleys.

The responsibility for providing public transportation in Allegheny County today rests with one of the nation's largest systems—PAT, Port Authority of Allegheny County. PAT's economic role goes beyond transporting people. It also assists with promoting the Port of Pittsburgh. The two functions are distinct but interwoven. The region's geographical assets pose difficult challenges to the transportation engineer and operator. From the earliest times into the twentieth century, river traffic might be slowed to a trickle when a dry summer dropped the water level.

On the other hand, periodic floods could play havoc with land transportation—and demanded, at the least, structurally powerful bridges.

Early in this century the federal government's "canalization" of the rivers by locks and dams assured their navigability in seasons of too little rainfall while flood-control dams greatly diminished the damage from too much. The result is that more than 50 million tons of cargo can move each year on Pittsburgh's three rivers, making the Port of Pittsburgh the nation's largest inland port. The famed Point of Pittsburgh connects to a remarkable 8,954 miles of navigable waterways that ultimately emerge into the Gulf of Mexico.

It's not widely realized today, but trolley companies built many of the early crossings in the "City of Bridges." They were needed to convey vehicles and riders across rivers. Intense interest in public transportation goes back to at least the mid-nineteenth century. Horsecars first appeared in Pittsburgh in 1859; the last survivor operated on the South Side until 1923. Cable cars appeared in 1888, but by 1897 they were replaced by the much more versatile electric trolley cars.

The earliest models were glorified four-wheel horsecars refitted with a "troller," or trolley pole, and electric motors to drive the wheels.

This fast and fashionable mode of travel—before the age of the automobile—spurred the formation of more than 100 private trolley ventures in Allegheny County. In 1902 the three largest of these merged to form Pittsburgh Railways Company, which would pro-

*Public transit plays an integral part in Allegheny County's economic well being. PAT carries approximately 90 million riders each year, including 60 percent of the people working in Downtown Pittsburgh. PAT services a more than 700-square-mile area with a 1.4-million population base.*

vide the bulk of service in the region for more than six decades. In 1964 Pittsburgh Railways and 32 other transit operations were consolidated into a countywide system: Port Authority Transit, or PAT.

As established by the state legislature on April 6, 1956, the authority's first responsibility was for port facilities. Not until October 7, 1959, did it acquire the mission of transporting the public. Before that, transit in the county had been highly fragmented. Each carrier had its own fares and schedules, and much equipment was outdated. Few operating companies earned a profit. PAT purchased all this—31 transit firms and two inclines—for $26 million.

The first tasks were to consolidate 38 garages (one of which had begun life as a coal mine's mule stable) into six operating divisions and to purchase a fleet of new buses. PAT went on to a pioneering role in development and technology.

The 4.3-mile South Busway opened in 1977, an exclusive right-of-way that removed 15 bus routes from congested Highway

51 and also is shared, part way, with streetcars. Rehabilitated equipment and a new transportation center went into service in 1982 on the PATrain, a commuter train serving the Monongahela Valley. The following year marked the opening of another major improvement: the Martin Luther King, Jr., East Busway. Significantly reduced travel times are the daily reward from this 6.8-mile concrete ribbon through eastern neighborhoods; it is used by 27 routes, including the EBA, a bus route dedicated exclusively to linking the five busway stations to Downtown. The historic Monongahela Incline also received a $3-million rehabilitation in 1983, improving its operating condition and enhancing its turn-of-the-century charm.

PAT has become the nationally

---

*The Martin Luther King, Jr., East Busway is one of two transit-only roadways operated by PAT. This 6.8-mile exclusive bus-only facility complements PAT's 4.3-mile South Busway, where both bus and rail vehicles share portions of the same right-of-way. When opened in 1977 the South Busway became the nation's first busway built entirely on its own right-of-way and not in conjunction with another highway project.*

acknowledged pioneer in ACCESS service. This door-to-door advance-reservation transportation system gives mobility to elderly and handicapped persons who cannot use a conventional bus and other fixed-route services.

The highlight in modern people-carrying convenience is the Light Rail Transit and Downtown subway system called the "T."

New cars, smooth track, and bright, safe stations drew more than a quarter-million curious riders into the subway during its four-day grand opening that began July 3, 1985. The completion of the system in late 1986 sparked a rediscovery of the economy and convenience of mass transit by thousands of South Hills residents and motorists.

The Port Authority of Allegheny County takes its dual roles seriously: providing superior public transportation; and attracting commerce, and ultimately jobs, to the region's versatile rivers, with their values for industry, trade, recreation, and aesthetic beauty. Two missions, seemingly separate, in fact flow together harmoniously for the benefit of the community.

# KAUFMANN'S
## A RETAILER THAT REFLECTS THE CITY'S DYNAMISM

"The store was small, the stock limited, but they had the most important stock a merchant can carry . . . faith, foresight, and fair-dealing."

As have many great enterprises, Pittsburgh's largest department store company sprang from humble beginnings.

The time was June 1871, within a few years of the end of the Civil War and in the early dawn of Pittsburgh's role as supplier of rails, cable, and girders for an America rapidly filling and building its continent. Two brothers, Isaac and Jacob Kaufmann, opened a one-room shop in Carson Street on the

*Edgar J. Kaufmann, son of the founder, whose flair for retailing set the style for Kaufmann's for years to come.*

industrial city's South Side. The store was gas-lit; the brothers had $1,500 between them.

Jacob Kaufmann, the son of a trader in horses, had come to Pittsburgh from the Rhenish village of Viernheim, Germany. In keeping with the name "kaufmann," which in German literally connotes a retailer, a "buy man," the young immigrant became a peddler with a pack on his back—selling household items in the villages around Pittsburgh. When he had saved enough, he was able to bring Isaac to America; then, a bit

later, 14-year-old Morris and 12-year-old Henry. Morris slept on the second floor of the shop. Legend has it—perhaps a family joke that acquired the authority of tradition—that the boy served as the store's burglar alarm. A piece of string tied to his toe dangled out the window and down to street level. A sharp yank woke him if he overslept.

The timing was right for the Kaufmann brothers. The coal and steel industries were creating jobs by the thousands, thereby boosting workers' economies. The Jones & Laughlin American Iron Works populated the South Side, and Carson Street teemed with shopping traffic. Menswear was a specialty with the Kaufmann merchants: They hand-tailored suits from fine imported fabrics. At the end of their first year, sales to-

*William T. Tobin, president and chief executive officer (left), and Elden Rasmussen, chairman.*

taled a creditable—in fact, a remarkable—$21,585. Six years and several expansions later, the brothers arrived at the site of the present store on Smithfield Street in the heart of the city's Golden Triangle. They continued to expand, opening the walls into one store after another until the entire block was occupied from Fifth Avenue to Diamond Street (now Forbes Avenue).

When Edgar J. Kaufmann, the son of Morris, took the reins in the 1920s, a new era began. Kaufmann's was on the way to ac-

*A Pittsburgh landmark.*

488

quiring the polished cosmopolitan image that it bears to this day.

Just one generation removed from the shop on the South Side, "E.J." (as department store people called him) was educated at Shady Side Academy and Yale. He cut a handsome, romantic figure (complete to an authentic saber scar from Heidelberg). Possessing a grand flair for retailing, he apprenticed at Marshall Field in Chicago and at stores in Germany and Paris; then, returning to the family business, he performed endeavors in every department, not excluding the warehouse, the garage, traffic, and packing.

A "merchant prince," people often called him, and E.J. was never known to take offense at the royal image. He meant to put Pittsburgh, and Kaufmann's, on fashion's world map. He set up business offices in no fewer than 27 foreign cities. When the first transatlantic telephone call was put through from Pittsburgh to Paris in 1928, it was Edgar Kaufmann at the stateside end: He wanted a first-hand report—and of course the attendant publicity—on what his buyer thought of the couturiers' latest showings. E.J. kept two private offices at the huge store. One was spacious and modern, the other a former monastery taproom that he had shipped intact from Europe. His home—one of his five homes— was "Fallingwater," overhanging Bear Run in rural Fayette County. Designed by Frank Lloyd Wright, it may be that great architect's masterpiece and is certainly one of the most photographed houses in the world.

Liliane Kaufmann, E.J.'s wife, was also closely involved with the store. She originated and supervised its elite Vendome Shops. Although short in stature, she had the poise and posture that enabled her to wear fashions like a model. It was said that she and E.J. were two of a kind, cut from the same cloth. In fact, they were. Liliane was

Expansion into the suburban areas of Pittsburgh and other communities began in 1961, and today there are 16 contemporary, service-oriented, regional Kaufmann's department stores. Shown here are stores in Charleston, West Virginia (above), and Kaufmann's in the Century III Mall, Pittsburgh (right).

the daughter of Isaac Kaufmann, and hence her husband's first cousin.

For Edgar Kaufmann the fate of his store was always tied to its larger community. He played a key role in the city's post-World War II renaissance. One of the six incorporators of the Allegheny Conference on Community Development, he also donated $1.5 million toward construction of the Civic Arena and financed the Civic Light Opera. The philanthropist set up the Kaufmann Multiple Fellowship at Mellon Institute and the University of Pittsburgh, and the bulk of his estate went to a charitable fund for cultural projects in his beloved hometown.

A connoisseur and collector of art, Edgar Kaufmann believed that creative beauty should be incorporated into industry and commerce. He had a chance to express this idea in Kaufmann's First Floor: a high point of Art Deco, widely copied elsewhere in the country, with black Carrara glass columns and a marble floor with inlaid wheel-and-

spoke motifs. The First Floor was opened in the "movie premiere" style of 1930, hosting 600 invited guests. Ten canvas murals lined the walls: Boardman Robinson's heroic figures depicting the history of commerce. Years later the murals were donated to the Pittsburgh History and Landmarks Foundation; however, the Arcade elevators and entrance doors remain gleaming examples of Art Deco.

In its 75th year of business, on October 1, 1946, Kaufmann's joined The May Company. The merger provided the solution to nonfamily managerial succession. Edgar Kaufmann's only child, Edgar Jr., had not sought an active role in the store and instead pursued an art career in New York. The store's owner retained its presidency after the merger, and became a vice-president of

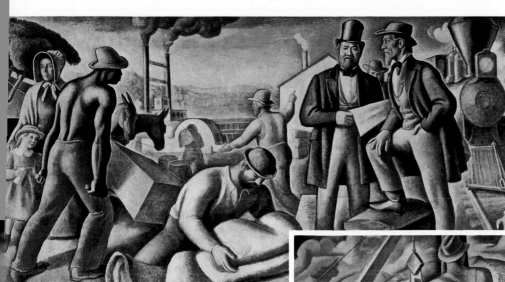

the corporate parent—which is based in St. Louis and is now the May Department Stores Company.

Kaufmann's "flagship" store generates more than 50 percent of all conventional department store sales in Pittsburgh's thriving Downtown area. Nonetheless, by the 1960s it was clear that the firm had to meet its suburban customers more than halfway.

Expansion began with its Monroeville unit in 1961; today there are 16 of these contemporary, service-oriented, regional Kaufmann's department stores. The latest is the Ross Park Mall store, opened in August 1986. At 220,000 square feet, it was the largest of seven new stores in The May Company capital program for the year. With the multibillion-dollar buying power of that firm behind it, Kaufmann's now serves a region embracing western Pennsylvania, northeastern Ohio, and West Virginia. Its large, well-stocked stores, which are at once keen to trends in fashion and home furnishings, are in tune as well with their respective local communities. A Kaufmann's operation—wherever—takes an active role in local economic and community life.

Kaufmann's in Downtown Pittsburgh continues to be the largest department store between New York and Chicago. A 13-story bazaar of music, color, and action, it's a retailing stage for everything up-to-the-minute in consumer preferences. In addition, the establishment houses beauty salons, a dental clinic, seven restaurants, and food bars.

A Kaufmann's charge account accommodates a vacation, theater tickets, a mink coat, or a bag of jelly beans. Lovers of homemade soup consume 50,000 steaming gallons a year at Kaufmann's, which also sells 220,000 hamburgers during that period. A half-million cookies are baked annually, as well as renowned pies from 15 tons of apples simmered in cinnamon.

Triangle Corner, Ltd., is Kaufmann's program for women in business. By the mid-1980s it was bringing in more than 7,800 persons for a year-round agenda of health, literature, current events, and travel lectures. B. Dalton Booksellers operates a large outlet in Kaufmann's Downtown. Some residents learn to drive a car at Kaufmann's, while others take full-credit college courses taught by local university faculty. And thousands traditionally welcome Santa Claus in the company's annual Christmas Parade on Fifth Avenue the day after Thanksgiving.

A great department store is a wonderfully complex world within itself. Before the day's first sale is rung up, it's a beehive of activity. At 10 a.m. the shining brass doors open to welcome the customers, but hundreds of employees may have been on the job for hours—including porters, maids, payroll clerks, computer operators, and electricians. Painters and display designers are already changing scenery, decorating windows, and dressing mannequins. Chefs have been baking, stirring, and seasoning. Floors are scrubbed, carpets swept, merchandise unpacked, ticketed, and arranged; escalators and elevators are inspected. Tailors have been letting seams out or taking them in. Even artists and copywriters have been preparing advertisements in the early hours before the customers' arrival.

These employees are drawn from every part of the community, and no one doubts that their commitment is the cement that holds Kaufmann's together as a great retailer in Pittsburgh's dynamic marketplace. "A block long and a world wide," it is said of Kaufmann's. Still, it remains a phenomenon rooted very much in the economic well-being of the city that welcomed four immigrant brothers with their touching belief in the business values of "faith, foresight, and fair-dealing."

# USAIR GROUP, INC.
## FLOURISHING IN A DEREGULATED ATMOSPHERE

On a spring morning in 1939, three small planes took off from Allegheny County Airport near Pittsburgh and skimmed across the rolling countryside toward Latrobe, 40 miles to the east in Westmoreland County, 18 minutes away. There, by a grassy landing strip, several hundred spectators waited.

The crowd jostled as the sound of propeller motors snuffled over the pastures. Then the planes appeared, insect-like on the horizon—single-engine Stinsons, boldly painted scarlet, with cabin spaces that would not have made a roomy closet. No matter. The premier flights of All American Aviation, Inc., were not going to be carrying passengers.

Edwin I. Colodny, chairman of the board and president of USAir Group, Inc.

In the lead plane, pilot Norman Rintoul descended to just 60 feet and flew over the strip at 100 miles per hour. Two cables hung down from the belly of his craft: One ended in a 50-pound container, the second in a grappling hook. The container, suddenly released, landed with a puff of dust and rolled. Rintoul headed the plane straight between, and a few

yards above, a pair of 30-foot stell masts that had been erected 60 feet apart (like football goalposts). Loosely slung from the masts was a limp rope, and another container hung from it. The plane's suspended cable hooked the rope and whipped the container aloft, drawing it into the belly of the craft. The crowd cheered and slapped backs.

Thus was the mail—official U.S. postal airmail—delivered and picked up from Latrobe Airport at 11 a.m. that historic day, May 12,

Several hundred flights a day operate from USAir's hub at Greater Pittsburgh International Airport.

1939.

It was the inaugural flight of what would become a few decades later, USAir Group, Inc., one of the nation's most successful transportation companies and, in several ways, "Pittsburgh's airline." USAir's history, as that of aviation itself, has been a continuing drama of enterprise and surprise.

Serving more than 19 million travelers annually by the mid-1980s, the firm went through its first 10 years of operation without transporting a single passenger. It was the first domestic airline to be certified by the Civil Aeronautics Board after the CAB came into existence in 1938, but the license was granted strictly for mail and express service.

Although USAir was an outspoken opponent of airline deregulation in 1978, no other carrier had flourished so well in the high winds of marketplace freedom. Most competitors dived at least temporarily into the red; 70 ceased operations; 35 went bankrupt.

"Think of the toughest business you can," wrote *Washingtonian Magazine* in 1984, "a business that changes radically because of deregulation, oil price increases, the run-up in interest rates, and severe labor problems . . . (in

which) almost every major company lost money. We're speaking of the airline industry." This was the preamble to the publication's naming of USAir board chairman Edwin I. Colodny as Businessman of the Year in Washington, D.C., for heading "what may be the best-run company in that industry."

The half-century contrast between All American Aviation and USAir is phenomenal. The pioneer firm had begun with seven pilots and four flight mechanics; USAir's 1986 employment neared 14,000. More than 7,000 worked in the Pittsburgh area, where USAir

Left: *Boeing 737-300, a twin-jet, fuel-saving craft whose specifications USAir helped create.*

Bottom left: *USAir's operations hub at Greater Pittsburgh International Airport, where scheduling becomes a fine science.*

Below: *The comfort, safety, and speed of air travel is discovered each year by thousands of Pittsburghers in a USAir 727-200.*

ranks among the half-dozen largest private employers. The company's maintenance and operations base had been centered since 1963 in huge hangars at Greater Pittsburgh International Airport; some 2,400 mechanical, engineering, and training experts there account for 11 percent of the airline's direct operating costs, performing more than 90 percent of the work needed to keep its planes aloft, on a budget topping $165 million a year. USAir's total inputs to the area economy of the 1980s was estimated at $620 mil-

lion annually—including salaries, landing fees, taxes, and purchases of fuel and food. Training in both flight and ground operations is focused at Pittsburgh; so is the firm's largest single reservations center.

From a passenger standpoint the airport figures most prominently as USAir's flight "hub." In the years since deregulation all the growth-minded carriers have found it most efficient to fly to multiple destinations from a single point. Consequently, they have added routes as "spokes" radiat-

ing from a central, frequently served airport. Travelers from all points of the compass can transfer quickly from inbound to outbound flights, while the airline gets the best odds of exceeding its all-important "breakeven load factor" on every outgoing flight.

The system works best for people who live near a hub: They get the most choices of nonstop destinations. USAir's Ed Colodny calls greater Pittsburgh a "megahub." Within five years of deregulation his firm and its Allegheny Commuter associates were running 328 daily departures from the Moon Township jetstrips, and a remarkable 111 nonstop destinations were reachable from Pittsburgh by USAir or a related Allegheny Commuter service. More than 88,000 times a year, USAir jets climbed skyward from greater Pittsburgh bearing 5.5 million enplaned travelers.

The universality of riding the sky could hardly be prophesied when young Richard C. DuPont, of Wilmington, Delaware, formed All American Aviation in 1938. The country's air transport system, a full 20 years after the advances made in World War I, still served just 210 of the 4,000 U.S. communities of more than 5,000 people. Only one-quarter of Americans had reasonable access to an airport. As late as 1928 an airline executive had predicted: "The day will never come when passengers will fly over the Alleghenies. It is too dangerous."

Passengers were less than top priority with DuPont himself. Not yet 30, an heir to the famed industrial family, he was a glider enthusiast, president of the Soaring Society of America, and had become fascinated with techniques for picking objects up and dropping them off while airborne. A serious potential market was thought to exist; few visionaries predicted a nationwide proliferation of real airports. Specifically, DuPont was excited by the work of Dr. Lytle S. Adams, of Irwin, an eastern suburb of Pittsburgh. Adams had invented a grappling-hook airmail

*All American Airways used a 24-seat DC-3 on its historic first passenger flight, March 7, 1949.*

pickup system and demonstrated it in daily stunt runs at the 1933 Chicago World's Fair.

When, a few years later, the U.S. Post Office advertised for an experimental service to fly 1,040 miles of sparsely traveled mail routes in Pennsylvania and three neighboring states, DuPont eagerly bid. He was the only bidder—and had to acquire planes and build an organization in less than six months. His firm manufactured the hook and mast equipment at Wilmington, while the flight operations that began that May morning in 1939 were swiftly catching the imagination of news media and the public. "Flying post offices," "Winged mailmen," the press romanticized the couriers that swooped down through Appalachia at five- to 20-mile intervals for the suspenseful deliveries and pickups. In four years the service spread, with no injuries to cargo or personnel, to 115 communities in six states; and DuPont's company employed 130 persons.

By that time the founder was serving in the war, as an expert in glider operations for the U.S. Army

*USAir's maintenance and operations base at Greater Pittsburgh International Airport employs some 2,400 technical personnel keeping a great fleet aloft. Photo by Mike Mitchell*

Air Corps. He was killed at age 33 while testing advanced equipment. The company adapted much of its technology to military use, and gliders saw service in the Burma and Germany campaigns, even at D-Day in Normandy. An adaptation of the pickup technique helped remove casualties from the Remagen beachhead on the Rhine; and human pickup still occasionally comes in handy in the rescue of agents and prisoners from remote spots.

In the years after World War II, the many innovations in airports and aircraft had made mail pickup a high-cost, obsolescent service. The CAB had turned to promoting conventional boarding for both passengers and postcards. It began awarding "feeder line" routes to smaller carriers, and in 1949 All American was awarded service to 25 cities in six mid-Atlantic states. Robert M. Love, the firm's president at that time, launched its passenger service on March 7 of that year, using dependable 24-seat Douglas DC-3s especially modified with fold-down doors and boarding steps for "two-minute stops." The company's name was trimmed to All American Airways, the corporate office moved to Washington from Wilmington, and a few months later the thrills of air pickup quietly passed into history.

However, passenger service flourished. A major reorganization in 1953 under president Leslie O. Barnes changed the corporation's name to Allegheny Airlines; expanded the fleet with larger, more powerful planes; and ushered in service innovations, such as the nation's first on-board ticketing, without reservations, on commuter flights between Pittsburgh and Philadelphia in 1959.

With the epoch-making marking arrival of the jets in 1965, Allegheny during one stretch was adding a new turbine-powered airplane at the rate of one every 18 days. The operations base moved

*USAir's maintenance base makes Pittsburgh an important center for the repair of jet engines.*

from congested Washington to Pittsburgh; 14 reservations offices were combined in a single computerized complex; and the Allegheny Cornmuter system, an industry first, was launched in 1967 to serve smaller communities by locally based airlines feeding a central airport with frequent turnaround service, Allegheny itself providing backup support reservations, ground handling, and interline ticketing.

Mergers with Lake Central Airlines in 1968 and Mohawk Airlines in 1972 gave Allegheny a territory from Montreal to Memphis, the Atlantic Ocean to the Mississippi, and more than nine million annual passengers. By 1974, although then the nation's sixth-largest passenger-carrying airline, Allegheny was still misperceived as being "small," a problem that market research traced in large part to its local-sounding name.

Management chose the new identity of USAir—but carefully kept it on the shelf until a broader geographical reach would give it credibility. The gates to greater, but also riskier, growth were thrown open by the Airline Deregulation Act of 1978, and the firm swiftly went for such long-denied markets as Orlando, Phoenix, and New Orleans. On October 28, 1979, at the height of a skillful media campaign to underline the new image in public conscious-

ness, Allegheny Airlines became USAir.

In the post-deregulation era the organization has invested one billion dollars to expand and improve its fleet, particularly stressing efficient, fuel-saving craft such as the twin-jet Boeing 737-300 (whose specifications it helped create, knowing well that two-thirds of all domestic travel is under 1,000 miles). In the first five years of a competition open to any new entrants with used planes, loss leader fares, and nonunion workers, USAir increased its revenues 96 percent; employment 22 percent; and added 25 cities, mostly in the Sunbelt, dropping only 12 (of which seven continued to be served by commuters).

The number of airline industry passengers continues to increase. The total will reach 400 million in 1987; and by the early 1990s, probably 500 million. Thus, America faces a major infrastructure issue: to increase the capacities of its airports and airways. USAir's Colodny says the price is manageable—an estimated $18 billion for the balance of the 1980s in federal, state, and local funding—while the payoff, in safety, convenience, and utilization of time is incalculable.

# OLIVER REALTY
## COMPLETE SERVICES FOR COMMERCIAL AND INDUSTRIAL REAL ESTATE

Oliver Realty leases and manages more major office buildings in metropolitan Pittsburgh than any other firm.

Nonetheless, its 16 million square feet of space under management and leasing contracts nationwide is only part of the firm's expertise. Its 190 employees also design office space for optimum client use, supervise construction, and conduct real estate investment brokerage, syndication, and consulting services coast to coast.

The company's history is rooted in the real estate investments left by Henry W. Oliver (1840-1904), a Pittsburgh developer of steel, railroad, and pre-mining properties. In 1976 veteran executive Ernest U. Buckman purchased the real estate management functions of Oliver Tyrone Corporation, and later brought in 40 key co-workers as shareholders. The organization enjoyed a decade of solid growth under employee ownership, becoming one of the country's 20 largest firms in real estate services.

In September 1985 the growth trail led to a strategic integration with the Grubb & Ellis Company. With strong positions in Pittsburgh, Philadelphia, Cleveland, Princeton, Tampa, and southeastern Michigan, Grubb & Ellis made a valuable acquisition in Oliver Realty. San Francisco-based Grubb & Ellis, formed in 1951 as a residential brokerage company, has evolved into the largest independent operation of its type in the nation, and is listed on the

New York Stock Exchange.

Oliver Realty's president and chief executive officer, Ronald M. Puntil, and Grubb & Ellis' hard-driving chairman, Harold E. Ellis, Jr., believe that real estate opportunities no longer can be served by a fragmented, local industry. Their merger brings Oliver Realty numerous advantages, says Puntil. He lists them as "first and foremost, more markets. We represent a number of major corporations and other clients who want to conduct real estate business nationally, and we now have the increased capability to do so. Second, we now have extensive training programs and other resources to help us provide better services for our clients and wider opportunities for our employees."

Although its horizons are nation-

*Oliver Realty corporate headquarters at Two Oliver Plaza.*

wide, Oliver Realty likes what it sees in Pittsburgh's real estate future: an orderly absorption of office space by growing, information-based firms, and a city whose location and quality of life keep major headquarters content. Oliver Realty no doubt will continue to play a major role in maintaining the quality of life for Pittsburgh's business headquarters. Recalls Ron Puntil with a smile, "One client recently told us that we seemed as concerned as he was with the bottom line."

*Oliver Realty property managers conduct an analysis of building operations systems.*

*Oliver Design Group personnel discuss various office interior finishes.*

# BEYNON & COMPANY
## GROWING, CHANGING WITH A RENAISSANCE CITY

The growth of Beynon & Company is woven into the patterns of Pittsburgh's transformation during the twentieth century.

From its beginning as C.C. McKallip & Company in 1912, Beynon has specialized in selling, renting, managing, and developing commercial and industrial real estate. It is one of the city's largest privately owned firms of its type.

It was McKallip that handled development of Oakland's Webster Hall as an exact copy of a Detroit hotel, and pioneered both percentage leases and long-term leases in Pittsburgh. During the Depression the company kept active in real estate for local investors who were accumulating income properties at foreclosure prices. In the 1950s renaissance McKallip brokered the strategic acreage that contains Downtown's Gateway Center.

In 1965 William J. Beynon purchased the firm and renamed it Beynon & Company. He had joined McKallip at 18 as a stock boy and attended the University of Pittsburgh at night, earning his real estate license in 1943. Returning from World War II as a decorated veteran, he quickly rose through the ranks to become head of the company's industrial development department, then vice-president in 1951.

Not missing a step in its first year under his aegis, Beynon & Company, in 1965, earned record profits; consulted on land acquisition for the U.S. Steel Building, the Urban Redevelopment Authority, and Ford Motor Company; helped initiate the revival of the Strip District; and acquired Logue Brothers and the Hess Company, to become one of Pittsburgh's major independent insurance agents.

The pace has not flagged since. Beynon's was one of the first private real estate firms to test the concept of a fully integrated industrial park, the Parkway West's Vista

*Thorne McKallip (left) and William J. Beynon signing the papers for Beynon & Company's takeover of C.C. McKallip & Company in January 1965.*

*The Grant-Liberty Center hotel/office/retail complex. Beynon & Company helped to develop this newest Pittsburgh commercial center.*

Industrial Park. The company took a large hand in Pittsburgh's subway development—consulting for U.S. Steel in the formation of the Grant Street station and selling the former Azen property for the Wood Street station.

Beynon also assembled land for One Mellon Bank Center, the Village Square Shopping Center on Fort Couch Road, and Fifth Avenue Place, Downtown. It managed one of the Downtown area's first conversions to office condominiums, the Benedum-Trees Building. It helped develop and is part owner of both the Hunt Stable Condominiums in Ligonier and Liberty Center, Pittsburgh's newest hotel/office/retail complex. It also served as broker and assembled additional land for the conversion of the Stanley Theater into the new gem of Pittsburgh's cultural cluster, the Benedum Center for the Performing Arts.

In 1986, following the death of William J. Beynon, leadership of Beynon & Company passed to his oldest son, Robert, who sees a wealth of opportunities in the years ahead for real estate creativity. "This firm was founded on family principles of service, honesty, and integrity," he states. "We're going to keep growing the same way."

# H.K. PORTER COMPANY, INC.
## A PITTSBURGH BUSINESS LEGEND

*Thomas Mellon Evans, who, in the midst of the Great Depression, took over the bankrupt H.K. Porter Company and saved it from almost certain extinction. Today he is still active in the firm as chairman of the executive committee.*

H.K. Porter Company, Inc., is a firm that has been founded twice: once in 1866, the second time in 1939. Each time by a man for his time, an entrepreneur. Each man seized upon a set of circumstances. Each took advantage of an opportunity, moved with confidence, and trusted in his ability. And each became enormously successful.

Strangely, there are few similarities in the men who built the two H.K. Porters and none in their respective companies, other than the fact that both businesses were formed to manufacture quality products that would serve industry.

Henry Kirke Porter was a reserved man, a New Englander. He studied for the ministry, served with the Massachusetts Volunteers during the Civil War, and at war's end, armed with a $20,000 bequest from his father, came to Pittsburgh and formed the Smith and Porter Company. The young

*The* Joshua Rhodes *steam locomotive is an example of one of the early products of the Smith & Porter Company, forerunner of today's H.K. Porter Company, Inc.*

enterprise manufactured steam locomotives of the type then used in factories, mills, and mines. The business was an immediate success. The year was 1866, and Porter was just 26 years old.

By the time the century drew to a close the Smith and Porter Company had become the H.K. Porter Company and had grown to become one of the largest manufacturers in the world in its highly specialized field. Porter locomotives were shipped all over the industrialized world. By 1920 Porter was producing 600 locomotives a year.

Unfortunately, the 1920s also brought a series of circumstances that would mortally wound the firm. In 1921, at the age of 81, Henry Kirke Porter died. His death rocked the company and came at a time when the nation was suffering massive growing pains. Inventions and progress came faster than many industries could keep pace. The H.K. Porter Company felt the impact as the steam locomotive was shunted aside in favor of electric and diesel engines. Everywhere the economic climate

was uneasy—finally, the stock market collapsed, and the Great Depression shrouded the nation. The H.K. Porter Company had begun what was to become a slow, steady decline.

In 1931, in the midst of the greyest days of the Depression, Thomas Mellon Evans was graduated from Yale University. Young Evans was a man of meager financial means, but he possessed an enormous determination and a

# MICROBAC LABORATORIES, INC.
## A HUNDREDFOLD GROWTH OF SERVICES

An ambitious couple, new to these shores, buys a small business and prospers. It's the quintessential American Dream, free enterprise in an antique frame—and yet it keeps coming true.

A. Warne Boyce and his wife, Doreen, formed Microbac Laboratories, Inc., in 1969 with a staff of 16 and a payroll that first year of $113,520. By the mid-1980s some 60 employees were earning three million dollars annually in 10 locations from Boston to Chicago.

Somewhere at a given moment a Microbac sample is being taken or a truck is gently clinking toward a company lab with swabs, scraps, computer readouts, and test tubes. Finding a noxious chemical in a factory's wastewater heads off one sort of disaster, a colony of germs at a dairy or supermarket another. At three Army posts a maintenance schedule for tanks and troop carriers waits upon Microbac's analysis of used crankcase oil. Sensitive to charges of "junk food," a chain of fried-chicken restaurants receives Microbac's count of the mineral and vitamin content in wings and drumsticks.

Boyce was trained as a metallurgist, his wife as an economist. They came to Pittsburgh in Britain's 1960s' "brain drain." He headed the U.S. arm of a British pump maker involved in wastewater technology. She joined the faculty of Chatham College, later becoming executive director of the Buhl Foundation.

Convinced of a sound business opportunity in analytical services to industries under environmental pressure, the couple purchased a small milk-testing firm on Pittsburgh's North Side. "It wasn't environmental, but we thought this could be a vehicle," recalls Warne. The deal was made with $15,000 family cash (all they could spare),

a friend's investment of $11,000, and $180,000 in loan repayments over the next 10 years.

Their timing was right—in at least two respects. Growth was rapid enough to require a new headquarters facility at 4580 McKnight Road, North Hills, in May 1972—just days ahead of the floods of Hurricane Agnes, which would have inundated records and

Directors of Microbac are (left to right) J. Trevor Boyce, A. Warne Boyce, and Dr. Doreen E. Boyce.

sensitive equipment in the original basement location.

Since 1982, by now U.S. citizens active in civic affairs, the Boyces have been sole owners of an oft-expanded business. They have made a dozen acquisitions,

typically of family-owned laboratories with an extra dividend of strong local management such as Bob Morgan, vice-president marketing, who heads the flourishing ETL Division in Erie, Pennsylvania. The Schiller lab, in Pittsburgh's North Hills, represents both past and future to Microbac. Founded in the 1890s by Dr. L. Ashman, pioneering forensic chemist, it's now headed by the Boyces' son, Trevor, the third member of its board of directors.

Warne Boyce estimates that the company's services have multiplied "a hundredfold," as he and his wife had hoped but hadn't quite predicted. Unforeseen was the proliferation of fast-food restaurants; the appearance of salad bars even in supermarkets; the national fascination with nutrition; and the alarming increase in liability insurance rates, resulting in a new Microbac product for the food-service industry: "risk assessment audits."

"Ironically, our environmental business, related to drinking water, hazardous waste, air, and asbestos, has developed about as we planned," says Boyce. "The dairy and food side continues to grow beyond expectations."

*Testing of milk and dairy samples is a Microbac specialty—and a growing market.*

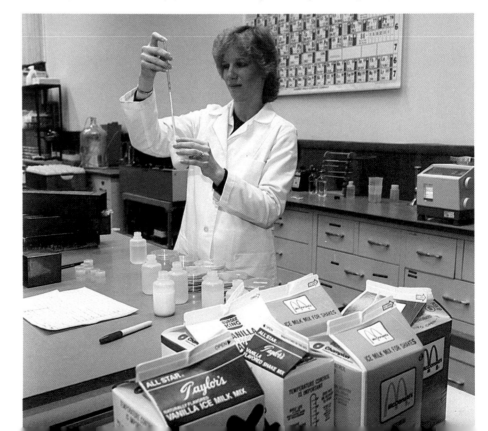

# EQUIBANK
## COMMITTED TO THE AREA'S BUSINESS AND CONSUMERS

Equibank, one of western Pennsylvania's strongest and largest financial institutions, carved out a special market niche in the mid-1980s—the needs of retail customers and small and medium-size businesses. With its nearly 2,000 employees and more than $2.25 billion in assets, this wasn't a new direction so much as a renewal and restoration of the institution's basic strength and purpose.

Equibank's regional roots go back to 1871. Like Pittsburgh, its larger neighbor to the north, the city of McKeesport was growing in commerce, population, and metal-based industry in the years of national ebullience following the Civil War. McKeesport needed its own bank, community leaders instinctively felt, to develop the independent possibilities of the river town at the confluence of the Youghiogheny and the Monongahela. The result was the Commercial Banking Company—cornerstone of the future Equibank, whose downtown McKeesport office still occupies the original site.

In 1875 came a conversion from a state-chartered bank to a federal charter, and the rather bland, generic name was changed to the more locally identifying First National Bank of McKeesport, which it retained for more than 80 eventful years.

Banking underwent several booms and "panics" in the late nineteenth century, an era that preceded regulation of any serious sort, when bank patrons had to have a "buyer beware" attitude like other shoppers. Always neighbors of their own customers, the men who operated First National of McKeesport built its strength slowly on public trust and on the underlying economic integrity of the Monongahela Valley—then America's unrivaled steelmaking center with McKeesport's own pipemaking mills making it famous worldwide as "The Tube City." The Depression of the 1930s

strained the company but did not break it, and toward the end of World War II, in 1944, the bank topped $20 million in assets for the first time.

A considerable amount of growth came from acquisitions of smaller community banks whose locations, customers, and deposits formed an expanding branch network for the McKeesport institution. Today's Equibank is the result of 33 such mergers.

The most momentous occurred in 1956, under then president M.A. Cancelliere, with the acquisition of Pittsburgh's Washington Trust Company in the city's wholesale district along Fifth Avenue just above Downtown. Lacking the large corporate customers of the city's major banks, the new competitor—which now gave itself the more regional identity of Western Pennsylvania National Bank—promptly became the most aggressive force in the "retail banking" market of Pittsburgh (with unsung benefits to the customers of many other institutions by the sheer dynamics of competition). WPNB—as it was called in that era—grew rapidly, and in 1964 moved its headquarters from McKeesport into Downtown Pittsburgh.

A holding company was established as Equimark Corporation, and the name of the banking subsidiary became Equibank in 1973. Two years later the headquarters relocated to one of the Golden Triangle's most striking new buildings, the multifaceted Two Oliver Plaza.

But the century-long growth track struck a detour—clearly a temporary one—in the recession of the early 1980s. Similar to many other important financial institu-

tions, Equibank was stung by defaults on substantial loans, many of them to basically sound projects whipsawed by lurching movements in interest rates and energy prices.

Asked by federal regulators to strengthen its capital position by $100 million within one year, the bank, under new management, launched a major recapitalization effort. Substantial investors, convinced of Equibank's solid relationships with customers in its home region, joined the board of directors. The asset base was trimmed, a number of offices sold at a profit (and others purchased for a foothold in the diversified Philadelphia market), and problem loans sharply reduced. Strategically, the marketing focus returned to Equibank's long-standing service to the consumer and small-to-medium business market.

The result was that $127.6 million in new capital flowed in, and a

---

*Commercial Banking Company, predecessor of Equibank, began in this building in 1871. Equibank's downtown McKeesport office still occupies this same site.*

major U.S. bank was restored to health—for the first time without assistance from the federal government or a forced merger with another institution.

Equibank chairman Alan S. Fellheimer and president Claire W. Gargalli, heading a virtually transformed management team, have targeted a return to solid profitability as the first priority of the last half of the 1980s and 1990s.

"Our plan is simple," says Fellheimer. "Stick to the basics: hard work, sound banking practices, and good service to customers and our communities; no quick fixes, no high-risk ventures." Bank management believes that the marketing niche of consumers and small and medium-size business establishments continues to be underserved by the financial industry as a whole, providing numerous opportunities for an institution that sees itself as "The Straight Talk Bank."

With western Pennsylvania offices spread through four counties—Allegheny, Westmoreland, Washington, and Beaver—Equibank has concentrated three "regional loan centers" in the North Hills, South Hills, and Monroeville to expedite and simplify the decision-making process in commercial banking transactions that do not have to "go Downtown." New checking and deposit products are coming into consumer banking, and Equibank's leaders say that other service improvements will follow apace with findings of continual market research.

"Our customers are the lifeblood of the region's economy," states Fellheimer. "We define ourselves as a regional bank; that's an important decision. It means support for economic growth here, not for loans in South America or the Sunbelt."

*Two Oliver Plaza—the Pittsburgh address of Equibank headquarters.*

# ALLEGHENY INTERNATIONAL, INC.
## TECHNOLOGY FOR A RISING STANDARD OF LIVING

The world's foremost producer of small electric appliances—with brand names including Sunbeam and Oster—is a Pittsburgh-based company. However, it did not start out to cater so directly to the home and the homemaker.

The corporate antecedent of Allegheny International, Inc. (AI), was a traditional western Pennsylvania "heavy industry" operation, a specialty steelmaker with roots practically as deep as the industrial revolution. Yet the firm also harbored leaders with the goal of contributing to the rising life-style of households around the globe, of reaching millions of potential customers.

Thus, an essentially new enterprise has emerged from the old. AI easily could be called one of America's youngest companies, remolded during the 1970s and early 1980s to achieve some 2 million dollars in annual sales. Some of its brand names prob-

*Oliver S. Travers, Jr., chairman and chief executive officer of Allegheny International, Inc.*

ably are better known than the company name. They include Sunbeam and Oster small appliances, Wilkinson Sword shaving products, Northern Electric blankets, Hanson scales, Springfield clocks, Vitamaster exercise equipment, and Almet/Lawnlite outdoor furniture. In the industrial area AI member companies are active in advanced technologies from pollution-control devices to sophisticated medical equipment. The connecting motif is meeting customer needs for quality and convenience through technology.

AI encourages inventiveness and the practical application of such discoveries. In the case of products for the home, AI's use of advanced technology has made it a transforming presence in the marketplace, opening up new opportunities for growth in products for which consumers will pay a premium.

AI's products that bring new technology home for consumers include the Sunbeam® Monitor® line of self-shut-off irons and hair care products, the Sunbeam®

Safe Idea™ hair dryer that protects the user against electric shock if it is dropped into water while in use, Northern Electric's PM™ electric blanket, which eliminates bulky thermostats and adapts to the sleeper's body temperature, and the Sunbeam® Freedom™ cordless appliances that combine high power with the convenience of a single-outlet recharging system.

In 1985 alone AI consumer companies introduced more than 50 new products. Consumer businesses account for about two-thirds of AI's sales. The company is organized into two main business groups: a worldwide consumer segment and an industrial and technology segment. AI's goal

*Sunbeam's Oskar® has taken the food-processing market by storm since its introduction in 1985 because of its smaller size, more attractive price, and ease of cleaning.*

"blanket with a brain," which adjusts to a sleeper's body temperature. Sunbeam's Oskar® food processor, "smaller, less expensive, easier to clean . . . took department stores, specialty shops and kitchen centers by storm," the *New York Times* reported after the introduction of Oskar® in 1985.

Another AI member company, United Kingdom-based Wilkinson Sword Company, traces its history from 1772. Still the world's leading ceremonial swordmaker, its considerably larger product line consists of razors and blades, matches and lighters, and home and garden products, all used worldwide. Wilkinson invented the safety razor in 1898, and stainless steel blades in 1961, forging the technical lead for the kind of world-class products that realistically epitomize AI's philosophy of putting technology to work for consumers.

And there's much more to Allegheny International. In the industrial sector AI's enterprises include John Zink Company (air pollution-control devices and specialized process combustion equipment, and systems to produce energy by burning garbage); Illinois Water Treatment (liquid treatment systems); AI Medical Technology, Inc. (computer-based patient monitoring systems); Thermco (microprocessing equipment for silicon chips); and Kennedy Company (computer peripheral equipment).

AI's commitment to technical leadership is exemplified by annual company awards to AI scientists and engineers from member companies all over the world. Their contributions range from automating an assembly process for coffeemaker heating elements to designing systems to monitor a surgical patient's recovery from anesthesia.

The awards are a fitting tribute to employees who have had a hand in transforming AI into an enterprise committed to breaking new ground.

is to be a corporation with key positions in growth markets for the 1990s and beyond.

A diversification strategy was already under way at AI in the early 1970s. The firm was then called Allegheny Ludlum Industries, and its chief subsidiary was Allegheny Ludlum Steel Corporation. Then, in the 1970s, AI intensified its participation in markets of above-average growth while moving the firm away from labor- and capital-intensive, cyclical businesses.

The year 1981 proved a milestone. Allegheny Ludlum Steel, the original core operation, was divested to private owners, while the parent firm charted its new course under the fresh identity, Allegheny

International, Inc. Key to the metamorphosis was that year's major acquisition, Sunbeam Corporation.

Founded in Chicago in 1897, Sunbeam had established an eminent brand name in mixers, irons, frypans, and food processors. John Oster Manufacturing Company, founded in 1924, originated the Osterizer® household blender; Northern Electric's appliances and personal care products—vaporizers, hair dryers, blankets, and heating pads, for example—are led by the P.M.™ system electric

# REED SMITH SHAW & McCLAY
## A PITTSBURGH INSTITUTION IN THE PRACTICE OF LAW

In the 1870s the Civil War had been over only a few years, and Pittsburgh was waking up to unprecedented growth—led by financial kingpins such as George Westinghouse, Andrew Carnegie, Henry Clay Frick, Thomas Mellon, and H.J. Heinz.

Their lawyers weren't far behind.

*James Hay Reed*

Attorneys James Hay Reed and Philander Chase Knox were 24 years old in 1877, the year they opened the humble legal practice at Fifth Avenue and Scrip Way that evolved into today's Reed Smith Shaw & McClay.

The founding partners litigated an epic battle between onetime business partners Frick and Carnegie. Paralleling the movers and shakers they represented, Reed and Knox kept busy. In 1901 Reed presided over the legal joining of several steel companies into U.S. Steel. The following year Knox left the firm to assume the position of U.S. Attorney General. He subsequently served a term as Secretary of State, then was named a U.S. Senator.

Reed Smith continued to grow, moving in 1917 to the old Union Arcade, later the Union Trust Building (known today as Two Mellon Bank Center), becoming the stately structure's first office tenant. The firm, which adopted its present name in 1922, attracted many able lawyers who worked on some of the most prominent cases in modern legal history.

One of the most memorable cases spanned two decades. From the 1930s to the 1950s, Reed Smith led the Pittsburgh & Lake Erie Railroad to victory in a dispute over construction of a canal from Lake Erie to the Ohio River, a project the trainmasters decried as a waste of taxpayers' money.

In 1948, after a number of deaths were blamed on noxious emissions from the U.S. Steel plant in Donora (south of Pittsburgh) during a freak atmospheric inversion, more than 100 lawsuits were filed against U.S. Steel. With Reed Smith's assistance U.S. Steel settled them all on the eve of the trial—for $265,000.

In another celebrated courtroom battle, Reed Smith represented the Jones & Laughlin Steel Corporation during a 1952 strike, when President Harry Truman issued a seizure order without invoking the Taft-Hartley Act. The case went all the way to the U.S. Supreme Court, which ruled that Truman had acted unconstitutionally in seizing a private industry's property.

Reed Smith left its mark on Downtown Pittsburgh when its experts in real estate, eminent domain, contract negotiation, and litigation helped to transform the blighted Point area into the Gateway Center complex of office skyscrapers, a development that sparked Pittsburgh's renaissance in the 1950s.

However, the firm's expansion has extended well beyond the Alleghenies. In 1970 Reed Smith merged with the Washington, D.C., firm of Whitlock & Tait, with a practice focusing on antitrust, se-

curities, and tax efforts. Later, in 1976, a merger with the firm of Gall, Lane & Powell expanded Reed Smith's D.C. practice to include a full labor law group. Two years later, in Philadelphia, a merger was made with Townsend, Elliott & Munson. Today Reed Smith has smaller offices in Harrisburg, McLean, Virginia, and

*Philander Chase Knox*

Delray Beach, Florida, as well as international representation in Paris, France.

By 1985 Reed Smith's continuing growth demanded larger quarters. So, after 68 years in the Union Trust Building, the firm moved a block away to what is now the James H. Reed Building, at Sixth Avenue and William Penn Way.

After a $15-million renovation—complete with a 35,000-volume law library, marbled lobby, and state-of-the-art communications system—the nine-story structure became the Pittsburgh office for 480 lawyers and support staff. Today Reed Smith has grown to include 250 attorneys, 112 of whom are partners.

In an age when many business clients are selecting lawyers on a transaction-by-transaction basis, Reed Smith still serves about half its clients as general counsel. Yet the firm has carved several niches for itself.

In major products liability litigation, for instance, Reed Smith became national and regional co-ordinating defense counsel for clients faced with potentially crippling massive litigation. Such clients represented include those in the asbestos, drug, propane distribution, hand-held tools, construction equipment, and other industries. In labor relations and employment discrimination litigation, the firm serves as national counsel in important industries—including retail food, steel, and the

*The Reed Smith Shaw & McClay executive committee (front row, from left): Bernard J. Casey, Washington; J. Sherman McLaughlin; Daniel I. Booker; and Dennis R. Bonessa. Second row (from left): William J. Smith; Thomas Todd; Norman W. Goldin, Washington; J. Tomlinson Fort; and James J. Restivo, Jr. Third row (from left): James A. Yard, executive director; Blair S. McMillin; Harry H. Weil; G. Donald Gerlach, managing partner; James H. Hardie; Robert J. Dodds, Jr.; Scott F. Zimmerman; and David C. Auten, Philadelphia.*

aerospace industry. In 1983 Reed Smith made a timely move on the high-tech front with the formation of the TECHLEX® team of lawyers to serve emerging advanced technology ventures in its local markets.

At the same time Reed Smith maintains a tax practice, serving banking and industrial clients. In general corporate and security law work—including the recent surge of leveraged buy-outs, acquisitions, mergers, and bankruptcies—the firm has been a catalyst for forging first-time ties between Pittsburgh and a broad array of

*The James H. Reed Building, with its 35,000-volume law library, marbled lobby, and state-of-the-art communications system, is the Pittsburgh home of Reed Smith Shaw & McClay and its staff of 480 lawyers and support staff.*

domestic and overseas clients.

More than a century after its founding, the practice begun by young Knox and Reed has become one of the nation's largest and most prominent law firms as well as a widely recognized Pittsburgh institution: Reed Smith Shaw & McClay.

# PRESBYTERIAN-UNIVERSITY HOSPITAL
## CARING FOR PATIENTS—AND THE FUTURE

Presbyterian-University Hospital of Pittsburgh has long been committed to excellence in patient care, medical education, and research. This commitment was inspired by its founder, Dr. Louise Wotring Lyle, a widow of a Presbyterian minister, who started the hospital in 1893.

Recognizing the need for medical care in Pittsburgh's ethnic and working-class North Side area (then the city of Allegheny), Dr. Lyle opened her hospital with just five rooms, and only five dollars of working capital. She charged $15 a week for a room and physician care. Two years later the Pittsburgh Presbytery—the local governing body of the church—took up support for her institution, which then became Presbyterian Hospital. Though Dr. Lyle left the active role of hospital management by the turn of the century, the institution continued to grow; by 1927 the hospital was affiliated with the University of Pittsburgh School of Medicine. The present 564-bed hospital was built in 1936 on the University of Pittsburgh campus, adjacent to the medical school. Through hard work, dedication, and commitment, Dr. Lyle's

*The original hospital was located on Sherman Avenue on Pittsburgh's North Side.*

tiny hospital evolved into one of the premier medical centers in the world.

"Presby," as Pittsburghers call the hospital, is best known as the world's leading center for organ transplantation. Presby surgeons now average one transplant every 24 hours, and the numbers continue to grow. The institution performed the Pittsburgh area's first kidney transplant in 1964, followed four years later by a pioneering heart transplant. The hospital now performs transplant procedures for hearts and heart/lungs, as well as kidneys, livers, and pancreas glands. Transplant surgeons also utilize the Jarvik-7 artificial heart as a temporary, life-saving device on patients who may not survive the wait for a human donor.

These advances in medical technology are possible only at an institution that offers a broad spectrum of medical and surgical specialties—which underscores the importance of Presby's affiliation with the University of Pittsburgh School of Medicine. The Pitt campus and Presby's main building on DeSoto Street dominate the Oakland area of Pittsburgh. These institutions, along with other Oakland hospitals, form one of the nation's most advanced centers for medical research and patient care. Since 1927 the hospital has served

as the clinical setting for the medical school's physician training programs. Every member of the hospital medical staff is a faculty member at the school. Each year, more than 400 physicians receive their postgraduate training at Presbyterian-University Hospital.

The hospital itself provides the full range of adult acute health care, and boasts many advanced medical/surgical programs, in-

*Louise Wotring Lyle, M.D., founded the hospital in 1893.*

cluding:

The Trauma Center—Presby is a founding member of the Center for Emergency Medicine of Western Pennsylvania (CEM), and STAT, the Specialized Treatment and Transport system. Presby's Trauma Suite can double as an operating room for emergency surgery, and contains an in-wall X-ray machine for on-the-spot diagnostics.

Neurosurgery—employing a uniquely equipped stereotactic operating room that houses a CT scanner and fluoroscope, as well as one of the nation's first "gamma knife" units, a noninva-

Dr. Lyle's tiny hospital has evolved into this 564-bed facility on the University of Pittsburgh campus, adjacent to the medical school.

from professionals to weekend joggers. The institute also is involved in research activities relating to prevention of injuries.

Critical care—Presby was the first hospital to offer fellowship training for physicians in intensive care units, and is now part of the country's largest training programs in critical care medicine.

Presby is an integral part of the Pittsburgh Cancer Institute, a consortium of health care facilities and research centers designed to provide new directions in the diagnosis and treatment of oncology patients.

The hospital has also developed innovative treatments in many

other areas, including the hyperbaric oxygen chamber for wound healing; treatments for heart arrhythmias (irregular heart beats that can lead to sudden death); and revolutionary treatments for fractured pelvic bones, which can cut the patient's recovery time in half.

With its threefold mission of patient care, research, and education, Presbyterian-University Hospital has grown from a five-room hospital into one of the world's leading medical centers. Presby's commitment to excellence, which has dominated its pioneering past, will now lead it into the challenges of the next century.

The hospital and staff are committed to excellence in patient care, medical education, and research.

sive radiation device that can eradicate deep-seated brain tumors that were previously considered inoperable.

Cardiology—Presby provides a range of cardiovascular services available nowhere else in the region, including a specialized treatment program for arrhythmic hearts and computer-enhanced scans of the heart chambers.

Orthopedic surgery—the Hospital's Joint Replacement Center offers a multidisciplinary approach for patients who need replacement of diseased hips or other bone joints.

The Sports and Preventive Medicine Institute of Pittsburgh—which provides medically supervised conditioning, training, and rehabilitation for athletes of all levels,

A dramatic scene in the surgery suite. Presbyterian-University Hospital is best known for advances in organ transplantation. Presby surgeons now average one transplant every 24 hours.

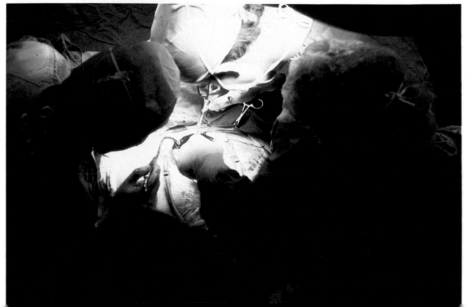

# EQUITABLE RESOURCES, INC.
## AN ENERGY INDUSTRY LEADER

Equitable Resources, Inc., began as one of the pioneers of natural gas development in western Pennsylvania about a century ago. Today it's a fully integrated energy company, Pittsburgh-based, with over 2,000 employees and annual revenues in the range of one-half billion dollars. The firm's beginnings involved one of the world's most famous industrial names—Westinghouse—and one that deserves at least an honored footnote—Haymaker.

It was the brothers Obediah and Michael Haymaker who discovered the vast deposits of natural gas east of Pittsburgh. They had begun drilling for oil in 1878 but struck gas instead in a meadow near Murrysville, Westmoreland County. The well came in with such force, it's said, that the coun-

*An Equitable rotary rig drills for natural gas. Equitable's energy resource activities are concentrated primarily in the Appalachian region, where drilling risk is minimal and development and operating costs are low.*

tryside shook. Local residents panicked; men in the drilling area were knocked off their feet. Gas thundered skyward in a geyser of vapor later estimated at 34 million cubic feet per day.

The Haymakers' wildcat bonanza catapulted the little town into world headlines, and Murrysville became the first commercially developed gas field in the United States. Among a swarm of new operations formed to drill more wells, lay pipelines, and transport the fabulous fuel to the homes and factories of Pittsburgh was Equitable Gas Company, chartered in 1888.

One of the first to recognize the commercial potential was industrialist George Westinghouse, then about 40 years old. The rising inventor-tycoon had drilled a well in the backyard of his home on Thomas Boulevard in Pittsburgh's East End in 1884. A reporter on tour for *Harper's Weekly* reported: "Mr. W. has a habit of entertaining his friends with experiments in

*Equitable's continued economic growth will come primarily from increased production and the sale of natural gas and oil.*

regulating the pressure of his well, known as 'Old Number One.' He shuts off the gas for a brief period and then releases it, when it shoots up in a volcanic flame and with a noise that arouses all his neighbors." The Westinghouse residence was the first in Pittsburgh to light and heat with gas.

Through one of his corporate holdings, The Philadelphia Company, Westinghouse began to buy up acreage in the Murrysville field. He swept a number of smaller gas producers, including Equitable, in under the capacious Philadelphia umbrella. An extensive network of production and distribution facilities resulted, and in the end those would be consolidated as Equitable Gas.

Marketing was no problem. Industrial Pittsburgh's reaction to a new source of cheap energy approached the ecstatic. *The Daily Messenger* reported on December 12, 1885:

*Staid Pittsburghers are fairly standing on their heads for excitement and joy. They see their busy, pleasant old town booming ahead at a rate which paralyzes the imagination. Fuel gas at their doors at a cost of not much more than the piping and valves to bring it into their furnaces. It means iron, glass, copper, and a thousand manufactured products at a rate so low that no other city in the Union can compete with it.*

Even before the turn of the century the soaring demand for gas had begun to deplete local supplies. Determined to protect and expand his market, Westinghouse pushed The Philadelphia Company's lines south to tap new fields in West Virginia and Kentucky. Field crews drove teams of horses and oxen hauling heavy sections of cast-iron pipe, tools, and equipment over hundreds of miles of mountain terrain, building the lines to carry gas to the Pittsburgh market.

By 1910 the organization had 440,000 acres under lease in Pennsylvania and West Virginia and was operating 902 wells. A subsidiary, Kentucky West Virginia Gas, acquired drilling leases in the 1920s on approximately one million acres in eastern and central Kentucky; it became one of the first to explore commercially in that region. Kentucky West is now a subsidiary of Equitable Resources, Inc.

Natural gas and oil deposits in the Appalachian Basin tend to be not only rich and long-lived but generally shallow; this means low-risk drilling opportunities. As a result, Equitable's success rate in exploration and development is well above the industry norms. The firm's strong position in Appalachian acreage also enables it to develop gas reserves at some of the industry's lowest costs. It holds a competitive advantage, too, in its access to major eastern markets.

Equitable separated from The Philadelphia Company in 1950, acquiring ownership of all of the parent firm's gas properties—including transmission and distribution facilities. That same year, by the sale of two million shares of common stock, Equitable became a publicly owned utility. Its primary business was selling gas at retail to customers in three states. Now a subsidiary of Equitable Resources, Inc., the firm continues to provide natural gas service to more than a quarter-million residential, commercial, and industrial customers. It is also the major gas supplier to Downtown Pittsburgh,

---

*A completed well in western New York State produces natural gas for delivery to Equitable's expanding markets in the eastern United States.*

and has played an important role in the city's renaissance.

By the mid-1980s Equitable's energy resources operations were accounting for more than three-quarters of its total operating income, and the corporation was applying its considerable skills in gas and oil production to new opportunities. Donald I. Moritz, president and chief executive officer, believes that Equitable's future growth will spring primarily from higher production and sales of gas and oil. That means in familiar Appalachia certainly, but also in new fields of investment such as the Southwest and the Rocky Mountains states. Something of the spirit of the Haymakers lives in Equitable Resources, Inc., one of the nation's first utilities to break out of the local mold and become an energy industry leader.

# DUQUESNE SYSTEMS, INC.
## BRIGHT STAR IN THE SOFTWARE UNIVERSE

Enter the world of computer software—an industry that bids fair to set the tone for Pittsburgh's economic future in the way that heavy manufacturing marked its past. Typically far smaller companies too, but many more, in place of the valley-filling giants of old. Fewer 30-ton steel coils may leave the mill gates on the backs of groaning tractor-trailers, but more one-pound reels of magnetic tape—valued at up to $100,000—are sent on their way by registered mail in a cardboard boxes. The sweaty, goggled hardhats of the open hearth will be missed; but there should be more well-paid analysts and programmers seated at keyboards in front of video-screens, doing the "development" work to tap the vast inherent power of computers.

Much of the economic hope of Pittsburgh is riding on such firms as Duquesne Systems, Inc., brightest star among the city's ascendant high-technology industries. From a level of $53,000 profit on less than one million dollars in sales in 1979, Duquesne Systems surged to $2.4 million profit on $11 million in sales in 1985—and was heading for $30 million in revenues a year later. *Business Week* magazine ranked Duquesne Systems 15th on its 1986 list of the "100 Best Small Growth Companies" in the nation.

"Our products are highly technical, but the benefits that they provide are easy to understand," says Duquesne Systems president Glen F. Chatfield. "We help our customers get greater productivity from their large data-processing installations—by making their computers process more efficiently and, in fact, making them easier to operate."

"Mainframe" manufacturers such as IBM market the strategic benefits of computer systems as a whole; but hardware is only one of three components for tapping the prowess of digital computers. The other two are both software. The most visible is the applications program but equally important is the "systems software," which transfers information to and from the applications programs as they perform their tasks. It is in the systems software for IBM mainframes (which account for more than 80 percent of free world computing capacity) that Duquesne Systems finds its marketing niches.

Notwithstanding that it already served more than 1,700 data centers by mid-1986, with more than 7,000 copies of its software products, Duquesne Systems believed it had not yet reached 10 percent of its possible market penetration.

A steady stream of new products—the firm directs 15 to 20 percent of its revenues into research and development—enabled Duquesne Systems to increase its potential sales of "one of each" from $69,000 per mainframe in 1981 to $177,000 by 1985, a 250-percent increase. Pricing its software on a per-mainframe basis, Duquesne Systems charges a license fee plus annual maintenance set at 15 percent of the purchase price. Its profit margins tripled from 7 percent in 1979 to 21 percent in 1985. Represented in 30 countries, the

*Duquesne Systems products are copied onto magnetic tape for shipment to customers.*

*S. Craig McKee, senior vice-president (left), Glen F. Chatfield, president (center), Neal M. Pollon, executive vice-president (right).*

Pittsburgh firm's exports have been roughly 35 percent of sales from 1984 through 1986.

Success has brought no sense of complacency to the company's brightly lit headquarters on upper floors of Two Allegheny Center in Pittsburgh's North Side. Difficult years followed the company's founding in 1970; a complete reorganization was needed in 1976; and not until 1979 did Duquesne Systems hit its growth stride. Beginning as a computer perform-

*TPX (Terminal Productivity Executive) is a software product that improves terminal user productivity by allowing the user to switch quickly from one on-line system or application to another.*

ance consulting firm, it began to click only after this people-intensive mode of operation was left behind for a strategy of marketing packaged, off-the-shelf system software products.

Computer hardware is, of course, no small investment. Duquesne System's own IBM mainframe used for product development cost two million dollars. Typically customer hardware and software investments run far higher. "Getting maximum productivity from that large investment is very important to our customers," says Chatfield. His firm's highly successful TPX (Terminal Productivity Executive) enables a standard display terminal to interact concurrently with an unlimited number of applications programs. A simple keystroke takes the user from one application to another providing a huge improvement in efficiency and cost-effectiveness.

"We're not afraid to let the customers try before they buy," says executive vice-president Neal M. Pollon, who heads Duquesne Systems sales and marketing ef-

*Using their IBM 4381 mainframe, Duquesne's development staff can simulate most customer environments for developing new products and enhancing current ones.*

fort. All potential customers clients are encouraged to put the company's products to the test in a 30-day free trial. All products are upgraded constantly, so that competitors are always shooting for a moving target.

Duquesne Systems acquired the Single Image Software product lines in early 1986—which added some $8 million in sales, 300 new customers, offices in New Jersey and Florida, and 30 percent to the company's sales force. Product development itself is performed painstakingly by teams of experts at terminals, a process that Chatfield likens to "writing a book."

In fact, a book is one result. The product documentation is illustrated, printed, and bound, and accompanies the magnetic tape reels that go out in the mail. With good documentation customers typically can install a product in a half-hour or so on their computers.

S. Craig McKee, Duquesne Systems senior vice-president, who heads the firm's financial and administrative functions, considers Pittsburgh ideal in several respects for the growth of the software industry. Computer science programs at the University of Pittsburgh, Carnegie-Mellon University, and other local institutions have created a rich field for personnel recruitment. McKee admires the fact that there is "less job-hopping" than in such other software meccas as Boston's Route 128 and California's Silicon Valley.

Unmistakable, too, is the sense of an industry at the beginning rather than the end of a life cycle. "Software is absolutely in its infancy," says Chatfield. "There's a strong foundation of good talent here. Pittsburgh, with a large number of start-up companies is becoming and exciting and important member of the international software community."

# DUQUESNE LIGHT COMPANY
## POWER FOR THE ECONOMY OF PITTSBURGH

Wesley W. von Schack, president and chief executive officer, Duquesne Light Company.

The electric power that makes a dazzling vista of Pittsburgh's Golden Triangle at evening is supplied by Duquesne Light Company, a public utility. As is the city itself, Duquesne Light is in the midst of an invigorating transition.

The corporation, which serves more than a half-million residential and commercial customers in Allegheny and Beaver counties, was a pioneer in nuclear power and in managing the immense flows of electricity demanded by steel plants and other basic manufacturers of the industrial heartland. With a mid-1980s sales level approaching one billion dollars annually, and 13 billion kilowatt-hours, it has virtually spanned the modern history of electricity.

Duquesne Light's earliest forerunner was Allegheny County Light Company, founded by Pittsburgh businessmen in 1880 with a capital of $90,000. Its first customer was the Pennsylvania Railroad, which needed lamps to discourage the pilfering of freight cars by night. The utility's original power plant, in Downtown's Virgin Alley, illuminated the Pennsy's glaring carbon arc lamps so effectively that more customers signed up.

In 1882 Thomas Edison's incandescent light bulbs came to Pittsburgh, and soon the little utility needed more capacity. Its Garrison Alley plant, built in 1886, provided power for some of George Westinghouse's pioneering efforts with alternating current. Within a few years small electric companies were springing up everywhere, none on a scale sufficient to earn consistent profits. A group of these enterprises consolidated in the two counties in 1903 to form Duquesne Light.

Thus began an era of expansion, new plants, acquisitions, and technologies. Duquesne Light became a subsidiary, for several decades, of the Philadelphia Company, a utilities holding organization. In 1915 the firm began building around Pittsburgh the nation's first metropolitan high-tension ring. In the 1920s Duquesne Light promoted electricity by selling appliances to customers. The Great Depression and, even more, the power plant shutdowns of the catastrophic March 1936 flood challenged the company severely, but practically every employee volunteered—and helped restore service in an amazingly few days.

The home-building, industrial, television, and shopping center

Massive cooling towers mark dramatic "Power Alley" along the Ohio River northwest of Pittsburgh. Beaver Valley Power Station (foreground) and Bruce Mansfield coal-fired generating stations in the distance are operated by Duquesne Light for itself and four other Pennsylvania and Ohio utilities in the CAPCO power pool.

booms of the post-World War II era greatly spurred electrical demand. President Dwight D. Eisenhower threw the switch to start Duquesne Light's—and the nation's—first commercial nuclear power plant at Shippingport, Beaver County, in 1954. Its mighty successor, the Beaver Valley Power Station, produced a record 5.9 billion kilowatt-hours in 1985, with an industry pace-setting 91.9 percent of availability.

"Our company's future," says Wesley W. von Schack, president and chief executive officer, "depends on how well we change with our marketplace. We have many good things going for us, especially the quality of the people who work here."

# PARKER/HUNTER INCORPORATED
## HELPING MEET REGIONAL FINANCIAL NEEDS

An investment banking and stock brokerage firm must be intimately involved with the financial needs of its clients, whether they are businesses or individuals, and these financial needs are continually changing and growing. An investment firm must also deal with present and future economic realities. Pittsburgh is a city of the future—a city with a large number of major corporate headquarters but also a rapidly expanding base of small and medium-size companies that are enjoying rapid growth. The economic and social outlook of the residents of southwestern Pennsylvania is continually brightening.

"It's hard to be anything but enthusiastic when you're as much a part of the fabric of the community as this firm is," says Robert W. Kampmeinert, president and chief executive officer of Parker/Hunter Incorporated. "We are exposed daily to the growth plans of businesses, institutions, and individuals. When you look at all this, you've got to project an outstanding future for southwestern Pennsylvania."

Parker/Hunter is the largest independently owned investment banking and stock brokerage firm based in Pittsburgh, and the second largest in the state. It was founded in 1969 by the merger of two regional firms of longstanding: Kay, Richards & Company, founded in 1902; and McKelvey & Company, 1928. Since 1969 the business has grown from 150 employees in 13 offices to 300 in 19 offices. Including the 600 Grant Street headquarters in Downtown Pittsburgh, there are 10 Pennsylvania offices; 5 in Ohio, 3 in West Virginia, and one on New York's Wall Street.

Parker/Hunter is engaged in the business of underwriting corporate and municipal securities, corporate and municipal finance, venture capital, equity research, portfolio management, mutual funds and in-

*Parker/Hunter is the largest independently owned investment banking/stockbrokerage firm based in Pittsburgh. In addition to its headquarters at 600 Grant Street and office on Wall Street, Parker/Hunter has 17 locations throughout Pennsylvania, Ohio, and West Virginia.*

surance, U.S. government securities, market making, and the handling of stock and bond transactions on most exchanges and in over-the-counter markets. The company's 140 investment executives are committed to handling the financial needs of their clients, who are primarily individuals. These investment executives rely heavily on the professional staff in Pittsburgh to help them plan and execute each client's financial program.

The primary function of the firm's investment banking department is to serve as financial advisor and consultant to a select number of corporations, municipalities, authorities, and hospitals

and to assist them in raising capital to meet their financing requirements, usually through the public underwriting or private placement of common stock or long-term debt. Over the past several years Parker/Hunter has acted as manager, co-manager, or financial advisor on nearly four billion dollars of financings. Recently it has focused its attention on raising equity capital for small and medium-size companies in the Pittsburgh area. Some of these equity financings were public offerings, most notably for the fast-growing Du-

quesne Systems Inc., a computer software manufacturer, but there has also been a great deal of activity in private placements of equity.

This is an era of proliferating

*As part of their commitment to personal financial service, Parker/Hunter's investment executives frequently hold seminars to discuss timely investment topics.*

nationwide financial giants; however, it is the regional investment firm's special, personal familiarity with the individuals, businesses, and institutions in a given area that is critical to providing service of the highest quality. "It is vital to our clients," says Kampmeinert, "that we understand their special needs and opportunities in order to deal with them more effectively."

# MSA
## PROTECTING WORKERS AND PLANTS AROUND THE WORLD

The work that made Pittsburgh great is hazardous—fierce heats, crushing forces in the slam and roar of steel plants, coal mines, rail yards, and heavy industry. The risks involved prompted the formation of a little two-man venture, which started as Mine Safety Appliances Company in 1914 and would grow to world leadership. No company on earth produces more equipment and systems for worker and plant protection than MSA of Pittsburgh.

The genesis of the firm traces to 1913, when a young rescue engineer from the newly formed Bureau of Mines was on temporary assignment with the U.S. Navy in Matanuskan, Alaska. As far out as he could see, the Alaskan snows glistened over the Matanuskan coal fields.

But John Thomas Ryan could not sleep. He was haunted with the memory of a dozen mine disasters. Since joining the Bureau in 1910, he had rushed into the mines in a rescue car to save lives

and had seen the devastation. Up to that point, much had been said about mine safety yet little had been accomplished. As the Alaskan expedition was ending, Ryan made a list of equipment that was so desperately needed in the mines—first aid items, protective clothing, resuscitators, and gas detectors. That was the beginning.

When he returned from Alaska, Ryan joined forces with another Bureau of Mines engineer, George Herman Deike. Deike's rescue experiences had sparked a similar intense desire to fight the tragedies underground. During Ryan's absence in Alaska, Deike, 4,000 miles away, was having similar thoughts—even of the same needed products. As a result, they

*This new corporate headquarters in O'Hara Township, north of Pittsburgh, serves as the focal point of MSA's worldwide operations. The three-story, granite-clad building houses offices for approximately 350 corporate, staff, and administrative personnel.*

formed their own business within months after Ryan's return.

On June 5, 1914, the partners watched a small sign go up over a doorway in a downtown Pittsburgh office building; it read "Mine Safety Appliances Company." From that one-room office and a basement storeroom, the partners began their crusade for safety.

One of their first achievements was to persuade Thomas A. Edison to scale down his heavy nickel-

*MSA's new Instrument Division complex in Cranberry Township, north of Pittsburgh, coordinates the direction and technology of the portable and continuous instrument lines and communications products.*

Firefighters wear Brigade® Helmets and Ultralite™ and Custom 4500™ Air Masks for state-of-the-art protection.

iron alkaline battery to a size small enough to be worn on a miner's belt. Soon open-flame lamps disappeared in favor of electric lamps, a step that made a giant advance toward eliminating accidents and saving lives.

It also launched a firm that found no limits to the need for its kind of expertise. Long ago MSA expanded its first horizon of mine safety into industrial plants, construction jobs, transportation, the military, and police and fire emergencies—in fact, everywhere that life and health is exposed to hazards. It is the world's largest company devoted exclusively to the development and manufacture of personal protection and environmental monitoring products. It has operations in nearly two dozen countries—from Singapore to Sweden, and Australia to Scotland—with 7,000 employees, about half of them in the United States, and annual sales in the range of $400 million.

The miner's lamp now has plenty of companions on the MSA shelf, literally thousands of products. Respirators, gas masks, and self-contained breathing apparatus enable crews to work amid gases and fumes, and firefighters to retrieve victims from burning homes. Today the "hardhat" takes many sophisticated forms. MSA's Skullgard®, favored in steel mills and foundries, retains protective integrity at high temperatures; the Brigade® Firefighter Helmet provides high-performance head protection in a unique design. Face shields, goggles, and welding helmets shield eyes and skin from flying particles, chemical splash, and glare, while Noisefoe™ ear muffs conserve the hearing of the traffic teams parking jets at the airport. Harnesses, belts, and securing lines lower workers into chasms, tanks, and pits, while a nearby rescue squad will certainly have an Oxygen Administrator to help in an emergency. A major cleanup job, such as a chemical spill, may call for a Chempruf® II Total-Encapsulating Suit for full body protection.

MSA's product lines aren't solely reactive—to protect, that is, against accidents and hazards that actually occur—they're also preventive. Environmental monitoring instruments, both portable and continuous, head off leaks and breakdowns in a host of manufacturing, mining, utility, transportation, and chemicals industries. Infrared analyzers swiftly detect gases or vapors, while an Explosimeter® Combustible Gas Indicator can draw a sample from a remote or nearby area to measure the combustibility of airborne gases.

MSA International, a division also headquartered in Pittsburgh, oversees MSA subsidiaries in 21 countries, and also offers customers in many nations extensive training in the use and care of MSA equipment through its global network. MSA Research Corporation in Evans City, north of Pittsburgh, is a division that develops foam-generating systems for fires and spills—and has done pioneering life-support work. Callery Chemical Company, also in Evans City, is a division that is a leader in boron and alkali metal chemistry. Catalyst Research Corp., a subsidiary in Baltimore, is a leader in battery technology, including sophisticated batteries for heart pacemakers.

Supporting more than 135 MSA sales representatives across the United States are 3,000-plus technical specialists, researchers, and production and administrative employees in offices, plants, laboratories, and test facilities throughout the country.

Approximately 1,300 of MSA's personnel are located at its headquarters and other installations in the Pittsburgh area, including a number of modern buildings constructed in the 1980s. Among them are a new 150,000-square-foot corporate headquarters at RIDC Industrial Park, O'Hara Township, and the new Instrument Division on 326 acres of rolling countryside by a man-made lake in Cranberry Township, 25 miles north of the city. At that location the 70,000-square-foot John T. Ryan Memorial Laboratory houses engineers and test equipment ceaselessly improving MSA's lines of respiratory, head, hearing, and body protectors—and renewing the pledge made by a young mining engineer long ago in an Alaskan coal field.

This photograph of John T. Ryan, Sr., was taken in 1911 just after he entered a mine following an explosion. Three years later he and George Deike founded MSA, today the world's leading manufacturer and supplier of equipment and systems for worker and plant protection.

# ROBERT MORRIS COLLEGE
## CONVERTING CAREER DREAMS TO REALITY

It was in 1921 that an enterprising group of students, faculty, and staff launched what was then called the Pittsburgh School of Accountancy. The venture was a success from the beginning, and yet it is unlikely that any of the pioneers could have predicted the extent of its growth over the next six decades and more. Today the little school has become Robert Morris College, named for one of the patriotic financiers of the American Revolution. And it ranks among the largest private four-year institutions in Pennsylvania.

"We have always remembered the spirit and drive of that founding group," says Charles L. Sewall, president of the institution and spearhead of the two most recent decades of its growth. "It's that dedication on the part of the entire college community that has enabled us to expand so rapidly."

Robert Morris College's current enrollment numbers more than 5,000 undergraduate and 800 graduate students. With some 350 full-time faculty and staff, it is also an institution that boasts:

*Two Pittsburgh area campuses. In the heart of the Downtown business district is the imposing red-brick Pittsburgh Center, with its convenient access to day and evening students from around the regional compass. Equally valid but different in atmosphere is the lush 230-acre campus in Moon Township, one mile from Greater Pittsburgh International Airport. It has grown to 22 buildings set amid impressive vistas of greenery.

*An undergraduate division that offers bachelor of science degrees in 11 disciplines. Also featured is a popular associate degree program in business administration and liberal arts.

*A graduate division. It awards master's degrees in business administration (including sport management), business education, and taxation. The latter serves as a key training ground for Pittsburgh's financial professionals.

*The Sewall Center for Leadership*

*Outstanding community service. Examples include the critically acclaimed Colonial Theater at the Moon Township campus; sponsorship of the Pittsburgh Folk Festival, an annual celebration of the area's numerous ethnic heritages, which draws as many as 50,000; and student campaigns to benefit the D.T. Watson Rehabilitation Hospital and the local Muscular Dystrophy chapter.

*A varied menu of the student activities, which range from a student government that operates as an actual business to a men's varsity basketball program that has earned a berth twice in the NCAA championship tournament.

The secret of the college's vitality seems to be its commitment to preparing students for rewarding careers that actually exist. This comes down to jobs in the business world. Hence the school's unblushing nickname: "Industry's College."

"If there were no Robert Morris College, the Pittsburgh business community would have to invent

one," says William J. Copeland, vice-chairman of the school's board of trustees and retired vice-chairman of Pittsburgh National Bank.

The institution's students receive exceptional preparation for leadership roles in business. For starters the college provides flexible scheduling to accommodate students who are already active in the working world, those whom the college calls "adult learners." It also insists that hands-on computer training be an integral part of every undergraduate's education. "We encourage our students to consider extensive computer training," explains Sewall. "But no student can graduate from here without, at the very least, a firm understanding of the fundamentals of computer technology and use."

The college faculty has developed an innovative teaching method called "ability-based learning." It allows students to advance at an individualized pace. As with flexible scheduling, ability-based

learning enhances the usefulness of Robert Morris to adult learners particularly.

The role of "Industry's College" involves other dimensions, such as the sponsorship of a "Free Enterprise Program." Its student members promote the values of private ownership and the market system, and present annual awards to notable corporate achievers.

The latest advancement of the college's commitment to students and business is embodied in the Sewall Center for Leadership. Completed in 1985 at the Moon Township campus, this 75,000-square-foot facility is designed for business seminars of regional and national scope.

"We also see it as a hub for important community events as well as a focal point for delivery of educational services to adult learners," says Sewall. "We've taken

*The Pittsburgh Center*

the leadership in serving adult learners, and this facility will keep us on the cutting edge."

In its first months the Center for Leadership hosted an appropriate diversity of events: a benefit for the Western Pennsylvania Heart Fund, the ECAC Metro basketball tournament, the Business Trade Fair of the Airport Area Chamber of Commerce, and a series of adult education programs.

For its Center for Leadership fund-raising drive, the college adopted the slogan, "Where American Dreams Get Down to Business." It's a description of what has been the school's mission since 1921, and its continuing mission on into the future of a changing Pittsburgh: to prepare serious-minded students for the exciting challenges that beckon the ambitious in a free enterprise economy.

Given the can-do history of Robert Morris College itself, an equally valid motto might be "Where the Dreams of American Business Become Reality."

# FORBES HEALTH SYSTEM
## AN INNOVATIVE APPROACH TO MEETING THE HEALTH CARE CHALLENGE

At the midpoint of the 1980s the Pittsburgh area employed 80,000 persons in health care—nearly 10 percent of its total labor force. Making people well, and helping them to stay well, has become a premier growth industry in western Pennsylvania.

That environment helps to explain the strong pulse of enterprise created in 1972 when two long-established hospitals merged to form Forbes Health System. (The name commemorates General John Forbes, whose troops carved the route through western Pennsylvania to Fort Duquesne in the French and Indian War in 1758. Both founding hospitals stood in the historic line of march along the Forbes Trail.)

The hospitals have evolved into a unique continuum of health facilities and services as more institutions have been added. Today Forbes Health System is a 763-bed multi-institutional system, providing care to more than 50 communities in Allegheny, Westmoreland, and Fayette counties. Services are now linked together by "vertical integration," so that a patient has

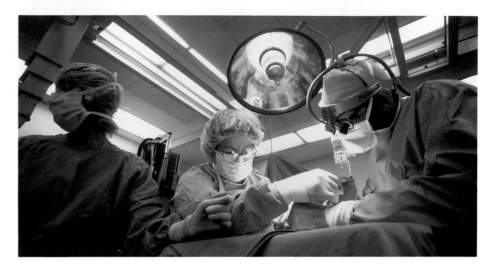

*Through modern technology and a medical staff committed to excellence, Forbes Health System offers quality patient care to more than 50 communities in three counties.*

access to the full continuum of care, from hospital to nursing facility to home care or hospice.

By linking various health facilities, Forbes Health System minimizes duplication and provides patient care in the most appropriate setting. This enables patient needs to be met effectively and at the lowest-possible cost.

Throughout its growth and development, Forbes Health System's priority has been meeting community needs for high-quality, affordable, personalized health care. The health system has made a commitment to deliver health care with compassion and hospitality, and has adopted a systemwide guest relations philosophy to assure that all its patients and visitors are treated as welcomed guests in all its facilities.

Forbes' health centers provide preventive and ambulatory care, patient and consumer education, and community outreach programs in addition to traditional hospital services. The facilities of Forbes Health System include Forbes Regional Health Center in Monroeville; Forbes Metropolitan Health Center, Forbes Center for Gerontology and Forbes Hospice in Pittsburgh's East End; and the latest addition to this regional network, Highlands Hospital and Health Center in Connellsville in Fayette County.

The system is also affiliated with

several free-standing urgent care centers called Urgi-Care® and the Forbes Life Style Center, an innovative fitness and rehabilitation program located within The Racquet Club of Pittsburgh.

The health centers of Forbes Health System target their services to meet the health needs of their specific markets. Forbes and its medical staff have made a joint commitment to medical excellence and modern technology in the effort to provide quality patient care.

Forbes' regional pediatric program specializes in pediatric endocrinology and diabetes, infectious disease, neurology, physical medicine, orthopedics, internal disorders, and nutrition. Other specialty areas include developmental and behavioral disorders, pediatric psychiatry, and physiatry provided by highly trained and diversified staff pediatricians.

Modern diagnostic imaging services include CT scanning, ultrasound, nuclear medicine, digital subtraction angiography, and sonography. The angiographic suites at Forbes Regional and Forbes Metropolitan contain the most sophisticated equipment available to health care providers.

*Forbes Regional Health Center has one of the most advanced pediatric departments in the region, with a special care nursery for seriously ill newborns.*

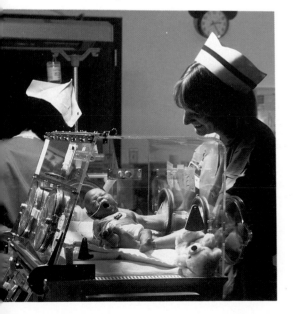

The Forbes Back Institute at Forbes Metropolitan Health Center is a new program to assist patients suffering from chronic back pain. The program uses the latest back testing and rehabilitation equipment in conjuction with aggressive screening and treatment protocols.

Forbes' orthopedic services and physicians are recognized among the most progressive in the country. Services include fracture treatments, joint replacement surgery, arthritis care, hand surgery, special care for the back such as microdisc surgery, and care for athletic injuries.

Through the major emergency departments at each of the acute care centers, patients are treated by a team of specially trained physicians and nurses experienced in providing emergency and critical care.

This health system approach to the delivery of health care enables these market-specific services to be enhanced by systemwide programs in occupational health, cancer care, and comprehensive health care services for the mature market (people age 55 and over).

The Forbes Center for Gerontology addresses the special needs of the aging population through skilled nursing care for the individual who is discharged from the hospital but still requires professional health care services, intermediate care for individuals who cannot function independently but do not require professional health care services, and residential living for self-sufficient individuals who prefer a structured living environment.

Forbes Health System initiated one of the first hospice programs in Pennsylvania in 1979. Adjacent to its gerontology center, Forbes Hospice provides comprehensive care for terminally ill patients and their families. An interdisciplinary team of professionals focuses on improving the patient's quality of life and relieving pain, while supporting the emotional and spiritual needs of everyone concerned.

The system's Urgi-Care centers extend Forbes' health services further into the communities served by the system. Urgi-Care was developed jointly by Forbes Health System and Western Pennsylvania Emergency Physicians, Inc., in 1982 to provide care for people who have medical problems that require the attention of a physician, but not the extensive services of a hospital emergency department or the primary care provided by a personal physician.

In June 1985 Forbes Health System joined with The Racquet Club of Pittsburgh to open the Forbes Life Style Center, a health and fitness facility blending sports medicine, physical therapy, physical testing and evaluation, and general fitness and health education. While these programs are offered in The Racquet Club of Pittsburgh, they use the sophisticated medical technology and the trained staff of a hospital.

To better meet future challenges, Forbes Health System reorganized in 1985 to become part of a multicorporation structure called Healthmark Corporation. This decision was made to provide for many long-term advantages: the continued delivery of cost-effective, quality medical care; continued growth; the ability to diversify into new health-related lines of business; enhanced fund-raising capabilities; and the ability to fully focus on each of those activities independently.

Forbes Health System, through Healthmark Corporation, is a shareholder in American Healthcare Systems, one of the largest health care networks in the world.

Basically, the new structure consists of four distinct corporations: Healthmark Corporation, the not-for-profit parent firm that has created a framework for selected providers, like Forbes, to link together; Forbes Health System, the full-service health care provider organization; Forbes Health Foundation, the fund-development organization; and Landmark Ventures, a separate holding company under which all of the national for-profit businesses are coordinated. Landmark Ventures assists Forbes in its efforts to diversify, a national trend aimed at reducing the traditional dependence of hospitals on acute inpatient revenues.

Forbes Health System believes that this new structure will assure its future strategic position, enabling it to respond to the community's health care needs in a rapidly changing marketplace.

® A registered service mark of Forbes Health System

*The facilities of Forbes Health System include (clockwise from upper left): Forbes Metropolitan Health Center, Forbes Center for Gerontology and Forbes Hospice, Forbes Regional Health Center, and Highlands Hospital and Health Center.*

# LA ROCHE COLLEGE
## TOMORROW'S TRADITIONS ARE BEING MADE TODAY

Pittsburgh's new economy of high technology and services is rising on a base of superb higher education resources.

One of the newest of these is La Roche College. In less than a quarter-century it has built a student body of 1,780, pursuing degrees in more than 25 fields attuned to present and future employment opportunities.

There is one advantage in not having a long history. It means fewer excuses for why something can't be done. Thus, La Roche has been able to pioneer a number of ground-breaking programs in liberal and professional education, retaining a high teacher-to-student ratio with a deep commitment to the uniqueness of every individual.

Like Pittsburgh itself, La Roche College has emerged stronger from a crisis. The difference is that the school's rocky period came early in its life rather than in maturity, as it has with the indus-

*Situated on 160 acres of woods and rolling hills, La Roche College is in the North Hills suburbs of Pittsburgh.*

trial city.

La Roche College was founded in 1963 by the Sisters of Divine Providence. It has since become a private, independent institution operated by a board of trustees composed primarily of lay persons. The Sisters' original goal in establishing the college was to prepare Catholic nuns for teaching vocations in the Pittsburgh area. However, within a few years the young school had fallen into financial distress and nearly closed.

*La Roche encourages its students to grow as individuals as well as professionals.*

The situation was remedied in 1970. A dynamic group of board members took charge and changed the institution's direction and its corporate identity. It became both independent and coeducational and the curriculum was broadened. As a result, the change in La Roche College's fortune has been nothing less than staggering. From an enrollment of less than 300, the student body grew sixfold during the ensuing 16 consecutive years of balanced budgets.

By the mid-1980s La Roche could realistically embark on an $18-million program of growth on its 160-acre campus along Babcock Boulevard in Pittsburgh's North Hills. The first phase of the capital campaign was launched in September 1985. It met with such success that the following spring La Roche broke ground for a $5-million College Center. The Center serves as the focal point of La Roche's dramatic hill-top East Campus. Other Phase One projects will renovate two existing buildings for conference and classroom use.

Later phases of the capital campaign—it will extend through 1995—will add a Fitness and Recreation Center and new academic and conference buildings. Endowments for faculty development, student scholarships, and general operations will also be strengthened. Due for completion in 1987, the College Center will house modern dining facilities, an

*La Roche is dedicated to a personalized approach to education.*

art gallery, a bookstore, offices, and student services.

Despite such significant physical growth, the college is committed to remaining relatively small in student population, and to maintaining a learning environment that is friendly and nurturing. With 36 full-time and 80 part-time faculty members, La Roche is able, in many classes, to provide a teacher for every 17 students.

A substantial percentage of students attend classes on a part-time basis. Many already hold outside jobs and are enrolled at the college to seek a degree or other professional enhancement. As a result, the average age of students is 28 in day classes and 32 in evening classes.

*The college has achieved a national reputation in the fields of graphic arts, graphic design, and interior design.*

natural and health-related sciences, the social sciences, and the humanities. The school's graduate programs include master of science degrees in human resources management and nursing management. La Roche is fully accredited by the Middle States Association of Colleges and Schools and is one of 10 members in the Pittsburgh Council on Higher Education.

The college's suburban setting combines the best of several worlds, since it is located 10 miles from Downtown Pittsburgh and two miles from North Park in the rolling countryside of western Pennsylvania. Its buildings include a large library, extensive computer facilities, and a learning center for tutoring and support services. Resident students live in spacious apartment suites with private baths and numerous amenities.

body & Co., several other trustees have held positions on the college's board since 1970. They include Pittsburgh industrial leaders Frank Schneider and Donald Peters; and former state labor secretary Charles Lieberth.

There is a particular thrill for students and faculty alike in this era of La Roche College's youthful development: the opportunity to put a personal stamp on the future. As Sister Margaret, president, has remarked, "If you do something twice here, it's an event. Three times, it's a tradition."

*La Roche's dynamic educational mission affords numerous personal growth experiences for its students.*

The diversity and maturity of the college's students is clearly one of its greatest strengths. In addition, the students represent strong Pittsburgh roots. More than 90 percent hail from western Pennsylvania and remain in the area after graduation. They take undergraduate degree programs in administration and management, graphics, design, and communications, the

There is an active social and cultural life, which includes varsity basketball and baseball teams for men, volleyball and softball for women, a variety of intramural sports and recreation opportunities, lectures, and cultural activities.

Along with chairman Thomas C. Ryan, who is vice-president of the Pittsburgh office of Kidder, Pea-

# ALLEGHENY GENERAL HOSPITAL
## A COMMITMENT TO EXCELLENCE

The steady, even sounds of hooves pounding and wooden wheels turning on cobblestone streets were common to Allegheny City residents, as large and often cumbersome horse-drawn ambulances carried the ill and injured to Allegheny General Hospital in the late 1800s.

A century later the whirring of blades and the roar of twin-engines preparing for take off signify something similar to residents of Pittsburgh's North Side. The sounds mean that one of Allegheny's Life Flight emergency medical helicopters may soon transport someone who is critically ill or injured to Allegheny General, which houses the nation's sixth-largest trauma center.

Allegheny City and Pittsburgh's North Side are the same now, barring a few adjustments in boundary. Likewise, the Allegheny General Hospital that stood three stories high amid Allegheny City 100 years ago now towers 18 stories over the North Side, and has more than 700 beds. A century's difference stands between the familiarity of the horse-drawn ambulance once considered modern and the current use of state-of-the-art, well-equipped emergency medical helicopters.

In spite of the obvious differences that time and change have brought, the mission of Allegheny General Hospital remains con-

*The strongly horizontal architectural design of Allegheny General's 13-story, 704-bed patient facility (background), completed in 1982, contrasts with the 1936 hospital in its new role as the Tower Building.*

stant, as do its commitment to excellence and the boldness with which its physicians, scientists, and other professionals pursue answers to the mysteries of medicine.

Celebrating its centennial anniversary in early 1986, Allegheny General's history has shown a long and consistent dedication to service and quality, one that began when a Ladies' Society worked to raise funds to establish the hospital in the early 1880s. From then until now Allegheny General has grown in services and sophistication, establishing itself early as a prominent force in area health care and building upon that reputation. From its very beginning the institution has measured success by the quality of life and the ability to preserve and enhance that precious gift.

The purchase of a microscope in 1890, for example, made possible more accurate detection and treatment of diseases. On the theory that disease might be spread by microscopic organisms, Allegheny General was among the first hospitals to install a water-filtration system, use sterilization techniques for operating rooms,

and use window screens. In that same era a Roentgen tube, the X-ray's forerunner, was also used routinely.

In 1918 the first director of the William H. Singer Research Laboratory, endowed three years earlier, established a relationship between air pollutants and pneumonia, silicosis, and tuberculosis. Allegheny established the tri-state area's first cardiopulmonary laboratory, a radiotherapy center, and one of the world's first high-quality, commercially available cobalt units to treat cancer. In the 1960s surgical research investigators created artificial heart valves.

In recent years, as in past ones, great strides have been made at Allegheny General in treating those diseases and injuries that most threaten mankind. The William H. Singer Research Laboratory has since been renamed the Allegheny-Singer Research Institute. It, like its predecessor, is a center for continued searching into the intricacies of the body.

For victims of trauma, the speed with which Life Flight transports the critically ill and injured to Allegheny General's trauma center

*The speed with which Life Flight transports the critically ill and injured to Allegheny's trauma center may mean the difference between life and death.*

may mean the difference between life and death, as does the deftness with which highly skilled trauma surgeons recognize and treat the multiple injuries suffered by patients.

Allegheny General researchers and cardiologists have used the body's own resources to give diseased hearts the strength to beat when they have become weak and tired. In the first successful muscle-flap operation in the United States, the institution's heart and plastic surgeons removed a patient's back muscle, wrapped it around her diseased heart and trained it to beat with a special pacemaker.

A few months later an Allegheny General neurosurgeon performed a new procedure that may one day greatly reduce inpatient surgery and the subsequent pain for hundreds who suffer herniated lumbar discs. The surgeon inserted a needle into the patient's back and removed damaged disc fragments by suction. In selected patients, the procedure, called percutaneous automated discectomy, can be performed on an outpatient basis and leaves an incision so small it can be covered with a bandage.

In a state-of-the-art procedure, Allegheny General orthopedic surgeons can now successfully implant ceramic hips into patients who have lost mobility due to arthritis, cancer, or other diseases. The ceramic hip is more permanent than other hip replacement devices and may eliminate the need for patients to undergo repeat surgery in later years.

Magnetic Resonance Imaging, introduced to Pittsburgh by Allegheny General, allows doctors to see inside the body, layer by layer, without invading it. MRI also allows physicians to isolate and use bold new procedures to remove previously inoperable tumors. It permits them to determine the nature of breast cancer tumors without surgery and to detect multiple sclerosis, a disease for which

there had been no definitive diagnostic test.

Allegheny Home Care Hospice registered nurses and volunteers comprise a team that makes a difficult situation easier by providing support to the terminally ill, their friends, and family. Hospice workers lend a caring ear or an extra hand when the burden seems heaviest and provide strength when families and patients are least able to cope with strains caused by the disease.

In line with Allegheny General's sophistication and its tradition of uniting experts in various specialities to solve complex medical problems, the department of dentistry and oral surgery has developed a comprehensive program

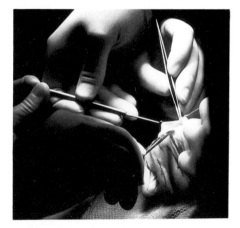

Surgeons at Allegheny General are renowned for being in the forefront of innovative techniques.

called Facial Oral Reconstructive Management (FORM) to enhance care for patients with unusual facial and oral health problems.

Ophthalmologists and neurosurgeons at Allegheny General use a carbon dioxide laser to remove eye tumors without damaging the nerve or surrounding tissue in a procedure that can preserve the gift of eyesight. It is an example of the institution's ongoing quest for knowledge about the human body, how it functions, why it ceases to do so, and how to repair it.

Allegheny General doctors today pass on to their successors the knowledge and dedication to excellence they inherited from doctors of yesterday. Through formalized teaching programs students of medicine learn from those skilled in the field. Physicians, scientists, nurses, and other professionals share their knowledge and spark a desire to excel in future generations. The institution's residency program draws qualified and committed young doctors, and many of its physicians are faculty members at major universities in the Pittsburgh area.

Allegheny General scientists hope to one day eliminate a major cause of paralysis among accident victims using a drug now being tested for its ability to reduce spinal cord swelling, a chief factor in accident-related paralysis. There also is encouragement that laser welding may soon replace suturing in many types of surgical procedures.

As medicine is practiced today, new laser treatment methods for cancer, gynecologic problems, and eye disorders are emerging for use tomorrow. By combining lasers with catheter techniques, it may soon be possible to eliminate cardiovascular blockages without surgery.

The mission of today's mature and technologically sophisticated Allegheny General was adopted from the mission of yesteryear's hospital, which was never afraid to be bold in its efforts to better the health and understanding of mankind. To do so, Allegheny General Hospital's mission has been and is to stretch the boundaries of medical knowledge through teaching and research; to provide high-quality, specialized health care for all patients, regardless of their ability to pay, through community service that now touches four states; and to fulfill that promise that surpasses all others—to give quality to life.

# THRIFT DRUG COMPANY
## A LEADER IN THE NATIONAL CHAIN DRUG INDUSTRY

In the middle of the Great Depression, two Pennsylvania pharmacists, Reuben Helfant and Philip Hoffman, had faith in their idea. Both were University of Pittsburgh graduates, both owned drugstores, and they shared a vision. They invested almost $10,000 in their new joint venture, a chain of stores they called Thrift Drug.

Helfant and Hoffman opened their first store in Sewickley in May 1935 and a second in Bellevue two weeks later. "My husband was a dreamer," says Mrs. Hoffman. "He had faith that Thrift would prosper." Helfant and Hoffman both died in 1968, but their chain of drugstores has continued to grow. Today Thrift Drug has over 370 stores in more than 20 states, with some 200 outlets in Pennsylvania alone. Its operating performance has consistently made it a leader in the national' chain drug industry.

The firm has grown both by opening new Thrift Drug stores and by acquisitions. In 1946 the eight-store Miller Drug chain of Ohio became part of Thrift, and West Virginia became the third Thrift Drug state. Expansion continued through the 1950s. The first store in eastern Pennsylvania opened in West Chester in 1959. That same year witnessed Thrift's transformation to a public corporation with its issuance of 75,000 shares of common stock.

Originally the only warehouse space required by Thrift Drug was the basement of the Bellevue store. As the chain expanded that space proved inadequate. The warehouse was moved to Pittsburgh's North Side, and then to Sharpsburg. In 1968 newly appointed president Louis L. Avner moved it to the site of the current distribution center and executive office complex in O'Hara Township. The original 175,000-square-foot facility now contains 285,000 square feet of floor space.

Under Mr. Avner's leadership Thrift Drug became a division of JCPenney in 1969. During the 1970s Thrift Drug pursued a policy of aggressive growth, including

*James B. Armor, president.*

launching its Treasury chain, first in Atlanta, then throughout the South. To complement the Pittsburgh distribution center, a 60,000-square-foot facility was built in Langhorne, Pennsylvania, in 1973. Two years later the Atlanta distribution center was built to help handle the accelerating needs of the expanding chain. Along with the increasingly complex distribution network came an electronic ordering system, bringing new efficiency to the entire system.

In 1980 J.B. Armor succeeded Avner as president. Armor began his career with JCPenney in 1948.

Under Armor's leadership Thrift Drug has achieved peak growth and operational efficiency. In an early reorganization, he developed a three-region structure with bases in Pittsburgh, Philadelphia, and Atlanta. He also consolidated the chain by acquiring new stores in Pennsylvania, Maryland, New Jersey, and Delaware, while divesting 20 stores in the Carolinas, Ten-

*The soda fountains of a bygone era have been replaced by effective merchandise displays, catalog desks and pharmacy computers.*

*A Thrift Drug store in the 1940s.*

nessee, and Alabama. His policy of aggressive, steady growth has resulted in continual expansion.

The Thrift Drug stores have also evolved over their half-century. During the early years stores were built at downtown locations. Later they opened mainly at suburban shopping malls. The smaller stores of the early days gave way to large, general merchandise centers in the 1970s. More recently Thrift has returned to a smaller facility, concentrating on more traditional drugstore merchandise.

Throughout its history the firm has continuously emphasized its prescription business—which still accounts for over 30 percent of Thrift Drug's total sales. Most store managers are pharmacists, guaranteeing that the emphasis on prescriptions will continue.

A nostalgic look at Thrift Drug

*Over the past half-century Thrift Drug stores have evolved with the times but still concentrate on traditional merchandise and policies.*

stores of the past would include elaborately trimmed windows and soda fountains, but those are gone now. In their place are durable medical equipment displays, catalog desks, and pharmacy computers. The durable medical equipment operation which began

in June 1982, is a new concept—a home medical equipment program that rents or sells such products as wheelchairs and hospital beds. Customers receive free home delivery, assistance from trained technicians, and a 24-hour emergency service.

Another innovative program is Express Pharmacy Services, Thrift's mail order pharmacy, which provides low-cost and efficient service to many group plans such as H.J. Heinz, Westinghouse, and Rockwell. Thrift is also moving to become a major contractor with nursing homes, currently providing prescription services to approximately homes in many states.

Thrift Drug demonstrates both a continued awareness of the traditional services and products required of the community pharmacy, and a willingness to accept innovation and technology to meet new demands. The firm remains aware of its rich heritage, proud of its current growth, and excited by the promise of its future.

# MON VALLEY TRAVEL, INC.
## HELPING PEOPLE TRAVEL WITH FORESIGHT

*Alex Zelenski (center), founder and president, with son Marc Zelenski, chief operating officer, and Bonnie Viverito, vice-president of operations.*

A journey of a thousand miles, according to an old Chinese proverb, starts with a single step. For Mon Valley Travel, which has grown into one of the 50 largest travel agencies in the United States, the journey began with a modest 1959 opening in a converted shoe-shine parlor. That was in the Monongahela River industrial town of Charleroi, south of Pittsburgh. By the mid-1980s, its headquarters long since moved to the Golden Triangle, Mon Valley was assisting more than 350 area companies with their travel budgets and serving over 100,000 travelers annually.

The company's founder and president, Alex Zelenski, credits this growth to a simple philosophy: "Provide the best travel services available anywhere." In the beginning, he recalls, the major marketing task was to explain what a travel agent actually did. "Travel in those days was straightforward. Prices and schedules were regulated."

Today the concept of full service involves considerably more, explains Zelenski's son, Marc, chief operating officer of the agency. "We once represented travel suppliers; now we represent the traveling public," he says.

Mon Valley Travel employs more than 85 persons. In 1985 it crossed the $35-million mark in sales, ranging from the everyday round trip air reservation for one or two persons to complicated itineraries for 200. Stressing the concept of "travel with foresight" (getting the most mileage, comfort, and convenience, whatever the budget for a given trip) the agency has made its mark by adapting to a constantly evolving marketplace. "Innovation," states Marc Zelenski, "is a way of life."

Thus, when the agency moved to Downtown Pittsburgh in 1964—it is now at 4 Smithfield Street—in order to assure the expertise of its staff, Bonnie Viverito, vice-president/operations, established one of the nation's first in-house travel schools. The firm pioneered computer software designed to expedite travel; its RATESCAN, developed in 1978 in anticipation of airline deregulation, is a computerized checklist for the best available fares. At Mobay Chemical Corporation the agency set up one of the nation's first in-plant travel operations. It also was a founding member of Associated Travel Nationwide, a consortium of the largest U.S. travel agencies with representation now worldwide. In 1982 Mon Valley began producing "The Business Traveler," a daily, two-minute program of advice and tips, which airs on regional radio stations.

Most of the organization's present clients are commercial travelers, but the agency earned its

*Alex Zelenski is backed by Mon Valley Travel's professional staff, which has provided full-service travel planning for commercial travelers and vacationers for over 25 years.*

start by helping people to plan vacations—and this remains a highly valued part of its activity. "Innovation and dollar savings are important to any business," says Marc Zelenski. "But our bottom line has always been based on personal service."

# PITTSBURGH ANNEALING BOX COMPANY
## A DIVERSIFIED NETWORK OF INDUSTRIAL SERVICES COMPANIES

Pittsburgh Annealing Box Company (PABCO) was founded before the turn of the century on the north bank of the Ohio River across from "the Point." As its name implies, the small manufacturing company first produced one specialized product, annealing covers, which are used in the heat-treating process of sheet steel. More than 90 years later PABCO is today a strong network of interrelated companies serving the energy, chemical, marine, and steel-producing industries.

Characteristically, the enterprise began by serving the growth market of its time, the steel industry. Since the company's first annealing box was forge-welded and riveted in 1893, PABCO has designed and introduced more innovations in annealing equipment than any other manufacturer in its field. For more than 20 years now, however, the firm has diversified its services to meet the changing needs of old and new customers.

While still the dominant supplier of annealing equipment to steel mills worldwide, Pittsburgh Annealing Box Company has derived new strength through diversified products manufacturing and related services to industry. The company's Special Products Divi-

*Ceramaloy, developed by PABCO's Daman Industries, is meticulously fired by hand.*

sion, located in McKees Rocks, Pennsylvania, produces industrial cylinders and pipe for special applications in the chemical, steelmaking, and nuclear fields, to mention just a few.

Inland Metal Fabricators, which was acquired by PABCO in 1971, represents another area of service to industry. The Indiana-based subsidiary is a leading fabricator of access steel and miscellaneous structural steel for utilities and power plants, chemical plants, refineries, and steel mills.

Daman Industries, based in East Brady, Pennsylvania, specializes in the mechanical repair and reconstruction of pumps, compressors, large fans, and numerous other mechanical components. This subsidiary company, acquired by Pittsburgh Annealing Box in 1979, is active in developing maintenance programs for a wide range of client-owned equipment. In this venture, Daman recently introduced new vibration analyzing equipment that can detect early warning symptoms in the rotating parts of costly industrial machinery. Also significant is the firm's development of Ceramaloy®, a

ceramic-powder coating for metals that are subject to high abrasion and corrosion. Today marine propulsion shafts are commonly treated with this product.

In 1985 PABCO purchased Capital Market Services of New York, a leasing company with over 20 years of experience in equipment leasing and financial services.

PABCO's most recent venture is in the area of service to our national security. Through the 1985 acquisition of NABCO, a former competitor, a new product was developed. This product, a total containment bomb disposal unit, is currently being utilized by the FBI, U.S. Army, U.S. Navy, and the Police Departments of New York City and Los Angeles.

President Sam Michaels is proud of PABCO's continuity of growth. "Although ours are relatively small companies, they are all major leaders in their respective fields. This is the niche we hope to expand in while looking for newer, more innovative ways of serving our customers."

*Pittsburgh Annealing Box Company products being manufactured by a licensee in São Paulo, Brazil.*

# SCHNEIDER GROUP OF COMPANIES
## TURNING PROBLEMS INTO OPPORTUNITIES

*Frank J. Schneider (seated), founder and chairman of the board, and Edward B. Schneider, president.*

"America is a greenhouse for people with entrepreneurial spirit," says Frank J. Schneider, whose business success bears out the metaphor. He established a one-man mechanical contracting firm in 1962, and today the Schneider Group of Companies employs over 7,000 persons (more than half of them in the Pittsburgh area) and has annual revenues that surpass one-half billion dollars.

The Schneider Group is a privately held conglomerate, with activities ranging from building power plants to operating nursing homes for the elderly. Its headquarters at 121 Seventh Street received the Building Owners and Manufacturers Association Building of the Year Award in 1975, in recognition of outstanding contributions to the continuing renaissance of the Pittsburgh area. The organization has approximately 1,900 administrative and engineering personnel in numerous Pittsburgh locations, from the city's North Side to Bridgeville, as well as 2,500 craftsmen at work on major projects such as the Beaver

Valley Nuclear Power Station, near Shippingport, in addition to the city's major new office buildings, hotels, and hospitals.

Frank Schneider was a division manager for another local contracting firm when he decided to go into business for himself. A $250 heating contract for St. John's Hospital was his first order. "My philosophy when I started was to be the most economical producer of services that my clients could obtain. This doesn't always mean providing the least expensive product on the market, but offering the best value for the money. Most of my business was built on satisfied customers—and on their willingness to have us back."

A list of Schneider Group activities demonstrates that while waiting for those callbacks the firm has tirelessly expanded into related fields. Its basic specialties are the design and construction of

nuclear, cogeneration, and fossil-fueled power plants, and mechanical contracting for the chemical, steel, refining, industrial, commercial, and institutional markets. Its engineers also serve environmental, utility, and municipal customers, and consult in energy-related ventures. Other corporate interests include operation of government facilities, insurance, real estate, construction equipment rentals, industrial supplies, energy exploration, die casting, financial, and health services.

Schneider personnel perform mission support services for the vast U.S. Air Force Arnold Engineering Development Center near Tullahoma, Tennessee; recover gas energy from garbage landfills, sewage sludge, and low-quality coal in California; pump Colorado River water across Arizona; build pumping stations in Arizona and New Mexico for the world's longest heated crude oil pipeline; and play a major role in the construction and maintenance of Pittsburgh's modern Light Rail Transit System. The magazine *Domestic*

*PPG Place, Pittsburgh. The Schneider Group installed HVAC systems in satellite buildings. Photo by Don Van Kirk*

*Engineering* ranks the corporation number one among this nation's specialty contractors.

Frank Schneider—who is chairman and chief executive officer—was joined in 1965 by his brother, Edward B. Schneider, who is president. Ed Schneider has made a specialty of labor relations.

Seeking opportunities for logical expansion of its success in contracting, the firm moved early into fabrication. "We were buying large quantities of metal, so we decided to create our own source of supply," recalls the founder of his operation. "Second was the insurance business. Construction requires a lot of insurance, so why not supply it ourselves? We purchased the suppliers to our parent business, enhancing the parent in the process." Next came moves outside the Pittsburgh market, first to Chicago, then to Arizona and the West Coast. By year-end 1985 the organization had offices in 15 states.

A dedicated supporter of Pittsburgh's arts, education, and charitable institutions, Frank Schneider

believes that while success is an individual achievement, "the individual needs the proper environment to be successful, and the entrepreneurial environment is what this country is all about." He feels that those who benefit from the American system accrue an obligation to contribute to it. "That means you become involved in the political arena, the educational and cultural arenas. You contribute your time, talent, and fortune as a slight repayment for the advantages this system gives you," he emphasizes.

Pittsburgh's economic future looks full of potential to the chairman of the Schneider Group. The decline in certain basic manufacturing industries resembles doomsday only where there is lack of historical perspective, he believes. "What happened to everybody who left the farm in the nineteenth century? What happened to harness makers and the people who made radio cabinets? Economies change as needs change. It's only a question of whether we'll use our imaginations to turn difficult situations into opportunities to move forward."

*County Sanitation Districts of Los Angeles (California) County. Schneider Inc. designed, procured, constructed, and started up the Puente Hills Energy Recovery from Gas (PERG) Power Plant. The Puente Hills landfill generates a substantial amount of gas that has been flared into the atmosphere. PERG, the largest facility of its kind in the world, is fired on the lost gas.*

Schneider believes Pittsburgh's strong suits include talent, willingness to work, and "a strong, positive, opportunistic attitude," combined with pleasant living conditions and plenty of financial and intellectual capital embodied in major banks, educational institutions, and research centers. "You put people, climate, and the right attitudes together," he states, "and you have the ingredients for success."

His term for his own organization is "an opportunity company," ceaselessly searching for ideas and idea people—"the adrenalin that makes the corporation move, that gives it energy. Our future is being capable of participating in the marketplace with new ideas."

"I don't know what products we're going to be involved with two or three years from now," admits the entrepreneur. "But I do know we'll be looking for opportunities. That's our nature; we turn problems into opportunities."

*Beaver Valley Power Station, Shippingport, Pennsylvania. The company engineers and craftsmen installed all mechanical equipment and piping systems on the 880 MWe nuclear unit. Photo by Don Van Kirk*

# ECKERT, SEAMANS, CHERIN & MELLOTT
## HITTING A HOME RUN IN A CHANGING LEGAL MARKETPLACE

For more than a quarter-century, Eckert, Seamans, Cherin & Mellott had handled major corporate litigation in Pittsburgh. Still, nothing brought the firm such prominence as a piece of public service it carried to fruition in 1985. The Pirates were saved for Pittsburgh!

Outside estimates range upward of $900,000 on the value of so much legal expertise donated *pro bono publico.* Insiders and news media alike give much of the credit to the law firm's tireless deal structuring and shuttle diplomacy. A $26-million "public/private partnership," completely new to major league sports, swung the team to solid local loyalists, with the sale-leaseback of Three Rivers Stadium providing a huge assist on the play.

The management committee (from left): W. Gregg Kerr; Carl F. Barger, chairman; and Donald C. Winson.

Cloyd R. Mellott, chairman of Eckert, Seamans, Cherin & Mellott.

Eckert, Seamans, Cherin & Mellott goes to bat for the Bucs.

The Pirates activity, spectacular as it was, was only a signal to many new strategies for the 1980s at Eckert Seamans. Pursuing both geographical and service diversification, the firm set up offices in Washington, D.C., Harrisburg, and at the University of Pittsburgh Applied Research Center (formerly Gulf Laboratories), where 12 attorneys spend rotating time to counsel emerging high-technology companies.

Founded in 1958, primarily to serve major corporate clients, Eckert Seamans won high marks for its handling of antitrust and product liability litigation. The late Frank Seamans led American Tobacco's defense against an early suit alleging the culpability of cigarettes in the cause of cancer. Price-fixing charges against corrugated-box manufacturers were beaten off in the famous Georgia-Pacific case. Eckert Seamans helped limit Gulf Oil's damage from a foreign payments scandal in the 1970s, assisted Westinghouse in settling a swarm of uranium supply cases, and coordinated for Firestone 20,000 claims against its "500" tires.

However, legal markets shifted in the 1980s, and the firm responded by diversifying to full service. Its attorneys practice in virtually every field of law, including banking, creditor's rights, environmental, estate trusts, general corporate matters, international trade, municipal finance and public law, transportation, nuclear law, real estate, antitrust, tax, family law, government contracts, patents and trademarks, securities, labor law, and general litigation.

Eckert Seamans in 1986 still admired the partnership mode of organization. Its 140 attorneys included 54 partners; they meet monthly to set major policy directions. Two of the founders are still active: Cloyd R. Mellott, who is chairman of the firm, and Carl Cherin. A management committee of three provides day-to-day direction: Carl Barger, chairman; W. Gregg Kerr; and Donald C. Winson. C. James Parks serves as executive director of the firm.

Barger, who became unpaid secretary and general counsel of the Pirates, seems proudest that the save-the-team project involved virtually everyone at Eckert, Seamans, Cherin & Mellott. "We got support from the partnership up and down the line, and no one grumbled that we were doing all of this nonbillable work," he says. "The payback we're hoping for is to make Pittsburgh a better community."

# WEAN UNITED, INC.
## AN INDUSTRY LEADER

Although Wean United wasn't created until 1968, the company's roots go back more than 100 years. Today the firm has more than 1,000 employees in plants and offices in five states and Canada. Its metal-producing, metal-working, rubber, plastics, and wood products machinery is at work in more than 100 countries.

Wean United's subsidiaries are Berkeley-Davis, Inc., which designs and builds welding equipment; Automated Production Systems Corporation (APROS), which designs metals-recycling systems; Stedman Machine Company, which supplies crushing and grinding equipment; Schaming Industries, which supplies fluid-control equipment; and Wean United Canada Limited, which manufactures machinery in Canada.

Wean United's modern history began in 1929, when R.J. Wean, Sr., a former sales engineer from Barto, Pennsylvania, decided to risk everything and form his own company in Warren, Ohio. Wean Engineering Company, Inc., specialized in the design of sheet, strip, and tinplate processing machinery. R.J. Wean, Sr., who died in 1980 at the age of 85, was the holder of numerous patents and was a leader in the conversion of sheet-steel processing to more efficient and economical coil processing. Today R.J. Wean, Jr., is

*A modern electrolytic tinning line mechanically handles what was done by hand dipping in a tin pot in the early 1900s.*

chairman and chief executive officer of Wean United, and R.J. Wean III is president and chief operating officer.

In July 1966 Wean Industries, Inc., was formed, and the first public offering of common stock was made. The corporation expanded rapidly with the acquisitions of the McKay Machine Company,

Youngstown Foundry and Machine Company, and Vaughn Machinery Company.

In 1968 Wean Industries acquired the United Engineering and Foundry Company of Pittsburgh as the result of an exchange offer. United Engineering designed and built rolling mills and manufactured mill rolls. That same year the parent company's name was changed to Wean United.

In 1970 the firm's corporate headquarters was relocated from Warren to Pittsburgh. Wean United, Inc., is proud to have played a role in Pittsburgh's progress and looks forward to continuing that involvement.

*A recently installed hot strip mill contrasts dramatically with the old, hard way of rolling tinplate.*

# GENERAL NUTRITION CENTERS
## PROMOTING A HEALTHY DIET AND WAY OF LIFE

In August 1935 David B. Shakarian, a young native of the city, opened a health food store at 418 Wood Street, Downtown. He called it Lackzoom; and he was his own manager, purchasing agent, sales clerk, stock boy, and janitor.

Shakarian's stock in trade was yogurt. His Armenian-born father had been one of the first to introduce the nutritious native dairy preparation to America, importing and later manufacturing yogurt in Pittsburgh's East End since 1910. His venture was forced to close during the Depression.

The enterprising spirit was strong in son David, however. Newly graduated from Peabody High School, he attended a free lecture at Soldiers and Sailors Memorial Hall given by health food popularizer Gayelord Hauser. Hauser attacked white sugar and white flour as being dietarily worthless, and his point of view struck a commercial chord in his young listener.

Although bad times had emptied many stores in Pittsburgh, Shakarian persuaded a mortgage-holding bank to let him open his health

food business and pay rent later. His first-day sales totaled an encouraging $35. The shop prospered, and soon he was planning another, not far away on Smithfield Street. Then came the devastating flood of March 17, 1936, filling the Smithfield basement and swamping the Wood Street store under four feet of water. Undaunted, he reopened with an improved store, and by World War II he had six operating in the Pittsburgh area.

In 1947 came the sort of accident that alters business history. A public employee's strike halted Pittsburgh's trolleys, then the chief mode of public transit. Customers could not get to the Lackzoom stores. Shakarian changed his approach overnight.

"Since you can't come in for your health food products," he publicly advertised, "send money and we'll mail them to you."

Thus was born the mail-order health foods business—so successful that in 13 years, by 1960, it had become national in scope, with a volume exceeding that of the stores. Renamed General Nu-

*There are more than 1,100 General Nutrition Centers in the United States, the largest chain of its kind.*

trition Centers—now known as GNC—the firm grew to more than 1,100 stores in the United States, the largest chain of its kind. To meet customer demand for quality products, GNC opened its own manufacturing plants in Pennsylvania and three other states and established a sizable research and development organization.

Since David Shakarian's death in 1984, General Nutrition Incorporated, still headquartered in Pittsburgh's Downtown, at 921 Penn Avenue, has been refining its concepts and also expanding its market. GNC now defines its mission as one of striving to become the leading provider of products, services, and information for self-care and personal health enhancement. A new management under Jerry D. Horn, president and chairman of the board, is dedicated to promoting the benefits of a healthy way of life for the greatest number of people.

# RYAN HOMES, INC.
## A RESTLESSLY CREATIVE MARKET FORCE

Innovation has been the hallmark of Ryan Homes, Inc., since its founding in Pittsburgh's post-World War II surge of building in 1948. Now one of the nation's largest caterers to the American dream—a home of one's own—the organization has led the way in imaginative techniques of construction, marketing, and financing. Challenged periodically by its industry's worst cyclical enemy—high interest rates—Ryan pioneered mortgage-backed bonds; and by year-end 1985 had issued more than $1.2 billion of them, providing 70 percent of the mortgage funds that its own financial services subsidiary made available to customers.

At the mid-point of the 1980s, Ryan Homes was grossing well

*This home is in the Ryan American Portfolio series, which the firm has designed to meet the taste of "move-up" buyers.*

over a half-billion dollars a year, actively building in 27 markets in 11 states, franchising in others, and setting new profit records. With a staff of more than 1,700 employees in a host of skills, the firm normally will "close" on 7,500 to 9,000 housing units per year and take orders for that many or more.

The company's founder, Edward M. Ryan, was driven by a deep fascination for the art of building.

No stranger to muddy boots, he worked out with his crews new ideas for economical construction that continue to evolve to this day. Eight company manufacturing plants in seven states now produce wall panels and structural

*The Shenandoah model is one of the largest homes Ryan builds in the Pittsburgh metropolitan area.*

components to varying stages of finish. Combined with additional materials, these high-quality sections are delivered to the building site as "house packages." The project is then completed by Ryan crews or independent subcontractors under the watchful eye of Ryan employees. A Research and Development Center near Pittsburgh, established in 1985, provides a year-round facility to construct entire houses indoors

for testing new methods and standards—enhanced as well by a computer-aided design system.

Ryan Homes stock became publicly traded in 1968, and ten years later was listed on the New York Stock Exchange.

Ryan Financial Services first began setting up financing for the firm's home buyers in the "tight money" era of 1969 and has become an aggressive participant in mortgage banking and servicing, with a $2-billion portfolio by year-end 1985. Ryan Building Systems, organized in 1973 to sell the corporation's "package designs" to independent builder/dealers, has since expanded as well into franchising.

A management transition that "Ed" Ryan initiated in 1970 placed the company on the path to become a large, integrated force in a market that has been traditionally small, local, and fragmented. Malcolm M. Prine has been chief executive officer of Ryan Homes, Inc., since 1971, and board chairman since 1973; Steven J. Smith is president and chief operating officer.

Its strikingly residential-looking headquarters of glass and timbers, tucked into a wooded hillside overlooking the Parkway West, states just what Ryan Homes, Inc., wants to say about Pittsburgh: Here's home.

# H.J. HEINZ COMPANY
## IN FOOD, THE WORLD IS ITS FERTILE FIELD

The town of Sharpsburg, Pennsylvania, is a community of homes, stores, and light industry on the north shore of the Allegheny six miles upstream of Pittsburgh. It is a pleasant place to live, the residents say, with a main street of modest storefronts along which commuters pass to and from their jobs in the city. Several homes in the hills that rise above the town are blessed with spectacular views at night down the curling river to the sparkling skyline of the Golden Triangle.

Sharpsburg holds a significant place in industrial history. It was the birthplace of a world-spanning enterprise and the boyhood home of the determined man who began the enterprise in 1869, when the area was still essentially rural.

Henry J. Heinz, born in 1844, was not yet out of his teens when he hit upon what modern students of business would call his "marketing niche." Horseradish, he knew, was a popular kitchen staple. But making it was a tedious job for the housewife! It fell to her to grate the pungent root, inevitably ending with reddened eyes and scraped knuckles. The term "convenience foods" had not yet entered the language, but surely here was the need.

Young Heinz was not the first to spot the opportunity; what distinguished his product, and set the

H.J. Heinz Company's Pittsburgh factory and headquarters complex on the north bank of the Allegheny River.

clear glass jars. "Missus" could see what she was buying before she paid for it. In later years the entrepreneur's flourishing venture would enshrine "The Little House Where We Began." It was floated downriver to serve as an inspiration to tourists and employees at the great factory site on Pittsburgh's North Side; and now for many years it has stood among the preserved relics of Henry Ford's Greenfield Village in Dearborn, Michigan—"a monument,"

Company chefs are continually working on new formulations.

tone for his company ever afterward, was its appeal to quality and purity. Others might conceal a flaw inside a dark green or brown bottle, or "stretch" the product with ground turnip and even sawdust.

Not Henry Heinz: He processed the harvest of the family's own garden outside the brick home in Sharpsburg, and did his packing in

Huge buckets of tuna are unloaded for Heinz' Star-Kist facility in Terminal Island, California.

as one commentator put it, "to American business acumen and the American dream."

Henry Heinz was 25 in 1869, when he and some partners launched the business that bears his name. Within a half-dozen years operations spread through the eastern United States—and brought bankruptcy. The young company had contracted to purchase certain crops, and was overwhelmed by bumper harvests that

Another Star-Kist canning plant amid the lush vegetation of Pago Pago, American Samoa.

were far too much to process; it could not even pay for such volume.

The years that followed were hard. However, Heinz insisted upon doing what the law did not compel him to do—that is, personally to pay back every cent of his 80-percent share in the firm's debts.

This scrupulous adherence to principle paid dividends. Restarted, the company earned people's trust, and again began to grow.

The founder's grandson, Henry J. Heinz II, once gave this brief summary of the pioneer's achievements:

*He was a remarkable man, an entrepreneur in the literal meaning of that word. He foresaw with a clarity virtually unknown in his time that there would be a market for processed pure food products in*

Greenery surrounds the Heinz factory in Venezuela.

the America that was taking shape after the awful fratricide of the Civil War. He quickly instituted research and quality control as vital functions in his new business. That same ethical passion animated his successful battle for the passage of the Pure Food Law of 1906.

Before there was national advertising or marketing, and without the benefit of the electronic media we use today, he made his brand name a household word through the sort of instinctive promotional sense that inspired him to coin the "57 Varieties" slogan.

Most importantly, at a time when his young venture was still struggling to stay afloat in the Pittsburgh area, his fertile mind

had conceived of an international market for his products. He was a man famous for his mottoes. One of those mottoes is preserved in a stained glass window that still stands in our Administration Building, completed in 1906, around the time we started production in England. The window shows a globe of the world. Beneath that globe, my grandfather had two words inscribed: "Our Field."

The beautifully landscaped Hayes Park facility near London is H.J. Heinz Company Ltd.'s headquarters in the United Kingdom.

Founder Heinz personally took the first multinational step a century ago. Wealthy enough by 1886 to tour Europe with his family, he thought to combine business with pleasure and paid a call on the venerable London provisioners, Fortnum & Mason. He knew no one there, and they did not know him. Nevertheless, he took a horse-drawn hansom to Piccadilly and strode through the store's Georgian doorway, perhaps unmindful that there was a service entrance for such missions. His American "push" was rewarded. After examining samples the man from Pittsburgh had thoughtfully brought from home, the head of grocery purchasing spoke the words that became company legend: "I think, Mr. Heinz, we will take all of them."

By the time of his death in 1919, Henry J. Heinz was an authentic folk hero. He had established strong foreign companies in Canada and England (where, slogan attests, "Beanz Meanz Heinz"), and he had made the keystone label familiar in millions of American kitchens. The astute businessman also bequeathed a corporation of rare stability, headed by only five chief executives—himself included—in a span of 12 decades.

Howard Heinz succeeded his father in the wake of World War I, consolidating the organization's gains and building steady growth in the Heinz brand name. He ex-

*A typical British double-decker bus passes a Heinz billboard advertising baked beans, the country's "staff of life."*

tended the founder's dream by dispatching his son, Henry J. Heinz II, to investigate the possibility of operations in yet another English-speaking country, Australia. The mission was accomplished—with the establishment of a company in the state of Victoria, its factory at Dandenong.

The second-generation owner took on numerous assignments related to food relief for the hungry of the world. At his death in 1941 he left the Howard Heinz Endowment, which continues to benefit Pennsylvania's charitable, educational, medical, and cultural institutions.

Henry J. Heinz II began his ten-

ure as chief executive by overseeing the conversion of a number of company facilities to World War II service. Heinz plants produced military rations, of course, but also glider parts for the United States and allies.

It was after the war that the firm first started to manufacture and market products other than those that carried the Heinz brand name—notably with the acquisition in 1963 of Star-Kist Foods, a leading supplier of tuna products for people and pets, and of Ore-Ida Foods in 1965. Ore-Ida is now the country's foremost producer of frozen foods for the grocery trade. "Jack" Heinz's 25 years of leadership also brought in more foreign operations: Holland, in 1958; Venezuela, 1959; Japan, 1961; Italy, 1963; and Portugal, 1965. Each has since grown in size, volume, and influence.

By 1966 president Heinz had become deeply involved in a variety of public service. He supervised the large endowment left by his father, and his global activities brought honors from several governments. For his "significant contribution in the furtherance of British-American relationships, especially in the cultural, educational, and economic fields," Queen Elizabeth II personally bestowed on H.J. Heinz II the title of Honorary Knight Commander of the Most Excellent Order of the British Empire (K.B.E.). He also helped to found the Agribusiness Council; The Nutrition Foundation; and the Allegheny Conference on Community Development, which spearheaded the Pittsburgh Renaissance. Still to come was the refurbishment of a faded Downtown movie palace into the glittering Heinz Hall for the Performing Arts, home of the Pittsburgh Symphony Orchestra.

With so many outside pursuits to engage his energies, Heinz felt it was time to relinquish direction of corporation operations. Thus,

*Tomatoes ready for ketchup making in the Heinz factory in Elst, the Netherlands.*

*Cans of* itarian sosu *and* biifu gureibi *for the Japanese consumer. Translated, they contain Italian sauce and beef gravy.*

R. Burt Gookin became the first person outside the founding family to be given that responsibility.

Gookin's period of stewardship was one of sustained growth. More business units entered the fold: Australia's Stanley Wine Company in 1971; The Hubinger Company, maker of corn-based sweeteners and other grain products, in 1975; and in 1978, Weight Watchers International and Foodways National. The latter firm manufactures many of the frozen products prescribed in the former's programs. Industry colleagues credit Gookin with pushing to completion the Universal Product Code, the system of bars and numbers that revolutionized super-

The familiar ketchup bottle moving along the assembly line at Tracy, California.

Millions of Plasmon biscuits move out of the Heinz Latina factory for the children of Italy.

market checkouts and facilitated inventory control and market analysis. Gookin retired in 1979, and the post went for the first time to a non-American.

Anthony J.F. O'Reilly had been general manager of the Irish Dairy Board, and managing director of the Irish Sugar Company and Erin Foods Ltd. when he joined Heinz in its centennial year, 1969, as managing director of the British operation. Dr. O'Reilly (his Ph.D. is in agricultural marketing) moved to Pittsburgh in 1971 as senior vice-president/North America and Pacific. The following year he was made executive vice-president and chief operating officer, becoming president in 1973. Today, with Henry J. Heinz II retaining the chairmanship, "Tony" O'Reilly is chief executive officer—managing some of the most dramatic developments in company history.

These obviously include acquisitions: Germany's Nadler-Werke, in 1979; Gagliardi Brothers, a Pennsylvania-based maker of portion-controlled meat products, 1980; Fratelli Sperlari, a confectionery manufacturer in Italy, and Ets. Paul Paulet, a French seafood processor, both in 1981; and Johma Holdings, the leading Dutch marketer of chilled salads and sauces, 1984. Others include

Chico-San, a California producer of rice cakes, and Cardio-Fitness Corporation, which operates executive health facilities.

It may be that future historians will find the chief contribution of the O'Reilly era to be the firm's outward reach into world markets still in the formative stage: for example, Zimbabwe, the African nation once known as Rhodesia. In 1982 Heinz reached a historic agreement for a 51-percent interest in Olivine Industries with a nation as its partner; Zimbabwe's government holds the remaining 49-percent share in this major manufacturer of edible oils and related products. A similar joint venture in China, Heinz-UFE, was set up to operate a new baby-food factory in Guangzhou (formerly Canton); and yet another, South Korea's Heinz-Seoul Food Ltd., serves one of the world's most rapidly growing economies.

Meanwhile, the Heinz U.S.A. Division continues to evolve, prosper, and grow. It is the core unit best known for its ketchup and

other tomato-based products, and is the direct descendant of the enterprise originated in 1869. The prosperity of Heinz U.S.A. stands as proof of a corporation that has not dissipated its capital strength in pursuit of expansion alone. Financially robust, the H.J. Heinz Company of the 1980s seems constantly ready to seek out and negotiate with the most attractive purchase candidates available.

The corporation has for 22 consecutive years set records in sales, operating profits, and earnings per share, and is determined to perpetuate these accomplishments. Headed by a lean staff at world headquarters in Pittsburgh's 600 Grant Street Building, the H.J. Heinz Company is an enterprise employing 45,000 persons full-time and thousands of others at seasonal peaks. It includes 21 firms with 41 factories in 14 nations and territories, representing all the inhabited continents and functioning—by design—with a high degree of local autonomy. Heinz managers around the globe enjoy broad latitude to direct their own operation, and handsome incentives to perform profitably. Today's hundreds of Heinz products and services (indeed, the famous "57 varieties" were exceeded long, long ago) reach consumers in at least 150 nations.

Still, that does not satisfy the organization.

"This company's program of new product development and territorial expansion will be the most extensive in its history," president O'Reilly has pledged. From his 60th-floor office in Downtown Pittsburgh, the view is spacious and seems to embrace a human society more healthfully fed than ever before in history.

"We have as part of our goal," he explains, "nothing less than the 85 percent of the world's billions of people who do not yet have access to Heinz products and services."

# SARGENT ELECTRIC COMPANY
## YOUTHFULNESS AT AGE 80

*It's 7:30 p.m. As people all over Pittsburgh finish their evening meals and turn toward their night's activities, a technician from Sargent Electric Company races toward Greater Pittsburgh International Airport to board a plane to respond to an urgent call from a West Coast defense facility that has a critical need for this man's specialty—fiber-optic cable and the electronic equipment associated with it.*

*En route to the airport he passes service vehicles also from Sargent Electric, where a crew has been called out to perform emergency work on traffic signals damaged during rush hour by an automobile collision at a busy intersection.*

*Not far beyond that point he comes across vans from Gray Communications, the telecommunications division of Sargent Electric, outside the offices of a major corporation. This evening the workers are placing into service a few hundred telephones that first thing next morning will be used by a department that has just relocated.*

*Meanwhile, the lights burn late at Sargent Electric's headquarters*

*as an electrical estimator puts the finishing touches on a proposal for the construction of a new, multimillion-dollar cogeneration plant in another state. It will supply steam from burning waste to an industrial park and help pay for itself by selling electricity to the local utility grid. Another estimator completes a companion proposal for the instrumentation and controls which will be essential to the operation of that facility.*

*Estimators do not usually work nights at the Sargent office, but someone is always there. For Sargent's headquarters facilities are manned by service personnel seven days per week, 24 hours per day, to respond at any time to customers' needs.*

That little vignette compresses in fictional form a picture of what in reality does occur at Sargent Electric Company on a routine, daily basis. For Sargent Electric is one of those Pittsburgh companies that participate in the nation's fastest-growing segment of the economy, the service industry. The firm is representative of the many Pittsburgh companies that have

evolved from decades-old, traditional activities into wholly new businesses.

Twenty years ago it would also have been very possible for Sargent's electrical workers to be seen pushing on after dark to meet a critical deadline on an important construction schedule, perhaps for the refurbishing of a blast furnace or some other basic industry facility. As one of the nation's 10 largest electrical contractors, with annual billings of $130 to $150 million, Sargent makes a gospel of honoring customers' deadlines. Meeting customers' demanding requirements has always been the mainstream of the firm's business.

But now instead of, for example, pressing to meet a construction schedule for the completion of a new high school facility before the beginning of the school year, Sargent employees may also be producing the computerized class schedules for the students. Indeed, providing data-processing support for educational institutions or other corporations is a regular activity of Sargent's newly formed Information Systems Division, representative of the firm's overall corporate direction to make a conversion that corresponds to the change in the region's business character.

Founded by 1907 by Edward B. Sargent, a native of Pittsburgh's South Side, the company for decades maintained a strong reputation in industrial construction in Pittsburgh and elsewhere, responsible for some of the largest electrical projects ever performed in the steel industry.

In recent years, when the postwar era yielded to the age of deregulation, Sargent Electric also had

*Gray Communications services and maintains telephone systems in the Mid-Atlantic region, which currently handle one million calls per day.*

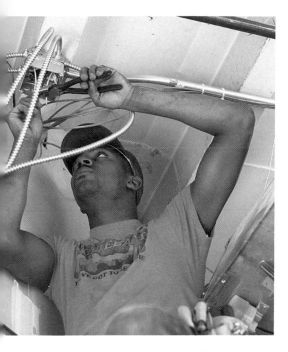

*Specialties of Sargent Electric Company include installation, maintenance, and service for commercial office buildings.*

to make a conversion. To that end, it has geared itself to a wider and more diversified range of services for its customers.

One of the more far-reaching changes in the firm's makeup began in 1978, when Sargent acquired a small locally based sound contracting business that had ventured into the new field of interconnect telephone systems. In 1973 Sargent purchased the first private telephone system ever sold by Gray Sound and Communications Company. In 1978 Fred Sargent, then president of the firm, decided to purchase a second telephone system from Gray. In his words, "I went to buy a phone system from them but ended up buying the company instead."

At that time Gray had about 30 employees and 200 customers. Today, with more than 260 employees and 3,000 customers, Gray is one of the most prominent private telephone companies serving the Mid-Atlantic region.

*Shown here making a fusion splice of fiber-optic cable, a technician from Sargent provides an example of the company's new emphasis on high-tech fields.*

In its 80th year Sargent Electric has maintained youthfulness by continuing to lead its industry in innovation. In the past decade, always counted among the very largest of firms of its type across the nation, Sargent has also stood out for its leadership in this respect.

More than a half-century after its founder patented the Sargent Wiring System to provide floor outlets for electrical and telephone receptacles (today known as underfloor duct in high-rise office buildings), Sargent Electric is engaged in installing unique fiber-optic cabling systems to create local area networks in offices.

In the 1920s workmen under Edward B. Sargent electrified the Liberty Tubes and Bridge during their original construction. Today, throughout the district, Sargent Electric crews can be found on a daily basis engaged in street lighting erection and maintenance, along with installation of state-of-the-art traffic signals, synchronized to speed the flow at rush hour.

While Sargent people recall with pride the firm's work installing the brilliant chandeliers for the conver-

sion of the old Penn Theater to Heinz Hall in 1970, today technicians from its Gray Communications division are busy installing the sound system in the city's newest theater, Benedum Center.

Outside the city Sargent has continued to hold a reputation for its performance on major projects of all kinds. In more than 15 states there can be found countless facilities installed for a large number of *Fortune* 500 companies, who have been repeat customers of the firm for years.

With an eye constantly on the future of not only his firm but the electrical industry itself, Edward J. Sargent, chairman of the board, has dedicated years to leadership in the field, serving as president of the Western Pennsylvania Chapter of the National Electrical Contractors Association. Devoting great time and attention to the industry's apprenticeship and scholarship programs as well, he has directed the concerted energies of the trade association's membership toward assuring that skilled craftsmen and trained technicians will be available in the future to deal with the ever-changing technology of electrical and electronic work.

As further evidence of the firm's interest in the future development of its industry's leadership, Ralph D. Vryenhoek, president of Sargent Electric Company, annually presents to a junior-year electrical engineering student at Carnegie-Mellon University the James M. Patterson Prize, recognizing outstanding citizenship and scholarship, while commemorating a former officer of the company who played a key role in its development for more than 20 years.

As the character of American business continues on its changing course, so too will Sargent Electric Company progress, to respond to the needs of a wide variety of customers in the electrical and electronic systems vital to their operations.

# ROCKWELL INTERNATIONAL
## A PROFITABLE MARRIAGE OF SCIENCE AND MARKETS

Rockwell International Corporation, with more than $12 billion in annual sales by the mid-1980s, is a firm whose products range from the ordinary, such as truck brakes and gas meters, to the farthest frontier of human adventure, the exploration of space itself.

If there is a unifying thread, it's in the application of high technology. In virtually all its businesses—aerospace, electronics, automotive, and general industries—the huge organization, with dual corporate headquarters at 600 Grant Street in the Golden Triangle and in El Segundo, California, is a leader in technology and market share. Rockwell, for example, does more business with the National Aeronautics and Space Administration than NASA's next four contractors combined. It has built more military aircraft than any other U.S. company, and supplies communications or navigation gear to nearly every jetliner in the Free World. Close to half the heavy-duty trucks and tractors in North America ride on Rockwell axles—and stop with Rockwell brakes. More than a million Rockwell gas and water meters are installed annually in the United States, and two out of three U.S. newspapers roll out of Goss presses—manufactured by Rockwell.

The corporation's roots go back to a predecessor firm founded before the turn of the century, but the modern enterprise dates from the 1967 merger of Pittsburgh's Rockwell-Standard and California's North American Aviation to form, first, North American Rockwell; in 1973 Rockwell International, its name more accurately reflecting worldwide interests, was organized.

Since 1975—the company's first full year under Robert Anderson as chief executive officer and now chairman of the board—sales have more than doubled, and earnings have increased almost fivefold. Reinforcing its reputation

Robert Anderson, chairman and chief executive officer.

Donald R. Beall, president and chief operating officer.

as the firm "where science gets down to business," Rockwell can count 19,000 engineers and scientists on its payroll, nearly one in every six of its 123,000 employees. Rockwell people built the Space Shuttle Orbiter and its main engines, support the operations of NASA's shuttle fleet, and expect to create key portions of the proposed permanently manned space station. They also are builders of the Air Force's Navstar satellites, as well as rocket engines, navigation and guidance systems, and electronic equipment for defense; and they've bid for a major role in developing the Strategic Defense Initiative.

Rockwell International and its predecessor companies have benefited from a number of strong-willed leaders. One was certainly Colonel Willard F. Rockwell, Sr., who in 1919 reorganized a bankrupt axle venture in Oshkosh, Wisconsin, in time to participate in the 1920s' boom in trucks as the freight carriers of the American road. Colonel Rockwell moved his

headquarters to the metalworking center of Pittsburgh, built Rockwell-Standard into the country's major independent producer of automotive components, and organized a strong separate firm in Rockwell Manufacturing Company—which made meters, power tools, and other products.

Meanwhile, another industrial phenomenon was evolving under the leadership of J.H. "Dutch" Kindelberger and J.L. "Lee" Atwood. They took little North American Aviation, Inc., from a Baltimore suburb in 1928 to the blue-sky spaces of Los Angeles in 1936—and during World War II produced 42,000 planes, including the workhorse B-25 Mitchell bomber and the famed P-51 Mustang fighter. After the war North American diversified into rocket propulsion and electronics. It manufactured the F-86 Sabre Jet of Korean War fame, the engines that boosted the first U.S. astronauts into space, and the XB-70 triple sonic research aircraft, among others.

*The B-1B, the Air Force's long-range strategic aircraft.*

In 1967 the commercial strengths of Rockwell-Standard were merged with the aerospace and government markets of the California firm. It was a strategic decision amply ratified by later events.

During the late 1960s and early 1970s the company began a program of diversification, acquiring or merging with a variety of firms including Miehle-Goss Dexter, a leading manufacturer of printing presses; Rockwell Manufacturing, a leading maker of water and gas meters and valves; and Collins Radio Company, a world leader in electronics.

In space activities Rockwell International played a historic role. The "giant step for mankind" of 1969 was taken from a Rockwell-built Apollo spacecraft that carried men to the moon and back. Presi-

dent Ronald Reagan's 1981 plan to revitalize the nation's defense featured as a major aspect the deployment of 100 B-1B long-range strategic bombers, manufactured by Rockwell International. The first production B-1B was rolled out of the firm's Palmdale, California, assembly plant in September 1984.

The organization continues restlessly to perfect its technology. In 1985 it significantly strengthened its role in industrial electronics through the acquisition of Milwaukee-based Allen-Bradley Company. Allen-Bradley is a leader in the manufacture and sale of industrial automation.equipment.

Today Rockwell chairman Robert Anderson and president Donald R. Beall head a multi-industry company performing in four major markets:

Aerospace, including military aircraft, manned and unmanned space systems, rocket engines, space-based surveillance systems, high-energy lasers, and other

"directed energy" programs.

Electronics, in part the legacy of Arthur A. Collins, founder of Collins Radio Company. Products include equipment for precision guidance and control, tactical weapons, avionics, navigation, and telecommunications—plus the systems, drives, components, and controls of Allen-Bradley.

Automotive, including components for heavy- and medium-duty trucks, buses, trailer, and heavy-duty off-highway vehicles, as well as for light trucks and passenger cars.

General Industries produces high-speed printing presses and related graphic arts equipment; flow control and measurement equipment for the utility, oil, gas, and nuclear industries; and industrial sewing machines.

Solidly based technically and financially, Rockwell International keeps making good on that catchy claim: " . . . where science gets down to business."

# EAT'N PARK RESTAURANTS, INC.
## LEADERSHIP THROUGH INNOVATION

On June 12, 1949, a group of Pittsburghers led by Larry Hatch, a successful executive of The Isaly Company of that era, opened the first Eat'n Park.

It began serving at 2 p.m. and had to close six hours later; the place was so busy it was creating a traffic jam! That situation soon cleared up, however, and in fact represented a popular vote of confidence in the new restaurant, which contained only 13 counter stools in a tiny two-tone yellow building along busy Saw Mill Run Boulevard in Pittsburgh's South Hills.

Just 37 years later in 1986, Eat'n Park Restaurants, Inc., has grown to be the leading full-service restaurant chain in the Pittsburgh area. Gradual changes over the past 37 years have dramatically transformed it. With 45 Eat'n Parks in western Pennsylvania and Ohio, and more than 3,000 employees, there are few reminders of the early years.

Eat'n Park has succeeded by growing and changing with the times. New trends in customer preferences have prompted shifts in dining style, exterior and interior building designs, menu selections, and training activities.

The secret to Eat'n Park's original success was also innovation. Apart from indoor service, it also employed 10 carhops. It was the city's first chain to feature food service to patrons in their autos. The concept caught on so quickly that in just four months the second unit opened in suburban Avalon. By 1960 Pittsburgh-area Eat'n Parks totaled 27. Then as now, they appealed to most everyone, but they were especially popular spots for teenagers who spent weekend evenings "cruising" from one to another.

Logically speaking, what the

*The original Eat'n Park Restaurant on Saw Mill Run Boulevard.*

*A modern Eat'n Park at South Hills Village.*

*The Bakery at Eat'n Park.*

customer actually did, of course, was to park first, then partake. However, "Park & Eat" was a common sign at food pickups and could not be copyrighted. Hence, the name "Eat'n Park." It is ironic that through the years "Park & Eat" signs have virtually disappeared, along with the carhop service itself, while Eat'n Park has become a Pittsburgh tradition—so much so that although the original concept no longer describes the chain's dining style, the catchy name has never changed.

Not so everything else. By the early 1970s McDonald's and other fast-food chains were on the move, and drive-in service was becoming passé. Management responded aggressively. It reoriented the company away from the parking lot and the back window to the front of the restaurant—the dining room. With a focus on breakfast and lunch, and a broader menu, Eat'n Park became what the trade calls a "coffee shop."

As a coffee shop chain, Eat'n Park once more began to thrive. In 1976 the Big Boy franchise for hamburgers was dropped in favor of Eat'n Park's own creation, the Superburger. Car service was gradually phased out, and by 1977

was gone. New locations opened, and outdated old ones closed. Twenty-four-hour operations were introduced in 1977, and the menu continued to expand in response to new opportunities in dinner and late-night service.

The transition from coffee shops to full-service, family-style restaurants came gradually—with the installation of soup and salad bars, additional selections on the dinner menu, further expansions, and remodelings of dining rooms and kitchens. The year 1983 brought breakfast buffets, then Sunday brunches and weekend midnight buffets.

The most recent innovation is the addition of in-house bakeries. "The Bakery at Eat'n Park" provides fresh baked goods for the dining room customers as well as for take-home service. Located near the front entrance, the bakery delights the customer with irresistible scents and displays. The whole concept of fresh homemade goodness is a dynamic symbol of the present-day Eat'n Park.

Parallel dramatic changes occurred in employee development. The two restaurants of 1949 employed only 40 persons. By 1986

more than 3,000 persons worked for Eat'n Park in 45 restaurants, making the chain one of the largest employers in Pittsburgh and one of the top 50 in western Pennsylvania.

The firm's employees are actively involved in the community, rallying to raise funds for Children's Hospital, the United Way and other charity drives, and events such as the Pittsburgh Marathon. This huge volunteer effort contributes much to the success of these drives, which benefit the entire Pittsburgh area. The restaurants are also involved in local events, making each Eat'n Park unique as it strives to meet the needs of its own surrounding community.

Since 1949, despite all the monumental changes in design, decor, food, and service, Eat'n Park has never lost sight of the importance of being affordable to everyone. Future growth and innovation will continue to reflect that philosophy, keeping Eat'n Park Restaurants, Inc., the leading full-service restaurant chain in the region.

*Friendly service at Eat'n Park makes customers feel at home.*

# COMMUNITY COLLEGE OF ALLEGHENY COUNTY
## BUILDING A NEW TRADITION OF HIGHER EDUCATION

Community College of Allegheny County is an institution that has grown in its first 20 years to become a powerful force in the changing economy of the Pittsburgh area.

More than 85,000 residents of the county attend at least one class at CCAC in a given year. Additionally, the college is in the forefront of the customized job training market, providing advanced technology and human service education to local business and industry. The school's "customized training program" has been utilized by General Motors, H.J. Heinz Company, the Forbes Health System, and Duquesne Light, among others, to prepare thousands of employees for new or upgraded jobs.

A 1985 economic study of the CCAC phenomenon found that for every dollar invested in the college by Allegheny County's taxpayers, the local economy received $3.50 in direct returns and $7.28 in indirect spending within the county. A study by the American Council on Education has indicated that the college's expenditures support the creation of 4,068 local jobs. However, more than economic rewards stem from the school's embodiment of "affordable, accessible, quality education."

Community College of Allegheny County is a two-year institution that brings the enrichment of general education to the lives of more than 27,000 full- and part-time credit students and 58,280 noncredit students. These numbers translate into a student body equivalent of more than 19,000 full-time students. CCAC is the largest community college in the state and one of the largest in the United States, as well as one of Pennsylvania's three largest colleges with enrollment just behind that of Penn State and the University of Pittsburgh. The college has four campuses and more than 200 neighborhood learning sites, which

helps to make higher education readily accessible to residents of Allegheny County.

Although the college is a commuter school, it has an active student life. Extracurricular activities include lecture series, films, and theater productions; varsity and intramural sports and personal fitness programs; campus newspapers and literary magazines;

*CCAC professors are experienced, knowledgeable, and committed to teaching. Faculty and staff are responsive to students' needs, and have years of practical experience gained through careers in business and industry. Here a professor gives some advice to a student.*

and student government groups and clubs.

CCAC president John W. Kraft notes two things in common about most of his students, however varied in age and background. "They are serious about educating themselves, and without CCAC it would be much more difficult or even impossible for them to attend college," he says. Low tuition, flexible class schedules, and an open admissions policy make the benefits of higher education available

to anyone willing to work for them.

There is no such thing as a typical CCAC student. Those in career-oriented programs obviously are pursuing occupational goals. Thousands are recent high school graduates from cities, suburbs, or rural areas, but 64 percent of credit course registrants are age 22 or older, and about 60 percent are women.

In 1966, its first full year of operation, CCAC offered fewer than 20 programs and awarded two as-

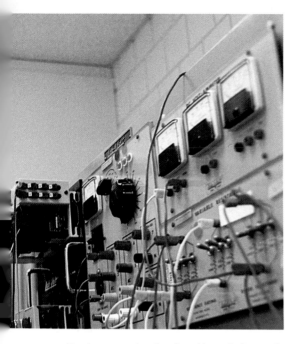

Students receive first-hand knowledge and experience on a variety of state-of-the-art equipment.

Historic West Hall on the site of the Allegheny campus.

sociate degrees. Today more than 150 credit programs help to prepare students for transfer to a four-year college or for immediate employment. Three types of degrees are offered—associate in arts, associate in science, and associate in applied science—as well as certificate and diploma programs for students seeking career or vocational training in a year or less.

The chef's apprenticeship program, for example, was begun in 1974 in cooperation with the Chefs and Cooks Association of Pittsburgh. Frank Ruta of McKeesport, a member of the second-year class, considers the program "the best in the country." Since 1980 he has been First Family Chef at the White House—one of the youngest ever hired, at age 22.

CCAC and 13 similar institutions in Pennsylvania came into being after passage of the Community College Act of 1963. Its mandate was and is to provide low-cost, open-door education—which means that College Board scores and other entrance tests are not

required. Student payments typically cover one-third of the total expenses of CCAC, whose annual budget by 1984-1985 topped $47.6 million.

The faculty includes 346 full-time professors and instructors and scores of part-time educators who are expert in their fields. Classes typically are small, averaging 20 students. Facilities include libraries, laboratories, studios, and one of the most accessible computer systems for education in the region. Governance is by a 15-member public board of trustees.

CCAC's first campus was purchased from the former Western Theological Seminary along historic Ridge Avenue on "Monument Hill" in Pittsburgh's North Side. Now the Allegheny Campus, it has been beautified and expanded. Boyce Campus, in Monroeville, serves the eastern portion of the county. South Campus began in temporary lodgings in 1967, and four years later moved to a 200-acre site along Route 885 in West Mifflin. Center-North, originated in a trailer on the grounds of a hospital in 1972, now occupies several facilities in the North Hills.

The growth of Community Col-

lege of Allegheny County continues, and with the region's economic transition so dependent on new technology, president Kraft is sure of one thing: "The need for higher education can only increase."

CCAC provides "hands-on" training. Here students learn procedures and instruments in an operating room setting.

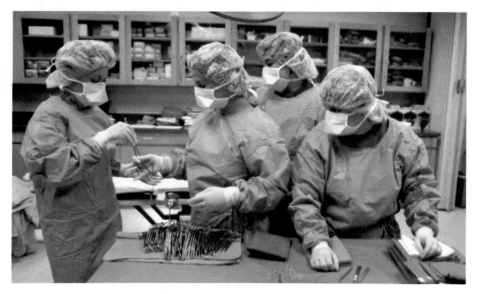

# COMPUNETICS, INC.
## MANAGING A HIGH-TECH BUSINESS FOR GROWTH

"Advanced."

That adjective applies not only to the products and markets of Compunetics, Inc., but also to management's approach. The firm has some strong ideas on how to run a small high-tech business.

Compunetics in 1986 was approaching an annual sales rate of $10 million. It had 150 employees and an expanding plant at 2000 Eldo Road, Monroeville. Long a producer of hardware and software used in military communications and simulation systems, the company more recently has forged into proprietary products.

The first of these was an image-processing system for the noncontact measurement of hot steel. Soon after came a cellular switching system to handle calls from automobile phone systems. Both are advanced—even novel—technological solutions to specific challenges.

Compunetics' management approach begins with president

Giorgio Coraluppi's belief that the key to success in business lies in fostering a satisfying environment for work. Coraluppi founded Compunetics in 1968, just a few years after he had moved from Italy with a doctorate in electrical engineering.

The little company pursued government business from the beginning. One early prize was a contract to design a tailor-made computer system for antisubmarine warfare, and Compunetics managed to win it ahead of some of the industry giants. From that experience Coraluppi developed certain convictions on how to open the gates to creative and profitable technological innovation by a small group.

From the start he believed that more compact organizations have unique competitive strengths to bring against the corporate titans. "A specialized niche, or knowledge area, is always going to be tackled by a team, whether within a small company or a large one,"

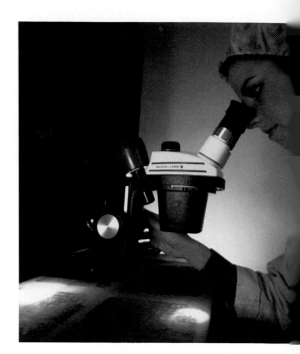

he points out. "In a genuine high-tech area, a single individual may well be the only person who can find a solution to a given problem."

Coraluppi reasoned that in a one-to-one or team-versus-team

approach, the advantage will swing to the group that has the edge in creativity, dedication, and independence.

Thus, Compunetics management gives extraordinary attention to providing an atmosphere in which people of talent have the room to take initiative and assume individual responsibility. To encourage common objectives among investors, employees, and managers, each and all share in the rewards of success through equity participation. From the start, management has promoted participatory capitalism. An employee stock-ownership plan—ESOP—now accounts for more than 40 percent of the company's shares. As one executive puts it: "Every person first reports to himself or herself."

Another factor that contributes to the creative ferment is a liberal use of consultants. Compunetics has put together a network of outstanding talents drawn from the academic riches of the Pittsburgh area and beyond.

The rate of product development shows that these approaches pay off. The image-processing system, for example, was derived from three years of development by a team of in-house scientists and selected consultants, and it was put into practical operation at a U.S. Steel plant. It makes use of cameras linked by computers to measure hot-steel slabs for cutting. The system's extreme accuracy improves the mill's operating flexibility and sharply cuts waste. In certain plants of the hard-pressed steel industry, Coraluppi believes that installations of this kind could make the difference between operation and shutdown.

The same team approach resulted in the firm's new cellular technology for mobile phones, which took two years and one million dollars in research and development; the result is a patented switching device that provides a

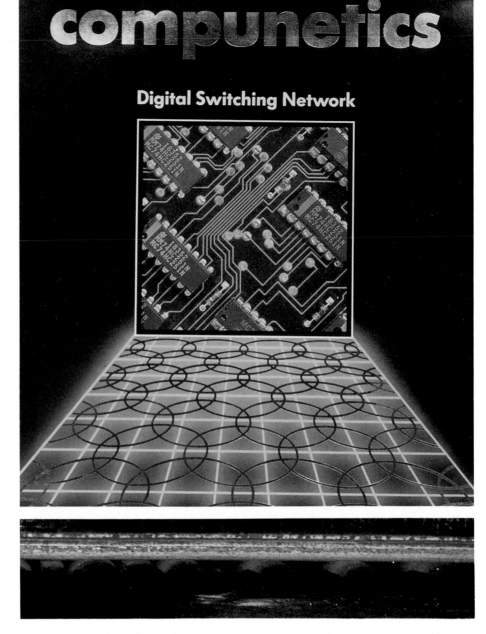

# compunetics

## Digital Switching Network

leap in capacity. It is equipped with a specially designed microchip that processes information faster than conventional data chips. Consequently, a greater volume of traffic can be serviced and at a faster, more efficient rate than could previously be handled. Importantly, too, the new system can be added to existing equipment.

Without such an advance telephone mobility would inevitably bump against limits to growth. The defense applications appear to be obvious, and Compunetics officials believe they have come up with a cost-effective answer to a potential communications snarl.

The firm is also growing physically. Facilities expanded to more than 50,000 square feet in early 1986 with the addition of 22,500 square feet of manufacturing space

for production of high-quality printed circuit boards. State-of-the-art equipment is now turning out boards able to meet the most stringent "MIL spec" standards.

Compunetics is helping other area high-tech firms as well with engineering and manufacturing services. Although the company remains active in tailor-made communications for the defense market, that segment now accounts for only 10 percent of total sales.

"In a high-tech market one is always in the business of surpassing oneself," says Giorgio Coraluppi. "Each new development leads to surprising applications." He implies that a safe prediction for the future is that more products and more growth lie ahead for Compunetics, Inc.

# THE CHESTER ENGINEERS
## PROVIDING SAFER WATER AND WASTE DISPOSAL

By 1910 the U.S. population had reached 92 million, and water treatment and sewage disposal plants had become public health necessities—certainly in any sizable community.

It was into this market of spreading opportunity that two young Pittsburgh engineers, John N. Chester and Thomas Fleming, Jr., launched a consulting firm. One of their first jobs was to design the main pumping and filtration plant of South Pittsburgh Water Company, a predecessor of the system that still serves the Pittsburgh area. Other projects of the early years supplied communities in 17 states, many of which continue as clients.

Fleming resigned in 1920, but Chester carried on through various partnerships until his retirement in 1942. By then the venture had become The Chester Engineers— and America was deeply involved in World War II. With most municipal improvements postponed "for the duration," the corporation shifted to water and waste treatment units for military bases and, significantly, designing synthetic rubber and ammunition plants— the launch of the firm's services to private industry.

Today The Chester Engineers is an organization of 200 professional and support people in six regional offices around the United States and a headquarters in Coraopolis,

*The main filter gallery of The K.R. Harrington Water Treatment plant designed by The Chester Engineers for Nashville, Tennessee. Capable of 60 million gallons per day of high-rate filtration, it is expandable by 50 percent as service area demand grows.*

near the Greater Pittsburgh International Airport. It is a wholly owned subsidiary of Mestek, Inc., itself a Pittsburgh holding company with high-technology interests in engineering and computer services. Chester's president, Alfred E. Baily, who joined the operation in 1949, and vice-president Anthony F. Lisanti, on board since 1964, are only two of numerous colleagues who have been with the company more than twenty years. Recorded clients now total more than 3,000 in 39 states.

Since the 1960s the corporation has provided systems of entire waste recycling for several industries—"Zero Discharge Plants." In

*Primary solids-removal facilities for the continuous caster water system at LTV Steel Corporation, Indiana Harbor, Indiana.*

the 1970s a Chester-designed site for industrial residual waste disposal was the first to receive a Pennsylvania permit. The firm performed vast area-wide planning studies for its home state's Schuylkill River Basin and Lower Delaware Valley, as well as Michigan's Saginaw Bay. Long an expert in the operating facilities of a water or sewage plant, Chester in 1977 expanded into general architectural design as well. Hazardous waste studies and designs for remedial action have subsequently become a major business.

Baily says, "We have seen more rapid changes in the 1980s than ever before." He cites the pace of growth in computer capabilities, public concerns over waste disposal and damage to groundwater, and the fierce drive by U.S. manufacturers to step up their worldwide competitiveness.

Today, utilizing Computer-Aided Drafting and Design (CADD) services, The Chester Engineers provides the design, construction review, and operation of water and wastewater treatment facilities to its clients.

# AMERICAN THERMOPLASTIC COMPANY
## LOOSE-LEAF PRODUCTS FOR THE NATION

A tiny enterprise that originated in Pittsburgh three decades ago has grown into one of the country's largest suppliers of custom-imprinted binders and loose-leaf products.

American Thermoplastic Company serves a huge market. The student who buys a "Boston College," "Pitt," or "Ohio State" notebook seldom realizes that it might come from a technologically

*Aaron Silberman founded American Thermoplastic Company in Pittsburgh in 1954.*

advanced Pittsburgh plant. However, not only students fill loose-leaf pages. Industry is a giant user, as well as research laboratories, hospitals, churches, and banks; in addition, salesmen call on customers with ringed catalogs of price lists and brochures. ATC president Steven Silberman says his firm's largest order was for 100,000 binders (for a fried chicken chain's back-to-school giveaway), but it has also supplied deluxe originals—to convey, for example, a major corporation's contract proposal to a foreign government.

"Thermoplastic" refers to heat-sealing. ATC, in fact, welds sheets

of brightly hued vinyl by means of electronic waves pulsing through metal dies. Heat-sealing, silk-screen printing, and other technologies are constantly being upgraded in the firm's strikingly remodeled plant at 622 Second Avenue.

Vinyl as a material for binders was relatively new when Aaron Silberman, ATC's chairman, launched the firm on May 25, 1954. The versatile Silberman—musician, accountant, salesman—had the idea that vinyl products imprinted with a corporate logo would enhance employee usage and status. Some of Pittsburgh's major organization's agreed and placed orders.

"Al" Silberman and his wife, Freda, and one other employee started production in a fifth-floor loft above a Downtown restaurant. Originally they only foil-stamped products, which had been purchased blank; later investments in heat-sealing and printing machinery put the young company into full-fledged manufacturing. By 1964 the move to larger quarters became urgent, and since then ATC has gradually taken over all seven floors of the Second Avenue property. This has been trans-

formed from a former liquor and linoleum warehouse into a beehive of design, production, office, and shipping facilities that gained 25 percent additional space in a neighboring stucture in the mid-1980s. The Silberman strategy to "do one thing really well" has created what is probably the country's top line of custom-imprinted loose-leaf and related products.

A specialty at ATC, says Steve Silberman—who succeeded his father as president in 1986—is its reaction time to deadline pressures for sales conferences, conventions, and sudden client needs. "QuickShip 10" is a unique service by which credit-worthy accounts are guaranteed shipment of binders within 10 working days of ATC's receipt of the artwork.

That means delivery to any of 16,000 current customers, as distant as California, a nationwide market that ATC finds well served by its home region's network of communications and transportation. "Pittsburgh," states Steve Silberman, "is good for us."

*American Thermoplastic manufactures custom loose-leaf products for businesses and schools all across the country.*

# BUCHANAN INGERSOLL PROFESSIONAL CORPORATION
## PITTSBURGH'S FASTEST-GROWING MAJOR LAW FIRM

Founded more than 130 years ago and rich in tradition, Buchanan Ingersoll nevertheless shows the vital signs of a young law firm. Its most dramatic period of growth has been during the 1980s, with its roster approximately tripling from 60 to 150 lawyers. It has become Pittsburgh's second-largest law office, serving more than 8,000 clients and handling a broad spectrum of transactions—from the financing of high-technology and cable TV companies to hospi-

*John G. Buchanan (left) and Frank B. Ingersoll, late partners of the Pittsburgh law firm which bears their names.*

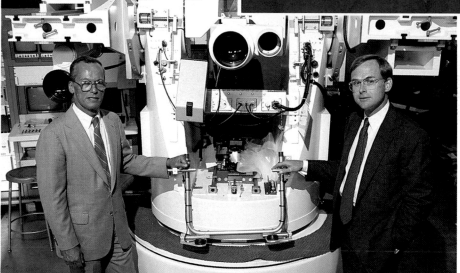

*Buchanan Ingersoll's managing director, William R. Newlin (right), with James Colker, president of Contraves Goerz Corporation and president of the Pittsburgh High Technology Council. Buchanan Ingersoll has played an instrumental role in the evolution and growth of Pittsburgh's high-technology community. Colker and Newlin are two of the founding directors of the Pittsburgh High Technology Council.*

tal reorganizations, international joint ventures, and leveraged buyouts.

Tracing its origins to Hampton and Son, founded in 1850, Buchanan Ingersoll is reputed to be western Pennsylvania's oldest law firm in continuous practice. When John G. Buchanan joined the office in 1912, it had only five other lawyers. Buchanan often walked to his Downtown office, four miles

from his home in Shadyside, until he was well into his seventies. His illustrious career included 17 consecutive victories in the Pennsylvania Supreme Court. He argued more cases in the U.S. Supreme Court than any member then active in the Allegheny County Bar Association. Buchanan died in June 1986 at age 97.

Frank B. Ingersoll, the other former partner after whom the firm is now named, practiced with the firm from his admission to the Pennsylvania Bar in 1917 until his death in 1977. Ingersoll was a noted corporate law practitioner who sat on the boards of directors of numerous companies including, among others, The Union National Bank of Pittsburgh, Armstrong World Industries, Inc., and the Na-

tional Mine Service Company. In 1973 his alma mater, The Cornell Law School, honored Ingersoll by establishing the Frank B. Ingersoll Professorship.

In the tradition advanced by Buchanan and Ingersoll, the firm has served many leaders of the corporate community. Over the years it has represented *Fortune* 500 and other New York Stock Exchange companies in their corporate finance and other complex business transactions. Such corporate work has intertwined with the law firm's service to notable industrial families. The Hunt family representation continues from the formation of the Pittsburgh Reduction Company (later the Aluminum Company of America) to the family's current involvement in business and philanthropy. It has long been counsel as well to The Union National Bank of Pittsburgh and, more currently, to the McCune Foundation.

While traditional industries continue to be highly valued clients, the newer sectors of Pittsburgh's economy have been the law firm's own "growth markets." High technology, health care, banking and financial services, real estate, and

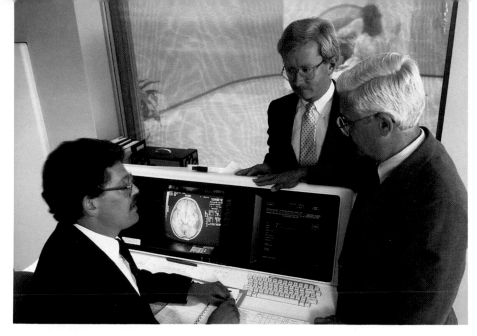

investment banking all increasingly demand the most acute legal attention.

The modern Buchanan Ingersoll represents more than 50 high-tech companies in the Pittsburgh area; it helped to found, and continues to represent, the Pittsburgh High Technology Council; and it was the city's first major law firm to open an office amid the hotbed of new company formations in Oakland.

Buchanan Ingersoll's health law practice is among western Pennsylvania's largest. As the industry has changed, hospitals, nursing homes, home health agencies, and health maintenance organizations have consulted the firm in regulatory disputes, mergers, financings,

Buchanan Ingersoll's contribution to the telecommunications industry has grown in step with the rise of cable television and related industries in the Pittsburgh community. Here, Buchanan Ingersoll attorneys John R. Previs and Pamela E. Rollings discuss issues concerning satellite communications.

and reorganizations.

Banking law is another growth area. Buchanan Ingersoll represents national, state, and foreign banks in all aspects of their business, including lending, acquisitions, and the formation of holding companies.

The organization's real estate practice is one of the largest in Pittsburgh, serving lenders, de-

velopers, and investors in a host of complex transactions. In recent years the firm has been actively involved in numerous important projects, including Fifth Avenue Place, Station Square, the Civic Arena, Two Mellon Bank Center, and CNG Tower.

A highly valued strength of the firm's experience is in representing active "dealmakers," such as Pittsburgh underwriters Parker/ Hunter Inc. and Russell, Rea & Zappala, Inc., as well as various New York underwriters. Tax and securities lawyers have helped to prepare numerous syndications in oil and gas, real estate, cable television, and energy projects. Communications and public finance have been other strong areas for the firm.

In order to help Pittsburgh companies pursue markets abroad, Buchanan Ingersoll was the first major law firm to form an international section with multilingual capability to help with exporting, licensing, and other foreign matters.

It is Buchanan Ingersoll's aggressive involvement in these developing sectors of the economy that has made it the fastest-growing major law firm in Pittsburgh in recent years. "Getting the deal done," effectively and timely, is the firm's pride—and it is clearly what the business world demands of lawyers today.

The same approaches infuse Buchanan Ingersoll's traditional areas of practice—litigation, labor, tax, and estate matters—all of which also have been expanding. An office was opened in Wash-

Buchanan Ingersoll health care attorneys Thomas E. Boyle (seated) and James A. Wilkinson (center) in the control room of the Pittsburgh NMR Institute with Geoffrey J. Suszkowski, president of the institute and president of Magee-Womens Health Corporation. Buchanan Ingersoll, which helped create the NMR Institute, regularly advises its health care clients on matters such as complicated financings, joint venture proposals, and innovative reorganizations.

ington, D.C., in 1977 to monitor regulatory, administrative, and international tax issues. A new office in Philadelphia is expanding the firm's statewide activity.

The commitment to Pittsburgh transcends day-to-day legal affairs. Buchanan Ingersoll people give substantial time and support to numerous philanthropic and nonprofit organizations.

The firm believes that its youth, its strong business orientation, and its community involvement make it something of a creative civic resource. Its 150 lawyers are in a position to support Pittsburgh's corporate and institutional move forward—in effect to advance the dramatic transition now occurring from an economy controlled by the cycles of heavy industry to one more solidly based on the effective combination of the rapidly growing high-technology, health, and financial services industries. Like the rest of Pittsburgh, Buchanan Ingersoll Professional Corporation has found strength in diversity and remains firmly committed and optimistic about the city's future.

# COMMUNITY SAVINGS ASSOCIATION
## ITS ROOTS ARE IN HEALTHY NEIGHBORHOOD VALUES

In the 1880s Pittsburgh's North Side was a proudly independent community, the City of Allegheny. It was a mixture of grand homes and undeveloped lots, filled with the potential to establish a neighborhood, a true sense of community. What was needed to realize the prospect was a larger provision of adequate family housing, and that in turn meant a requirement for home construction money.

The forerunner of today's Community Savings Association was born in that practical, neighborhood-enhancing vision. East Park Building and Loan Association opened in 1890 on West Diamond Street, close to the present Allegheny Center. It provided the thrifty families and investors of its day a safe place to deposit their savings, while giving others in the area a source of mortgage loans to fulfill the dream of home ownership.

Thus was set the solid foundation of what would become, nearly a century later, Community Savings

Association, one of Pittsburgh's fastest growing thrift institutions, with 12 offices, 100 employees, and $200 million in assets by the second half of the 1980s. Those totals would have seemed incredible in the formative era of the typical neighborhood building and loan, a financial institution that has evolved in roughly the same proportion as the cornerstore to a modern shopping mall.

It took a full generation and a leap of several neighborhoods for the next link in the Community Savings chain to be forged. That took place following World War I, in Lawrenceville—a settled area of homes, stores, and factories along the south bank of the Allegheny. Lawrenceville people, then as now, enjoyed a reputation for hard work and a profound sense of family and community. In such fertile soil Foster Building and Loan Association planted its office on thriving Butler Street in January 1922. Not everything changes. Community Savings' modern Lawrenceville and North

Side branches flourish just a few doors from the original Foster and East Park locations.

By the 1950s, however, Pittsburgh was stretching its urban limitations. Prosperity and mobility summoned families to the open spaces of suburbia—and stores, factories, and financial institutions followed.

East Park opened its first suburban office in the North Hills' Northway Mall in 1957; that same year Foster Federal started a New Kensington office to serve savers and borrowers in Pittsburgh's northeastern suburbs and northern Westmoreland County. It was obvious that East Park and Foster held similar views on both the region and the thrift industry, and on July 1, 1969, they merged to form Community Savings Association, which soon entered its most spec-

*Community Savings Association's corporate headquarters and Monroeville office at 2681 Moss Side Boulevard.*

tacular era of growth.

The energetic developments sparked by Greater Pittsburgh International Airport and the Parkway West made the northwestern suburbs a prime market. Community Savings arrived there April 1, 1972, with the opening of its Moon Township office on Narrows Run Road. The bicentennial summer of 1976 brought the Forest Hills office; the next summer two more branches completed the service compass around Pittsburgh. The Baldwin Borough office in the Baldwin Shopping Center established the association for the first time in the spirited South Hills market, while construction of the strikingly modern Community Plaza East building in Monroeville placed Community Savings in the midst of the fastest growing eastern suburb. Another ribbon was cut in the summer of 1978, when the first Washington County office opened its doors in Millcraft Center, near the heart of the historic courthouse and college town.

Kenneth J. Tyson, who has been president of Community Savings since 1971, said that with the ring of facilities established around Pittsburgh, the next logical step was to expand within the circle. As had its sister institutions, South View Savings had started in a small way in the settled, healthy community of Carrick, on Brownsville Road, and later had begun its own branch network in Bethel Park and Finleyville. Since the merger of South View, the Carrick and Bethel Park offices have undergone complete remodelings, providing for expansion and additional services in an airy and pleasant atmosphere.

More progress came in 1986. Community Savings moved its busy Forest Hills office to the Great Valley Shopping Center along Route 30 in North Versailles. The transfer permitted the association to expand services and provide convenient parking for customers along the traffic corridor that is known as Lincoln Highway in that heavily traveled stretch.

"Our pattern of growth—you can trace it for almost a century now—has fairly well mirrored the growth and spread of Pittsburgh and its suburbs," says Ken Tyson. "We think our people bring not only a sense of history but a sense of service, the fulfillment of an obligation to help people grow and prosper and move on to better homes and communities for their families.

"There's no question about it, the opportunities to serve are still here. We're very optimistic about the Pittsburgh area's economy. The recession that occurred in a number of manufacturing industries hurt, no doubt, but we never really saw it in loan delinquencies. People are able to make their payments, and they are borrowing on a number of new services our industry is able to offer—consumer loans, car loans, student and commercial loans. Our own association's policy is not to invest outside this area. We have 40,000 savings accounts and 8,000 to 10,000 loan customers, a very healthy base. From our perspective, Pittsburgh's strength in research and universities is going to create new industries, and we'll be better off with the diversification."

---

*Community Savings Association is one of Pittsburgh's fastest growing thrift institutions. The North Side office, at 401 East Ohio Street, adds a modern twist to the older architecture and surroundings.*

# ST. MARGARET MEMORIAL HOSPITAL
## FINDING BETTER WAYS TO SERVE PEOPLE

Pittsburgh grew fast in the last third of the nineteenth century. The region's iron and steel furnaces and foundries, as well as its manufacturing, trade, and shipping found insatiable markets in a continent whose vast spaces beckoned the ambitious, the immigrant, and the adventurous. An arsenal of the recent Civil War, the Pittsburgh of 1870 was already a vital community of 86,000 residents. In the next 30 years it nearly quadrupled. The census of 1900 found 321,616 persons inhabiting the 11th-largest U.S. city—a "boom town" before the term was originated.

Among the pragmatic and far-seeing men of Pittsburgh, but of an age just predating the greatest empire-builders, was John Hopson Shoenberger. His forebears had been in steel long before Andrew Carnegie, and had certainly made

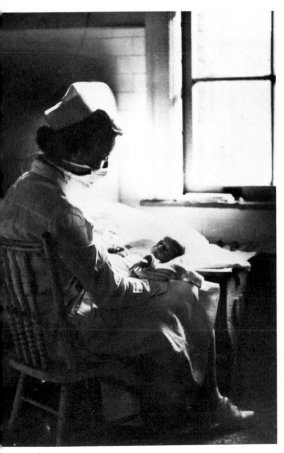

*A nurse spends a quiet moment with her precious charge, circa 1910.*

*Imposing iron gates and twin copper-sheathed domes distinguished the original hospital building constructed in Lawrenceville in 1898.*

a fine fortune for their time. It was Shoenberger's father, Peter, who operated central Pennsylvania's historic Juniata Iron Works and established a branch of it on the banks of the Allegheny at "Pittsburg" between 14th and 16th streets. One of the country's first steam-run rolling mills operated there, and the firm remained in the control of the Shoenbergers from 1824 to 1900.

Enlightened and charitable, John Shoenberger envisioned what today is called "quality of life," as well as industrial prosperity. In the years before his death in 1889, he often talked about plans to endow a hospital for the chronically ill and the poor. In fact, he explained himself in such detail that there would be little doubt how to forward his aims. All this occurred well before Mary Schenley bequeathed land for a great city park, or Carnegie had made his first gift of a public library, or Andrew Mellon had created his institute for industrial research.

In Shoenberger's era, hospitals were few in number and primitively equipped—popularly thought to be places to die. To think about a hospital was to think about morbid matters; hospitals were not a nice subject for discussion in the best parlors.

Shoenberger evidently had an idea that improvements in medical science would surely follow industrial progress, that someday there would be a great demand for health services. His will, dated March 10, 1887, donated in trust a 3.273-acre plot plus $550,000 for the construction and maintenance of a hospital in memory of his wife, Margaret. The site was at 46th and Davison streets in Pittsburgh's Lawrenceville section.

A copper box was lodged in the cornerstone at ceremonies on October 17, 1896, when construction of St. Margaret Memorial Hospital was launched before an assemblage of dignitaries and invited guests. Inside the box, carefully wrapped in foil, were placed a Bible, the hospital's charter, photographs of John and Margaret Shoenberger, and copies of the city's numerous daily newspapers. Episcopal Bishop Cortland Whitehead was the eloquent speaker.

Construction proceeded quickly. The handsome red-brick building was finished in 1898—and then not opened for 12 years. The

*John H. Shoenberger applied the same vision and foresight used to build an empire of iron and steel to endow a hospital in memory of his wife.*

Shoenberger will, despite the philanthropist's oft-expressed wishes, was protractedly contested.

It was not until October 1, 1910, that the first patients were admitted to the care of St. Margaret's 9 physicians and 12 nurses. The facility contained 16 private rooms for medical and surgical patients, and "free wards" for the care of 75 to 100 charity patients. Broad neighborhood support gave the fledgling hospital a healthy start.

Soon after opening, the new institution began a school of nursing, which graduated its first class in 1913. Alumni of this diploma school have put their skills into practice at hospitals throughout the Pittsburgh area, and more than 1,100 registered nurses are counted today among the graduates.

*In 1912 Drs. Keeler and McGinley, interns, posed with the first ambulance outside the hospital's main entrance.*

St. Margaret in the 1920s introduced numerous advances in treatment, research, and medical education. Dr. Paul Titus, an internationally known obstetrician and gynecologist, was the institution's commanding personality of the era. He was chief of the departments of obstetrics and gynecology for more than 20 years and performed research in the toxemia of pregnancy, intravenous dextrose therapy, and human sterility. Medical students the world over consulted his textbooks on obstetrical difficulties, published in the 1940s. Ob-Gyn departments in most of Pittsburgh's hospitals were headed by Titus-trained specialists.

With funding from the John C. Oliver Memorial Foundation, St. Margaret became one of the nation's first independent hospitals to operate an endowed research laboratory.

The institution's growth and reputation advanced its standing with the people of Lawrenceville and the city, drawing support from many generous Pittsburgh philanthropists. The hospital at one time had more board-certified physicians on its staff than any other in Pittsburgh. The original building was many times expanded, although in patchwork fashion.

With World War II and Pittsburgh's much-needed renaissance that followed, a period of transformation came to St. Margaret. Externally, the main building looked much as it had during its first half-century. Then, in 1952, with broad community support, a major addition opened. Capacity increased by more than 70 beds. There were spacious new facilities for surgery, pathology, maternity, and the X-ray department.

In addition to money, the community gave countless volunteers.

With the help of the Women's Auxiliary Board, a voluntary services department began operating in 1956. The thriving program now involves more than 600 adult and student volunteers, who work with patients, visitors, and staff in nearly every hospital area. A previous group had formed the Dispensary Board in 1923; its dedication was to providing funds for vital projects. The board's annual Cinderella Ball to benefit St. Margaret Hospital has highlighted Pittsburgh's holiday social season with its elegant presentation of debutantes, for well over 60 years.

In the 1950s the hospital began building its reputation as a pacesetter in arthritis treatment. It was in that decade that Dr. Harry M. Margolis came to St. Margaret from the Mayo Clinic; and as he watched the Lawrenceville institution grow, he envisioned a regional center for the full-service treatment of chronic illnesses. His ideas for a comprehensive treatment facility took form in the rehabilitation unit that St. Margaret opened as the 1960s began. Focusing a systematic team approach on the multiple problems of the person with arthritis, the unit has grown to become a referral center for the tri-state area, and one of America's model treatment facilities, providing advanced programs of rehabilitation, joint replacement, and education.

The 1960s were marked by an even quicker pace of scientific advances—and they found St. Margaret ready. From the institution's earliest days it had performed actively in medical education, and in 1965 it became a teaching hospital, offering residencies in surgery and pathology and internships on a rotating basis. In 1968 the American Medical Association took a forward step that dramatically affected education at St. Margaret. Responding to the desire of medical students to engage in a more personalized form of care, the

A gentle hug from nurse Joanne Mascara is good medicine for this young patient.

with 267 beds, state-of-the-art technology throughout, and an accessible location offering grand views from the patients' windows of the river and surrounding green hills.

Its first years in the new building enabled St. Margaret to become a health resource for thousands of families, while enhancing its reputation for the teaching and delivery of arthritis care and family practice medicine, a renown that extends far beyond the Pittsburgh area.

No sooner was St. Margaret in its new home, however, than the 1980s brought another set of imperatives, with government regulation, consumer resistance to rising health care costs, and increasingly

*Front entrance view of the new St. Margaret facility, opened in Aspinwall in 1980, and its Outpatient Pavilion (right), added in 1985.*

AMA created a new specialty: family practice.

This was a natural for St. Margaret. The addition of a residency in family practice fulfilled its own traditional standard of caring for the person, not just the illness.

In 1971 the hospital opened its Family Health Center. This facility not only served as a physician's office-training setting for family practice residents, it alleviated a serious shortage of family doctors in Lawrenceville. Today more than 100 family practice specialists in the Pittsburgh area trace their professional roots to the residency at St. Margaret. The program is Pennsylvania's oldest and largest of its kind, attracting some of the nation's most gifted medical school graduates.

The Lawrenceville Family Health Center, at 5150 Penn Avenue, still operating on the original hospital grounds, formed the pattern for an additional center to serve the Bloomfield and Garfield neighborhoods.

The hospital itself, however, long ago outgrew its original location. By the mid-1970s cramped space and the expressed wish of a majority of patients for a more central and accessible location prompted the planning of an entirely new facility.

The site selected was an "island" of the city of Pittsburgh: its former water-filtration plant on the north shore of the Allegheny River, surrounded by the borough of Aspinwall. Many younger city dwellers had moved to the North Hills; yet the new site remained convenient to the old neighborhood via the Highland Park Bridge, and was therefore the optimum choice.

In March 1980 the new St. Margaret Memorial Hospital opened,

sophisticated medical technology. The hospital's board of directors, led by chairman W. Walter Braham, Jr., and its administration, under president Stanley J. Kevish, worked in concert with the staff of more than 350 physicians to bring about a progressive evolution. Innovations in treatment have moved in a direction from traditional overnight hospital care to convenient,

*Modern medicine retains a personal touch at St. Margaret's, as shown here by Paul W. Dishart, M.D., with his patient.*

economical outpatient treatment.

The results have been impressive. A highlight of 1985 was the opening of a two-story outpatient pavilion to accommodate rapid growth in the numbers of surgical operations and medical procedures now being performed on a same-day basis. Years of experience in arthritis treatment culminated in the opening of The Doris Palmer Arthritis Center, a regional outpatient diagnosis and treatment facility, which includes a division dedicated to research and education—for arthritis patients, their families, and area health professionals.

The spirit of community outreach has also spurred new programs in industrial health, sports medicine, the training of community ambulance crews, home health care, and an array of health education services.

The modern hospital environment, in short, bears little resemblance to John Shoenberger's "country estate" in Lawrenceville—except in one vital particular,

the founding philosophy of "personal care and concern for each patient."

A new corporate structure came into being in 1986 to enable the institution to remain economically strong even as it provides quality programs. The reorganization set up a new parent firm, St. Margaret Health System, Inc., with two subsidiary corporations: St. Margaret Memorial Hospital and St. Margaret Memorial Hospital Foundation.

The hospital, nonsectarian and neither owned nor operated by the church, although valuing that long association, remains the anchor of the system.

States chairman Braham: "The restructuring makes better use of the talents of the board, medical staff, more than 1,100 employees, and all the volunteers and auxiliaries in building on this institution's great strengths. We intend to continue to be one of the Pittsburgh area's finest providers of health care."

*Warm water exercise in the hospital's heated therapy pool is part of the daily regimen for arthritis patients. Here physical therapist Chris Dolnack (far right) helps patients during pool class.*

# LA NORMANDE
## PITTSBURGH'S SUPREME RESTAURANT

It is the first place that comes to mind at any conjunction of the words "great" and "restaurant."

La Normande has won so many accolades that the food critic of the *Pittsburgh Press,* Robert M. Bianco, summed it up this way in a January 2, 1986, review: "From appetizer to dessert, no other restaurant can match its consistent quality . . . A place to take people who are special to you to show

*The ambience of La Normande is reflected in its table setting, which won the 1985 First Place Tabletop Award from* Restaurant Hospitality *magazine. Courtesy,* Restaurant Hospitality

them how special they are."

La Normande is the only exemplar in the city, and for hundreds of miles around, of that ideal of French dining to which *Le Guide Michelin* pays its supreme tribute. Three stars. The map of France is dotted with perhaps 20 such restaurants. Reuben Jacob Katz's goal was to establish one in Pittsburgh.

"I don't mean continental," says Katz. "Pittsburgh has several fine continental eating places, which represent various countries and styles. I mean a serious French restaurant."

Katz's office is up a concrete stairway from the kitchen of his 12 chefs. The bookshelves are loaded with histories, atlases, and encyclopedias of food and wine. "In France there is a sense of dining as a complete evening's entertainment," he says, "not only the food but all the elements of decor, setting, and method of service. It's the ultimate dining experience that we chose to emulate. Most people thought we were crazy."

La Normande is located at 5030

*La Normande's yearly black-tie anniversary dinner menus warrant special presentations. The 1983 menu cover featured some of the restaurant's awards. Courtesy, Wiilliam Kolano/Irene Pasinski Associates*

Centre Avenue, Shadyside, in the ground level of an apartment building. *Travel Holiday* magazine, in its 1986 Fine Dining Awards, likened the atmosphere to that of a chateau; others find the ambience of a provincial inn in the two intimate, darkly paneled dining rooms. Each room seats 35 patrons. Candlelight flickers on crystal stemware, china, and linen. "If a table top talked, this one would speak French," said *Restaurant Hospitality* magazine in the citation of its 1985 Top of the Table Award to a Katz arrangement of flowers, napery, crystal, and imported silver and china.

But it is through its menu that La Normande speaks French most unmistakably. Calligraphed each day to reflect what is best in the markets, it contains such specialties as Homard en Choux (poached lobster wrapped in a blanched cabbage leaf with caviar and pimiento butter); Sole de la Manche Grillee a la Ciboulette (grilled Dover sole with chives, white wine, and cream); Mignons de Veau a l'Estragon (medallions of veal loin with tarragon). And the wines!—a cellar of 500 labels, exclusively from the vineyards of France.

La Normande opened on Wednesday, November 8, 1978, in space formerly occupied by a failed fast-fooder. A troubling omen, but Katz and his then-partner, Norman Schlesinger, preferred a kitchen and dining space already built. Both were mindful that no true French restaurant had ever succeeded in Pittsburgh, much less a dream of amateurs.

Reuben Katz had been an economist, college instructor, and president of a manufacturing firm when he decided at age 40 to open his ideal restaurant. He was and is a gourmet cook, traveler, Francophile, and connoisseur of French wines.

The first crisis came when the restaurant's third partner, one of Pittsburgh's most prominent chefs,

backed out at the 11th hour. Desperately Katz interviewed a score of candidates and on a flash of faith hired Lawrence Timothy Ryan, then newly out of the Culinary Institute of America, a sous-chef at a suburban restaurant, and only 19 years old. Later a member of the 1984 U.S. Culinary Olympics Team, Ryan stayed for four years and established the unique direction of La Normande.

As the kitchen became known for its dedication to the three-star standard, it attracted apprentice "externs" from leading culinary schools. Cathy Armburger arrived in that role in 1979. A social worker who had switched careers when she realized that for her cooking was kismet, Armburger succeeded Ryan as executive chef.

An award-winning poster was La Normande's gift to the guests at its 1985 anniversary dinner. The poster commemorates La Normande's new logo. Courtesy, William Kolano/Irene Pasinski Associates

As Pittsburgh's chief proponent of the creative in cuisine never mind the cost, La Normande offers opportunities akin to those of a premier art gallery. Four times a year Katz stages what he calls "symphonies." Eight to 10 wines accompany a planned succession of courses, enabling guests to seek their own optimum harmony of tastes. A yearly black-tie anniversary dinner introduces the kit-

chen's newest dishes, the event typically ending in a standing ovation for Armburger and her white-toqued minions. Conversely, any Monday through Friday, a "Menu Degustation" provides a retrospective sampling of menu items that have pleased through the years.

For imparting such pleasures La Normande has won the Cartier Gold Plate, the Ambassador 25, and De Montal Armagnac awards; inclusion in too many "best restaurants in America" lists to mention; and the only "five forks" so far bestowed by *Pittsburgh Post-Gazette* critic Mike Kalina, who does not lightly hand out four.

One sort of praise La Normande has never received. It has yet to be called inexpensive.

Katz maintains that his Monday-through-Thursday Table d'Hote Menu is certainly reasonable and that food and drink on a par with La Normande's would probably command twice the check in New York, Chicago, or San Francisco. "It comes down to a question of quality versus quantity," he says. The costs of raw materials (40 percent air-freighted from France) and of talented labor inevitably come high.

However, to widen the market, on November 8, 1983, La Normande's fifth anniversary, Katz opened Le Bistro. It is a sister restaurant, immediately adjacent, seating 65 persons, and served from Armburger's kitchen. With its casual aura of a Parisian cafe, Le Bistro features a "country" French menu at more moderate prices than the haute cuisine of La Normande.

Reuben Katz says his greatest satisfaction is that "we didn't compromise; we stayed French.

"The ultimate kick is having guests who've eaten at great French restaurants all over the world come up and say that what we do at La Normande is as good as anything they've ever seen."

# BERKMAN RUSLANDER POHL LIEBER & ENGEL
## A COMMITMENT TO EXCELLENCE IN THE PRACTICE OF LAW

Berkman Ruslander Pohl Lieber & Engel is a Pittsburgh law firm with roots reaching back to the turn of the century. It first built a reputation in corporate, tax, and related fields of law as Ruslander, Ruslander & Lieber. In the mid-1960s a merger with the equally prestigious Glick, Berkman & Engel extended the firm's capabilities in litigation and labor law. Soon afterward Frank J. Pohl and G.C. Burgwin III joined the firm, bringing in a well-regarded municipal finance and securities practice.

Located for many years in the landmark Frick Building, Berkman Ruslander Pohl Lieber & Engel established itself as a leading law firm, emphasizing service to the business community in western Pennsylvania and portions of Ohio and West Virginia. By 1986 the professional staff had grown to more than 60 lawyers.

Commitment to Pittsburgh's cultural, civic, and charitable activities has long been the firm's hallmark. Its attorneys have given time and talent to the Pittsburgh Association for the Blind, the Pittsburgh Symphony, Pittsburgh Trust for Cultural Resources, World Affairs Council, the United Way, YMCA, Salvation Army, Association for Retarded Citizens, and a variety of schools and hospitals.

Berkman Ruslander joined the spirit of Pittsburgh's Renaissance II in 1984 by relocating its offices to three upper floors of One Oxford Centre—a move that also reflected other modern directions. While continuing its professional work of the highest quality in traditional areas of the law, the firm has been developing new ideas, skills, and approaches to address the challenges posed by rapid technological and economic change. Its own facilities incorporate advanced technical systems. Computerized legal research, word processing, and telecommunications are essential to the delivery of modern legal services. Nevertheless, the firm believes that the practice of law continues to be a profession of people serving people.

Today's Berkman Ruslander Pohl Lieber & Engel is a full-service law firm. It represents businesses of all kinds, including public and privately held corporations; charitable, educational, and nonprofit organizations; and individual clients. It handles matters of corporate and public finance; corporate acquisitions and mergers; real estate development and financing; federal, state, and local taxation; labor and employment relations; litigation before state and federal courts and administrative agencies; health care; bankruptcy and creditors' rights; estate planning and probate; executive compensation and employee benefits; and entrepreneurial development of high-technology and emerging companies.

Berkman Ruslander Pohl Lieber & Engel holds an expectation that business in the Pittsburgh and tri-state regions will enjoy a new era of vitality and growth. It is committed to assisting clients to achieve a full share in that prosperity.

# COOPERS & LYBRAND
## HELPING CLIENTS TO GROWTH, ECONOMIC HEALTH

The public accounting profession was in its infancy when Walter Staub set out from the Philadelphia headquarters of Lybrand, Ross Bros. & Montgomery in 1908. He had a directive to establish the third office of the firm in Pittsburgh.

Staub rented quarters in the Union National Bank Building and hired a small staff composed of business school graduates and bookkeepers. Together they launched pioneering efforts in auditing. For a fee as low as seven dollars per day, a client had access to the firm's full services. These consisted mostly of checking postings to handwritten journals, comparing canceled checks to the cash book, comparing vouchers, and verifying footings.

Since then Coopers & Lybrand has become one of the world's premier accounting organizations. It has offices in 90 U.S. cities and in every major country. The Pittsburgh staff numbers more than 200 and occupies the entire 35th floor and part of the 33rd in the

*Now one of the world's premier accounting organizations, Coopers & Lybrand's Pittsburgh office occupies the entire 35th floor and part of the 33rd in the 600 Grant Street Building.*

*Coopers & Lybrand's very first office in Pittsburgh was in the Union National Bank Building in 1908. For a fee as low as seven dollars per day a client had access to the firm's full services.*

600 Grant Street Building, in the heart of the city's business district.

Coopers & Lybrand has been at the forefront of bringing the accounting profession to its present sophistication. The firm offers a broad range of services—in addition to accounting and auditing—bringing a well-rounded, business-oriented approach to client activities that has become a hallmark of the C&L practice.

A partner oversees each of the firm's engagements. Specialists, who are residents in the Pittsburgh office, provide support in such disciplines as accounting and auditing; taxes; management consulting; actuarial, benefits, and compensation consulting; and computer and information systems.

Although some of the area's major enterprises are C&L clients, the practice is not limited to corporate giants. "We take great pride," says James H. Weber, managing partner, "in meeting the special needs of smaller, growing clients. That's the mission of our Emerging Business Services Group."

Health care providers, manufacturers, retailers, and wholesalers all figure prominently in the client list. Lockhart Iron & Steel Company is the firm's oldest client relationship in Pittsburgh, continuous now for more than 60 years. Overall, C&L's office delivers audit and related services to approximately 600 diverse clients.

Coopers & Lybrand also encourages partners and staff members to give time and talent to local service organizations as volunteers. Among the chief commitments of this kind are the Family & Children's Service, Boy Scouts of America, HELPLINE, Junior Achievement, Inroads, and Parental Stress Center.

"We believe that our people—their breadth, depth, and experience—and our clientele are our greatest strengths," states Weber. "All of us basically want what the community wants: growth and economic health."

# DRAVO CORPORATION
## TECHNOLOGY SHAPES ITS MODERN COMPETITIVE EDGE

Dravo Corporation is rounding out its first century in a state of energetic change. The economic doldrums of the early 1980s put the diversified, international firm to a severe trial, but it has emerged in many ways a "new" company.

Technology is steering Dravo's traditional engineering and construction activities into various other channels. Typical of the redirection is Dravo Automation Sci-

Dravo developed this lime plant, of one million tons per year capacity, and a companion limestone mine at Maysville, Kentucky, in the mid-1970s to supply a special "Thiosorbic" lime to electric utilities.

ences, Inc. That unit was formed in the mid-1980s, initially to develop information and control systems for management of process industries, and rapidly expanded. Now it is turning out software systems and products for factory automation in manufacturing industries.

By acquiring proven combustion technology from Germany, and coupling this to its own expertise in power engineering, Dravo has become a major factor in other strong markets: waste-to-energy and power cogeneration. Technologies for continuous casting, ladle metallurgy, and other modern pro-

cesses have given the firm a substantial role as well in updating the North American steel industry.

Even the most earthy of Dravo's businesses—natural resources—feels the technology impact. The company has long led at helping the electric power industry comply with pollution control regulations, which grow ever more stringent. Dravo's large new mining and calcining complex in Kentucky furnishes utilities with a special lime. It is sold under long-term contract to more than a dozen coal-burning power plants in the Ohio Valley. Used in wet scrubbers, the lime removes virtually all the sulfur dioxide from stack emissions.

Difficult periods such as the early 1980s are never really new to a long-lived company. Dravo Corporation, in fact, was born in hard times.

That was back in 1891. Francis R. "Frank" Dravo was a young mechanical engineer. Just a few years after graduation, he found himself unemployed during an economic slump. With no work available, Dravo took the typical American entrepreneur's approach to adversity: He went into busi-

This rolling mill control "pulpit" is part of a system developed by Dravo Automation Sciences for a new steel plant in Ohio. The facility incorporates $30 million of computer hardware and Dravo-developed software.

A huge crowd on September 11, 1943, midway through World War II, cheered the launching of the USS Jenks 2,000 miles from the open sea. It was the first destroyer escort to slide down the ways at Dravo's Neville Island shipyard on the Ohio River.

ness for himself. Two years later his brother, Ralph, joined him.

F.R. Dravo & Company began as a sales agency for steam power plants and industrial machinery; however, business soon expanded into installation services. By 1898 the enterprise was into general construction. Four

*Dravo is a leading designer-builder of waste-to-energy and other alternate power facilities. This 55-megawatt geothermal unit is one of two completed for Northern California Power Agency north of San Francisco at The Geysers—the world's largest source of power from the earth's internal heat.*

gineering construction expertise, Dravo has been in the forefront of the trend toward "privatization" of industrial services in the 1980s. Long-term assignments to operate geothermal, waste-to-energy, and other facilities now represent a significant portion of the firm's backlog.

Dravo's natural resource business expanded in 1976 to include lime. It opened a complex in Maysville, Kentucky, to produce one million tons annually for stack gas scrubbing at electric plants. The later purchase of Southern Industries Corporation expanded both the lime and aggregate operations into the Gulf Coast states.

*Thomas F. Faught, Jr., president and chief executive officer of Dravo Corporation.*

years later it began dredging sand and gravel from Pittsburgh's rivers to assure a reliable source of concrete aggregates for its construction work. Subsequently, Dravo began building barges for the sand and gravel business.

Growth came slowly but steadily in the firm's first half-century. It tackled construction projects in many parts of the country. On the rivers, the company pioneered in welded steel fabrication for barges and towboats and the switchover to diesel power. It also entered the transportation industry directly by purchasing a barge line.

In World War II, the firm concentrated almost entirely on producing fighting ships for the Navy. Dravo served as the "lead yard" for building LSTs—tank loading ships; it launched about 150 of them. The product list also included sub chasers, auxiliary mine sweepers, medium landing ships (LSMs), and destroyer escorts.

The return to a peacetime economy dropped the company's employment abruptly from a high of nearly 30,000 to just 4,500, but three major growth strategies soon unfolded—technological development, geographic expansion,

and acquisitions.

In the early 1950s Dravo built its first large electric generating plants, then enhanced its position in 1964 by acquiring Gibbs & Hill, Inc., a New York engineering firm long experienced in serving utilities. This background led to Dravo's prominence as a designer-builder of the specialized generating facilities that characterize the power industry today—waste-to-energy plants fueled by municipal refuse, cogeneration plants that furnish multiple energy supplies for industry and utilities, and geothermal plants that harness the energy potential of subterranean steam and hot water.

Dravo's industrial construction work spread into a broad range of process facilities. By licensing German sintering and pelletizing technology, it became the premier designer-builder of iron ore processing projects in North America. The purchase of Blaw-Knox Chemical Plants, Inc., provided entry to the chemical, petroleum, and synthetic fuels industries, while a combination of licenses and internal developments made the firm a leader in the design of coal-handling systems.

Building upon its traditional en-

The old regional limitations long ago disappeared. Sizable facilities for engineering or production on the East, Gulf, and West coasts now complement the Pittsburgh headquarters. Even by the 1960s Dravo was taking on mammoth engineering/construction projects in Australia, Africa, the Mideast, and Latin America; today overseas subsidiaries and affiliates handle these numerous activities.

Thus, on the threshold of its second century, a much-changed Dravo Corporation has charted its strategic course for continued growth and achievement.

# RUSSELL, REA & ZAPPALA, INC.
## THE FAST RUNNER IN CREATIVE INVESTMENT BANKING

Russell, Rea & Zappala, Inc., has been major league in its management from the start, literally. Less than a decade after its founding by a onetime star of the Pittsburgh Steelers and his partners, the investment banking firm also achieved major league status the way investment bankers count it: in the dollar volume of its securities underwriting.

In 1985 RR&Z placed more than $1.34 billion of tax-exempt municipal bonds with investors. The box score on such heroics is kept by *Institutional Investor* magazine, which ranked the company, just eight years old at that point, as the 20th-most-active performer in the nation's marts for municipals, well ahead of any of its veteran Pittsburgh-based rivals. The high standing was derived in part from $229 million of educational financing, $227 million in public power projects, and a remarkable $402 million in water and sewer facilities for eighth place nationally in that field.

Since all that flow of dollars into bricks and mortar is an activity traditionally dominated by the major houses of New York, RR&Z has come to be viewed as one of the fastest growing regional invest-

*Two North Shore Center, overlooking the Golden Triangle, is the Pittsburgh headquarters for the investment banking firm of Russell, Rea & Zappala, Inc.*

ment banking firms in the United States, comparable to the "young lions" that roam the canyons of lower Manhattan.

How did it happen? "Creativity" is how the firm's principals explain it.

From the company's first phone call in 1978, "we tried to erase the mind set that said that you had to access Wall Street to get anything done," says RR&Z president Charles R. Zappala. "Those Wall Street organizations were geared to operate in only one way. We knew that there was more than one way to go."

A Pittsburgh-born lawyer with an investment banking background and a family prominent in politics, Zappala formed RR&Z with C. Andrew Russell and Donald Evans Rea, who today are the firm's chairman and secretary/treasurer, respectively.

Andy Russell played professional football for 14 years with the Steelers, winning All-Pro honors nine times. Holder of an economics degree and a master's degree in

business administration, Russell foresightedly spent his off-seasons pursuing a career in securities and real estate. He set up a flourishing practice in tax shelter syndications, and by 1978 was looking for diversification as well as an entry into the institutional market.

Meanwhile, Don Rea had also previously helped organize a predecessor firm; its specialty was the use of industrial revenue bonds to finance shopping center development, spearheaded by a blue-chip retailer with a solid credit rating. The rapidly expanding K mart proved to be Rea's chief corporate vehicle.

What Russell, Rea, and Zappala hoped to put together was a combination of expertise that would be more than the sum of its parts. The results have amply borne out that desire.

More than 500 governmental

bodies and private- and public-sector organizations in 22 states have become clients. Tax-exempt underwriting continues to be the company's bedrock business, but the pursuit of allied opportunities has carried RR&Z into corporate finance, secondary trading of debt securities, real estate development, and even resource recovery.

In addition to the investment banker's primary mission of putting together packages of financing, RR&Z has become an aggressive investor on its own account. It is a direct developer of three shopping centers in Maryland and Delaware; it has begun the purchase of $30 million of real estate in North Carolina and Virginia; and it owns a hydroelectric power plant near Atlanta. The firm also has drilled 450 producing oil wells, managing them as well. And it has acquired five cable television systems in western Pennsylvania and Ohio. Prospectively, in late 1986 the company was looking for landfills and waste energy projects to acquire. Unlike many investment bankers, RR&Z will often take an equity position in lieu of fees on some of the projects for which it rounds up the financing.

The firm has established offices in Philadelphia, Atlanta, and West Virginia—additional operations are foreseen in Florida—to complement Russell, Rea & Zappala's headquarters in Pittsburgh's Two North Shore Center, with its dramatic view of the Golden Triangle that fills the windows of the offices of more than 30 professional staff members.

Rea, who serves as the company's director of project finance, successfully managed its financing of a $300-million solid-waste-to-energy facility in eastern Pennsylvania—the largest private development of its type anywhere so far—and he believes that opportunities for similar creative activity in the 1990s will be even more attractive. However, he also points out that

*The principals in the firm are (left to right) Andy Russell, Charles Zappala, and Donald Rea.*

modern financial and regulatory complexities make it imperative for the people who bring in the money to have detailed technical knowledge. "There is no deep pocket in project finance," says Rea. "Every deal must stand on its own."

Although RR&Z has completed tax-free financings for some of Pittsburgh's largest enterprises—USX, Heinz, Alcoa, and Rockwell

among them—one of its new subsidiaries, RRZ Capital Group, Inc., is designed to work specifically with small to medium-size firms in acquisitions, divestitures, mergers, and leveraged buyouts. The Wall Street giants might be too big to pay attention; Russell, Rea & Zappala is not.

The firm's 1985 municipal underwritings did average more than $30 million per issue; and one of its largest pieces of business ever was to serve as lead and co-lead underwriter for $800 million of Pennsylvania Turnpike bonds. But Charlie Zappala says the partners of Russell, Rea & Zappala, Inc., take particular pride in working closely with issuers of securities

*Some of the professionals who have made Russell, Rea & Zappala one of the fastest growing regional investment banking firms in the United States.*

for projects of any size, ranging from $500,000 up in such fields as health care, education, municipal and utility services, and resource recovery.

"Investment banking is an extraordinarily exciting business," says Zappala. "It is gratifying to be part of the creation of a facility that provides construction jobs and permanent employment—and to be part of a process that creates the modern environment for work and for play."

# CALGON CORPORATION
## WORLDWIDE LEADERSHIP IN WATER TREATMENT

Water, people, technology: Like the confluence of three mighty rivers at The Point, they uniquely converged in Pittsburgh to establish it as one of the nation's premier cities. Appropriately, those same vital resources have been crucial to the success of Calgon Corporation—a Pittsburgh-born and -based company whose people are recognized worldwide for leadership in the development and application of innovative water-treatment technology.

Calgon's singular commitment to assuring that water works for its clients, not against them, evolved simultaneously with the firm's founding as Hagan Corporation in 1918 by Pittsburgh natives John Hopwood and Tom Peebles.

Originally focused on developing automatic combustion controls for industrial, utility, and marine boilers, they quickly recognized a more critical client need—preventing the costly system failures caused by calcium scales that water deposited in boiler tubes. Their response would set the company's future direction and establish its tradition of science-based, results-oriented technology.

Recruiting a young Pittsburgh scientist, Dr. Ralph Hall, Hopwood and Peebles funded a five-year boiler water research program at the U.S. Bureau of Mines' Pittsburgh Experimental Station. Their farsighted investment paid off handsomely with Dr. Hall's discovery of the unique water-conditioning properties of sodium hexametaphosphate.

Trademarked Calgon for "calcium gone," it was quickly adopted as the standard treatment for preventing scale in boilers—an application where it is still used. This versatile chemical became the raw material for a variety of products used to solve water-related problems in industrial systems, in commercial operations such as restaurants and laundries, and in the home. Its wide-ranging useful-

ness was formally recognized in 1935 when Calgon® was named Chemical of the Year at the British Industries Fair.

Concomitant with the success of its flagship chemical, Calgon was earning a reputation for technical problem solving and engineering excellence. Its Hall Laboratories Division, chartered to expand and exploit Dr. Hall's pioneering research in water science, was soon

V. James Gregory (left), president of Calgon Water Management Division, confers with A. Fred Kerst, Ph.D., vice-president.

acknowledged as industry's water-treatment consultant. First in the steel mills, power stations, and chemical plants that lined Pittsburgh's rivers, then across the country, and finally around the globe—wherever water was used—Hall consultants were the first called to solve the problems it caused.

Although Calgon's controls business also flourished, there was ultimately little doubt but that its most promising future was to be in water treatment. That perception became a reality in 1963, when the company sold its Controls Division and the Hagan name

Calgon Center, the company's headquarters complex, is situated midway between Greater Pittsburgh International Airport and the city's Golden Triangle business section.

to Westinghouse and adopted the name of its most famous product as its new identity, becoming the Calgon Corporation.

While Calgon is still most commonly associated in the public mind with the popular bath and home laundry products that bear that name, the firm sold that part of its business in 1977 to Beecham Products, a British pharmaceutical company. Calgon itself is now a subsidiary of Merck & Co., Inc., a U.S. pharmaceuticals firm.

Today, at Calgon's Pittsburgh headquarters, in its manufacturing plants, and at its offices in major U.S. cities and around the world, more than 1,200 Calgon people continue to build on a long tradition of technical innovation and value-added service.

In countless ways, every day, Calgon people and technology affect everyone's life directly and beneficially. Understandably so, since water has been accurately termed our most essential resource. In our homes and schools,

offices and plants, hospitals, hotels, and restaurants, we take it for granted that the quantity and quality of water we need will always be there when we open the faucet. To assure this, local utilities work closely with Calgon Corporation.

Calgon produced the first cationic organic polyelectrolyte approved for potable water treatment. These polymers are used to remove suspended matter from water and to enhance the operation of water clarifiers and filters. Calgon technology is also used to protect the pipes that bring water to users—preventing them from being plugged by scale or eaten away by corrosion.

The electricity used by consumers is generated by boiling water into steam to drive a turbine. Thousands of power plants around the world depend upon Calgon expertise to assure the ultrapure water needed to protect equipment

and the miles of water and steam lines that make up a typical steam-generating unit. Specialized Calgon technology also maintains the integrity of its water-based air pollution control systems. In many

*Calgon clients have access to one of the world's largest and most sophisticated laboratories devoted exclusively to water science. Here an atomic absorption spectrophotometer is used to analyze one of the tens of thousands of water and deposit samples received annually from around the world.*

*Employing advanced, innovative systems such as this scanning electron microscope, Calgon research scientists explore the fundamental nature of water-related problems and investigate the effects of Calgon technology in controlling them.*

*Since paper starts out as pulp, which is 97-percent water, papermakers are major Calgon clients. Here a Calgon paper chemicals specialist explains how the company's polymers optimize sheet formation. Other Calgon products control chemical and biological deposits to maximize paper machine runnability.*

cases, the firm even treats the fuel power plants use—to enhance residual oil combustion, for example, or to prevent coal pile freezing in winter and dusting in summer.

The page you're reading started out as pulp—about 97-percent water. Paper of the proper sheet strength, formation, and quality must form during the scant seconds it takes to pass over the wet end of a modern high-speed papermaking machine. Polymeric drainage and retention aids manufactured by Calgon help make this possible. It also supplies biological and chemical deposit control technology to prevent problems that can ruin paper quality and shut down papermaking equipment. Consider all the books and magazines, boxes and bags, newspapers and catalogs, and the avalanche of other sundry paperwork that innundates us all each day—and you'll appreciate why papermakers are among Calgon's most important clients.

In one way or another, in fact, water is essential to virtually every manufactured product. Clothes, automobiles and the gasoline that fuels them, furniture, carpets, and appliances. The cans, bottles, jars, and boxes on consumers' shelves—plus the processed foods and beverages, cosmetics and medicines, cleaners and grooming aids they contain. Even the plastic credit cards that pay for it all.

Each year U.S. plants require hundreds of trillions of gallons of usable, trouble-free water to heat and to cool, to generate power, to convey process materials and waste products, and as an integral component of many finished goods. Thousands of those plants—among them most of the *Fortune* 500—depend on Calgon people and technology to prevent water from damaging equipment, impairing product quality, and threatening productivity.

A revolutionary new Calgon technology called CalGUARD® lets these plants optimize the performance of their critical cooling systems for the first time. The result of a five-year, multimillion-dollar research and development effort, CalGUARD has been hailed as a major advance in water treatment—elevating it from an art to a science. Using sophisticated computer modeling, CalGUARD realistically simulates the operation of plant cooling systems under any conceivable combination of operating variables (up to $8 \times 10^{47}$ possibilities). Then it precisely predicts the extent of corrosion, scale, and other water-related problems that will be encountered. Finally, it selects the most cost-effective treatment to accomplish operating objectives.

*United States power plants use over 30 trillion gallons of water annually. They depend upon Calgon technology to protect their boilers (lit in background), which convert water into steam to drive turbines, and their cooling systems, which help condense the steam back into water for reuse. Here a Calgon engineer collects a sample from the plant reservoir, which supplies its hyperbolic cooling towers.*

The latest advance in cooling water-treatment chemistry was also developed by Calgon. Called pHreeGUARD®, it lets plants operate their cooling systems safely, efficiently, and economically under a much broader range of conditions than ever before possible.

Once water has served its essential roles in our plants and homes, of course, it must be cleaned up before it can be safely returned to rivers and lakes. There, too, Calgon technology is invaluable—helping municipal and industrial plants transform sewage and wastewater back into literally drinking-quality water, ready to be reused.

Efficient water recycling, in fact, has become an urgent challenge. Increasing demands on limited supplies, along with years of abuse and neglect, are already resulting in more frequent shortages of usable water. To assure that industries, farmers, utilities, and the public will always have the quantity and quality of water needed, all users must squeeze more value from every drop.

While many plants already recycle much of their water, most will

*Mineral processors use millions of gallons of water daily—much of it in processes that separate valuable ore from the soil containing it. At this coal preparation plant, Calgon products are used on a dewatering filter to accelerate drying of the processed fine coal.*

*Virtually every type of industrial plant requires large volumes of trouble-free water. The Calgon engineer atop the cooling tower at this steel mill monitors the effectiveness of Calgon treatment in protecting its BOF systems. Calgon polymers are used in the thickener (lower right) to speed removal of particulates from a gas scrubbing system that controls air pollution from the BOF.*

ultimately have to close their plantwide water loop entirely. That will exacerbate the threat water problems pose to plant efficiency and reliability. Calgon scientists and engineers are now working to develop the advanced technology that will make such zero-discharge operation practical.

As important as technology is, it's the application expertise and creativity of Calgon's people that the firm's clients most value. Engineering and science graduates for the most part, they undergo extensive classroom and on-the-job training at Calgon in what is virtually a postgraduate course in the science of water treatment. Those who make the grade literally become "Industry's Water Doctors."

Wherever water is used, these skilled and dedicated men and women are at work: out in plants, examining critical client systems and diagnosing water-related problems; back in laboratories, developing a course of treatment; and, in client offices, counseling management about their prescriptions.

While their work is sometimes long, hard, and dirty, they respond to the challenge of developing their professional skills in an arena that so dramatically benefits the public good. And, like all members of the family of companies that make up Merck, Calgon employees share in the rewards and satisfaction that come from being part of an organization acknowledged by *Fortune* magazine as one of America's best managed, most admired firms.

# MONTEFIORE HOSPITAL
## PROMOTES THE COMMUNITY'S HEALTH AND EDUCATION

Montefiore Hospital, a corporate member and teaching hospital of the University Health Center of Pittsburgh (UHCP), is an Oakland-based medical complex that has gained international recognition for its leading-edge contributions to health care.

As a member of the health center—a consortium of six university-affiliated hospitals—Montefiore plays a key role in a national medical resource, offering leadership in patient care, education, and scientific and technological development. An affiliate of the University of Pittsburgh Schools of Medicine and Dentistry and the Health Sciences, Montefiore provides comprehensive medical, surgical, and dental care, as well as a broad range of educational and community outreach programs.

Montefiore was founded in 1908 by the Jewish community of Pittsburgh as its gift to the total community. Its roots, however, date back 10 years earlier, when 17 dedicated women formed the Hebrew Ladies Aid Society—forerunner of today's Ladies Hospital Aid Society. It was their pursuit of the dream of establishing a Jewish hospital that led to its creation, and their ideals still guide Montefiore.

The Auxiliary, and the men who would later join with it to form the Montefiore Hospital Association, saw the hospital as a place where Jewish doctors could practice, where Jewish patients could receive caring treatment in a familiar setting, and where others in the community could come for care, regardless of their religion, race,

or ethnic origin.

By 1908 their dream had become a reality. Housed in a converted mansion on Centre Avenue in the Hill District, the original Montefiore Hospital stood in the heart of the city's Jewish community boasting 60 beds, surgical facilities, kosher kitchens, and the latest equipment available.

As the scope of services expanded and the number of patients increased, a larger facility was needed. The hospital's

*Founded by the Jewish community of Pittsburgh in 1908, Montefiore Hospital, a full-service adult health care facility has a 520-bed capacity, and the most modern technology for complete, high-quality patient care.*

supporters began a drive for funds that culminated in 1929 with the dedication of a new Montefiore building at its present location on Fifth Avenue.

From its beginning Montefiore's growth and development have provided a unique opportunity to extend the benefits of a teaching hospital into the community to assure the residents of its immediate neighborhoods—as well as those of the broader regions it serves—of ready access to high-quality care.

As a full-service adult health care facility, today's 520-bed Montefiore Hospital offers medical, surgical, neurosurgical, and coronary intensive care units; an emergency room with rapid critical care transport capabilities; and state-of-the-art laboratory, diagnostic, and therapeutic services. Included in Montefiore's programs are specialties in cardiovascular services, gastroenterology, hematology, oncology, oral and maxillofacial surgery, orthopedics, plastic surgery, and rheumatology.

As part of the UHCP's internationally recognized transplant program, Montefiore directs a comprehensive bone marrow transplant center, which provides area residents with convenient access to the latest techniques. As a national leader in brain tumor treatment and research, Montefiore is one of only seven university-affiliated medical centers partici-

pating in the National Cancer Institute-sponsored Brain Tumor Cooperative Group. By introducing high technology such as lithotripsy, a nonsurgical and painless method of treating kidney stones, and the use of the carbon-dioxide laser for cancer and other operations, Montefiore provides the optimum in patient care.

Utilizing modern technology, the hospital's physicians have developed research programs that have resulted in new treatments, surgical and diagnostic techniques, and equipment advances. Montefiore researchers have developed a system for detecting cardiac disease through changes in blood enzymes, offering physicians greater accuracy in diagnosis. The hospital and other University Health Center of Pittsburgh researchers pioneered the use of high-frequency jet ventilation, which offers safe respiratory support for patients in surgery, those suffering from injury to breathing passages, and victims of lung failure.

Since its creation, Montefiore Hospital has served as an educational center for the area's medical community. The hospital included three interns on its original staff, as well as a School of Nursing that operated for 68 years.

Montefiore's medical staff, who number more than 400, has blended those early ideals with the benefits of today's research, medical advances, and other resources of

a university-affiliated teaching hospital.

In its affiliation with Pitt's Schools of Medicine and Dental Medicine, Montefiore participates in the education of more than 250 undergraduate students annually. The hospital also acts as a primary educational resource for Pitt's Schools of the Health Sciences, and the nursing and paramedical programs of several area colleges and universities. In all, almost 1,000 students engage in educational activities at Montefiore each year.

Montefiore Hospital was founded on a concept that emphasizes community service and involvement. The hospital continues that commitment through a unique and diverse offering of community outreach programs.

Each year the hospital receives more than 68,000 ambulatory care visits through its network of facilities and programs, including an outpatient department treating more than 16,000 patients in programs covering 24 medical specialities. As a leader in the home care field—the hospital's program was established in 1952 as the first in Pennsylvania and one of only four in the nation—Montefiore recently introduced new high-technology services into the home.

These services, as well as the hospital's policy of providing care outside the hospital setting, make Montefiore's approach to this growing trend toward increased community outreach programs truly unique in the area. Montefiore Hospital's future will continue to mirror its past and present—the work of bringing care and science together in a way that offers a healthier and fuller life.

*A leader in patient care, education, and scientific and technological development, Montefiore uses advanced medical developments such as this carbon dioxide laser for cancer and other operations.*

# MAGEE-WOMENS HOSPITAL
## OASIS OF HOPE FOR WOMEN AND INFANTS

Little in the life of Christopher Magee suggested he might have an interest in the health of women. Born in 1848, he filled active roles as a civic leader, industrialist, politician, and newspaper founder. Yet, at the time of his death in 1901, his will disclosed a $5-million bequest for a hospital to serve "all females . . . for lying-in purposes . . . without any questions asked as to their lives or names."

Magee's own mansion—The Maples, on the family estate in Pittsburgh's Oakland section—would serve as the first hospital facility, although he provided that his widow could live out her days there. After she died in 1909, his trustees began organizing the Elizabeth Steel Magee Hospital, named for his mother.

Two years later the doors opened on what would grow to be a model for American hospitals. Medical graduates would vie for coveted residencies in obstetrics and gynecology, and patients would find a quality of specialized care and knowledge that only a handful of institutions can impart. On the property where the Magees once lived, at Forbes Avenue and Halket Street, now stands a full-fledged medical center for women and infants.

Innovation has flourished there from the beginning. It was Dr. Charles E. Ziegler, the hospital's first medical director, who introduced early in the century the concept of free clinics in needy neighborhoods. (He also invented the obstetrical bed, an umbilical clamp, and—the coffee percolator!) Dr. John B. Josimovich's research in the 1960s earned worldwide attention for advancing the understanding of fetal malnutrition and prenatal disease. Magee-Womens was among the first U.S. hospitals to perfect intrauterine transfusions and to contribute to a cure for Rh disease. In the 1980s it opened the tri-state area's first specially designed birthing suite

*From infant to adult, Magee-Womens Hospital is a matchless source of specialized health care and information for women.*

and the area's most utilized same-day surgery unit. Dr. Thomas Gill discovered a method to immunize the growing fetus against childhood diseases. Dr. Mark Scher's studies of sleep provide a window into the neurological problems of the newborn and their impact on future development.

The first Magee patients in 1911 numbered just 14 women and their babies, but soon a new hospital building was going up alongside The Maples. When it was completed in 1915, the old family home became a nurses' residence and later a teaching facility; it was finally razed to make room for an

expansion in 1954. Christopher Magee's legacy grew over the decades to become the largest private obstetrical service in the United States, with more than 10,000 births annually by the mid-1980s. The modern Magee-Womens Hospital contains 290 adult beds, 181 bassinets, and employs some 1,500 professional and support personnel.

The facility's physicians in private practice and hospital-based specialists survey the entire range of maternal concerns; they also set the stage for the practice of modern gynecology and the care of patients with breast and abdominal cancer. The hospital's low mortality rates testify to the skill of its staff.

Research specific to women and infants is conducted at Magee, with the result that the newest

The focus of Magee-Womens Hospital is the healthy woman.

proven information is brought directly to bedside. Its specialists teach at the University of Pittsburgh School of Medicine, conveying the latest developments in obstetrics, gynecology, cancer management, and high-risk newborn care. They also teach doctors on staff at other area institutions.

However, the chief beneficiaries of this vast bank of knowledge are the patients at one of only 13 such specialty hospitals in the country. Older Pittsburghers will remember a Woman's Hospital, founded in 1939 as part of Presbyterian Hospital; Magee merged with Woman's in 1962 to become Magee-Womens Hospital.

The focus of Magee-Womens is the healthy woman. Its emphasis is on illness prevention, consumer education, and counseling. The hospital setting is viewed as a backup when necessary. Staff members conduct health screen-

ing and educational programs in new satellite centers in Pittsburgh's suburbs, as well as at the hospital itself and in Oakland. The institution's consumer education programs sparked a trend among local women to seek out more health information as a guide to physical well-being and to the choice of a doctor. Both at the hospital and in the satellites, Magee instructors work with parents-to-be, with parents and teenagers concerned about sexuality and reproductive development, and with women who intend to be prepared for menopause, osteoporosis, premenstrual syndrome, and cancer. Registered nurses prepare and deliver the programs; they also address women's groups and female employees at local firms.

The modern Magee-Womens Hospital, its facilities sharply upgraded by a $41-million restructuring completed in 1982, takes seriously the broad mission of a "medical center for women." The range is enormous: infertility treatment, including in-vitro fertilization;

genetic studies and counseling; management of diabetes and other conditions that may affect pregnancy; therapy for substance abuse problems and physical violence, including rape; treatments for cancer, including laser surgery; intervention in complicated pregnancies and deliveries; and counseling for couples who have lost a baby or have had a premature infant.

Magee-Womens Newborn Intensive Care Unit is the referral center for the tri-state area, a 40-bassinet facility for premature infants and those born with other life-threatening problems. Physicians encourage the high-risk pregnant woman to be delivered at Magee—thereby avoiding transfer from another facility if the baby should need intensive care, and increasing the chance of recovery.

Whatever the problems or the questions, from infant to octogenarian, Magee-Womens Hospital is a matchless source of specialized health care and information for women.

# JOHN M. ROBERTS & SON COMPANY
## A JEWEL IN PITTSBURGH FOR MORE THAN 150 YEARS

When a 23-year-old Scottish immigrant named John M. Roberts began his watchmaking and jewelry business in a log cabin at the corner of Fifth Avenue and Market Street, Downtown, horse-drawn wagons were a common sight on the unpaved streets. It was 1832.

Today, more than a century and a half later, the John M. Roberts & Son Company stands a couple of blocks away, at 429 Wood Street. The four-story Grecian edifice, occupied since 1925, is still run by the fourth and fifth generations of the founding family. In fact, the Roberts company is Pittsburgh's oldest family-owned enterprise in continual operation. Further, it is one of the few retail stores in the United States that has been in business for over 150 years and owned successively from father to son throughout that long span.

In the beginning the log cabin shop sold watches, diamonds, ivory miniatures, Bohemian garnets, and glassware. The bearded Scot would personally transport these valuables on an arduous annual trek to New York City. At a time when Pittsburgh was already sporting an "Iron City" reputation with numerous metalworks, textile, and glass factories, Roberts pioneered the retailing spirit. He was the first merchant west of the Alleghenies to install glass-paned windows, and later his store became the first in Pittsburgh to be lighted with electricity. The entrepreneur was one of the city's premier art dealers offering oil and watercolor works on his walls.

The Roberts firm has catered to a long list of famous customers. Such businessmen and industrialists as Andrew Carnegie, Thomas Mellon, and George Westinghouse purchased from the founder and his son. The legendary "Diamond Jim" Brady bought gems to dazzle his girlfriend, Pittsburgh actress Lillian Russell. The business has also served some spectacularly loyal clients. One man rowed a boat to the front door during the flood of 1936. He waded in and explained that it was his anniversary—and his wife would have been crushed without a gift from Roberts.

Two mandates at the store may be responsible for its longevity. One is that at least one family member must be available to serve customers at any hour the doors are open. The other is that an expert salesman be willing to explain to clients whatever they want to know about gems and jewelry. Potential diamond buyers, for example, are shown into a specially lighted room where thay receive a worthwhile lesson on the steps taken to cut a high-quality stone.

Pittsburgh has changed profoundly during the past century and a half, and Roberts is one of the few businesses to have witnessed the transformation from the presidency of Andrew Jackson to Renaissance II. The fathers and sons who have managed the store have retained the principles of the founder, at the same time contributing continually with updated expertise.

*The original log cabin where John M. Roberts began his watchmaking and jewelry business in 1832.*

*John M. Roberts, founder.*

*Mayor Richard S. Caliguiri (third from left) presents the fourth and fifth generation of the Roberts family with a commendation for their service to the Pittsburgh area over 150 years. From left: Steele M. Roberts, Jr., Joseph L. Roberts, Jr., Mayor Caliguiri, William D. Roberts, Steele M. Roberts, and E. Dexter Roberts.*

# II-VI, INC.
## WORLD LEADERSHIP IN INFRARED OPTICS AND COMPONENTS

World leadership in infrared optics, components, and material.

It is meaningful to have the unique name "Two-Six" in the markets where the company operates. Its infrared (IR) materials, optics, and components serve vital functions in surgery with lasers and in weather satellites. Metals are cut and welded using them, and millions of miles from earth they spear through our universe aboard deep space probes. The company's products are based to a large extent on II-VI semiconductor materials technology.

Infrared (IR) laser and instrument markets are expanding briskly today—for industrial, medical, aerospace, and defense applications.

II-VI, Inc., was founded in 1971. By 1986 the company employed 140 persons at its facility in Saxonburg, 25 miles north of Pittsburgh. Annual sales are approaching $10 million. In its very specialized field, II-VI, Inc., is the world's leading manufacturer and respected pioneer in research and development.

II-VI produces high-purity cadmium telluride, which is used in infrared detectors and in laser modulators. It also is one of three producers of laser grade zinc selenide worldwide. These materials are key in $CO_2$ laser and other IR defense programs.

The company has developed innovative techniques for fabricating optics and for applying specialized thin-film coatings to optical surfaces. Quality control at every production stage ensures that customer specifications or military standards are met or exceeded. When $CO_2$ laser or IR system designers and manufacturers stress their optics or components to the limit, it is II-VI, Inc. that they rely on to eliminate device failures by pushing quality and reliability frontiers ahead.

The company believes that the world is its marketplace. In addi-

*Final laser test for specific infrared application.*

tion to extensive direct and telemarketing sales activities in North America, II-VI, Inc., has nurtured a growing presence in the high-technology export markets. Japan and West Germany in particular have emerged as leading $CO_2$ laser manufacturers and users. Exports presently account for 30 to

*Optics and components for high-powered laser instrumentation.*

40 percent of the company's sales.

Today, II-VI products are key to IR laser technology emergence for
- Next generation military/ aerospace detection and guidance
- Factory of the future implementation (along with robots and microcomputers)
- Medical procedures from microsurgical tumor removal to laser vaporization of plaque in blocked arteries.

Dedication to research and engineering, advanced manufacturing, quality assurance, and marketing will keep the company at the forefront in its infrared technology speciality.

# EASTERN AIRLINES
## IT BROUGHT AMERICA THE JOY OF FLIGHT

No name in the corporate world symbolizes the romance of travel like Eastern Airlines. From its beginnings in 1928 Eastern was a company that made ordinary people want to fly. Although its most famous executives have been living symbols of the daring adventure of flight, Eastern has persuaded millions of Americans to experience the exhilaration of being airborne.

Eastern, which more than any other carrier accustomed business people and tourists of the eastern United States to do their traveling six miles above the earth, today—with its own wings unfettered by deregulation—has become a major East-West airline, criss crossing the nation. It covers 25 cities throughout the West and Southwest. In total, the airline serves 145 cities in 25 countries. While it was Eastern that pioneered the quintessential service for business travelers—the famed Air-Shuttle linking Boston, New York, and Washington, D.C., with hourly flights more than a quarter-century ago—it is also the same Eastern that saw the vast possibilities in family fun, which made it the official airline of Walt Disney World.

Eastern Airlines is a huge enterprise. Even at the beginning of 1986, not counting the effect of a projected merger with Texas Air International, it was a company with annual sales approaching five billion dollars; nearly 300 jet aircraft; four operating hubs at Atlanta, Miami, Kansas City, and San Juan, Puerto Rico; more than 44,000 employees (the vast majority of whom are also stockholders); and 4,000 pilots. In 1985 it carried approximately 42 million passengers some 25.2-billion revenue passenger miles, not to mention 241-million revenue ton miles of freight and 202-million revenue ton miles of mail.

Mail was how it all started. That was on May 1, 1928. The company's first name was Pitcairn

Aviation, Inc., and it had a government contract to haul mail at under three dollars per pound. Its route system stretched 792 miles from New Brunswick, New Jersey, to Atlanta, Georgia, and was soon extended another 641 miles to Miami. Airplane manufacturer Harold F. Pitcairn was the founder, and the first fleet consisted of his own products—Pitcairn Mailwings, single-engine biplanes with open cockpits. The pioneering Pitcairn decided to concentrate on airplane manufacturing, however, and sold the airline in July 1929 to North

*Eastern inaugurated jumbo-size aircraft with the first big order for Lockheed L-1011's in 1968.*

*Eastern Airlines' Miami, Florida, terminal.*

American Aviation, Inc., which changed its name to Eastern Air Transport, Inc.

The new owners launched their first passenger service on August 18, 1930, between what is now LaGuardia Airport and North Beach, Long Island, and Richmond, Virginia, 310 miles south, with stops at Camden, Baltimore, and Washington. Ten-passenger Ford Trimotors were the first "wings of man," soon augmented by 18-passenger Curtiss Condors and, when service was extended to Florida on New Year's Day, 1931, by 120-mile-per-hour Kingbirds.

In 1932 Eastern made it possible to fly from New York to Miami—"from frost to flowers," as a radio jingle merrily advertised, "in 14 hours." Today's non-stop time is two and a half hours.

Edward V. "Eddie" Rickenbacker came aboard at North American Aviation's behest in the early 1930s. The famed former racing driver and World War I flying ace became a vice-president in charge of Eastern, and took over as general manager January 1, 1935, after a year in which the carrier had lost $700,000. Rickenbacker's stringent financial controls and operational acuteness turned the company around to a $90,000 profit his first year. He shifted the operations and maintenance quarters from Atlanta to Miami, where they remain; and he began replacing the patchwork airfleet with Douglas DC-2s and the sharply improved DC-3. Soon the singing

commercial was caroling, "from frost to flowers in only eight hours."

"Captain Eddie," as he was known, purchased the airline with a group of associates in 1938 for $3.5 million and became president of what was then an enterprise of 1,032 employees, 34 daily scheduled flights, 4,518 route miles, and steady yearly profits without benefit of federal subsidy. Fifteen years later, when he stepped up to board chairman, the visionary Rickenbacker looked at $136 million in annual sales and cracked,

*Eastern Airlines' A-300.*

*Eastern's B-757.*

"We haven't begun to grow."

By the dawn of the 1960s Eastern was entering the jet age. Its hourly Air-Shuttle first flew on April 30, 1961; and it inaugurated jumbo-size aircraft with the first big order for Lockheed L-1011s in 1968. Meanwhile, Captain Eddie had retired in 1963, and acquisitions were extending Eastern's route reach to Canada, Bermuda, and the Caribbean.

Eastern, which began service to Greater Pittsburgh International Airport in 1955, now operates 15 flights from there daily, including non-stops to Miami; Walt Disney World, Orlando, Florida; Toronto; and San Juan, Puerto Rico. More than 10,000 passengers are boarded at the airport each month.

It was under the leadership of another well-known aviator and former astronaut, Colonel Frank Borman, that Eastern weathered some of its most challenging financial clouds in the 1970s: first, the crises brought on by skyrocketing fuel prices and economic recession, and later the price-cutting competition of new entrant carriers invited into the fray by deregulation after 1978. Blessed with one super advantage, low labor rates, many a neophyte airline looked for prime pickings in Eastern's well-traveled Northeast-Florida route concentration. Borman's management team fought back with imaginative campaigns of employee participation—including the variable earnings and wage investment programs—and by significant operational changes. In 1982 Eastern aggressively purchased the Latin American routes previously operated by Braniff, and in 1984 inaugurated Miami to London service.

With Frank Borman's retirement in mid-1986 and the possibilities opened by a major consolidation with Texas Air International, a new era looms for Eastern Airlines, the company that gave Americans the confidence to fly.

# SHADYSIDE HOSPITAL
## MISSION: TO BE IN THE FOREFRONT OF HEALTH CARE

When the Civil War ended Pittsburgh had only three hospitals—Mercy, Passavant, and Western Pennsylvania—struggling to care for returning soldiers and the population of a burgeoning industrial region.

Eleven physicians who saw the need raised $22,000 to buy the three-story James B. Murray house on Second Avenue near Smithfield Street, Downtown. This became the site of the city's fourth medical institution—the Homeopathic Medical and Surgical Hospital and Dispensary of Pittsburgh, forerunner of the modern Shadyside, dedicated on August 1, 1866.

Just 16 years later the 38-bed structure had to be demolished. "Its soul had outgrown its body," observed benefactor William Thaw. In its place arose a 180-bed facility. "Too commodious," said the critics, but within three decades it too was outgrown.

A new six-story building of 200 beds opened on March 10, 1910, on Centre Avenue in Shadyside. The six-floor Pavilion Wing, added in 1924, increased the bed total to 325.

Shadyside's first 70 years were marked by a close alliance with Philadelphia's Hahnemann Medical College, which taught the homeopathic approach to treatment of illness, relying on minute doses of very powerful medicines. When Hahnemann changed its medical philosophy in 1938, the Pittsburgh institution dropped its original name in favor of Shadyside Hospital.

Due to expansion dictates, ground was broken in 1940 for a six-story nurses' residence and dispensary; the South Wing was added in 1954, as well as the Bailey Memorial Wing—a subsidized facility for women on limited incomes.

*The original Homeopathic Medical and Surgical Hospital and Dispensary of Pittsburgh on Second Avenue was formerly the James B. Murray residence. Drawing circa 1866*

In 1968, at age 102, Shadyside launched its second century project: to finance a new main building, the addition of the Aiken Professional Building, a parking garage, and the remodeling of existing facilities. Five years later the endeavor was completed, and Shadyside had a capacity of 426 beds. However, change is inherent in a living institution. An 18-bed in-

*The front entrance of the contemporary Shadyside Hospital.*

tensive care unit came into service in 1976, a second parking garage in 1981, and the East Wing Building in 1982.

In line with its tradition as a teaching hospital, Shadyside joined La Roche College in a baccalaureate program for registered nurses. Its school of nursing also led the way for the institution's dietetic internship venture in 1926 and its nurse anesthesia and perfusion services in 1971, the same year in which the radiologic technology program graduated its first class.

Shadyside boasts a proud history of enhancements to education and patient care services. Among the more recent of these are the Family Health Center, a nine-bed, medical/surgical intensive care unit opened in 1984; the Katz Non-Invasive Peripheral Vascular Laboratory; the Richard McLeod Hillman Non-Invasive Cardiac Laboratory; and the endocrinology, gastrointestinal, cardiac catheterization, and pulmonary function laboratories. Other additions to the complex are the Mary Hillman Jennings Oncology Center, the Cardiopulmonary Rehabilitation Center, the Sports Medicine Center, the Ambulatory Surgery Center, and the Medical Short Stay/Day of Admission Surgery unit. To provide financial support for the development of such facilities, the Shadyside Hospital Foundation was formed in 1975.

The new Second Avenue facility, which was dedicated April 15, 1884.

Today's Shadyside is a 474-bed progressive teaching institution, a modern hospital with a medical staff of 357, and a substantial force in its city's economy, with approximately 1,900 employees.

Shadyside Hospital's history has been one of breaking new ground in medicine. The institution opened the first school for nurses west of the Alleghenies in 1884. It operated the first successful X-ray machine in Pittsburgh in 1896, the year after its invention in Germany. More recently Shadyside became the city's first hospital to establish cardiac care units and to develop a pacemaker clinic. It is a leader in fighting the major "killers:" cancer, stroke, heart disease, and diabetes. The most active endocrinology program in Pittsburgh is another distinction cited by Henry Mordoh, president of the hospital and of its parent firm, SHERCORP.

The most recent innovation to

the hospital at 5230 Centre Avenue is a specialized PTCA laboratory, another Pittsburgh first, opened in 1986. PTCA stands for percutaneous transluminal coronary angioplasty—which translates into an additional weapon against heart disease.

The new laboratory is next door to three existing cardiac catheterization labs. In the PTCA procedure, the patient is mildly sedated, and a catheter insertion site is anesthetized. The catheter, a thin flexible tube, is guided into the coronary artery. Then an even narrower catheter, tipped with a tiny balloon, is inserted through

plaque against the arterial wall. Depending on the number of vessels to be opened, the process might take anywhere from a half-hour to four hours. Utilizing this procedure since 1978, Shadyside has found it to be an almost pain-free—and a far less expensive—alternative to open-heart surgery.

The "Cardio-Beeper," a Shadyside innovation believed to be the first of its type in the world, keeps watch on cardiac patients outside the hospital by remotely monitoring their cardiac rhythms. The patient is equipped with an electronic device similar to a transistor radio. The device tracks the person's heart performance and transmits this information by phone to the hospital. To report in—either by prearranged schedule or as needed—the patient

The hospital staff with young patients in the children's ward.

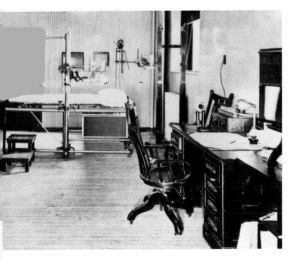

the first. A cardiologist uses X-rays to position the balloon at the point where the artery is blocked by cholesterol-laden plaque. Inflation of the balloon reopens the blood vessel by compressing the

Left: Among many other Shadyside Hospital "firsts" was its Roentgen Ray Department, the first X-ray facility in Pittsburgh. Photo circa 1900.

Right: The children's ward.

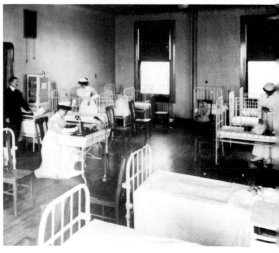

places electrodes wired to the beeper under each arm. Then he or she dials a special hospital phone connected to a recorder. Electronic impulses are received and printed out as an electrocardiograph, ready for analysis by the nurse taking the call.

The beeper offers two important advantages: The patient is given the "psychological comfort" of checking in; and the hospital's ability to respond to an emergency sharply increases. For example, some heart patients carry "Lido-Pens," disposable hypodermic syringes resembling felt-tip writing pens, which can save a life in the early stages of a heart attack. Instead of ink the "pens" contain lidocaine, a medicine that calms the erratic heart rhythm that often precedes a coronary emergency. When a patient checks in on the beeper, and a problem is detected, the

Shadyside has become a major cardiac center, performing thousands of catheterizations in its fight against heart disease.

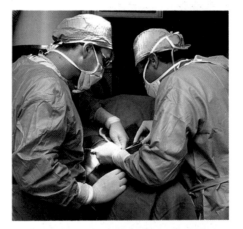

development of yet another specialization—the diagnosis and management of disorders of the nervous system. Neurosurgery has been a traditional service; now microsurgical techniques are enhancing the ability to treat brain tumors, and to perform such sophisticated feats as "through the nose" surgery for pituitary disorders.

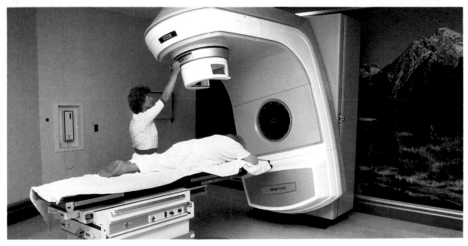

The six-million-volt linear accelerator at the Mary Hillman Jennings Oncology Center is capable of very specific targeting, safeguarding healthy tissue during radiation therapy.

nurse dispatches an ambulance— and also advises the patient how to make a lidocaine injection to stabilize the heartbeat until help arrives.

Shadyside has evolved into one of western Pennsylvania's major cardiac centers. By the mid-1980s one-third of its annual patient days related to the treatment of cardiovascular disease. The hospital also had performed more than 3,000 catheterizations, PTCAs accounting for 19 percent of those.

The early 1980s witnessed the

Stereotactic neurosurgery is a procedure that comes into play when all other treatments have failed to help such conditions as epilepsy, intractable pain and tremors caused by Parkinson's Disease, multiple sclerosis, strokes, and various forms of spasticity. The process employs X-ray sys-

tems, electronic stimulation of the brain, and three-dimensional geometry.

The surgeon gains access to the brain by drilling a small hole, no larger than a fingernail, in the skull. Then an X-ray device is used to zero in on the trouble spots. Amazingly, the patient receives only a local anesthetic and remains conscious throughout the operation. Thus, he or she can assist the surgeon during the electrical stimulation to locate the area of the brain in which the tremor originates. Once the target is pinpointed, the physician destroys the diseased tissue or implants a stimulator to eliminate chronic pain.

During this era Shadyside also has expanded its role in the fight against cancer, with the opening of the Mary Hillman Jennings Oncology Center. It is the first outside affiliate of the Joint Radiation Oncology Center at the University Health Center of Pittsburgh. The unit, which occupies renovated space in Shadyside's South Wing, provides comprehensive radiation therapy for both inpatients and outpatients.

In 1982 Shadyside Hospital officials answered the demands of health care changes with a decision to reorganize the institution into Shadyside Health, Education, and Research Corporation— SHERCORP. The restructuring

*Ground was broken in March 1986 for the Heritage Nursing Center.*

*Shadyside neurosurgeons regularly employ advanced microsurgical techniques in the treatment of a range of disorders of the nervous system.*

created five subsidiaries, giving SHERCORP an edge in providing service that is at once high-quality and cost-effective—in line with the growing demands of employers, government, and others responsible for medical payments.

Hospitals today are necessarily concerned regarding cost-effectiveness. The federal government has imposed stringent guidelines on Medicare reimbursement, and insurance premiums have soared.

"The mission of Shadyside Hospital has been expanded," explains a statement of institutional goals, "to include a renewed emphasis on using the resources made available to it for serving its community . . . in less costly, more convenient, and more accessible ways." The cost-containment efforts range from health maintenance and prevention-of-illness programs to a strong emphasis on outpatient care.

Henry Mordoh lays stress on his institution's "total approach" to health care. "You don't just treat the part that's sick," he states. "You have to understand the dynamics of the patient." Mordoh sees the hospital holding the fore-

*Automated endocrine testing using a radioimmunoassay technique is among the many resources that keeps Shadyside at the forefront of endocrinology.*

front in such key areas as heart disease, neurosurgery, and endocrinology; and he is excited about its development of an infertility center. "We're entering the area of genetics, and this is really a pioneering field," he says.

The mission, in sum, becomes one of recognizing all the changes that are revolutionizing health care nationally and applying them where appropriate to the Pittsburgh area.

Shadyside Hospital leaders broke ground in early 1986 in Squirrel Hill for the Heritage Nursing Center, a 159-bed skilled nursing facility. Not specifically a hospital project, it is the creation of two SHERCORP subsidiaries—Keystone Health Resources Corporation and Keystone Diversified Services Corporation—a demonstration of SHERCORP's commitment to a "continuum of care" for patients. The result should be a valuable and positive linkage between the acute care services of Shadyside Hospital and the aftercare offered by Heritage Nursing Center.

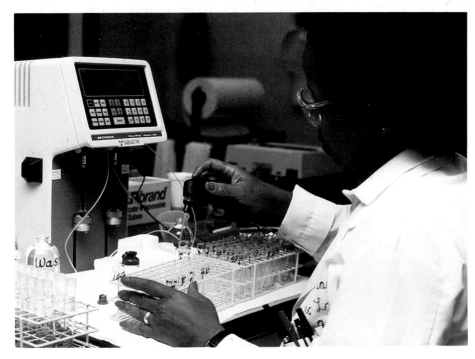

# DUDRECK DePAUL FICCO & MORGAN INC.
## MEETING THE CHALLENGE OF A CITY IN TRANSITION

*DDF&M partners, who form the advertising agency's management team, are (top, left to right) Al Dudreck and John DePaul and (bottom, left to right) James V. Ficco and Paul Morgan.*

If ever there was a perfect fit between an advertising agency and the market it serves, it's Dudreck DePaul Ficco & Morgan Inc. and Pittsburgh—an agency in transition in a city in transition.

Now in its second renaissance, Pittsburgh is rapidly diversifying from a basic industries economy to one of service and high technology. DDF&M, in its formative years, served the marketing and advertising needs of primarily smaller industrial clients, but has grown in size to become one of the top five agencies in the Pittsburgh market, with a diversified client base that includes consumer, retail, financial, and business-to-business accounts in local, regional, national, and international markets.

The agency recently made its second move in 26 years, this time to the heart of Pittsburgh's Downtown renaissance area. In renewing its commitment to Pittsburgh, DDF&M consolidated its operations in the city's redeveloped Firstside area. It owns and occupies about one-third of the 45,000-square-foot, newly restored former Oil Well Supply-Oliver Steel building at 200 First Avenue.

"Serving the communications needs of Pittsburgh and its business community means being at the center of the community," notes DDF&M chairman Al Dudreck. "Not only are we close to both clients and suppliers, but with our newly renovated building, we've made our own modest contribution toward making Downtown Pittsburgh a better place to be.

"While others may choose to desert a city such as ours in the midst of a tough and challenging transition in its economic base, we think that's all the more opportunity to get down to work and bolster our city," Dudreck says.

Adds DDF&M president John DePaul, "It's fitting that our agency is based in a building that played a clear role in the growth of this city during the industrial revolution. Instead of being demolished, it's been fully restored and equipped to continue its contribution to the city in a new and totally different era. As such, the building is in keeping with our philosophy as an advertising agency, and in itself typifies the special vitality and resilient character of Pittsburgh."

The agency began its modern era in 1970, when DePaul and Paul Morgan, both Pittsburgh advertising executives, joined Dudreck to form Dudreck DePaul & Morgan. When Jim Ficco joined the agency as a partner in 1976, the firm assumed its present name.

Growth with its clients has been a trademark of DDF&M throughout its history. The agency has been a long-term participating partner in the growth and success of a wide variety of clients. Several, in fact, began as both fledgling enterprises and fledgling clients to become the recognized leaders in their respective industries.

A pattern of steady, consistent growth has also marked the progress of DDF&M itself. In the past 10 years the agency's staff has more than quadrupled, while its total billings have quintupled. The firm's public relations division has emerged as one of the city's strongest. And a branch office, established in Boca Raton, Florida, in 1983, is serving the growing communications needs of clients in that part of the country.

But Pittsburgh has been and always will be home to Dudreck DePaul Ficco & Morgan Inc. "This 'city in transition' is exciting and challenging," concludes Dudreck, "and we're the perfect agency to meet that challenge."

# JOHNSON/SCHMIDT AND ASSOCIATES
## A HALF-CENTURY OF ARCHITECTURAL EXCELLENCE

In 1939 architects Roy L. Hoffman and Kenneth Crumpton stood at a career crossroads. The prestigious firm that employed them, Janssen & Cocken, was about to break up with the retirement of Benno Janssen, its principal. But that was the organization that had built some of Pittsburgh's finest landmarks—Mellon Institute, the William Penn Hotel, and Longue Vue Country Club among them—products of a grand tradition of "gentlemen architects" who expressed the classic European and Wren colonial styles in stone, steel, wood, and leaded glass. It was too valuable a practice to see disappear.

And so with Janssen's blessing the two younger men spun off their own firm, Hoffman and Crumpton, Architects, and continued to serve Richard K. Mellon and his bank, Edgar Kaufmann and his department store, Ben Fairless and U.S. Steel, Westinghouse, and other growth-minded clients.

From these beginnings came Johnson/Schmidt and Associates, a corporation whose name since 1980 reflects generational change at the top, but whose growth has been a model of sound professional evolution.

Thus a direct line traces from JSA's long experience in office and bank architecture (including several dozen Mellon and Pittsburgh National branches) to a strong current activity in interior planning and design. Its major achievements have included the Rockwell International and Heinz world headquarters, the new executive suites of PNC Financial Corporation, and the 21 directors' suites, as well as a Security Operations Center, at the World Bank, Washington, D.C. In late 1986 Federated Investors, Inc., moved its headquarters into 165,000 square feet of offices planned and designed by Johnson/Schmidt and Associates on 10 floors of Pittsburgh's new Liberty

*A new type of project for JSA—and equally as successful as its others—involved the transformation of the old Duquesne Light headquarters into the modern James H. Reed Building.*

Center.

The growing list of JSA's completely new headquarters and data center structures (Carnegie Natural Gas, Bessemer & Lake Erie Railroad, and the award-winning H.H. Robertson Company Building in Green Tree) has now been extended by a striking transformation in downtown Pittsburgh. It was JSA that created the modern James H. Reed Building out of the old Duquesne Light headquarters.

Its client for that project was Oxford Development Company, for which it had previously designed the pioneering South Hills Village and Monroeville Mall, among dozens of major retail facilities in several states. But this fits a pattern. More than 60 percent of a typical year's work comes from clients previously served, says JSA president James B. Johnson.

Other members of the firm's senior management are Thomas W. Schmidt, executive vice-president; James V. Eckles and Gary Gardner, vice-presidents; and Terence Miller, Susan Dunlap, William Gray, Gregory Katanick, and Edward Shriver, associate professionals.

*JSA's award-winning H.H. Robertson Company Building in Green Tree.*

Jim Johnson believes that Johnson/Schmidt and Associates' expertise has been enriched through the years by the creative tension between historic form and detail and the opportunities constantly being engendered by electronics, new construction materials, energy systems, and unornamented function. The current staff is "the best in our history," says Johnson, "a marvelous mix of professionals from different places and various schools, with fresh, challenging ideas."

# HARMARVILLE REHABILITATION CENTER
## RETURNING PEOPLE TO PRODUCTIVE ROLES IN LIFE

Harmarville Rehabilitation Center is one of the largest free-standing rehabilitation centers in the United States, located just 15 miles from Downtown Pittsburgh. The facility led the way for medical rehabilitation services and today serves physically disabled adults in southwestern Pennsylvania and the tri-state region.

As does its host city, the center represents a long history of change and growth. It opened in 1913 as a convalescent home for women, operated by graduates of independent schools in the eastern United States known then as The Federation of Girls' School Societies of Pittsburgh. In 1919 it was recognized as the most outstanding convalescent home in the nation.

The transition began in 1954, when the facility became western Pennsylvania's first comprehensive rehabilitation hospital for men and women. Within a year The Federation initiated a program to advance the level of rehabilitative care, including the addition of a hydrotherapy department, a work-testing shop, a speech-therapy unit, and a vocational-counseling unit. Due to lack of space—every year more patients were seeking treatment—the hospital relocated to a 69-acre site in Indiana Township northeast of the city. The new building opened June 28, 1975, and doubled Harmarville's capacity.

Within a few years even more space was needed, and in 1981 Phase II of the 10-year renovation was completed. Inpatient capacity increased from 120 to 200 beds, and outpatient and educational services widened. Outreach and educational programs continued to grow as the center restructured in 1983 to become one of three sub-

*Northeast of the city, Harmarville Rehabilitation Center offers the best in rehabilitation services in a beautiful, sylvan setting.*

sidiaries governed by a holding company, Harmarville Affiliates, Inc. "As in the past," said Mrs. Robert L. (Nancy) Whitney, Federation president, "the members of The Federation of Independent School Alumnae, as we are known today, continue to be involved in the operation of the specialty hospital and its affiliates."

*A quadriplegic patient learns movement, coordination, and balance in a physical therapy program designed specifically for him. A leader in rehabilitation for spinal cord injuries, Harmarville offers services tailored to the individual's needs.*

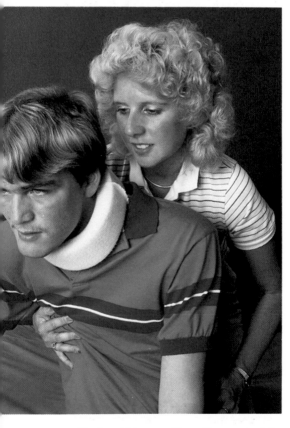

Today Harmarville offers rehabilitation for stroke, amputee, spinal cord injury, chronic pain, and head injury. It also provides hand therapy and general rehabilitation, outpatient services, and occupational health and rehabilitation services.

Following the team approach, each patient is assigned a physiatrist, a physician who specializes in rehabilitative medicine, to coordinate the services of specialists on the rehabilitation team. These professionals deal with nursing, physical therapy, occupational therapy, hand therapy, home management, nutritional services, speech/language pathology, audiology, orthotics/prosthetics, psychology, driver education, social services, vocational/educational services, and recreational therapy. The therapists meet with the team's physiatrist for weekly or biweekly staff conferences to discuss the treatment goals and progress for each patient. The team-approach philosophy, combined with the expertise of the staff, produces a high rate of success in returning patients to an independent life-style.

With its 200 beds, satellite centers, and 900 employees, Harmarville admitted 1,801 patients in 1985 and performed 32,083 outpatient treatments. Ninety-five percent of the chronic-pain patients experienced improved physical functioning and decreased pain medication, and more than 80 percent of the spinal-cord injury patients in a recent evaluation were able to acquire independent living skills. Another study revealed that nearly 90 percent of all inpatients with stroke were able to return to their own homes; only 2 percent required long-term care in a nursing home. This success rate is approximately 10 percent higher than national indicators.

"The real value of rehabilitation is returning people to a productive role in society," states Robert E. Henger, chief operating officer of the center. "We continue to ensure a positive outcome for our patients by applying technological advances to treatment and evaluating its benefits."

He pointed out, for example, that research suggests a reduction in risks associated with heart attack for spinal-cord patients if they remain physically active, and that biofeedback helps patients to control their pain. Electrical stimulation of the muscles of recently paralyzed people has given them a better return of function. Current projects include further refinements in the dosage of electrical stimulation and an application of this treatment for patients with multiple sclerosis.

Funding for these projects and for further improvements in patient care is the responsibility of a new subsidiary, the Harmarville Foundation, under the direction of Fred A. Giuliano.

"Harmarville is also investing in the future by reaching into the community to provide high-quality health care," notes William J. Hetrick, chief operating officer of HRC Community Outreach. One outreach program, Occupational Health and Rehabilitation Services (OHRS), helps to return employees to work after an injury on the job; thus, it is an aid to controlling compensation costs. The key to this approach is involving the patients in rehabilitation as soon as possible. Since the program's inception in 1978, 85 percent of the injured workers with whom it has dealt have returned to work. OHRS' central office is located a quarter-mile from the center at the Rehabilitation Outreach Center; satellite centers are operating in Greensburg, at Allegheny Center Mall in Pittsburgh, and in Washington, Pennsylvania.

Harmarville Rehabilitation Center is serving as a model for future rehabilitation centers in West Virginia and possibly in the United Kingdom through the efforts of Lee H. Lacey, president and chief executive officer of Harmarville Affiliates. As chief executive officer of the center for nearly 30 years, Lacey has been a champion of independence for disabled persons. "The challenge of the future," he states, "is to remove social and architectural barriers in our communities and foster the fullest integration of disabled citizens and their families into the mainstream of social and civic participation."

# MCI
## THE PITTSBURGH CONNECTION

What do the Pittsburgh Pirates, Fisher Scientific, and Westinghouse have in common? MCI® in their offices.

These well-known Pittsburgh business leaders are among a growing number of business and residential customers who have selected MCI Telecommunications Corporation for its service, innovation, and ability to provide quality telecommunications services.

From high-tech companies to athletes, MCI has dedicated its people and advanced technology to deliver a full range of voice, data, telex, and video services demanded by the most sophisticated customers. That same dedication has launched MCI's rise from an "upstart" who dared to challenge a telecommunications institution—AT&T—to the second-largest long distance company in America.

MCI's success in an intensely competitive industry, and the growth of its Pittsburgh operations since 1973, is evidence of the kind of entrepreneurial spirit, vision, and gritty aggressiveness so often attributed to it.

A look at the company's history offers some insight.

MCI's battle to compete as a long-distance carrier began in 1968. The firm's mission was to offer a lower-cost alternative in long-distance telephone service to AT&T.

But it wasn't until 1972, after four years of federal regulatory battles and AT&T attempts to crush any competition, that MCI actually

began offering long-distance service—between St. Louis and Chicago. By the following year MCI had grown rapidly and had begun its operations in Pittsburgh. Service consisted of point-to-point private lines for area businesses who required direct telecommunications with their various locations.

At that time the Pittsburgh operation was staffed by 10 employees, and MCI's local network capacity was limited to 500 simultaneous calls. Realizing that its growth and future success rested on its ability to provide all types of telecommunications services, MCI instituted its residential long-distance service in 1980.

Over the next four years the firm rapidly gained a significant foothold in the telecommunications market. However, the real turning point came with the court-ordered divestiture of AT&T and its local operating companies in 1984. The era of equal access has enabled MCI to rapidly expand the scope and range of its services, as well as implement better local system-connections to its domestic and international networks.

"The Information Age isn't coming. It's here," says MCI chairman William G. McGowan. In recent years a quiet revolution has been

*Through a combination of in-place and rapidly expanding transmission facilities—microwave, fiber optic, and satellite—MCI provides network capacity for the growing telecommunications market at the greatest efficiency and lowest cost possible.*

sweeping through the business world, bringing basic changes in the way organizations operate. The driving forces behind this revolution are information technologies—the combination of advanced data processing and telecommunications.

Recognizing that the future belongs to the most effective and creative users of these technologies, MCI has invested billions in its products, people, and organization to be the leading telecommunications company for the Information Age.

Its decision to decentralize in 1985 to locate closer to customers represented a major—and unprecedented—step toward this goal. Headquartered in Washington, D.C., MCI is now organized into seven divisions, their multistate boundaries coinciding with those of the regional Bell operating companies. Pittsburgh is one of the many MCI business centers serving major business and residential customers in the Mid-Atlantic Division, headquartered in Arlington, Virginia.

*An MCI engineer at work in the Network Management and Administrative System (NEMAS) national center, located in Arlington, Virginia. NEMAS allows MCI to monitor the network to assure that traffic is moving in an optimal fashion.*

In 1986 the company offered service to every telephone in the United States and provided telecommunications services to more than five million business, governmental, and residential customers. Its international direct-dial service extended to most major foreign countries.

To run the second-largest communications network in the world, MCI had, through 1986, nearly 15,000 employees, and had invested four billion dollars in its network since 1983. The network spans 28,000 route miles and employs the most modern digital technologies. They include such critical technologies as fiber optics, satellite, and total digital capacity—the keys to reliable, high-volume voice and data transmission.

For business customers, including 80 percent of the *Fortune* 500, MCI's services are tailored to meet a variety of needs—from the small business operation to the multinational corporation. Among the services offered are Banded WATS, a customized service for businesses with monthly bills of $1,500 or more; MCI PRISM℠ a flexible alternative to WATS, which offers a family of outbound long-distance services designed for various size business operations to control telecommunications costs as their calling patterns change; and Hotel WATS, which provides the lodging industry with economical national and international calling service.

Data services include MCI Data-Transport℠, a high-volume data service offering worldwide packet switching service; MCI Corporate Account Service℠, for businesses with multiple locations, offers maximum volume discounts and monthly management traffic summary reports to increase cost control among company locations; MCI Data Network Services, which offers corporate customers all digital terrestrial and satellite-based services to carry data, voice, and

image applications; and MCI Mail®, a time-sensitive message delivery system.

All of the firm's services are available to Pittsburgh customers through four local locations. Penn Center West, along Campbell's Run Road, is MCI's major site for administration, sales, and marketing. In 1986 the company employed 120 people in sales, engineering, and operations to serve more than 70,000 customers in the area. Trained representatives from MCI's National Accounts and Government Systems departments are also available to consult and assist large commercial users.

Two major electronic switching centers and a microwave and fiber-optics transmission center in Bairdford, northern Allegheny County, link the city to MCI's network. They serve as the major junctions for telecommunications traffic through the area—providing the network link from the Northeast to major cities in the Midwest, South, and overseas via MCI International's "gateway" switch at Crystal Lake, New Jersey.

Fiber-optics transmission will continue to play a major role in the future of telecommunications tech-

*A project engineer tests a 565-megabit optical fiber at MCI's laboratory in Richardson, Texas. MCI routinely tests the products of independent suppliers from around the world in its facilities in Texas and Washington, D.C.*

nology—and at MCI. At year-end 1986 MCI's 5,500-mile fiber-optic network ran from Chicago through Pittsburgh to Washington, D.C., and from New York to Atlanta and west to Dallas.

True to its advertising slogan, MCI is continuing to develop its technology and services to be the "communications company for the next 100 years." It expects to be a full partner in the Pittsburgh area's growth as a center of high technology.

*An electronic specialist tests new equipment to ensure quality operation prior to installation in MCI's network. All equipment is quality tested before it leaves the warehouse and retested at field locations.*

# INTERNATIONAL CYBERNETICS
## AN ENTREPRENEUR IN IMPROVING PRODUCTIVITY

Launched in 1982, International Cybernetics Corporation had burgeoned to 110 employees and $20 million in annual sales when it was sold to Gould, Inc., in late 1985—and it is still growing. President Donald H. Jones expects the firm to reach an employment goal of more than 500 in its first five years as the stand-alone Cybernetic Controls Division of Gould, a $1.5-billion Chicago-based supplier of electronics and computer systems.

Jones explains that cybernetics are flexible automated controls. In effect, it is what gives "intelligence" to a robot—the sequence of instructions that manipulate the tireless arms, fingers, and tools to weld, cut, flip, twist, tighten, assemble, and inspect. However, Gould's CCD Division products move more than robots. They serve an ever increasing array of industrial processes—not just to make production lines faster but to enable plants to shift quickly from one product to another, mini-

*Don Jones, founder of International Cybernetics Corporation, directed its growth from a start-up venture in 1982 to one of the world's leading automation companies. ICC was acquired by Gould in 1985.*

mize inventory, avoid retooling, and cut costly down-time.

The productivity gains even on existing facilities not uncommonly reach 30 to 70 percent, says Jones. The total market for such equipment was approaching three billion dollars per year midway in 1984, when ICC captured what it believes was the largest single order for robot controls to that time—100 systems, for a consortium of the major American automakers: Chrysler, General Motors, and Ford.

When Gould went shopping for a company to fill its demand for intelligent motion-control devices, it interviewed the people who know best: customers. Recalls Michael Bernath, Gould vice-president: "There was no doubt that he (ICC's Jones) had the best tech-

nology and the most respect of anyone in the marketplace. He's classically entrepreneurial. Instead of sitting in an ivory tower creating products that may be needed, he's creating things that are needed."

*ICC headquarters, located in the R.I.D.C. Industrial Park in the northern suburbs of Pittsburgh. There engineers develop new products that automate factories and complete production lines.*

ICC was the third substantial business established, grown, and sold at a profit by the restless Jones. "The dean of Pittsburgh's high-tech entrepreneurs," the *Pittsburgh Business Times-Journal* called him when bestowing its annual Enterprise Award early in 1986.

A 1959 engineering graduate of the University of Pittsburgh, Jones worked only four months at Westinghouse Electric before joining a small, local division of an optical company. It was his first involvement with compact, loosely structured firms that tend to produce hard work, morale, and inventiveness.

En route to founding ICC in 1982, Jones designed and patented an "angiographic injector" (used to detect heart diseases) as a consultant for another Pittsburgh firm, Medrad, Inc., and launched and sold two other companies, Control Systems Research (200 employees, $10 million in sales) and Technology Recognition Corporation, which created and published *Who's Who in Technology Today.*

His original plan for ICC, established with one million dollars in financing from four private investors who had backed him before, was the manufacture of robots; but on reflection that "didn't seem like quite the right thing for a small company," Jones says. The ultimate focus came down to "the intelligent part—the controls, the brain of the robot."

Before the new firm had sold a single product, when it had just 10 employees and $80,000 in the bank, it risked $30,000—payment in advance—for a booth at an international trade show. A worthwhile investment, as Jones recalls: "We walked away with 1,000 leads." A marketing blitz directed at 60 major robotics firms produced one million dollars in business for ICC in its first fiscal year. By year-end, operations were in the black. By 1985 ICC was selling to about half of the top 100 U.S corporations and heading for its 1,000th system sale.

The company's busy headquarters is in RIDC Industrial Park, O'Hara Township, just northeast of Pittsburgh. What actually goes out the door is a highly advanced "programmable automation controller," about the size of a personal computer, with some compact related gear. When retrofitted to an existing production line, such equipment is meant to increase output. A bearings manufacturer, for example, boosted production by 40 percent, as well as an increase in quality, from a $500,000 retrofit, according to Jones.

Very little manufacturing takes place at ICC itself, which makes it a point to subcontract most manufacturing to local electronics suppliers. That way it concentrates its skills on engineering and product development, testing, and assembly. Forty percent of ICC's technical staff consists of cum laude university graduates, of whom president Jones frankly expects much.

"Sure, he can be demanding at times," says a longtime employee. "Don sets a goal, and we have to meet it. That means some long hours. But he's right there with us—and he's the one that goes and gets the pizza when we take a break."

Jones has, in fact, been known to calculate the size of a venture by the quantity of pizza needed to sustain the after-hours people. ICC started as a "5 large pizzas" business; by the time of the Gould merger it had hit 30.

Having fended off an average of two acquisition bids per month since its early days, ICC agreed to go with Gould for its "dedication to the factory automation market," as Jones put it. "Our product fits perfectly with theirs."

The agreement called for Jones to stay on as president of Gould's new Cybernetics Control Division—to keep developing markets and retaining the small company, entrepreneurial environment, even as Gould's superior cash resources could be made available for equipment expansion and product development. "If I'm doing my job right," said Don Jones, "nobody should want to leave."

---

*The Flexible Automation Controller, developed by International Cybernetics Corporation in 1983, is the "brains" of industrial robots and other advanced automation systems.*

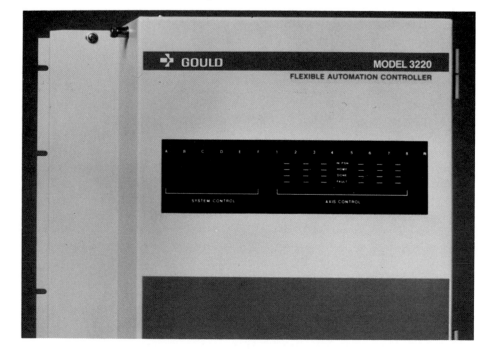

# KETCHUM COMMUNICATIONS INC.
## A PITTSBURGH SUCCESS STORY IN MARKETING COMMUNICATIONS

Pittsburgh-based Ketchum Communications Inc. is a worldwide marketing communications firm comprised of five operating units: Ketchum Advertising U.S., Ketchum Public Relations, Ketchum Direct, Ketchum Yellow Pages, and Ketchum International.

In 1923 George Ketchum organized an advertising and public relations agency with an initial capital of $5,000. He had been doing publicity for Colonial Trust Company, which asked Ketchum to take on advertising as well. Pittsburgh National Bank, a Colonial Trust descendant, remains a client today. The new agency, occupying three small rooms in the old Keenan Building, billed $100,000 its first year and soon outgrew its quarters.

Through both client growth and acquisitions, billings have grown every year since, and strongly of late: $180 million in 1975 to $450 million in 1986. After several moves and expansions, the firm arrived in 1985 at Six PPG Place, where it occupies three and one-half floors. The handful of names on the door in 1923 has grown to 300 employees in Pittsburgh and 1,000 worldwide. There are 13 U.S. offices, 6 overseas locations, and affiliates in 34 countries.

Major clients of Ketchum Communications include Westinghouse, Heinz, PPG, Du Pont, Digital Equipment Corporation, Bell Atlantic, American Honda, Dow Chemical, Pittsburgh National Bank, Pittsburgh Pirates, Bayer USA, Dravo Corporation, Mine Safety Appliances, and many more. It is the 11th-largest fully independent U.S. ad agency and the largest in Pennsylvania.

Ketchum Yellow Pages started autonomous life in the 1960s. Servicing more than 140 clients, it has become the largest yellow page service owned by a general agency.

In the early 1980s Ketchum Public Relations—now the nation's

*The Ketchum Communications office in Pittsburgh. As the 11th-largest fully independent U.S. ad agency and the largest in Pennsylvania, Ketchum has come a long way since 1923, when George Ketchum organized his company with $5,000 and three small rooms in the old Keenan Building.*

10th-largest public relations firm—developed its publicity tracking model, a computerized system that analyzes and measures the effect and value of publicity campaigns. Ketchum PR's Food Centers in New York and San Francisco offer food industry clients research, development, and marketing facilities rarely available at an agency level. In fact, Ketchum is believed to be responsible for promoting more food to American consumers than any other agency.

Ketchum people have traditionally volunteered their professional talents and personal commitments to Pittsburgh civic and cultural affairs. In 1986, under chairman William H. Genge and president Gerald J. Voros, the agency joined leading law and accounting firms in donating professional services to the investor group that kept the Pirates in Pittsburgh. Ketchum is now assisting the effort to broaden its community support.

The many facets of Ketchum Communications' growth and success have a common denominator that possibly explains the firm's extraordinary enterprise. The agency is owned by 130 stockholders, and they all work there.

# CARLOW COLLEGE
## PREPARING WOMEN FOR LEADERSHIP ROLES

Atop a hillside campus in Oakland, along green, upward-curving walks, stands Carlow College. While offering undergraduate and graduate programs for 1,200 traditional-age and adult students, it is a broader educational complex as well. Its Center for Business, Society, and Ethics has become a valued resource for major corporations, while a campus building houses a prestigious grade school for girls and boys.

Such a provision for all ages would have surprised, but no doubt pleased, seven pioneering Sisters of Mercy who arrived in Pittsburgh in 1843 from Carlow, Ireland. Their mission was simple and boundless: to serve the poor, the sick, and the uneducated. In 1844 they opened their first school, and in 1847 the first hospital west of the Alleghenies—Mercy Hospital of Pittsburgh. St. Paul's Orphanage, St. Xavier Academy, Our Lady of Mercy Academy, Cathedral High School, and St. Bridget's School were later harvests of the Sisters' determination.

During Pittsburgh's economic boom in the 1920s, prominent laymen urged the order to establish a Catholic college for women. Mount Mercy College, as it was first known, opened September 24,

*Carlow College serves nearly 1,200 students who represent more than 10 states and 13 foreign countries.*

1929, with 24 freshmen, 7 faculty members, and classrooms borrowed from Oakland's St. Mary's Convent. Within a few weeks came the stock market crash. It was questioned whether a tuition-charging school with no tradition, and no alumnae, could possibly survive. The doubters did not know Sisters Ireneaus Dougherty and Regis Grace. Somehow the two founding Sisters drew on faith, experience, and administrative skill—whatever might have been lacking in the mere bank account.

From its origination the college strove to graduate "the true scholar and the true woman with the ability for real service." The idea of women's rights, responsibilities, and leadership has always been central to this purpose.

A private institution sponsored by the Sisters of Mercy, the modern Carlow ranks as one of the best small, comprehensive colleges in the eastern United States,

according to a *U.S. News & World Report* survey of college presidents. *Everywoman's Guide to Colleges and Universities* finds it one of the best women's colleges anywhere. The key to such excellence is faculty. Nearly 70 percent of the women and men who teach at Carlow possess either doctorates or the highest degrees available in their particular discipline.

Carlow's Weekend College was a response to the demand for bachelor's degree opportunities for adult learners in accounting, management, communications and journalism, and nursing. There is also a Tuesday College, Evening College, and Hill College. On the childhood side of the educational spectrum, a Montessori program and the Campus School exemplify progressive education.

Mount Mercy College's name change to Carlow College in 1968 was significant. It renewed a link to the past and a promise to the future.

*Carlow College—educational excellence in the tradition of the Sisters of Mercy.*

# PITTSBURGH HISTORY & LANDMARKS FOUNDATION
## PRESERVATION OF THE PAST WITH A FINE PRACTICALITY

*Station Square is a preservation triumph. Against expert advice and public disbelief, the Pittsburgh History & Landmarks Foundation began working with subdevelopers in 1976 to adapt five historic railroad structures for new uses to create a lively urban environment on the south shore of the Monongahela River opposite Pittsburgh's Golden Triangle.*

As aging structures become old-fashioned and deteriorate, many are obliterated in the name of progress. Irreplaceable links between yesterday and today have been severed by visionary planning goals and by economic demand—often short-term demand, and often enough that even that is misread. The developers and planners err not only aesthetically but economically. Something splendid, valuable, and reusable is wiped out and replaced with mediocrity.

In Pittsburgh, public planning in the 1950s and 1960s called for the widespread demolition of significant historic neighborhoods such as the Mexican War streets and Manchester, the razing of Central North Side including its Market House and Old Post Office, the (ill-conceived) replanning of East Liberty, and the demolition of potentially good historic housing stock on the Lower Hill for an arts acropolis that was never developed. In protest to these plans, the Pittsburgh History & Landmarks Foundation was formed in 1964. The historic preservation organization came to the rescue of the architectural heritage of this city and has grown to become the largest local preservation group in the United States.

"The Pittsburgh History & Landmarks Foundation (PHLF) is big business in a big business town," national magazine *Architectural*

*Record* reported in October 1983, hailing the city's "virtuoso preservationists." With a shrewd sense of economic realities as well as the values inherent in charm, style, and a sense of tradition, PHLF has made itself the preserving as well as progressive spearhead in the "livable" quality of Pittsburgh.

The organization was established by architectural historian James D. Van Trump; Arthur P. Ziegler, Jr., then a college English instructor; lawyer Charles C. Arensberg; and Barbara D. Hoffstot, a trustee of the National Trust for Historic Preservation. Their idea was to reverse the slide into decay of older, inner-city neighborhoods—not by tearing them down, scattering the residents, and starting over but by purchasing, restoring, and renting houses whose basic architectural integrity was masked by flaking paint or crumbling shingles.

The founding nucleus enlisted other individuals and organizations, and PHLF came into being as a nonprofit catalyst for some of Pittsburgh's most exciting commercial developments of modern times. Its largest project to date is Station Square, which by the mid-1980s was en route to more than $150 million of new—and renewal—investment.

PHLF's small staff in the 1960s and early 1970s worked hand in hand with the local citizenry to begin revitalization in the Mexican War streets, Manchester, and other urban areas, partly by use of a $.5-million revolving fund for property renovations, rentals, and sales. Government money and incentives were tapped into for "renovation without displace-

*It was a sad spectacle that the 1300 block of Liverpool Street in Manchester presented in the early 1960s that led to the idea of a preservation organization for Allegheny County. The identical double houses in the Second Empire style, all with delicately detailed wooden entrance porches, have now been restored.*

Hundreds of students and teachers participate in the Foundation's education programs each year. By developing the skills of a "detective," students and teachers learn how to explore the local community and discover the history and architecture of Pittsburgh and its neighborhoods.

ment."

Most visible to many people was the rescue of historic properties on the endangered list. The North Side's "useless" Old Post Office became the inspiriting, chock-full Pittsburgh Children's Museum. Other one-of-a-kind structures, such as Downtown's Union Station and Springdale's Rachel Carson Homestead, received hard-headed feasibility analyses by the PHLF staff. In 1976 the foundation joined with a volunteer committee and the City of Pittsburgh to spark a $7-million restoration of Schenley Park's famed Phipps Conservatory. The park itself is now the focus of a major restoration effort initiated by PHLF.

Station Square was the triumph that convinced the skeptics. Imagine trying to add another 10 percent, in effect, to the land area of Pittsburgh's Downtown, but across a river—and in ramshackle railroad structures and yard areas to boot!

In 1976 PHLF leased 41 acres, from the Pittsburgh & Lake Erie Railroad, on the south side of the Monongahela River. The property included five buildings dating from

the turn of the century, some 650,000 square feet of ill-used space. "The foundation wanted to prove that a lively, economically viable urban environment could be developed out of the historic remains of a railroad terminal," says Louise King Ferguson, PHLF executive director. Vital to the effort was five million dollars in seed money (later considerably augmented) from the Allegheny Foundation, headed by Richard M. Scaife, publisher of the Greensburg *Tribune-Review.*

The P&LE's grand, high-vaulted Edwardian waiting room was restored and refitted as the main dining room of the hugely successful Grand Concourse restaurant; a sprawling, deserted industrial shed became the Freight House Shops, a 55-unit mall of boutiques and eating places that later extended into a cavernous warehouse that was given new life as the light-filled Commerce Court office and retail building. There are also a Sheraton Hotel, multilevel parking facilities, and a colorful berth for the Gateway Clipper Fleet that conducts river excursions. The result of those efforts is a weekend and evening "festival center" that attracts crowds of visitors and residents, employs at least 3,000 persons, and generates two million dollars annually in parking and real estate taxes alone.

In addition to the $71 million of investments plowed into Station Square by 1986, at least that much more is on the drawing boards, says Art Ziegler, who is the PHLF president. Future phases of the phenomenon will include clusters of housing, office, retail, and cultural projects.

Meanwhile, PHLF has been focusing its attention on the development of educational programs, tours, lectures, publications, and architectural surveys which broadly promote the value of historic preservation. Since 1982 the foundation has educated thousands of

Beginning in 1966 the Pittsburgh History & Landmarks Foundation worked with the neighborhood residents in Manchester on Pittsburgh's North Side to create the first historic preservation district for blacks.

teachers and students through such workshops as "An Eye for Architecture," "Pittsburgh Heritage," "Hands-On History," and "Exploring Your Neighborhood." More than 6,000 structures in Allegheny County should be saved, the PHLF has found, by a block-by-block survey, and over 300 of these are the subject of an extensive publication titled *Landmark Architecture: Pittsburgh and Allegheny County.*

Preservation has become a national trend, but Pittsburgh is considered particularly well endowed with sources of seed money, corporate and private foundations, and the civic tradition needed to solidify dreams in brick and mortar. It is also a community whose colorful past has bequeathed the sort of neighborhoods that could make historian Van Trump exclaim:

"From that moment when one has fallen in love with the street, one could not help but be dedicated to its renewal. It is a poetic vision in the end that saves."

# CHAMBERS DEVELOPMENT COMPANY, INC.
## APPLYING SCIENTIFIC KNOW-HOW TO WASTE MANAGEMENT AND SECURITY

When Chambers Development Company, Inc., went public in late 1985, investors learned what only sanitation insiders had known before: that relieving society of its trash burden, under the drumbeat of constantly tightening budgets, is more than an essential service business. It can be an exciting growth industry.

Since 1980 Chambers has built a six-year string of annual sales increases averaging 36 percent. Its first year of public reporting, 1985, showed $20 million in revenues and net profits of $3 million.

Chambers' stock-in-trade is to improve a customer's waste management service while also saving municipalities and industries money. Its first disposal contract for Pittsburgh cut the city's costs from $11.21 per ton to only $3.70.

The paradox of waste is that rising living standards constantly generate more of it, but allow less and less space for its disposal. Pennsylvania had 1,100 landfills in 1980; it is estimated that only 30 will still meet standards to operate by the mid-1990s.

Chambers Development operates three landfills in western Pennsylvania—at Monroeville, Johnstown, and Washington. Each is "geotechnically" engineered, and has sufficient airspace to last well into the next century; and as

John Rangos, Sr., chief executive officer and president of Chambers Development Company, Inc.

all are being reclaimed and re-seeded even as they conceal more than 555,000 tons of waste per year, they have futures as developable real estate as well.

Chambers is the creation of John G. Rangos, Sr., an Ohio Valley native and industrial sales whiz who started establishing small companies to handle electric power plant wastes in the 1960s. In 1971 he consolidated into one parent firm, Chambers Development, to construct environmentally sound landfills and, in the 1980s, to bid for the hauling contracts to fill them. After successfully serving Pittsburgh and a number of other western Pennsylvania communities, the company, since 1984, has opened operations in a number of Sunbelt communities in the Southeast.

President Rangos flatly claims "the most productive collection operations in the waste disposal industry." Computer software lays out the most cost-efficient route structure, which the company follows up by strict monitoring of equipment and employees.

A Chambers subsidiary, Security Bureau, Inc., provides uniformed guard and investigative services that not only account for 35 percent of corporate revenues today but also open a lot of cross-marketing doors with customers.

The firm's 1,100 employees include two of Rangos' sons, John Jr. and Alexander, as vice-presidents, as well as a number of non-family officers. Only the sixth waste firm in the nation to go public, Chambers Development Company, Inc., celebrated 1986 with a move to a new corporate headquarters in Penn Hills. It is an attractive grouping of ranchlike buildings around a central plaza, spacious, spread out, and boldly planned—like the future the company sees for itself.

*An artist's rendering of Chambers' new headquarters in Penn Hills.*

# ST. CLAIR HOSPITAL
## SERVING THE GROWING SOUTH HILLS AREA

What started in 1954 as a 104-bed hospital has nearly quadrupled in the decades since. St. Clair Hospital, now a 363-bed facility that serves many communities, has since expanded on its 35-acre tract of greenery in Mt. Lebanon, at 1000 Bower Hill Road.

The idea for a hospital to serve the growing "South County" area came from Dr. A.S. Haines, a local physician who argued that such a facility would head off lengthy—and often life-threatening—journeys to the nearest hospitals in Downtown Pittsburgh, the South Side, or McKees Rocks.

South Hills community leaders worked hard for 10 years to raise money and construction materials. Several fund-raising campaigns were conducted and at least two building plans commissioned by the time St. Clair Hospital opened in 1954. However, its growth has been constant ever since, reflecting its burgeoning surroundings. "This area has always been on the move," said Benjamin E. Snead, president, St. Clair Health Corporation. "It's been our goal over the years to meet increasing needs for health services."

*In order to bring medical care to Mt. Lebanon, St. Clair Hospital was opened in 1954. Today it is a 363-bed facility with 361 physicians serving nearly 200,000 residents with a wide variety of medical and surgical skills.*

With that in mind the board of directors, medical staff, and administration spent two years developing a strategic plan to continue providing "skillful, caring, cost-effective, and comprehensive health care services." The plan established a new St. Clair Health Corporation as a tax-exempt parent company with three tax-exempt subsidiaries—St. Clair Hospital, St. Clair Hospital Foundation, and St. Clair Health Ventures—and one taxable, for-profit subsidiary, St. Clair Management Resources, Inc.

"All the corporations must be entrepreneurial, opportunistic, and willing to take risks," noted Snead. He adds that all 1,500 employees of St. Clair are expected to work in concert toward innovative, economically motivated venture opportunities.

The institution's programs, specialties, and technologies are kept continually updated with the input of 361 physicians on staff. It serves an area of approximately 200,000 residents with a wide variety of medical and surgical services. The inpatient facilities for adults and children also contain state-of-the-art critical care services for coronary care, intensive care, and intermediate care units. In addition, 24-hour emergency care is provided to approximately 45,000 patients per year.

St. Clair's progressive, family-centered maternity care program includes a full range of prenatal, postpartum, and family maternity education. Complete outpatient diagnostic facilities employ modern laboratory and medical imaging techniques; and there is a 12-bed outpatient surgical unit.

It takes many caring hands to provide the services offered at St. Clair Hospital.

"We think it is fitting that a pair of hands—surrounding a family group—are symbolically portrayed in our hospital logo," said Snead. "It's one way of saying that patients and their families can obtain the best treatment possible whenever they need it."

# WILLIAMS TREBILCOCK WHITEHEAD
## ARCHITECTS, PLANNERS, INTERIOR DESIGNERS

The direction taken by Williams Trebilcock Whitehead over the years has strikingly paralleled that of Pittsburgh itself. It has been a case of being in the right place at the right time, and being there with the right skills and standards—a talent for high-quality design combined with a determination to complete projects on time and within budget.

When the suburban exodus threatened to cover the countryside with cement and sprawl, WTW created some of the region's most beautiful assemblages of site and structure. When the civic conscience began to rebel against the wrecking ball approach to what seemed old-fashioned and run-down, WTW answered with surprising revitalizations of historic buildings. Now, as Pittsburgh leans toward a future of high-tech industrial development, the firm is again on the cutting edge with expertise in the design of sophisticated research, manufacturing, and data-processing facilities.

The enterprise was founded by G. Thomas Williams and Thomas B. Trebilcock, who had met while working for a large Pittsburgh construction firm. In 1959 they opened their first office in the old Republic Building on the North Side's East Ohio Street and were soon joined by Paul A. Whitehead.

The young venture received welcome early boosts from Mobay Corporation and Calgon Corporation, which were setting up headquarters along the Parkway West, and from Western Pennsylvania National Bank (Equibank). The busy corridor from Downtown to the Greater Pittsburgh International Airport was just beginning to develop with the opening of the Fort Pitt Tunnels, and continues as a scene of ceaseless activity. WTW has been responsible for a sizable share of the architecture visible to thousands of Parkway motorists: hill-topping Foster Plaza, the tree-shaded headquarters

*Once the Schenley Hotel, it is now the William Pitt Union at the University of Pittsburgh.*

of Ryan Homes, Inc., the Mobay research and administrative complex, Automatic Data Processing's regional headquarters, and the daring glass cubes of Park Ridge Office Center.

When urban renewal crossed the Allegheny River in the mid-1960s, it leveled the North Side Market area—including WTW's office—to make way for Allegheny Center Mall. The three partners then moved to an imposing, 90-room mansion on Ridge Avenue, sharing the facility with other professional firms.

By that time civic-minded people, determined to save architectural treasures, had grown more vocal, organized, and effective. The Pittsburgh History and Landmarks Foundation hired WTW to give new life to the Allegheny City Post Office, built in 1894, and scheduled for demolition in 1968. It became the Landmarks Museum, visited by thousands annually and a gem of classical charm in a viable neighborhood. WTW also initiated the era of renovation and

adaptive reuse in Pittsburgh's First Side district when it converted a turn-of-the-century riverfront warehouse into the Fort Pitt Commons office building with an exposed timber structure, bridges, and landscaped space that dramatizes a basement-to-roof atrium.

WTW has completed a number of these "extended-use" projects.

*Mine Safety Appliances Company's Research and Manufacturing Complex overlooks a man-made lake in Cranberry Township north of Pittsburgh.*

*Foster Plaza Building Six and one of its boardrooms (inset).*

The Commerce Court offices and shops in Station Square, with their glass-enclosed elevators reaching up into the exciting seven-story atrium, were recycled from a musty and cavernous liquor warehouse. The Hartley-Rose Building once housed a Downtown factory engaged in the manufacture of steam engine belts. The University of Pittsburgh's William Pitt Union occupies the elegant but long-since-faded Schenley Hotel of 1898.

In 1983 Williams Trebilcock Whitehead created its own headquarters by converting a vacant, 1920s-era lumber mill into Timber Court. A sky-lit mezzanine was added, red brickwork was cleaned, and the heavy timber structure was exposed, sandblasted, and sealed. The result is a dramatic 30,000-square-foot office building on Pittsburgh's North Shore oppo-

site the Golden Triangle. WTW's architects, planners, and interior designers occupy the upper levels, while several medical groups share the lower floors.

The firm, with its accumulated experience of more than 700 projects, is intimately tied to Pittsburgh's economic transition. The change from heavy industry to high-tech industrial development provides a multitude of new construction opportunities for area architects. Notable among WTW projects is the 326-acre Mine Safety Appliances Research and Manufacturing Complex. It was specifically designed to respond to the client's concern for environmental priorities and for a livable work environment. This type of involvement suggests that, for architects, the city's greatest days lie ahead.

As of 1986 Williams Trebilcock

Whitehead designed an annual construction volume of approximately $100 million; had a staff of 65, including 35 registered architects and 5 interior designers; and operated offices in Pittsburgh and Orlando. It has performed work throughout the United States and in several foreign countries. The major reason behind the firm's success, in president Tom Williams' opinion, has been strict adherence to a design philosophy. He sums it up as "high-quality design, efficient project management—and client service with a personal touch."

# PITTSBURGH & LAKE ERIE RAILROAD
## FIRING UP THE ENGINES OF INNOVATION

No enterprise has been more challenged by the restructuring of the steel industry than the "Little Giant" of railroads. "Serves the Steel Centers" was the proud slogan that flashed along the river valleys for decades on the boxcars of the Pittsburgh & Lake Erie Railroad.

For the P&LE, the steel plant closings of the early 1980s could have been the financial equivalent of "bridge out!" Instead, the feisty carrier went scouting for new business. By 1986 new management, private ownership, and a tightened team of 950 employees had hopes of reaching a new level of prosperity.

It was in 1875 that a small group of risk-takers led by William H. McCreery (grain and iron dealer), restless under the domination of the Pennsylvania Railroad, received a charter for a line out of Pittsburgh on the south bank of the Ohio River to Youngstown, Ohio. However, the start-up dollars —three to four million—proved too much to raise. Overtures went out to the Vanderbilts, whose New York Central and Lake Shore railroads already reached south to Youngstown.

When William H. Vanderbilt purchased $300,000 of P&LE stock, other investors were heartened to subscribe; and construction began in earnest in late 1877. On February 12, 1879, the first train out of Pittsburgh took 14 hours to travel to Youngstown; but the first year's profit (which modern accounting methods might have amended) totaled $157,500 on revenues of $335,300.

Encouraged by its profits, Vanderbilt continued to invest in the company. By the mid-1880s his stock controlled the P&LE and tied it to the New York Central system, to which it remained attached for nearly a century—dutifully moving mountains of coal and steel to Youngstown, and often earning more than $10 a share an-

*The historic P&LE Terminal Building in the heart of Station Square.*

*A 2,000-horsepower diesel locomotive utilized in main line freight service.*

nual profits. Only in the aftermath of the Penn Central bankruptcy was the "Little Giant" finally set free under private ownership, in 1979.

A specialist in hauling massive loads (three times the national railroad average by 1903) the P&LE built the first all-steel hopper car in 1898 and pioneered development of heavier locomotives at its historic McKees Rocks shops, which still serve as its maintenance center. It also ran as many as 60 passenger trains daily from the high-vaulted terminal on Pittsburgh's South Side that survives as an elegant part of Station Square.

Challenged to overcome the decline in steel, the P&LE has vigorously branched out into new

business. In 1986 it won the *Modern Railroads* magazine's Golden Freight Car Award for promoting hundreds of thousands of tons of barge-rail movements of coal of varying sulfur content for environmentally critical markets. Other innovations were afoot as well.

Quality, efficient service, and an extensive fleet of railcars available to customers are Pittsburgh & Lake Erie Railroad's strong points in board chairman Gordon E. Neuenschwander's program to "continue serving the Pittsburgh industrial community as a viable, competitive railroad."

# FRANKLIN INTERIORS
## OFFICE PLANNERS FOR A MORE PRODUCTIVE FUTURE

Saul Franklin borrowed $3,000 in 1945, leased space on Smithfield Street, and opened a retail carpet and drapery business. He had learned that business as an employee at the old Frank & Seder department store and decided to take a chance on his own.

The gamble—and hard work—paid off. Two expansions later, in 1955, Franklin had his own store on the Boulevard of the Allies and a sufficient reputation with architects and designers that he was gaining more and more commercial work. In 1960, not long after his son, Charles, began helping in the store, commercial business had become so dominant that the firm moved to 100 Ross Street to open a spacious showroom featuring commercial furnishings.

Charles Franklin graduated from Pratt Institute in 1965 with a degree in interior design and a perception that no one in Pittsburgh was properly marketing the kind of contemporary, international style of furniture that he admired—the work of Mies van der Rohe, Marcel Breuer, Charles Eames, and Le Corbusier. He saw this as an opportunity, but realized that it demanded an exclusive showroom for proper presentation to the architectural and design community. Launching the first serious introduction of this genre to the Pittsburgh market featuring Knoll International products, by 1969 Charles had established Franklin Interiors solidly with architects and their clients seeking a contemporary look in their offices. To better serve this market niche, Franklin Interiors began to develop a capability in office planning. The firm became a Steelcase dealer in 1974, and later that year installed Pittsburgh's first major systems furniture project—for Equibank's corporate headquarters.

Systems furniture necessarily implied a substantial service capability; merely selling goods as a merchant was not enough. In 1977

*This office layout is typical of the executive office space Franklin Interiors develops for its clients.*

the firm reorganized as a new corporate structure, with officers, departments, computer systems, and all the administrative functions to serve a complex and growing market in office furnishings.

Today Franklin Interiors is one of the largest and most experienced companies in the area providing planning, furnishings, and installation to industrial, financial, and institutional clients. Representing a select group of furniture manufacturers, the firm has completed installations for Pittsburgh-based organizations throughout the United States.

Franklin Interiors' 35 full-time employees and its field installation technicians have served many of Pittsburgh's blue-ribbon companies. Its 1985 sales level was 40 times the volume of 1965—and the region's transition to a predominantly white-collar work force promises further growth.

"The days of supplying the employee just a desk and a chair are

*Franklin Interiors technicians have become specialists in planning and installing complex furniture systems for corporate clients in Pittsburgh and throughout the United States.*

over," says Charles Franklin, who has succeeded his father as president of Franklin Interiors. "More small and medium-size companies are concerned with creative, productive offices. Studies show that intelligently planned office environments are a key to higher productivity—and that's exactly where we are."

# JOHNSON & HIGGINS
## A FIRM WITH A TRADITION OF EXCELLENCE PROSPERS AND LOOKS TO THE FUTURE

Johnson & Higgins is the nation's and world's largest privately held insurance broker and human resource consultant. The firm was begun in 1845 on Wall Street during the time of tall ships and the beginnings of international trade. Henry W. Johnson and A. Foster Higgins plied the ancient trade of "average adjusting," the sharing of losses from cargoes sacrificed at sea by ships in distress. As the industrial revolution took hold, the firm followed its clients' needs on shore and helped bring insuring capacity to an industrializing America. History records that after the 1906 San Francisco earthquake and fire, it was Johnson & Higgins that saw that "every loss was serviced with satisfactory payments to its clients." In 1912 it was Johnson & Higgins and its Lloyd's partner that placed the insurances on the *Titanic.* Amazingly, in view of today's litigious society, "all claims were collected within less than 30 days."

Since the end of World War II American business has concerned itself more and more with the retirement and health care needs of its employees. Because of that fact Johnson & Higgins has become a leader in the human resource consulting field. Today, with 60 U.S. and Canadian offices and scores of others overseas, Johnson & Higgins is a globally recognized expert in all aspects of insurance brokering and human resource consulting.

As a firm long accustomed to serving the nation's largest corporations, Johnson & Higgins opened its Pittsburgh office in 1946. Under such leaders as David H. Winton, Richard I. Purnell, Benedict A. Collins, and current managing partner George F.B. Owens, Jr., the Pittsburgh office acquired a growing list of the city's most esteemed corporations. In October 1983 it moved into spacious new quarters at One PPG Place. The office has grown to over 140 professionals.

It was the Pittsburgh office that promoted perhaps the most innovative insurance concept of the century—the Capital Asset Protection Plan (CAPP)—placing a corporation's insurable risks under a single financial arrangement. Such pioneering is characteristic of Johnson & Higgins, still privately held, service minded, and entrepreneurial after more than 140 years.

Henry W. Johnson

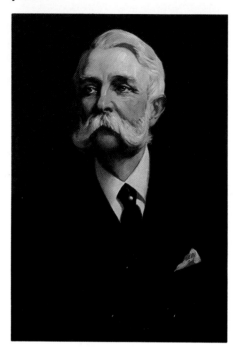

A. Foster Higgins

George F.B. Owens, Jr., chairman of Johnson & Higgins of Pennsylvania, Inc.

# THE BIGLER-KETCHUM GROUP
## PREVENTION OF LOSS IS MORE VALUABLE THAN RECOVERY OF LOSS

Its members are insurance brokers, seemingly a prosaic enough business. However, to Chandler G. Ketchum, chairman, The Bigler-Ketchum Group is "typical of the unique organizations that will make the Pittsburgh area regain its economic leadership."

Based on the belief that well-managed businesses should not be diverted from their prime function by costly losses and interruptions, Bigler-Ketchum incorporates the consulting assistance of "risk management" to the traditional broker's function of simply placing a client's insurance with an appropriate carrier.

"Our philosophy is to provide a client with virtually his own insurance staff," states president Harold S. Bigler. "We're known for our ability to spot hidden loss potentials. Bigler-Ketchum encourages the establishment of 'risk review' teams within client companies, consisting of operations, legal, financial, sales, and risk management officials, to identify and protect against needless exposure. We serve as the independent consultant, utilizing our own professional loss control staff."

Chan Ketchum and Hal Bigler had worked together in corporate insurance for 25 years when they created their own firm in 1976. Their spectrum of professional service has steadily widened ever since. By 1986, when The Bigler-Ketchum Group moved to the Ketchum Center Building, contributing to the rebirth and viability of Pittsburgh's Uptown, it had a staff of more than 30 people and was exceeding two million dollars in annual commissions and consulting fees.

In addition to its corporate risk-management approach, Bigler-Ketchum seeks to spur clients' sales growth, both nationally and internationally, by the utilization of credit insurance, and, should foreign governments blow hot or cold on overseas contracts, political

risk insurance. Concern for the financial health of its clients has led The Bigler-Ketchum Group to become expert in guaranteeing long-term and long-distance financial obligations.

One of Bigler-Ketchum's subsidiaries works to reduce massive insurance settlements in liability cases, while also ensuring that money is regularly received tax-free by the victim. Structured Annuities, Inc., arranges to convert huge lump-sum awards into regular income, spaced prudently over a lifetime—with obvious benefits to recipient, payer, and society.

Other skills of the versatile organization include the designing, administering, and communication of employee benefits programs; compensation plans for key employees; student health insurance at universities; and worker's compensation for a 2,300-member Pennsylvania trade association.

Renaissance Realty, its development organization, has created marketing strategies to lease shopping center space and to turn

*Bigler-Ketchum is unique in the level of loss control expertise that it can offer to clients. Here, Phil Metz, manager of Loss Control Services (right), inspects special maps to evaluate the risk that mine subsidence poses to a client.*

underutilized and underdeveloped real estate into successful ventures.

Chan Ketchum and Hal Bigler see their company effectively promoting sales for western Pennsylvania marketers, whether through credit or political risk insurance on overseas business, or "due diligence" studies for European buyer or American investor groups. Bigler emphasizes: "We go beyond insurance to preserve our clients' asset bases."

*Hal Bigler (left) and Chan Ketchum, the co-founders of The Bigler-Ketchum Group, an organization that provides corporate insurance, structured settlement, and commercial real estate services to business in the western Pennsylvania area.*

# CENTRAL MEDICAL CENTER AND HOSPITAL
## BETTER ALTERNATIVES IN HEALTH CARE DELIVERY

Tradition has its merits; so too does youth—youth even as an institution. The organizational joints are more limber, the managerial link freer of shalt nots. Change is not only something to respond to, but to initiate.

A vigorous example in Pittsburgh is Central Medical Center and Hospital. It is the city's youngest institutional provider of health and medical services, just founded in 1974. Today nearly 400 physicians practice or attend there, a true one-stop center for almost all adult medical and surgical needs. The total full-time staff is 560, the annual payroll above $11 million.

Physicians, mostly, started Central Medical. The pioneering group of 58 organizers possessed a predominance of medical degrees

*The Central Medical Center and Hospital at 1200 Centre Avenue in Pittsburgh.*

along with certain necessary business and legal expertise. They were ahead of a trend. Their sense that health care services ought to be organized more effectively to meet the needs of the public has been amply ratified by a

*The officers of the Central Medical Center and Hospital board of directors (from left): John W. Hannon; Harold E. Ciccarelli, M.D.; Thomas M. Gallagher; James G. Zangrilli, M.D.; and John F. Horty, Esq.*

swarm of changes in delivery systems and financing since the mid-1970s.

Central Medical's first major physical impact on the city was the construction of its imposing Downtown hospital at 1200 Centre Avenue, near Chatham Center and the Civic Arena. The big sand-toned building contains 205 beds for inpatient care of adults (there are outpatient services for pediatric and obstetrical care as well) along with offices for 54 physicians in private practice, covering well over a dozen medical specialties. These doctors are augmented by 325 others on the attending medical hospital staff. Dr. James G. Zangrilli is medical director.

The array of surgical and diagnostic services available at CMC is vast and sophisticated. The facility also addresses the tensions of everyday life as well as health crises. Thus it features a fitness and wellness center for the general public. Its mental health and chemical dependency programs embrace the treatment of eating disorders, and detoxification for alcohol and drug abuse. Facilities for diabetes edu-

cation and treatment include an insensitive (diabetic) foot clinic. Occupational and industrial medicine and women's health services are large and growing activities.

According to Thomas M. Gallagher, who has been president of CMC&H since its beginning, the thrust of recent innovations has been in the expansion of outpatient wellness and educational services. Satellite health centers, four of them by the mid-1980s, were serving outpatients in the Mt. Washington, Brookline, and Century III Mall areas and at Greater Pittsburgh Airport. More are planned. In terms of education,

*The Louis Tambellini Health Center Outpatient Urgent Care Facility. Family practice medicine is practiced here.*

many smokers free themselves of the habit through tuition courses at Central Medical, while public audiences attend free twice-a-year seminars on health issues conducted in layman's language by hospital staffers. CMC&H also trains health care workers, and participates in medical education through teaching associations at universities and other hospitals.

The Central Medical Health Plan was born with the hospital. It is a nonprofit subsidiary of the parent Central Medical Health Corporation, itself a nonprofit, tax-exempt entity. Operating since 1974, CMHP is Pittsburgh's oldest health maintenance organization (HMO). It began in 1986 with 12,300

subscribers. For a fixed premium each is entitled to a full range of medical and surgical services. The latter are provided by 180 physicians at any of four hospitals and nine satellite centers. The financial "risk" of a major medical problem—costing perhaps $25,000 or more for surgery and intensive care—is borne by the HMO, in keeping with the insurance principle of guarding against the catastrophic rather than the routine. Institutionally this insurer does best when folks stay well, not when they "fully occupy the facilities."

John F. Horty, a Pittsburgh attorney who specializes in national health law and who has served as Central Medical's board chairman since 1975, says the goals of CMHP is high-quality care in an environment of dignity and privacy, with a stress on preventive medicine. "A viable alternative," he calls it, "to traditional health insurance."

It is also a dollar-saving alternative. Tom Gallagher notes that HMOs nationally have shown a pattern of less than 10 percent annual premium increases in the same era that saw conventional health plan charges jump closer to 20 percent.

Subscribers benefit because the most mischievous barrier—the worry that a doctor to see means a bill to pay—is removed in favor of the incentive to seek medical attention in a timely manner. The encouragement is on the side of

going in for routine health care services to prevent or minimize a problem. Yet when serious problems arise, there is deep comfort in CMHP's established network of primary and specialty care physicians.

The employers' advantage is cost savings; plus, no doubt, whatever psychological fallout derives from a better contented work force. Approximately 250 Pittsburgh area companies now provide benefits through CMHP in preference to, or alongside of, the older "hospitalization." Checks and balances, such as pre-admission reviews, ensure that health care is a fringe benefit to be used, not abused. "It is an economically practical alternative-care system," says Gallagher, a 25-year veteran of the health industry who served as chief financial officer of a Washington, D.C., hospital before joining CMC&H.

For the future, Central Medical Center and Hospital believes its flexibility of design will enable it to provide the services and technology, facilities, and sensible economics demanded by a public that learned a valuable lesson in the 1970s and 1980s. Health care, no less than other goods and services, responds to the most knowledgeable consumers.

*Cardiac catheterization procedure being performed in the hospital's cardiac catheterization laboratory.*

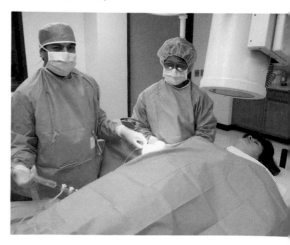

# IBM
## A COMMITMENT TO PITTSBURGH SINCE 1917

International Business Machines Corporation has been a part of the Pittsburgh business community since 1917. In the early days of the century the company contributed products and services that helped support the region as a center of heavy industry. Today, as Pittsburgh gains leadership in high technology, finance, health, and services, IBM people are helping it to meet the challenges of the future.

In IBM's 10-story, 250,000-square-foot building at Four Allegheny Center, nearly 600 employees are concentrating on solutions to Pittsburgh's needs for advances in information processing. These sales, service, and support people help bring to the Pittsburgh area the wide variety of products, services, ideas, and solutions created by IBM research, development, and manufacturing facilities throughout the world.

In Pittsburgh as elsewhere, business, industry, and the public sector require new products and technologies for computer processing, which has become a fundamental part of virtually every organization's daily operations. Over many years IBM and its people have built a strong reputation for quality information systems products and support.

Another key ingredient in Pittsburgh's future is the requirement for further application of information processing to areas such as office productivity and engineering/scientific advancement. IBM marketing, systems engineering, and service representatives are working to bring to Pittsburgh customers the latest in products and services for speeding and streamlining a broad variety of office activities from financial analysis and word processing to graphics and printing. IBM is also addressing an increasing need for capacity and sophistication in engineering/scientific and industrial computing.

Telecommunications is an emerging area of very rapid growth. A changing environment, combined with new technologies in voice data and graphic information, makes this area an important priority for investment with IBM customers.

IBM's long and successful association with Pittsburgh is reflected not only by its close alliance with business and industry, but also by its commitment to the entire community. The Allegheny Center

*People—dedication to excellence.*

*IBM Pittsburgh area headquarters.*

building is one demonstration of this commitment. It was completed in 1977 as part of an intensive effort to restore the city's North Side, and today IBM management continues to serve actively in North Side restoration activities.

This location is one of many in IBM's long Pittsburgh history. It dates back to 1917, when IBM's predecessor, the Computing-TabulatingRecording Company, occupied three rooms in the Union Trust Building with eight employees who sold primarily time-recording equipment and computing scales. The C-T-R Company had been formed in 1911 by a

merger of three companies, all of which dated back to the nineteenth century. One was the Tabulating Machine Company, founded in 1896 by Herman Hollerith, the father of modern data processing. Another was the International Time Recording Company of Endicott, New York, site of IBM's oldest manufacturing and development facility.

In 1924 the firm changed its name to International Business Machines Corporation and moved its Pittsburgh office to 209 Ninth Street, which housed 20 employees. By 1935 IBM's Pittsburgh representation had grown to 55 employees, with offices in the Koppers Building. The company's product line had expanded to include electronic accounting machines and typewriters—the forerunners of today's office productivity tools.

Growth continued for the company in Pittsburgh and throughout the world—in 1947 there were 125 employees housed at 421 Seventh Avenue, and by 1964 that number had grown to 350 at a new location at Gateway Center. Then, in 1977, the IBM offices were moved to the present location. Today the Pittsburgh office represents a corporation of more than 400,000 employees in more than 130 countries, developing, manufacturing, marketing, and servicing computer systems ranging from the large-scale processors to the mid-range systems to the IBM Personal

Computer, along with offerings that include software, telecommunications products, storage devices, printers, typewriters, copiers, robotics, industrial systems, education, and a broad range of professional services.

The IBM commitment to Pittsburgh is demonstrated through its people. Graduates of Pittsburgh

*IBM Customer Center.*

colleges and universities join IBM in significant numbers for careers nationwide. Other employees, many of them Pittsburgh area natives, have devoted most of their careers to the local IBM operations. For example, more than 60 percent of today's IBM Pittsburgh employees have worked 10 or more years at the facility; some employees have spent more than 40 years with IBM in Pittsburgh.

Local IBM people and their counterparts worldwide have benefited from a wide number of IBM programs. The company is an

*Bidwell Training Center—community job training and placement.*

equal opportunity employer, and ensures that all employees have the same chance to succeed. All personnel programs are administered without regard to race, color, religion, sex, national origin, handicap, or age. Hiring is based on business need, job-related requirements, and an individual's qualifications; advancement depends on job performance and the individual's demonstrated ability to assume greater responsibility. Affirmative action programs, such as recruiting, training, and providing accommodations for the handicapped, also are in place to ensure that all can compete on an equal basis. A merit system of pay and promotion rewards superior performance. In nearly 50 years no person employed on a regular basis by IBM has lost as much as one hour of working time because of a layoff.

The skills of IBM employees are continually expanded through specialized education and on-the-job experience. The results are mutually beneficial: Employees improve their knowledge and their opportunities for advancement, and IBM improves its ability to succeed with its customers in a fast-growing and highly competitive industry.

Wherever it does business, IBM contributes significantly in money, equipment, and employee services to support education, social programs, and the arts.

In Pittsburgh, for example, IBM has played a significant role in supporting the Bidwell Training Center, which has given job training and job placement to more than 2,000 disadvantaged people since 1968. The firm began a partnership with the Bidwell Center in 1983, and in January 1985 a Bidwell/IBM Information Sciences Center began full operation, training people for careers in data processing and computer operations. An IBM manager is on the board, and two IBM people are on loan from their regular jobs to teach at and help run the center. The company has invested a half-million dollars in equipment, supplies, and employee services in the center, which currently services more than 120 students annually.

IBM people are also involved in the Greater Pittsburgh Chamber of Commerce, the United Way, the Red Cross, and other community activities. In the academic arena, IBM supports a variety of programs at such institutions as Carnegie-Mellon University and the University of Pittsburgh.

IBM's partnership with Pittsburgh businesses and public-sector agencies is based on commitment, dedication, excellence, and good will. This partnership is the foundation from which IBM employees strive together in forging new directions and a better life for the firm, the city of Pittsburgh, and its people.

# HYATT PITTSBURGH
## A MOST LIVABLE AND ELEGANT HOTEL

*Hyatt Pittsburgh—after dark.*

Location is everything, some folks say, but location is just the first thing at the Hyatt Pittsburgh. The beautiful hotel dominates a five-acre site at the top of the city's Golden Triangle near the domed Civic Arena. It faces a park-like plaza of fountains, trees, and flowers and is the centerpiece of bustling, modern Chatham Center—a cluster of real estate that includes The Towers, with its fashionable condominiums, and 17 floors of offices in Chatham Two, all served by a multilevel underground garage.

From their hotel windows, Hyatt guests can glimpse the Allegheny River with its bridges to the north and a sweep of the Monongahela to the south. The city's dramatic Downtown, formed by the meeting of the rivers, awaits nearby. Hyatt guests readily understand why Rand-McNally found Pittsburgh

to be the "Most Livable City in America."

Once the site of St. Peter's Church, the development of Chatham Center formed a fascinating chapter in the Pittsburgh renaissance of the 1950s and 1960s.

The Urban Redevelopment Authority acquired the site from the Diocese of Pittsburgh, which was quite willing to sell it. However, that did not prevent a protracted legal struggle which ended only when the Pennsylvania Supreme Court upheld the transfer. Present at nearly all the court proceedings was an elderly woman carrying a sign: "Save St. Peter's Church." It was obvious that she disagreed, as did a number of St. Peter's parishioners, with the Bishop's decision that the neighborhood needed only one church, Epiphany. Legend has it that when the legal battle ended, the lady cast a curse on the property.

Undeterred, Pittsburgh philanthropist and civic leader Leon Falk, Jr., and Chatham Management, Inc., moved forward to develop the important tract, then regarded as an "extension" of the city's compact Downtown. The most promising first-phase structure was a much-needed modern hotel designed by Edward D. Stone and Associates.

In 1976 Prudential Insurance purchased the development and designated Chicago-based Hyatt Corporation to manage the hotel, a firm that about a decade earlier had practically revolutionized the industry. It had built the Hyatt Re-

*Concierge Bobbi Galloway serves guests in the Regency Club.*

*Executive chef Justin Wagner approves Hugo's award-winning Sunday brunch.*

gency in Atlanta—instantly famous for its soaring atrium, consisting of balconied floor upon floor of guest rooms looking down into the great well of the lobby. While Hyatt had no part in the original design of the hotel at Chatham Center, it brought to Pittsburgh the first-class concepts of management and service for which it was so respected.

Soon after its reopening as Hyatt Pittsburgh, the hotel's general manager—genial, courtly Horst Schulze—observed a strange sight in the newly redecorated lobby: a black-garbed woman motioning with her arms and chanting sotto voce. Schulze politely inquired if he could be of help. "No," said the mysterious one, "I like what you have done with the place, and I'm taking off a curse I cast on it many years ago."

Perhaps that is why the hotel's fortunes have soared since Hyatt took over; more likely, it is because Hyatt puts the comfort of its guests above all else and because of its community involvement. "A touch of Hyatt" means one thing—dedication to excellence!

Lunch, dinner, and Sunday Brunch at the award-winning Hugo's restaurant became famous. Hyatt Pittsburgh soon became the host hotel for a number of worthwhile charities and civic projects—such as the Pittsburgh Marathon, the Jazz Festival, the International Poetry Forum, CMU's "Carnegie Salutes Carnegie," and the American Heart Association's "Heart Throb '86."

Hyatt has invested millions of dollars in an ongoing program of restoration and decorating. The mirrored lobby featuring floral design; splendid ballrooms and flexible, businesslike meeting rooms; and overnight accommodations decorated in soft, pleasing tones generate an ambience of hospitality and gracious comfort.

Building and furnishings alone are not enough, however. According to Klaus Peters, present general manager of Hyatt Pittsburgh, "Our people are our most valuable asset, from the concierge who serves guests on our Regency floors to every desk clerk, bellperson, door attendant, room attendant and wait staff. We all share the Hyatt view—that service is the ultimate hallmark of excellence in the hotel industry."

Hyatt Pittsburgh is host hotel for National Hockey League teams and the flight crews of several major airlines. Among the many famous names recorded in its registers are the late Princess Grace of Monaco, Sophia Loren, Count Basie, Bill Cosby, Beverly Sills, Princess Caroline, Itzhak Perlman, Joan Rivers, Bob Hope, Yo Yo MA, Robin Williams, and Sarah Vaughn. The guest list continues with explorer Thor Heyerdahl; composer Gian Carlo Menotti; comedians Jerry Lewis and Sid Caesar; tennis champions Billie Jean King, John McEnroe, and Arthur Ashe; media personalities Phil Donahue and Howard Cosell; singers Mel Torme, Diana Ross, and Andy Williams; medical pioneer Jonas Salk; athletes Mario Lemieux, Joe Montana, ex-heavyweight champ, Larry Holmes, and O.J. Simpson; and actors Art Carney, Tony Randall, and Karl Malden.

Whether a guest walks in the bright light of celebrity or in the subdued glow most business and pleasure travelers share, Hyatt Pittsburgh offers accommodations and service fully in keeping with a most livable hotel in America's most livable city.

*Klaus Peters hosting his monthly general manager's luncheon, toasts special guest Pierre LaRouche of the New York Rangers hockey team.*

# KDKA RADIO
## THE WORLD'S FIRST BROADCAST STATION

Imagine your world without the communications industry. There would be no radio, television, or cable. No up-to-the-minute news, weather, and sports reports. No music, discussion, or commercials to inform, entertain, reassure, or intrigue you.

Such was the world of only the day before yesterday. Quieter, no doubt; but more isolating to individuals and communities. However, the advent of radio broadcasting would result in millions of people "connecting" with each other through the shared knowledge of current events, new ideas, and music.

In the history of communications, Pittsburgh occupies an unforgettable moment. It was a Pittsburgher who had the curiosity and imagination to develop radio as a broadcasting mechanism—the beginning of instant mass communications.

And it all started with a bet!

Dr. Frank Conrad was chief engineer of Pittsburgh's Westinghouse Electric in 1912. Determined to prove to a doubting friend that his $12 watch kept accurate time,

he built a small receiver to pick up signals from the Naval Observatory in Arlington, Virginia. Conrad won his $5 bet.

He also became fascinated with radio as a hobby. Conrad constructed a small transmitter on the roof of a garage behind his home in Wilkinsburg. The first official record of this station—licensed 8XK—appeared in the August 1, 1916, edition of the U.S. Department of Commerce, then the government's radio licensing agency. For security reasons during World War I, however, all American amateur radio licenses were cancelled.

On May 1, 1920, 8XK was relicensed and soon became a powerhouse among amateur transmitters. Its program messages were heard in widely separated locations, although they chiefly consisted of discussions of radio equipment and test results. Boredom with such transmissions prompted Conrad to place his phonograph before the microphone on October 17, 1919, and play a song. The music amazed radio "hams," and song requests poured in. Conrad

announced he would "broadcast" records for two hours each Wednesday and Saturday evening—the first recorded use of the word *broadcast* to describe a radio service.

The Westinghouse Company soon became convinced that radio represented a new industrial opportunity. The firm applied for its own license on October 16, 1920. Presidential election night, a little more than two weeks away, was selected for the station's debut. Construction had been started only a month before the election and entrusted to Frank Conrad.

The KDKA license was issued October 27, 1920. The now-familiar call letters were not derived from painstaking tests of thousands of alphabetical combinations. Apparently they just came next on the list from a roster that was used to

*Radio's first broadcast was the Harding-Cox election returns on November 2, 1920. The coverage on KDKA Radio was the beginning of the communications industry.*

identify ship and shore stations.

The world's first election broadcast, which reported the presidential victory of Warren G. Harding over James Cox, originated from a tiny shack atop a Westinghouse factory building in East Pittsburgh. Its single room accommodated transmitting equipment, a turntable for records, and the broadcast staff. Announcer Leo Rosenberg kept requesting: "Will anyone hearing this broadcast communicate with us, as we are anxious to know how far the broadcast is reaching and how it is being received."

It proved to be a national sensation. Newspapers acclaimed the phenomenon of instant information, and mail flowed in telling of reception in numerous states.

KDKA's technology and programming developed rapidly after that initial triumph. The station's industry "firsts" included the nation's first regular programming, religious service, sports broadcast, baseball and football play-by-play, farm service report, and presidential inaugural address. In addition, Conrad's experiments with short wave led to the development of static-free FM radio, television, low-power long-distance

communications, and radar.

Innovation continues to this day. In July 1982 KDKA became the nation's first station to broadcast a talk show in AM stereo; on November 2, 1985, it became a full-time AM stereo station. Its state-of-the-art studios enable KDKA to transmit and receive network broadcasts via satellite. This satellite broadcasting is the fastest and most flexible means of broadcasting today, and offers listeners the finest in quality reception.

KDKA's 50,000 watts reach 140 counties in Pennsylvania and five nearby states. At night this powerful signal carries to 35 states and into Canada. Having millions of listeners imposes a responsibility that the station takes very seriously. From its origin, KDKA Radio has adhered to some self-imposed standards: to provide programs of interest and benefit to the greatest number of listeners, to assign distinctive features at regular times for the convenience of listeners, and to offer news reports that inform and enlighten.

These goals have been supplemented by a strong commitment to public service. The station's volunteer-run "Call for Action" program recovers hundreds of

*A familiar Pittsburgh sight and sound since 1946—KDKA's annual Children's Hospital campaign. A remote broadcast from a downtown department store window enables a KDKA Radio personality to accept donations and make some new friends.*

thousands of dollars each year for victims of consumer fraud. Nonprofit agencies benefit from KDKA's public service announcements and hands-on involvement. And KDKA's annual Children's Hospital campaign in December is nationally recognized as the most successful charity drive in radio history. Since 1946 KDKA and Pittsburghers have raised millions of dollars in free medical care for local children.

KDKA Radio's mission will continue to be to provide information and entertainment, and to keep Pittsburghers informed about what is occurring in their neighborhoods, their country, and their world. KDKA Radio and Pittsburgh: a station and a city committed to helping each other grow, improve, and communicate for more than 65 years.

**KDKA** RADIO 1020

# THE GAGE COMPANY
## DEEP IN THE INDUSTRIAL BASE OF PITTSBURGH

From its nineteenth-century beginnings The Gage Company has specialized in flow control—that hidden world of valves, pipes, and meters that keep chemicals, gases, oil, and water running safely through the veins of industry.

With a $75-million annual business and 17 sales offices and warehouses scattered through the country's manufacturing heartland, "The Gage" of today is well diversified. However, it still shares deep entrepreneurial connections with its hometown. The firm served the factories of Carnegie and Westinghouse, and countless of its products are imbeded in the walls, floors, and control rooms of a metropolis at work. "We're right in the guts of what has made Pittsburgh," says Robert A. Chute, the company's owner and chairman since 1979.

William L. Rodgers founded the enterprise in 1892 as Pittsburgh Gauge & Supply Company, and began manufacturing quality gauges in a store building at 308 Water Street, Downtown. In 1896 Rodgers published a catalog (the forerunner of today's thick tome circulated to 30,000 plant storerooms) and, when a printer's error changed the "Gauge" of the title to "Gage," the economical enterprise trimmed the company name rather than recall the book.

Business prospered. A handsome six-story brick plant was opened in 1907 in the busy Strip District at 3000 Liberty Avenue, still the organization's headquarters. By 1913 the ambitious firm was producing automobiles. A luxury car, the Duquesne, was intended to sell for more than $3,000. Only seven were ever completed. The Gain-A-Day washing machine of the 1920s did better. More than a half-million were made and sold before the Great Depression ended the dream of manufacturing.

Since then Gage has concentrated on the distribution (with

*Headquarters of The Gage Company since 1907.*

some fabrication) of industrial supplies. The company has clearly fared better serving Detroit than fighting it. The corporation operates seven branches in Michigan, and auto plants are major customers.

The Gage Company's sales, still under two million dollars as late as 1940, have grown sharply under a series of managers determined to keep the entrepreneurial, small-business style of operation. When Pittsburgh's great mill supply market began shrinking, the firm successfully expanded services to mechanical and plumbing contractors. A user of computers since 1960, Gage has honed its inventory management to the point where

95 percent of the items in most critical demand—from its catalog of thousands—can be shipped directly off the shelf. Engineering services, in-house and on-the-road repairs, and equipment rentals round out the skills of a very flexible organization.

"We're a highly visible company to the people who manage plants," states Chute. "The great spirit of our employees is that they're part of the mechanical and industrial base of Pittsburgh."

# Patrons

The following individuals, companies and organizations have made a valuable commitment to the quality of this publication. Windsor Publications and The Greater Pittsburgh Chamber of Commerce gratefully acknowledge their participation.

Alcoa*
Alexander & Alexander Inc.
Allegheny General Hospital*
Allegheny International, Inc.*
Allegheny Ludlum Corporation*
The Alternative Employment Service
Amcom Office Systems
American Business Center
American Thermoplastic Company*
Mark B. Aronson Law Offices
AT&T*
Bell of Pennsylvania*
Berkman Ruslander Pohl Lieber & Engel*
Beynon & Company*
The Bigler-Ketchum Group*
Blahnik and Associates, Inc.
Blue Cross of Western Pennsylvania*
Buchanan Ingersoll Professional Corporation*
Burt Hill Kosar Rittelmann Associates*
Calgon Corporation*
Carlow College*
Central Medical Center and Hospital*
Chambers Development Company, Inc.*
The Chester Engineers*
Colonial Gallery Furniture Inc.
Community College of Allegheny County*
Community Savings Association*
Compunetics, Inc.*
Consolidated Natural Gas Company*
Consolidation Coal Company*
Coopers & Lybrand*
Deloitte Haskins & Sells*
Dravo Corporation*
Dudreck Depaul Ficco & Morgan Inc.*
Duquesne Light Company*

Duquesne Systems Inc.*
Duquesne University*
Eastern Airlines*
Eastman Kodak Company
Eat'N Park Restaurants, Inc.*
Eckert, Seamans, Cherin & Mellott*
Elkem Metals Company
Ellis Real Estate Company
Engineering Mechanics, Inc.
Equibank*
Equitable Group & Health Insurance Company*
Equitable Resources, Inc.*
Executive Report
First Federal of Pittsburgh*
Fisher Scientific*
Forbes Health System*
Franklin Interiors*
The Gage Company*
Gateway Center*
General Nutrition Centers*
GMAC Mortgage Corporation
Gold & Company, Inc.
Hall Industries Inc.
Harmarville Rehabilitation Center*
The Harris/Duddy Agency*
H.J. Heinz Company*
Heyl & Patterson, Inc.*
Joseph Horne Co.
Horne's*
Hussey Copper, Ltd.*
Hyatt Pittsburgh*
IBM*
International Business Associates
International Cybernetics*
Fred S. James and Co., Inc. of Pennsylvania
Johnson & Higgins*
Johnson/Schmidt and Associates*
Joy Manufacturing Company
Kaufmann's*
KDKA Radio*
Ketchum Communications Inc.*
Kidder, Peabody & Co., Inc.*
Kirkpatrick & Lockhart*
Landmark Savings Association*
La Normande*
La Roche College*
Magee-Womens Hospital*
Marsetta Lane Temp-Service, Inc.
Matthews International Corporation*
MCI*
Mellon Bank*
Mellon Stuart Company*
Microbac Laboratories, Inc.*
Montefiore Hospital*

Mon Valley Travel, Inc.*
Robert Morris College*
MSA*
The Murray Agency, Inc.
National Intergroup, Inc.*
Neville Chemical Company
Oliver Realty*
#1 Cochran Pontiac-GMC Trucks*
Oxford Development Company*
Parker/Hunter Incorporated*
Penstan Supply Inc.
The Peoples Natural Gas Company*
Pittsburgh & Lake Erie Railroad*
Pittsburgh Annealing Box Company*
Pittsburgh History & Landmarks Foundation*
Pittsburgh National Bank*
Port Authority of Allegheny County*
H.K. Porter Company, Inc.*
PPG Industries, Inc.*
Presbyterian-University Health*
Price Waterhouse*
Mr. Michael F. Ragan
Reed Smith Shaw & McClay*
John M. Roberts & Son Company*
Rockwell International*
Russell Industries, Inc.
Russell, Rea & Zappala, Inc.*
Ryan Homes, Inc.*
St. Clair Hospital*
St. Clair, Inc. Realtors
St. Francis Health System*
St. Margaret Memorial Hospital*
Sargent Electric Company*
Schneider Group of Companies*
Shadyside Hospital*
Thorp, Reed & Armstrong*
Thrift Drug Company*
Tucker Arensberg P.C.
II-VI, Inc.*
Union National Bank of Pittsburgh*
University of Pittsburgh
USAir Group, Inc.*
USX Corporation*
Wean United, Inc.*
The Western Pennsylvania Hospital*
Westinghouse Electric Corporation*
The Westin William Penn*
Williams Trebilcock Williams*
Zane's Inc.

*Partners in Progress: Profiles appear in Chapter 9.

# Index

# Books in the Windsor Series

1984, 192 pp., $22.95
ISBN 0-89781-114-3

DELAWARE
The First State: An Illustrated History of
Delaware
by William Henry Williams
1985, 216 pp., $24.95
ISBN 0-89781-158-5

DISTRICT OF COLUMBIA
Washington, D.C.: The Making of a Capital
by Charles Paul Freund
1987
ISBN 0-89781-205-0

FLORIDA
Fort Lauderdale and Broward County: An
Illustrated History
by Stuart McIver
1983, 236 pp., $24.95
ISBN 0-89781-081-3
Palm Beach County: An Illustrated History
by Donald W. Curl
1986, 224 pp., $24.95
ISBN 0-89781-167-4

GEORGIA
Columbus: Georgia's Fall Line "Trading
Town"
by Dr. Joseph Mahan
1986, 256 pp. $24.95
ISBN 0-89781-166-6
Eden on the Marsh: An Illustrated History
of Savannah
by Edward Chan Sieg
1985, 224 pp., $24.95
ISBN 0-89781-115-1

IDAHO
Boise: An Illustrated History
by Merle Wells
1982, 208 pp., $22.95
ISBN 0-89781-042-2
Idaho: Gem of the Mountains
by Merle Wells and Arthur A. Hart
1985, 256 pp., $24.95
ISBN 0-89781-141-0

ILLINOIS
Chicago: Center for Enterpise
by Kenan Heise and Michael Edgerton
1982, 600 pp. (2 Vols), $39.95
ISBN 0-89781-041-4
Des Plaines: Born of the Tallgrass Prairie
by Donald S. Johnson
1984, 136 pp., $19.95
ISBN 0-89781-095-3
Prairies, Prayers, and Promises: An Illustrated History of Galesburg
by Jean C. Lee
1987
ISBN 0-89781-194-1
Prairie of Promise: Springfield and Sanga-
mon County
by Edward J. Russo
1983, 112 pp., $19.95

ISBN 0-89781-084-8

INDIANA
At the Bend in the River: The Story of
Evansville
by Kenneth P. McCutchan
1982, 144 pp., $22.95
ISBN 0-89781-060-0
The Fort Wayne Story: A Pictorial History
by John Ankenbruck
1980, 232 pp., $22.95
ISBN 0-89781-015-5
Indiana: An Illustrated History
by Patrick J. Furlong
1985, 232 pp., $24.95
ISBN 0-89781-152-6
Muncie and Delaware County: An Illustrated Retrospective
by Wiley W. Spurgeon, Jr.
1984, 144 pp., $22.95
ISBN 0-89781-104-6
Terre Haute: Wabash River City
by Dorothy J. Clark
1983, 112 pp., $19.95
ISBN 0-89781-089-9

IOWA
Cedar Rapids: Tall Corn and High Technology
by Ernie Danek
1980, 232 pp., $19.95
ISBN 0-89781-021-X

LOUISIANA
River Capital: An Illustrated History of Ba-
ton Rouge
by Mark T. Carleton
1981, 304 pp., $21.95
ISBN 0-89781-032-5
So Mote It Be: A History of Louisiana Free-
masonry
by Glenn Jordan
1987
ISBN 0-89781-197-6
New Orleans: An Illustrated History
by John R. Kemp
1981, 320 pp., $24.95
ISBN 0-89781-035-X
The History of Rapides Parish
by Sue Eakin
1987
ISBN 0-89781-201-8

MARYLAND
Baltimore: An Illustrated History
by Suzanne Ellery Greene
1980, 325 pp., $19.95
ISBN 0-89781-009-0
Maryland: Old Line to New Prosperity
by Joseph L. Arnold
1985, 256 pp., $24.95
ISBN 0-89781-147-X
Montgomery County: Two Centuries of
Change
by Jane C. Sween
1984, 232 pp., $24.95
ISBN 0-89781-120-8

MASSACHUSETTS
Boston: City on a Hill
by Andrew Buni and Alan Rogers
1984, 240 pp., $24.95
ISBN 0-89781-090-2
The Valley and Its Peoples: An Illustrated
History of the Lower Merrimack River
by Paul Hudon
1982, 192 pp., $22.95
ISBN 0-89781-047-3
South Middlesex: A New England Heritage
by Stephen Herring
1986, 248 pp., $24.95
ISBN 0-89781-179-8
Heart of the Commonwealth: Worcester
by Margaret A. Erskine
1981, 208 pp., $19.95
ISBN 0-89781-030-9

MICHIGAN
Battle Creek: The Place Behind the
Products
by Larry B. Massie and Peter J. Schmitt
1984, 136 pp., $19.95
ISBN 0-89781-117-8
Through the Years in Genesee: An Illustrated History [Flint]
by Alice Lethbridge
1985, 144 pp., $22.95
ISBN 0-89781-161-5
In Celebration of Grand Rapids
by Ellen Arlinsky and Marg Ed Conn
Kwapil
1987
ISBN 0-89781-210-7
Jackson: An Illustrated History
by Brian Deming
1984, 148 pp., $19.95
ISBN 0-89781-113-5
Kalamazoo: The Place Behind the Products
by Peter J. Schmitt and Larry B. Massie
1981, 304 pp., $19.95
ISBN 0-89781-037-6
Out of a Wilderness: An Illustrated History
of Greater Lansing
by Justin L. Kestenbaum
1981, 192 pp., $19.95
ISBN 0-89781-024-4
Michigan: An Illustrated History of the
Great Lakes State
by George S. May
1987
ISBN 0-89781-181-X
Muskegon County: Harbor of Promise: An
Illustrated History
by Jonathan Eyler
1986, 200 pp., $22.95
ISBN 0-89781-174-7
Saginaw: A History of the Land and the
City
by Stuart D. Gross
1980, 200 pp., $19.95
ISBN 0-89781-016-3

MINNESOTA
Duluth: An Illustrated History of the Zenith
City

by Glenn N. Sandvik
1983, 128 pp., $19.95
ISBN 0-89781-059-7
*City of Lakes: An Illustrated History of Minneapolis*
by Joseph Stipanovich
1982, 400 pp., $27.95
ISBN 0-89781-048-1
*Saint Cloud: The Triplet City*
by John J. Dominick
1983, 168 pp., $22.95
ISBN 0-89781-091-0
*St. Paul: A Modern Renaissance*
by Virginia Kunz
1986, 200 pps.,
$29.95
ISBN 0-89781-186-0
*St. Paul: Saga of an American City*
by Virginia Brainard Kunz
1977, 258 pp., $19.95
ISBN 0-89781-000-7

## MISSISSIPPI

*The Mississippi Gulf Coast: Portrait of a People: An Illustrated History*
by Charles L. Sullivan
1985, 200 pp., $22.95
ISBN 0-89781-097-X

## MISSOURI

*From Southern Village to Midwestern City: Columbia, An Illustrated History*
by Alan R. Havig
1984, 136 pp., $19.95
ISBN 0-89781-138-0
*Joplin: From Mining Town to Urban Center, An Illustrated History*
by G.K. Renner
1985, 128 pp., $19.95
ISBN 0-89781-153-4
*At the River's Bend: An Illustrated History of Kansas City, Independence and Jackson County*
by Sherry Lamb Schirmer and Richard D. McKinzie
1982, 352 pp., $24.95
ISBN 0-89781-058-9
*Kansas City: The Spirit, The People, The Promise*
by Patricia Pace
1987
ISBN 0-89781-211-5
*Springfield of the Ozarks*
by Harris and Phyllis Dark
1981, 240 pp., $19.95
ISBN 0-89781-028-7

## MONTANA

*Montana: Land of Contrast*
by Harry W. Fritz
1984, 200 pp., $24.95
ISBN 0-89781-106-2

## NEBRASKA

*Lincoln: The Prairie Capital*
by James L. McKee
1984, 192 pp., $24.95

ISBN 0-89781-109-7
*Omaha and Douglas County: A Panoramic History*
by Dorothy Devereux Dustin
1980, 200 pp., $19.95
ISBN 0-89781-011-2

## NEVADA

*Reno: Hub of the Washoe Country*
by William D. Rowley
1984, 128 pp., $22.95
ISBN 0-89781-080-5

## NEW HAMPSHIRE

*New Hampshire: An Illustrated History of the Granite State*
by Ronald Jager and Grace Jager
1983, 248 pp., $27.95
ISBN 0-89781-069-4

## NEW JERSEY

*Hudson County: The Left Bank*
by Joan F. Doherty
1986, 168 pp., $22.95
ISBN 0-89781-172-0
*Morris County: The Progress of Its Legend*
by Dorianne R. Perrucci
1983, 216 pp., $24.95
ISBN 0-89781-075-9
*The Hub & the Wheel: New Brunswick & Middlesex County*
by Gary Karasik
1986, 136 pp., $22.95
ISBN 0-89781-188-7
*New Jersey: A History of Ingenuity and Industry*
by James P. Johnson
1987
ISBN 0-89781-206-9
*A Capital Place: The Story of Trenton*
by Mary Alice Quigley and David E. Collier
1984, 160 pp., $22.95
ISBN 0-89781-079-1

## NEW MEXICO

*New Mexico: The Distant Land*
by Dan Murphy
1985, 184 pp., $24.95
ISBN 0-89781-119-4

## NEW YORK

*Albany: Capital City on the Hudson*
by John J. McEneny
1981, 248 pp., $24.95
ISBN 0-89781-025-2
*Broome County Heritage*
by Lawrence Bothwell
1983, 176 pp., $24.95
ISBN 0-89781-061-9
*A Greater Look at Greater Buffalo*
by Jim Bisco
1986, 480 pp., $35.00
ISBN 0-89781-198-4
*Buffalo: Lake City in Niagara Land*
by Richard C. Brown and Bob Watson
1981, 336 pp., $27.95

ISBN 0-89781-036-8 [Hard Cover] $12.95
ISBN 0-89781-062-7 [Soft Cover]
*The Hudson-Mohawk Gateway: An Illustrated History*
by Thomas Phelan
1985, 184 pp., $22.95
ISBN 0-89781-118-6
*A Pictorial History of Jamestown and Chautauqua County*
by B. Dolores Thompson
1984, 128 pp., $19.95
ISBN 0-89781-103-8
*Between Ocean and Empire: An Illustrated History of Long Island*
by Dr. Robert McKay and Carol Traynor
1985, 320 pp., $24.95
ISBN 0-89781-143-7
*Harbor and Haven: An Illustrated History of the Port of New York*
by John G. Bunker
1979, 302 pp., $25.00
ISBN 0-89781-002-3
*A Panoramic History of Rochester and Monroe County, New York*
by Blake McKelvey
1979, 264 pp., $24.95
ISBN 0-89781-003-1
*Syracuse: From Salt to Satellite*
by Henry W. Schramm and William F. Roseboom
1979, 244 pp., $19.95
ISBN 0-89781-005-8
*The Upper Mohawk Country: An Illustrated History of Greater Utica*
by David M. Ellis
1982, 224 pp., $22.95
ISBN 0-89781-054-6

## NORTH CAROLINA

*Asheville: Land of the Sky*
by Milton Ready
1986, 136 pp., $22.95
ISBN 0-89781-168-2
*Greensboro: A Chosen Center*
by Gayle Hicks Fripp
1982, 216 pp., $24.95
ISBN 0-89781-056-2
*Made in North Carolina: An Illustrated History of Tar Heel Business and Industry*
by David E. Brown
1985, 248 pp., $24.95
ISBN 0-89781-157-7
*Raleigh: City of Oaks*
by James E. Vickers
1982, 128 pp., $22.95
ISBN 0-89781-050-3
*Cape Fear Adventure: An Illustrated History of Wilmington*
by Diane Cobb Cashman
1982, 128 pp., $22.95
ISBN 0-89781-057-0

## OHIO

*Butler County: An Illustrated History*
by George C. Crout
1984, 128 pp., $19.95

ISBN 0-89781-123-2
*Springfield and Clark County: An Illustrated History*
by William A. Kinnison
1985, 152 pp., $22.95
ISBN 0-89781-146-1

OKLAHOMA
*Oklahoma: Land of the Fair God*
by Odie B. Faulk
1986, 344 pp., $29.95
ISBN 0-8978-173-9
*Heart of the Promised Land: An Illustrated History of Oklahoma County*
by Bob L. Blackburn
1982, 264 pp., $24.95
ISBN 0-89681-019-8

OREGON
*Lane County: An Illustrated History of the Emerald Empire*
by Dorothy Velasco
1985, 168 pp., $22.95
ISBN 0-89781-140-2
*Portland: Gateway to the Northwest*
by Carl Abbott
1985, 264 pp., $24.95
ISBN 0-89781-155-0

PENNSYLVANIA
*Allegheny Passage: An Illustrated History of Blair County*
by Robert L. Emerson
1984, 136 pp., $22.95
0-89781-137-2
*Erie: Chronicle of a Great Lakes City*
by Edward Wellejus
1980, 144 pp., $17.95
ISBN 0-89781-007-4
*Life by the Moving Road: An Illustrated History of Greater Harrisburg*
by Michael Barton
1983, 224 pp., $24.95
ISBN 0-89781-064-3
*The Heritage of Lancaster*
by John Ward Willson Loose
1978, 226 pp., $14.95
ISBN 0-89781-001-5 [Hard Cover]
              $ 9.95
ISBN 0-89781-022-8 [Soft Cover]
*The Lehigh Valley: An Illustrated History*
by Karyl Lee Kibler Hall and Peter Dobkin Hall
1982, 224 pp., $24.95
ISBN 0-89781-044-9
*Pennsylvania: Keystone to Progress*
by E. Willard Miller
1986, 640 pp., $35.00
ISBN 0-89781-171-2
*Pittsburgh: Fullfilling Its Destiny*
by Vince Gagetta
1986, 624 pp., $35.00
ISBN 0-89781-189-5
*Never Before in History: The Story of Scranton*
by John Beck
1986, 144 pp., $22.95  0-89781-190-9

*Williamsport: Frontier Village to Regional Center*
by Robert H. Larson, Richard J. Morris, and John F. Piper, Jr.
1984, 208 pp., $22.95
ISBN 0-89781-110-0
*The Wyoming Valley: An American Portrait*
by Edward F. Hanlon
1983, 280 pp., $24.95
ISBN 0-89781-073-2
*To the Setting of the Sun: The Story of York*
by Georg R. Sheets
1981, 240 pp., $22.95
ISBN 0-89781-023-6

RHODE ISLAND
*Rhode Island: The Independent State*
by George H. Kellner and J. Stanley Lemons
1982, 208 pp., $24.95
ISBN 0-89781-040-6

SOUTH CAROLINA
*Charleston: Crossroads of History*
by Isabella G. Leland
1980, 136 pp., $17.95
ISBN 0-89781-008-2
*Columbia, South Carolina: History of a City*
by John A. Montgomery
1979, 200 pp. $17.95
ISBN 0-89781-006-6
*Greenville: Woven from the Past*
by Nancy Vance Ashmore
1986, 280 pp., $24.95
ISBN 0-89781-193-3

SOUTH DAKOTA
*Gateway to the Hills: An Illustrated History of Rapid City*
by David B. Miller
1985, 136 pp., $19.95
ISBN 0-89781-107-0

TENNESSEE
*Chattanooga: An Illustrated History*
by James Livingood
1981, 206 pp., $19.95
ISBN 0-89781-027-9
*Metropolis of the American Nile: Memphis and Shelby County*
by John E. Harkins
1982, 224 pp., $24.95
ISBN 0-89781-026-0

TEXAS
*Abilene: The Key City*
by Juanita Daniel Zachry
1986, 128 pp., $22.95
ISBN 0-89781-150-X
*The Golden Spread: An Illustrated History of Amarillo & the Panhandle Plains*
by B. Byron Price & Frederick Rathjen
1986, 168 pp., $22.95
ISBN 0-89781-183-61986
*Austin: An Illustrated History*
by David Humphrey

1985, 376 pp., $27.95
ISBN 0-89781-144-5
*Beaumont: A Chronicle of Promise*
by Judith W. Linsley and Ellen W. Rienstra
1982, 192 pp., $22.95
ISBN 0-89781-053-8
*Corpus Christi: The History of a Texas Seaport*
by Bill Walraven
1982, 136 pp., $22.95
ISBN 0-89781-043-0
*Dallas: An Illustrated History*
by Darwin Payne
1982, 400 pp., $29.95
ISBN 0-89781-034-1
*City at the Pass: An Illustrated History of El Paso*
by Leon Metz
1980, 126 pp., $19.95
ISBN 0-89781-013-9
*Where the West Begins: Fort Worth and Tarrant County*
by Janet L. Schmelzer
1985, 152 pp., $22.95
ISBN 0-89781-151-8
*Houston: Chronicle of the Supercity on Buffalo Bayou*
by Stanley E. Siegel
1983, 296 pp., $29.95
ISBN 0-89781-072-4
*In Celebration of Texas*
by Archie P. McDonald
1986, 488 pp., $29.95
ISBN 0-89781-165-8
*Waco: Texas Crossroads*
by Patricia Ward Wallace
1983, 136 pp., $22.95
ISBN 0-89781-068-6

UTAH
*Ogden: Junction City*
by Richard C. Roberts and Richard W. Sadler
1985, 288 pp., $24.95
ISBN 0-89781-154-2
*Salt Lake City: The Gathering Place*
by John S. McCormick
1980, 130 pp., $19.95
ISBN 0-89781-018-X

VERMONT
*Vermont: An Illustrated History*
by John Duffy
1985, 264 pp., $24.95
ISBN 0-89781-159-3

VIRGINIA
*Norfolk's Waters: An Illustrated Maritime History of Hampton Roads*
by William Tazewell
1982, 224 pp., $22.95
ISBN 0-89781-045-7
*RICHMOND: An Illustrated History*
by Harry M. Ward
1985, 544 pp., $29.95
ISBN 0-89681-148-8

*Virginia Business and Industry* 1987

WASHINGTON
*King County And Its Queen City: Seattle*
by James R. Warren
1981, 314 pp., $24.95
ISBN 0-89781-038-4
*Where Mountains Meet the Sea: An Illustrated History of Puget Sound*
by James R. Warren
1986, 288 pp., $24.95
ISBN 0-89781-175-5
*A View of the Falls: An Illustrated History of Spokane*
by William Stimson
1985, 160 pp., $22.95
ISBN 0-89781-121-6
*South On The Sound: An Illustrated History of Tacoma and Pierce County*
by Murray and Rosa Morgan
1984, 199 pp., $22.95
ISBN 0-89781-0474-0
*Vancouver on the Columbia: An Illustrated History*
by Ted Van Arsdol
1986, 200 pp., $22.95
ISBN 0-89781-194-1

WEST VIRGINIA
*Charleston and the Kanawha Valley: An Illustrated History*
by Otis K. Rice
1981, 136 pp., $19.95
ISBN 0-89781-046-5
*Huntington: An Illustrated History*
by James E. Casto
1985, 160 pp., $22.95
ISBN 0-89781-101-1
*Wheeling: An Illustrated History*
by Doug Fethering
1983, 120 pp., $19.95
ISBN 0-89781-071-6

WISCONSIN
*The Fox Heritage: A History of Wisconsin's Fox Cities*
by Ellen Kort
1984, 256 pp., $22.95
ISBN 0-89781-083-X
*Green Bay: Gateway to the Great Waterway*
by Betsy Foley
1983, 168 pp., $22.95
ISBN 0-89781-076-7

WYOMING
*Cheyenne* 1987